VISUAL QUICKSTART GUIDE

QuarkXPress 4

FOR WINDOWS

Elaine Weinmann

Peachpit Press

Visual QuickStart Guide
QuarkXPress 4 for Windows
Elaine Weinmann

Peachpit Press
1249 Eighth Street
Berkeley, CA 94710
510/524-2178
800/283-9444
510/524-2221 (fax)

Find us on the World Wide Web at: www.peachpit.com

Peachpit Press is a division of Addison Wesley Longman

Cover design: The Visual Group
Interior design and illustrations: Elaine Weinmann

Colophon
This book was created with QuarkXPress 4.0 on a PowerTower Pro 200 and a Power Macintosh 8500. The primary fonts used are New Baskerville, Gill Sans, Franklin Gothic, Lithos, Officina, and Futura from Adobe Systems Inc.

Permissions
Definitions on page vi from *The Oxford Encyclopedic English Dictionary,* 1991, edited by Joyce M. Hawkins and Robert Allen, reprinted by permission of Oxford University Press.

ISBN 0-201-69699-1

9 8 7 6 5

Printed and bound in the United States of America

♻ Printed on recycled paper

Introduction

At last! Por fin. Enfin. Επι τέλοσ. Até que enfim. Endlich...

Bear with me while I do a tiny bit of whining. I usually whine about how fast applications upgrade, especially in this, The Year of the Big Upgrades. Heck, there's even a sequel to Myst. In the case of QuarkXPress, I hated to see a great program lying stagnant, and meanwhile, my wish list was getting longer and longer. With the release of Four-Oh, are there still features left on my wish list? You betcha: A layers palette, a navigation palette, style sheets for items, Web export capability, and more. (Quark headquarters, are you listening?)

Now for a nice round of applause. XPress 4.0 incorporates most of the features that were on my original wish list as well as a few delightful surprises, including the ability to create Bézier shapes; enter text on a path; make all sorts of conversions, such as from a text box into a picture box or a line; create clipping paths; create custom dashed and multi-line frames, lines, and paragraph rules; find and change style sheets; selectively append style sheets, colors, H&Js, and lists; resize whole groups; turn XTensions off and on from within the application; synchronize style sheets and other specifications across multiple documents; and—hoot, holler, jump in the aisles—create and apply character-based style sheets.

Some of the enhancements are smaller and won't engender a lot of media fanfare, but are nevertheless welcome to a daily QuarkXPress user like myself. Take smart space, for example. If you copy and paste a text passage, XPress figures out whether a space is needed before and/or after the pasted text and inserts it automatically for you.

Should you toss out your drawing application, now that QuarkXPress has its own Bézier tools? No, you'll still need that drawing application for some tasks. But what you'll like about XPress' Bézier tools is that you can draw right in your layout program and see how your text path or irregularly-shaped picture box looks in your layout. What's more, QuarkXPress' anchor points and curve handles are easy to see (less squinting). And you can convert a corner anchor point into a curve using a keyboard shortcut or with a quick click on an icon on the Measurements palette—elegant maneuver.

Is 4.0 more difficult for a beginner to learn? Not really. There are more features to learn, but the basics are the basics. Here's my advice: Think of yourself as a visitor in a foreign country, and use this volume as your guidebook. But don't try to see the whole country all at once. Give yourself time to get acquainted with the turf, with where the various menus, features, screen icons, and commands are located, and with the new QuarkXPress language. This Visual QuickStart Guide will help direct you down the main thoroughfares, with its step-by-step instructions, hundreds of illustrations, and oodles of tips to help you avoid getting lost.

How difficult will it be for you to upgrade your skills if you already know the program? The new folder tab interface is a bit different, but the basic methods used to create documents haven't changed significantly. If you're an experienced QuarkXPress user, the beauty of this application upgrade is that you can add to your store of knowledge in bits and pieces—learn how to use character style sheets, for example, or fiddle with the text path tools—without turning your life upside down or substantially interrupting your normal work flow.

You may have already noticed that I can never resist improving my books. In this very thoroughly revised edition you'll find an updated design, new illustrations, many more tips,* and more thorough introductory paragraphs and instructions. In fact, you'll find new tips and info bites on almost every page. So even if you memorized the previous edition, take some time to read the fine print in this one. In addition to the spanking new instructions for all the latest features, you'll find tips that will save you time and revised instructions that will hopefully shed light on the older features—some of which until now you may have been avoiding like the plague. I extend to you a warm welcome to the new and improved *QuarkXPress 4.0 for Windows: Visual QuickStart Guide* ■

**Speaking of tips, I'd love to hear from you if you've come up with any tips that you think might help other readers of this book or any corrections that you think I should make. I can be reached at Pixbill@aol.com. Don't ask me for advice on hardware, though. To say it's not my forté is a gross understatement.*

I'm grateful to

First and foremost, *Peter Lourekas,* co-author, teacher, artist, and computer wizard, for his top-notch testing, suggestions, insights, hardware know-how (thank goodness!), and general all-'round brilliance.

Nancy Aldrich-Ruenzel, publisher of Peachpit Press; *Corbin Collins,* my editor; *Gary-Paul Prince,* publicist; *Keasley Jones,* foreign rights manager; *Amy Changar* and *Mimi Heft,* production coordinators, and the rest of the terrific staff at Peachpit.

The following pre-press specialists for their "input" on output and trapping: The Electronic Pre-press Department at *Malloy Lithographing, Inc.* (Ann Arbor, Michigan), *Wayne Van Acker,* pre-press production specialist (New York City), and *Ken Harris* (New York City).

Lois Thompson, Chris Boughton, and the staff at Malloy Lithographing, Inc., for a fine print job.

Amy Snetzler, Brian Gillespie, Steve Musgrove, and all the anonymous tech support people at Quark, Inc. who e-mailed me with helpful answers to my many questions.

XChange, Inc. for providing me with resources.

Adam Hausman, Macintosh systems specialist, for his layout and testing services.

Judy Susman, proofreader, and *Elliot Linzer,* indexer.

Ted Nace, the founder and original publisher of Peachpit Press, for taking a chance with me as a first-time writer and for giving me the freedom to design and write a QuickStart Guide *my* way.

My parents, *Bert* and *Richard Weinmann,* for being both my parents and an inspiration. ■

A ***character*** *style sheet*

A ***paragraph*** *style sheet*

First and foremost, *Peter Lourekas,* co-author, teacher, artist, and computer wizard,

quark[1] /kwa:k/ *n. Physics* any of a group of (originally three) postulated components of elementary particles Quarks are held to carry a charge one-third or two-thirds that of the proton Many predictions of this theory have been corroborated by experiments but free quarks have yet to be observed. In a sense, quark theory recapitulates at a deeper level efforts earlier this century to explain all atomic properties in terms of electrons, protons, and neutrons [coined by M Gell-Mann, 1964, from phrase 'Three quarks for Muster Mark!' in James Joyce's *Finnegans Wake* (1939)]

quark[2] /kwa:k/ *n.* a type of low-fat curd cheese.

From The Oxford Encyclopedic English Dictionary, 1991, Oxford University Press

Table of Contents 

The basics 1

"Beauty! I've starved myself since you forgot about me. Now at least I shall die in peace..."
"Live!" cried Beauty. "And let us marry. How could I live without you, my dearest Beast?"

1 *A text box with a frame.*

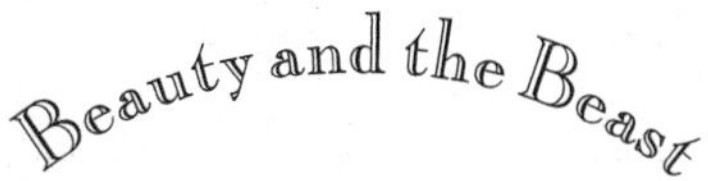

2 *Text on a path.*

3 *A picture in a picture box. This box has a delicate .5 point frame applied to it.*

4 *A picture in a box without a frame.*

What is QuarkXPress?

QuarkXPress is a page layout application. A page layout application is a central gathering place for text, pictures, lines, and other graphic elements, all of which together compose a page or a series of pages. QuarkXPress can be used to produce anything from a tiny hang tag for a line of apparel to a multiple-volume encyclopedia. A finished document can be output on a home laser printer (newsletter, party invitation, etc.), output on a high-end imagesetter for final printing by a commercial printer (book, magazine, brochure, etc.), or exported for on-line viewing.

This chapter is a reference guide to the basic QuarkXPress features. In the remaining chapters you'll learn how to actually build pages and page elements.

The QuarkXPress building blocks

- To place text on a page, you must type or import text into a rectangular or irregularly-shaped ***text box*** **1** or along the edge of a Bézier ***text path*** **2**.

  Similarly, to place a picture on a page, you must first create a container for it, whether it's a simple retangular or intricate Bézier ***picture box***. Then you can import a picture into it. If you want the border of a text or picture box to print, you must apply a frame to it **3**–**4**.

  A fourth type of page element, a ***line***, can be straight or curved.

- A text box, text path, picture box, or line is called an ***item***. The picture or text a box contains is called its ***contents***. A picture or text box can also be rendered ***contentless***, after which it functions strictly as a colored shape.

- Tool selection is the first step in many of the instructions in this book. To create an item, for example, you'll use an item creation tool (logically), like the Line tool or the Rectangle text box tool.

  To move a whole item or a group of items across a page, you'll use the ***Item*** tool 1, since you'll be working with the overall container.

  To copy/paste, delete, or restyle text or a picture after it's input or imported, you'll use the ***Content*** tool 2, since you'll be working with the contents of, not the outside of, the container.

  For some tasks the Item and Content tools are interchangeable. For example, the Content tool can be used to reshape or resize items, or select multiple items. The Item tool can be used to import a picture.

- An item or its contents must be ***selected*** before either one can be modified 3–4.
- The readouts on the ***Measurements*** palette will vary depending on which tool and which kind of item are currently selected (1, next page). The left side of the Measurements palette displays information pertaining to an item—a picture box, text box, text path, or line—if that item and the Item or Content tool are selected. Item information includes dimensions and location on the page.

  The right side of the Measurements palette displays content information about a picture or text, such as its size, if that item and the Content tool are selected (2, next page). The right side of the Measurements palette displays line style and width information if a line and the Item or Content tool are selected. The palette is blank when no items are selected (3, next page).

The two workhorse tools

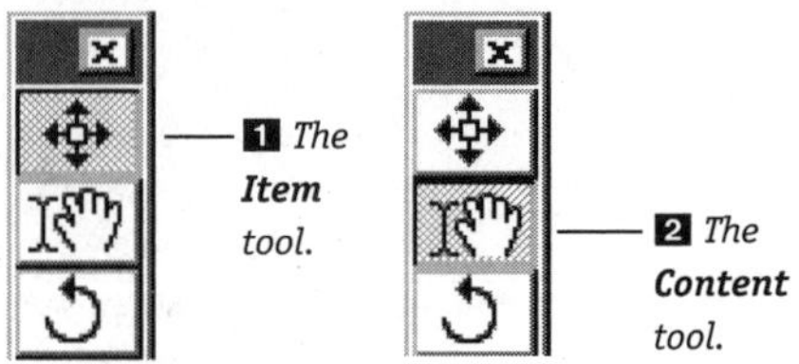

1 *The **Item** tool.*

2 *The **Content** tool.*

3 *A picture box that is **not selected.***

4 *Eight handles display when a box is **selected.***

1 *The Measurements palette when the **Item** tool and a **text box** are selected.*

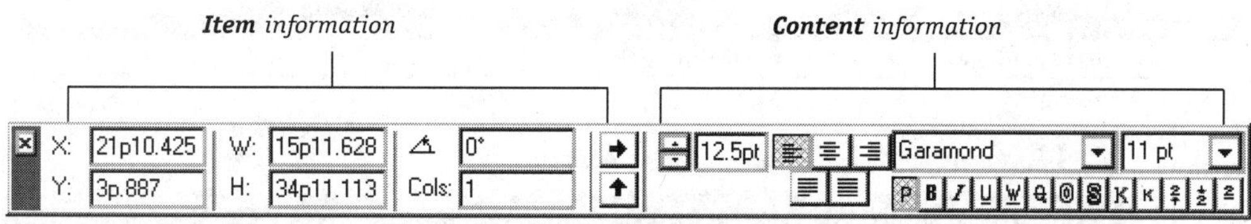

2 *The Measurements palette when the **Content** tool and **text** are selected.*

3 *The Measurements palette is **blank** when **no** items are selected. Select an item to make the palette light up.*

If it's not one thing it's another

My first encounter with QuarkXPress was in 1988 (ancient history, in the software world), and I was impressed with its precision, but frustrated by the inflexibility of its parent/child architecture. New items were drawn inside—and were constrained by—existing items.

Now QuarkXPress is as flexible as it originally was brittle. Not only can you place an item anywhere, you can turn just about anything (text box, text path, picture box, or line) into something else **4**–**5**. If you're brand new to QuarkXPress (or are chronically indecisive), just ignore this aspect of QuarkXPress for the moment. But just to whet your appetite, these are a few of the easy conversions you can make:

- Change a text box into a picture box, a line into a box or a text path, and vice versa.
- Make a text or picture box contentless—capable only of being recolored or resized (the contents of either kind of box are deleted during the conversion).
- Change a standard box into a Bézier box or Bézier line, or vice versa.
- Change a text character into a picture box.

4 *Via the Item menu > **Shape** submenu, you can change a box into a line or a standard box into a Bézier box, and perform other conversions.*

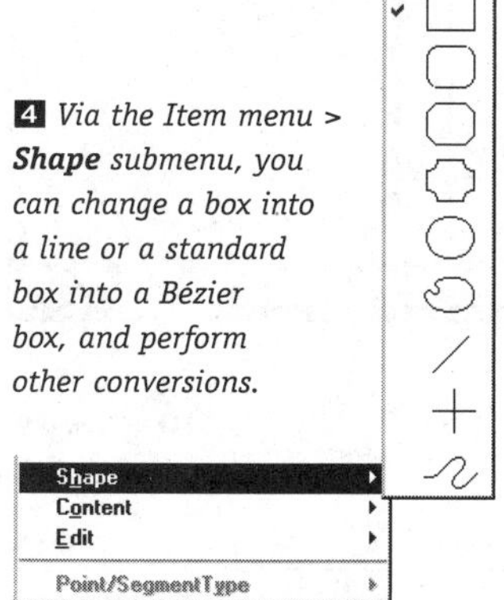

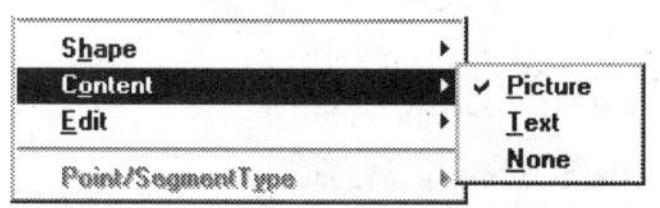

5 *Using the Item menu > **Content** submenu, you can change a text box into a picture box, or vice versa, or make either one contentless.*

The QuarkXPress screen

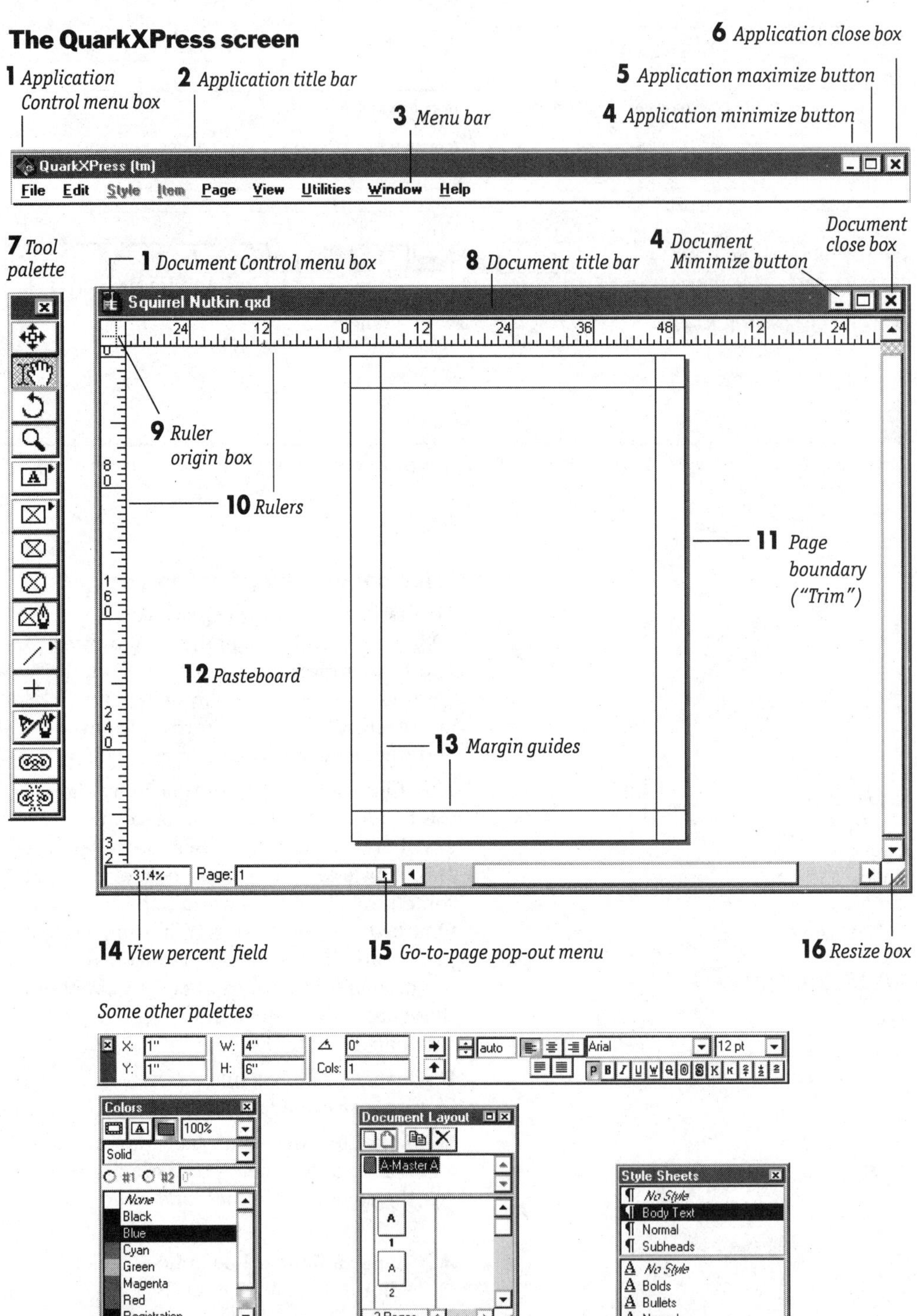

1 Application Control menu box
2 Application title bar
3 Menu bar
4 Application minimize button
5 Application maximize button
6 Application close box
QuarkXPress (tm)
File Edit Style Item Page View Utilities Window Help
7 Tool palette
1 Document Control menu box
8 Document title bar
4 Document Mimimize button
Document close box
Squirrel Nutkin.qxd
9 Ruler origin box
10 Rulers
11 Page boundary ("Trim")
12 Pasteboard
13 Margin guides
31.4%
Page: 1
14 View percent field
15 Go-to-page pop-out menu
16 Resize box
Some other palettes
X: 1"
Y: 1"
W: 4"
H: 6"
0°
Cols: 1
auto
Arial
12 pt
Colors
100%
Solid
#1
#2
None
Black
Blue
Cyan
Green
Magenta
Red
Registration
Document Layout
A-Master A
2 Pages
Style Sheets
No Style
Body Text
Normal
Subheads
No Style
Bolds
Bullets
Normal

The QuarkXPress Screen

Key to the QuarkXPress screen

1 ***Application (or document) Control menu box***
The application Control menu box commands are: Restore, Move, Size, Minimize, Maximize, and Close. The document Control menu box commands are: Restore, Move, Size, Minimize, Maximize, Close, and Next.

2 ***Application title bar***
The application title bar contains the name of the application. If a document is maximized, the document name will appear in the application title bar.

3 ***Menu bar***
Press any menu heading to access dialog boxes, submenus, and commands. XTensions are also accessed via the menu bar.

4 ***Application (or document) minimize button***
Click the application minimize button to shrink the application to an icon on the task bar. Click the icon on the task bar to restore the application window to its previous size.

Click the document minimize button to shrink the document to an icon at the bottom left corner of the application window. Click the icon to restore the document window to its previous size.

5 ***Application (or document) maximize/restore button***
Click the application or document restore button to restore a window to its previous size. When a window is at the restored size, the restore button turns into the maximize button. Click the maximize button to enlarge the window.

6 ***Close box***
To close the application or a document, dialog box, or palette, click its close box.

7 ***Tool palette***
One of many moveable palettes. The Tools, Measurements, Document Layout, Style Sheets, Colors, Trap Information, Lists, and Index palettes open from the View menu. Open a library palette via File menu > Open.

8 ***Document title bar***
The document's title appears here. Press and drag the title bar to move the document within the application window (this won't work if the document is maximized).

9 ***Ruler origin box***
Press and drag from the ruler origin box to reposition the intersection of the horizontal and vertical rulers (the "zero point"). Click the ruler origin box again to reset the zero point to the uppermost left corner of the page.

10 ***Rulers***
Ruler increments can be displayed in one of eight measurement systems: inches, inches decimal, picas, points, millimeters, centimeters, ciceros, or agates. Choose View menu > Show Rulers or Hide Rulers. Non-printing guides can be dragged from the vertical and horizontal rulers to aid in the layout process.

11 ***Page boundary***
The edge (trim size) of the page.

12 ***Pasteboard***
The pasteboard functions as a scratchboard for creating page elements or as a holding area for storing page elements for later use.

13 ***Margin guides***
The non-printing margin guides are displayed for layout purposes only. Choose View menu > Show Guides or Hide Guides.

14 ***View percent field***
The view size of a document is displayed, and can be modified, via this field.

15 ***Go-to-page pop-out menu***
Display a document or master page by choosing it from this menu.

16 ***Resize box***
Press and drag this box to resize the document window.

The Tool palette

The Tool palette contains 28 tools for item creation, editing, and linking. To open the Tool palette, choose View menu > Show Tools (F8). Choose a visible tool by clicking on it; choose a hidden tool from a pop-out menu.

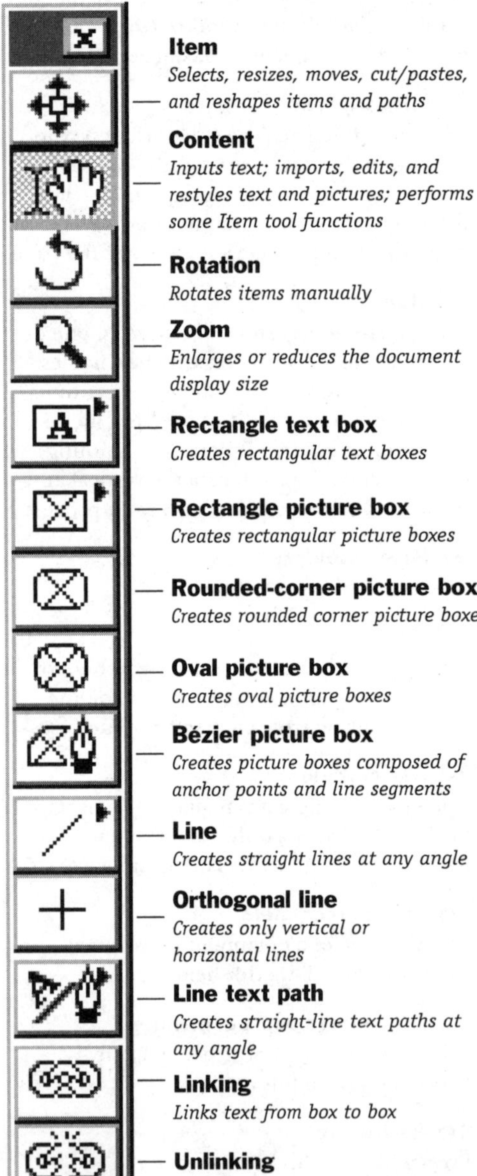
Item
Selects, resizes, moves, cut/pastes, and reshapes items and paths
Content
Inputs text; imports, edits, and restyles text and pictures; performs some Item tool functions
Rotation
Rotates items manually
Zoom
Enlarges or reduces the document display size
Rectangle text box
Creates rectangular text boxes
Rectangle picture box
Creates rectangular picture boxes
Rounded-corner picture box
Creates rounded corner picture boxes
Oval picture box
Creates oval picture boxes
Bézier picture box
Creates picture boxes composed of anchor points and line segments
Line
Creates straight lines at any angle
Orthogonal line
Creates only vertical or horizontal lines
Line text path
Creates straight-line text paths at any angle
Linking
Links text from box to box
Unlinking
Unlinks text boxes

TOOL TIPS

- When you select a tool from a pop-out menu, it becomes the tool of that type that is displayed on the toolbar. To add a tool from a pop-out menu to the tool bar as a separate, visible tool, hold down Ctrl as you choose the tool. Ctrl-click a tool to restore it to its pop-out menu. The last-used Tool palette configuration will remain in effect when you re-launch QuarkXPress.
- To select the next tool in the Tool palette using the keyboard, hold down Ctrl-Alt and press Tab. To select the previous tool, hold down Ctrl-Alt-Shift and press Tab.
- Hold down Alt and select any item creation or linking tool to keep it selected. To deselect a tool, click on another tool.
- Double-click a tool to set preferences for it (see page 284).
- Speaking of tool tips, if the Show Tools Tips box is checked in Edit menu > Preferences > Application > Interactive folder tab, you can rest the pointer on a visible tool or palette icon and its name will appear on the screen.

Tools on the default pop-out menus

Text box tools

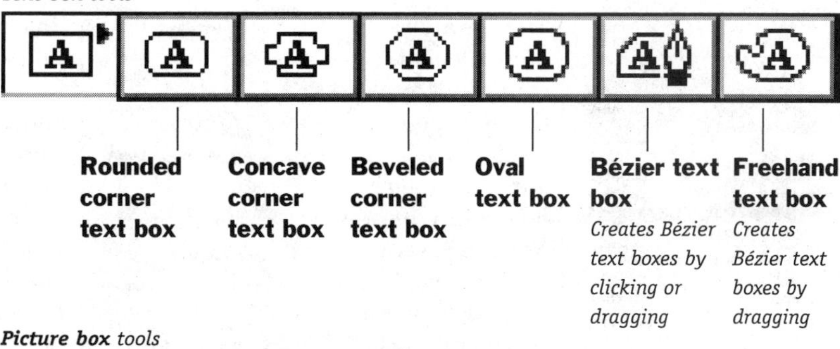

Picture box tools

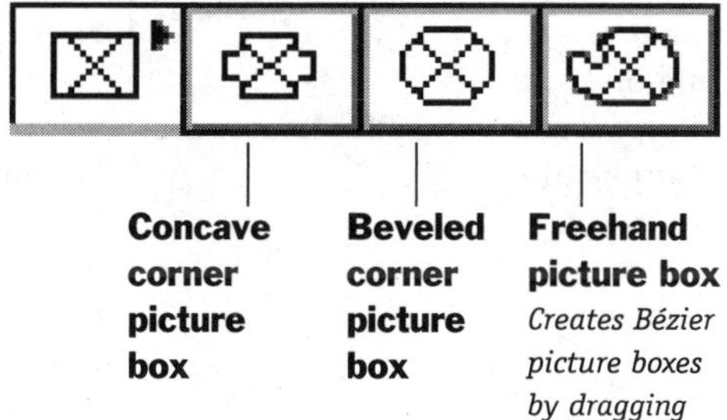

Line tools

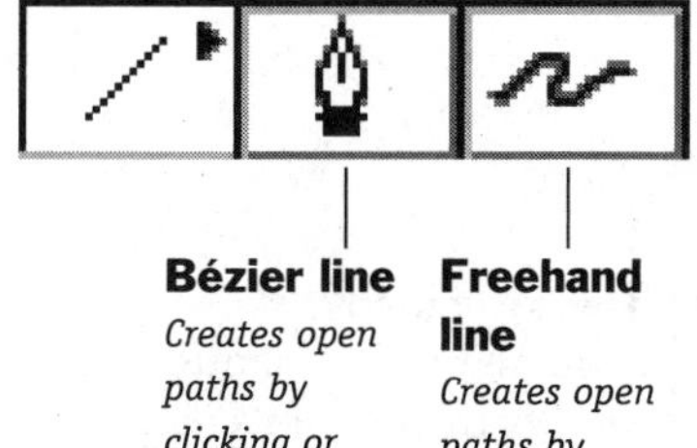

Text path tools

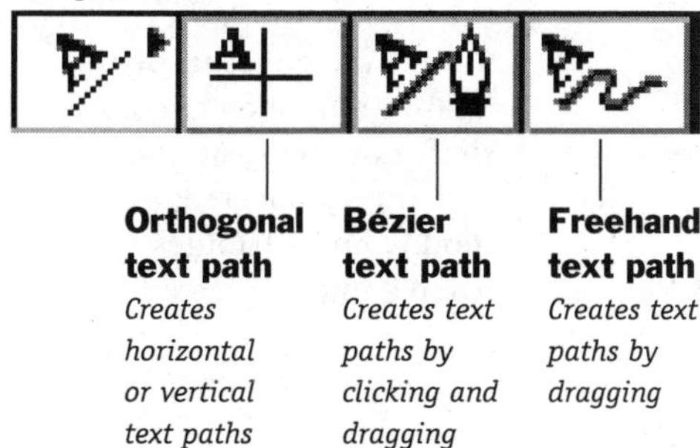

The QuarkXPress menus

File
New
Open... Ctrl+O
Close
Save Ctrl+S
Save as... Ctrl+Alt+S
Revert to Saved
Get Text... Ctrl+E
Save Text... Ctrl+Alt+E
Append... Ctrl+Alt+A
Save Page as EPS... Ctrl+Alt+Shift+S
Collect for Output...
Document Setup... Ctrl+Alt+Shift+P
Page Setup... Ctrl+Alt+P
Print... Ctrl+P
Exit Ctrl+Q

The File menu

Most File menu commands apply to the document as a whole, such as creating, opening a file, library, or book or closing, saving, or printing a file. Other File menu commands include exporting text, importing text and pictures, and exiting the application.

Edit
Undo Drag Move Ctrl+Z
Cut Ctrl+X
Copy Ctrl+C
Paste Ctrl+V
Paste Special...
Delete
Select All Ctrl+A
Links...
Object
Insert Object...
Show Clipboard
Find/Change Ctrl+F
Preferences
Style Sheets... Shift+F11
Colors... Shift+F12
H&Js... Ctrl+Shift+F11
Lists...
Dashes & Stripes...
Print Styles...

The Edit menu

Edit menu commands include Select All and Delete, the Clipboard functions, Find/Change for searching and replacing text and/or attributes, Preferences for setting defaults, Style Sheets, Colors, H&Js (hyphenation and justification settings), Lists, and Dashes & Stripes. The Undo command will undo the last modification made. Choose Redo if you change your mind again.

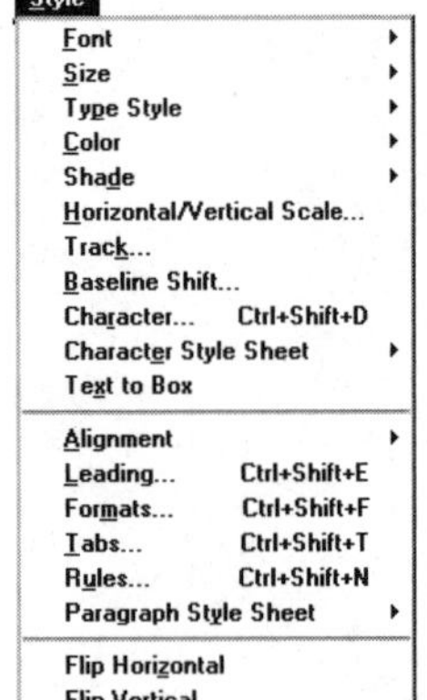

***Text** selected.*

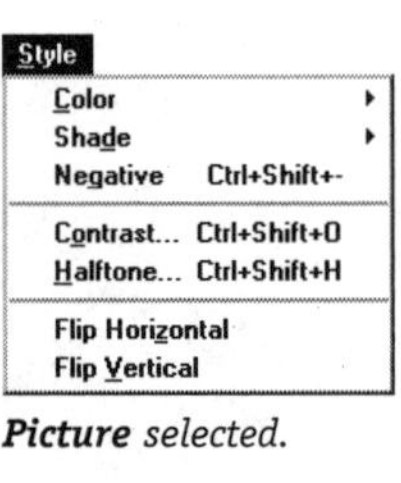

***Picture** selected.*

Style
Line Style
Arrowheads
Width
Color
Shade

***Line** selected.*

The Style menu

Style menu commands modify the contents of a text box, including typographic specifications and paragraph formatting when text is selected using the Content tool; they modify the contents of a picture box, such as color, shade, or contrast, when a picture is selected; they modify line attributes when a line is selected.

Item	
Modify...	Ctrl+M
Frame...	Ctrl+B
Runaround...	Ctrl+T
Clipping...	Ctrl+Alt+T
Duplicate	Ctrl+D
Step and Repeat...	Ctrl+Alt+D
Delete	Ctrl+K
Group	Ctrl+G
Ungroup	Ctrl+U
Constrain	
Lock	F6
Merge	▸
Split	▸
Send Backward	Ctrl+Shift+F5
Send to Back	Shift+F5
Bring Forward	Ctrl+F5
Bring to Front	F5
Space/Align...	Ctrl+,
Shape	▸
Content	▸
Edit	▸
Point/SegmentType	▸

The Item menu
Item menu commands modify items—text boxes, pictures boxes, and lines. Deleting, framing, grouping, duplicating, locking, aligning, and layering are some Item commands. The Item menu is available only when an item is selected.

Page	
Insert...	
Delete...	
Move...	
Master Guides...	
Section...	
Previous	
Next	
First	
Last	
Go to...	Ctrl+J
Display	▸

The Page menu
Page menu commands are used to add, delete, and number pages, move through a document, and modify master guides.

View	
Fit in Window	Ctrl+0
50%	
75%	
✔ Actual Size	Ctrl+1
200%	
Thumbnails	Shift+F6
Hide Guides	F7
Show Baseline Grid	Ctrl+F7
✔ Snap to Guides	Shift+F7
Hide Rulers	Ctrl+R
Show Invisibles	Ctrl+I
Hide Tools	F8
Hide Measurements	F9
Show Document Layout	F4
Show Style Sheets	F11
Show Colors	F12
Show Trap Information	Ctrl+F12
Show Lists	Ctrl+F11
Show Index	

The View menu
View menu commands control document view sizes and the display of guides, rulers, invisibles, and palettes.

Utilities	
Check Spelling	▸
Auxiliary Dictionary...	
Edit Auxiliary...	
Suggested Hyphenation...	Ctrl+H
Hyphenation Exceptions...	
Usage...	
XTensions Manager...	
PPD Manager...	
Build Index...	
Use CPSI Fixer	
Tracking Edit...	
Kerning Table Edit...	

The Utilities menu
Utilities menu commands include miscellaneous functions, such as checking spelling, hyphenation, picture and font usage, the XTensions and PPD Managers, indexing, and tracking and kerning tables.

Dialog boxes

Dialog boxes are like fill-in forms with multiple choices. The various methods of indicating one's choices are shown in the illustrations on this and the next page. Numbers can be typed into fields in any of the seven measurement systems used in QuarkXPress. Click OK or press Enter to exit a dialog box and implement the indicated changes.

A dialog box can be opened from a menu or via its assigned keyboard shortcut. A dialog box will open when any menu item that is followed by an ellipsis (…) is selected.

TIP In any dialog box, press Tab to highlight the next field. Hold down Shift and press Tab to highlight the previous field.

TIP For some dialog boxes, you can use the Ctrl-Z shortcut while the dialog box is open to reset its values to those that were in effect when it was opened.

Unfortunately, many of the QuarkXPress 4.0 dialog boxes are larger than before, which makes it difficult to preview changes in a document. To ***move*** *a dialog box out of the way, press and drag its title bar. Click the Apply button, if there is one, to preview.*

A downward-pointing arrowhead opens into a drop-down menu.

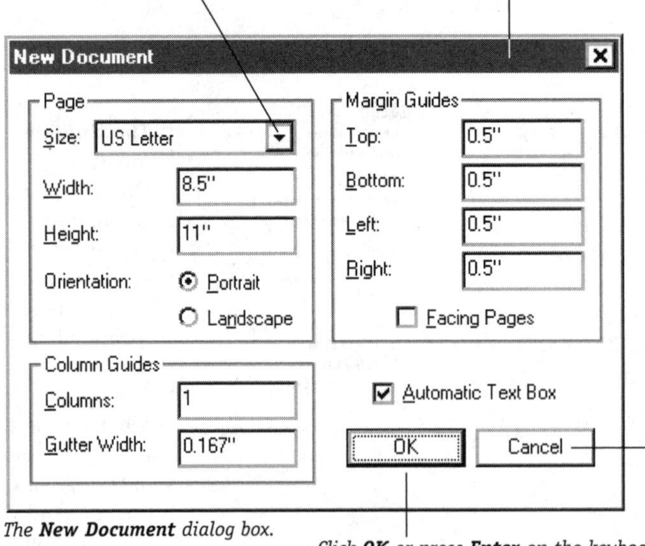

Click ***Cancel*** *(or press* ***Esc****) to exit a box with no changes taking effect.*

The ***New Document*** *dialog box.*

Click ***OK*** *or press* ***Enter*** *on the keyboard to exit a box and accept the new settings. You can press Enter for any button that has a double border, like Save.*

Folder tabs: while you're at it...

In QuarkXPress 4.0, related dialog boxes are housed under one roof. For example, if you choose Item menu > Modify, the Modify dialog box will open, of course, but at the top of the dialog box, you'll also see folder tabs for related dialog boxes lined up across the top. Click a folder tab to access a related dialog box. With the Modify dialog box open for a picture, for example, you may see the Box, Picture, Frame, Runaround, and Clipping folder tabs. It's like one-stop shopping: Change the Vertical Alignment for a text box first, click the Frame folder tab, choose frame specifications, click the Box folder tab, and add a background color—all from one convenient central hub. Oversized and in the way, but convenient.

*Click a **folder tab** to access a related dialog box. Once a dialog box is open, you can press Ctrl-Tab to cycle through related folder tabs.*

*A **Check box** option can be clicked on or off. A "√" in a check box indicates that option is turned on.*

*If more than one value exists within the currently selected text or items, the corresponding field will be **blank** (as in the Left Indent field in this screen shot). For example, if highlighted text contains 8 pt. and 12 pt. leading, the Leading field will be blank.*

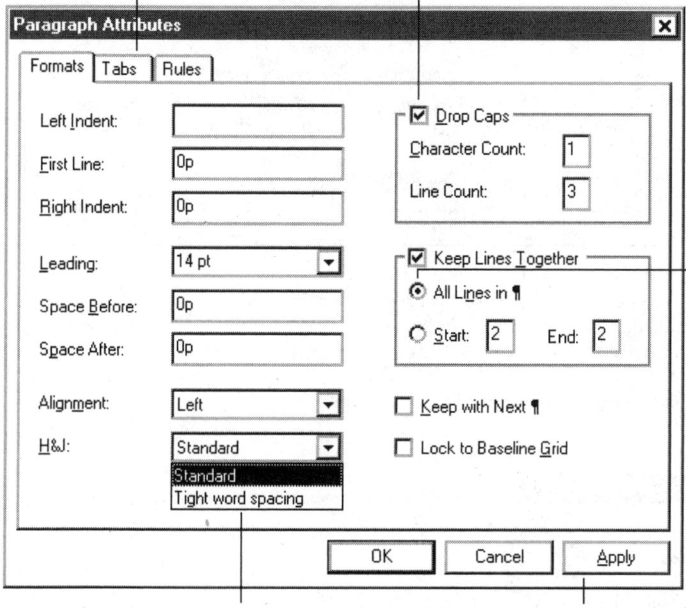

*A radio **button** can be clicked on or off. Only one button can be selected per group.*

Press and drag to choose from a drop-down or pop-up menu.

*Click **Apply** (Alt-A) to preview modifications in the document while the dialog box is open. Hold down Alt and click Apply to turn on continuous Apply mode. Hold down Alt and click Apply again to turn off continuous Apply mode.*

SPEEDTIP

Folder Tabs

The QuarkXPress palettes

The Measurements palette

The Measurements palette contains some of the commands and options that are available under the menus. The information on the Measurements palette changes depending on what kind of item and tool are selected. The palette is blank when no items are selected.

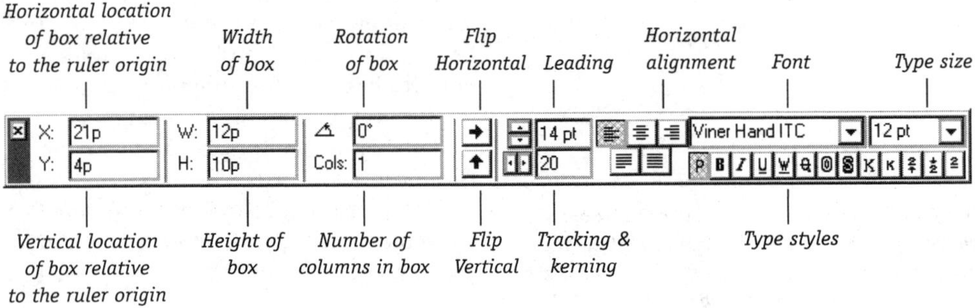

*The Measurements palette with the Content tool and a **text box** selected.*

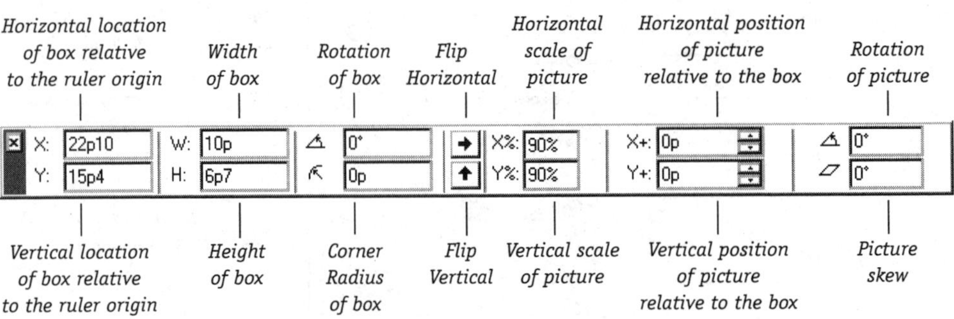

*The Measurements palette with the Content tool and a **picture box** selected.*

MEASUREMENTS PALETTE SHORTCUTS

Open the palette	F9
Highlight the first field	Ctrl-Alt-M
Highlight Font field	Ctrl-Alt-Shift-M
Highlight next field	Tab
Highlight previous field	Shift-Tab
Exit palette without applying changes	Esc

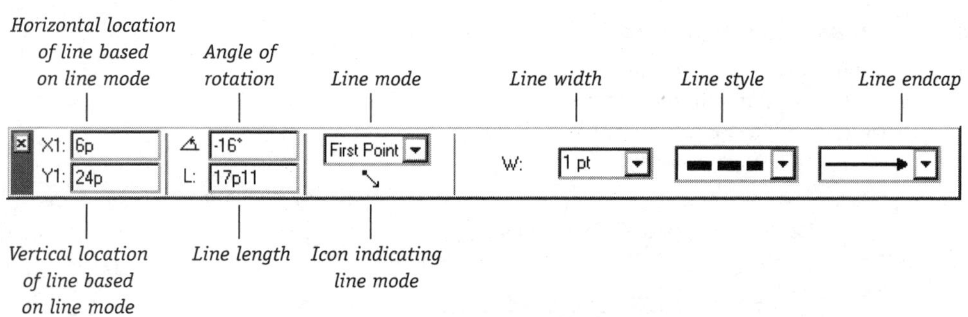

The Measurements palette with the Content tool and a ***line*** *selected.*

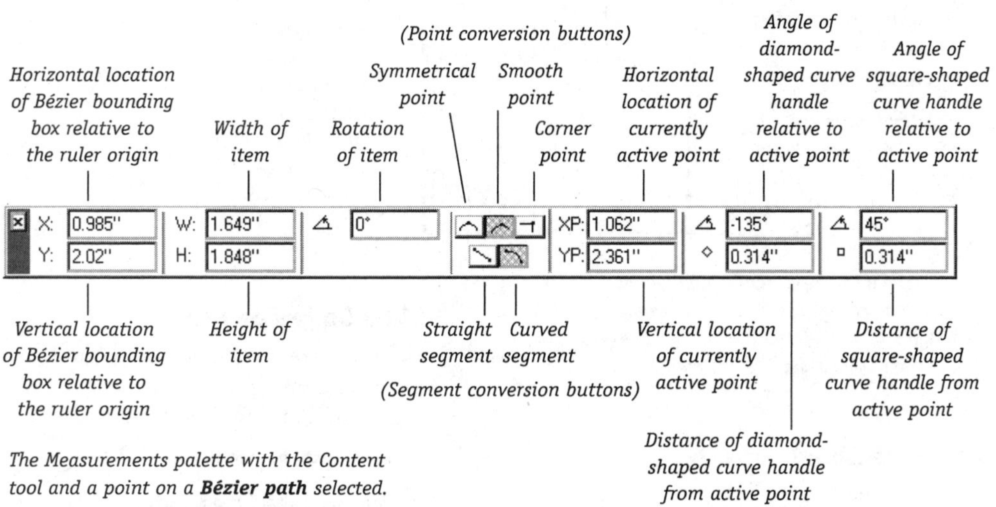

The Measurements palette with the Content tool and a point on a ***Bézier path*** *selected.*

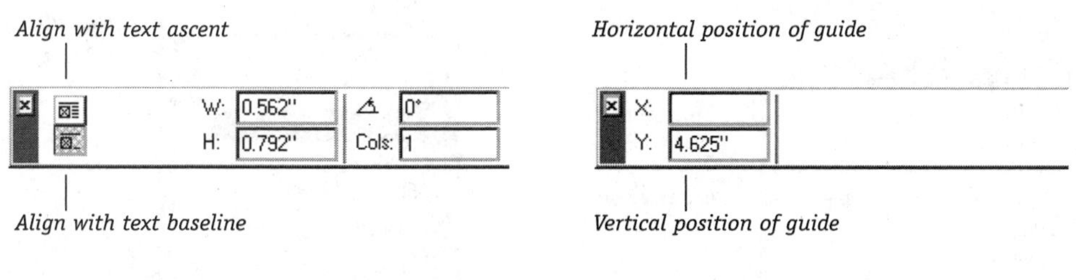

The left side of the Measurements palette with the Content tool and an ***anchored box*** *selected.*

The left side of the Measurements palette as a guide is dragged from the top (horizontal) ruler.

Measurements Palette

The Document Layout palette

The Document Layout palette is used to rearrange, insert, and delete document pages, move through a document, and create, modify, and apply master pages.

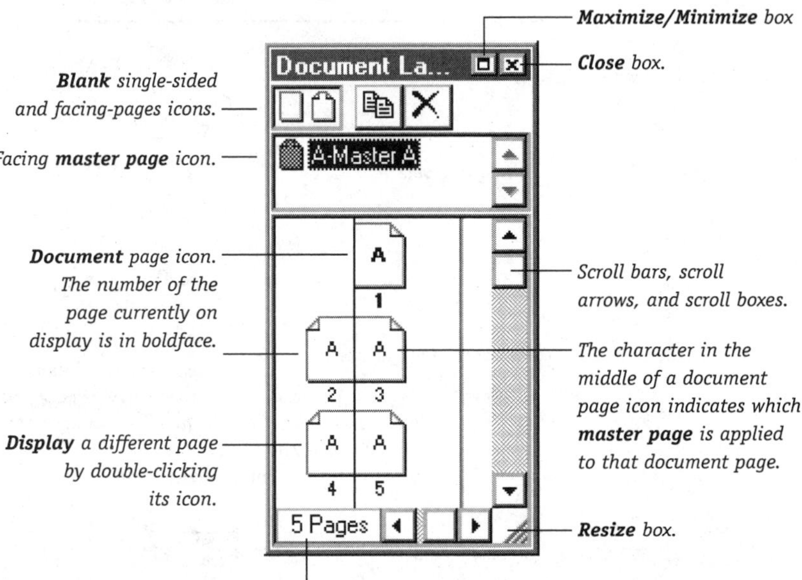

The Style Sheets palette

The Style Sheets palette is used to apply style sheets, which are sets of multiple character or paragraph specifications.

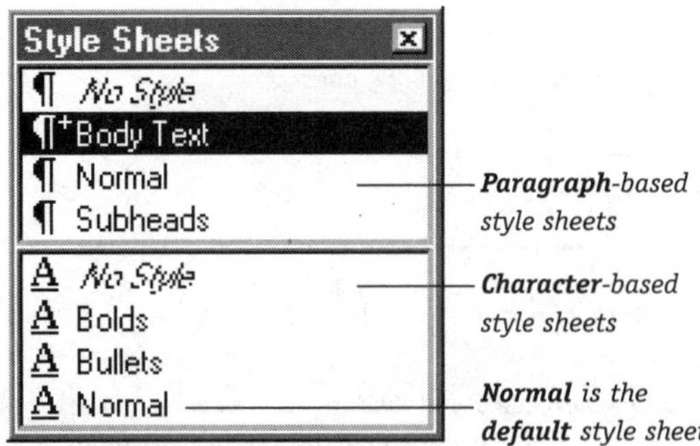

The Colors palette

The Colors palette is used to apply colors to text, pictures, boxes, and lines, and to create blends.

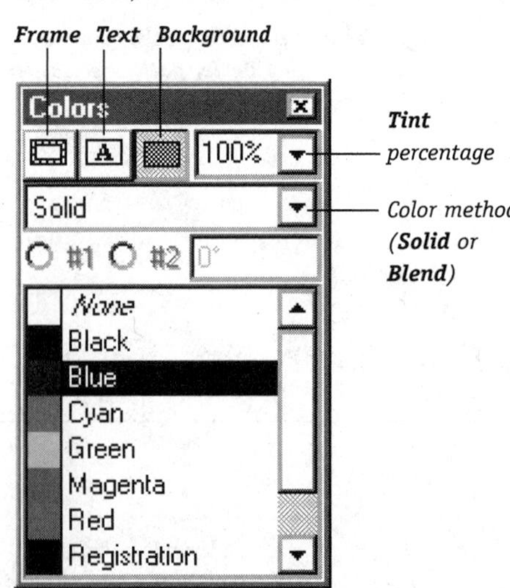

The Index palette

An index is constructed by marking each individual entry for indexing in the actual document, and then using the Index palette to assign formatting specifications for how each entry will appear in the index, such as its style and level of indentation.

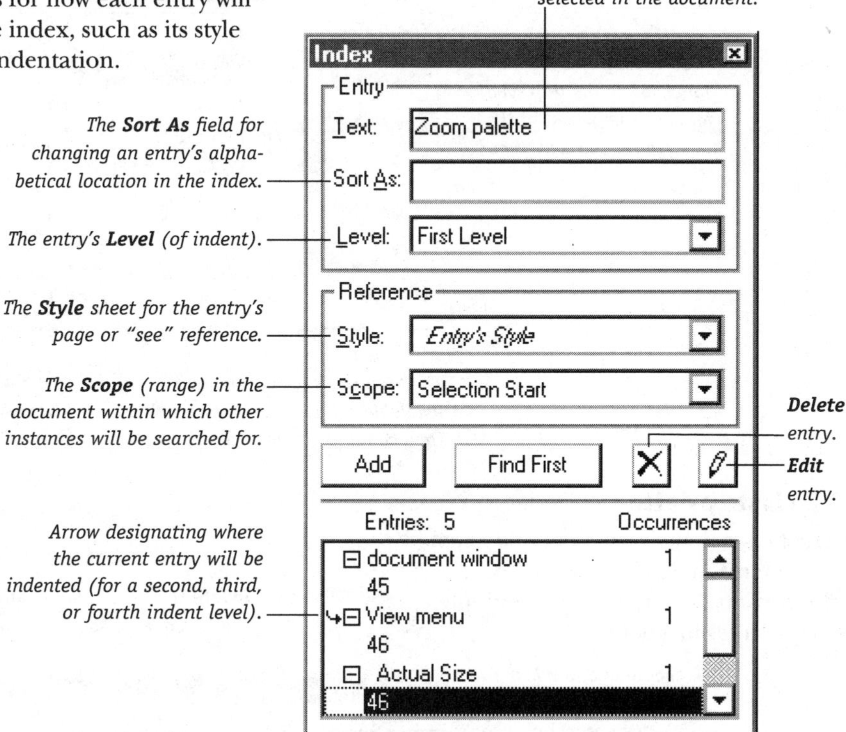

The Profile Information palette

The Profile Information palette is used to display the current characteristics of a selected picture and/or change its color profile for color management.

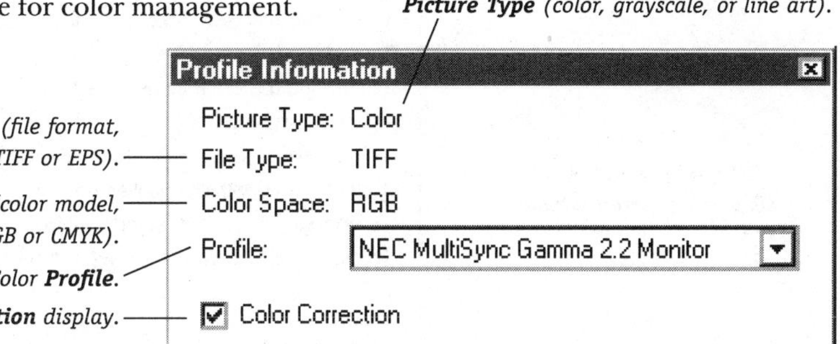

Index Palette

The Trap Information palette

The Trap Information palette is used to assign trapping specifications on an object-by-object basis.

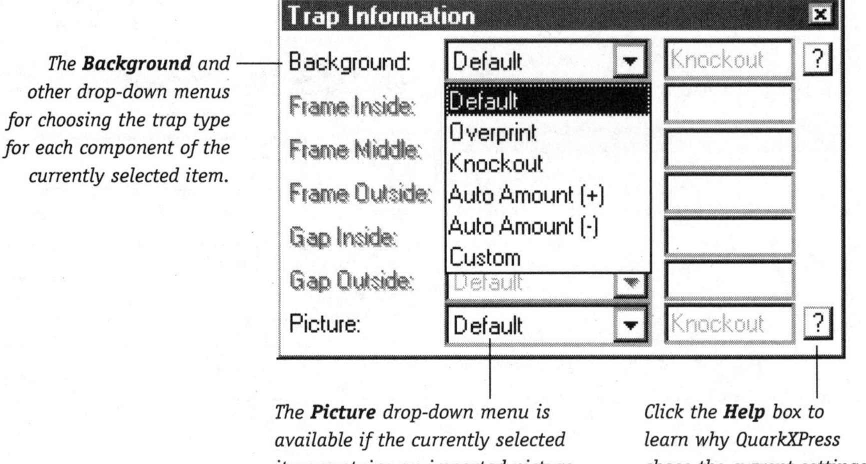

*The **Background** and other drop-down menus for choosing the trap type for each component of the currently selected item.*

*The **Picture** drop-down menu is available if the currently selected item contains an imported picture.*

*Click the **Help** box to learn why QuarkXPress chose the current settings.*

The Lists palette

The Lists palette is used to build a table of contents or an alphabetized list in the current document or for multiple chapter files in a book.

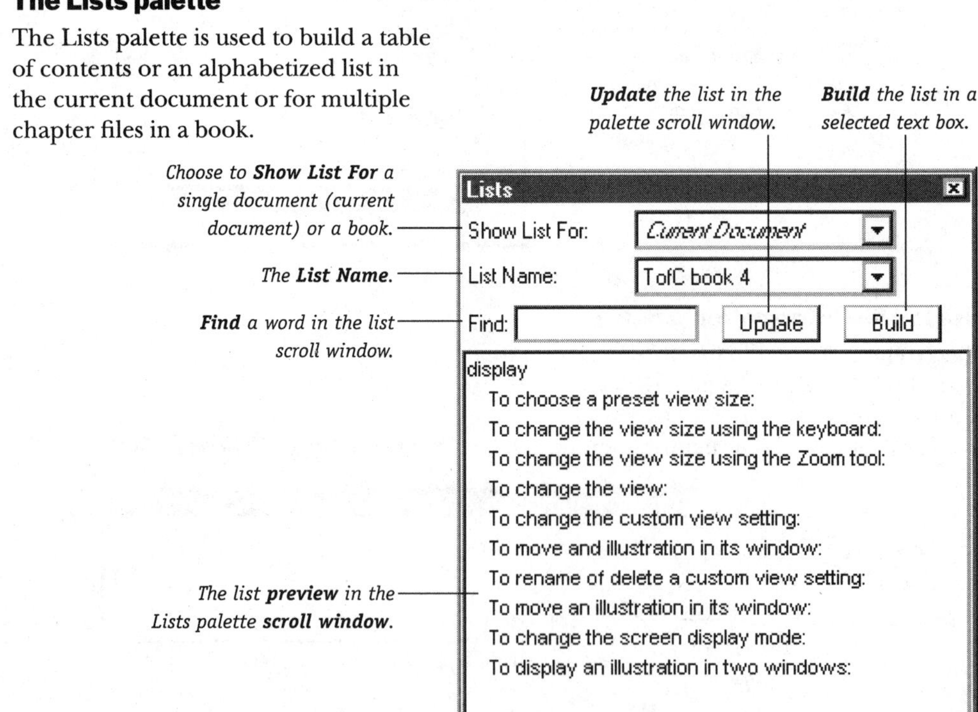

***Update** the list in the palette scroll window.*

***Build** the list in a selected text box.*

*Choose to **Show List For** a single document (current document) or a book.*

*The **List Name**.*

***Find** a word in the list scroll window.*

*The list **preview** in the Lists palette **scroll window**.*

Trap Information Palette; Lists Palette

The Find/Change palette

The Find/Change palette is used to search for and replace text characters, paragraph- or character-based style sheets, fonts, point sizes, or type styles.

The text, style sheets, and attributes to be searched for are entered or chosen in the ***Find What*** *area.*

The text, style sheets, and attributes to be changed to are entered or chosen in the ***Change To*** *area.*

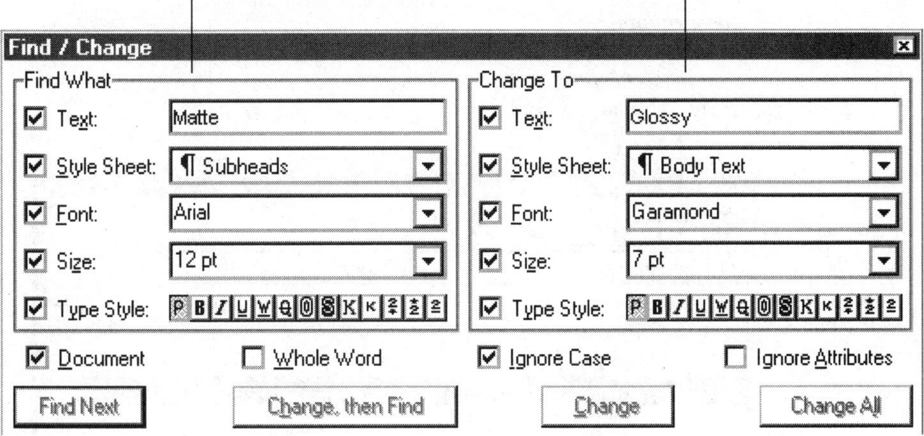

A library palette

An unlimited number of library palettes can be created by the user, and more than one palette can be open at a time. The palette is used to store any page elements—picture boxes (with or without pictures), text boxes (with or without text), lines, text paths, or groups. To add an entry to a library, simply drag it into the palette. To retrieve an item or group from a library, drag it from the library onto your document page.

You can assign a ***label*** *to each entry in a library, and then display all the entries at once or display them selectively by label category via this drop-down menu.*

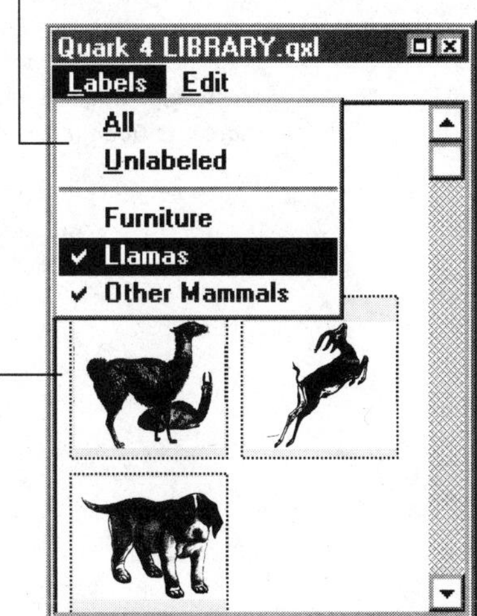

Library entries display as thumbnails on a library palette.

A book palette

A book is a collection of individual chapter files in which style sheets, colors, H&Js, lists, and dashes & stripes are synchronized. For each book there is a book palette that's used to add/delete, reorder, and print chapters.

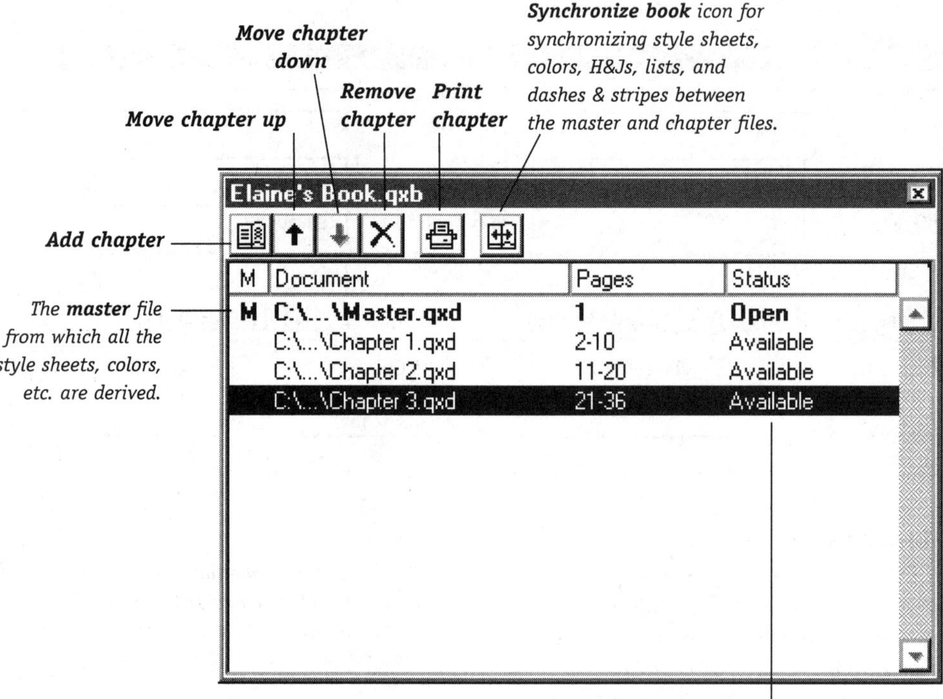

*The **Status** column indicates whether a chapter is currently **Available, Modified,** or **Missing.** This column also indicates to all the members of a network whether a chapter is **Open** at the current station or open on **another station.***

SHRINKING PALETTES

To conserve screen space, any palette or window that you're not using can be shrunk down to a gray bar. Double-click the window or palette title bar to shrink; double-click it again to enlarge.

A library palette shrunk down by double-clicking its title bar.

WHERE TO BUY 'EM

For a list of XTension distributors, visit the Quark web site: www.quark.com. You can download the free TypeTricks XTension from this site.

You can purchase extensions from ThePowerXChange (thepowerxchange.com), 877-940-0600

Some XTensions are sold directly by the manufacturer. For example, you can purchase QX-Effects and QX-Tools from Extensis (800-796-9798).

XTending XPress with Xtensions

What is an XTension?

QuarkXPress doesn't do everything. In fact, one of its great selling features is that third-party developers have written software modules for the program, called XTensions, that extend or enhance its features. Some XTensions are sold individually; others are sold as part of a collection.

Quite a few XTensions are mentioned in this book, but they are a few in a very big bucket full of useful tools. You can start to explore them by browsing through one of the on-line or printed XTension catalogs.

Where should I install them?

In order to use an XTension in XPress, it must be installed in the XTension folder inside the QuarkXPress application folder. Some XTensions come with an installer that will do the job for you; others must be copied manually into the XTension folder. If an installer places an XTension in the QuarkXPress folder but not in the XTension folder, make sure to drag it into the XTension folder yourself.

Once an XTension has been correctly installed on your hard drive, you can use the XTensions Manager feature within the application to enable or disable it (see pages 285–287). The program must be re-launched for a newly enabled XTension to be available.

To control whether the XTensions Manager will open upon launching QuarkXPress, use Edit menu > Preferences > Application > XTensions folder tab (see page 280).

On-screen help

To access on-screen help, choose Help menu > Help Topics (F1). Click Contents to choose from a list of general topics, or click Index to choose from a more detailed index **1**, or click Find to search for a topic by entering a key word or phrase. Double-click a topic to read about it **2**.

TIP To bring up a Help screen for any visible item, choose Help menu > What's This. A question mark appears next to the cursor. Click on any visible object.

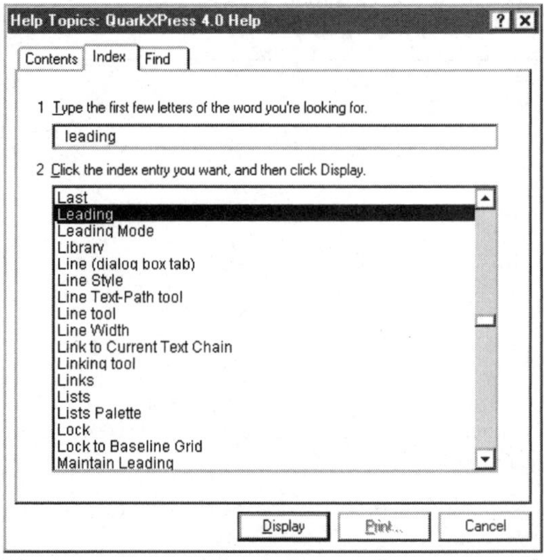

1 *Click **Contents, Index,** or **Find** in QuarkXPress 4.0 Help.*

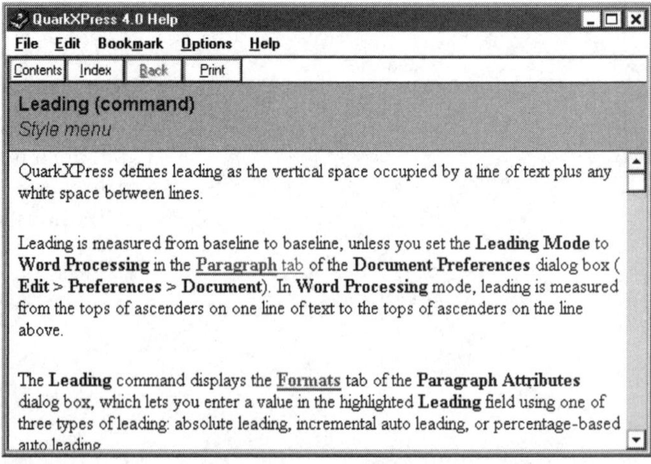

2 *A Help window. Use the scroll bar, if visible, to access further information (or use the mouse wheel, if your mouse has one).*

ABBREVIATIONS

Inches/ Inches Decimal	"
Picas	p
Points	pt *or* p followed by a number (i.e. p6)
Millimeters	mm
Centimeters	cm
Ciceros	c
Agates	ag
quarter of a millimiter	q

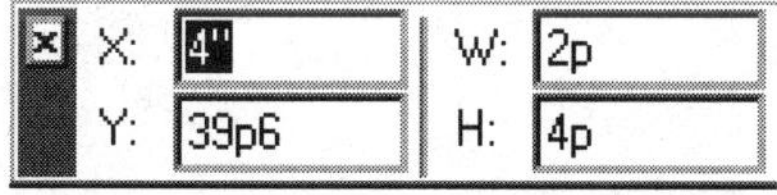

1 *Enter a number in any measurement system used in QuarkXPress.*

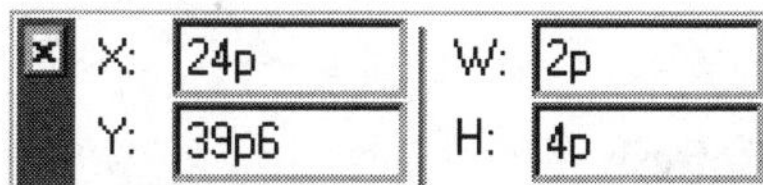

2 *When the Enter key is pressed, the number will convert into the file's current default measurement system.*

The QuarkXPress measurement systems

While numbers in fields are displayed in the current default measurement system, numbers can be entered in any of the other measurement systems used in QuarkXPress.

Any one of these measurement systems can be chosen for a file: inches, inches decimal, picas, points, millimeters, centimeters, and ciceros **1**–**2**. If you enter a value in a measurement system that isn't the current default system, use one of the abbreviations listed at left. You can change the horizontal or vertical measure in Edit menu > Preferences > Document > General folder tab.

TIP Don't enter "pts" for points or "in" for inches—it just won't work.

Picas and points

A pica is a standard unit of measure used in the graphic arts. Six picas equals 1 inch; 1 pica equals 12 points.

Regardless of the current measurement system, points are always used to measure type sizes, leading, rules, frame widths, and line widths.

Picas and points can be combined in the same entry field. For example, to indicate four picas and six points, enter "4p6."

Agates, in case you're wondering, are commonly used for measuring the vertical column length in classified ads.

Using math in a field

To **add**, enter + after the current number, then the amount you want to add. To **subtract**, enter -, then the value you want to subtract. To **multiply**, enter *, then the multiplier. To **divide**, enter /, then the divider. (To divide 38 by 3, for example, enter "38/3".) In each case, press Enter or Tab to perform the math.

Preferences—a sneak preview

Preferences are the default settings that can be chosen for an individual document or for the application as a whole. Chapter 19 is devoted entirely to the Preferences dialog boxes, and some preferences are discussed in individual chapters, where relevant. As you learn QuarkXPress, you may change a preferences setting here or there, and thus gradually familiarize yourself with them. Below is a list of some of the settings that can be changed.

TIP If you add, delete, or edit style sheets (including the Normal style sheet), colors, hyphenation exceptions, H&Js (settings for hyphenation and justication), or an auxiliary dictionary when no documents are open, those specifications will become the new defaults for any subsequently created documents. The same holds true for any Document Preferences that you change while no document is open, such as Ruler units, or Auto Page Insertion or Auto Picture Import on or off. Don't underestimate this enormous time-saver!

SPEED TIP

ONE HAS IT, THE OTHER DOESN'T

Turn on Runaround and/or define a frame for one of the picture box tools, and turn those settings off for a second picture box tool. Change the Corner Radius to zero if you want to create a second rectangular box.

SPEED TIP

A partial listing of preferences

- Margin, ruler, or grid guide colors
- Preview resolution for imported pictures
- Scroll speed
- Smart quotes
- Drag-and-drop text
- Pasteboard width
- Auto save and auto backup
- Auto library save
- Save document position
- Show XTensions manager
- Measurement increment for rulers, dialog boxes, and Measurements palette
- Auto page insertion
- Guides in front or behind
- Auto picture import
- Keep or delete master page items
- Live Refresh
- Baseline grid increment
- Hyphenation method
- Auto kerning
- Flex space width; standard em space
- Text inset, runaround, line width, etc.
- Trapping
- Tool preferences, including style, width, color, shade, and Runaround settings for the Line or text path tools; background color, angle, frame, and Runaround settings for the picture box tools or Bézier tools; background color, number of columns, frame, and Runaround for the text box tools; and the Zoom percentage for each click of the Zoom tool

Startup 2

To launch QuarkXPress:

In Windows 95, click the Start button on the Taskbar **1**, choose Programs, choose QuarkXPress, then click QuarkXPress for Windows.

or

In Explorer, double-click a QuarkXPress file icon. The application will launch and that file will be maximized on screen **2**.

TIP To create a shortcut icon for QuarkXPress on your desktop, open the QuarkXPress folder in Explorer, then drag the QuarkXPress icon to the desktop. (You can create a shortcut for any QuarkXPress document using the same technique.) Right click on the icon to rename it. Double-click on the icon to launch the program.

TIP Once QuarkXPress is running, you can choose it (or any other open application) from the Taskbar at the bottom of the screen **3**

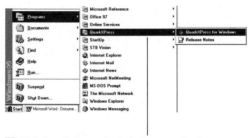

1 *Click **QuarkXPress for Windows** on the **Start** menu.*

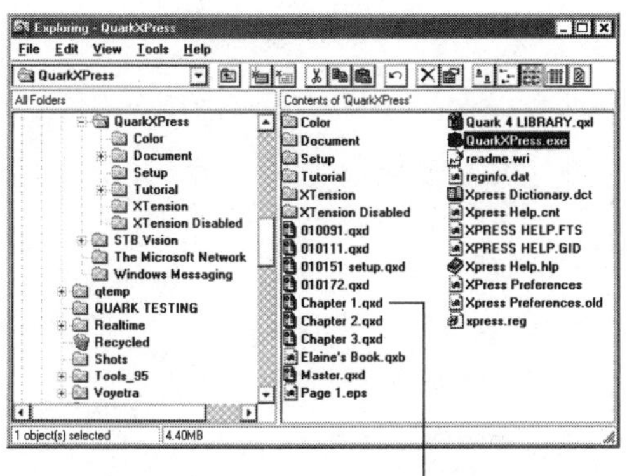

2 *Or double-click any QuarkXPress file icon to launch the application and open that file simultaneously.*

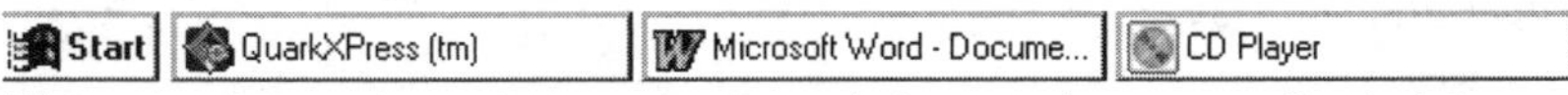

3 *Once QuarkXPress is running, you can choose it (or any other open application) from the Taskbar at the bottom of the screen.*

While the New Document dialog box is open, take a minute and make sure you're satisfied with the current settings before clicking OK. Your choices aren't irrevocable, but it's easier to make them at the outset than it is to fix them later on.

To create a new file:

1. Launch QuarkXPress (instructions on previous page).
2. Choose File menu > New > Document (Ctrl-N). (*Don't* choose File menu > Open—that command opens existing, already saved files.)

Change any of the following settings (press Tab to move from field to field):

3. Choose a preset size from the Size drop-down menu (**1**, next page).
   or
   Enter numbers in the Width and Height fields to create a custom size document. (This is the document size, not the paper size.) You can enter values in any measurement unit used in QuarkXPress.
4. Change the number of Columns.
   and
   Change the Gutter Width if the number of columns is greater than 1.
5. Change any of the Margin Guides. If you turn on Facing Pages, the Left and Right Margin Guides fields will convert to Inside and Outside and the document pages will be stacked in pairs.
6. *Optional:* Click the un-highlighted Orientation button to swap the document's width and height values.
7. Turn on Automatic Text Box to have a text box appear automatically within the margin guides on Master page A and on every document page with which Master page A is associated.
8. Click OK or press Enter. The last used settings in the New Document dialog box will reappear next time it's opened.

1 *Choose a preset **Page Size** or enter a number between 1" and 48" in the **Width** and **Height** fields. A4 Letter is 210 mm x 297 mm, B5 Letter is 182 mm x 257 mm, and Tabloid is 11" x 17". Numbers can be entered in any measurement system used in QuarkXPress.*

***Margin Guides** don't print, but they're useful in the layout process. The **Left** and **Right** fields convert to the **Inside** and **Outside** fields when Facing Pages is turned on.*

*Click the Portrait or Landscape **Orientation** button.*

*Enter a number between 1 and 30 in the **Columns** field.*

*If the number of columns is greater than 1, enter a **Gutter Width** between 3 and 288 points (4").*

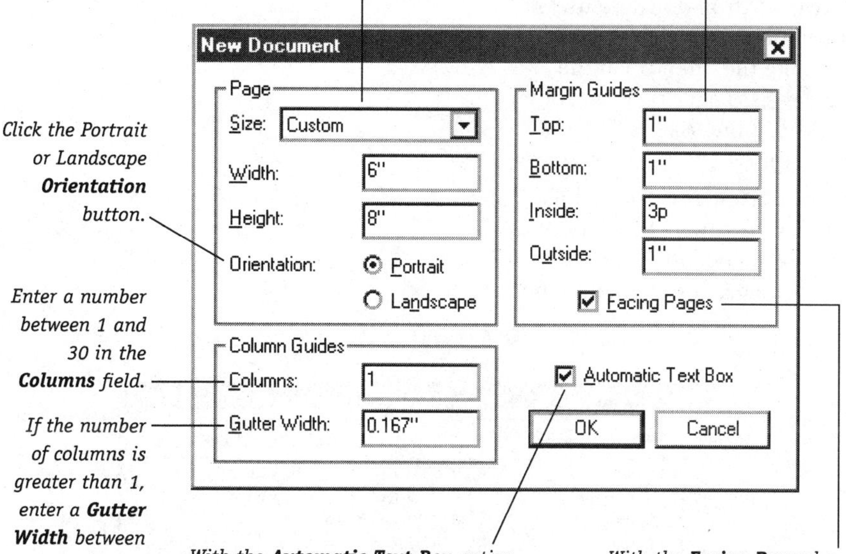

*With the **Automatic Text Box** option checked, a text box containing the number of columns and gutter width specified in the Column Guides fields will appear on the default Master A page and on any document pages that are associated with it.*

*With the **Facing Pages** box checked, document page 1 will appear by itself on the right-hand side and any additional pages will be stacked below it in pairs. The Facing Pages format is used for books and magazines.*

Margin ***Column*** ***Gutter***

First of all he said to himself: "That buzzing-noise means something. You don't get a buzzing-noise like that, just buzzing and buzzing, without its meaning something. If there's a buzzing-noise, somebody's making a buzzing-noise, and the only reason for making a buzzing-noise that I know of is because you're a bee.

Then he thought another long time, and said: "And the only reason for being a bee that I know of is making honey."

And then he got up, and said: "And the only reason for making honey is so I can eat it." So he began to climb the tree. *A.A. Milne*

To save a new file:

1. Choose File menu > Save (Ctrl-S).
2. The "File name" field will highlight automatically. Type a name for the document **1**.
3. On the "Save in" drop-down menu **2**, double-click the drive in which you want to save the file, then open the desired folder **3**. That drive and folder should appear in the "Save in" box (**5**, next page).

   Optional: Open a folder or sub-folder in which to save the file. Or, to create a new folder for the document, click the New Folder icon **4**, enter a name, then press Enter.

2 *Then click on the arrow in the* ***Save in*** *box.*

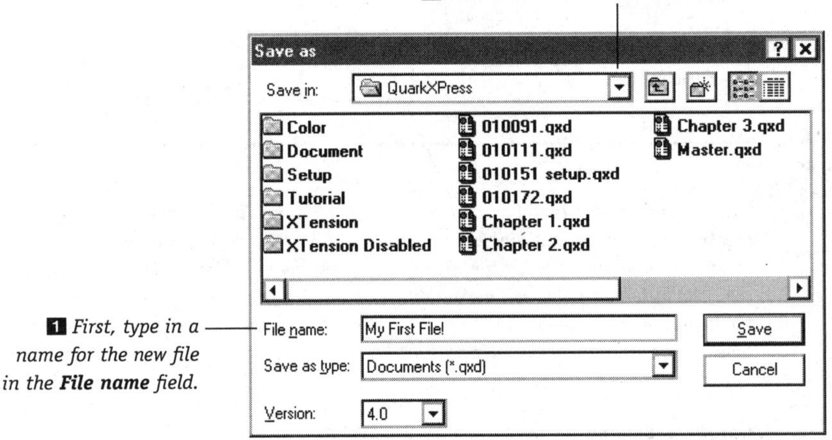

1 *First, type in a name for the new file in the* ***File name*** *field.*

4 ***Optional:*** *Click the* ***New Folder*** *icon to create a new folder.*

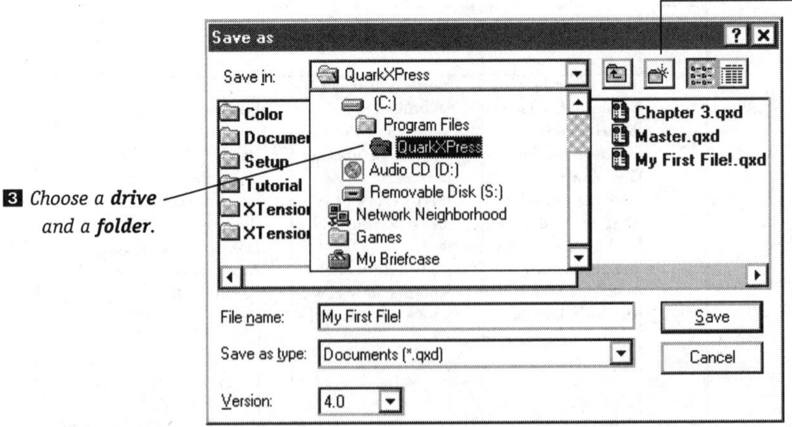

3 *Choose a* ***drive*** *and a* ***folder.***

5 *Make sure the name of the drive or folder into which you have chosen to save the document is displayed here.*

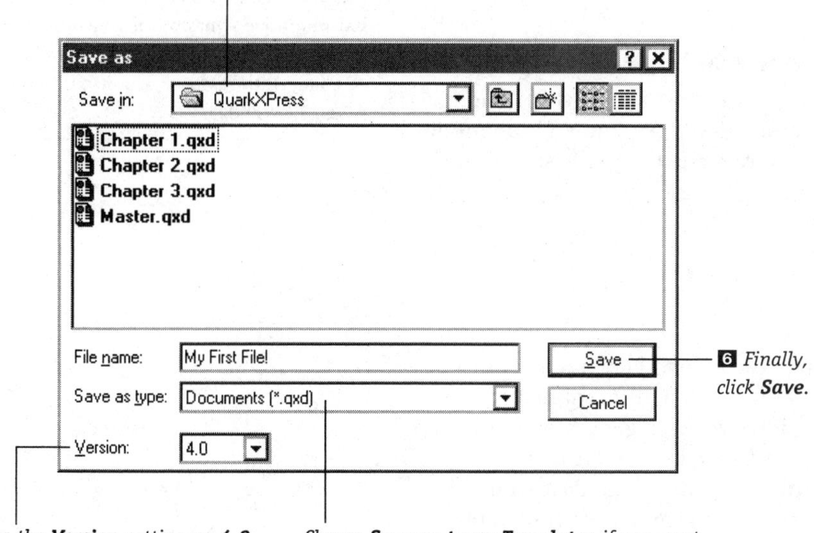

6 *Finally, click* ***Save****.*

Leave the ***Version*** *setting on* ***4.0*** *unless you have a particular reason to save in the version 3.3 format.*

Choose ***Save as type: Templates*** *if you want to create a save-proof file (see page 29). Otherwise, leave this setting on* ***Documents****.*

Save frequently, or use Auto Save or Auto Backup (see sidebar at right). If your computer freezes, at least you can reopen the document with most of the latest changes.

To save an existing file:

Choose File menu > Save (Ctrl-S). The Save command will be dimmed if no modifications were made to the file since it was last saved.

AUTO SAVE OR AUTO BACKUP?

Auto Save is like system-freeze insurance—in the event of a freeze, you'll be able to rescue the last mini-saved version of your document. Auto Backup is a method for creating multiple backups of a file. Both features are discusssed fully on pages 279–280.

The Save As command creates a copy of a document under a different name, and is useful if you want to generate multiple variations of a document. Or if you're having trouble saving a file or it seems to be corrupted, you can try rescuing it by saving a new version of it using Save As.

To save a new version of a file:

1. Open the file to be duplicated.
2. Choose File menu > Save As (Ctrl-Alt-S).
3. Enter a new name in the File name field or modify the existing name **1**.
4. *Optional:* If you need to save the document in a prior application version, choose Version: 3.3.
5. Choose a location in which to save the duplicate file.
6. Click Save or press Enter. The new version of the document will remain open; the original version of the document will close.

TIP If the title of the active file is *not* altered in the Save as dialog box and you click Save, a warning prompt will appear. Click Yes to save over the original file or click No.

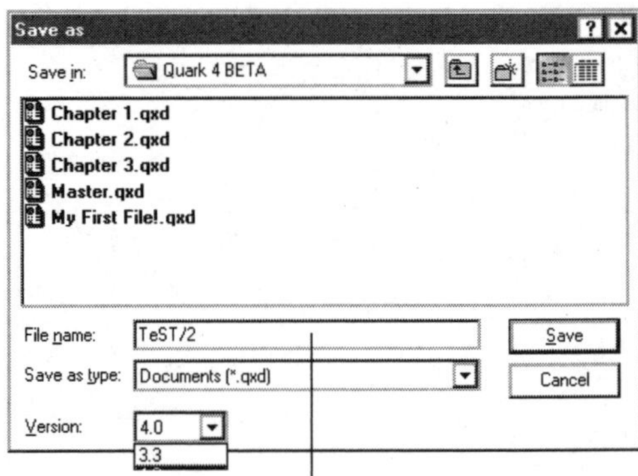

1 *Enter a new **name** for the duplicate file or alter the existing name, then click **Save**.*

What is a template?

If you choose Type: Template in the Save or Save As dialog box, your document will be save-proof. If you try to save over a template, the Save As dialog box will open automatically, at which time you can enter a name for and save a non-template version of the document. The template can contain, of course, master page items, style sheets, custom colors, H&J settings—anything you'll need again.

If you want to edit the template itself and then resave it, reenter the exact same name of the template when the Save As dialog box opens, choose its current location, click Save, then click Yes when the prompt appears.

Here's another way to prevent a document from being overwritten: Highlight its icon in the Explorer, choose File menu > Properties (or right-click the file and choose Properties), then check the Read-only box.

*Click on Details to see the file's type and **storage size**, and the **date** it was last modified.*

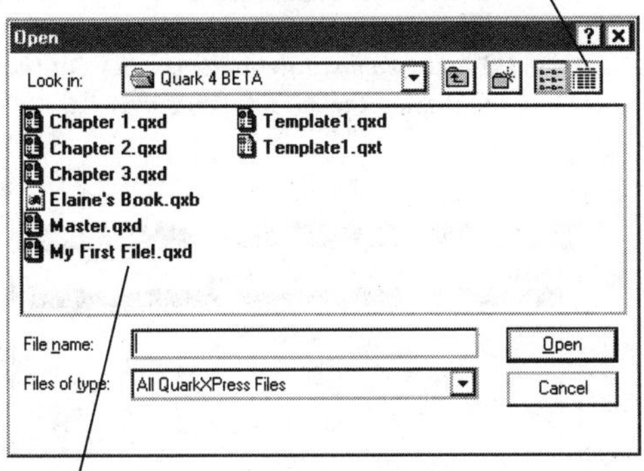

1 *Double-click the name of the file that you want to open.*

To open a QuarkXPress file from within the application:

1. Choose File menu > Open (Ctrl-O).
2. Locate and double-click a file name **1**.
   or
   Click a file name once, then click Open.
   or
   Type the path name (if necessary) and file name in the File name box, then click Open or press Enter. The number of QuarkXPress files that can be open at a time is limited only by available memory.

   Note: Read "Things that can happen when you open a file" on the next two pages.

To open a file from Windows Explorer:

Double-click a QuarkXPress file icon in Windows Explorer. The application will launch, if it isn't already open, and that file will appear on screen.

THINGS THAT CAN HAPPEN WHEN YOU OPEN A FILE

Non-matching preferences prompt

Kerning and tracking table settings, hyphenation exceptions, and custom frame data are stored in individual documents and in the QuarkXPress folder in a file called XPress Preferences. If, upon opening a file, the document settings do not match the XPress Preferences settings, a prompt will appear **1**. Click **Use XPress Preferences** (or press Alt-U) to apply the Preferences currently resident on that machine. Click **Keep Document Settings** (or press **Enter**—the *reverse* of Version 3.3) to leave the document as is.

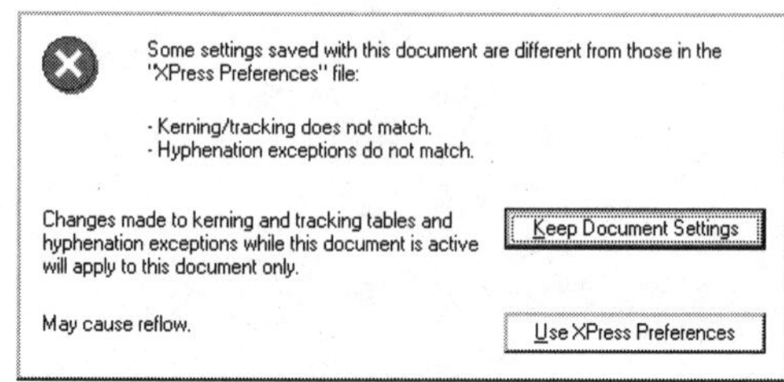

1 *The* ***XPress Preferences*** *prompt.*

Fonts are missing

If you open a document that uses fonts that are not installed or currently available in your system, a prompt will appear:

1. Click List Fonts to see a list of missing fonts **2**. *Note:* If you click Continue and the missing fonts subsequently become available, they will display properly.
2. To replace a font, click on a Missing Font **3**. An asterisk in the Replacement Font column indicates that font has *not* been replaced.
3. Click Replace.
4. Choose a font from the Replacement Font drop-down menu **4**.
5. Click OK.
6. Repeat steps 2–5 for each missing font you want to replace. If you change your mind after choosing a replacement font, click the replacement font, then click Reset.
7. Click OK or press Enter.

TIP If you click Continue for step 1, above, and you subsequently open the document on a system in which a missing

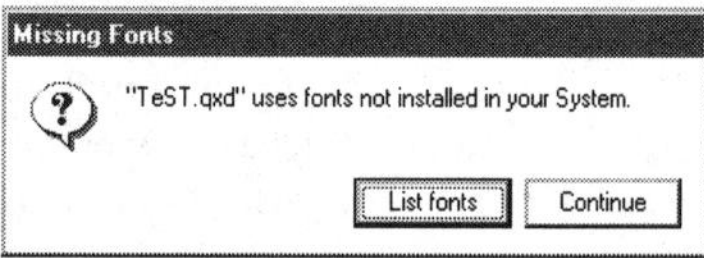

2 *The missing fonts prompt. Click* ***List Fonts*** *to substitute fonts. Or click* ***Continue*** *to display the missing fonts in Arial.*

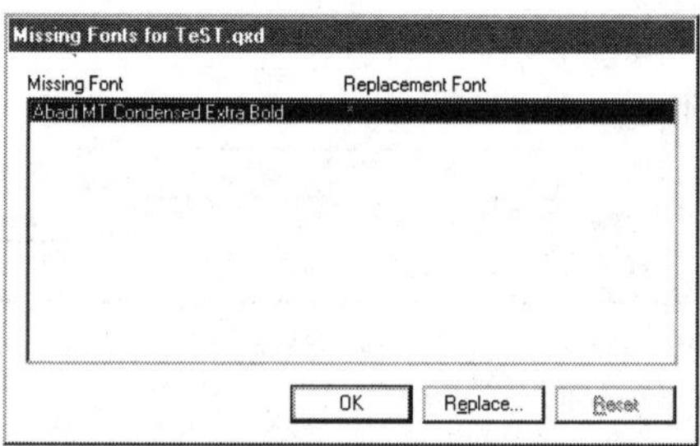

3 *In the Missing Fonts dialog box, click a font name, click* ***Replace****. . .*

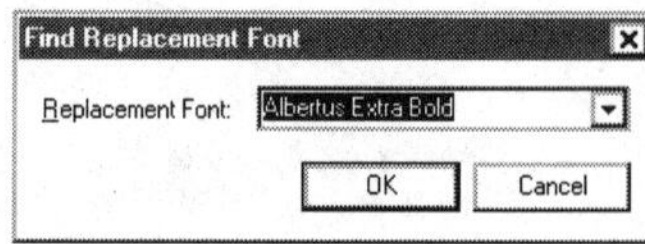

4 *. . . then choose from the* ***Replacement Font*** *drop-down menu.*

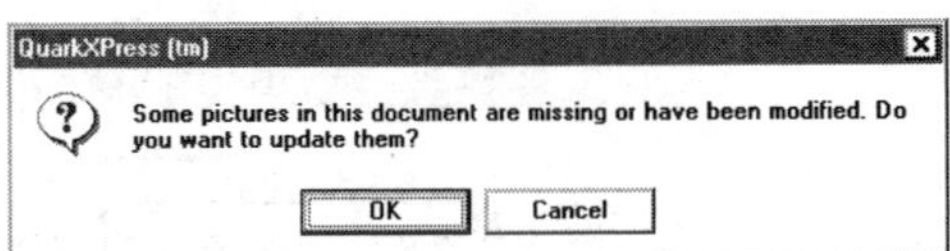

1 *This prompt will appear if, when you open a document, the original picture files for that document are missing or modified.*

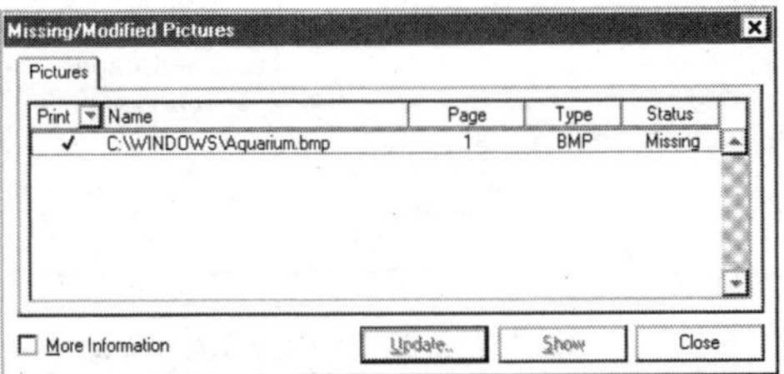

2 *In the* ***Missing/Modified Pictures*** *dialog box, double-click the name of a missing picture, locate and highlight the picture file name, then click Open.*

3.3 TO 4.0

To convert a file from a previous version of QuarkXPress to 4.0, open the document using the Open command (instructions on this page)—not by double-clicking its file icon—then immediately after the document opens and you've responded to the XPress Preferences prompt, choose File menu > Save, choose 4.0 from the Version drop-down menu, click Save or press Enter, then click Yes. If Expanded is the Hyphenation Method currently chosen in Edit menu > Preferences > Paragraph folder tab, the text may reflow.

If the document contains an EPS picture in a box with a background color of None, it may not display properly or at all. To remedy this, click on the picture, choose Item menu > Clipping, and choose Type: Item. I've found that some pictures display properly only in Actual Size view (Ctrl-1). Go figure.

If you downsave a 4.0 file back to 3.3, document elements that were created using 4.0 features will revert back to their 3.3 equivalents. For example, Bézier boxes will revert to polygon boxes, text paths will revert to text boxes, dashes and stripes will revert to solid lines, etc.

font is available or you install the font via the Font Control Panel, the font will display properly.

Pictures are missing

If pictures are used in the document that were moved or modified since the document was last opened and Auto Picture Import (Verify) is turned on in the General Preferences dialog box, yet another prompt will appear **1**. Click OK to proceed, and then to update the picture-document linkage, double-click the name of one of the missing or modified pictures **2**, locate and highlight the picture file name, then click Open or click OK. Repeat for other missing or modified pictures. Click Close when you're done. See pages 151–152.

If a "No XTension" prompt appears, the document contains a PCX, JPEG, PhotoCD, or LZW TIFF picture for which an import XTension filter must be enabled.

Note: If additional missing pictures are located in the same folder as the first missing picture, you'll get a prompt indicating that you can update them all at once. This works for pictures missing only—not modified pictures.

XTensions Manager opens

Whether the XTensions Manager opens depends on the Show XTensions Manager at Startup setting in Edit menu > Preferences > Application > XTensions folder tab. You can choose to Always show the XTensions Manager during launch, only show the XTensions Manager if an XTension was added or removed from the XTension folder, or only show the XTensions Manager if QuarkXPress encounters a loading error during launch. Read more about the XTensions Manager on pages 285–287.

To change a document's page size:

1. Choose File menu > Document Setup (Ctrl-Alt-Shift-P).
2. Choose a preset page Size.
   or
   Change the numbers in the Width and/or Height fields **1**.
   or
   Click the opposite page Orientation button.

   Note: Smaller page size values or the opposite Orientation setting won't be accepted if any items in the current file are positioned below, or to the right of, or are too large to fit within the new pasteboard dimensions **2**. If this is the case, you can move those items upward or to the left, reopen the Document Setup dialog box, then choose the desired settings. You could also move those items into a new document that has the desired dimensions.
3. *Optional:* To convert a single-sided document into a facing-pages document, check the Facing Pages box (more about facing pages on page 215).

   Note: To convert a facing-pages document into a single-sided document, first delete all the facing master pages in the document, then open the Document Setup dialog box and uncheck Facing Pages. Or drag the blank single-sided master page icon over each facing-pages master and release the mouse button. If you do this, any unmodified master items on document pages to which that master has been applied will be removed.
4. Click OK or press Enter. Any text box that fits exactly within the margin guides (like the automatic text box) will resize automatically to fit within the new margins.

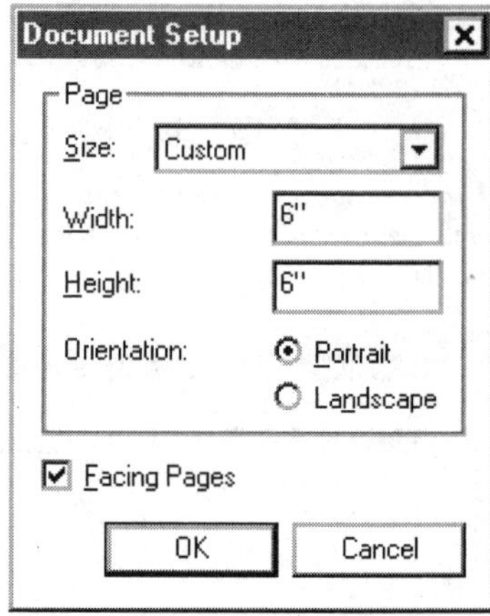

1 *Change the **Width** and/or **Height** of a document and check or uncheck the **Facing Pages** option in the **Document Setup** dialog box.*

2 *This prompt will appear if any items on a document page won't fit within the new page dimensions.*

GUIDES ON, GUIDES OFF

Use the **F7** shortcut to turn guides on or off. With guides off, margin guides, ruler guides, column guides, the X in empty picture boxes, and the edges of unselected boxes will disappear from view. Turn guides on to position objects; turn them off to judge the overall compositional balance of a page.

Column and margin guides are modified in the **Master Guides** dialog box, which can be opened from the Page menu only when a master page is currently displayed (see page 215).

Change Document Page Size

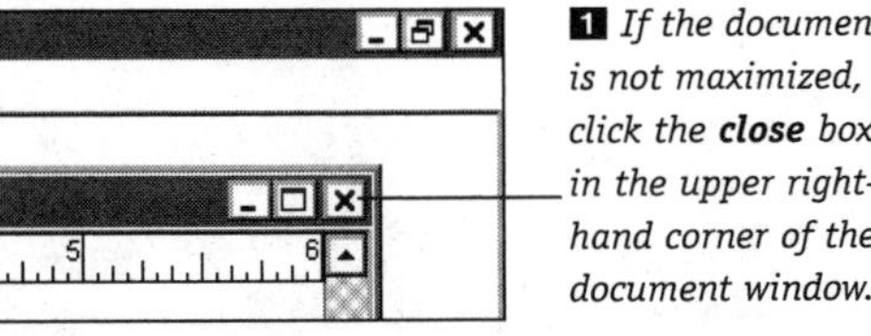

1 *If the document is not maximized, click the* ***close*** *box in the upper right-hand corner of the document window.*

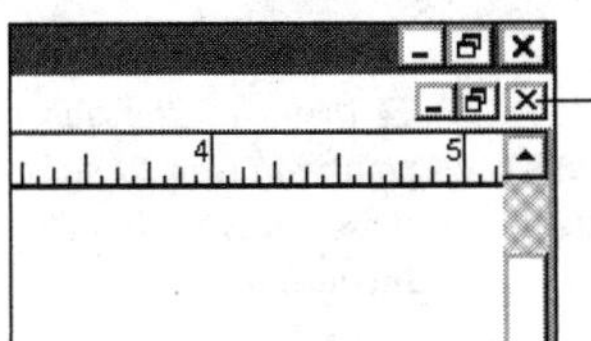

2 *If the document is maximized, click the close box directly below the application close box.*

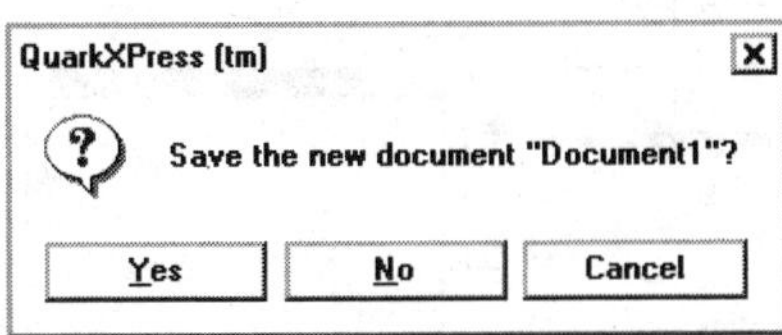

3 *If you attempt to close a file that has never been saved, this prompt will appear.*

To close a file:

If the document is not maximized, click the document close box in the upper right-hand corner of the document window **1**. If the document is maximized, click the document close box directly below the application close box **2**.

or

Choose File menu > Close (Ctrl-F4).

TIP If you try to close a file that has never been saved, a prompt will appear giving you the option to save or discard the file, or cancel the close operation **3**.

TIP To close *all* open files, choose Window menu > Close All.

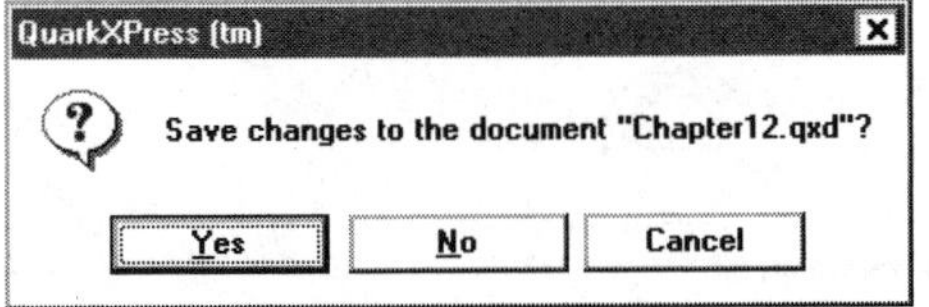

4 *If you attempt to exit the application and modifications were made to the file since it was last saved, this prompt will appear.*

To exit the application:

Choose File menu > Exit (Ctrl-Q).

TIP Exiting the application will close all open QuarkXPress files. If changes have been made to any open file since it was last saved, a prompt will appear offering you the option to save again before exiting or cancel the exit operation **4**.

The Append feature, which was previously accessible only in the individual Style Sheets, Colors, or H&Js dialog box, is now housed under one roof: The Append dialog box. This new system is simpler and easier, and offers a great enhancement: You can *selectively* pick and choose which document components will append.

To append style sheets, colors, H&Js, lists, or dashes & stripes from one file to another:

1. Open the file to which you want to append the style sheets, colors, H&Js, lists, or dashes & stripes.
2. Choose File menu > Append (Ctrl-Alt-A).
   or
   Click Append in the Style Sheets, Colors, H&Js, Lists, or Dashes & Stripes dialog box.
3. Locate and highlight the name of the file containing the components that you want to append, then click Open. You can append from a library.
4. Click the Style Sheets, Colors, H&Js, Lists, or Dashes & Stripes folder tab.
5. Locate and click on the name of the style sheet, color, H&J, list, or dashes & stripe style that you want to append **1**.

   To append multiple components, click on the first component in a series of consecutively-listed components, then Shift-click on the last in the series. Or Ctrl-click to select/deselect individual components.
6. Click the right-pointing append-items arrow **2**.
7. Click OK or press Enter. If a warning prompt appears, click OK again **3**. Check the Don't Show This Warning Again box if you don't want to see it again.
8. If an appending component has the same name as a component in the

1 Click the name of the ***style sheet*** *(or* ***color, H&J, list,*** *or* ***dashes & stripes****) you want to append.*

2 Then click the ***right-pointing*** *arrow to move those items to the* ***Including*** *column.*

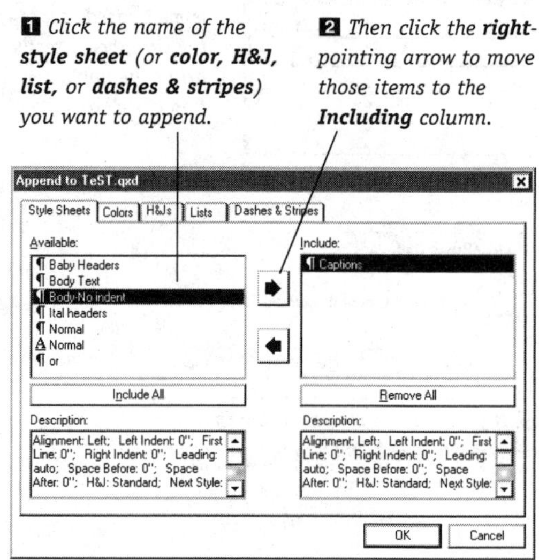

Appending ***style sheets.***

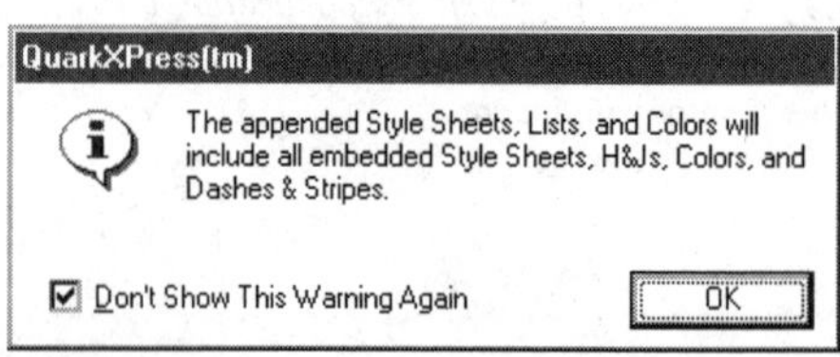

3 Click ***OK*** *when this warning prompt appears.*

Append

QUICK-AND-DIRTY APPEND

If text to which a style sheet or sheets have been applied is pasted from another document using the Clipboard, copied from another document, or retrieved from a library, the style sheet or sheets will be appended, with a name conflict being the only exception. Colors can also be appended this way.

SPEED TIP

4 *Click **Rename** or **Auto-Rename** if you want to keep the existing item **and** append the new.*

5 *Or click **Use New** to replace the existing item with the appending item.*

6 *Or click **Use Existing** if you don't want to append the item with the same name.*

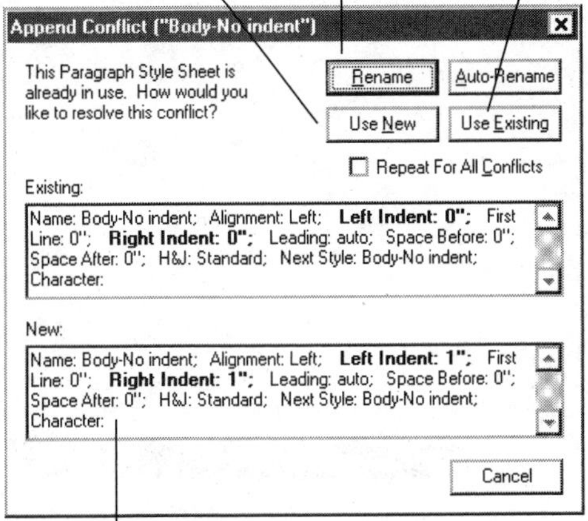

Append Conflict ("Body-No indent")

This Paragraph Style Sheet is already in use. How would you like to resolve this conflict?

Rename | Auto-Rename | Use New | Use Existing

☐ Repeat For All Conflicts

Existing:

Name: Body-No indent; Alignment: Left; **Left Indent: 0";** First Line: 0"; **Right Indent: 0";** Leading: auto; Space Before: 0"; Space After: 0"; H&J: Standard; Next Style: Body-No indent; Character:

New:

Name: Body-No indent; Alignment: Left; **Left Indent: 1";** First Line: 0"; **Right Indent: 1";** Leading: auto; Space Before: 0"; Space After: 0"; H&J: Standard; Next Style: Body-No indent; Character:

Cancel

*In the **Append Conflict** dialog box, any specification in the appending style sheet that doesn't exactly match that specification in the document to which you are appending will be highlighted in **boldface**.*

open, destination document, the Append Conflict dialog box will open. Do one of the following for each conflict that arises:

Note: To apply the same response automatically to any remaining conflicts, check the Repeat For All Conflicts box before clicking Rename, Auto-Rename, Use New, or Use Existing.

To keep the existing component, append the new component, and rename an individual component yourself, click Rename **4**, type a new name, then click OK.

or

To have an asterisk be inserted automatically next to the name of any appending component that has a match in the open, destination document, click Auto-Rename.

or

To replace the existing item with the appending component, click Use New **5**.

or

To cancel the append of that item, click Use Existing **6**.

9. Click OK or press Enter.

TIP To append all the components listed, don't highlight any of them, and click Include All. Click Remove All to delete the whole appended list.

TIP If a style sheet that you are attempting to append has the same keyboard equivalent as a style sheet in the active file to which you are appending, the style sheet will append, but the keyboard equivalent will not.

(Illustrations on the following page)

Append

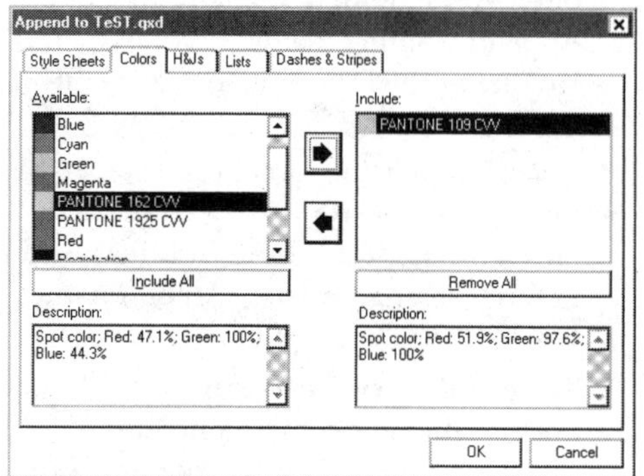

Appending **colors.**

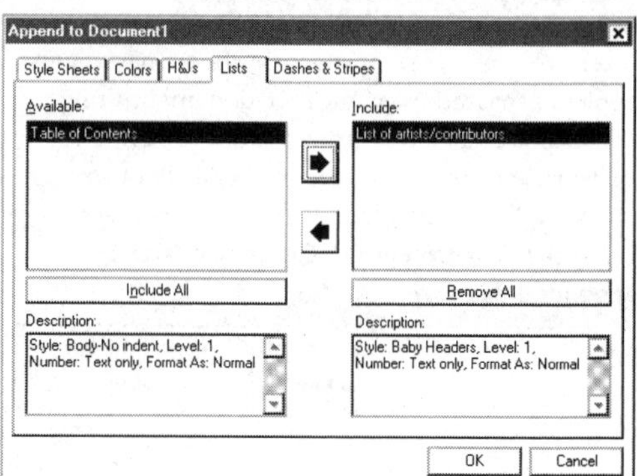

Appending **lists.**

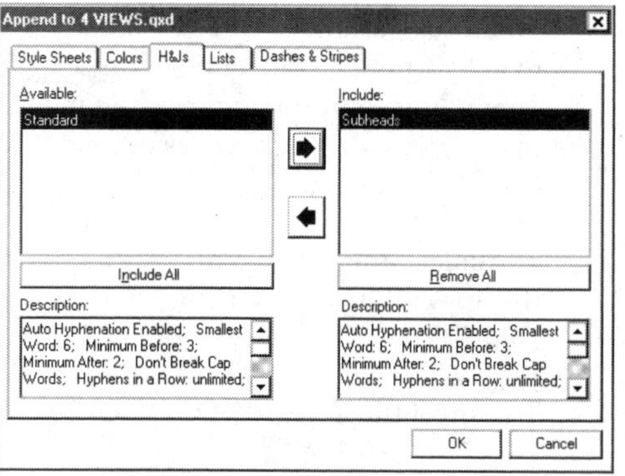

Appending **H&Js.**

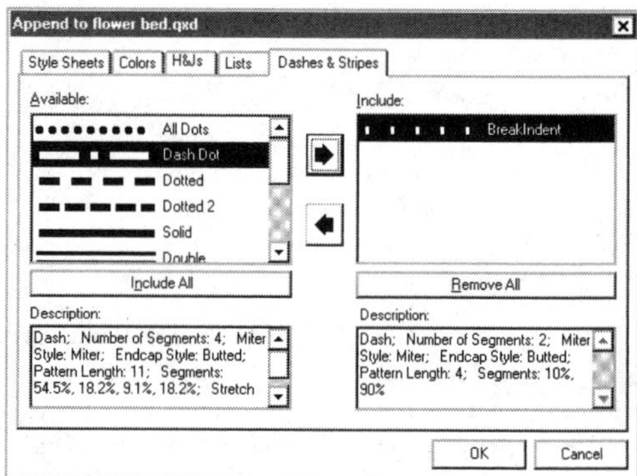

Appending **dashes & stripes.**

You can use the Revert to Saved feature to revert to an earlier saved version of a file while experimenting with multiple design variations, or to restore a file that has been modified by a household pet walking across your keyboard (it happens!).

To revert to the last saved version:

1. Choose File menu > Revert to Saved.
2. When the prompt "Revert to the last version saved?" appears, click OK or press Enter **1**.

TIP Choose Revert to Saved with Alt held down to revert to the last Auto-Saved version of the file (see page 279).

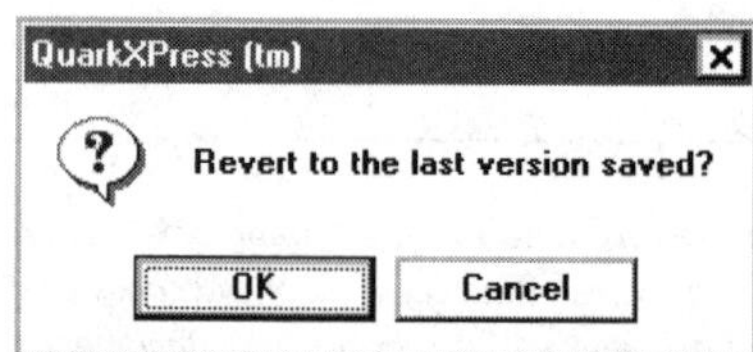

1 *If you choose File menu >* ***Revert to Saved****, this prompt will appear. Click OK to restore the last saved version of the file.*

Get around 3

DISPLAY SIZE SHORTCUTS

Fit in Window	Ctrl-0 (zero) *or* right-click and choose Fit in Window
Actual Size	Ctrl-1 (one) *or* right-click and choose Actual Size
Thumbnails	Shift-F6 *or* right-click and choose Thumbnails
Make all open windows Thumbnails	Alt-Shift choose Window menu > Tile Horizontally *or* Tile Vertically
Fit in pasteboard	Alt-choose View menu > Fit in Window *or* Ctrl-Alt-0 (zero)
Highlight view percent field	Ctrl-Alt-V
Zoom in	Ctrl-space-click
Zoom out	Ctrl-Alt-space-click
Zoom in/out	Turn mouse wheel, if your mouse has one
Zoom in on area	Ctrl-space-drag *or* Ctrl-Alt-space-drag
Toggle between 100% and 200%	Ctrl-Alt-click

SPEED TIP

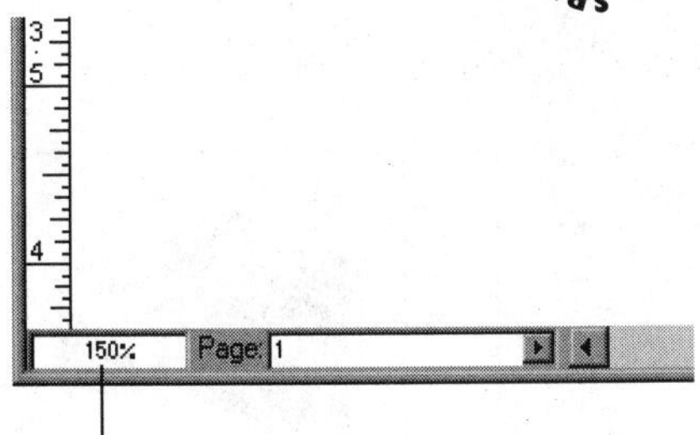

1 *The* ***view percent*** *field.*

There are many ways to move from page to page and to switch between small and large display sizes. To minimize eye and neck strain, it's essential to learn how to switch display sizes, from a large display size to edit a small detail, back to Fit in Window or a smaller view size to check out the overall layout, and so on. Changing a document's view size doesn't alter its page or print size, it only changes the size at which it is displayed.

To change a document's display size:

Choose View menu > Fit in Window, 50%, 75%, Actual Size, 200%, or Thumbnails.

or

Double-click in the view percent field in the lower left-hand corner of the document window **1** (Ctrl-Alt-V), enter a number between 10 and 800, then press Enter. You don't have to enter the % symbol. Type "T", then press Enter, for Thumbnails view.

TIP Page elements cannot be modified in Thumbnails view. Pages within a file *can* be rearranged in Thumbnails view, however (see page 68), and whole pages can be drag-copied from one file to another if both documents are in Thumbnails view (see page 73).

TIP For an almost-thumbnails view in which page elements are editable, choose a very small view size, like 25%.

Accessing the Zoom tool from the keyboard is much speedier than selecting and then deselecting the Zoom tool from the Tool palette. Get used to this shortcut as quickly as you can.

To change the display size using the Zoom tool from the keyboard:

Ctrl-Space bar-click on the page to enlarge the view size **1**.

or

Ctrl-Alt-Space bar-click on the page to reduce the view size **2**.

or

Ctrl-Space bar-drag a marquee around the area that you want to enlarge **3**.

TIP If your mouse has a mouse wheel, press Ctrl and turn the wheel to zoom in or out.

TIP If the Zoom tool doesn't work (its pointer doesn't display), make sure your pointer isn't over a Bézier point.

TIP Click a document window zoom box to enlarge the document window; click again to restore its former size. Alt-click the zoom box to enlarge the document window to its maximum size for your screen; Alt-click again to restore its former size.

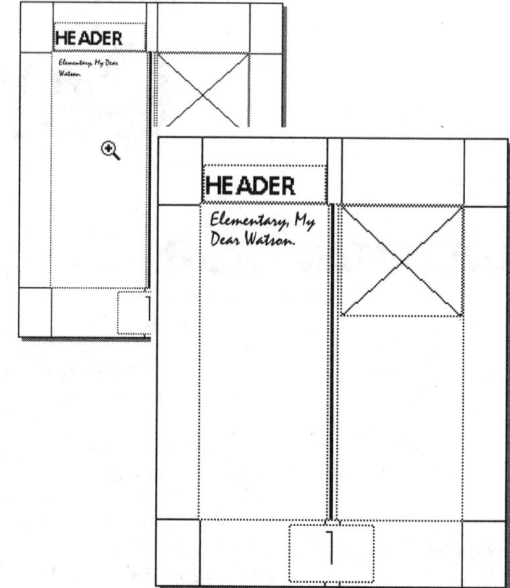

1 ***Ctrl-Space bar-click*** *on a page to enlarge the view size.*

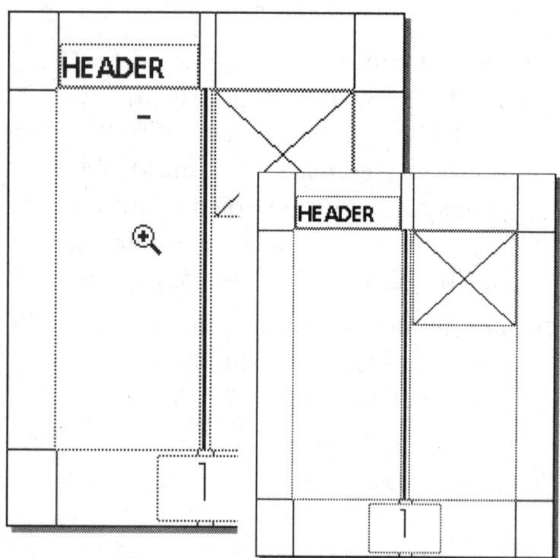

2 ***Ctrl-Alt-Space bar-click*** *on a page to reduce the view size.*

3 ***Ctrl-Space bar-drag*** *over a section of a page to magnify that chosen area.*

Change Display Size

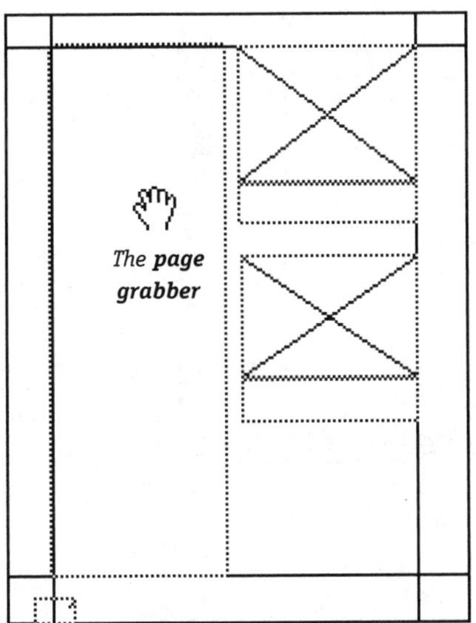

1 ***Alt**-drag with the mouse to move a page in the document window.*

SCREEN REDRAW SHORTCUTS

Forced redraw	Ctrl-Alt-. (period)
Stop redraw	Ctrl-. (period) *or* Esc *or* perform another action (select an item, choose another command, etc.)

Note: When the Zoom tool is selected, use Alt-drag to marquee an area for enlarging.

To move a document in its window using the page grabber hand:

Alt-drag to move a page in the document window. The cursor will temporarily turn into a hand icon **1**. The document will redraw as you scroll. If Speed Scroll is turned on (Edit menu > Preferences > Application > Interactive folder tab), pictures and blends may be greeked (grayed out) as you scroll.

TIP The Edit menu > Preferences > Application > Interactive folder tab options, including Scrolling, Speed Scroll, Live Scroll, Show Contents, and Live Refresh, are discussed on page 278.

To move a document in its window using the scroll arrows, bars, or boxes:

Click on a scroll **arrow** to scroll a short distance through a document in the direction in which the arrow is pointing **1**.

or

Move a scroll **box** to move through a document more quickly.

or

Click on a grey scroll **bar** to move through a document a full screen at a time. Click in the gray area above the scroll box to move a full screen upward or click below the box to move a full screen downward. Click to the left of the scroll box to move a full screen to the left, or click to the right of the scroll box to move a full screen to the right.

TIP If your mouse has a wheel between the left and right buttons, turn it to scroll through your document.

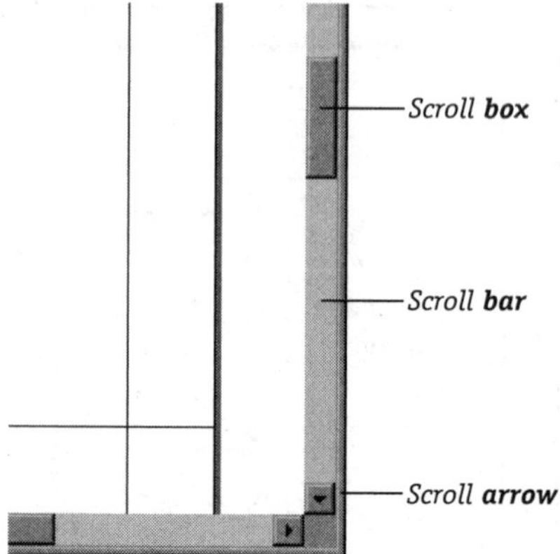

1 *The standard windows features: scroll boxes, bars, and arrows.*

To move through a document using the extended keyboard:

Press Page Up or Page Down to move up or down a full screen **2**–**3**.

or

Press Ctrl-Page Up to display the top of the first page in the document.

or

Press End to display the bottom of the last page (or the blank space to the right of the last page) in the document.

or

Press Ctrl-PageDown to display the top of the last page in the document.

or

Press Shift-Page Up to display the top of the previous page.

or

Press Shift-Page Down to display the top of the next page.

or

Press Alt-Page up to display the top of the previous spread.

or

Press Alt-Page Down to display the top of the next spread.

Insert	Home	Page Up
Delete	End	Page Down

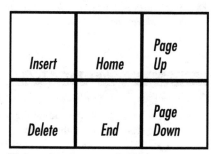

2 *A section of an extended keyboard.*

3 *The page that's currently showing in the upper left hand corner of the document window is the page that QuarkXPress considers to be displayed, even if only a small part of that page is in view.*

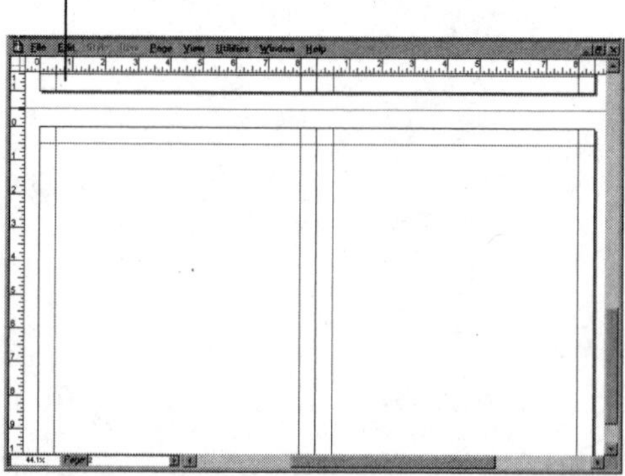

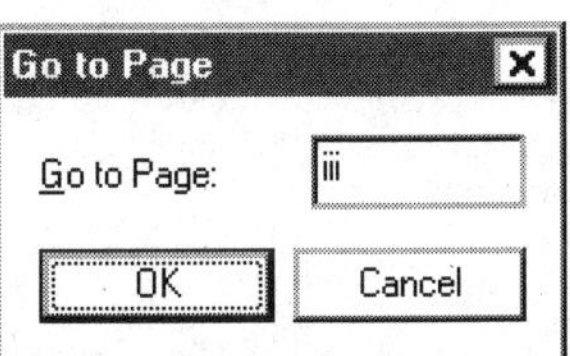
Go to Page
Go to Page:
iii
OK
Cancel

1 *Use the Ctrl-J shortcut to access the* ***Go to Page*** *dialog box quickly.*

To go to a page using a dialog box:

Choose Page menu > Previous, Next, First, or Last.

or

Choose Page menu > Go to (Ctrl-J), enter the desired page number in the Go to Page field, then click OK or press Enter **1**.

TIP If the page you want to display has a prefix that was applied using the Section command, be sure to enter the prefix along with the number in the Go to Page field. Also make sure to enter the number in the correct format (i.e. lowercase Roman, numeric). To display a page based on its position in the document rather than its applied Section number, enter "+" before the number (see page 74).

2 *The* ***Document Layout*** *palette.*

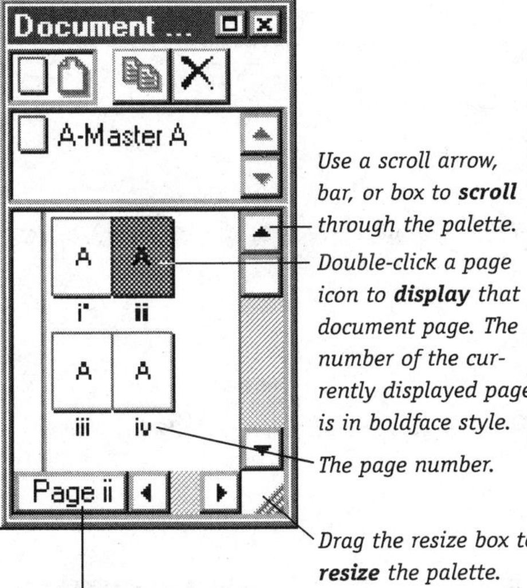
Document ...
A-Master A
A
A
i*
ii
A
A
iii
iv
Page ii
Use a scroll arrow, bar, or box to **scroll** through the palette.
Double-click a page icon to **display** that document page. The number of the currently displayed page is in boldface style.
The page number.
Drag the resize box to **resize** the palette.

3 *The number of the currently* ***highlighted*** *page icon (this is not necessarily the page that is currently displayed on screen).*

To go to a page using the Document Layout palette:

1. Choose View menu > Show Document Layout (F4).
2. Double-click a document page icon **2**.

TIP If a page icon is currently highlighted, its number will display in the lower left corner of the Document Layout palette **3**. If a page is the start of a section, its number will have an asterisk. If no page icon is highlighted, the total number of pages the document contains will display instead (i.e. "4 pages").

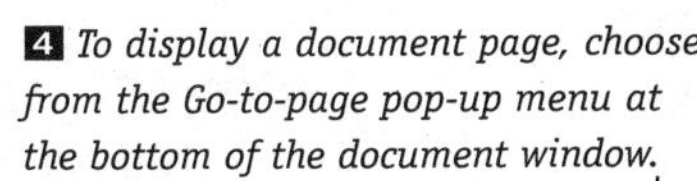

4 *To display a document page, choose from the Go-to-page pop-up menu at the bottom of the document window.*

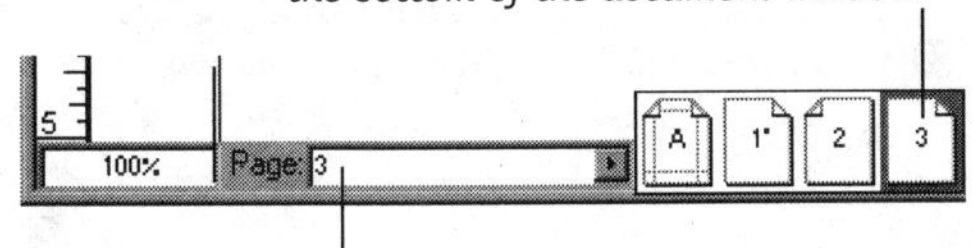
100%
Page: 3
A
1*
2
3

5 *Or double-click the current page number, enter the desired page number, then press Enter.*

To go to a page using the Go-to-page menu or field:

Press the arrowhead for the Go-to-page pop-up menu at the bottom of the document window **4**, and choose the number of the document page or master page (lettered page) that you want to display.

or

Double-click the current page number **5**, enter the desired page number, then press Enter.

Stack, tile, or activate open document windows:

Choose Window menu, then choose:

Cascade to stack document windows at full size, one in front of one another in a stair-step arrangement **1**.

or

Tile Horizontally to arrange document windows next to each other in horizontal strips **2**.

or

Tile Vertically to arrange document windows next to each other in vertical strips **3**.

or

The name of an open document to activate it.

TIP If you have more than one monitor hooked up and you choose Tile Documents, the currently open documents will be divided up among the monitors.

TIP Hold down Alt and Shift and choose Cascade, Tile Horizontally or Tile Vertically from the Window menu to stack or tile all currently open documents into Thumbnails view. Hold down Ctrl and Alt to stack or tile into Actual Size view, or hold down Ctrl and Shift to stack or tile into Fit in Window view. SPEED TIP

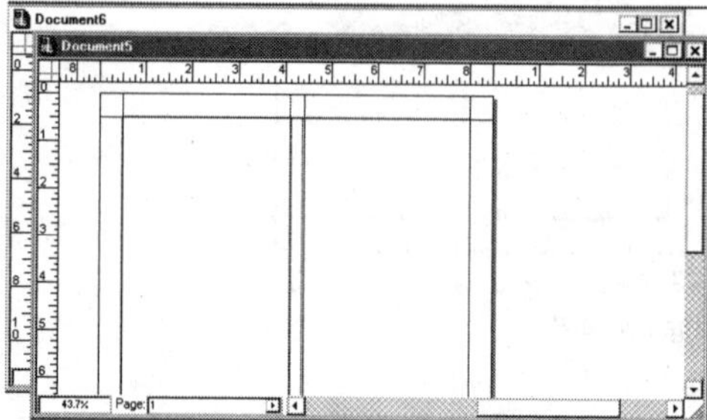

1 *Documents in a* ***Cascade*** *formation.*

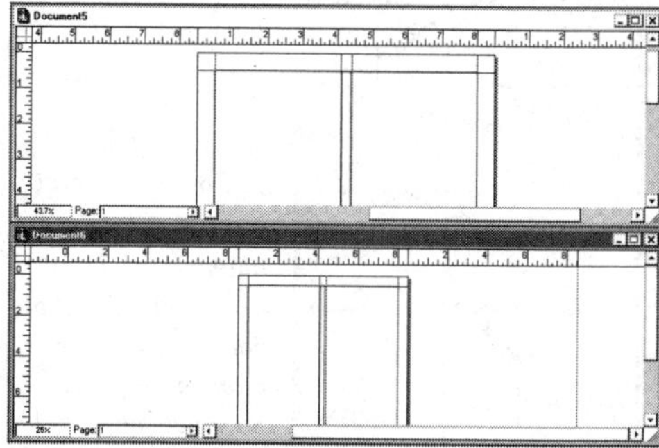

2 *Documents in a* ***Tile Horizontally*** *formation.*

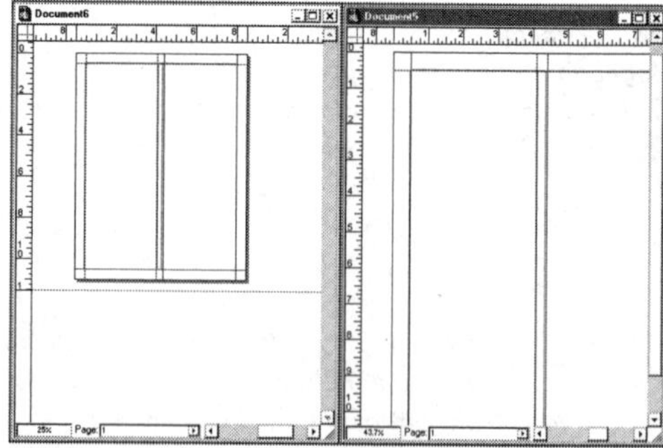

3 *Documents in a* ***Tile Vertically*** *formation.*

Text input 4

How does text get onto a page?

To input or import text in QuarkXPress, you have to first create a box to put it in or a text path to put it on. QuarkXPress has five tools that are expressly used for creating different-shaped text boxes, two Bézier text box tools, and four text path tools. What's more, you can convert any item into a text box or text path.

Once you've learned the rudiments of manipulating text from this chapter—getting it into a box, highlighting it, and rearranging it—you'll want to learn about paragraph formatting (Chapter 6) and explore the many ways to give it some flair (Chapter 7). To learn how to flow long text passages through multiple boxes, see Chapter 5, Text Flow.

Once you're comfortable with the basic typographic controls in QuarkXPress, you'll appreciate the beauty of character and paragraph style sheets, which are covered in Chapter 13. Bézier text paths are covered in Chapter 12.

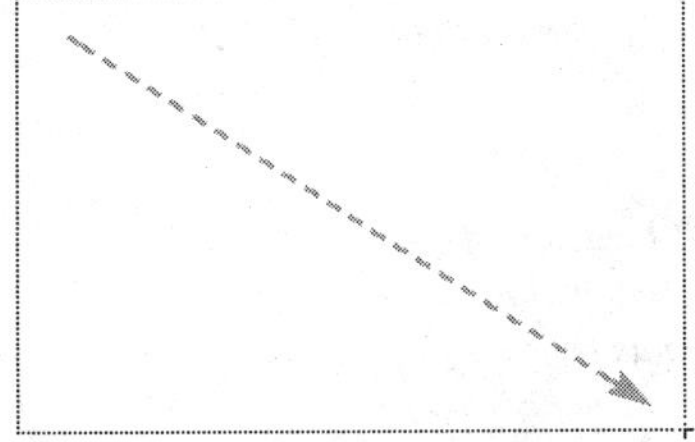

1 *Click and drag with a text box tool.*

2 *A new text box is created.*

To create a text box:

1. Choose any text box tool except a Bézier text tool (they're covered in Chapter 11). The cursor will turn into a crosshair.
2. Press and drag in any direction **1**. When the mouse is released the finished box will be selected and ready for inputting **2**.

To resize a text box manually:

1. Choose the Item or Content tool (Shift-F8).
2. Click on a box.
3. Press and drag any handle **1**–**2**.
   or
   To resize the box and preserve its original proportions, hold down Alt and Shift while dragging. (Hold down Shift without Alt to turn the box into a square.) Release Shift or Alt and Shift after you release the mouse.

TIP Make sure the point of the cursor arrow is directly over one of the box handles before pressing the mouse. The cursor will change into a pointing hand icon.

TIP If Live Refresh is turned on in Edit menu > Preferences > Application > Interactive folder tab and you pause before dragging a handle of a text box, the text wrap will update continuously as you drag **3** (the pointer will turn into a cluster of arrows).

1 *Resize a box by dragging any of its four corner handles (note the hand pointer).*

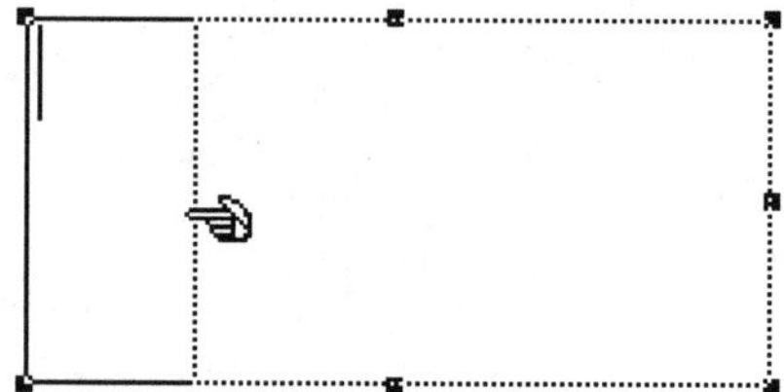

2 *Or drag any of its four midpoint handles.*

After a brief shower of orange juice, low clouds of sunny-side up eggs moved in followed by pieces of toast.

—Judi Barrett

3 *Pause-dragging with* ***Live Refresh*** *on.*

To resize a text box using the Measurements palette:

1. Choose the Item or Content tool.
2. Click on a box.
3. Enter a new number in the W field on the Measurements palette to modify the width of the box (press Enter) **4**. A number can be entered in any measurement system used in QuarkXPress. Be sure to include the proper abbreviation, such as "p" or "mm," if the number is in a measurement system other than the default (see page 21).
   and/or
   In the H field on the Measurements palette, enter a number to modify the height of the box (press Enter).

The ***horizontal location*** *of the box. This number can be replaced, or a plus or minus sign and then a specified amount can be entered to the right of the current number to add to or subtract from it.*

The ***width*** *of the box.*

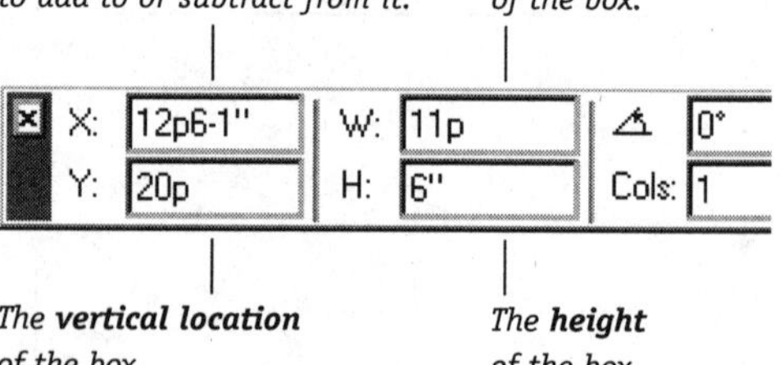

The ***vertical location*** *of the box.*

The ***height*** *of the box.*

4 *Note that in this illustration of the Measurements palette, numbers in the fields have been entered in different measurement systems.*

SNAP TO IT

If View menu > Snap to Guides is turned on (Shift-F7) and you drag the handle of a box or an anchor point near a guide, the handle or point will snap to the guide with a little tug. Turn Snap to Guides off if you want to drag an item manually without the little tug.

Mrs. Trenor was a tall, fair woman whose height just saved her from redundancy. Her rosy blondness had survived some forty years of futile activity without showing much trace of ill-usage except in a diminished play

Edith Wharton

1 *Make sure the cursor turns into an Item tool icon before dragging. A text box, like any other item, can be dragged from one page to another.*

Mrs. Trenor was a tall, fair woman whose height just saved her from redundancy. Her rosy blondness had survived some forty years of futile activity without showing much trace of ill-usage except in a diminished play

2 *If you don't pause for the text to redraw, only the outline of the box will be displayed as it's moved. Use this method if you've got a slow machine.*

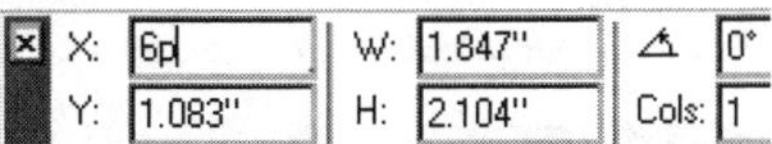

3 *To position an object very precisely, enter a new value in the X or Y field on the Measurements palette.*

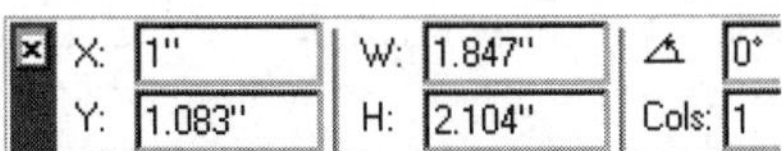

4 *After pressing Enter, the X pica value is converted into its equivalent in the default measurement system, which in this case is inches.*

To move a text box manually:

1. Choose the Item tool. Or hold down Ctrl to temporarily use the Item tool if the Content tool is selected.
2. Press inside a text box, pause briefly for the text to redraw, then drag the item to a new location on the same page or to a different page **1**–**2** (the cursor will be a cluster of arrowheads). The *x/y* position numbers on the Measurements palette will update as you drag. Touch the bottom of the document window to force scrolling, if necessary.

TIP Hold down Shift as you drag to constrain the movement to a horizontal or vertical axis. Release the mouse before releasing Shift. To use ruler guides to position an item, see page 135.

TIP Remember the Undo command, which undoes most operations: Ctrl-Z.

Use the Measurements palette to nail an item to a precise *x/y* location.

To reposition a text box or any other item using the Measurements palette:

1. Choose the Item or Content tool.
2. Click on the item you want to reposition.
3. Enter a number in the X field on the Measurements palette to change the horizontal position of the box relative to the ruler origin **3**, which, unless you change it, is located at the uppermost left corner of the document.
   and/or
   Enter a number in the Y field on the Measurements palette to change the vertical position of the box relative to the ruler origin.
4. Press Enter **4**.

TIP To use arithmetic in the X or Y field, enter "+" after the current number, then the amount you want to add. To subtract, enter "-"; to multiply, enter "*", to divide, enter "/".

To input text:

1. Choose the Content tool.
2. Click in a text box (or click on a text path) to create an insertion point.
3. Start typing **1**. Press Enter whenever you want to begin a new paragraph.

TIP Choose View menu > Show Invisibles (Ctrl-I) to reveal paragraph returns, spaces, and other non-printing characters **2**.

TIP To move the first line of text downward from the top of its box by a specified distance, choose Item menu > Modify, click the Text folder tab, then enter a number in the First Baseline: Offset field. To move the text inward from *all* sides of its box, enter a number in the Text Inset field.

As soon as they were gone, Elizabeth walked out to recover her spirits; or in other words, to dwell without interruption on those subjects that must deaden them more. Mr. Darcy's behavior astonished

1 *Text is typed into a text box with the Content tool selected.*

As•soon•as•they•were•gone,•Elizabeth• walked•out•to•recover•her•spirits;•or•in• other•words,•to•dwell•without•interruption• on•those•subjects•that•must•deaden•them• more.•Mr.•Darcy's•behavior•astonished• and•vexed•her.¶
"Why,•if•he•came•only•to•be•silent,•
Jane Austen

2 *Press **Enter** to begin a new paragraph. Choose View menu > Show Invisibles to display paragraph returns and other non-printing characters.*

What is the text overflow symbol?

If a text box is too small to display all the text that it contains, a text overflow symbol will appear in the lower right-hand corner of the box **3**. The text overflow symbol will disappear if the text box is enlarged enough to display all the type that it contains or if the box is linked to another box for the text to spill into.

The text overflow symbol doesn't print; it's merely an indicator that there is hidden text in the buffer. Only the text that is visible in a box will print.

TIP If pages are mysteriously added to your document when a text box becomes full, it means Auto Page Insertion is turned on (Edit menu > Preferences > Document > General folder tab).

TIP The maximum number of paragraphs per story is higher in QuarkXPress version 4.0 than it was in 3.3.

As soon as they were gone, Elizabeth walked out to recover her spirits; or in other words, to dwell without interruption on those subjects that must deaden them more. Mr. Darcy's behavior astonished ⊠

3 *The **text overflow symbol** appears when a box is too small to display all the text that it contains.*

KEEP THE CASE OPEN

Lowercase characters can be converted into caps or small caps with a flick of a switch on the Measurements palette, but characters input with the Caps lock key pressed can't be converted back to lowercase—so don't type with the Caps lock key pressed down. (Or use the Case Conversion or Enhanced Conversion XTension in the Windows TeXT ColleXTion by Visions Edge, Inc.)

On an exceptionally hot evening early in July, a young man came

1 *Double-click anywhere in the middle of a **word** to highlight it **without** including any punctuation.*

On an exceptionally hot evening early in July, a young man came

2 *Double-click between a **word** and a **punctuation mark** to select both. Read more about **smart space** on page 122.*

On an exceptionally hot evening early in July a young man came out of the garret in which he lodged in S. Place and walked slowly, as though in hesitation, towards K. Bridge.

He had successfully avoided meeting his landlady on the staircase. His garret was under the roof of a high, five-storied

3 ***Triple-click** to highlight a **line**.*

On an exceptionally hot evening early in July a young man came out of the garret in which he lodged in S. Place and walked slowly, as though in hesitation, towards K. Bridge.

He had successfully avoided meeting his landlady on the staircase. His garret was under the roof of a high, five-storied

4 *Click **four** times to highlight a **paragraph**.*

To highlight text:

1. Choose the Content tool.
2. Press and drag over the text you want to highlight.
   or
   Use a fast-clicking method **1**–**4**:

Number of clicks	*What gets highlighted*
1 click	Creates an **insertion point**
2 clicks on word	A **word** (but *not* the space following it)
2 clicks between word and punctuation	A **word** *and* the punctuation following it (but *not* the space following it)
3 clicks	A **line**
4 clicks	A **paragraph**
5 clicks	A whole **story** (all the text in a box or in a series of linked boxes)

   or
   To highlight a **whole story**, click in a text box, then choose Edit menu > Select All (Ctrl-A). Hidden, overflow text, if any, will be included in the selection. ***Note:*** If the Item tool is selected when you choose Select All, all items on the currently displayed page or spread and surrounding pasteboard will become selected instead.
   or
   Click in a text box at the beginning of a **text string**, then Shift-click at the end of the text string.
   or
   To select from the current **cursor position** to the **end of a story**: Ctrl-Alt-Shift-down arrow. (See page 330 for more shortcuts.)
   or
   To select a **series of words**, double-click the first word, keep the mouse button down on the second click, then drag. Triple-click, then drag downward to highlight a **series of lines**.

To delete text:

1. Choose the Content tool.
2. Click to the right of the character to be deleted **1**, then press Backspace. (Press the left or right pointing arrow key on the keyboard to move the insertion point one character at a time.)
   or
   Highlight the text that you want to delete **2** (see the previous page), then press Delete or Backspace, choose Edit menu > Delete or right-click and choose Delete.

TIP To delete the character to the right of the cursor, press the Delete key.

To delete a text box:

1. Choose the Item or Content tool.
2. Click on a text box.
3. Choose Item menu > Delete (Ctrl-K).

TIP Other ways to delete a box selected with the Item tool: Press Delete or Backspace on the keyboard; choose Edit menu > Delete; or right-click on the box and choose Delete.

The Line text path tool and Orthogonal text path tool are discussed here. The Bézier text path and Freehand text path tools are discussed in Chapter 12.

To create a straight text path:

1. Choose the Orthogonal text path tool to draw a straight horizontal or vertical text path.
   or
   Choose the Line text path tool to draw a straight line path at any angle with no corners or bends.
2. Press and drag to draw the path, and leave it selected.
3. Choose the Content tool.
4. Start typing **3**–**4**. The text will march along the path.

SAME OL' SELECTION

If you deselect and then reselect a box with the Content tool, the last group of characters that were highlighted, if any, will re-highlight. To create a new insertion point, click once more in the text box.

1 *Pressing the Backspace key with the cursor at this insertion point would delete the "S."*

2 *Pressing the Delete or Backspace key with this selection highlighted would delete the "HES."*

3 *Press and drag vertically or horizontally with the **Orthogonal text path** tool.*

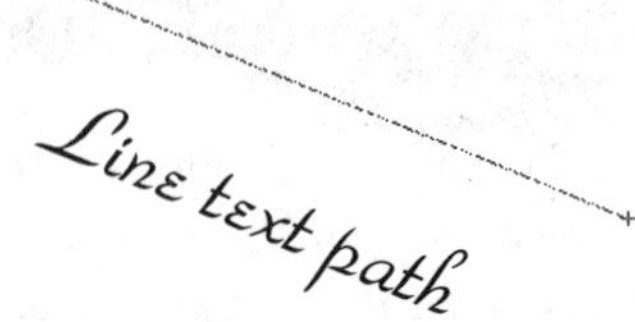

4 *Press and drag at any angle with the **Line text path** tool.*

Hip.	Well shone, moon—Truly, the moon shines with a good grace.
Dem.	Well roared, lion.
The.	Well run, Thisbe.
The.	Well moused, lion.

1 *To move text, highlight it, then choose Edit menu > **Cut**.*

Dem.	Well roared, lion.
The.	Well run, Thisbe.
The.	Well moused, lion.

2 ***Click** to create a new insertion point.*

Dem.	Well roared, lion.
The.	Well run, Thisbe.
Hip.	Well shone, moon—Truly, the moon shines with a good grace.
The.	Well moused, lion.

William Shakespeare

3 *Choose Edit menu > **Paste**.*

The Clipboard is a holding area that stores one cut or copied selection at a time. The current contents of the Clipboard can be retrieved an unlimited number of times via the Paste command. The Clipboard contents are purged when you exit QuarkXPress or shut down your computer.

To rearrange text using the Clipboard:

1. Choose the Content tool.
2. Highlight the text that you want to move **1**.
3. Choose Edit menu > **Cut** (Ctrl-X) or right-click and choose Cut to place the highlighted text on the Clipboard and *remove* it from its current location.
   or
   Choose Edit menu > **Copy** (Ctrl-C) or right-click and choose Copy to place a copy of the highlighted text on the Clipboard and *leave* the highlighted text in its current location.
4. Click in a text box to create a new insertion point **2**
5. Choose Edit menu > **Paste** (Ctrl-V) or right-click and choose Paste **3**.

TIP The Clipboard can also be used to cut or copy a text box, picture box, line, or group when the Item tool is selected, or a picture if the Content tool is selected. Be sure to Paste using the same tool that was used to Cut or Copy.

You can use the Drag and Drop Text feature to move or copy text quickly without having to execute any Clipboard commands. You can drag-and-drop text within the same box or between linked boxes (a story), but not between unlinked boxes. This is a very handy feature for doing quick copy edits.

Note: In order to drag-and-drop, the Drag and Drop Text box must be checked in Edit menu > Preferences > Application > Interactive folder tab **1**.

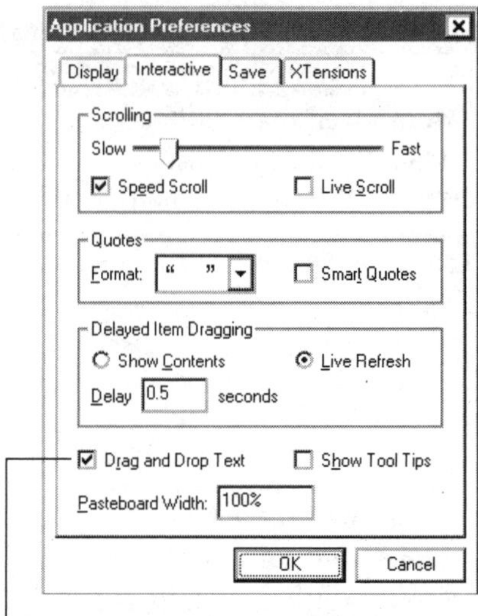

1 *Check the* ***Drag and Drop Text*** *box in Application Preferences > Interactive folder tab.*

To drag-and-drop text:

1. Choose the Content tool.
2. Highlight the text that you want to move or copy (see page 47) **2**.
3. Release the mouse.
4. To move the text, press on the highlighted text, drag the blinking cursor to a new location, then release the mouse **3**.
   or
   To move a copy of the text, press on the highlighted text, then hold down Shift and drag the blinking cursor to a new location (a box and a plus sign will display as you drag).

TIP The drag and drop text **is** automatically placed on the Clipboard, but you won't be aware of it unless you use the Paste command or choose Edit menu > Show Clipboard.

If you want to get somewhere else, you must run at least twice as fast as that. Now, *here*, you see, it takes all the running *you* can do, to keep in the same place.

Lewis Carroll

2 *To move (drag-and-drop) text, highlight it and release the mouse. Then press on the highlighted text and drag the blinking cursor to a new position.*

"Now, *here*, you see, it takes all the running *you* can do, to keep in the same place. If you want to get somewhere else, you must run at least twice as fast as that..."

Lewis Carroll

3 *The sentences are now in reverse order.*

■1 *The **Text Inset** field in the Modify (Text) dialog box.*

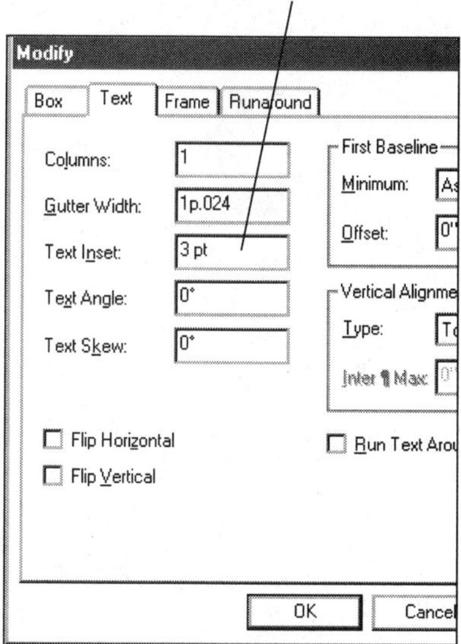

The Text Inset is the blank space between text and the four edges of the box that contains it. A Text Inset value greater than zero should be applied to any box that has a frame to create breathing space between the text and the frame.

To change the text inset:

1. Choose the Item or Content tool.
2. Click on the text box.
3. Choose Item menu > Modify (Ctrl-M) or right-click and choose Modify, then click the Text folder tab.
4. Enter a value in the Text Inset field ■1. If you're entering a value in points, you don't have to reenter the "pt."
5. *Optional:* Click Apply to preview.
6. Click OK or press Enter ■2–■3.

TIP If you want to apply a different inset value to each side of a box, use the Insets & Align palette in the Windows TeXT ColleXTion XTension by Vision's Edge.

PROMOTE THEN AS AN OBJECT OF PRIMARY IMPORTANCE, INSTITUTIONS FOR THE GENERAL DIFFUSION OF KNOWLEDGE. IN PROPORTION AS THE STRUCTURE OF A GOVERNMENT GIVES FORCE TO PUBLIC OPINION, IT IS ESSENTIAL THAT PUBLIC OPINION BE ENLIGHTENED.

■2 *A text box with a Text Inset of 0 pt.*

PROMOTE THEN AS AN OBJECT OF PRIMARY IMPORTANCE, INSTITUTIONS FOR THE GENERAL DIFFUSION OF KNOWLEDGE. IN PROPORTION AS THE STRUCTURE OF A GOVERNMENT GIVES FORCE TO PUBLIC OPINION, IT IS ESSENTIAL THAT PUBLIC OPINION BE ENLIGHTENED. *George Washington*

■3 *A text box with a Text Inset of 8 pt.*

MOVE DOWN THE LINE

To move the first line of text downward from the top of its box, select the box, choose Item menu > Modify (Ctrl-M), click the Text folder tab, then enter a number greater than 0 in the First Baseline: Offset field. This value will be added to the current Text Inset value. From the Minimum drop-down menu, choose whether the first baseline will start at the largest Cap Height, Cap + Accent (mark), or Ascent (top of highest letter, like an "l"or a "t") ■4–■5. Or, use the Insets & Align palette XTension instead (see the tip on this page).

Once upon a time there was a Pussy-cat called Ribby, who invited a little dog called Duchess to tea.

■4 ***First Baseline** 0.*

Once upon a time there was a Pussy-cat called Ribby, who invited a little dog called Duchess to tea.

Beatrix Potter

■5 ***First Baseline** 1p6.*

To apply a frame to a text or picture box:

1. Choose the Item or Content tool.
2. Click on a box (Bézier or standard).
3. Choose Item menu > Frame (Ctrl-B).
4. Choose a preset width from the Width drop-down menu **1** or enter a custom width in the Width field.
5. Choose a style from the Style drop-down menu. (To create a custom dashed or multi-line (striped) frame, see pages 169–170.)
6. Choose a color from the Color drop-down menu.
7. Choose a shade from the Shade drop-down menu or enter a percentage in the Shade field.
8. *Optional:* To recolor the white areas in a multi-line or dashed style, choose a Gap: Color and Shade.
9. Click Apply to preview, make any adjustments, then click OK or press Enter (illustrations on the next page).

TIP Enter 0 in the Width field to remove a frame.

TIP Enter a Text Inset greater than zero in Item > Modify > Text folder tab so the text won't touch the frame.

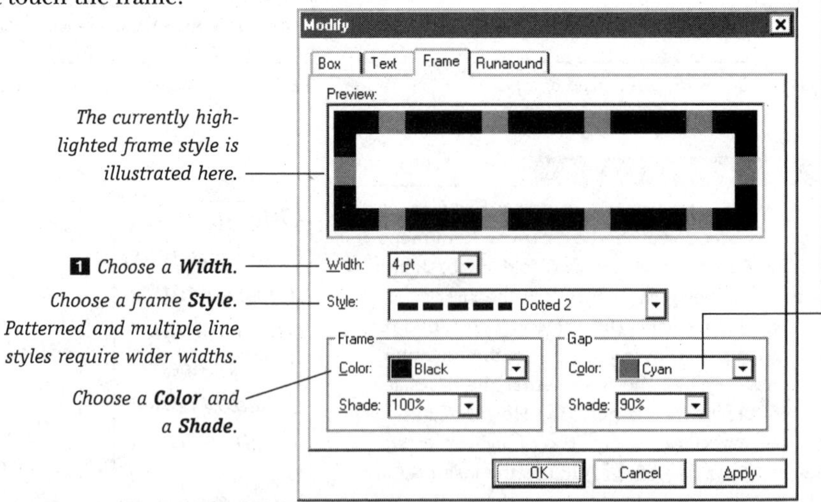
You can recolor the gaps in a multi-line or dashed frame by choosing a **Gap: Color** and **Shade**.
The currently highlighted frame style is illustrated here.
1 Choose a **Width**.
Choose a frame **Style**. Patterned and multiple line styles require wider widths.
Choose a **Color** and a **Shade**.
Modify
Box
Text
Frame
Runaround
Preview:
Width:
4 pt
Style:
Dotted 2
Frame
Color:
Black
Shade:
100%
Gap
Color:
Cyan
Shade:
90%
OK
Cancel
Apply

*The Item menu > Modify > **Frame** folder tab.*

Frames illustrated

Speak what you think now in hard words, and to-morrow speak what to-morrow thinks in hard words again, though it contradict every thing you said to-day.—"Ah, so you shall be sure to be misunderstood."—Is it so bad, then, to be misunderstood? Pythagoras was misunderstood, and Socrates, and Jesus, and Luther, and Copernicus, and Galileo, and Newton, and every pure and wise spirit that ever took flesh. To be great is to be misunderstood.

Ralph Waldo Emerson

Fish, like guests, smell after three days.

If you have built castles
in the air,
your work need not be lost;
that is where they should be.
Now
put the foundations under them.

Henry David Thoreau

DO I CONTRADICT MYSELF?

VERY WELL THEN...

I CONTRADICT MYSELF;

I AM LARGE...

I CONTAIN MULTITUDES.

Walt Whitman

Split pea soup

1 T. extra virgin olive oil
1 large onion, chopped
1 T. fresh ginger, minced
1 lb. dried split peas
3 carrots, diced
6 cups water
¼ t. dried mace
¼ t. dried coriander
1 T. parsley, minced
Freshly ground pepper

1. Heat the oil in a large soup pot, then saute the onions and ginger until soft.
2. Add the split peas, carrots, and water, and bring to a boil. Lower heat and simmer 30 minutes, or until the split peas are soft.
3. Add the dried and fresh herbs, and simmer 5 minutes more.
4. Puree the soup in a blender or food processor, and add freshly ground pepper to taste.

Text boxes can be made see-through so they can be layered on top of each other.

To make a text box transparent:

1. Choose the Item or Content tool.
2. Click on the text box that is to be on the top layer. If it's not on the top layer, choose Item menu > Bring to Front (F5).
3. Choose Item menu > Runaround (Ctrl-T).
4. Choose Type: None **1**.
5. Click OK or press Enter.
6. If the Colors palette isn't already open, choose View menu > Show Colors (F12).
7. Click the Background color icon on the Colors palette **2**.
8. Click None **3**. (Black with a 0% shade won't produce the desired result.) See the illustrations on next page.

TIP To select an item that is behind another item without changing its layer, hold down Ctrl, Alt, Shift and click. Each click will select the next item behind in succession (more about this on page 125).

1 *Choose Type:* ***None.***

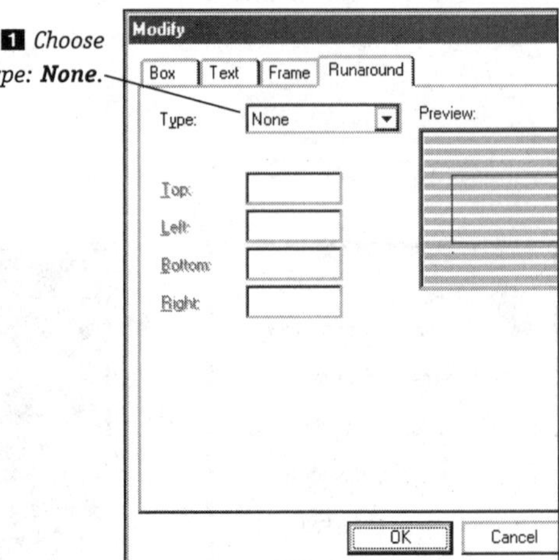

2 *First click the* ***background color*** *icon.*

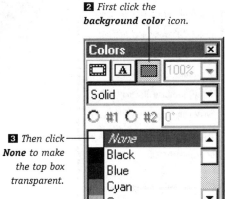

3 *Then click* ***None*** *to make the top box transparent.*

The ***Colors*** *palette.*

Script Script

SIDEWAYS

Bold

A variety of effects can be created by making boxes see-through. The shadow was created using the I Shadow XTension.

Italic

Roman

type in any direction

Piling up

Boxes can be layered to create an illusion of depth.

Text boxes can be layered on top of a picture box.

To rotate a text box using the Measurements palette:

1. Choose the Item or Content tool.
2. Click on a text box.
3. In the rotation field on the Measurements palette, enter a positive number between 0° and 360° to rotate the box counter-clockwise **1** or a negative number to rotate it clockwise.
4. Press Enter.

TIP Text can be modified in a rotated position.

1 *The **rotation angle** of a text box.*

X: 10p W: 5p3 30°
Y: 12p H: 2p5 Cols: 1

To rotate a text box using the Rotation tool:

1. Choose the Rotation tool.
2. Click on a text box.
3. Press to create an axis point for rotation, then drag the mouse away from the axis to create a "lever" **2**. The further you drag away from the axis before rotating, the easier the rotation will be to control.
4. Drag clockwise or counterclockwise **3**.

TIP Hold down Shift while dragging to rotate at a 0°, 45°, or 90° angle.

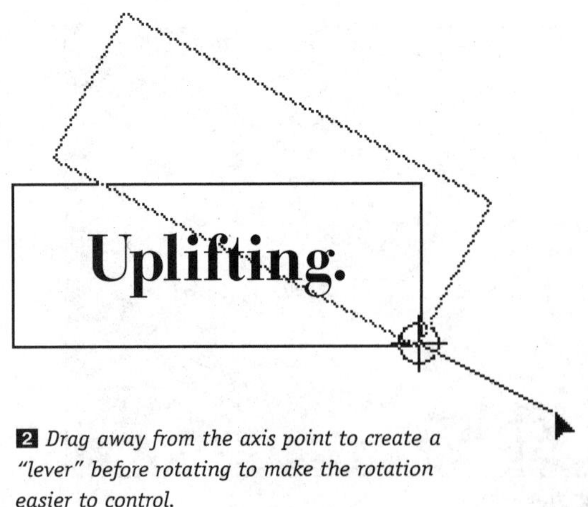

2 *Drag away from the axis point to create a "lever" before rotating to make the rotation easier to control.*

3 *A text box rotated -90.°*

WRAPPING ALL AROUND

Normally, text will only wrap around three sides of a box within a column. To wrap text around all sides of a box within a column, select the box that contains the text that's doing the wrapping, choose Item menu > Modify, click the Text folder tab, check the Run Text Around All Sides box, then click OK. See page 162.

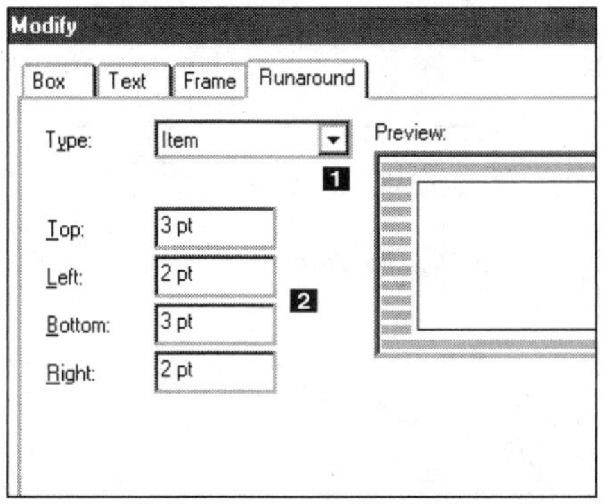

To wrap text around another box:

1. Arrange one text box on top of another. The box that you want to wrap text around must be on the topmost layer. A new box will automatically be on the topmost layer in the document. If you're using an existing box and it's not on top, select it and choose Item menu > Bring to Front (F5).
2. With the new box still selected, choose Item menu > Runaround (Ctrl-T).
3. Choose Type: Item **1**.
4. Enter a number in the Top, Left, Bottom and Right fields to adjust the space between the text box and the type wrapping around it **2**. If you're entering a value in points, you don't have to reenter the "pt". Press Tab to move quickly from field to field.
5. Click Apply to preview, make any adjustments, then click OK or press Enter **3**–**4**.

We thus learn that man is descended from a hairy, tailed quadruped, probably arboreal in its habits, and an inhabitant of the Old World. This creature, if its whole structure had been examined by a naturalist, would have been classed amongst the Quadrumana, as surely as the still more ancient progenitor of the Old and New World monkeys.
The Quadrumana and all the higher mammals are probably derived from an ancient marsupial animal, and this through a long series of diversified forms, from some amphibian-like creature, and this again

We thus learn that man is descended from a hairy, tailed quadruped, probably arboreal in its habits, and an inhabitant of the Old World.
Charles Darwin

3 *Normally, text will only wrap around three sides of a box that is placed within a column (unless Run Text Around All Sides is turned for the text that is wrapping–see the sidebar, above).*

We thus learn that man is descended from a hairy, tailed quadruped, probably arboreal in its habits, and an inhabitant of the Old World. This creature, if its whole structure had been examined by a naturalist, would have been classed amongst the Quadrumana, as surely as the still more ancient progenitor of the Old and New World monkeys. The Quadrumana and all the higher mammals are probably derived from an ancient marsupial animal, and this through a long series of diversified forms, from some amphibian-like creature, and this again from some fish-like animal. In the dim obscurity of the past we can see that the early progenitor of all the Vertebrata must have

We thus learn that man is descended from a hairy, tailed quadruped, probably arboreal in its habits, and an inhabitant of the Old World.
Charles Darwin

4 *Text will always wrap around all four sides of a box if the topmost box straddles two columns.*

The Vertical Alignment options affect the entire text box. Leading and inter-paragraph spacing, which are paragraph formatting commands, are discussed in Chapter 6.

To change vertical alignment:

1. Choose the Item or Content tool.
2. Click on a text box or select multiple boxes.
3. Choose Item menu > Modify (Ctrl-M) or right-click and choose Modify.
4. Click the Text folder tab.
5. Choose one of the four Vertical Alignment options from the Type drop-down menu **1**.
6. Click Apply to preview, if desired, then click OK or press Enter **2**.

TIP In vertically justified text with an Inter ¶ Max value of 0, space is added evenly between lines and paragraphs. An Inter ¶ Max value greater than 0 is the maximum space that can be added between paragraphs before leading is affected.

TIP Make sure there is no return at the end of the last line in a box to which bottom, centered, or justified Vertical Alignment has been applied.

TIP Vertical justification won't work if another box for which Runaround is turned on overlaps the text box to which justification has been applied. Choose a Runaround of None (Item menu > Runaround) for the topmost box, and vertical justification will work.

TIP With the Item tool selected, you can double-click a text box to quickly open the Modify dialog box. Ctrl-double-click if you're using the Content tool.

SPEED TIP

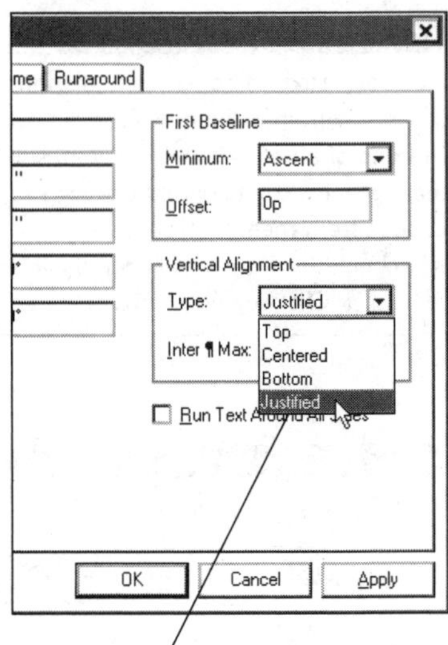

1 *The four **Vertical Alignment** options.*

2

Never put off till tomorrow what you can do the day after tomorrow.

***Top** vertical alignment.*

Never put off till tomorrow what you can do the day after tomorrow.

***Bottom** vertical alignment.*

Never put off till tomorrow what you can do the day after tomorrow.

***Centered** vertical alignment.*

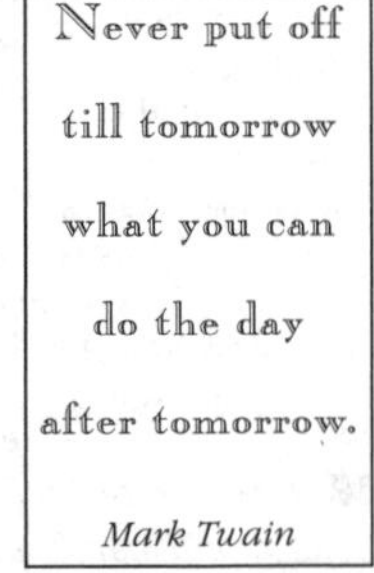

***Justified** vertical alignment.*

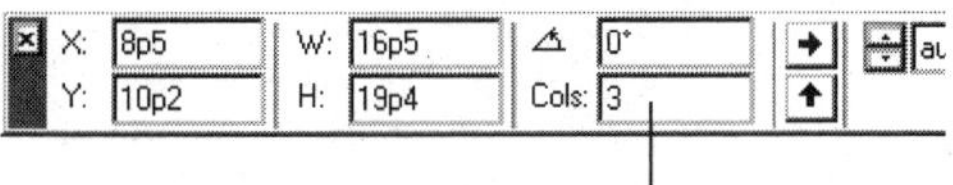

1 *The number of **columns** in a text box can be changed using the Measurements palette.*

There was a nice hot singey smell; and at the table, with an iron in her hand, stood a very stout short person staring anxiously at Lucie. Her print gown was tucked up, and she was wearing a large apron over her striped petticoat. Her little black nose went sniffle, sniffle, snuffle, and her eyes went twinkle, twinkle, twinkle; and underneath her cap—where Lucie had yellow curls—that little person had PRICKLES!

Beatrix Potter

2 *A two-column text box…*

There was a nice hot singey smell; and at the table, with an iron in her hand, stood a very stout short person staring anxiously at Lucie. Her print gown was tucked up, and she was wearing a large apron over her striped petticoat. Her little black nose went sniffle, sniffle, snuffle, and her eyes went twinkle, twinkle, twinkle; and underneath her cap—where Lucie had yellow curls—that little person had PRICKLES!

3 *…is converted into a three-column text box.*

Follow either set of instructions on this page to change the number of columns and/or gutter width in an individual box. To change the non-printing margin and column guides or to change the number of columns in a box originating from a master page, see page 215.

To change the number of columns using the Measurements palette:

1. Choose the Item or Content tool.
2. Select a text box.
3. Enter a number in the "Cols" field on the Measurements palette **1**.
4. Press Enter **2**–**3**.

To change columns and/or gutter width using a dialog box:

1. Choose the Item or Content tool.
2. Select a text box.
3. Choose Item menu > Modify (Ctrl-M) or right-click and choose Modify, and click the Text folder tab.
4. Enter a new number between 1 and 30 in the Columns field **4**.
   and/or
   Enter a new number in the Gutter Width field for the blank space between the columns.
5. Click OK or press Enter.

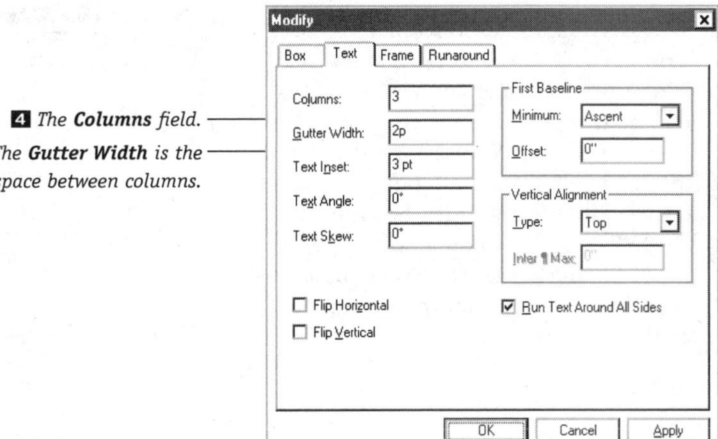

4 *The **Columns** field.*
*The **Gutter Width** is the space between columns.*

You can save a copy of text from a QuarkXPress file into a number of different word processing file formats. If you apply style sheets to text in QuarkXPress and then export the text in the Microsoft Word format, the style sheets will save with the file and will be useable in Word.

To save text as a word processing file:

1. Choose the Content tool.
2. Highlight the text to be saved.
   or
   Click in a story.
3. Choose File menu > Save Text (Ctrl-Alt-E).
4. Type a name for the text file in the File name field **1**.
5. If text is highlighted in the document, you can click Entire Story or Selected Text. If you merely clicked in a story, only the Entire Story option will be available.
6. Choose a file format from the "Save as type" drop-down menu. (The import/export filter for a file format must be enabled for it to appear on the list. Use the XTensions Manager to turn a filter on or off. See page 285.)
7. Choose a location in which to save the text file.
8. Click Save or press Enter.

TIP Text saved in the ASCII format will be stripped of all formatting. Text saved in a word processing application format may be stripped of some formatting. Text saved in the XPress Tags format will retain all formatting, but it will display with special codes. See the QuarkXPress documentation or David Blatner's *The QuarkXPress Book* (Peachpit Press) for more information about XPress Tags.

1 *Type a name in the **File name** field.*

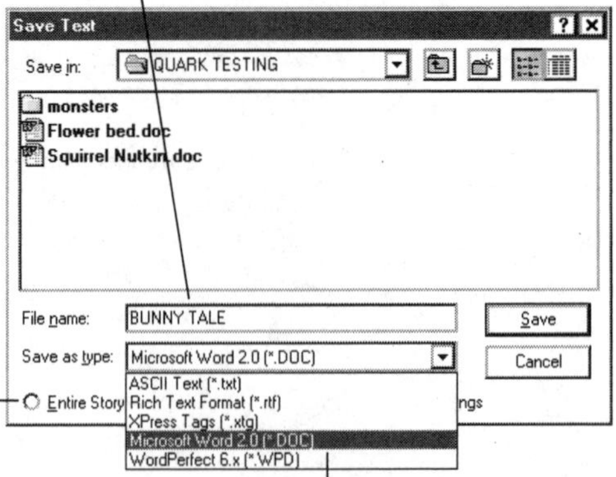

Save Text
Save in: QUARK TESTING
monsters
Flower bed.doc
Squirrel Nutkin.doc
File name: BUNNY TALE
Save as type: Microsoft Word 2.0 (*.DOC)
ASCII Text (*.txt)
Rich Text Format (*.rtf)
XPress Tags (*.xtg)
Microsoft Word 2.0 (*.DOC)
WordPerfect 6.x (*.WPD)
Entire Story
Save
Cancel

*Click **Entire Story** or click **Selected Text** (if available).*

*Choose a file format from the **Save as type** drop-down menu.*

Text flow 5

WHAT IF

If you forgot to turn on Automatic Text Box when you first created your document, you can add an auto text box later on. See the instructions on page 226.

If the Auto Page Insertion option is turned on in the General Preferences dialog box and your document contains an automatic text box, and then text is imported *or* input into an automatic text box, new pages will be added, if necessary, to contain any overflow text and text boxes will be linked from page to page. A document can contain up to 2,000 pages.

To turn on auto page insertion:

1. Choose File menu > New (Ctrl-N) to create a new document.
2. Check the Automatic Text Box box. With this option on, a text box will appear automatically on every document page.
3. Define the Page Size, Orientation, Margin Guides, and Column Guides.
4. Click OK or press Enter.
5. Choose Edit menu > Preferences > Document (Ctrl-Y).
6. Click the General folder tab.
7. Choose Auto Page Insertion: End of Story, End of Section, or End of Document **1** (the location where you want new pages to be added).
8. Click OK or press Enter.

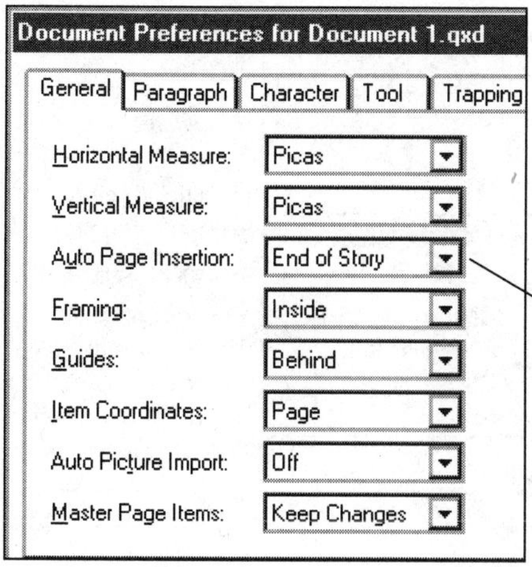

1 *Choose* ***Auto Page Insertion: End of Story, End of Section****, or* ***End of Document*** *in Document Preferences > General folder tab.*

A text file that is created in a word processing program (i.e. Microsoft Word) or a spreadsheet program can be imported into a text box in QuarkXPress. To import text, the import/export filter for the file's format must be enabled (see page 285).

To import text:

1. *Optional:* Turn on Auto Page Insertion (see steps 5–8 on the previous page).
2. Choose the Content tool.
3. Click in a text box. Click in an automatic text box for auto page insertion. (If Auto Page Insertion is off, the imported text will flow into a box or a series of linked boxes, but new pages won't be added.)
4. Choose File menu > Get Text (Ctrl-E).
5. Make sure the Convert Quotes box is checked **1**.
6. *Optional:* Check the Include Style Sheets box if the file contains style sheets that you want to import.
7. Highlight a text file, then click Open.
   or
   Double-click a text file (**2**–**5**, next page).

FORMATS YOU CAN IMPORT

WordPerfect, AmiPro, MS-Word, XPress Tags, MS-Works, and ASCII text with or without XPress tags.

WORD STYLES

- To import style sheets applied to text in Microsoft Word, check the Include Style Sheets box in the Get Text dialog box. If any style sheet names in the word document match style sheet names in the QuarkXPress document, a prompt will appear. Click Rename New Style to import that style. Also turn on Include Style Sheets if you want ASCII text with XPress tags to import as styled text.
- If Include Style Sheets is turned off, XPress' No Style will be applied to the imported text (unless it's a text-only file with no applied styles), which means it will be stripped of any local formatting if you then apply a style sheet to it.
- The XPress Tags filter must be enabled for the Include Style Sheets box to be available. Use the XTensions Manager to enable/disable this import/export filter.

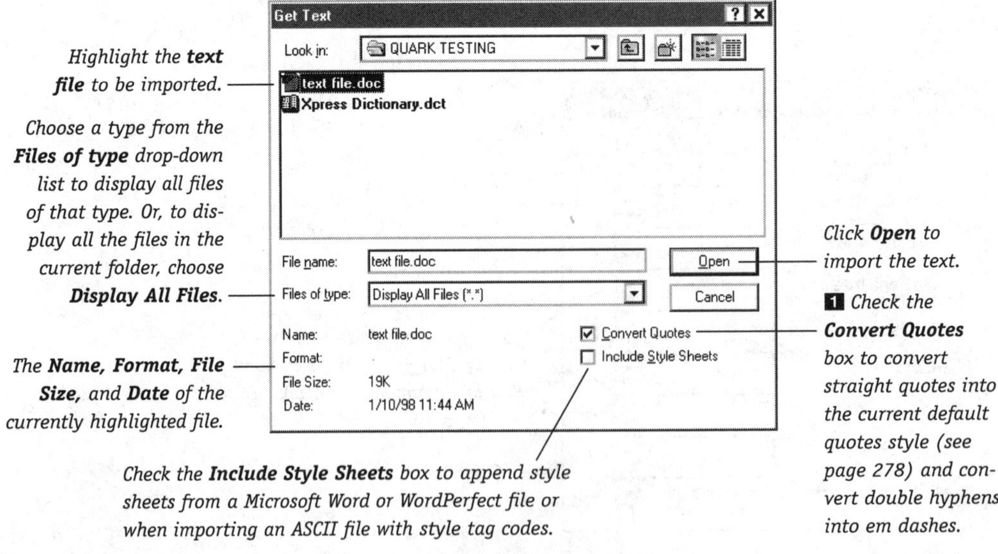

*Highlight the **text file** to be imported.*

*Choose a type from the **Files of type** drop-down list to display all files of that type. Or, to display all the files in the current folder, choose **Display All Files**.*

*The **Name, Format, File Size,** and **Date** of the currently highlighted file.*

*Check the **Include Style Sheets** box to append style sheets from a Microsoft Word or WordPerfect file or when importing an ASCII file with style tag codes.*

*Click **Open** to import the text.*

1 *Check the **Convert Quotes** box to convert straight quotes into the current default quotes style (see page 278) and convert double hyphens into em dashes.*

Auto Page Insertion on

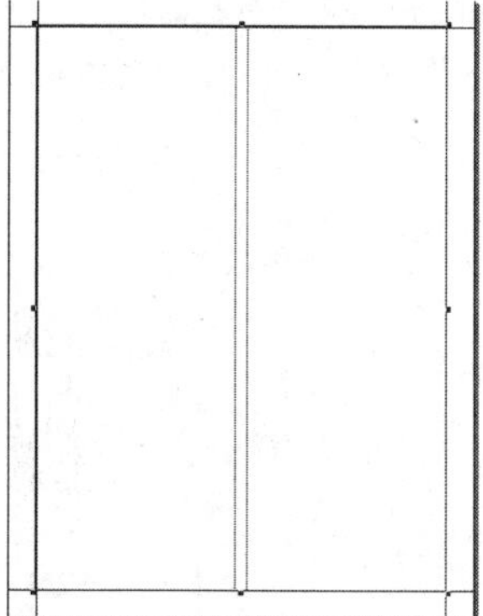

2 *Auto Page Insertion is on and an automatic text box is selected. Then a word processing file is imported.*

3 *New pages are created automatically to accommodate the imported word processing file, and the text is linked in a continuous flow.*

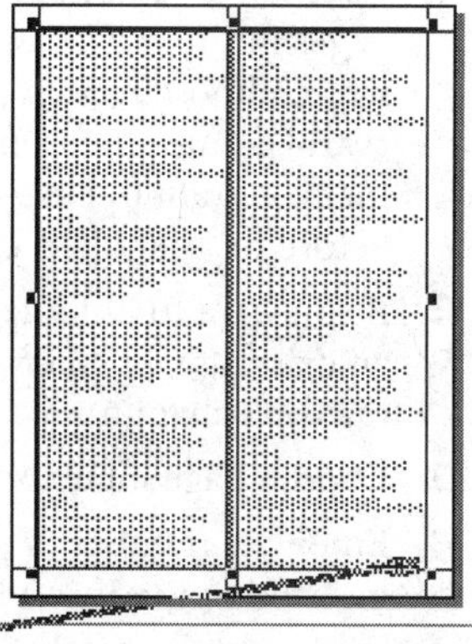

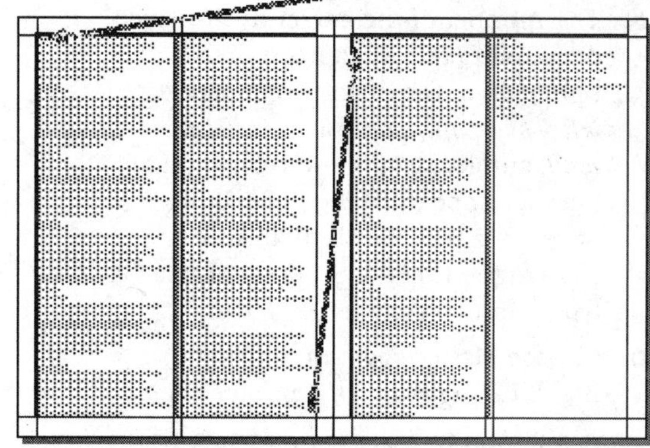

Auto Page Insertion off

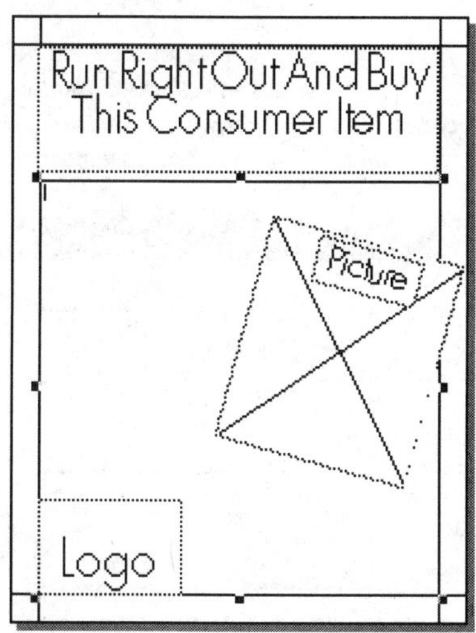

4 *Auto Page Insertion is off, and a text box is selected.*

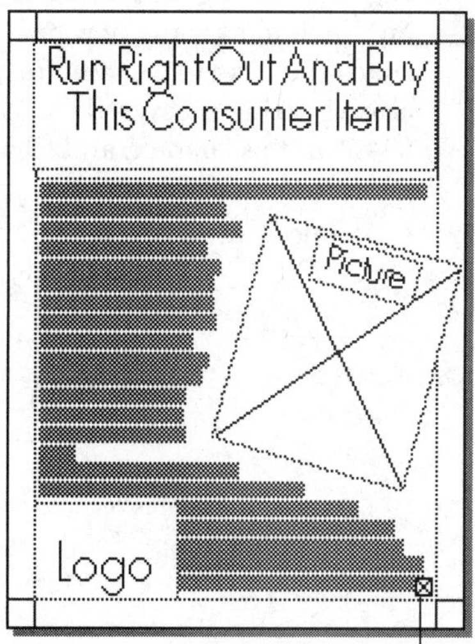

5 *The text overflow symbol appears after the text is imported.*

To insert pages using a dialog box:

1. *Optional:* To make sure you're inserting pages in the correct spot in your document, choose Page menu > Go to (Ctrl-J), enter the number of the page that you want to have text inserted before or after, then click OK.
2. If you want to link the new pages to an existing text chain, click in a box in that text chain now.
3. Choose Page menu > Insert.
4. Enter the number of pages to be inserted in the Insert field **1**.
5. The number of the currently displayed document page will appear on the right side of the dialog box. Click *before page, after page,* or *at end of document,* and make sure the correct page number appears in the field. If the page has a prefix or Roman style that was assigned via the Section command, type it in that manner.
6. Choose Master Page: Blank Single, Blank Facing Page, or a master page.

   If you want to link the new pages using an automatic text box, choose a Master Page containing an automatic text box on which to base the new page(s), and check the Link to Current Text Chain box. (Linking is covered on pages 69–71 in this chapter, and Chapter 14 is devoted entirely to master pages.)
7. Click OK or press Enter.

HOW MANY?

Need to know the total number of pages in a document? Make sure no page icons are highlighted on the Document Layout palette—the total page count readout will appear in the lower left-hand corner of the palette **2**.

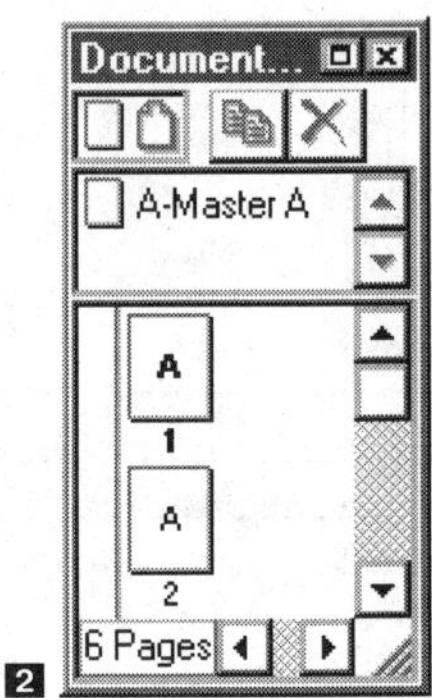

2

*Choose a **location** for the inserted pages.*

The number in this field initially reflects the currently displayed page. You can enter a different number.

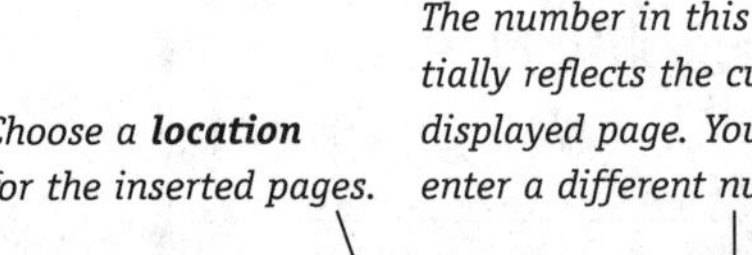

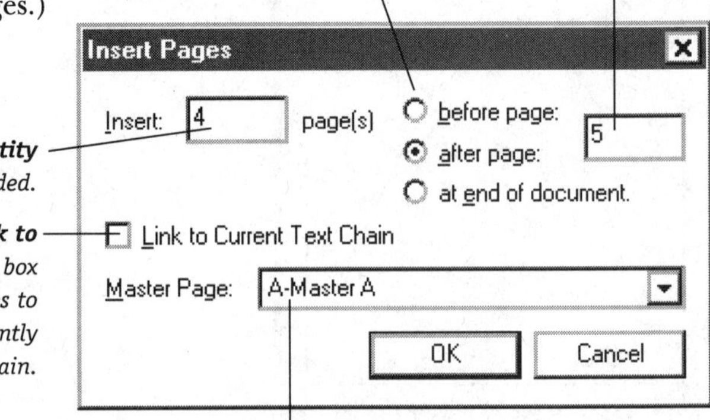

1 *Enter the **quantity** of pages to be added.*

*Check the **Link to Current Text Chain** box to link the new pages to the end of the currently selected text chain.*

*Choose whether the inserted pages will be based on an existing **master** page or a **blank** master page.*

Insert Pages Using a Dialog Box

1 *Press and drag a blank page icon to insert a new page.*

Blank single-sided page

Blank facing page

2 *Or press and drag a master page icon.*

Master page

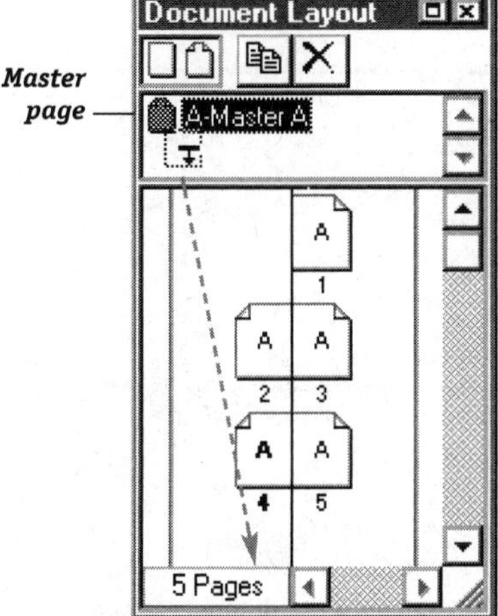

Note: Changes made using the Document Layout palette, such as adding, deleting, or rearranging pages, cannot be undone with the Undo command, so it's a good idea to save your document before performing any of those operations. Then, if something goes awry, you can choose File menu > Revert to Saved to rescue your document.

To insert pages using the Document Layout palette:

1. Choose View menu > Show Document Layout (F4).
2. Press and drag a blank or master page icon into the document icon area (**1**–**2**, this page and **3**–**6**, next page).

TIP A blank page will have no master page applied to it. You can apply a master page to it later (see page 219).

Note: If you add an uneven number of pages to a facing-pages document (unless you drag it manually to a spread by itself), the master page will reapply automatically from the inserted pages forward. Whenever possible, try to add an even number of pages to this type of document.

TIP A page cannot be placed to the left of the first page in a facing-pages document, unless the document begins with an even section number (see page 74).

TIP If you Alt-drag a blank or master page (step 2, above), the Insert pages dialog box will open.

(Continued on the following page)

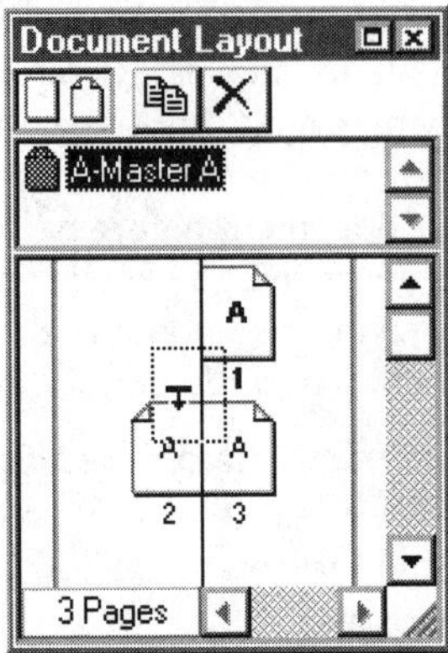

3 *To insert a page between spreads in a facing-pages document, release the mouse when the* ***Force Down*** *pointer is displayed.*

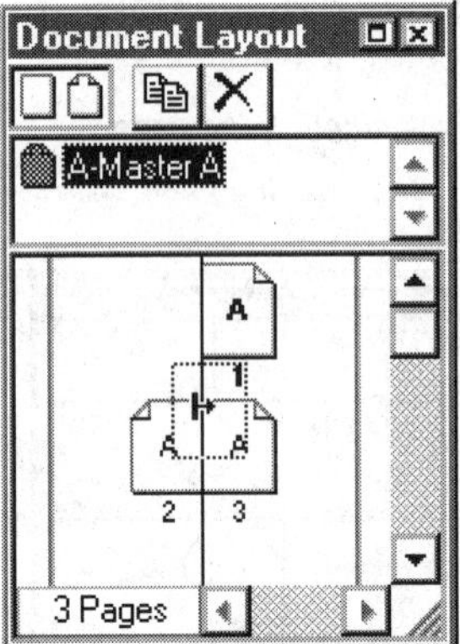

4 *In a facing-pages document, if you release the mouse when the* ***Force Right*** *pointer is displayed, subsequent pages may reshuffle. Pages won't reshuffle in a single-sided document.*

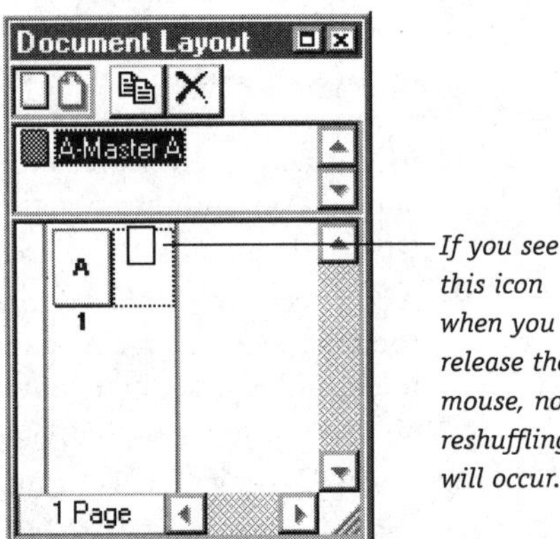

5 *To create a* ***spread*** *in a single-sided document, drag a new page next to an existing page. Choose a very small view size for your document so you can see how the new arrangement looks.*

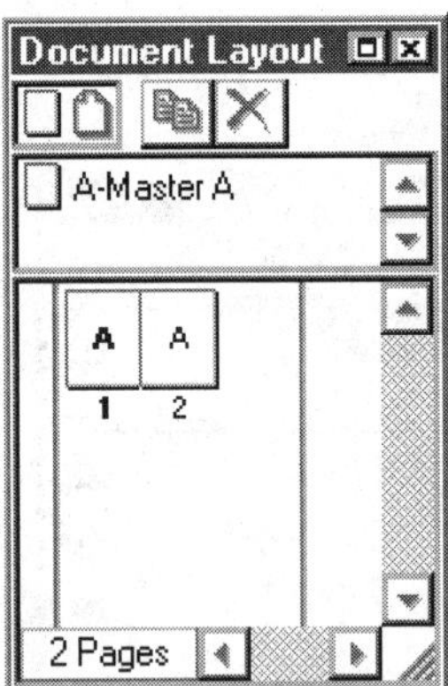

6 *Pages 1 and 2 will display side-by-side on the screen. 48" is the maximum width. Pages will print separately unless the Spreads box is checked in the Print dialog box (Document folder tab).*

PAGES KEEP COMING BACK

If, when you delete document pages, Auto Page Insertion is on (Edit menu > Preferences > Document > General folder tab), the master page has an intact (not broken) chain icon (an automatic text box is present), and all the text in a linked chain does not fit on the pages that remain, new pages will be added automatically to accommodate the overflow text. If Auto Page Insertion is off, the overflow symbol will appear, and new pages will not be added. Either way, the overflow text won't be deleted.

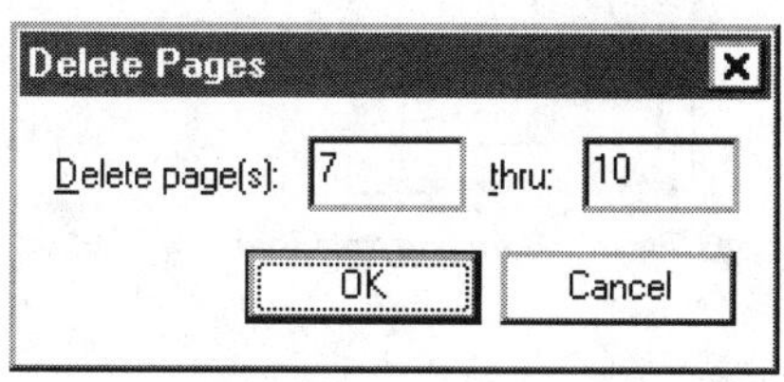

1 *Enter starting and ending page numbers to delete a series of pages.*

3 *Then click the brushstroke-X icon.*

2 *To delete a page, click its icon.*

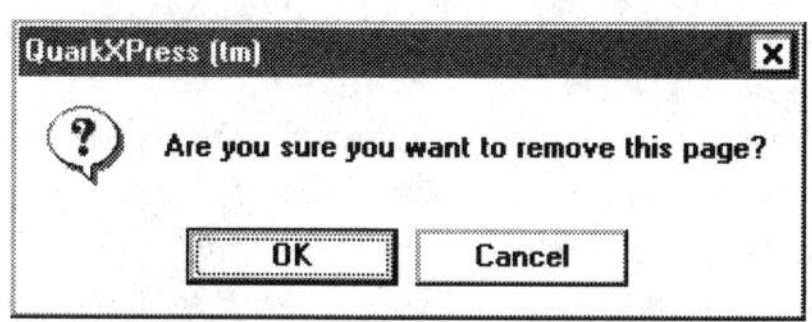

4 *Click OK when this prompt appears.*

To delete pages using a dialog box:

1. Choose Page menu > Delete.
2. Enter a number in the first field to delete a single page.
   or
   Enter numbers in both fields to delete a range of pages **1**. If a page has a prefix or Roman style that was assigned via the Section command, type it in that manner. You can enter "end" in the second field.
3. Click OK or press Enter.

To delete pages using the Document Layout palette:

1. On the Document Layout palette:
   Click on a document page icon **2**.
   or
   Click on the icon of the first page in a series of pages to be deleted, then Shift-click on the icon of the last page in the series.
   or
   Ctrl-click on non-consecutive page icons. (Ctrl-click a selected page icon if you want to deselect it.)
2. Click the brushstroke-X icon on the palette **3**.
3. When the prompt "Are you sure you want to remove these pages?" appears, click OK or press Enter **4**.

TIP Alt-click the brushstroke-X icon on the palette (step 2, above) to bypass the prompt.

If you rearrange pages in thumbnails view, you'll be able to see what the actual pages look like as they're moved, which means less room for error.

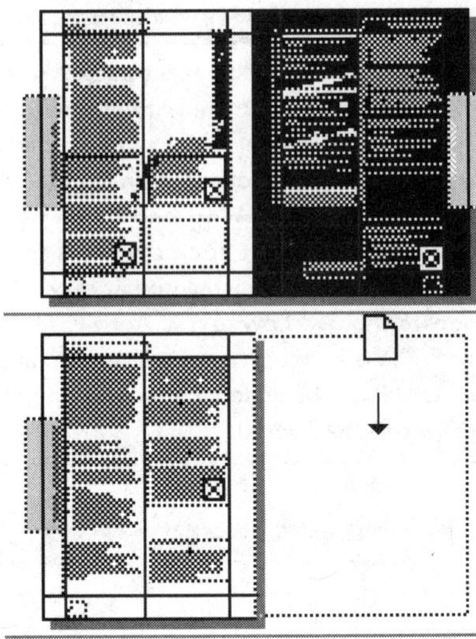

1 *Press and drag a page to a new location.*

To rearrange pages in Thumbnails view:

1. Choose View menu > Thumbnails (Shift + F6).
2. Press and drag a page icon to a new location in the document window **1**. If automatic page numbering was applied to the document, the numbers will update to reflect their new position.

TIP To move more than one page at a time, click on the first page in a series of consecutive pages, Shift-click on the last page in the series, then press and drag. Ctrl-click instead to select non-consecutive pages.

To rearrange pages using the Document Layout palette:

1. Choose View menu > Show Document Layout (F4).
2. Press and drag a document page icon to a new location **2**–**3**.
   or
   Click on the icon of the first page in a series of pages to be moved, hold down Shift and click on the icon of last page in the series, release Shift, then drag the pages to a new location. Ctrl-click to select non-consecutive pages. (See also the figures on page 66.)

TIP You can also rearrange pages using the Page menu > Move dialog box.

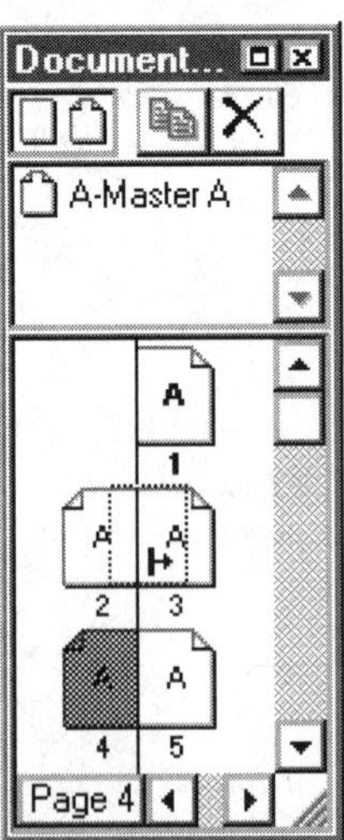

2 *If you force a page between two pages in a facing-pages document, the remaining pages may reshuffle. Note the* ***Force Right*** *pointer.*

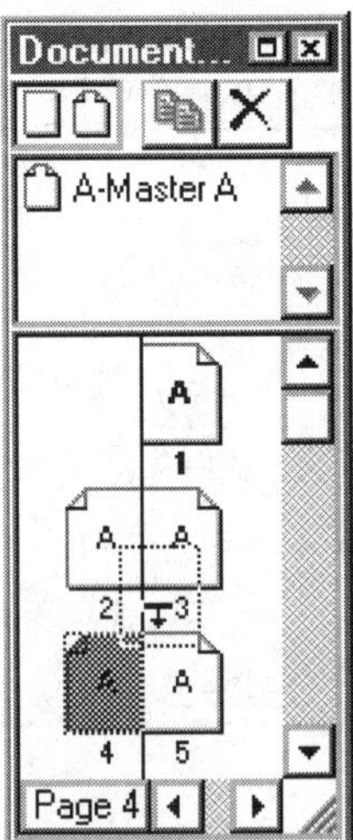

3 *If you force a page between two spreads in any kind of document, the remaining pages won't reshuffle. Note the* ***Force Down*** *pointer.*

KEEP ON LINKIN'

Alt-click the Linking tool to keep it selected so as to link multiple boxes. Click on another tool when you're done linking. This works with the Unlinking tool, too.

The text that is contained in one box or in a series of linked boxes is called a story. Text in a linked chain flows in a continuous stream from box to box, even if characters are added or deleted. Manual linking can be used in addition, or as an alternative to, automatic page insertion. Use it to flow text between non-consecutive pages, as in a newsletter or a magazine, or from box to box on the same page.

To link text boxes or paths manually:

1. Choose the Linking tool.
2. Click on a text box or text path. It can contain text or it can be empty. A moving marquee will appear **1**.
3. Click on an **empty** text box or path. An arrow will appear briefly, showing the new link **2**–**3**. A new box can be added at any juncture in an existing chain.

TIP If you inadvertently click on the wrong box with the Linking tool, to stop the box from flashing, just choose a different tool or click outside the box.

Again I see you're about to pounce,
alas, my poor computer mouse.

And losing this page I cannot afford,
but there you march across the keyboard.

You can't be hungry again so fast
Why the time's just barely passed.

Oh maybe I'll give you just a nibble,
just so you'll stay out of trib'l.

1 *Click on a text box.*

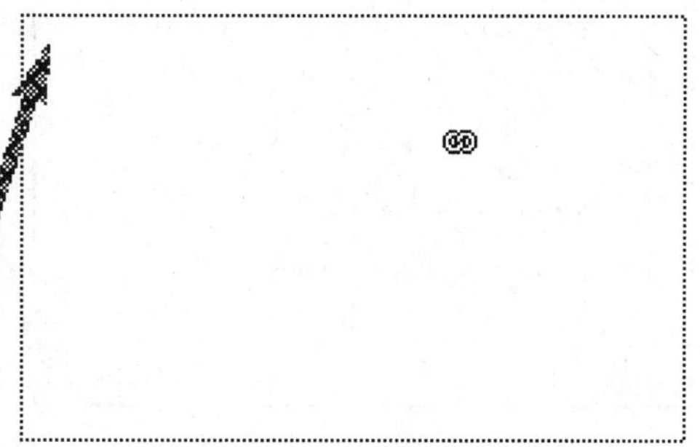

2 *Then click on an empty text box.*

Again I see you're about to pounce,
alas, my poor computer mouse.

And losing this page I cannot afford,
but there you march across the keyboard.

You can't be hungry again so fast
Why the time's just barely passed.

Oh maybe I'll give you just a nibble,
just so you'll stay out of trib'l.

I know it's warmer than my lap,
but the printer's not the place to nap.

And I don't need your claws to catch,
the printer's pages as they hatch.

To keep you from my papers chew'n
I guess I shouldn't leave them strew'n.

I just wish you wouldn't eat'm
before I've had a chance to read'm.

3 *These boxes are linked.*

To unlink text boxes or paths:

1. Choose the Unlinking tool.
2. Click on one of the two text boxes or paths that are to be unlinked.
3. Click on the head or tail of the arrow between them **1**. Links preceding the break will remain intact; the link to succeeding boxes or paths will be broken **2**.

TIP If you are unable to unlink with the Unlinking tool, make sure there are no other items obstructing the one that you are trying to click on.

TIP If you click in a linked box with the Content tool, you can use the up or down arrow on the keyboard to jump from the first line in the box to the last line of the previous box in the chain or from the last line in the box to the first line in the next box in the chain.

TIP If you rearrange pages in a text chain, the links will stay intact.

FIND THE LINKS

To see where the links are in a document, choose a small display size (around 30%), then click on one of the boxes in the link chain with the Unlinking tool. Choose a different tool when you're finished.

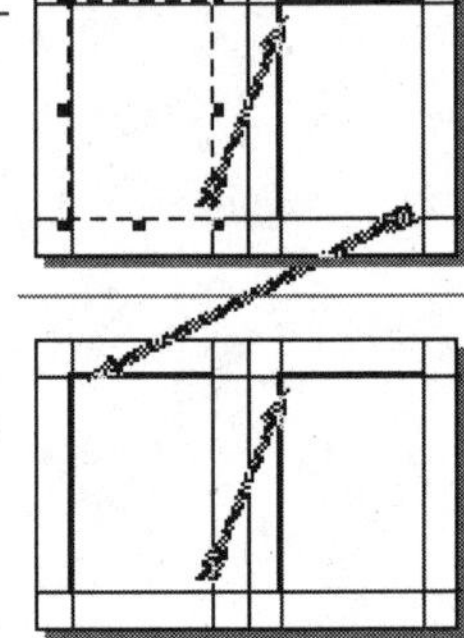

Ah, what can ever be more stately and admirable to me than mast-hemm'd Manhattan?

River and sunset and scallop-edg'd waves of flood-tide?

The sea-gulls oscillating their bodies, the hay-boat in the twilight, and the belated lighter?

What gods can exceed these that clasp me by the hand, and with voices I love call me promptly and loudly by my nighest name as I approach?

What is more subtle than this which ties me to the woman or man that looks in my face?

Which fuses me into you now, and pours my meaning into you?

Walt Whitman

1 *Click on one of the two text boxes, and then click on the head or tail of the arrow between them.*

Ah, what can ever be more stately and admirable to me than mast-hemm'd Manhattan?

River and sunset and scallop-edg'd waves of flood-tide?

The sea-gulls oscillating their bodies, the hay-boat in the twilight, and the belated lighter?

2 *The link is broken.*

Oronte. Do you find anything to object to in my sonnet?

Alceste. I do not say that. But, to keep him from writing, I set before his eyes how, in our days, that desire had spoiled a great many very worthy people.

Oronte. Do I write badly? Am I like them in any way?

Alceste. I do not say that. But, in short, I said to him: What pressing need is there for you to rhyme, and what the deuce drives you into print? If we can pardon the sending into the world of a

badly-written book, it will only be in those unfortunate men who write for their livelihood. Believe me, resist your temptations, keep these effusions from the public, and do not, how much soever you may be asked, forfeit the reputation which you enjoy at

Molière

1 *Choose the **Unlinking** tool, then **Shift**-click inside the box to be unlinked from the chain.*

COPY/PASTE/DUPE LINKED BOXES

You can copy, paste, or duplicate a linked text box. You can also drag-copy a linked box between documents or into a library. Text preceding the box in the chain will not copy. Overflow text will copy, but it will be hidden.

Linked boxes in a group or a multiple-item selection can be copied using any method described in the previous paragraph, as long as **all** the boxes in the chain are in the group or selection.

To delete a box or a path from a text chain and preserve the chain:

1. Choose the Item or Content tool.
2. Select the box or path to be deleted.
3. Choose Item menu > Delete (Ctrl-K).

To unlink a box or a path from a text chain and preserve the box and the chain:

1. Choose the Unlinking tool.
2. Shift-click **inside** the text box that you want to remove from the chain **1**–**2**.

TIP Using The Missing Link XTension in the Windows TeXT ColleXTion from Vision's Edge, Inc., you can perform magic tricks, like unlink a chain but leave the text exactly where it is.

Oronte. Do you find anything to object to in my sonnet?

Alceste. I do not say that. But, to keep him from writing, I set before his eyes how, in our days, that desire had spoiled a great many very worthy people.

Oronte. Do I write badly? Am I like them in any way?

Alceste. I do not say that. But, in short, I said to him: What pressing need is there for you to rhyme, and what the deuce drives you into print? If we can pardon the sending into the

2 *The middle box has been taken out of the chain.*

When text is linked between non-consecutive pages, as in a newsletter or magazine, there is usually an indicator to guide the reader to the continuation of the story or article. These "Continued on" and "Continued from" indicators are referred to as "jump lines." When the Next Box Page Number command is inserted, it instantly converts into the page number of the next linked box in the chain. If that text is re-linked to a box on a different page, the page number will update automatically.

To insert a "Continued on" command:

1. Choose the Rectangle text box tool. Or, if you want to get fancy, choose a Bézier text box or text path tool.
2. Create a separate, small box or path that overlaps the main text box of the story, and keep it selected.
3. Choose Item menu > Runaround (Ctrl-T).
4. Choose Type: Item.
5. Click OK or press Enter.
6. Choose the Content tool.
7. Type any desired text into the small box (or on the path), such as "Continued on page," or use a graphic symbol, like an arrow.
8. Hold down Ctrl and press "4" to insert the Next Box Page Number command **1**–**3**. Don't enter the actual page number yourself—it will appear automatically.

To insert a "Continued from" command:

Follow the above instructions, but for step 8, hold down Ctrl and press "2" to insert a Previous Box Page Number command **4**.

Elizabeth here felt herself called on to say something in vindication of his behaviour to Wickham; and therefore gave them to understand, in as guarded a manner as she could, that by what she had heard from his relations in Kent, his actions were capable of a very different construction; and that his

Continued on page 3

1 *A text box containing the* ***Next Box Page Number*** *command is positioned so that it overlaps the main text box.*

Continued from page <None>

2 *If the characters* ***<None>*** *appear instead of a page number, either the text box or path containing the Previous or Next Box Page Number command is not overlapping a linked text box or the text box it overlaps is not linked to a box on another page.*

Continued on page 3

3 *You can create a jump line on a text path.*

4 *The* ***Previous Box Page Number*** *command is inserted here.*

Continued from page 1

character was by no means so faulty, nor Wickham's so amiable, as they had been considered in Hertfordshire. In confirmation of this, she related the particulars of all the pecuniary transactions in which they had been connected, without actually naming her authority, but stating it to be such as might be relied on.

Jane Austen

RESCUE AN UNSAVEABLE FILE

If you get an error message that your file can't be saved, DON'T CLOSE IT! Create a new document or open a template that has the same dimensions, use the method on this page to drag pages from the old document to the new, save the new file, and then close and do not save the corrupted file.

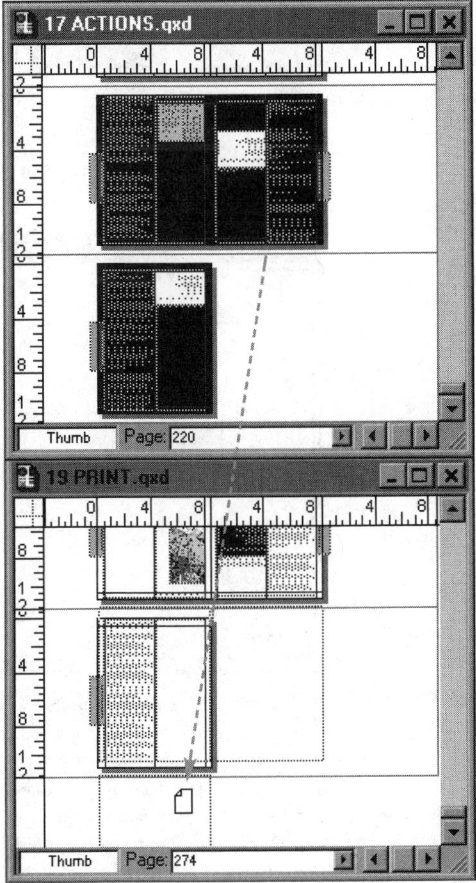

1 *Drag-copying pages in **Thumbnails** view from one document to another.*

Note: You can't copy a page to a document that has a smaller page size. And a page to which a facing-pages master has been applied cannot be copied to a single-sided document. Any style sheets, colors, dashes and stripes, lists, H&Js, or master pages on the appending pages will be added to the destination document.

To drag-copy pages from one document to another:

1. Open the document you want to copy from and the document you want to copy to.
2. Hold down Alt and choose Window menu > Tile Horizontally or Tile Vertically to tile both documents into Thumbnails view.

   Here's a trick I use to make room for new pages if I'm adding them at the end of a document: In the document window I'm copying to, I drag the resize box (lower right corner) upward, click the down scroll arrow to scoot the document pages upward, then drag the resize box to lengthen the document window again (see the bottom window in the illustration at left).
3. Drag a page icon from one document window into the other. A copy of the page will appear in the destination document. Pages will reshuffle depending on where you release the mouse (Force Right pointer or Force Down pointer).
   or
   To drag multiple pages at a time, click on the first page in the series of pages that you want to move, Shift-click on the last page in the series **1**, then drag. Or Ctrl-click to select non-consecutive pages. If the pages that you want to move contain linked text, move all the pages at once. Otherwise, the text from the linked boxes itself will move, but all the links from the first box in the chain forward will be broken.

Use the Section command to renumber all or some of the pages in any document with a user-specified starting number. You can choose a different page numbering format for each section. For example, in this book, the lowercase Roman format is used for the Table of Contents and the numeric format is used for the pages that follow.

Note: A document that is comprised of more than one file usually requires special starting page numbers. You can use the Book feature for that kind of publication to number the sections automatically (see Chapter 18).

To number a section of a file:

1. Display the page where the new section is to begin by double-clicking its icon on the Document Layout palette.
   or
   Choose Page menu > Go to (Ctrl-J), enter the number of the page that is to begin the new section, then click OK or press Enter.
2. Click the page number in the lower left corner of the Document Layout palette.
   or
   Choose Page menu > Section.
3. Check the Section Start box **1**.
4. Enter the desired starting Number for the section.
5. *Optional:* Enter a maximum of four characters in the Prefix field.
6. *Optional:* Choose a different numbering Format.
7. Click OK or press Enter.

TIP If you section-number a facing-pages document starting with an even number, the first page will become a left-hand page. The remaining pages won't necessarily follow suit and switch their right or left-hand positions, however.

1 *First check the **Section Start** box. Then enter a **Prefix**, if you need one, enter the starting **Number**, and choose a numbering **Format**.*

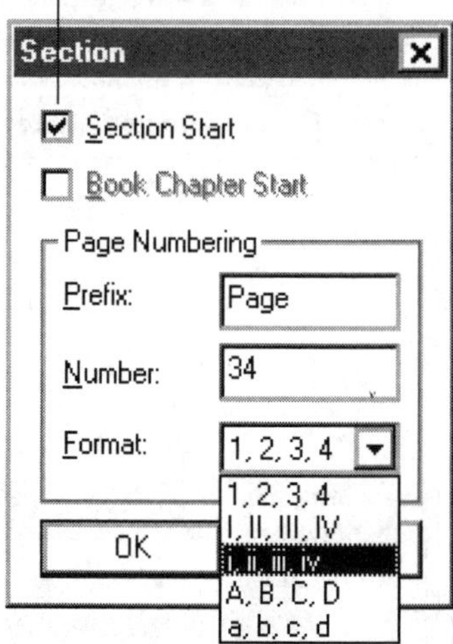

Note: The Book Chapter Start box is available only when a chapter is open independently of its book.

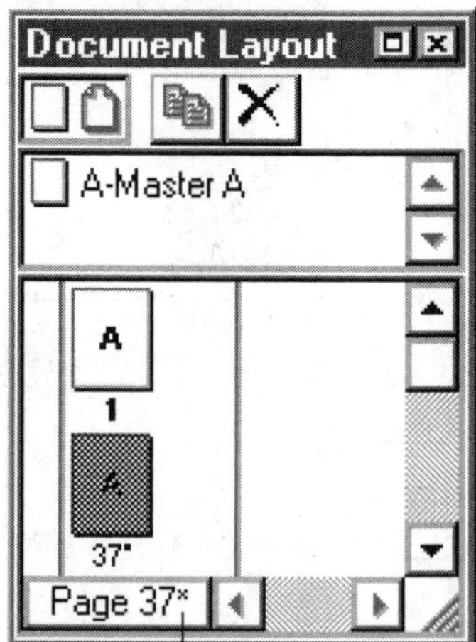

*The number of the **first page** in a section will be marked with an **asterisk** in the current page number field at the bottom of the document window and below the corresponding page icon on the Document Layout palette. (See also the first tip on page 41.)*
Tip: Alt-click a document page icon to display its absolute page number (relative position in the document).

Number a Section

Next Box and Next Column characters

The Next Box character pushes text to the next box in a linked chain. The Next Column character pushes text to the next column within the same box (or in some cases the next text box in the chain).

I come from haunts of coot and hern,
I make a sudden sally,
And sparkle out among the fern,
To bicker down a valley.

By thirty hills I hurry down,
Or slip between the ridges,
By twenty thorps, a little town,
And half a hundred bridges.

Till last by Philip's farm I flow
to join the brimming river,
For men may come and men may go,
But I go on for ever.

I chatter over stony ways,
In little sharps and trebles,
I bubble into eddying bays,
I babble on the pebbles.

With many a curve my banks I fret
By many a field and fallow,
And many fair foreland set
With willow-weed and mallow.

I chatter, chatter, as I flow
To join the brimming river,
For men may come and men may go,
But I go on for ever.

—Alfred Tennyson

The original text boxes.

I come from haunts of coot and hern,
I make a sudden sally,
And sparkle out among the fern,
To bicker down a valley.

By thirty hills I hurry down,
Or slip between the ridges,
By twenty thorps, a little town,
And half a hundred bridges.

Till last by Philip's farm I flow
to join the brimming river,
For men may come and men may go,
But I go on for ever.

I chatter over stony ways,
In little sharps and trebles,
I bubble into eddying bays,
I babble on the pebbles.

With many a curve my banks I fret
By many a field and fallow,
And many fair foreland set
With willow-weed and mallow.

I chatter, chatter, as I flow
To join the brimming river,
For men may come and men may go,
But I go on for ever.

—Alfred Tennyson

*Instead of shortening the text box to push the text to the next box, a **Next Box** character (**Shift-Enter** on keypad) is inserted. Remove a Next Box character as you would any text character: Click to the right of it with the Content tool, then press Delete.*

*The **Next Box** character (Shift-Enter on keypad). (Turn on View menu > Show Invisibles to see it.)*

I come from haunts of coot and hern,
I make a sudden sally,
And sparkle out among the fern,
To bicker down a valley.

By thirty hills I hurry down,
Or slip between the ridges,
By twenty thorps, a little town,
And half a hundred bridges.

Till last by Philip's farm I flow
to join the brimming river,
For men may come and men may go,
But I go on for ever.

I chatter over stony ways,
In little sharps and trebles,
I bubble into eddying bays,
I babble on the pebbles.

*The **Next Column** character (**Enter,** on keypad).*

One header over two columns

Ruler guide

The Night in Isla Negra

The ancient night and the unruly salt
beat at the walls of my house;
lonely is the shadow, the sky
by now is a beat of the ocean,
and sky and shadow explode
in the fray of unequal combat;
all night long they struggle,
nobody knows the weight
of the harsh clarity that will go on opening
like a languid fruit;
thus is born on the coast,
out of the turbulent shadow, the hard dawn,
nibbled by the salt in movement,
swept up by the weight of night,
bloodstained in its marine crater.

Pablo Neruda

You can align text baseline-to-baseline in separate boxes using a ruler guide. Make sure the leading is the same in both boxes. Tip: Choose the Item tool and press the up or down arrow key to nudge a box upward or downward one point at a time; press Alt-arrow to nudge in 1/10-point increments.

The Night in Isla Negra

The ancient night and the unruly salt
beat at the walls of my house;
lonely is the shadow, the sky
by now is a beat of the ocean,
and sky and shadow explode
in the fray of unequal combat;
all night long they struggle,
nobody knows the weight
of the harsh clarity that will go on opening
like a languid fruit;
thus is born on the coast,
out of the turbulent shadow, the hard dawn,
nibbled by the salt in movement,
swept up by the weight of night,
bloodstained in its marine crater.

Pablo Neruda

Or place the header in a separate box and put the text in a two-column box.

Formats 6

COMMANDS THAT AFFECT WHOLE PARAGRAPHS

Horizontal alignment

Hyphenation and justification

Indents

Leading

Space Before/After

Keep Lines Together

Rules

Tabs

Paragraph style sheets

All the commands described in this chapter affect entire paragraphs rather than individual characters, and they are grouped together under the Style menu. A paragraph consists of any number of characters or words followed by a paragraph return (a paragraph return looks like this when Invisibles are turned on: ¶). Paragraph formats can be changed manually or using a style sheet (see Chapter 13).

To indent a whole paragraph:

1. Choose the Content tool.
2. Click in a paragraph or press and drag through a series of paragraphs.
3. Choose Style menu > Formats (Ctrl-Shift-F).
4. Enter a number in the Left Indent and/or Right Indent fields **1**.
5. Click Apply to preview. (Alt-click Apply to turn on continuous apply.)
6. Click OK or press Enter (see **2**–**4**, next page).

You can access an individual format dialog box from the bottom of the Style menu or by clicking the ***Formats, Tabs,*** *or* ***Rules*** *folder tab in the Paragraph Attributes dialog box.*

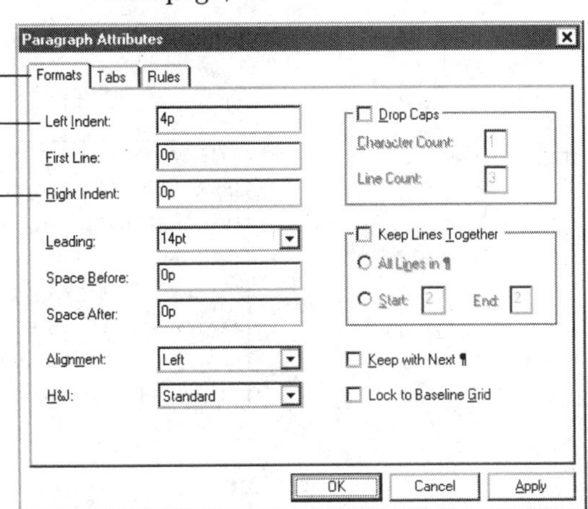

1 *Enter numbers in the* ***Left Indent*** *and/or* ***Right Indent*** *fields in the Paragraph Attributes (Formats) dialog box in any measurement system used in QuarkXPress.*

Paragraph Indents

THE MAIN CONCLUSION ARRIVED AT IN THIS WORK, NAMELY, THAT MAN IS DESCENDED FROM SOME LOWLY ORGANISED FORM, WILL, I REGRET TO THINK, BE HIGHLY DISTASTEFUL TO MANY. BUT THERE CAN HARDLY BE A DOUBT THAT WE ARE DESCENDED FROM BARBARIANS.

2 *A paragraph with 0 indents.*

THE MAIN CONCLUSION ARRIVED AT IN THIS WORK, NAMELY, THAT MAN IS DESCENDED FROM SOME LOWLY ORGANISED FORM, WILL, I REGRET TO THINK, BE HIGHLY DISTASTEFUL TO MANY. BUT THERE CAN HARDLY BE A DOUBT THAT WE ARE DESCENDED FROM BARBARIANS.

3 *A paragraph with a left indent of 2p.*

THE MAIN CONCLUSION ARRIVED AT IN THIS WORK, NAMELY, THAT MAN IS DESCENDED FROM SOME LOWLY ORGANISED FORM, WILL, I REGRET TO THINK, BE HIGHLY DISTASTEFUL TO MANY. BUT THERE CAN HARDLY BE A DOUBT THAT WE ARE DESCENDED FROM BARBARIANS.

Charles Darwin

4 *A paragraph with a right indent of 2p.*

1 *The* ***First Line*** *indent field in the Paragraph Attributes (Formats) dialog box.*

Paragraph Attributes
Formats | Tabs | Rules
Left Indent: 0p
First Line: p10
Right Indent: 0p
Leading: 14pt
Space Before: 0p
Space After: 0p
Alignment: Left
H&J: Standard
Drop Caps
Character Cou
Line Count
Keep Line
All Lines ir
Start: 2
Keep with N
Lock to Bas
OK | Can

To indent the first line of a paragraph:

1. Choose the Content tool.
2. Click in a paragraph or press and drag through a series of paragraphs.
3. Choose Style menu > Formats (Ctrl-Shift-F).
4. Enter a number in the First Line field **1**. If you're not sure what value to use, start with the point size of the text you're indenting.
5. Click Apply to preview (Alt-A).
6. Click OK or press Enter **2**.

TIP Indents and tab stops can be adjusted by pressing and dragging the indent and tab stop markers in the ruler that displays when the Paragraph Formats dialog box is open. Insert a new tab stop by clicking in the ruler **3** (more about tabs later in this chapter).

TIP The first paragraph in a story, particularly following a headline or subhead, looks better flush left than indented.

TIP Paragraph indent values are in addition to any Text Inset value applied to the text box (see page 51).

Oronte. [To Alceste] But for you, you know our agreement. Speak to me, I pray, in all sincerity.

Alceste. These matters, sir, are always more or less delicate, and every one is fond of being praised for his wit.

But I was saying one day to a certain person, who shall be nameless, when he showed me some of his verses, that a gentleman ought at all times to exercise a great control over that itch for writing which sometimes attacks us, and should keep a tight rein over the strong propensity which one has to display such amusements; and that, in the frequent anxiety to show their productions, people are frequently exposed to act a very foolish part.

Molière

2 *A* ***first line indent*** *enhances readability.*

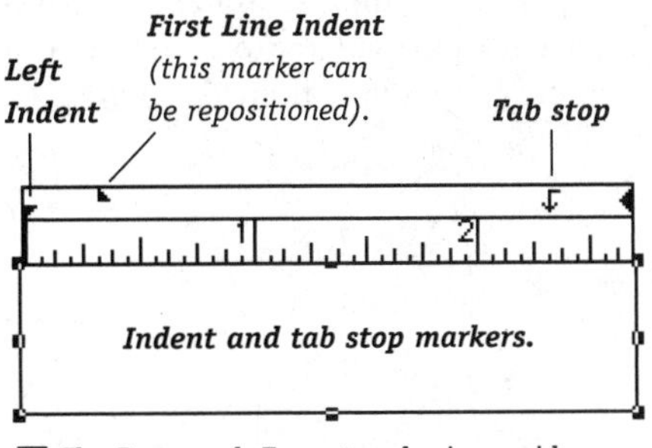

3 *The Paragraph Formats ruler is as wide as the currently selected text box.*

Leading

Leading is the distance from baseline to baseline between lines of type, and it's measured in points. Three types of leading are used in QuarkXPress:

Absolute leading is an amount that remains fixed regardless of the point size of the type to which it is applied **1**.

Percentage-based auto leading is a percentage above the point size of the largest character on each line **2**.

Incremental auto leading is calculated based on the point size of the largest character on each line plus or minus a specified number of points, such as +2 or –2. Both varieties of auto leading can be problematic, so I never use them. If you want to use them, you can specify a percentage or an increment in the Edit menu > Preferences > Document > Paragraph folder tab.

> But the moment that she moved again he recognized her. The effect upon her old lover was electric, far stronger than the effect of his presence upon her. His fire, the tumultuous ring of his eloquence, seemed to go out of him. His lip struggled and trembled under the words that lay upon it; but deliver them it could not as long as she faced him. His eyes, after their first glance...
>
> *Thomas Hardy*

1 *A paragraph with 11 pt.* ***absolute*** *leading. Note that the leading is consistent regardless of the differences in point size.*

> But the moment that she moved
>
> again he recognized her. The effect upon her old lover was electric, far stronger than the effect of his presence upon her. His fire, the tumul-

2 *The same paragraph with* ***auto*** *leading.*

To change paragraph leading using the Measurements palette:

1. Choose the Content tool.
2. Click in a paragraph or press and drag through a series of paragraphs.
3. Enter a number in the Leading field on the Measurements palette **3**.
   or
   Click the up arrow on the Measurements palette to increase the leading or the down arrow to reduce the leading in 1-point increments. Hold down Alt while clicking an arrow to increase or reduce leading in .1-point increments.

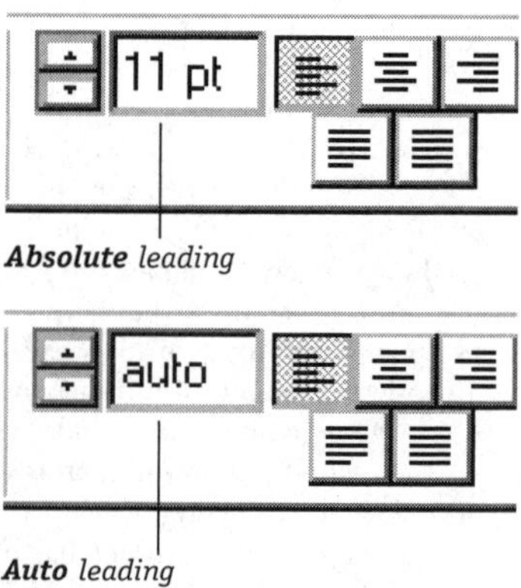

3 *The leading section on the Measurements palette.*

He put some sticking plaster on his fingers, and his friends both came to dinner. He could not offer them fish, but he had something else in his larder.
Sir Isaac Newton wore his black and gold waistcoat.
And Mr. Alderman Ptolemy Tortoise brought a salad with him in a string bag.
And instead of a nice dish of minnows they had a roasted grasshopper with lady-bird sauce, which frogs consider a beautiful treat; but I think it must have been nasty!
Beatrix Potter

Use spacious leading to enhance readibility in body text set in a wide column, in a sans serif or bold font, or in a font that has a large x-height or tall ascenders and descenders. This is 8 pt. Gill Sans Regular, 11 pt. leading.

He put some sticking plaster on his fingers, and his friends both came to dinner. He could not offer them fish, but he had something else in his larder.
Sir Isaac Newton wore his black and gold waist-coat.
And Mr. Alderman Ptolemy Tortoise brought a salad with him in a string bag.
And instead of a nice dish of minnows they had a roasted grasshopper with lady-bird sauce, which frogs consider a beautiful treat; but I think it must have been nasty!

You can use tighter leading for serif body text or multiple-line headlines or subheads. This is 8 pt. Bauer Bodoni, 10 pt. leading.

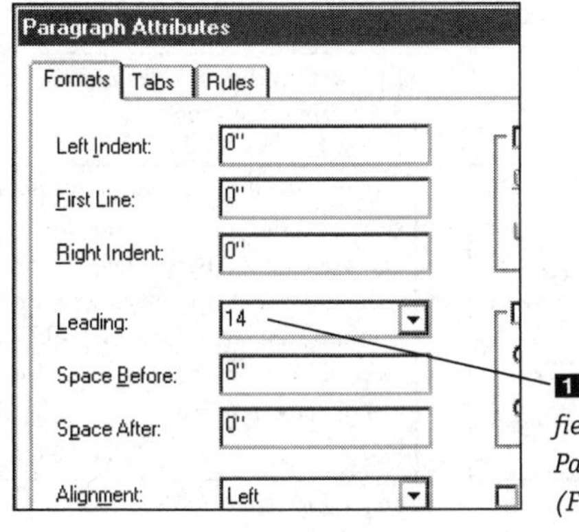

1 *The* ***Leading*** *field in the Paragraph Attributes (Formats) dialog box.*

To change paragraph leading using the keyboard:

1. Choose the Content tool.
2. Click in a paragraph or press and drag through a series of paragraphs.
3. Hold down Ctrl and Shift and press ' to increase leading or ; to decrease leading in 1-point increments. If the leading was on auto, it will switch to absolute when you use this shortcut.

TIP Add Alt to the above keystroke to modify leading in .1 increments.

TIP When point size and leading are notated traditionally, the two values are divided by a slash. For example, "8/11" signifies 8-point type with 11-point leading.

To change paragraph leading using a dialog box:

1. Choose the Content tool.
2. Click in a paragraph or press and drag through a series of paragraphs.
3. Choose Style menu > Leading (Ctrl-Shift-E).
4. The Leading field will highlight automatically. Type an amount in an increment as small as .001 **1**. You don't need to enter the "pt".
5. Click OK or press Enter.

TIP Leading has no affect on the position of first line of text in a box. To lower text from the top of its box, select the box, choose Item menu > Modify, click the Text folder tab, then change the number in the First Baseline: Offset field.

To change horizontal alignment:

1. Choose the Content tool.
2. Click in a paragraph or press and drag through a series of paragraphs.
3. Click one of the five horizontal alignment icons on the Measurements palette **1**.

TIP Only one alignment option can be applied per paragraph.

TIP The horizontal alignment options can also be applied using the Style menu > Alignment submenu or via the Alignment drop-down menu in the Style menu > Formats dialog box.

TIP Forced Justified alignment justifies all the lines in a paragraph—including the last line. For this alignment option, make sure the paragraph has a paragraph return character (¶) at the end.

TIP Justified text looks better with hyphenation on (see page 97).

HORIZONTAL ALIGNMENT SHORTCUTS

Flush left, ragged right	Ctrl-Shift-**L**
Centered	Ctrl-Shift-**C**
Flush right, ragged left	Ctrl-Shift-**R**
Justified	Ctrl-Shift-**J**
Forced Justified	Ctrl-Alt-Shift-**J**

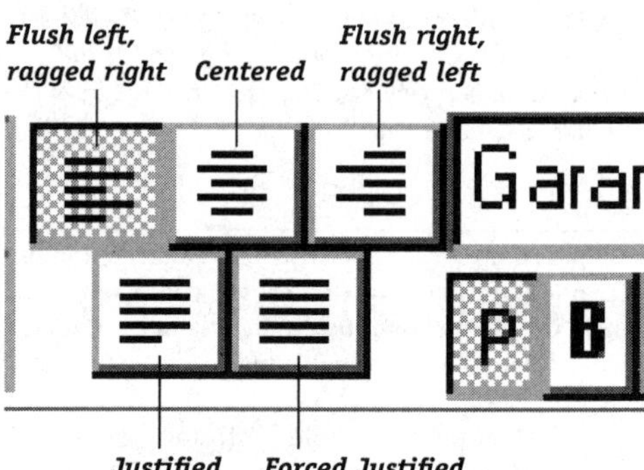

1 *The five **horizontal alignment** icons on the Measurements palette.*

So we was all right now, as to the shirt and the sheet and the spoon and the candles, by the help of the calf and rats and the mixed-up counting; and as to the candlestick, it warn't no consequence, it would blow over by and by....

Flush left, ragged right

So we was all right now, as to the shirt and the sheet and the spoon and the candles, by the help of the calf and rats and the mixed-up counting; and as to the candlestick, it warn't no consequence, it would blow over by and by....

Centered

So we was all right now,
as to the shirt and the sheet and
the spoon and the candles,
by the help of the calf and rats
and the mixed-up counting;
and as to the candlestick, it
warn't no consequence, it would
blow over by and by....

(Tip: Centered text looks better with varied line lengths.)

So we was all right now, as to the shirt and the sheet and the spoon and the candles, by the help of the calf and rats and the mixed-up counting; and as to the candlestick, it warn't noconsequence, it would blow over by and by....

Flush right, ragged left

So we was all right now, as to the shirt and the sheet and the spoon and the candles, by the help of the calf and rats and the mixed-up counting; and as to the candlestick, it warn't no consequence, it would blow over by and by....

Justified

So we was all right now, as to the shirt and the sheet and the spoon and the candles, by the help of the calf and rats and the mixed-up counting; and as to the candlestick, it warn't no consequence, it would blow over by and by.

Mark Twain

Forced Justifed

Use one of these methods to adjust a headline or fix an awkward break in ragged left or ragged right copy.

To break a line without creating a new paragraph:

1. Choose the Content tool.
2. Click just to the left of a word that you want to bring down to the next line.
3. If it's a hyphenated word, hold down Ctrl and press "-" (hyphen) **1**–**3** to insert a discretionary hyphen. (To remove a discretionary hyphen, click at the beginning of the next line, then press Backspace.)
   or
   If the word isn't hyphenated, press Shift-Enter.

1 *This is an awkward break.*

The night so luminous on the spar-deck,
but otherwise on the cavernous ones
below—levels so very like the tiered galleries in a coal-mine—the luminous
night passed away. Like the prophet in
the chariot disappearing in heaven and
dropping his mantle to Elisha, the with-
drawing night transferred its pale robe
to the peeping day.

The night so luminous on the spar-deck,
but otherwise on the cavernous ones
below—levels so very like the tiered¶

galleries in a coal-mine—the luminous
night passed away. Like the prophet in
the chariot disappearing in heaven and
dropping his mantle to Elisha, the with-
drawing night transferred its pale robe
to the peeping day.

2 *A paragraph return creates a new paragraph—no good.*

The night so luminous on the spar-deck,
but otherwise on the cavernous ones
below—levels so very like the tiered
galleries in a coal-mine—the luminous
night passed away. Like the prophet in
the chariot disappearing in heaven and
dropping his mantle to Elisha, the with-
drawing night transferred its pale robe
to the peeping day.

Herman Melville

3 *A discretionary hyphen creates a different line break within a paragraph.*

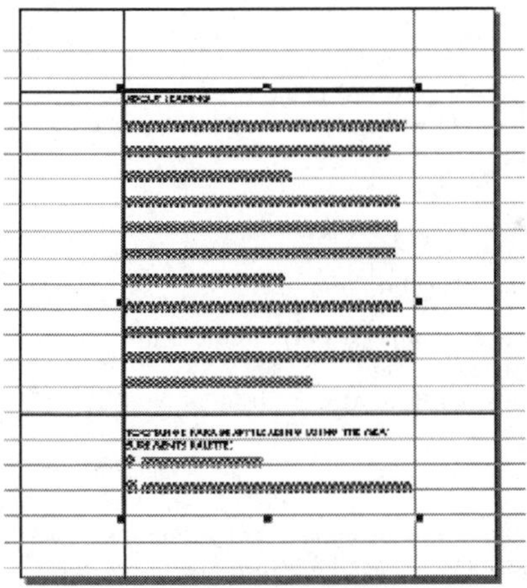

ALIGNING TEXT TO A GRID

For each paragraph you want to align to the grid, check the Lock to Baseline Grid box in the Paragraph Formats dialog box. You can do this via a style sheet (see Chapter 13). You might not want to lock subheads. In Edit menu > Preferences > Document > Paragraph folder tab, enter a Baseline Grid Increment that is equal to or a multiple of the text leading. To display the non-printing grid lines, choose View menu > Show Baseline Grid (Ctrl-F2).

To add space between paragraphs:

1. Choose the Content tool.
2. Click in a paragraph or press and drag through a series of paragraphs.
3. Choose Style menu > Formats (Ctrl-Shift-F).
4. Enter a number in the Space Before or Space After field **1**.
5. Click Apply to preview (Alt-A).
6. Click OK or press Enter **2**.

TIP The numbers entered into the Space Before and Space After fields add together, so you should be consistent and use one most of the time and the other for special circumstances. For example, I use Space After for most paragraphs and use Space Before for special instances, such as to add extra space above a subhead.

TIP The Space Before command has no effect on the first line of text in a box. To move text downward on a page, the simplest thing is to move the box itself—an obvious solution that's easy to forget! If you don't want to move the box, use First Baseline (see page 51).

COPY FORMATS IN THE SAME STORY

Click in a paragraph or press and drag through a series of paragraphs that you want to modify, then Alt-Shift-click in the paragraph whose formats you would like to copy. Both paragraph style sheet and local formatting specifications will copy. This trick works within one text box or between linked text boxes—but not between unlinked boxes. Character attributes (font, size, etc.) are not copied.

SPEED TIP

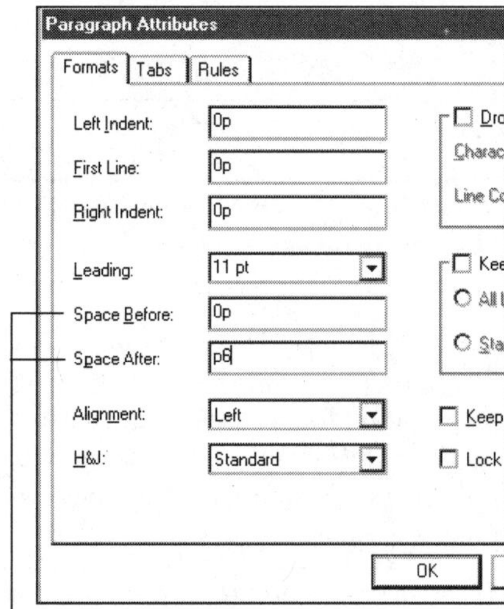

1 *The **Space Before** and **Space After** fields in Paragraph Attributes > Formats folder tab.*

O to be a Virginian where I grew up! O to be a Carolinian!
O longings irrepressible! O I will go back to old Tennessee
and never wander more.

Mannahatta

I was asking for something specific and perfect for my city,
Whereupon lo! upsprang the aboriginal name.

Now I see what there is in a name, a word, liquid, sane, unruly,
musical, self-sufficient,
I see that the word of my city is that word from of old,
Because I see that word nested in nests of water-bays, superb...

Walt Whitman

2 *If you want to fine tune the spacing between paragraphs, use the Space Before or Space After field. Don't insert extra returns.*

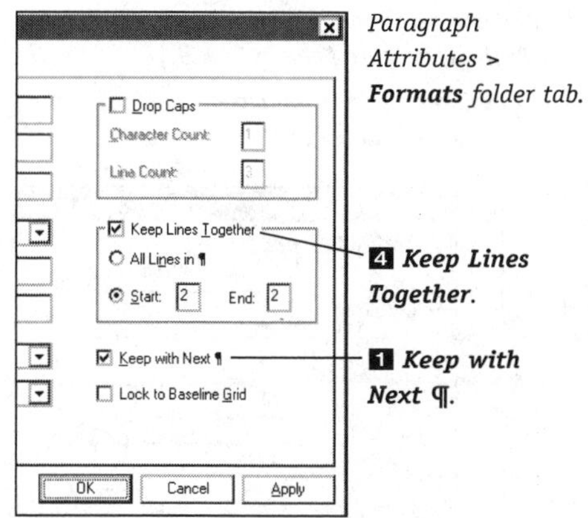

Paragraph Attributes > ***Formats*** *folder tab.*

4 ***Keep Lines Together.***

1 ***Keep with Next ¶.***

Apply the Keep with Next ¶ command to a subhead to ensure that it always remains attached to the paragraph that follows it. Like all paragraph formats, it can be applied manually or via a style sheet. Don't apply Keep with Next ¶ to body text.

To keep paragraphs together:

1. Choose the Content tool.
2. Click in a paragraph.
3. Choose Style menu > Formats (Ctrl-Shift-F).
4. Check the Keep with Next ¶ box **1**.
5. Click OK or press Enter.

2 *An unsightly* ***widow.***

"I am dreadfully afraid it *will* be mouse!" said Duchess to herself—"I really couldn't, *couldn't* eat mouse pie. And I shall have to eat it, because it is a party. And *my* pie was going to be veal and ham. A pink and white pie-dish! and so is mine; just like Ribby's dishes; they were both bought at Tabitha Twitchit's."

Duchess went into her larder and took the pie off a shelf and looked at it.

"Oh what a good idea! Why shouldn't I rush along and put my pie into Ribby's oven when Ribby isn't there?"

Beatrix Potter

"I am dreadfully afraid it *will* be mouse!" said Duchess to herself—"I really couldn't, *couldn't* eat mouse pie. And I shall have to eat it, because it is a party. And *my* pie was going to be veal and ham. A pink and white pie-dish! and so is mine; just like Ribby's dishes; they were both bought at Tabitha Twitchit's."

Duchess went into her larder and took the pie off a shelf and looked at it.

"Oh what a good idea! Why shouldn't I rush along and put my pie into Ribby's oven when Ribby isn't there?"

3 *An unsightly* ***orphan.***

A widow is the last line of a paragraph that's stranded at the top of a column **2**. An orphan is the first line of paragraph that's stranded at the bottom of a column **3**. Both are typesetting no-no's. The Keep Lines Together command can be used to prevent orphan and widow lines. It can also be used to keep *all* the lines in a paragraph—like a subhead—together.

To prevent orphan and widow lines:

1. Choose the Content tool.
2. Click in a paragraph.
3. Choose Style menu > Formats (Ctrl-Shift-F).
4. Check the Keep Lines Together box **4**.
5. Click the All Lines in ¶ button to keep all the lines of a paragraph together. Use this for subheads or any other paragraphs that musn't be broken at all.
   or
   Click the Start button to turn on orphan and widow control. Enter "2" in the Start and End fields to ensure that no less than two lines of a paragraph are stranded at the bottom or top of a column, respectively.
6. Click OK or press Enter.

A format in which the first line of a paragraph is aligned flush left and the remaining lines are indented is called a hanging indent. Hanging indents can be used to make subheads, bullets, or other special text more prominent or to hang punctuation (see page 112). A hanging indent created using the Formats dialog box can be applied via a style sheet. To style bullets or other repetitive text, use a character style sheet.

To create a hanging indent using the Formats dialog box:

1. Choose the Content tool.
2. Click in a paragraph or press and drag through a series of paragraphs.
3. Choose Style menu > Formats (Ctrl-Shift-F).
4. Enter a number in the Left Indent field **1**.
5. In the First Line field, enter a value that is equal to or less than the number you entered for step 4, preceded by a minus (-) sign **2**.
6. Click Apply to preview (Alt-A), make any adjustments, then click OK or press Enter **3**–**4**.

2 *And enter a negative number in the* ***First Line*** *field.*

1 *Enter a positive number in the* ***Left Indent*** *field.*

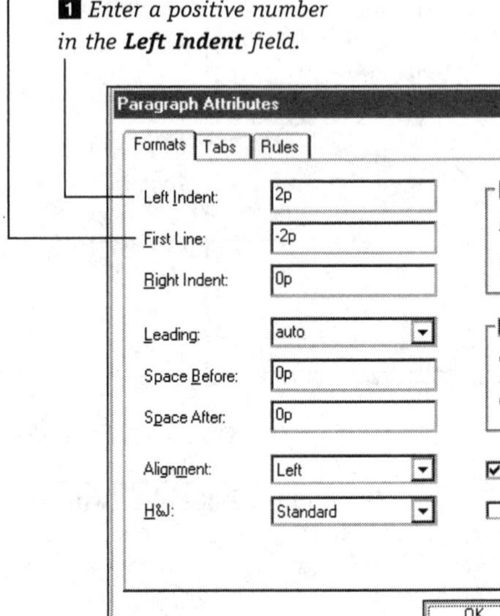

The Paragraph Attributes > ***Formats*** *folder tab.*

I mean in singing; but in loving—Leander the good swimmer, Troilus the first employer of panders, and a whole book full of these quondam carpet-mongers, whose names yet run smoothly in the even road of a blank verse, why, they were never so truly turned over and over as my poor self in love.

Marry, I cannot show it in rhyme; I have tried; I can find out no rhyme to lady but baby—an innocent rhyme;

3 *In this example, a positive Left Indent and a negative First Line creates a hanging indent formation in each paragraph.*

A ***tab*** *stop is automatically created at the location of the indent.*

D. Pedro. He is in earnest.

Claud. In most profound earnest; and I'll warrant you for the love of Beatrice.

D. Pedro. And hath challenged thee?

Claud. Most sincerely.

D. Pedro. What a pretty thing man is when he goes in his doublet and hose, and leaves off his wit!

Claud. He is then a giant to an ape: but then is an ape a doctor to such a man?

William Shakespeare

4 *In this example, after the hanging indents were created via a positive Left Indent and a negative First Line, a tab character was also inserted manually following the bold text in each paragraph to align the text to the automatically-inserted tab stop.*

THESEUS. Now, fair Hippolyta, our nuptial hour draws on apace; four happy days bring inanother moon: but, oh, methinks, how slow this old moon wanes! She lingers my desires, like to a step-dame or a dowager, long withering out a young man's revenue.

1 *To insert the **Indent Here** character, click in the text, then hold down Ctrl and press \.*

THESEUS. Now, fair Hippolyta, our nuptial hour draws on apace; four happy days bring in another moon: but, oh, methinks, how slow this old moon wanes! She lingers my desires, like to a step-dame or a dowager, long withering out a young man's revenue.

2 *A hanging indent is created.*

On the positive side, the Indent Here character instantly creates a hanging indent wherever your cursor happens to be positioned, so it's useful for quickly formatting a unique paragraph here or there.

On the minus side, the Indent Here character has to be manually inserted in each paragraph, it can't be incorporated into a style sheet, and it can't be added or removed using Find/Change. Follow the instructions on the previous page to create a hanging indent in multiple paragraphs.

To create a hanging indent using the Indent Here character:

1. Choose the Content tool.
2. Click in a paragraph where the indent is to be inserted **1**.
3. Hold down Ctrl and press \ (backslash) **2**.

3 *The **Indent Here** character displays as a vertical dotted line when Show Invisibles is turned on (View menu). Choose a large view size to see it.*

THESEUS. Now, fair Hippol hour draws on days bring in oh, methinks,

To remove an Indent Here character:

1. Choose the Content tool.
2. Click just to the right of the Indent Here character **3**. If you're having trouble locating the correct spot, you can use the left or right arrow key on your keyboard to move the insertion point one character at a time.
3. Press Backspace.

A drop cap at the beginning of a story can add pizazz to a page and spark a reader's interest. *Note:* Because they're so easy to create, it's tempting to use drop caps here, there, and everywhere. Like hot chilies, they're best used sparingly.

To insert an automatic drop cap:

1. Choose the Content tool.
2. Click in a paragraph.
3. Choose Style menu > Formats (Ctrl-Shift-F).
4. Check the Drop Caps box **1**.
5. Click Apply to preview, and move the dialog box out of the way, if necessary.
6. *Optional:* To "drop cap" more than one character, enter that number in the Character Count field. (The width of the text box determines the maximum character count.)
7. *Optional:* To adjust the height of the drop cap, change the number in the Line Count field. The drop cap will adjust to fit the line count. The maximum line count is 16.
8. Click OK or press Enter **2**–**3**.
9. *Optional:* Highlight the drop cap and change its color, shade, or font. Be bold and imaginative!

TIP To anchor a picture box or text box as a drop cap, see pages 127 and 130.

__Line Count:__ The number of vertical lines of text the drop cap will adjust to fit into.

1 *Check the __Drop Caps__ box in Paragraph Attributes > Formats folder tab.*

__Character Count:__ The number of characters to be "dropped."

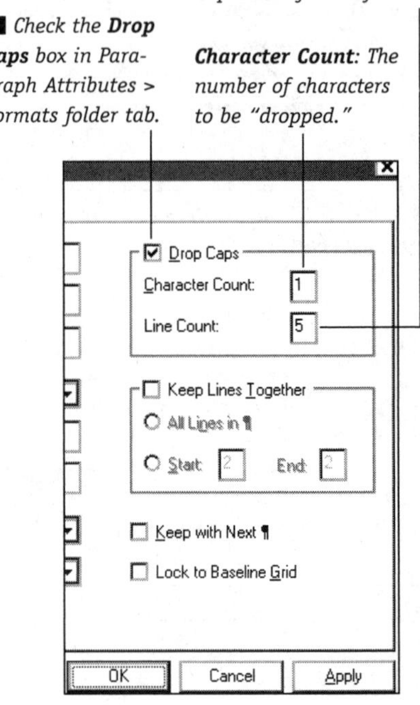

Not only was her first-floor flat invaded at all hours by throngs of singular and often undesirable characters but her remarkable lodger showed an eccentricity and irregularity in his life which must have sorely tried her patience. His incredible untidiness, his addiction to music at strange hours, his occasional revolver practice within doors, his weird and often malodorous scientific experiments, and the atmosphere of violence and danger which hung around him made him the very worst tenant in London. On the other hand, his payments were princely...

2 *A __drop cap__ with a character count of 1 and a line count of 5.*

NOT only was her first-floor flat invaded at all hours by throngs of singular and often undesirable characters but her remarkable lodger showed an eccentricity and irregularity in his life which must have sorely tried her patience. His incredible untidiness, his addiction to music at strange hours, his occasional revolver practice within doors, his weird and often malodorous scientific experiments, and the atmosphere of violence and danger which hung around him made him the very worst tenant in London. On the other hand, his payments were princely...

3 *A __drop cap__ with a character count of 3 and a line count of 2.*

An anomaly which often struck me in the character of my friend Sherlock Holmes was that, although in his methods of thought he was the neatest and most methodical of mankind, and although also he affected a certain quiet primness of dress, he was none the less in his personal habits one of the most untidy

1 *Highlight a drop cap.*

2 *Change the **size percentage** on the Measurements palette.*

An anomaly which often struck me in the character of my friend Sherlock Holmes was that, although in his methods of thought he was the neatest and most methodical of mankind, and although also he affected a certain quiet primness of dress, he was none the less in his per-

3 *A drop cap enlarged to 125%.*

For those who like this sort of thing, this is the sort of thing they like.

4 *The cursor correctly positioned for kerning next to a drop cap.*

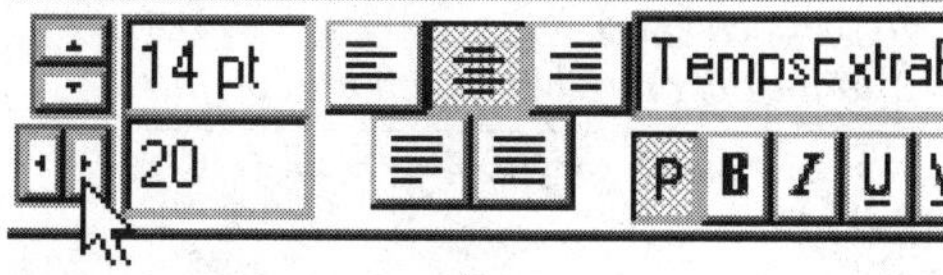

5 *The **tracking/kerning** section of the Measurements palette.*

To resize an automatic drop cap manually:

1. Choose the Content tool.
2. Press and drag to highlight the drop cap character or characters **1**.
3. In the point size field on the Measurements palette, enter a percentage above 100% to enlarge the drop cap or a percentage below 100% to shrink the drop cap. The minimum is 16.7% and the maximum is 400% **2**–**3**.

To kern next to a drop cap:

1. Choose the Content tool.
2. Click in the first line of the paragraph between the drop cap and the character to the right of it. A long blinking insertion cursor will appear when the cursor has been inserted correctly **4**.
3. In the tracking/kerning section of the Measurements palette, click the left arrow to delete space or the right arrow to add space **5**. Alt-click the left or right arrow to kern in finer increments.
   or
   To kern using the keyboard, use the Ctrl-Shift-[or Ctrl-Shift-] shortcut. Include Alt in the shortcut to kern in finer increments.

To remove an automatic drop cap, just back out the same way you came in.

To remove an automatic drop cap:

1. Choose the Content tool.
2. Click in the paragraph that contains the drop cap.
3. Choose Style menu > Formats (Ctrl-Shift-F).
4. Uncheck the Drop Caps box.
5. Click OK or press Enter.

There are many reasons to use a paragraph rule. First, a paragraph rule stays anchored to its paragraph even if the paragraph is moved or reflows, unlike a line that's created with a line tool. Second, a paragraph rule can be applied using a style sheet. And finally, unlike the Underline type style, a paragraph rule can be modified in its appearance and position.

To insert a paragraph rule:

1. Choose the Content tool.
2. Click in a paragraph or press and drag through a series of paragraphs.
3. Choose Style menu > Rules (Ctrl-Shift-N).
4. Check the Rule Above or Rule Below box (**1**, next page).
5. Choose a width from the Width drop-down menu or enter a custom width in the Width field (**2**, next page).
6. Choose Indents or Text from the Length pop-up menu. If you choose Text, the rule will be the width of the first line of text in the paragraph for a Rule Above or the width of the last line of text in the paragraph for a Rule Below (**3**, next page). If you choose Indents, the rule will be the width of the paragraph, unless you enter a number other than 0 in the From Left or From Right field (see step 8).
7. Highlight the entire Offset field, and enter the fixed distance in any measurement system that you want to offset a Rule Above upward from the baseline of the first line of the paragraph or offset a Rule Below downward from the baseline of the last line of the paragraph. For a Rule Above, use an Offset that is at least as large as the point size of the type.
   or
   Enter a percentage Offset (0–100%). A Rule Below with a 20% Offset, for

Hey! diddle, diddle,
The cat and the fiddle,
The cow jumped over the moon;
The little dog laugh'd
To see such sport,
And the dish ran away with the spoon.

A 2-pt Rule Above, Length: ***Indents****, Offset p10.*

Hey! diddle, diddle,
The cat and the fiddle,
The cow jumped over the moon;
The little dog laugh'd
To see such sport,
And the dish ran away with the spoon.

A 2-pt Rule Above, Length: ***Text****, Offset p10.*

H*ey! diddle, diddle,*
The cat and the fiddle,
The cow jumped over the moon;
The little dog laugh'd
To see such sport,
And the dish ran away with the spoon.

A 2-pt Rule Above, Length: Text, ***From Left*** *1p10, Offset p10.*

Hey! diddle, diddle,
The cat and the fiddle,

In this example, the first line of the paragraph is indented, which causes the rule to indent as well.

Hey! diddle, diddle,
The cat and the fiddle,

To align the rule with the left edge of the rest of the paragraph, as in this example, I entered the paragraph's Left Indent (1p) with a minus sign in front of it in the From Left field (-1p). Note that in this illustration, the text box itself has a Text Inset value (3 pt), which an anchored rule can't extend into.

example, would position the rule closer to the bottom of the currently selected paragraph than would an 80% offset. If this method is used and the spacing between the paragraphs is altered, the rule position will adjust automatically.

8. *Optional:* Change the number in the From Left and/or From Right field to indent, and thus shorten, the rule.
9. Choose a style from the Style drop-down menu **4**. To create a custom style, see pages 169–170.
10. Choose a color from the Color drop-down menu.
11. Choose a preset Shade percentage or enter a shade value.
12. Click Apply to preview (Alt-A), then click OK or press Enter.

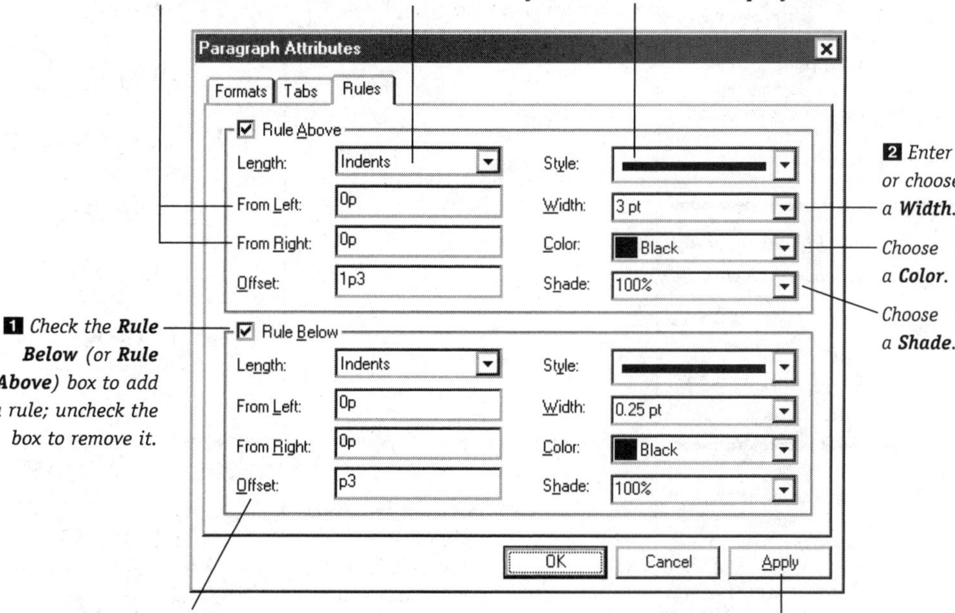

The amount a rule is indented is equal to the number in the From Left and/or From Right fields, plus any existing paragraph indents and text inset values.
3 Choose Length: Indents or Text.
4 Choose a Style. To create a custom style, use the Dashes & Stripes feature.
Paragraph Attributes
Formats
Tabs
Rules
Rule Above
Length:
Indents
From Left:
0p
From Right:
0p
Offset:
1p3
Style:
Width:
3 pt
Color:
Black
Shade:
100%
Rule Below
Length:
Indents
From Left:
0p
From Right:
0p
Offset:
p3
Style:
Width:
0.25 pt
Color:
Black
Shade:
100%
OK
Cancel
Apply
2 Enter or choose a Width.
Choose a Color.
Choose a Shade.
1 Check the Rule Below (or Rule Above) box to add a rule; uncheck the box to remove it.
Enter a number to Offset a Rule Above upward from the baseline of the first line of the paragraph or to Offset a Rule Below downward from the baseline of the last line of the paragraph.
Click Apply to preview.

(Illustrations on the following page)

E T H A N F R O M E

By Edith Wharton

I had the story, bit by bit, from various people, and, as generally happens in such cases, each time it was a different story.

If you know Starkfield, Massachusetts, you know the post-office. If you know the post-office you must have seen Ethan Frome drive up to it, drop the reins on his hollow-backed bay and

To create a reverse rule, color the text white and use a negative Offset and a wide width (the point size of the type plus a few points) for the rule. A negative value of up to half the width of the rule can be used. This is a 16-point black Rule Above, Length: Indents, Left and Right Indents of 0, and an Offset of -p4. The headline text is 9 pt.

Rules can be used to jazz up subheads.

Rules can be used to jazz up subheads.

Rules of varying lengths and weights.

Need to fill up a page with horizontal lines? Apply a paragraph rule, then keep hitting the Enter key.

Norton Thorpe clapped the young Frenchman on the shoulder and, with a hearty smile, shook his hand. "My dear chap! How could I possibly object to my daughter becoming not only the new Countess d'Auvergne but also the wife of an up-and-coming electronics genius!" Lisa, her

"How could I possibly object to my daughter becoming not only the new Countess d'Auvergne but also the wife of an up-and-coming electronics genius..."

eyes moist with tears of joy, not only because of her future marriage but also because of her restored relationship with her father, threw her arms around Nancy in a warm embrace exclaiming: "Oh, Nancy, none of this could ever have happened if you hadn't worked so hard to solve

Paragraph rules used to separate a pull quote from body text.

ALL

THE

REALLY GOOD

IDEAS

I EVER HAD

CAME

TO ME

WHILE I WAS

MILKING

A COW.

Grant Wood

Rules can be used as decorative elements or for emphasis. In this example, a paragraph return was inserted after every line, making every line a separate paragraph.

*A **decimal-aligned** tab with a dot leader.*

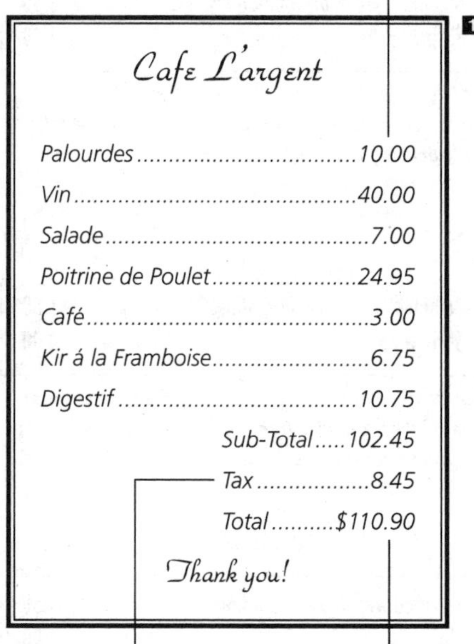

Cafe L'argent
Palourdes.................................10.00
Vin..40.00
Salade..7.00
Poitrine de Poulet......................24.95
Café...3.00
Kir á la Framboise........................6.75
Digestif....................................10.75
Sub-Total.....102.45
Tax.................8.45
Total..........$110.90
Thank you!

*A **left-aligned** tab.* *An **outrageous** tab.*

Ocean
Body more immaculate than a wave,
salt washing away its own line,
and the brilliant bird
flying without ground roots. ☾

Pablo Neruda

2 *One of many uses for a right indent tab: To position an end-of-story marker.*

Tabs are commands that are used to align columns of text or figures **1**. Using spaces to create columns would result in uneven spacing due to variable character widths. If no custom tabs are set and you press Tab, text will jump to the nearest default tab stop. The default tab stops are ½ inch apart. Before you can set custom tab stops (next two pages), you must insert the tab characters into your text. You can set a virtually unlimited number of custom stops per paragraph (one tab per point).

To insert tabs into text:

1. Choose the Content tool.
2. Press Tab as you input copy before typing each new column. The cursor will jump to the next default tab stop. Don't keep pressing the Tab key to move the type over. If you're not happy with the location of the default stops (I rarely am), you can set custom stops (next page).
   or
   To add a tab to already inputted text, click to the left of the text that is to start each new column and press Tab.
   or
   Press Shift-Tab to set a right indent tab flush with the right indent of the box **2**. (You won't see a marker on the Tabs ruler for this kind of tab.)

Endangered vs. non-Endangered Bears

	1930	**1992**	**2000** (Projected)
Pandas	1 million	4 thousand	0
Koalas	6 million	3 thousand	7
Poohs	1 million	2 billion	3 billion

*Use **tabs** to align columns of text.*

Endangered·vs.·non-Endangered·Bears¶

→ **1930** → **1992** → **2000**·(Projected)

*Choose View menu > **Show Invisibles** to reveal tab symbols and other non-printing characters.*

Insert Tabs Into Text

To set custom tab stops:

1. Choose the Content tool.
2. Zoom in on your document, but make sure you still see the full width of the text column. Zooming in will make the tabs ruler increments easier to see.
3. Highlight **all** the copy for which the tab stops are to be set.
4. Choose Style menu > Tabs (Ctrl-Shift-T), and move the dialog box if it's in the way.
5. Click the Left, Center, Right, Decimal, or Comma, or Align On icon (**1**, next page). Use the Decimal or comma if some of the numbers are in parentheses.
6. *Optional:* To create a leader, enter one or two keyboard characters in the Fill Characters field. Enter a period (.) to create a dot leader (all the illustrations on this page and **2**, next page).
7. Click in the tabs ruler to insert a tab stop (**3**, next page). If you need to move the marker, just drag it to the left or the right.
   or
   Enter a position number (location on the ruler) in the Position field using any measurement system, then click Set (**4**, next page).
8. *Optional:* Repeat steps 5–7 to create additional tab stops.
9. Click Apply (or turn on continuous apply by Alt-clicking the Apply button), make any adjustments, then click OK or press Enter.

TIP Tabs, like all paragraph formats, can be part of a style sheet. I usually create a style sheet based on a paragraph that already contains custom tabs in the right spots.

TIP To set a series of tabs by specifying the distance between them, enter "+" and then the gap distance in the Position field (i.e. "p10+p12").

Steamed vegetable dumplings 3.50
Shrimp rolls 4.00

To create a dot leader with extra space between the dots, enter a period and a space in the Fill Characters field.

Steamed vegetable dumplings - - - - - - - - 3.50
Shrimp rolls - - - - - - - - - - - - - - - - - 4.00

To create a dashed line with extra space between the dashes, enter a hyphen and a space in the Fill Characters field.

Steamed vegetable dumplings _ _ _ _ _ _ _ 3.50
Shrimp rolls _ _ _ _ _ _ _ _ _ _ _ _ _ 4.00

To change the point size, tracking, color, or other attributes of a tab leader, you must do it manually. The tab leader in this example is tracked out, horizontally scaled, and baseline shifted downward. Tip: You can copy-and-paste a tab from one line of text to another. Double-click the tab character—the whole leader will select along with it.

Steamed vegetable dumplings ≈ ≈ ≈ ≈ 3.50
Shrimp rolls ≈ ≈ ≈ ≈ ≈ ≈ ≈ ≈ ≈ 4.00

You can use any character as a fill character. Be creative! This is Alt-0187 in the Symbol font with a space.

Set Custom Tab Stops

To insert a ***new tab stop****, choose an Alignment option from the Tabs dialog box, then click on the tabs ruler. Or enter a number in the* ***Position*** *field (see the figure below), then click* ***Set****. Click* ***Apply*** *to preview. (Alt-click Apply to turn on continuous apply.)*

First Line Indent marker.

Right Indent marker.

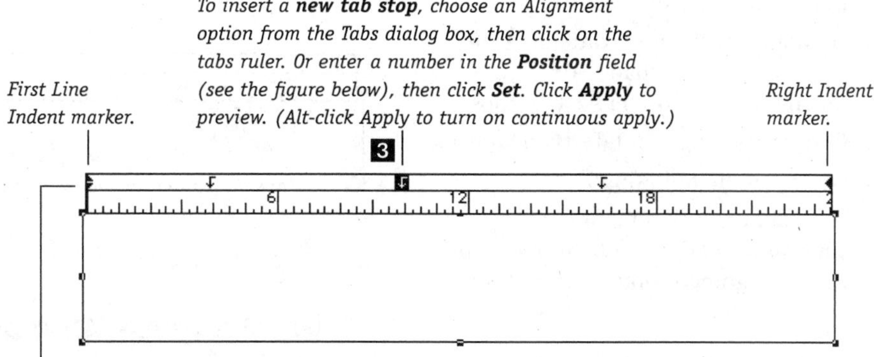

Left Indent marker. You can move these indent markers to change the paragraph indents. To enter indents numerically, use the Paragraph Attributes > Formats folder tab (see pages 77–79).

To align columns to a specific character, click the ***Align On*** *alignment icon, then type a character in the* ***Align On*** *field.*

1 *Choose an* ***Alignment*** *option first.*

4 *To insert a tab stop, click on the tabs ruler. Or enter a location in the* ***Position*** *field, then click* ***Set****.*

2 *Up to two characters can be entered in the* ***Fill Characters*** *field. Enter a period to create a dot leader.*

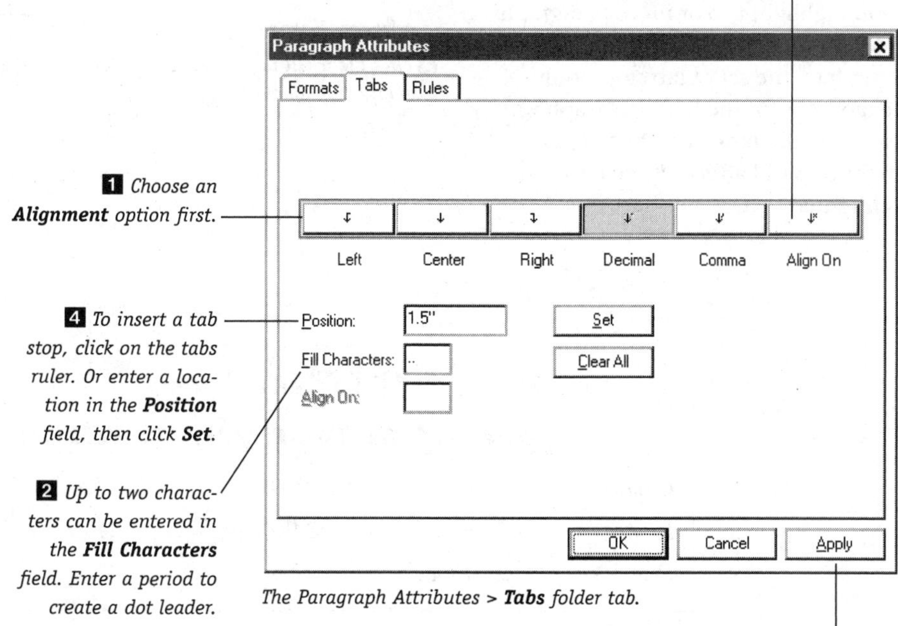

The Paragraph Attributes > ***Tabs*** *folder tab.*

Alt-click Apply to turn on continuous apply. Alt-click Apply again to turn it off.

Set Custom Tab Stops

To edit or remove custom tab stops:

1. Choose the Content tool.
2. Highlight *all* the text containing the stops you want to change or from which you want to remove tab stops.
3. Choose Style menu > Tabs (Ctrl-Shift-T).
4. Do any of the following:

   To change the alignment of a stop, click on its marker, then choose a different Alignment option. Ditto for a Fill character.
   or
   To move a tab stop, drag it manually. Or click on, it, then change the number in the Position field, then click Set.
   or
   To remove one tab stop, press and drag its marker upward or downward out of the ruler **1**.
   or
   To remove *all* the tab stops, click Clear All **2** or Alt-click the ruler.
5. Click OK or press Enter.

TIP If you highlight two or more paragraphs and the highlighted text contains more than one set of tab stops, only the tab stops for the first paragraph will display on the tabs ruler, but any new tab settings will affect *all* the currently highlighted text.

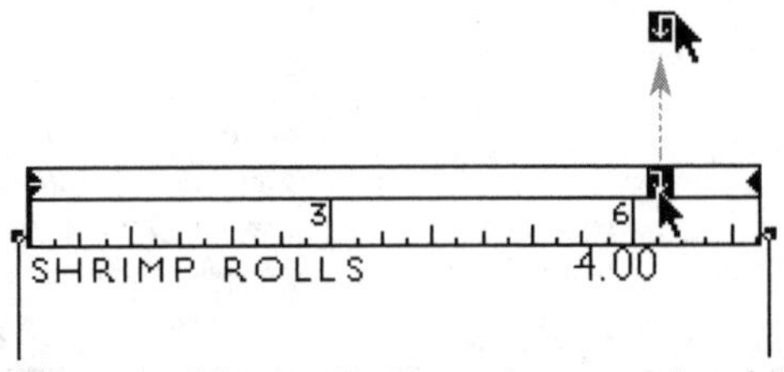

1 *Press and drag a tab stop marker out of the ruler to remove it.*

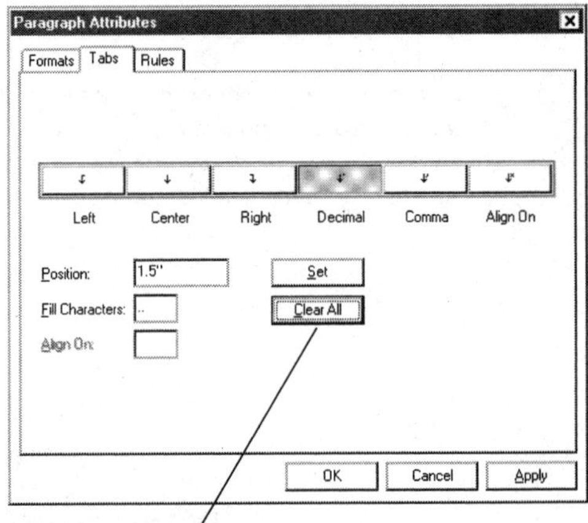

2 *Click* ***Clear All*** *to remove all the stops from the currently highlighted text.*

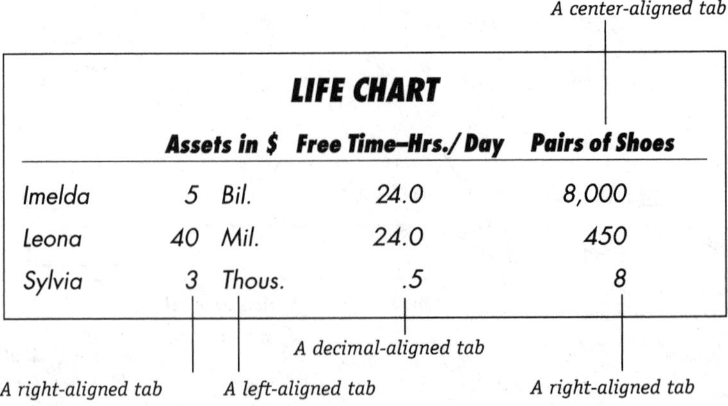

A center-aligned tab
LIFE CHART
Assets in $
Free Time–Hrs./Day
Pairs of Shoes
Imelda 5 Bil. 24.0 8,000
Leona 40 Mil. 24.0 450
Sylvia 3 Thous. .5 8
A decimal-aligned tab
A right-aligned tab
A left-aligned tab
A right-aligned tab

Hyphenation lessens gaps between words in justified type and smooths ragged edges in non-justified type. Auto Hyphenation (instructions below) can be turned on or off. Use manual hyphenation (see the tip on page 100) only for unique circumstances. A set of hyphenation and justification specifications is called an "H&J." A document can contain up to 1,000 H&Js, and they are applied on a paragraph-wide basis using Style menu > Formats.

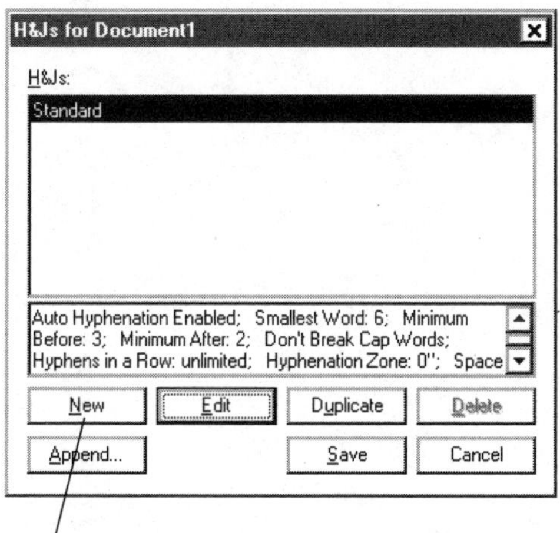

1 *Click **New**. Or choose an existing H&J and click **Edit**. Click **Append** to append an H&J from another document.*

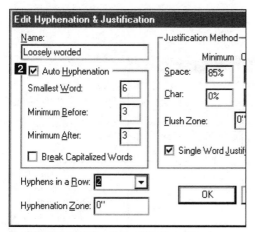

*The **Edit Hyphenation & Justification** dialog box.*

To create or edit an H&J:

1. Choose Edit menu > H&Js (Ctrl-Alt-H or Ctrl-Shift-F11).
2. To create a new H&J, click New **1**, then enter a name.
   or
   Choose an existing H&J, then click Edit. The Standard H&J can be modified.
3. Check the Auto Hyphenation box **2**.
4. Change any of these hyphenation settings:

   In the **Smallest Word** field, change the minimum number of characters a word must contain to be hyphenated.

   In the **Minimum Before** field, change the minimum number (1–6) of a word's characters that must precede a hyphen.

   In the **Minimum After** field, change the minimum number (2–8) of characters that can follow a hyphen. For the sake of readability, I use 3 rather than the default 2.

   Check or uncheck the **Break Capitalized Words** box for words that begin with an uppercase character.

   Change the number of consecutive lines that can end with a hyphen in the **Hyphens in a Row** field. More than two hyphens in a row can impair readability.

   Enter a higher number than zero in the **Hyphenation Zone** field to create a more ragged edge (less hyphenation).

(Continued on the following page)

5. To tighten word spacing in justified paragraphs, enter lower values in the **Space: Minimum** and **Space: Maximum** fields **3**. The subheads and thumb tabs in this book have slightly tightened word spacing. Headlines usually have tighter-than-normal word (and character) spacing. To loosen word spacing, enter higher values.

   To tighten character spacing in justified paragraphs, enter lower values in the **Char.: Minimum** and **Char.: Maximum** fields. To loosen character spacing, enter higher values. Experiment. The effect can vary depending on the font.

   To change word or character spacing in non-justified paragraphs, change the values in either **Optimum** field.
6. Click OK or press Enter.
7. Click Save. To apply an H&J, follow the instructions on the next page.

TIP To delete an H&J, click its name, then click Delete. If the H&J is currently applied to text in your document, you'll be prompted to choose a replacement H&J for the deleted one.

TIP To append an H&J from one document to another, see pages 34–36. An H&J created when no documents are open will appear on the H&J list of all subsequently created documents.

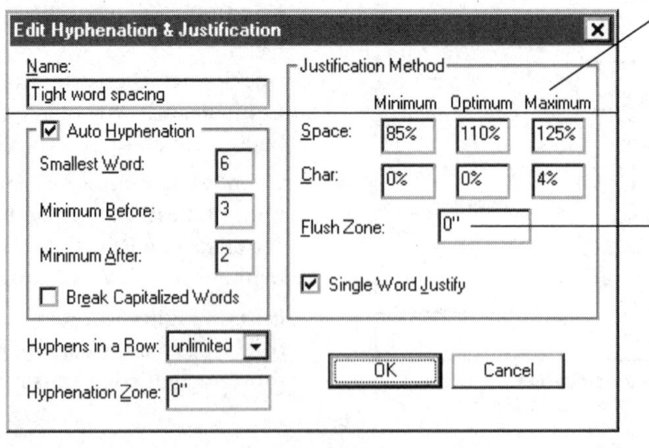

3 *The **Space** fields affect inter-word spacing; the **Char.** fields affect character (letter) spacing.*

*The **Flush Zone** is the horizontal area within which the last word in a justified paragraph must fall in order to be jusitifed. Forced Justify alignment nullifies the Flush Zone setting.*

> **SEASONINGS FOR WHITE SAUCE, FRICAS-SEES, AND RAGOUTS**
> White pepper, nutmeg, mace and lemon-peel, pounded together.
>
> **CATSUPS**
> Mushroom is most esteemed; but the difficulty in our country of obtaining the right kind of plant (some are poisonous), renders a recipe of little consequence. It is better to buy this catsup at the shops.

In this illustration, hyphenation is turned on for the subheads (a no-no) and turned off for the justified body text (another no-no, because it creates rivers of white space).

> **SEASONINGS FOR WHITE SAUCE, FRICASSEES, AND RAGOUTS**
> White pepper, nutmeg, mace and lemon-peel, pounded together.
>
> **CATSUPS**
> Mushroom is most esteemed; but the difficulty in our country of obtaining the right kind of plant (some are poi-sonous), renders a recipe of little con-sequence. It is better to buy this catsup at the shops.

Here hyphenation is turned off for the sub-heads and turned on for the justified body text—an improvement.

H&Js are applied to individual paragraphs using the Paragraph Formats dialog box. If you're using more than one H&J setting in a document, the most efficient way to apply them to your text is via a style sheet (see Chapter 13). The Normal style sheet will have the Standard H&J associated with it unless a different H&J is chosen for it.

To apply an H&J:

1. Choose the Content tool.
2. Click in a paragraph or press and drag through a series of paragraphs.
3. Choose Style menu > Formats (Ctrl-Shift-F).
4. Choose from the H&J drop-down menu **1**.
5. Click OK or Press Enter.

TIP The Expanded Hyphenation Method, which uses a new built-in hyphenation dictionary, creates better word breaks (turn on Auto Hyphenation). Choose Edit menu > Preferences > Document > Paragraph folder tab (Ctrl-Y), then choose Hyphenation Method: Expanded. Choose Standard or Enhanced to use a method built into an earlier version of QuarkXPress.

TIP If you want a word to *always* hyphenate but never break at the end of a line (a compound word like "e-mail" or "on-screen," for example), use a non-breaking hyphen: Ctrl-=.

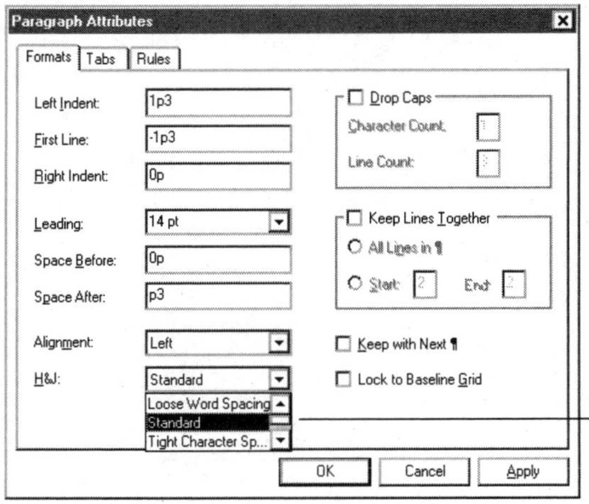

1 *To apply an H&J manually or to include it in a style sheet, choose from the **H&J** drop-down menu in the Paragraph Attributes > **Formats** folder tab.*

To prevent a word from hyphenating or specify where a word will hyphenate:

1. Choose Utilities menu > Hyphenation Exceptions.
2. Type a word that you *don't* want hyphenated **1**. Don't enter spaces, punctuation marks, or capital letters.
   or
   Specify how a word *will* be hyphenated by typing it with the hyphen.
3. Click Add or press Enter.
4. *Optional:* To edit an entry, click on it, edit it in the field, then click Replace.
5. Repeat steps 2 and 3 for any other words, then click Save. Hyphenation exceptions are saved in the XPress Preferences file.

TIP If, for some reason, you want to hyphenate a word manually, don't use a regular hyphen, which would stay in your text if the text reflows. Instead, use a discretionary hyphen (Ctrl-hyphen), which will disappear if the text reflows (though the invisible marker for it will remain).

If you're not sure where the proper spot is to enter a hyphen in a particular word, choose the Content tool, click in the word, then choose Utilities menu > Suggested Hyphenation (Ctrl-H). If no hyphens display in the dialog box, the word should not be hyphenated at all.

Line Check, which is part of Type Tricks, a free XTension, identifies hyphenated words. It also performs other tasks, like identifying loose lines in justified text.

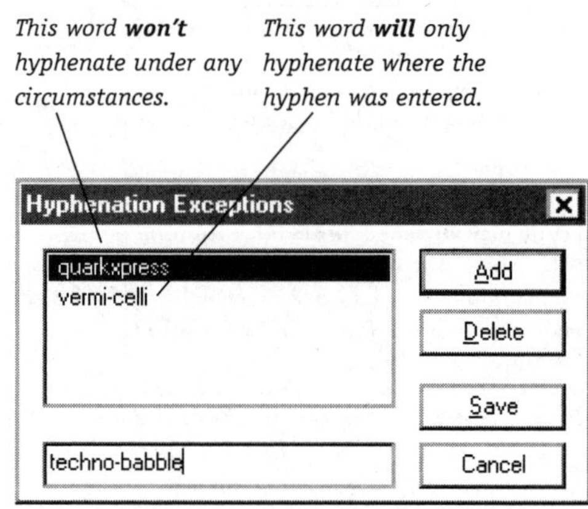
This word **won't** hyphenate under any circumstances.
This word **will** only hyphenate where the hyphen was entered.
Hyphenation Exceptions
quarkxpress
vermi-celli
Add
Delete
Save
techno-babble
Cancel

1 *Using the **Hyphenation Exceptions** dialog box, you can specify how a word **is** to be hyphenated and also specify which words you **don't** want hyphenated.*

Typography 7

*Choose a preset point size from the **Size** drop-down menu.*

*Or enter a point size between 2 and 720 in the **Size** field.*

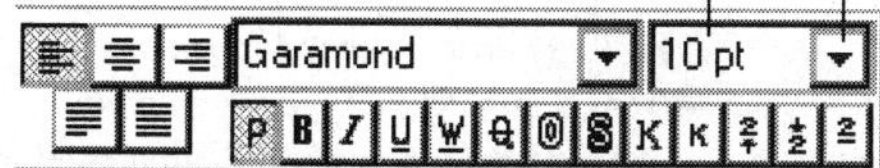

1 *The right-hand side of the Measurements palette.*

E
45 pt.

O H L M
25 pt.

T L S V Q
20 pt.

N Y I D X B
14 pt.

E U A F M G O
11 pt.

G I P H T R Q S
10 pt.

M X Q J U Z D L E
8 pt.

Once you learn the rudiments of changing type attributes (point size, font, etc.), I urge you to read Chapter 13, Style Sheets. Most of the type specifications that are discussed in this chapter can be applied and changed most efficiently using style sheets.

To resize type using the Measurements palette:

1. Choose the Content tool.
2. Highlight the text to be resized.
3. Choose a preset size from the Size drop-down menu on the right side of the Measurements palette **1**.
   or
   Double-click the Size field on the Measurements palette, enter a number between 2 and 720 in an increment as small as .001 point, then press Enter. You don't have to enter the "pt".

TIP You can also use the Ctrl-Shift-\ shortcut to open the Character Attributes dialog box—the Size field will highlight automatically.

Use this method to resize type if your highlighted text contains more than one point size—all the type will resize at once.

To resize type using the keyboard:

1. Choose the Content tool.
2. Highlight the text to be resized.
3. Hold down Ctrl and Shift and press "<" to reduce the text or ">" to enlarge the text to preset sizes.
   or
   Hold down Ctrl, Alt, Shift and press "<" to reduce the text or ">" to enlarge the text in 1-point increments.

To change a font:

1. Choose the Content tool.
2. Highlight the text to be modified.
3. Choose a font from the Font drop-down menu on the Measurements palette **1**.
   or
   Click in the Font field to the left of the current font name, type the first few characters of the desired font name, then press Enter **2**. (Ctrl-Alt-Shift-M highlights the Font field on the Measurements palette.)

TIP You can also choose a font from the Style menu > Font submenu.

TIP If you hold down Shift as you scroll through a font menu, fonts will display as they actually appear. Without Shift held down, fonts display in the default, plain-face font.

TIP Once text is highlighted, apply the next font on the menu to it by pressing Alt-F9. For the previous font, press Alt-Shift-F9.

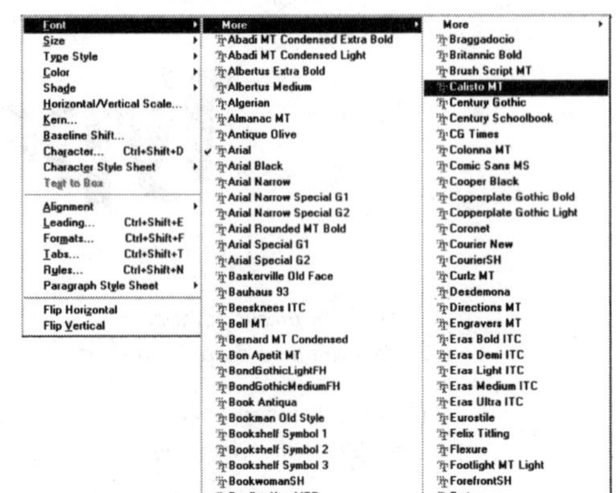

1 *Press an arrowhead to choose a font from a related group on a submenu. The font that is currently being used in the highlighted text has a checkmark.*

Click just to the left of the current font name, then start typing a new font name.

*Or press this arrowhead to choose from the **Font** drop-down menu.*

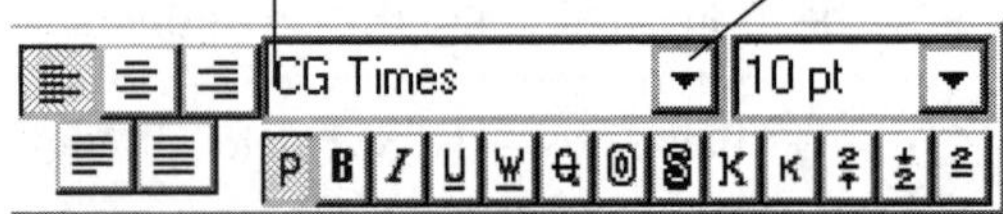

2 *The **Font** field is located on the right side of the Measurements palette.*

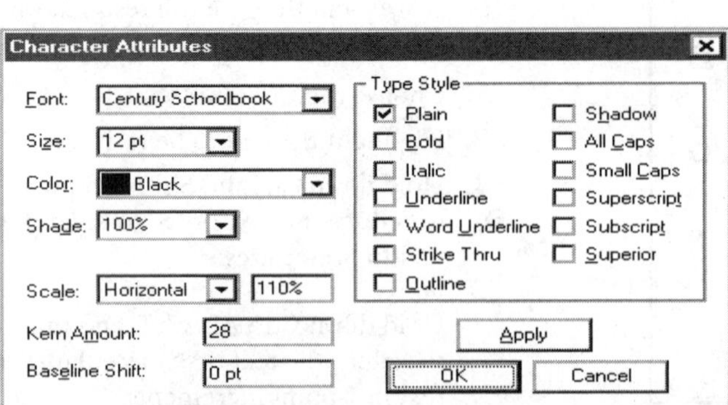

ONE-STOP SHOPPING

If you'd like to make all your Font, Size, Color, Shade, Scale, Track Amount, Baseline Shift, and Type Style choices from one dialog box, choose Style menu > Character (Ctrl-Shift-D). Don't forget to click Apply to preview!

Change Fonts

TYPE STYLE SHORTCUTS

First highlight the type. Then hold down **Ctrl** and **Shift** and press one of the following keys:

Plain	**P**
Bold	**B**
Italic	**I**
Underline	**U**
Word Underline	**W**
Outline	**O**
Shadow	**S**
All Caps	**K**
Small Caps	**H**
Superscript	**0** (zero)
Subscript	**9**
Superior	**V**

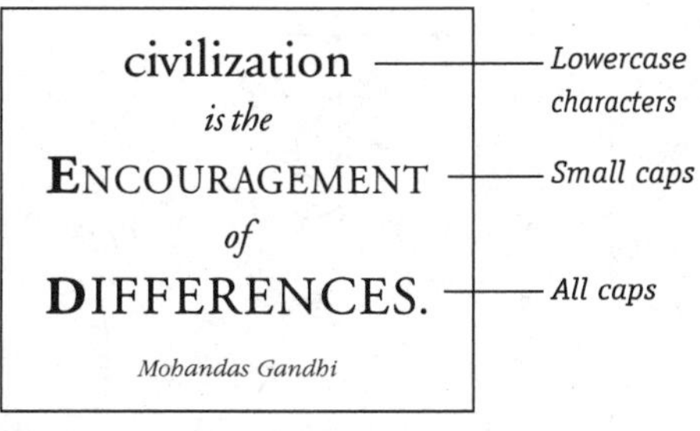

Note: Looking for boldface or italics? Choose the actual bold or italic font from the Font menu—it's less likely to cause a printing error.

To style type:

1. Choose the Content tool.
2. Highlight the text to be styled.
3. Click one or more of the style icons on the Measurements palette **1**.

TIP To remove *all* styling from highlighted type, click the "P" on the Measurements palette. To remove one style at a time, click any already highlighted style icon on the Measurements palette.

TIP Don't input text with the Caps lock key down; lowercase characters can easily be converted into caps or small caps, but characters input with Caps lock down can't be converted back to lowercase (unless you use a case-conversion XTension). When the small caps style is applied, uppercase characters remain uppercase and lowercase characters become small caps.

TIP Superscript type sits above the baseline (as in ^{B}). Subscript type sits below the baseline (as in $_{B}$). Superior type aligns with the cap height of the type and is reduced in point size (as in 14th or Lycra®).

1 *The **style** icons on the Measurements palette.*

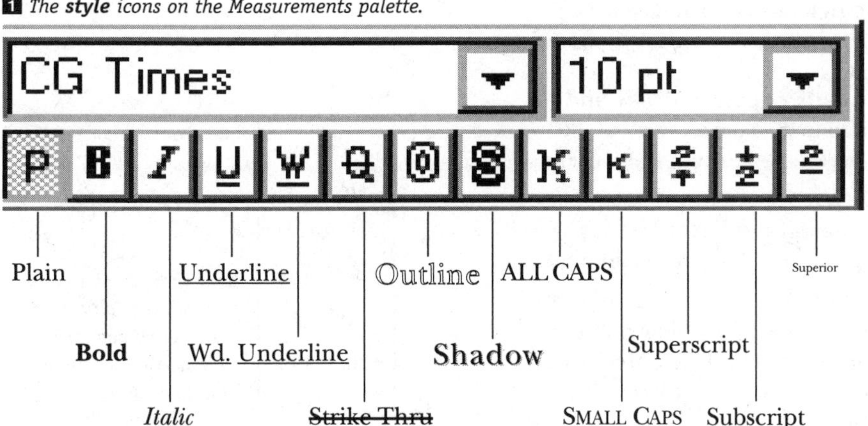

Style Type

Kerning is the manual adjustment of space between a pair of characters when the cursor is inserted between them. Tracking is the adjustment of the space to the right of one or more highlighted characters. The same section of the Measurements palette is used for tracking and kerning. (Make sure auto kerning is turned on in Edit menu > Preferences > Document > Character folder tab for the type size you're using before you start manually kerning. See page 283.)

T|omorrow

1 *Click between two characters to kern them.*

To kern type manually using the Measurements palette:

1. Choose the Content tool, and zoom in (Ctrl-Space bar-drag) on the type you're going to kern.
2. Click between two characters **1**.
3. Click the right Tracking & Kerning arrow to add space or the left arrow to remove space **2**–**3**.
   or
   Enter a number between -500% and 500% in an increment as small as .001 in the Tracking & Kerning field, then press Enter.

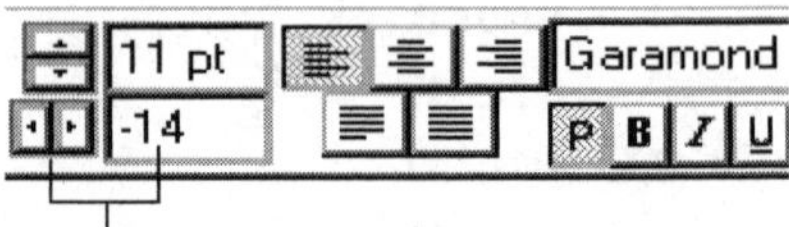

2 *The Tracking & Kerning arrows and field on the Measurements palette.*

Tomorrow

3 *Now the "T" and the "o" are closer together.*

To track type manually using the Measurements palette:

1. Choose the Content tool.
2. Highlight any number of characters.
3. Click the right arrow to add space or the left arrow to remove space **2**, **4**–**5**.
   or
   Enter a number between -500% and 500% in an increment as small as .001 in the Tracking & Kerning field, then press Enter.

TIP Alt-click the right or left arrow to track or kern in finer increments.

TIP To apply tracking (or kerning) values via a dialog box, choose Style menu > Track (or Kern). The Track Amount (or Kern Amount) field will highlight automatically.

C I V I L I Z A T I O N
is the
E N C O U R A G E M E N T
of
D I F F E R E N C E S.
Mohandas Gandhi

4 *A phrase with positive tracking values.*

Nothing
great was
ever
achieved
without
enthusiasm.
Emerson

5 *A phrase with a negative tracking value of -6. Positive and negative tracking values can be used to create a variety of typographic effects.*

To Tr Ta Yo Ya
Wo Wa We Va Vo

1 *These are a few of the character pairs that often need extra kerning, particularly if they're set in a large point size.*

THE TALE OF MRS. TIGGY-WINKLE
THE TALE OF MRS. TIGGY-WINKLE

2 *Wide letterspacing is popular nowadays, especially since it's so easy to achieve. Use it for small bits of type, as it can be tiring to read in large quantities. Small caps, as in this illustration, look nice "tracked out." Type that is very chunky or very thin may also require extra letterspacing.*

Style is self-plagiarism.

3 *A phrase with a normal word spacing.*

Style is self-plagiarism.
Alfred Hitchcock

4 *The same phrase with a word space value of -10. Negative word space tracking can improve the appearance of headlines and other large-sized text.*

To kern or track using the keyboard:

1. Choose the Content tool.
2. Click between two characters or highlight any number of characters.
3. Hold down Ctrl and Shift and press left bracket ([ ) to remove space, or right bracket ( ]) to add space **1**–**2**. To kern or track in finer increments, include the Alt key in the shortcut.

Note: To use the Word Space Tracking or Remove Manual Kerning command, you must install and enable the free Type Tricks XTension. Download it from the Quark web site (http://www.quark.com).

Use the shortcut described in the following instructions to adjust inter-word spacing in a unique phrase, like a headline. To adjust inter-word spacing in repetitive text, like subheads, or in a larger body of text, create an H&J with tighter word spacing and apply it via a style sheet. The word spacing of the subheads in this book was ever-so-slightly tightened that way.

To adjust inter-word spacing:

1. Choose the Content tool.
2. Highlight one or more words.
3. Hold down Ctrl and Shift and press left bracket ([ ) to remove space or right bracket ( ]) to add space **3**–**4**. For finer word space adjustments, include the Alt key.

To remove kerning and word space tracking:

1. Choose the Content tool.
2. Highlight the kerned text.
3. Choose Utilities menu > Remove Manual Kerning. This command has no effect on tracking values.

Some character pairs, because of their shape and how they fit side by side, have noticeable gaps between them. To ameliorate this problem, fonts have hundreds of built-in kerning pairs—character duos that are nudged together slightly. This pair kerning is turned on via the Auto Kern Above box in Edit menu > Preferences > Document > Character folder tab.

If you're unhappy with the spacing in a particular kerning pair or pairs that appear repetitively in your documents, you can use the Kerning Table Editor to specify your own kerning values. Your overall goal as a typesetter, though, should not be to equalize every single space between every single character, but rather to correct any particularly large, toothy gaps so they don't stand out in the crowd. Gaps are usually more noticeable in large point sizes. Overall letterspacing, by the way, should be adjusted via an H&J (see page 98). And headlines should be adjusted manually.

To use the Kerning Table Editor:

1. Choose Utilities menu > Kerning Table Edit. If it's unavailable, enable it via the XTensions Manager.
2. Highlight the name of the font that you want to edit **1**, then click Edit.
   or
   Double-click the name of the font you want to edit.
3. Click a kerning pair on the list.
   or
   Type the kerning pair that you want to edit in the Pair field.
4. Enter a new kerning Value or click the up or down arrow. A negative value will bring characters closer together. Alt-click an arrow for fine tweaking.
5. Note the Preview **2**, and when you're satisfied with the new kerning value, then click Replace to replace the existing pair or click Add if it's a new pair.
6. Click OK, then click Save.

KEEP DOCUMENT SETTINGS

Kerning table changes are made on a font-by-font basis, but they apply on an application-wide basis. Click Keep Document Settings when you open a document if you don't want it to be affected by new kerning table values. To restore a font's original, manufacturer-defined kerning values for all pairs, click Reset in the Edit Kerning Table dialog box. QuarkXPress' Kerning Table Edits don't affect font usage in any other application.

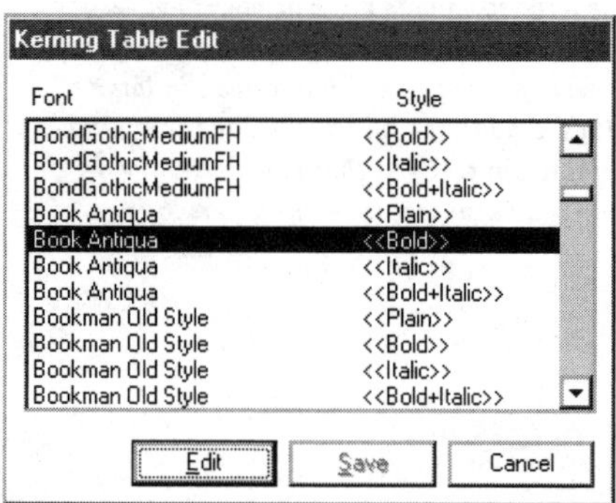

1 *Highlight the name of the font whose kerning you want to edit, then click **Edit**.*

2 *Note the **Preview** as you change a kerning pair's **Value**. The most accurate preview, of course, is high-resolution output.*

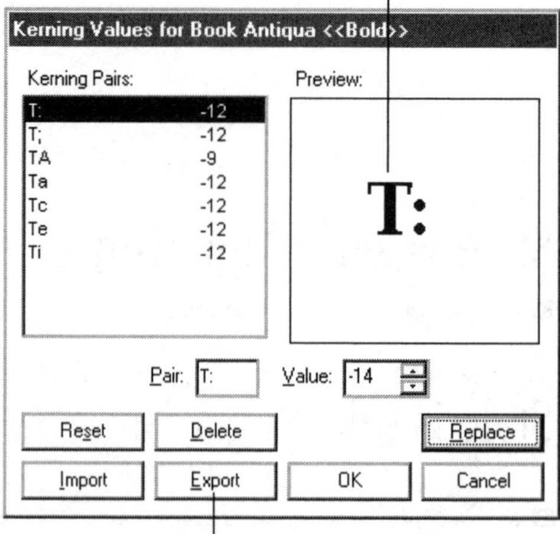

*If you want to export the kerning pairs you've adjusted for one font to use with another font, click **Export**, choose a different font, then click **Import**.*

Alligator

1 *Futura Regular, normal scale.*

Alligator

2 *Fudging a condensed font: Futura Regular, condensed 30%.*

Alligator

3 *Futura Condensed Regular, normal scale—a true condensed font—has more balanced proportions.*

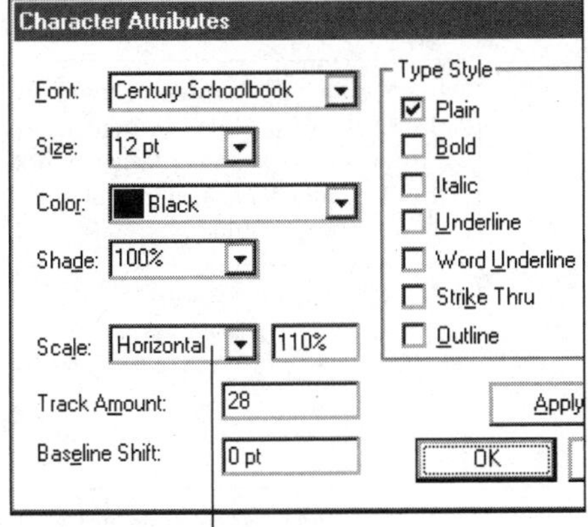

4 *The* ***Scale: Horizontal*** *field in the Character Attributes dialog box.*

Whale

Extended type.

Giraffe

Condensed type.

5 *Horizontal scaling is a way to stylize type.*

Normal text has a horizontal scale value of 100%. Horizontal scaling is the extending (widening) or condensing (narrowing) of type. Horizontal scaling only affects a character's width; vertical scaling only affects a character's height.

Note: Since the Scale command affects only the vertical parts of letters—not the horizontals (or vice versa)—it distorts letter shapes. If you're looking for narrow characters, it's better to use a condensed typeface than it is to fudge a condensed typeface by horizontally scaling a normal typeface 1–3. The true condensed font will look more balanced. The same holds true for an extended typeface. To enlarge characters without distorting them, change their point size.

To scale type using a dialog box:

1. Choose the Content tool.
2. Highlight the text to be scaled.
3. Choose Style menu > Horizontal/Vertical Scale. The Scale field will highlight automatically.
4. For horizontal scaling, choose Scale: Horizontal, then enter a percentage between 25 and 99 to condense type (make it narrower than normal) or a percentage between 101 and 400 to expand type (make it wider than normal) 4. A Horizontal Scale percentage of 60%, for example, will condense type 40%. A Horizontal Scale percentage of 125% will expand type 25%.

   or

   Choose Scale: Vertical, then enter the desired percentage.

   Note: You can scale type in only one direction—horizontally or vertically.
5. Click OK or press Enter 5.

To scale type horizontally or vertically using the keyboard:

1. Choose the Content tool.
2. Highlight the text to be scaled.
3. Hold down Ctrl and press left bracket ([ ) to condense or shorten in 5% increments, or right bracket ( ]) to expand or lengthen 1–4. Include the Alt key to scale in 1% increments. Scaling will be horizontal or vertical depending on which option is currently selected in the Character Attributes dialog box.

"It was much pleasanter at home," thought poor Alice, "when one wasn't always growing larger and smaller, and being ordered about by mice and rabbits."

1 *Normal (100%) horizontal and vertical scale.*

"It was much pleasanter at home," thought poor Alice, "when one wasn't always growing larger and smaller, and being ordered about by mice and rabbits."

2 *75% vertical scale.*

"It was much pleasanter at home," thought poor Alice, "when one wasn't always growing larger and smaller, and being ordered about by mice and rabbits."
Lewis Carroll

3 *80% horizontal scale.*

"It was much pleasanter at home," thought poor Alice, "when one wasn't always growing larger and smaller, and being ordered about by mice and rabbits."

4 *110% horizontal scale.*

This method for resizing type interactively rather than by specifying an exact point size is appropriate when you're working visually—trying to make a headline or a logo look just so.

To resize type interactively:

1. Choose the Item or Content tool.
2. To resize type while preserving its horizontal/vertical scale and the proportions of its box, Ctrl-Alt-Shift-drag a handle 5–6. The leading will readjust proportionately.
   or
   To resize type while changing its scale and the proportions of its box, Ctrl-drag a side midpoint handle to scale horizontally or a top or bottom midpoint handle to scale vertically. The type will condense or expand to fit the box.

TIP Type in a linked box cannot be resized using this technique.

TIP To restore normal scaling to the type, highlight it, choose Style menu > Horizontal/Vertical Scale, then enter 100 in the Scale field.

"Oh, I'm not particular as to size," Alice hastily replied; "only one doesn't like changing so often, you know."

5 *The original text.*

"Oh, I'm not particular as to size," Alice hastily replied; "only one doesn't like changing so often, you know."

6 *To resize text while preserving both its own proportions and the proportions of its box, Ctrl-Alt-Shift-drag a handle.*

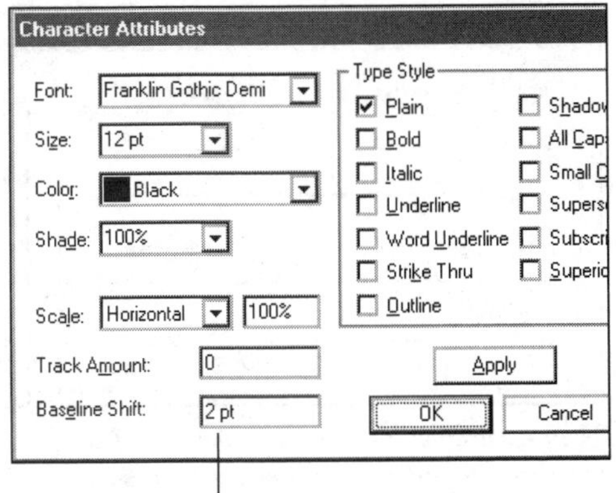

1 *A positive* ***Baseline Shift*** *value shifts characters above the baseline; a negative Baseline Shift shifts characters below the baseline.*

The baseline

Country

2 *The "C" was baseline shifted downward. Baseline Shift is useful for creating signs or company logos.*

Using the Baseline Shift command, one or more characters can be raised above or lowered below the baseline. Don't use this command to shift a whole paragraph—that's the job of leading. Use Baseline Shift only to fiddle with a little type nugget—to nudge a bullet or a dash slightly upward or downward, for example, or shift the position of text on a Bézier path. A Baseline Shift value can be incorporated into a paragraph or character style sheet.

To vertically shift type using a dialog box:

1. Choose the Content tool.
2. Highlight the characters to be shifted.
3. Choose Style menu > Baseline Shift. The Baseline Shift field will highlight automatically.
4. Enter a number up to three times the point size of the type to be shifted. Precede the number by a minus sign (-) to shift the type below the baseline **1**–**2**.
5. Click OK or press Enter.

To vertically shift type using the keyboard:

1. Choose the Content tool.
2. Highlight the characters to be shifted.
3. Hold down Ctrl, Alt, Shift and press left parentheses [(] to lower the type below the baseline in 1-point increments, or right parentheses [)] to raise the type above the baseline.

It's easy to input the curly, smart quotation marks that professional typesetters use or foreign language quotes, like guillemets (« »). With the XPress Smart Quotes feature on, press ' to produce a single quotation mark in the style currently specified in the Application Preferences dialog box (' for English) or press Shift-' (") to produce a double quotation mark (").

To turn on Smart Quotes:

1. Choose Edit menu > Preferences > Application (Ctrl-Alt-Shift-Y).
2. Click the Interactive folder tab.
3. Check the Smart Quotes box.
4. Choose a style for the quotes from the Format drop-down menu **1**.
5. Click OK or press Enter **2**.

TIP Uncheck the Smart Quotes box to produce inch and foot marks when you type ' and ". To produce a single smart quote when the Smart Quotes box is unchecked or to produce a foot mark when the Smart Quotes option is checked, hold down Ctrl and press '. To produce a double smart quote when the Smart Quotes box is unchecked or to produce an inch mark when the Smart Quotes option is checked, hold down Ctrl and Shift and press '.

TIP If you import text with the Convert Quotes box checked in the Get Text dialog box, smart quotes will be substituted for straight quotes.

TIP Sometimes you should intentionally make a quotation mark curve in the opposite direction from the way it's inserted automatically when Smart Quotes is on. A date is an example: '94. The quote should always curve toward the absent letter: '94. Press Alt-Shift-] or Option-] (Alt-Shift-] for double-quotes) to enter it manually. Here's another example: Sugar 'n' spice.

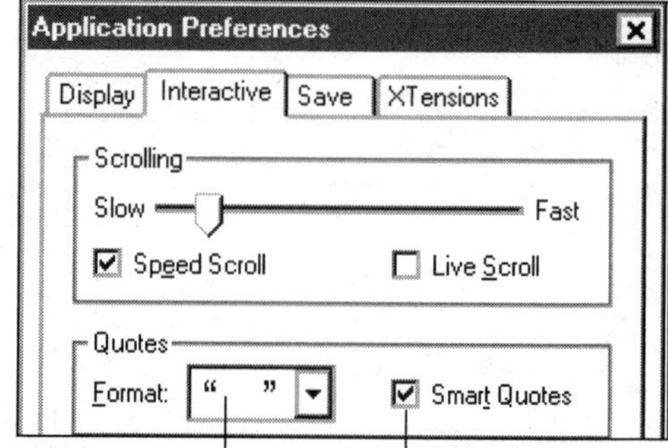

1 *In Application Preferences > Interactive folder tab, check the* ***Smart Quotes*** *box and choose a quotes* ***Format.***

"HATE THE SIN
and
LOVE THE SINNER"

Mohandas Gandhi

2 *Use Smart Quotes for quotation and apostrophe marks.*

PRIME TIME

Please—I beg of you—use straight quotes *only* for foot and inch marks **3** (not for quotation marks). Or better yet, use oblique foot and inch marks, called prime marks. To produce a foot mark, choose the ZappedPiFH font, then hold down Shift and press "M" **4**. To produce an inch mark, hold down Shift and press "N". If the ZappedPiFH font isn't available or you don't like the way it looks, you can use the italic inch or foot mark in your current font instead.

The woman is 5'6" tall.

3 *Use straight quotes only for foot and inch marks or minute and second marks.*

The woman is 5′6″ tall.

4 *Or better yet, use the ZappedPiFH Font: Shift-M for a foot mark, Shift-N for an inch mark.*

1 *A few WingedBat characters.*

> **SIR ISAAC NEWTON** wore his black and gold waistcoat.
>
> And Mr. Alderman Ptolemy Tortoise brought a salad with him in a string bag.
>
> And instead of a nice dish of minnows they had a roasted grasshopper with ladybird sauce, which frogs consider a beautiful treat; but I think it must have been nasty! ✿
>
> *Beatrix Potter*

2 *You can use a WingedBat or other dingbat to mark the end of a story or article.*

A FEW SPECIAL CHARACTERS

©	Alt 0169	*Hold down the Alt key while typing the numbers on the keypad, then release Alt.*
®	Alt 0174	
™	Alt 0153	
é	Alt 0233	
¢	Alt 0162	
¶	Alt 0182	
°	Alt 0176	

FONT FONTASY

You can use Character Map **3** to insert special characters, but inserting special characters is quicker and easier with the Fontasy XTension from Vision's Edge, Inc. **4** It's part of the Windows TeXT ColleXTion. Just click in a text box, then click on a character on the palette—that character will appear where your cursor is inserted.

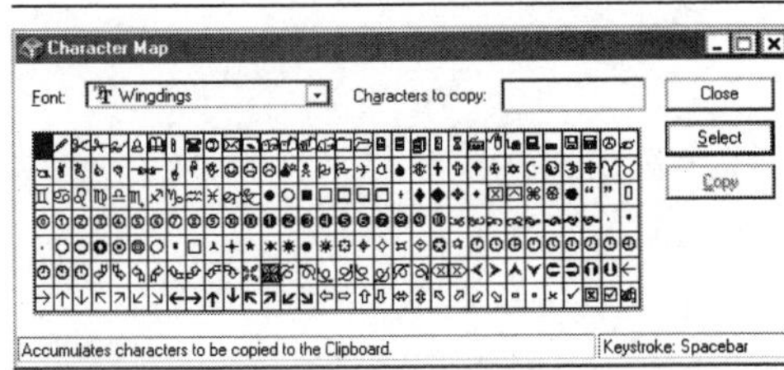

3 ***Character Map.***

Note: To insert dingbats repetitively, as in a bulleted list, use a character style sheet.

To insert one Zapf Dingbat or Symbol character:

1. Choose the Content tool.
2. Click in a line of text to create an insertion point.
3. For a Zapf Dingbat character, hold down Ctrl and Shift and press "Z". For a Symbol character, use the Ctrl-Shift-Q shortcut.
4. Press any key or keyboard combination to produce the desired Zapf Dingbat character **1**–**2**. When you continue to type, the original, non-Dingbat typeface will reappear automatically.

TIP Try making the Zapf dingbat, or any other dingbat, ever so slightly smaller than the surrounding text, or make it huge, so it functions like a graphic.

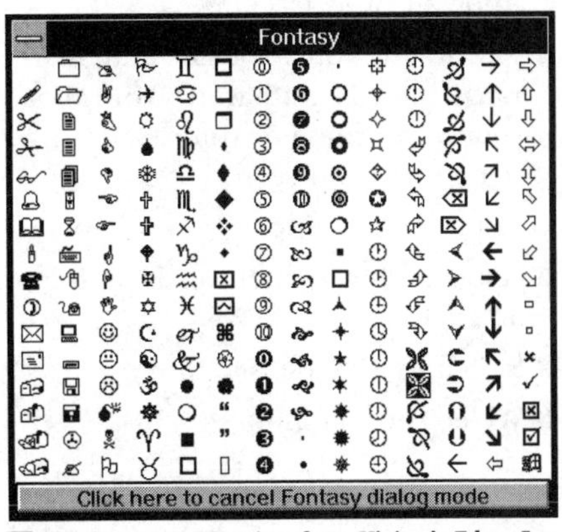

4 *The **Fontasy** XTension from Vision's Edge, Inc.*

Hanging punctuation

If you're setting text that starts or ends with punctuation and that is larger or more noticeable than standard body text (a pull quote in an article, for example, or a quotation on a book jacket), the paragraph alignment will look more correct and more pleasing if the punctuation hangs outside the main body of the text.

How to do it. Unfortunately, it's not a flick-of-the-switch operation, like a drop cap. Here are a couple of methods: Create a hanging indent using either positive or negative indents (see page 86), or use the Indent Here character (see page 87) **1**–**3**. (You could also use this technique to hang a large initial cap.)

Here's one more way to hang punctuation: Type a space before the punctuation mark, then negative kern backwards **4**–**5**. The first character will print, even though it may be partially or completely hidden outside the box if the box doesn't have a text inset.

Copyfitting

If you need to squeeze text into a tight space or bring up a stubborn orphan word or hyphenated word (horrors!) from the end of a paragraph, use whichever of these techniques you think your readers are least likely to notice:

- Apply –1 or –2 tracking.
- Rewrite the copy—delete, add, rearrange, or substitute words (only if it's your own writing or you're authorized to do so, of course!)
- Apply 99% scaling.
- Apply slightly tighter word spacing using an H&J.
- Switch to a condensed font.
- Widen the column.

"There is no such thing
as a non-working mother."

1 *Non-hanging punctuation.*

"There is no such thing
as a non-working mother."

2 *Hanging punctuation created using a hanging indent. The left alignment of the paragraph looks cleaner.*

"There is no such thing
as a non-working mother."

3 *Even better. The second line is aligned with the stem of the "T."*

"There is no such thing
as a non-working mother."

4 *To create hanging punctuation using kerning, insert a space to the left of the first character in the paragraph and then apply negative kerning.*

"There is no such thing
as a non-working mother."

Hester Mundis

5 *It may look peculiar on screen, but it will print just fine.*

BREAK THE RULE

Draw lines using the Orthogonal Line tool. Use the Step & Repeat feature (Ctrl-Alt-D), 0 Vertical Offset, to duplicate them. I wish there was an easier way.

Early American Cookery

PUMPKIN PIE	Stew the pumpkin dry, and make it like squash pie, only season rather higher. In the country, where this *real yankee pie* is prepared in perfection, ginger is almost always used with other spices.

To create side-by-side paragraphs, anchor a text box on the left side (Align with Text: Ascent), and create a hanging indent in the main paragraph (see page 87). Baseline Shift the anchored box upward, if necessary.

HOW TO GET ATTENTION

- Make the text you want to stand out larger (or make it much smaller, and surround it with lots of white space).
- Use **boldface** or ***italics*** in the same font family as the body text, or in a **contrasting** font or color.

What *not* to do: Don't use the underline or ALL CAPS style, both of which make type harder to read.

Type in reverse

There's no one-step method for creating reversed type. You have to change the type color to white (see page 233) and change the background of the text box to black (see page 234). To create reversed type in subheads or other repetitive text, use a black or colored paragraph rule (see page 92). The reverse headline on the sidebars in this book was created using such a rule.

Get your dashes straight

When to use a regular hyphen: To write a compound word, as in "three year-old."

When to use an en dash (Ctrl-Alt-Shift-hyphen): Between a range of numbers, as in "Figures 4–6," a time frame, as in "4–6 weeks," or a distance, as in "4–6 miles."

When to use an em dash (Ctrl-Shift-=): To break up a sentence, as in "Bunny rabbit—excuse me—stay here." Don't add a whole space around an em dash — it will be too noticeable (as in this sentence). Instead, you can add a little bit of space by kerning—as in this sentence—or use a narrow flex space. Specify a Flex Space Width percentage in Edit menu > Preferences > Document > Character folder tab. Or use an em dash with built-in thin spaces around it from an expert font set.

Dot, dot, dot

To create an ellipses (…), hold down the Alt key, type 0133 on the keypad, then release Alt. If those dots are too close together for your comfort, you can type periods instead and then track them out (. . .). Or you can alternately type period (.), then flex-space (Ctrl-Alt-Shift-5), then period (. . .), and so on.

The Character Preferences are discussed on page 283.

Fractions

There are several ways to produce fractions in QuarkXPress:

- Use any character set, press Alt-0190 to produce ¾ (Press Alt-0188 for ¼ or Alt-0189 for ½).
- Install and enable Quark, Inc.'s Type Tricks XTension, type the numerator, a slash, and the denominator, highlight all the characters, then choose Style menu > Type Style > Make Fraction. You'll produce a fraction that looks like this: ¾. You can kern between the characters in this type of fraction. Choose Fraction/Price preferences in Edit menu > Preferences > Fraction/Price.
- A third method—building a fraction by hand—requires more steps. Type the numerator, type Alt-0164, type the denominator, apply the Superior style to the numerator, select the symbol between the numbers and change the font to Symbol (it turns into a virgule), and finally, divide the point size of the denominator in half. This is what you get: ¾.

MAKE YOUR RAGS LOOK PRETTY

When all the copy is in place and ready for imagesetting, stop for a moment to fine-tune the right edge of your left-aligned paragraphs. Try to make the second-to-last line longer than the third-to-the-last line:

Every child is an artist.
The problem is how to remain
an artist once he grows up.

Or make the last line the longer than the second-to-last line:

Every child is an artist. The
problem is how to remain
an artist once he grows up. *Picasso*

But don't let the whole thing cave inward:

Every child is an artist. The problem
is how to remain an artist once
he grows up.

Typographic terms

***Sans serif** font*

***Serif** font*

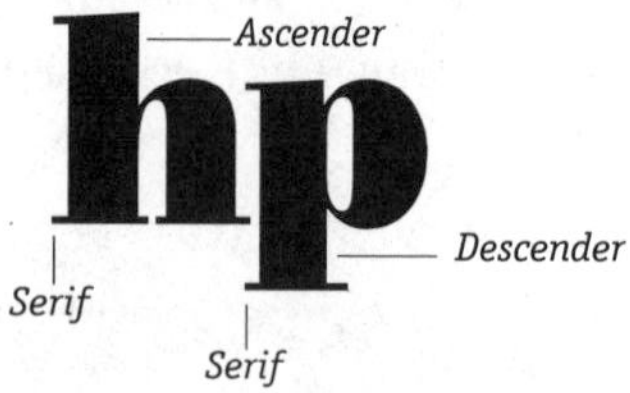

NON-PRINTING CHARACTERS

The character		*The keystroke*
Tab	→	Tab
Word Space	.	Space bar
New Paragraph	¶	Enter
New Line	↵	Shift-Enter
Next Column	↓	Enter (on keypad)
Next Box	⇣	Shift-Enter (on keypad)
Indent Here	⁞	Ctrl \

For other non-printing characters, see "Special text characters" on pages 333–334.

Multiple items 8

The position, size, angle of rotation, background color, and other specifications can be modified for a multiple-item selection. Modification options will vary depending on whether the items are all text boxes, picture boxes, lines, text paths, or a combination thereof. Two methods for creating a multiple-item selection are described below. Note that either tool can be used—Item or Content.

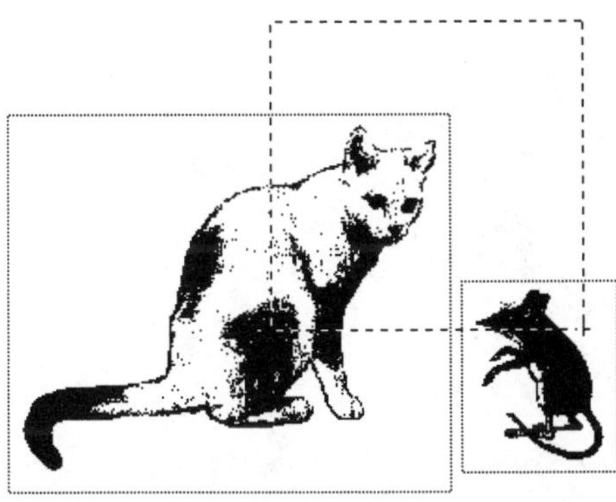

1 *Drag a marquee over multiple items with the **Item** tool.*

2 *Both picture boxes are selected, and the handles on both boxes are visible.*

To select multiple items:

1. Choose the Item or Content tool.
2. Shift-click on each item to be selected. (Shift-click any inadvertently selected item to deselect it.)
   or
   Position the cursor outside all the items to be selected, then press and drag a marquee around them. You only need to include a portion of each item in the marquee **1**–**2**.

TIP To quickly deselect all the currently selected items, choose the Item tool, then press Tab or click on a blank area in your document.

TIP Moving and constraining a multiple-item selection is a little tricky. Once all the items are selected, start dragging the selection, then hold down Shift and continue dragging to constrain the movement to the horizontal or vertical axis. Release the mouse, then release Shift.

Grouped items remain associated as a unit unless they're ungrouped. You might want to group such items as a picture and its caption so they will move as a unit. Individual items within a group can be modified, and multiple groups can be nested inside a larger group.

1 *A dotted **bounding box** surrounds a group when it's selected with the Item tool.*

To group items:

1. Choose the Item or Content tool.
2. Shift-click on each item to be included in the group. (Shift-click any inadvertently selected item to deselect it.)
   or
   Position the cursor outside all the items to be included in the group, then press and drag a marquee around them. You only need to drag over a portion of all the items—just make sure to grab at least one handle of each item.
3. Choose Item menu>Group (Ctrl-G) **1**.

To move an item in a group:

1. Choose the Item or Content tool.
2. Hold down Ctrl, press on the item to be moved, pause briefly for the item to redraw, then drag **2**.

TIP Use the Content tool to modify the size or contents of an item in a group.

TIP If you want to edit the contents of a box in a group and the group is already selected, deselect it by clicking outside it, then click on the item you want to edit with the Content tool.

2 *To move an item in a group, **Ctrl-drag** the item with the Content tool.*

To delete an item from a group:

1. Choose the Content tool.
2. Click on the item to be deleted.
3. Choose Item menu > Delete (Ctrl-K). This command *can* be undone.

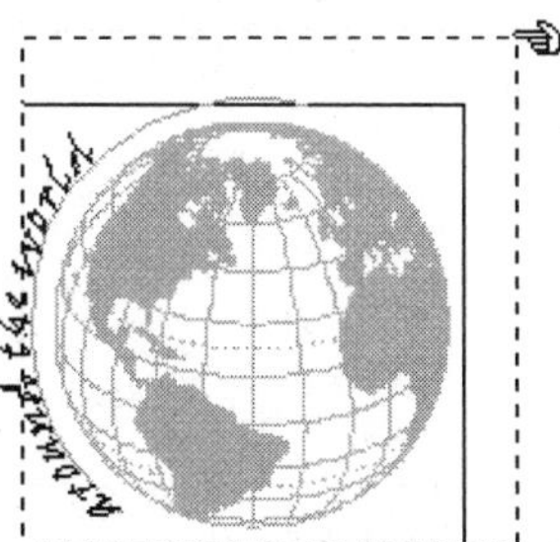

1 *If you resize a group while holding down **Ctrl, Alt,** and **Shift**...*

2 *...the items and their contents will resize proportionately.*

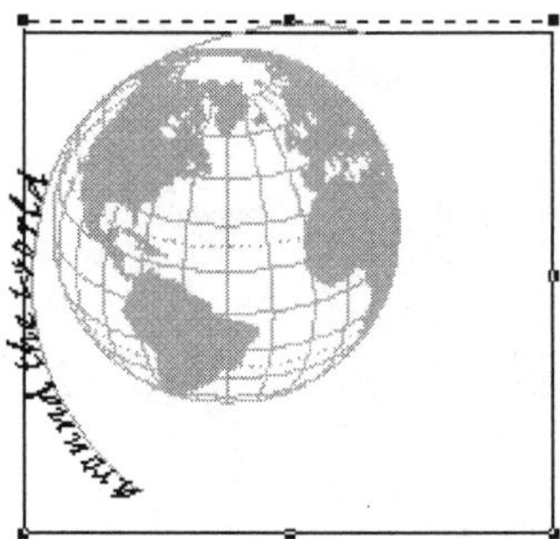

3 *If you resize a group with **no** keys held down, the items (containers) will reshape, but not their contents (text or picture).*

This method for resizing multiple items is a great time-saver.

SPEED TIP

To resize a whole group:

1. Choose the Item tool.
2. Click on the group.
3. To resize the grouped items as well as their contents (text or picture), frame widths, and line weights (if any) proportionally, Ctrl-Alt-Shift drag a handle **1**–**2**. You *can't* undo this! I smell a bug fix.
   or
   To change the shape of the grouped items but not their contents, drag a handle with no modifier keys held down **3**. You *can* undo this.

To ungroup items:

1. Choose the Item tool.
2. Click on the group you want to ungroup.
3. Choose Item menu > Ungroup (Ctrl-U).

TIP To change a group's overall dimensions, angle, background color, or shade, or to apply a blend across a whole group, use Item menu > Modify > Group folder tab (Ctrl-M) or right-click and choose Modify. Runaround options must be chosen individually for each item in a group.

Locking is a safety command that can be applied to any item—a line, a box, or a text path—to prevent it from being moved, resized, reshaped, or rotated manually. Locking does not prevent the *contents* of a locked text or picture box or the attributes of a line, such as its style and width, from being edited. Locking is particularly useful for securing items on a master page so they're not inadvertently moved or resized on a document page to which that master has been assigned.

Note: A locked item *can* be moved or resized using the Measurements palette or a dialog box, such as the Space/Align command. And **beware:** A locked item *can* be deleted.

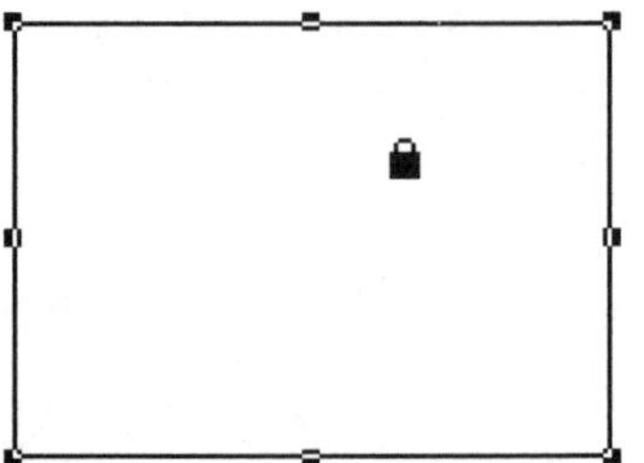

1 *The padlock icon displays if a locked item is selected with the Item tool.*

To lock an item:

1. Choose the Item or Content tool.
2. Select the item to be locked (or select multiple items to be locked).
3. Choose Item menu > Lock (F6) **1**. Choose the same command again to unlock the item.

Undoing a multiple-item delete

If you delete a group or choose Delete when more than one item is selected, you can choose Edit menu > Undo to undo it. You may encounter, however, either of these two gliches after the undo: First, if you delete multiple text boxes that are linked to other text boxes that you don't delete, a prompt will warn you that the links to and from the deleted boxes cannot be reestablished using the Undo command **2**. If you delete all the text boxes in a linked chain and then choose the Undo command, the entire chain will be restored. Second, the layering position of the deleted items may be different when they reappear.

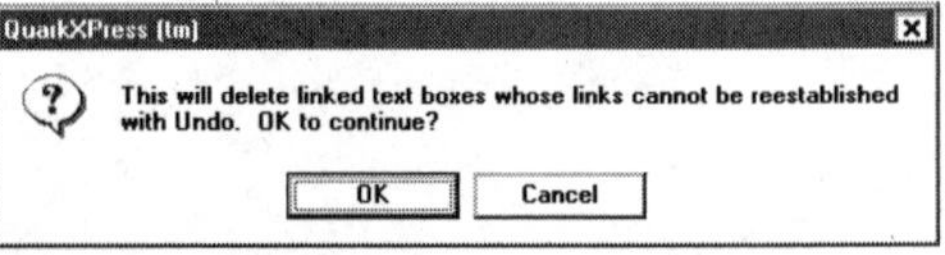

2 *This prompt will appear if you delete multiple linked text boxes but you don't delete all the boxes in the chain.*

To duplicate an item:

1. Choose the Item or Content tool.
2. Select the item or group that you want to duplicate **1**.
3. Choose Item menu > Duplicate (Ctrl-D) **2**.

TIP Duplicates are positioned according to the offsets last used in the Step and Repeat dialog box (see the next page).

1 *Select the item to be duplicated, then choose Item menu >* ***Duplicate****.*

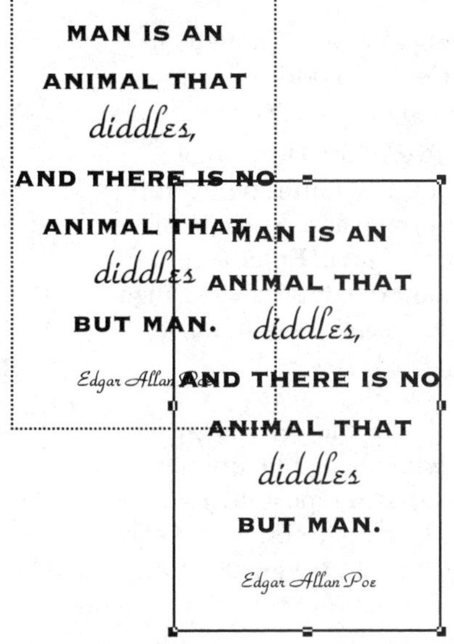

2 *A duplicate is made.*

Using the Step and Repeat command, multiple duplicates can be made at one time and the duplicates can be placed at a specified distance from each other. The Offset distance is calculated from the upper left corner of each item (or the bounding box, in the case of a Bézier box, line, or text path). You can use this command to reproduce, among other things, multiple picture and caption groups in perfect horizontal or vertical rows.

1 *Select an item.*

To step and repeat an item:

1. Choose the Item or Content tool.
2. Select an item or a group **1**.
3. Choose Item menu > Step and Repeat (Ctrl-Alt-D).
4. Enter a number between 1 and 99 in the Repeat Count field for the number of duplicates to be made **2**.
5. Enter a number in the Horizontal Offset field. Enter a minus sign before the number to step and repeat items to the left of the original. Enter 0 in this field if you want the duplicates to align along their left edges, but not move horizontally.
   and
   Enter a number in the Vertical Offset field. Enter a minus sign before the number to step and repeat items above the original. Enter 0 in this field if you want the duplicates to align along their top edges, but not move vertically.

   Enter positive numbers in both Offset fields to create a stair-step arrangement.
6. Click OK or press Enter **3**.

TIP If an alert prompt appears, reduce the Repeat Count and/or Offset values so the duplicated items will fit within the confines of the pasteboard.

Step and Repeat

Repeat Count: 5

Horizontal Offset: 0

Vertical Offset: 5p5

OK Cancel

2 *The* ***Step and Repeat*** *dialog box.*

3 *This item was duplicated using these values: Repeat Count 3, Horizontal Offset 0, and Vertical Offset 5p5.*

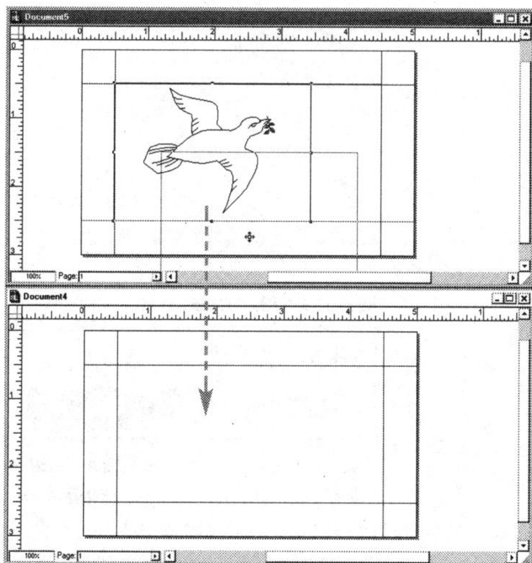

1 *Open two files, choose the **Item** tool, then press and drag an item from one document window into the other.*

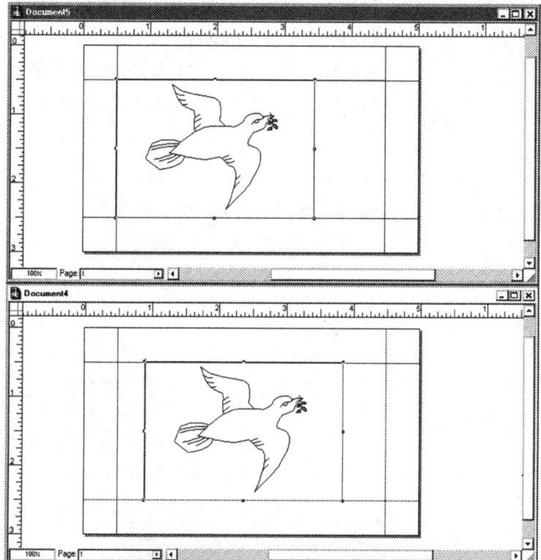

2 *A **duplicate** is made automatically as the item is dragged; the original item is unchanged.*

Note: This drag-copy method of copying items between documents doesn't use the Clipboard.

To drag-copy an item between documents:

1. Open two QuarkXPress files, and resize or move both document windows so they are side-by-side (choose Window menu > Tile Horizontally), or at least arrange them so they don't completely overlap each other.
2. Choose the Item tool, or hold down Ctrl if the Content tool is chosen.
3. Press and drag an item or group from one document window into the other. A duplicate will be created automatically **1**–**2**. Any style sheets, H&Js, or custom colors that were applied to the copied item will append to the destination document.

TIP If you drag-copy a box containing linked text, the text in that box will duplicate, along with any hidden overflow text from that point to the end of the story.

TIP Individual items cannot be copied between documents in Thumbnails view, but entire pages can (see page 73).

TIP If you think you're going to copy an item or a group more than once, instead of drag-copying it, put it in a library and then retrieve it from the library whenever you need it. This will save you time in the long run.

Use this method to copy and paste an item along with its contents instead of drag-copy (previous page) if you don't want to bother tiling or moving document windows.

To copy an item between pages or documents:

1. Choose the Item tool.
2. Select the item or group that you want to copy.
3. Choose Edit menu > Copy (Ctrl-C) or right-click and choose Copy.
4. Click in the destination page or destination document.
5. Make sure the Item tool is still selected, then choose Edit menu > Paste (Ctrl-V) or right-click and choose Paste. ***Beware:*** If you copy with the Item tool and paste with the Content tool, you'll create an anchored box!

To cut or copy contents (picture or text) between pages or documents:

1. Choose the Content tool.
2. Click on the picture or highlight the text that you want to copy or cut.
3. Choose Edit menu > Copy (Ctrl-C) or Cut (Ctrl-X) (or right-click and choose Copy or Cut).
4. Click on the destination page or in the destination document window.
5. Make sure the Content tool is still selected, then click in the picture box, text box, or text path into which you want to paste.
6. Choose Edit menu > Paste (Ctrl-V) or right-click and choose Paste.

TIP If you copy-and-paste or drag-copy text or a text box between documents, any style sheet that is applied to that item will also copy, providing the appending style sheet name doesn't match an existing style sheet name in the destination document; if there is an exact match, the style sheet won't append.

What smart space is

Cloudy With a
Chance of Meatballs.

*Double-click **inside** a word (or double-click, then drag), and only that word or text string are selected, not any adjacent spaces or punctuation.*

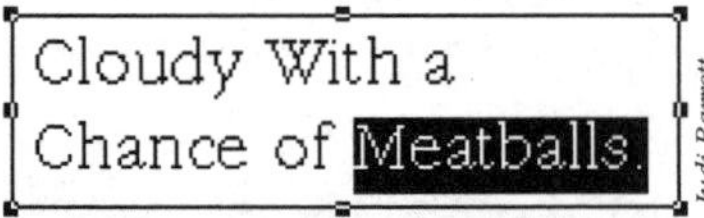

*Double-click **between** a word and punctuation, and both are selected. Paste the text, and extra spaces are added where needed.*

What smart space isn't

It isn't perfect.

Cloudy With a
Chance of .

If you cut text, extra spaces are deleted automatically, but not if the gap occurs between a word and punctuation.

Cloudy (With) a
Chance of Meatballs.

Double-click between a word and closing punctuation (i.e. parentheses or quotation marks)—only the closing punctuation selects. In this case, you're better off selecting by dragging.

WHO'S AFRAID OF SPACE/ALIGN?

Space/Align is one of my favorite QuarkXPress features, but it seems to confuse many people. This might help: When you choose between the Vertical and Horizontal options, think of the direction in which the items will move. If you want to align objects along their topmost edges, for example, check the Vertical box, click Space, leave the Space value at 0, and choose Between: Top Edges. To align objects along their left edges, on the other hand, check the Horizontal box and choose Between: Left Edges. Try it.

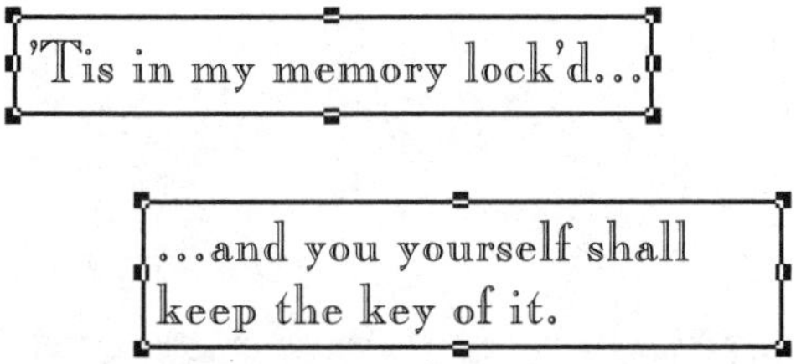

'Tis in my memory lock'd...

...and you yourself shall keep the key of it.

1 *Select two or more items.*

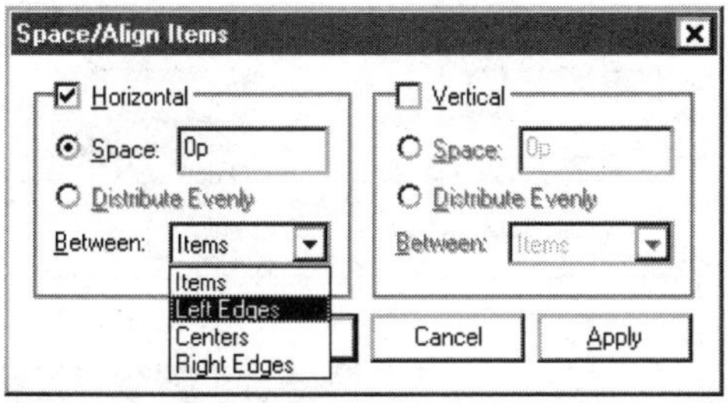

Space/Align Items

Horizontal — Space: 0p — Distribute Evenly — Between: Items (Items, Left Edges, Centers, Right Edges)

Vertical — Space: 0p — Distribute Evenly — Between: Items

Cancel — Apply

2 *Choose options in the* ***Space/Align Items*** *dialog box.*

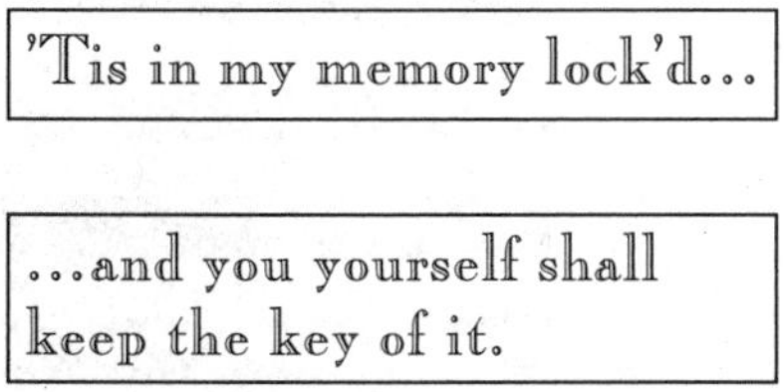

'Tis in my memory lock'd...

...and you yourself shall keep the key of it.

3 *These two text boxes are now aligned along their left edges.*

Note: The Space/Align feature aligns items according to the position of the leftmost or topmost of the currently selected items, depending on which option you choose from the Between drop-down menu. The results may be contrary to what you'd expect if you choose Between: Bottom Edges for the Vertical option. Items will align to the bottom of the topmost item—not to the bottom of the bottommost item.

To align items:

1. Choose the Item or Content tool.
2. Shift-click on each of the items that are to be aligned **1**.
   or
   Position the cursor outside the items to be aligned, then press and drag a marquee around them. The Space/Align command *will* move a locked item.
3. Choose Item menu > Space/Align (Ctrl-,).
4. Check the Horizontal or Vertical box **2**.
5. Click the Space button.
6. In the Space field, enter a positive or negative number between 0" and 10" in any measurement system in an increment as small as .001 to move the items to the left or the right if Horizontal is checked or upward or downward if Vertical is checked. Think of the Space field as an offset field.
   or
   Enter 0 to align the items along their edges or centers.
7. Choose from the Between drop-down menu.
8. Click Apply to preview.
9. Click OK or press Enter **3**.

TIP If you align a picture and an accompanying caption, remember to account for any Text Inset value above zero, which would push the text slightly inward from the left edge of its box.

If items are Space/Aligned horizontally using the Distribute Evenly option, the leftmost and rightmost of the selected items will remain stationary and the remaining selected items will be evenly dispersed between them. If you choose the Vertical and Distribute Evenly options, on the other hand, the topmost and bottommost items will remain stationary.

To distribute items:

1. Multiple-select three or more items or groups **1** (if you don't know how to do this, follow steps 1 and 2 on the previous page).
2. Choose Item menu > Space/Align (Ctrl-,).
3. Check the Horizontal or Vertical box **2**.
4. Click Distribute Evenly.
5. Choose an option from the Between drop-down menu.
6. Click Apply to preview.
7. Click OK or press Enter **3**.

I celebrate myself,

And what I assume

you shall assume,

For every atom

belonging to me

as good belongs to you.

Walt Whitman

1 *Select three or more items.*

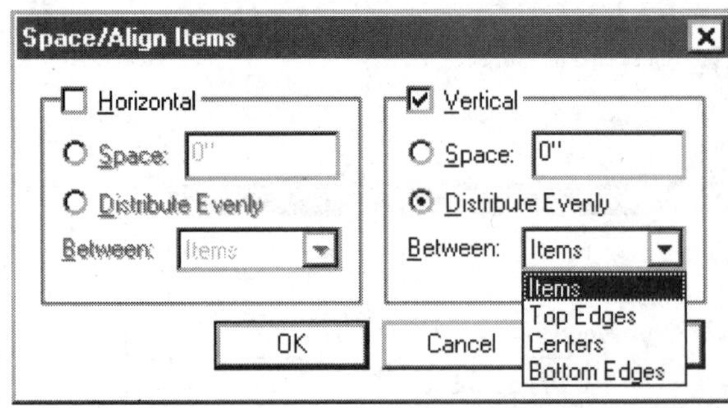

2 *The **Space/Align Items** dialog box.*

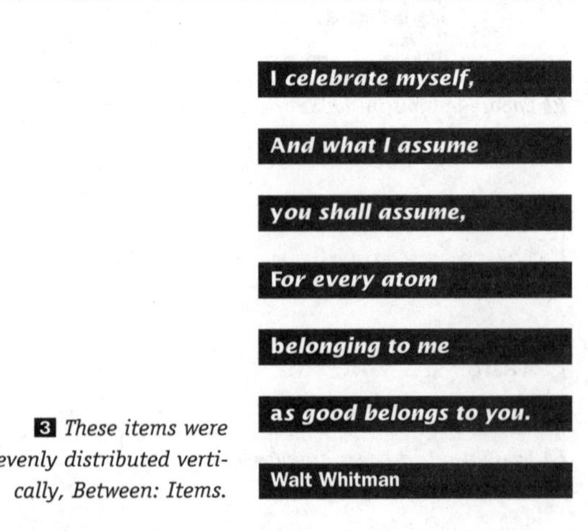

3 *These items were evenly distributed vertically, Between: Items.*

1 *The first click selects the text box, which is in front.*

2 *A second click selects the black cat. A third click would select the gray cat in the back.*

4 *The light gray cat is the backmost object.*

5 *The backmost object is **moved** in its layer.*

The most recently created item is automatically placed in front of all the other items in a document.

To select an item that is behind another item:

1. Choose the Item or the Content tool—whichever tool you're planning to use to edit the item you want to select.
2. Ctrl-Alt-Shift-click on an item **1**. Repeat to select the next item behind in succession, and so on **2**. After the backmost item is selected, the next click will reselect the topmost item.

TIP For more extensive layer-handling controls, use the Layer It! XTension by Vision's Edge, Inc. **3**.

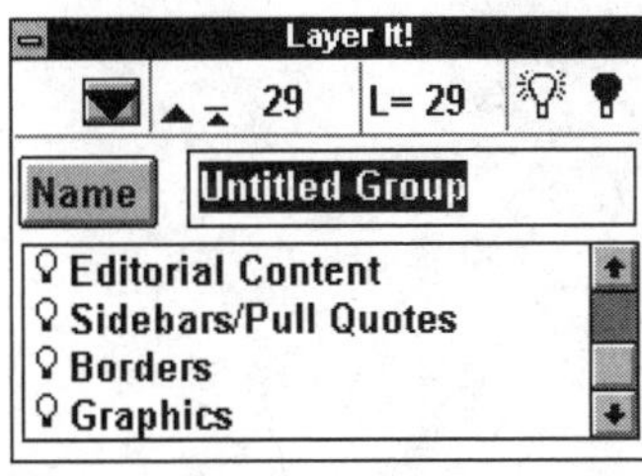

3 *The **Layer It!** palette.*

To move an item that's behind other items:

1. Choose the Item tool.
2. Keep clicking with Ctrl, Alt, and Shift held down. When you reach the item you want to move, don't release the mouse, just press and drag **4**–**5**. This little maneuver takes a bit of practice.

TIP Turn on Live Refresh in Edit menu > Preferences > Application > Interactive and pause before dragging to see the item as it truly looks in its layer as you drag it.

You can use the Send to Back, Bring to Front, Send Backward, or Bring Forward command to change the stacking position of any item.

To send an item to the back or bring an item to the front:

1. Choose the Item or Content tool.
2. Select an item **1**.
3. Choose Item menu > Send to Back (Shift-F5) or Bring to Front (F5) **2**.

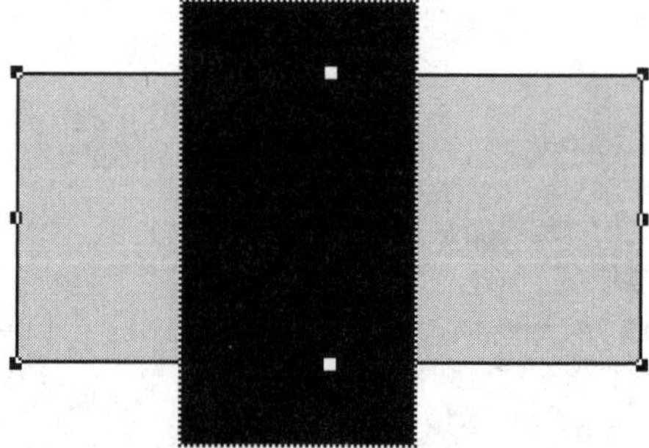

1 *A gray box (in back of a black box) is selected, as indicated by the eight handles.*

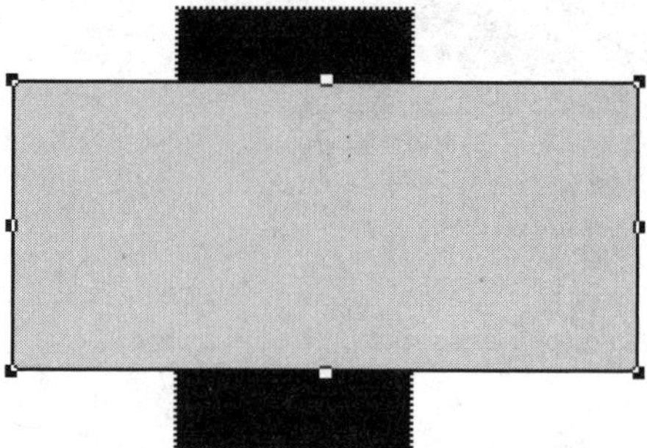

2 *The gray box is now in front of the black box.*

The Send Backward and Bring Forward commands move an item backward or forward one layer at a time (as opposed to moving it all the way to the front or all the way to the rear).

To send an item backward or bring an item forward:

1. Choose the Item or Content tool.
2. Select an item.
3. Hold down Ctrl and choose Send Backward (Ctrl-Shift-F5) or Bring Forward (Ctrl-F5) from the Item menu. Repeat this command, if necessary, until the item reaches the desired layer.

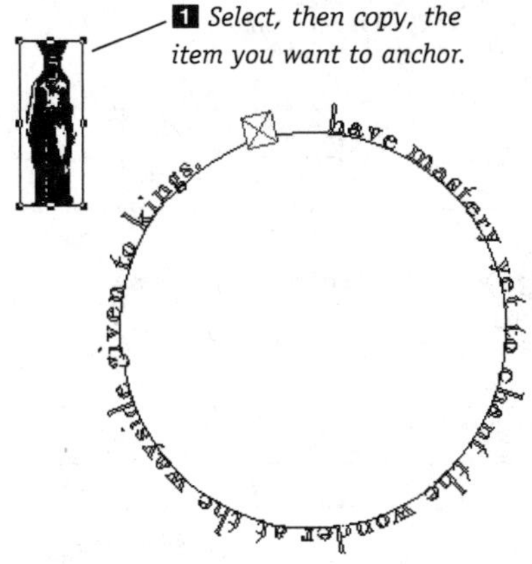

1 *Select, then copy, the item you want to anchor.*

You can paste a line, picture box, or text box of any shape into a text box or onto a text path as an inline graphic. It thereafter will function sort of like a character, in that it will remain anchored to the text if the text reflows, but unlike a normal character, its contents can be edited. Alas, you can't anchor a group or a text path.

Note: Be sure to choose the right tools for these instructions!

To anchor an item into text:

1. Choose the Item tool.
2. Select the item that you want to anchor 1.
3. Choose Edit menu > Copy (Ctrl-C) or Cut (Ctrl-X) or right-click and choose Copy or Cut.
4. Choose the Content tool.
5. Click in a text box or on a text path to create an insertion point 2.
6. Choose Edit menu > Paste (Ctrl-V) or right-click and choose Paste 3. You can do almost anything to an anchored item: Reshape it, recolor it, resize it, add a frame to it, change its content from picture to text, or vice versa, convert it into a Bézier shape, or make it contentless. The remaining pages in this chapter are devoted to adjusting anchored items.

2 *Choose the Content tool, then click in the text to create an insertion point.*

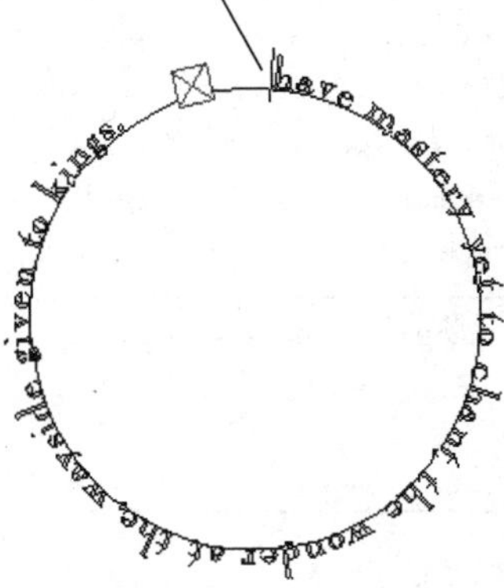

3 *Choose Edit menu > Paste.*

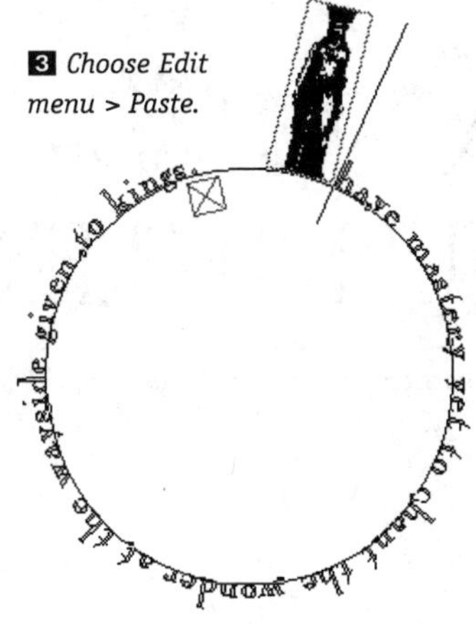

To align an anchored item:

1. Choose the Item or Content tool.
2. Click on an anchored item.
3. Click the Align with Text: Ascent icon on the Measurements palette to align the top of the anchored item with the ascent of the adjacent character to its right **1**–**2**.

   or

   Click the Align with Text: Baseline icon to align the bottom of the anchored item with the baseline of the line of text in which it is anchored **3**. (To vertically Offset a baseline-aligned anchored item, see the next page.)

TIP You can change the Runaround for an item after it's anchored. Click on it, then choose Item menu > Runaround (Ctrl-T).

TIP To move an anchored item to a new location, highlight it, cut it, and paste it using the Content tool.

*The **Align with Text: Ascent** icon.*

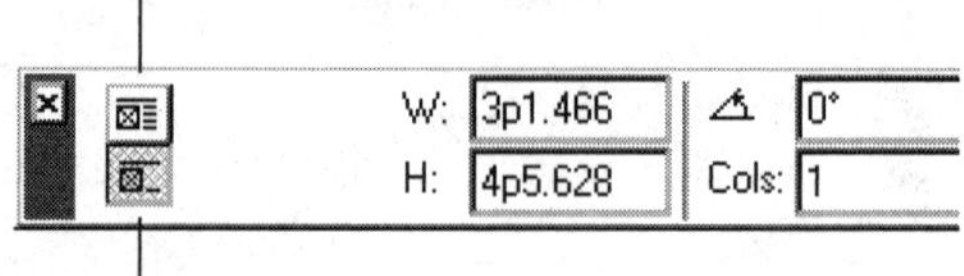

1 *The **Align with Text: Baseline** icon on the Measurements palette.*

have mastery yet to chant the wonder at the wayside given to kings. Still by God's grace there surges within me singing magic grown to my life and power, how the wild bird portent hurled forth the Achaeans' twin-stemmed power single hearted, lords of the youth of Hellas, with spear and hand of strength to the land of Teucrus. *Aeschylus*

2 *An anchored picture box, **Ascent** aligned.*

3 *An anchored picture box, **Baseline** aligned.*

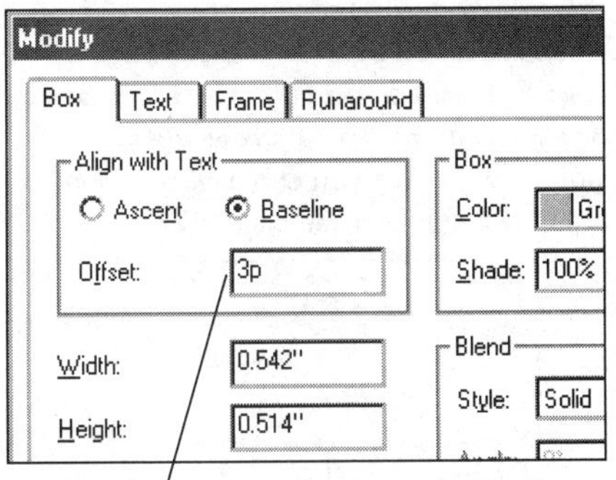

■1 *Enter a number in this field to* ***Offset*** *a baseline aligned-anchored item.*

The Offset option is only available for an anchored item that's baseline aligned—not an item that's ascent aligned.

To offset a baseline aligned anchored item:

1. Choose the Item or Content tool.
2. Click on the anchored item.
3. Choose Item menu > Modify (Ctrl-M) or right-click and choose Modify, then click the Box folder tab.
4. Enter a positive value in the Offset field to shift the anchored item upward or a negative value to shift the anchored item downward ■1.
5. Click OK or press Enter.

have mastery yet to chant the wonder at the wayside given to kings. Still by God's grace there surges within me singing magic grown to my life and power, how the wild bird portent hurled forth the Achaeans' twin-stemmed power single hearted, lords of the youth of Hellas, with spear and hand of strength to the land of Teucrus. *Aeschylus*

■2 *Resizing an anchored picture box.*

have mastery yet to chant the wonder at the wayside given to kings. Still by God's grace there surges within me singing magic grown to my life and power, how the wild bird portent hurled forth the Achaeans' twin-stemmed power single hearted, lords of the youth of Hellas, with spear and hand of strength to the land of Teucrus. *Aeschylus*

■3 *The anchored box enlarged.*

To resize an anchored item:

1. Choose the Item or Content tool. If the anchored item is a Bézier, make sure Item menu > Edit > Shape is turned off (F10).
2. Click on the anchored item.
3. Ctrl-Alt-Shift drag a handle (or drag an endpoint, if it's a line) ■2–■3.

TIP To reshape an anchored Bézier item, turn on Item menu > Edit > Shape (F10), then edit the shape as usual.

To delete an anchored item:

1. Choose the Content tool.
2. Click just to the right of the anchored item. The blinking cursor will be as tall as the anchored item.
3. Press Backspace.

TIP Duplicate an anchored item (Ctrl-D) to create an un-anchored copy of it.

DROP ANCHOR

To anchor highlighted text at its current location and convert it into a picture box at the same time, hold down Alt as you choose Style menu > Text to Box **1**–**3** (also see page 192).

1 *Standard text characters are highlighted.*

2 *After choosing Style menu > Text to Box with Alt held down, the text is simultaneously converted into a picture box and anchored at its current location.*

3 *The newly anchored picture box is filled with a picture.*

diddle diddle,

The cat  *and the fiddle,*

The cow  *jumped over*

the moon, 

The little dog  *laugh'd*

To see such sport,

And the dish  *ran away with the spoon.* 

Pictures 9

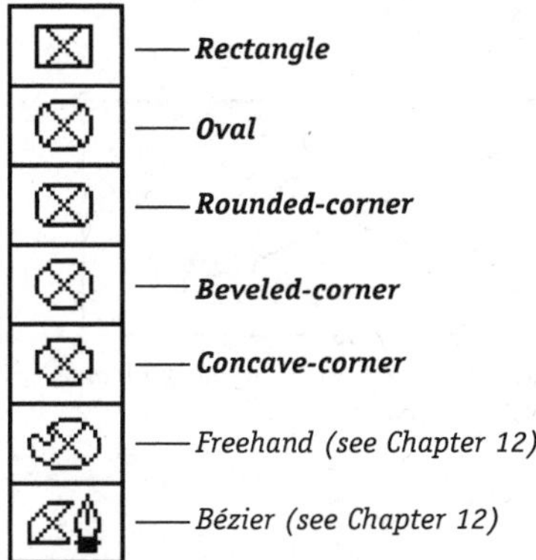

1 *The **picture box** tools.*

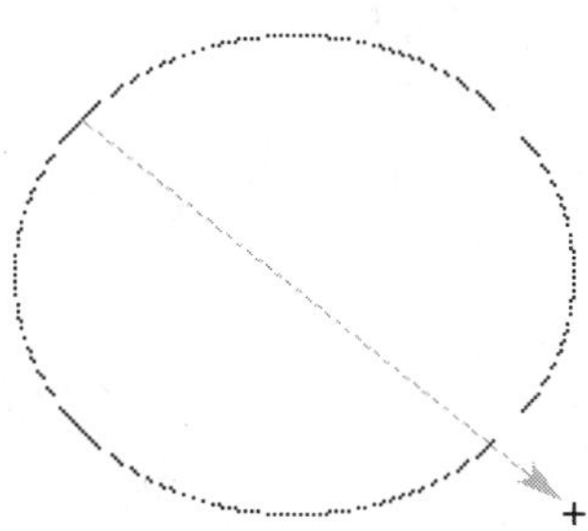

2 *Press and drag to create a picture box.*

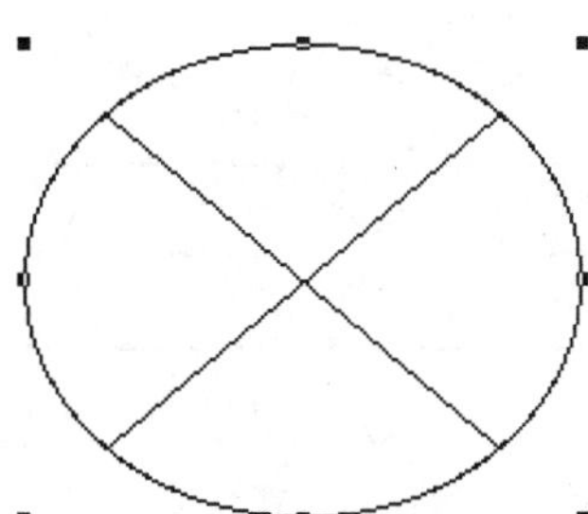

3 *An empty picture box has an "x" through its center.*

In QuarkXPress, a picture can be imported into a variety of different-shaped picture boxes. First you create a box using one of the picture box tools (Bézier or non-Bézier), then you import a picture into it. File formats that can be imported include .PCX, .GIF, Scitex CT (.CT, .SCT), JPEG (.JPG), TIFF (.TIF), PAINT, PICT (.PCT), EPS, Windows Metafile (.WMF), and Bitmap (.BMP). If the PhotoCD Import XTension is enabled (use the XTensions Manager), you can also import a Kodak PhotoCD (.PCD) picture from a PhotoCD. Béziers are covered in Chapter 12. Most of the commands that are discussed in this chapter can be applied to a Bézier picture box, in addition to a standard picture box.

To create a picture box:

1. Choose any picture box tool **1** except the Bézier or Freehand picture box tool. The cursor will temporarily turn into a crosshair icon.
2. Press and drag in any direction **2**–**3**.

TIP Shift-drag a handle to turn a rectangular picture box into a square or an oval picture box into a circle. This also works with a text box.

TIP To apply a frame to a picture box, use Item menu > Frame (Ctrl-B).

TIP Need more than one? Use Duplicate (Ctrl-D) or Item menu > Step and Repeat to create multiples of any item.

To resize a picture box manually:

1. Choose the Item or Content tool.
2. Click on a picture box. For a Bézier picture box, turn off Item menu > Edit > Shape (F10).
3. Press and drag any handle 1–2. Hold down Alt and Shift while dragging to preserve the original proportions of the box.

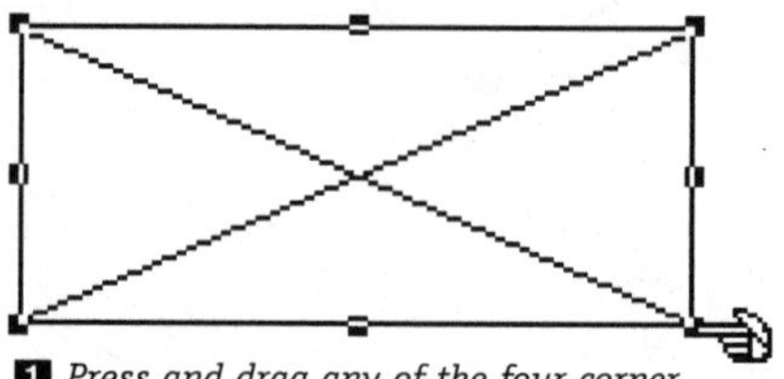

1 *Press and drag any of the four corner handles of a box.*

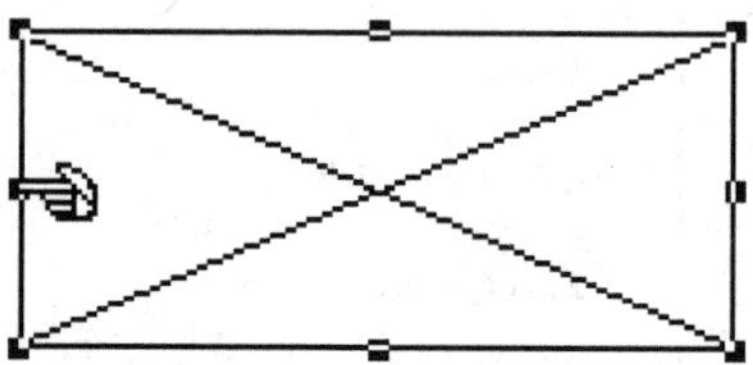

2 *Press and drag any of the four midpoint handles of a box.*

To resize a picture box using the Measurements palette:

1. Choose the Item or Content tool.
2. Click on a picture box.
3. Double-click the W field on the Measurements palette, enter a number in an increment as small as .001 to modify the width of the box 3, then press Enter.
   and/or
   Double-click the H field on the Measurements palette, enter a number to modify the height of the box, then press Enter.

TIP To enlarge or reduce the dimensions of a box by a specified amount, insert the cursor after the current value in the W or H field, enter a plus (+) or minus (-) sign, then enter the amount you want to add or subtract in any measurement system used in QuarkXPress. You can also use / (backslash) to divide the current value or * (asterisk) to multiply it.

*The **Width** field with two inches being added to the existing four pica width of a box.*

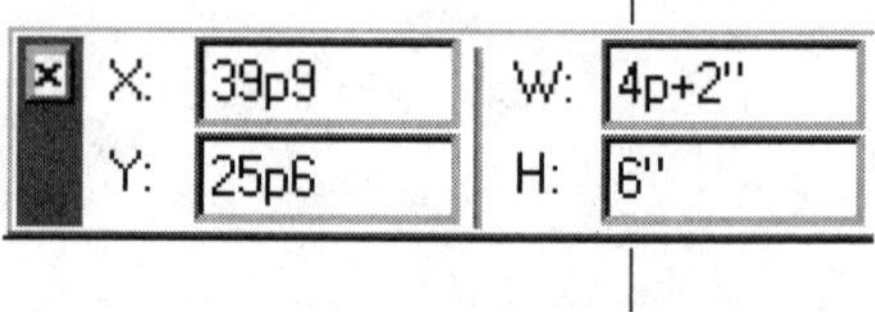

*The **Height** of a box.*

3 *You can enter a value in the Width and Height field (or in any other field) in any measurement system used in QuarkXPress.*

To delete a picture box:

1. Choose the Item or Content tool.
2. Click on a picture box.
3. Choose Item menu > Delete (Ctrl-K) or right-click and choose Delete.

TIP A picture box that is selected with the Item tool can also be deleted by pressing Delete or Backspace on the keyboard or by choosing Edit menu > Delete or by right-clicking on the box and choosing Delete.

1 *To move a box, press and drag inside it with the Item tool. Pause before dragging to display the picture as it's moved (the four-headed arrow cursor will change into a cluster of arrows if Live Refresh is chosen in Edit menu > Preferences > Application > Interactive folder tab.).*

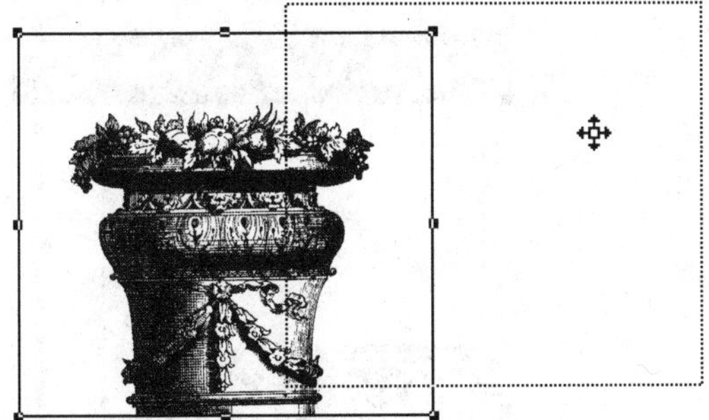

2 *Or drag without pausing to display only the outline of the box as it's moved.*

To move a picture box manually:

1. Choose the Item tool or hold down Ctrl if the Content tool is currently chosen.
2. Press on the inside of a picture box, then drag in any direction. Pause before dragging to display the picture as it is moved **1**. Or drag without pausing to display only the outline of the box as it's moved **2**.

TIP You can drag a picture box or any other item from one page to another. Knock into the edge of the document window to force scrolling, if necessary, to help you get to the desired page.

To reposition a picture box using the Measurements palette:

1. Choose the Item or Content tool.
2. Click on a picture box.
3. To change the horizontal position of the box relative to the ruler origin, which is normally located in the uppermost left corner of the document, double-click the X field on the Measurements palette, enter a new number, then press Enter **1**.

   and/or

   To change the vertical position of the box, double-click the Y field, enter a new number, then press Enter.

TIP To move a box a specified horizontal or vertical distance, insert the cursor to the right of the current number in the X or Y field, type a plus (+) or minus (-) sign, and then enter a number in any measurement system used in QuarkXPress **2**–**3**.

TIP To nudge a picture box or any other item one point at a time, select it with the Item tool, then press any arrow key on the keyboard. Alt-press an arrow key to move an item in .1-point increments.

*The **horizontal** location of a picture box.*

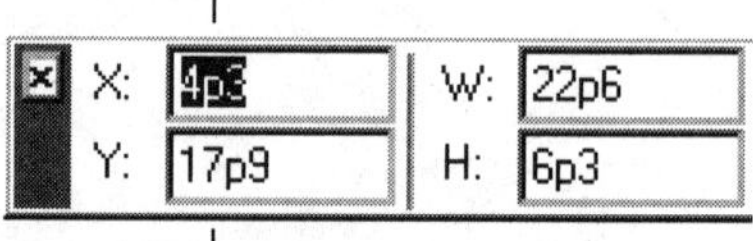

*The **vertical** location of a picture box.*

1 *The Measurements palette.*

2 *Add a positive or negative number to the right of the current value in the X or Y field, then press Enter.*

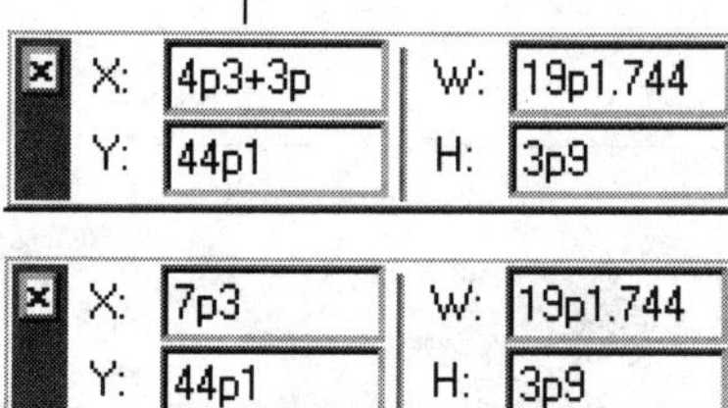

3 *The two numbers add together and the box is repositioned.*

A bleed is an item that runs off the edge of the page. The overhanging portion is trimmed by the print shop after the page is printed.

To create a bleed:

To create a bleed, position any item so that part of the item is on the page and part of the item extends onto the pasteboard **4**. An item that is completely on the pasteboard will not print.

TIP Change the width of the bleed area that you want to print in the Bleed field in the Print dialog box > Document folder tab. Read about the Quark's Bleed Redefine XTension on page 297.

4 *These items are positioned for a bleed.*

1 *Press and drag from a ruler to place a **guide** on a document or master page. (Tip: If you release the mouse over the Pasteboard as you drag a guide, the guide will straddle facing pages and extend onto the Pasteboard.)*

2 *An item will **snap** to a guide if it's dragged within the specified Snap Distance of the guide.*

To position items precisely, use ruler guides (this page) or use the X and Y fields on the Measurements palette.

To create a ruler guide:

1. If the rulers aren't visible, choose View menu > Show Rulers (Ctrl-R). If the margin guides aren't visible, choose View menu > Show Guides (F7).
2. Press and drag a guide from the horizontal or vertical ruler onto a document or master page. As you drag, the position of the guide will be indicated by a marker on the ruler and in the X or Y field on the Measurements palette **1**.

   If you press and drag an item to the guide, the item will snap to the guide if View menu > Snap to Guides is on **2**. Choose a Snap Distance in Edit menu > Preferences > Document > General folder tab (6 pixels is the default).

TIP Ruler guides will display in front of or behind page elements depending on whether Guides: Behind or In Front is chosen in Edit menu > Preferences > Document > General folder tab.

TIP To make a ruler guide visible only at or above a certain zoom percentage, choose that percentage, then hold down Shift as you create the guide.

To remove ruler guides:

To remove one ruler guide, choose the Item tool (or hold down Ctrl with the Content tool if the guide is over an item), then drag the guide back onto either ruler. You can use the same technique to move a guide.

or

To remove *all* horizontal or vertical guides, make sure no pasteboard is visible between the edge of the page and the corresponding ruler, then Alt-click the horizontal ruler to remove all horizontal guides or the vertical ruler to remove all vertical guides.

When a picture is imported into a picture box, a screen preview version of it is saved with the QuarkXPress file for display purposes. Also saved with the QuarkXPress file is information about changes made to the picture within the QuarkXPress file, such as cropping or scaling. The original picture file is not modified by such changes. Instead, a link is created to the original picture file, which the QuarkXPress file accesses when the document is printed. If the link to the original picture file is broken (the original picture is moved) or the picture itself is modified, you must update it, otherwise it won't output properly (see pages 151–152).

To import a picture:

1. Choose the Item or Content tool.
2. Click on a picture box (use the Content tool to select a box in a group).
3. Choose File menu > Get Picture (Ctrl-E).
4. *Optional:* Check the Preview box to display a thumbnail of the picture (the picture needs to have been saved with a preview). Skip the preview if you've got a slow machine.
5. Highlight a picture file name, then click Open, or just double-click the file name **1**–**4**.

__1__ Click on a picture box. If you click on a box that contains a picture, the existing picture will be replaced by the one you're importing.

*__2__ The picture is imported—but where **is** it? If it has a large white background, it may be off to the side.*

*__3__ You can use the **Ctrl-Alt-Shift-F** shortcut to fit the picture into its box or move the picture using the **Content** (hand) tool.*

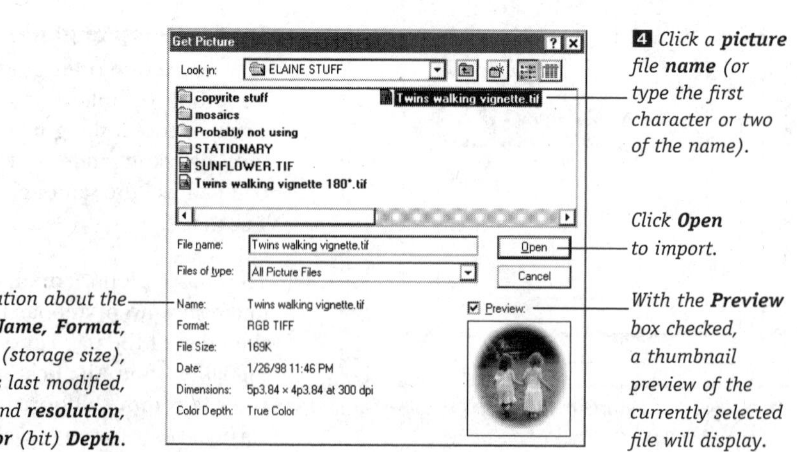

*__4__ Click a **picture** file **name** (or type the first character or two of the name).*

*Click **Open** to import.*

*With the **Preview** box checked, a thumbnail preview of the currently selected file will display.*

*Information about the picture: Its **Name, Format, File Size** (storage size), **Date** it was last modified, **Dimensions** and **resolution**, and **Color** (bit) **Depth**.*

FILE FORMATS YOU CAN IMPORT

You can import a TIFF (.TIF), EPS, JPEG (.JPG), DCS, PAINT, PICT (.PCT), OS/2 bitmap (.BMP), PCX, PhotoCD, Scitex CT, GIF, or Windows Bitmap picture into QuarkXPress. QuarkXPress can color separate an RGB or CMYK TIFF.

Note: To import a picture in the PCX, JPEG, PhotoCD, or LZW TIFF format, make sure that format's import filter is enabled. If the required filter is disabled, you will get an error message that reads "This file requires XTensions software to be read properly." Use the Utilities menu > XTensions Manager to enable/disable filters.

Pictures come in two basic flavors

A picture that is created in a bitmap program, like Photoshop, Painter, or Live Picture, or that is scanned, is actually composed of tiny pixels. You'll only see the individual pixels if you zoom way in on the image. The important thing to remember about a bitmap image is that enlarging it above 100% in QuarkXPress will diminish its resolution and output quality, whereas shrinking it will actually increase its resolution and output quality. If you're preparing an image in a bitmap program or scanning it for output from QuarkXPress, you should plan ahead and be sure to save it at the appropriate resolution, orientation, and size. You can make simple color changes to a bitmap picture in QuarkXPress, like applying a Pantone tint to it (this won't produce a Duotone).

A picture that is created in a drawing program, like Illustrator or FreeHand, is actually composed of mathematically defined objects. These types of pictures are called "vector," or "object-oriented." A vector picture can be moved, resized, recolored, and yes, enlarged, without affecting its output quality at all. It will be crisp at 20% and crisp at 120% (though enlarging it much beyond 100% may lengthen its print time). The higher the resolution of the output device, the sharper a vector picture will print. A vector picture can't be edited in QuarkXPress, however. It can be resized, rotated, or skewed, but not recolored.

TIP Rotate, crop, or scale your picture in its native application rather than in QuarkXPress—it will redraw and print more quickly.

Choosing the right resolution for a bitmap picture

For on-line display, you merely need to match the resolution of the most common monitor that your viewers will use, which in most cases is 72 ppi. For print output, choose one-and-a-half to two times the lpi (lines per inch) your commercial printer plans to use. For example, your printer says they're going to use a 133 line screen. You'll be saving a color picture at twice the line screen. 133 times two equals 266, so you should save the picture in its original application at 266 ppi. For a grayscale picture, one-and-a-half times the line screen is sufficient (200 ppi, in our example).

Every rule has its exceptions, however. A bitmap image that contains sharp linear elements will require a higher resolution (600 ppi or higher). For a very painterly picture that contains amorphous shapes, on the other hand, a resolution below twice the output line screen may suffice.

A vector-based picture from a drawing application is resolution independent, which means it will print at the resolution of the output device. Just make sure it's saved in a file format that XPress can read.

TIP A picture's file size, dimensions, color depth, and other information are listed in the Get Picture dialog box. For information about an already imported picture, click on it, choose Utilities menu > Usage > Pictures folder tab, and check the More Information box.

Enlarge or shrink?

Scaling a bitmap picture in XPress affects its output resolution. Shrink a bitmap picture in XPress, its output resolution will increase; enlarge a bitmap picture, its output resolution will decrease. Here's an example: Take a 150 ppi image and shrink it by half. It's ppi will increase to 300. Why should you bother to pay attention to this? Because enlarging a bitmapped picture above 100% in QuarkXPress will diminish its print quality. A vector-based image (i.e. an Illustrator EPS) won't be degraded in quality if it's enlarged in XPress, but it may take longer to print. And if you shrink a picture down significantly, its file size will be much larger than required and it will

HERE, SPOT

If you import an EPS picture into a QuarkXPress document, spot colors that were assigned to the picture will automatically append to the QuarkXPress document's Colors palette. (In previous versions, if you imported an EPS picture containing a spot color, in order to color separate the picture, you had to create a spot color with the same name in the QuarkXPress document.)

TIP To *prevent* applied colors from importing with an EPS picture, hold down Ctrl as you click Open in the Get Picture dialog box.

Picture Resolution; Scale

LOOKS LIKE GREEK TO YOU

To speed up screen redraw, turn on Greek Pictures in Edit menu > Preferences > Document > General folder tab (Ctrl-Y). Greeked pictures look solid gray on screen, but they print normally. To display a greeked picture, just click on it.

also take longer to print. So the moral of the story is…plan ahead.

Picture preview options

Every EPS picture has a TIFF preview built into it (unless it's specifically saved without one) so you can see it on screen or print it on a non-PostScript printer. The higher a picture preview's bit depth, the longer it may take to render on screen and the larger will be the file storage size of the document into which it's imported. Choose display options for imported TIFF pictures in Edit menu > Preferences > Application > Display folder tab (see page 277). In some applications (i.e. Illustrator) you can choose a bit depth for the preview. When you save an image for export to QuarkXPress, save it with a preview, if that option is available.

Saving a picture for QuarkXPress

Illustrator	Illustrator EPS with a preview
FreeHand	EPS with a preview
Painter	Painter TIFF
Live Picture	TIFF (RGB or CMYK) or EPS
Photoshop	TIFF (RGB or CMYK), DCS, or EPS (ask your printer)
Scanner	TIFF
PhotoCD	Open in QuarkXPress using the PhotoCD XTension

For on-screen display (not color separation), leave the image in RGB color mode. To color separate a bitmap picture from QuarkXPress, convert it to CMYK Color mode in Photoshop, then save it in the EPS, DCS, or TIFF file format. A DCS picture is pre-separated, which means it will output more quickly. Ask your print shop which format to choose.

A PhotoCD file contains multiple resolution versions of the image. For screen display, QuarkXPress uses the 3 x 5-inch version; for printing, QuarkXPress uses the highest resolution version that's appropriate for the output device.

To resize a picture:

1. Choose the Item or Content tool.
2. Click on a picture.
3. Hold down Ctrl, Alt, Shift and press the > key to enlarge the picture 5% at a time or the < key to shrink the picture.
   or
   On the Measurements palette, enter a new number in the X% and/or Y% picture size field, then press Enter **1**–**5**.

TIP Press Tab to move from field to field on the Measurements palette (press Shift-Tab to go backwards).

TIP If you're having trouble getting a picture to become selected, make sure you're clicking on a positive area in the image—not on a blank or white area.

TIP You can copy values from one field on the Measurements palette and paste them into another, such as from the X% field into the Y% field, or vice versa.

***Horizontal scale** of a picture.*

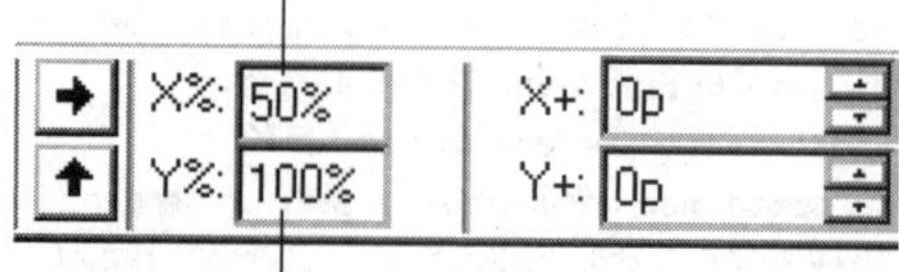

***Vertical scale** of a picture.*

1 *When the X and Y scale percentages differ from each other, it means the picture's proportions have been altered relative to the original.*

X%: 75%
Y%: 75%
X+: p5.438
Y+: p2.472

2 *When the X and Y scale percentages match, it means the picture's proportions are the same as those in the original.*

3 *A picture with an X coordinate of 55% and a Y coordinate of 55%.*

4 *A picture with an X coordinate of 40% and a Y coordinate of 60%.*

5 *A picture with an X coordinate of 60% and a Y coordinate of 40%.*

GET AN ASSEMBLY LINE GOING

If you're planning to import several pictures to which you will be applying the same scaling, offset, or other attributes, first apply those attributes to an *empty* picture box and then duplicate the box for each picture you import. Place a copy of the box in a library or on a master page so you'll be able to access it quickly.

SPEED TIP

To fit a picture into its box:

1. Choose the Item or Content tool.
2. Click on a picture.
3. Hold down Ctrl, Alt, Shift and press "F" 1–2. If you don't include the Alt key, the picture will fit into its box, but its proportions will change relative to the original picture 3.

1 *A picture before being resized.*

2 *After applying the **Ctrl-Alt-Shift-F** keystroke, the picture fits into the vertical dimension of the box and its proportions are maintained.*

3 *The original image (1), after applying the **Ctrl-Shift-F** keystroke. The image is stretched to fit the box.*

To resize a picture and its box simultaneously:

1. Choose the Item or Content tool.
2. For a Bézier picture box, turn off Item menu > Edit > Shape (Shift-F4).
3. Hold down Ctrl, Alt, Shift, pause briefly for the picture to redraw, then press and drag any handle 4.

TIP To quickly duplicate a picture and its box: Ctrl-D.

TIP Ctrl-drag to reshape a picture as you reshape its box.

4 *Hold down **Ctrl, Alt, Shift** and drag a handle to resize a picture and its box simultaneously.*

Resize a Picture

Note: If you're going to substantially crop a bitmapped picture, do it in the picture's original application. This will reduce the picture's file size and make it print faster.

To crop a picture by moving it within its box:

1. Choose the Content tool.
2. Press on a picture, pause briefly until the hand icon appears, then drag **1**.

TIP Click on a picture and press an arrow key to nudge a picture 1 point at a time. Alt-press an arrow key to nudge a picture .1-point at a time.

1 *A picture being **moved** within its box. Note the hand icon. Tip: You can also use a clipping path to prevent part of a picture from printing (see Chapter 10).*

To crop a picture by resizing its box:

1. Choose the Item or Content tool.
2. Press and drag any handle of a picture box **2**–**3**. For a Bézier box, turn off Item menu > Edit > Shape (F10).

To delete a picture (and keep the box):

1. Choose the Content tool.
2. Click on a picture.
3. Press Delete.

2 *Press and drag any handle to crop a picture.*

3 *After cropping.*

The ***picture and box angle.***

	X:	8p5	W:	16p3		0°
	Y:	7p8	H:	12p		0p

1 *The left side of the Measurements palette.*

Note: Whenever possible, rotate, crop, or scale a picture in its original application—it will redraw, process, and print more quickly.

To rotate a picture and its box using the Measurements palette:

1. Choose the Item or Content tool.
2. Click on a picture box.
3. In the picture and box angle field on the left side of the Measurements palette, enter a positive number between 360° and 360° to rotate the picture and box counterclockwise or a negative number to rotate them clockwise **1**, then press Enter.

TAKE YOUR PICK

With Delayed Item Dragging: Show Contents chosen in Edit menu > Preferences > Application > Interactive folder tab, if you move or rotate an item that's behind other items, its contents will be visible as you move it. If Live Refresh is chosen instead, you'll see the item as it actually looks in its layer as you move it. You won't see a lever as you rotate an object in Live Refresh mode, but it works just the same.

To rotate a picture and its box using the Rotation tool:

1. Choose the Rotation tool.
2. Click on a picture box.
3. Press to create an axis point, pause briefly for the picture to redraw (if desired), drag to reposition the cursor away from the axis point to create a lever **2**–**3**, then drag the lever clockwise or counterclockwise.

TIP Hold down Shift while dragging with the Rotation tool to rotate an item to a 0°, 45°, or 90° angle.

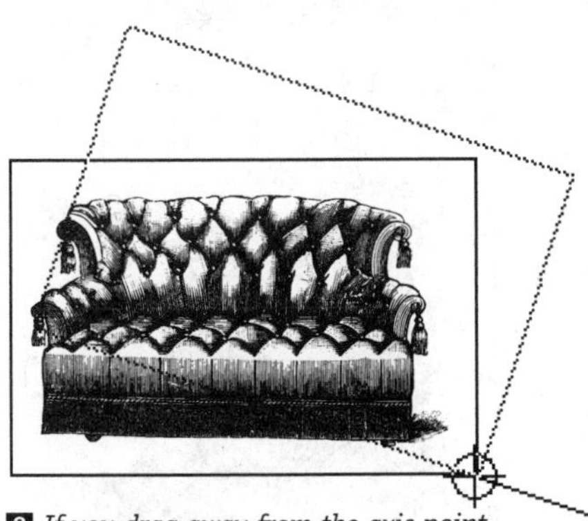

2 *If you drag away from the axis point before rotating, you will create a lever, and the rotation will be easier to control. If you don't pause before dragging, only the outline of the box will be displayed as it is being rotated.*

3 *A picture and its box rotated together.*

To rotate a picture (and not its box):

1. Choose the Item or Content tool.
2. Click on a picture.
3. In the picture angle field on the right side of the Measurements palette, enter a positive number to rotate the picture counterclockwise or a negative number to rotate it clockwise **1**.
4. Press Enter **2**–**5**.

TIP To rotate the picture box and *not* the picture, first rotate the box with the picture, then rotate the picture alone the negative amount. For example, if the picture with its box is rotated 20°, rotate the picture back –20°.

1 *The* ***picture angle****.*

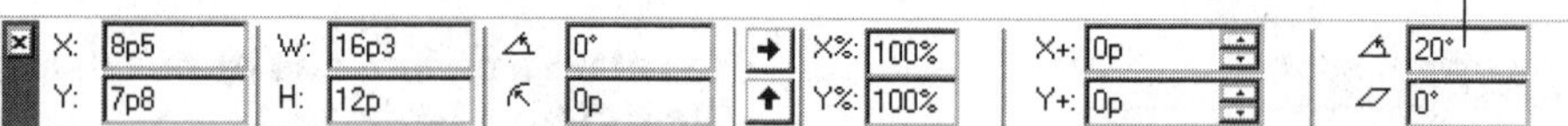

2 *0° rotation.*

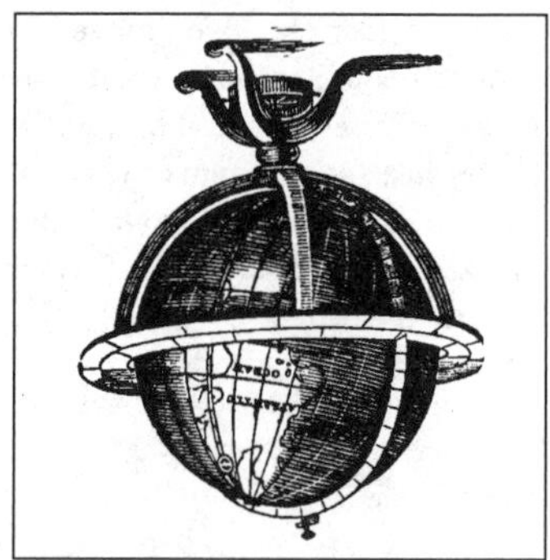

3 *180° rotation.*

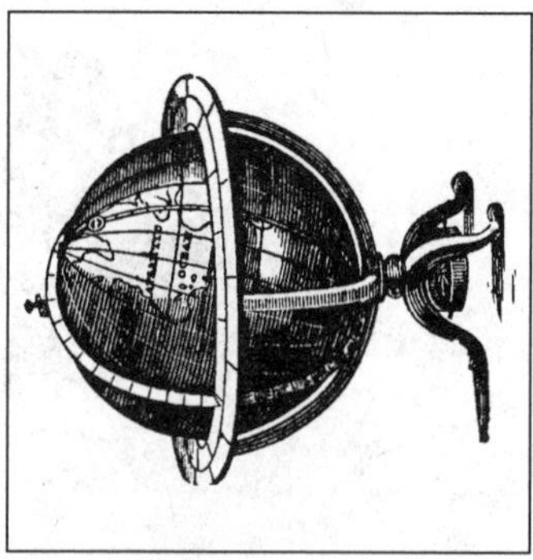

4 *90° rotation.*

5 *40° rotation.*

Modify

Box | Picture | Frame | Runaround | Clipping

Origin Across: 27p11
Origin Down: 14p2
Width: 10p6
Height: 13p3
Angle: 0°
Skew: 40°
Corner Radius: 0p
Suppress Printout

Box — Color: Wh — Shade: 100%
Blend — Style: Solid — Angle: 0° — Color: Wh — Shade: 100%

OK | Cancel

1 *To skew a text or picture box, choose Item menu > Modify, click the Box folder tab, then enter a number in the* ***Skew*** *field.*

To skew text or a picture and its box:

1. Choose the Item or Content tool.
2. Click on any shaped text or picture box. You can only skew one item at a time.
3. Choose Item menu > Modify (Ctrl-M) or right-click and choose Modify, and click the Box folder tab.
4. Enter a number between -75 and 75 in the Skew field **1**. Enter a positive number to skew to the right or a negative number to skew to the left.
5. Click OK or press Enter **2**–**4**. You can edit text or a picture after it's skewed.

TIP To skew a picture and not its box, choose the Content tool, then enter a number between -75 and 75 in the Skew field on the Measurements palette (lower right corner).

Sometimes I've believed as many as six impossible things before breakfast.

Lewis Carroll

2 *A rectangular text box skewed 40%.*

3 *A picture box.*

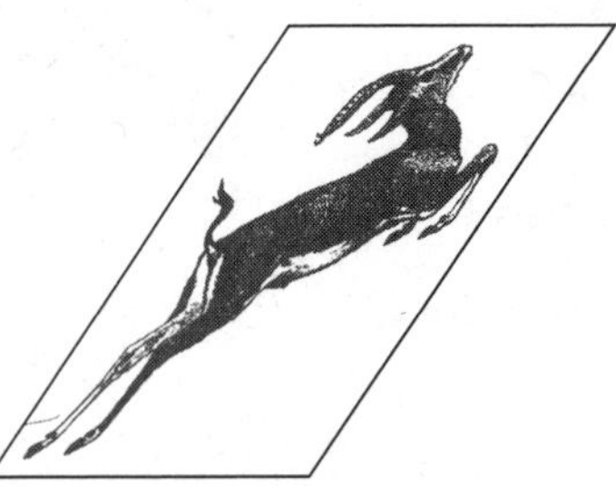

The same box skewed 35%.

4 *The Box Skew feature was used to produce the top and side portions of this cube.*

You can do more than convert a picture from one shape to another using the Shape submenu—you can also convert a standard picture box into a Bézier picture box or convert any kind of picture box into a line.

Note: If you convert a picture box that contains a picture into a line (any of the last three icons on the Shape submenu), the picture will be deleted. If you convert a text box into a line, it will become a text path.

To convert an item's shape:

1. Choose the Item or Content tool.
2. Click on one picture box (not multiple boxes).
3. Choose a shape from the Item menu > Shape submenu **1**–**5**.

TIP To make the corners of any of the first four shapes found under the Shape submenu more or less convex, choose Item menu > Modify (Ctrl-M) or right-click and choose Modify, click the Box folder tab, then enter a number in the Corner Radius field. 2" is the maximum.

Duplicate Ctrl+D
Step and Repeat... Ctrl+Alt+D
Delete Ctrl+K
Group Ctrl+G
Ungroup Ctrl+U
Constrain
Lock F6
Merge
Split
Send Backward Ctrl+Shift+F5
Send to Back Shift+F5
Bring Forward Ctrl+F5
Bring to Front F5
Space/Align... Ctrl+,
Shape
Content
Edit
Point/Segment Type

Rectangular box
Rounded-corner box
Beveled corner box
Concave corner box
Oval box
Bézier box
Line
Orthogonal line
Bézier line

1 *A picture box can be converted into any of the other shapes found under the Item menu >* ***Shape*** *submenu.*

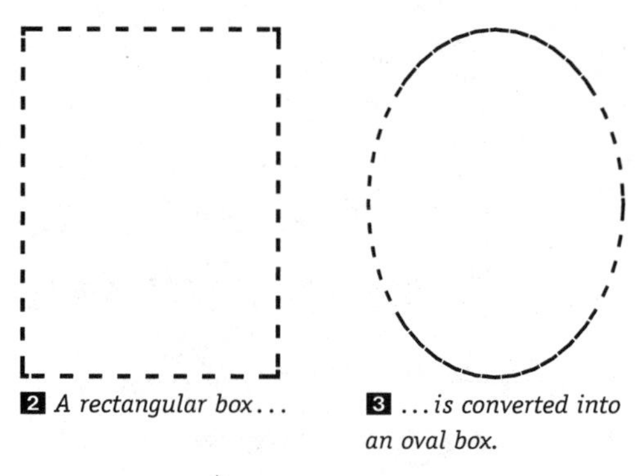

2 *A rectangular box...*

3 *...is converted into an oval box.*

Dinner one night consisted of lamb chops, becoming heavy at times, with occasional ketchup. Periods of peas and baked potatoes were followed by gradual clearing, with a wonderful Jell-O setting in the west.

—Judi Barrett

4 *A text box...*

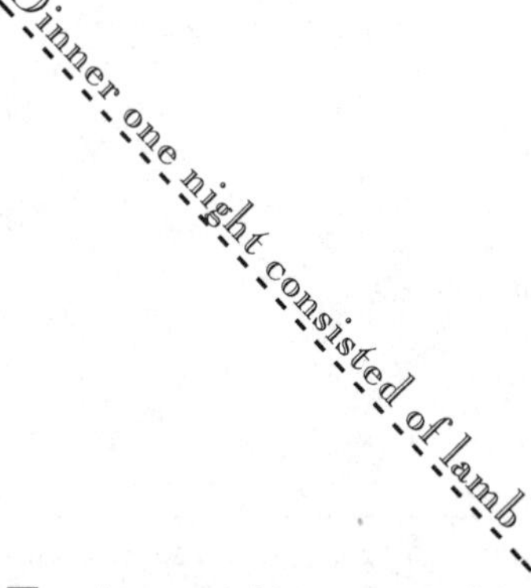
Dinner one night consisted of lamb

5 *...is converted into a text path by choosing the Line icon.*

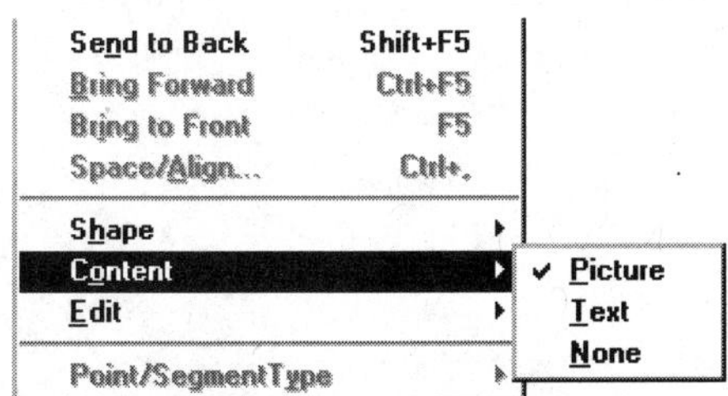

■1 *Choose **Picture, Text,** or **None** from the Item menu > **Content** submenu.*

■2 *A picture box.*

Suddenly
from somewhere far away
comes the sound of a fish jump-
ing, and the moon's reflection
ripples across the lake.
—*Tejima*

■3 *Is converted into a text box.*

■4 *A contentless box can contain a frame and a flat color or a blend—period.*

You can make a box or text path contentless, or change a box from a picture box to a text box, or vice versa, or change a line into a text path. Any text or picture the item originally contained will be removed; a frame will remain. A content conversion can't be undone.

The only thing you can do to a contentless box is change its background color or shade. It can contain a blend, but it cannot contain text or a picture. Contentless boxes function strictly as decorative elements.

To convert an item's contents:

1. Choose the Item or Content tool.
2. Click on a text box, picture box, line, or text path.
3. Choose Picture, Text, or None from the Item menu > Content submenu ■1–■4.
4. Click OK or press Enter if a warning prompt appears.

A few of the basic picture contrast adjustments that can be accomplished within QuarkXPress are outlined here. Use an application dedicated to image manipulation (i.e. Photoshop) for elaborate masking or color correction. Keep in mind that modifications made to a picture in XPress don't affect the original picture file, they only affect how it displays and prints. To colorize a picture, see page 235.

To apply a custom contrast setting to a picture:

1. Choose the Item or Content tool.
2. Click on a color bitmap picture or a color or grayscale TIFF, JPEG, PICT, Windows bitmap (BMP), PCX, PhotoCD, or Scitex CT picture.

   You can't adjust the contrast of an EPS, a 1-bit (black-and-white) picture, or a color TIFF imported with the 16- or 32- bit Color TIFFs setting in Edit menu > Preferences > Application > Display folder tab. (If you've imported the picture already using that setting, choose 8-bit Color TIFFs, and then reimport the picture.)
3. Choose Style menu > Contrast (Ctrl-Shift-C).
4. Alt-click the Apply button to turn on continuous Apply.
5. For a color picture, choose a color Model (HSB, RGB, CMY, or CMYK). Uncheck any individual box for a Color if you don't want it to be modified.
6. Make any of the following adjustments, or use any of the other tools on the left side of the dialog box to make adjustments (see 6, next page).

   To posterize the picture, click the second-to-last icon 1–2.
   or
   To adjust the contrast manually, click the hand icon, then drag the entire

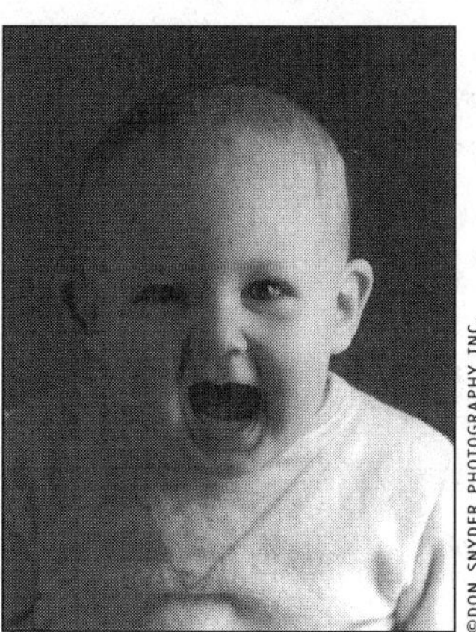

©DON SNYDER PHOTOGRAPHY INC.

1 *Normal Contrast.*

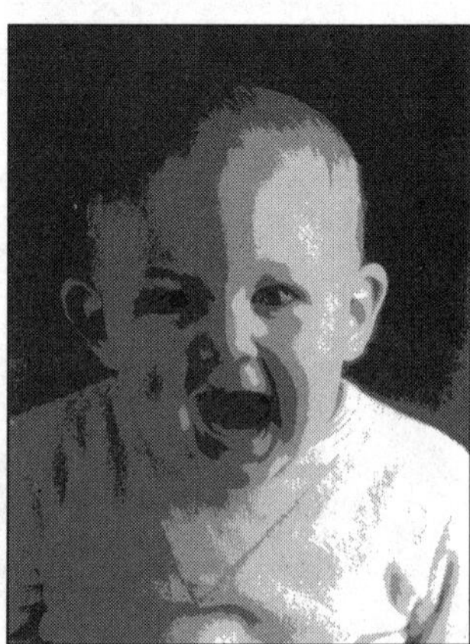

2 *Posterization reduces the number of grays in a picture to black, white, and four gray levels in between.*

Adjust Picture Contrast

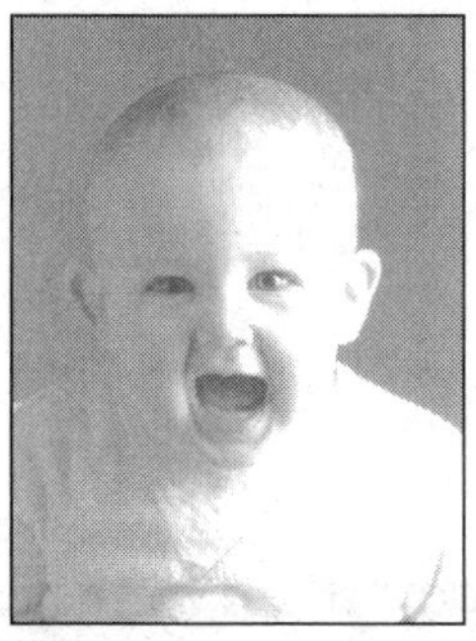

3 *A picture with the contrast curve shown in* **4**.

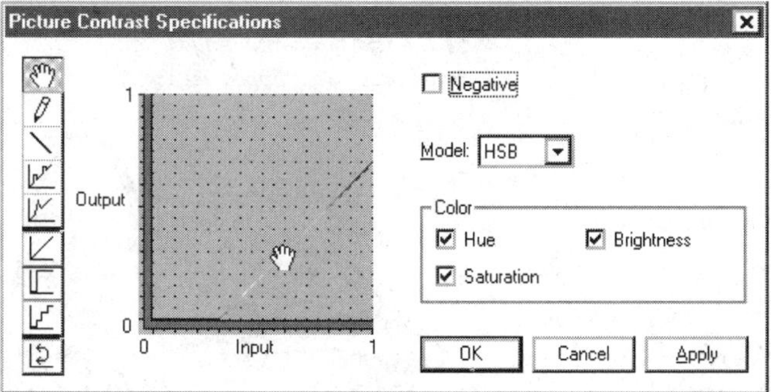

4 *The contrast curve moved with the* ***hand*** *tool.*

contrast curve toward the upper left or lower right corner **3**–**4**. To restore the picture's original contrast values, click the sixth (normal contrast) icon.
or
Choose the pencil tool, and draw a custom curve **5**–**6**.
or
Click the Negative box to create a negative of the picture.

7. Click OK or press Enter.

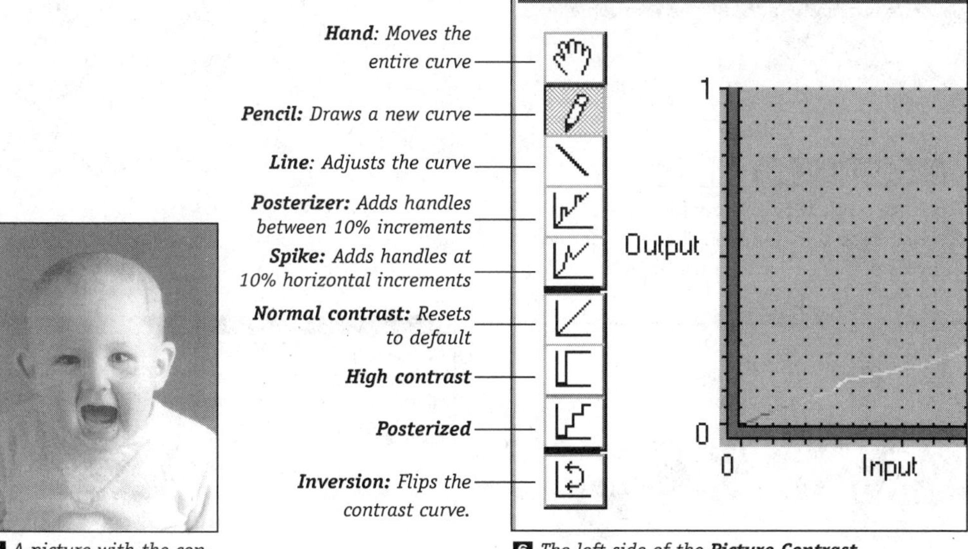

5 *A picture with the contrast curve shown in* **6**.

6 *The left side of the* ***Picture Contrast Specifications dialog box.***

Note: As with cropping and rotating, it's better to flip a picture in its original application than in XPress—it will print and redraw more quickly. The flip commands flip the contents of a box. The text or picture can be modified in its flipped position. (To flip a Bézier box, and not its contents, see page 198.)

To flip a picture or text:

1. Choose the Content tool.
2. Click on a picture box or text box.
3. Choose Style menu > Flip Horizontal or Flip Vertical.
   or
   Click the Flip Horizontal and/or Flip Vertical icon on the Measurements palette **1**–**4**.

It's a poor sort of memory
that only works backwards

Lewis Carroll

3 *The word "backwards" was typed into a separate text box, and then flipped horizontally.*

***Flip Horizontal** icon.*

1 ***Flip Vertical** icon.*

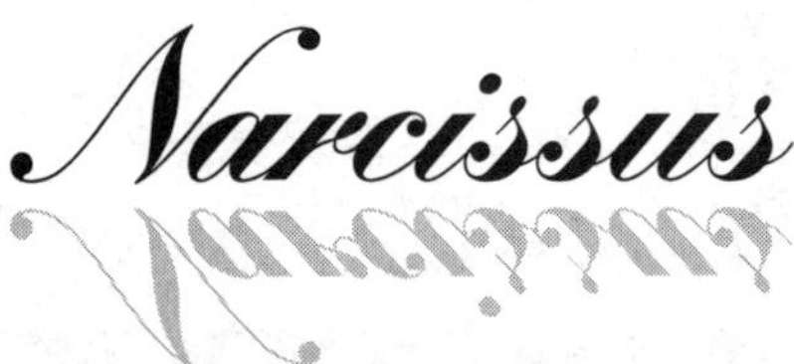

2 *The text box containing the gray "Narcissus" was flipped vertically.*

4 *A flipped picture.*

CAST A SHADOW

To create a soft drop shadow for any QuarkXPress item, use the I Shadow XTension from Vision's Edge, Inc., illustrated below and right.

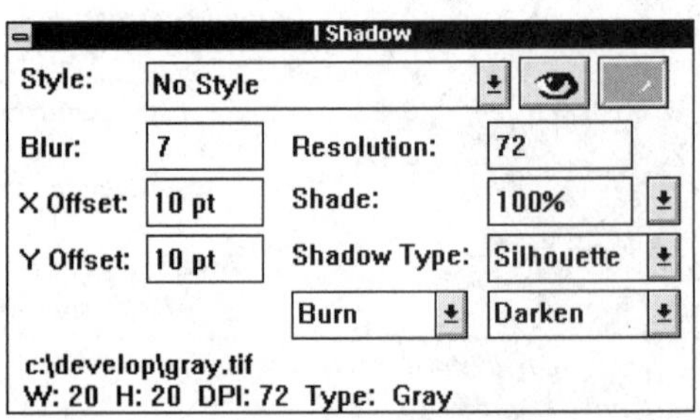

STATUS IS EVERYTHING

Modified	The picture was modified in another application (but not moved).
Missing	The picture was moved or renamed.
Wrong Type	The picture's file format was changed (or the picture was compressed using a utility; you can't update this type).
No XTension	The import filter for the picture's file format is disabled.

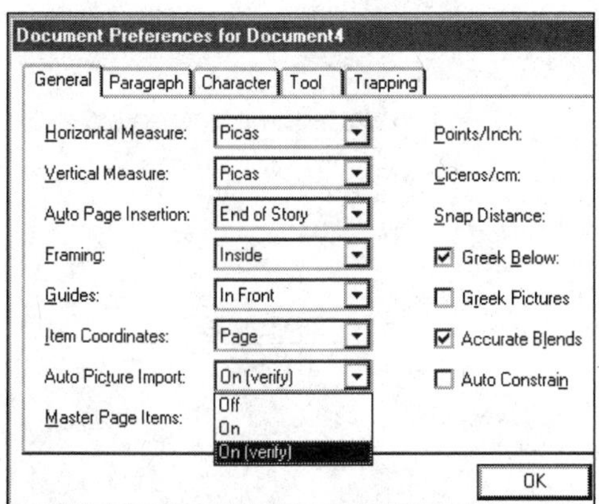

1 *Choose **Auto Picture Import: Off, On,** or **On (verify)** in Document Preferences > General folder tab.*

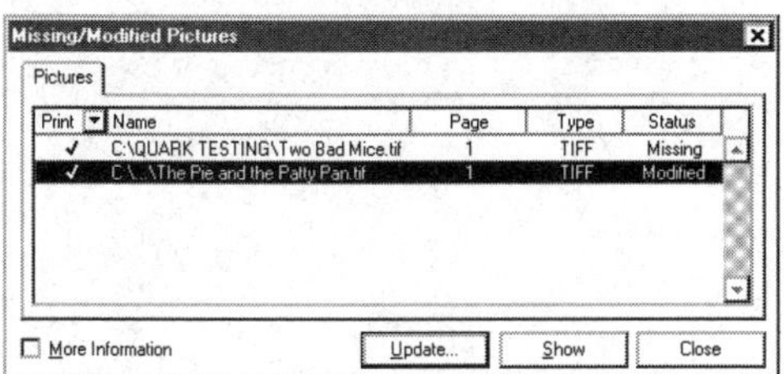

2 *Click on a picture file, then click **Update**.*

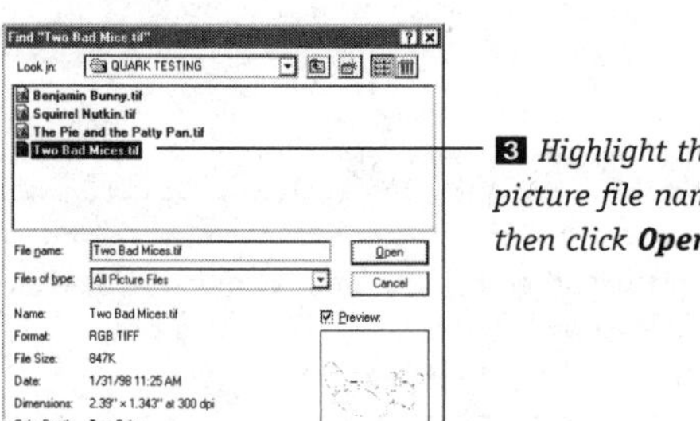

3 *Highlight the picture file name, then click **Open**.*

When a picture is imported into a QuarkXPress file, the original picture file's name and location information is stored in the QuarkXPress file. If the original picture file is then modified, renamed, or moved, its path to the QuarkXPress file must be updated for it to print properly.

To update the path to a picture upon opening a file:

There are three default settings for updating modified and missing picture files when you open a document, and they are chosen from the Auto Picture Import drop-down menu in Edit menu > Preferences > Document > General folder tab **1**.

If you open a document that was last saved with Auto Picture Import Off, the path to a missing or modified picture will not be updated; if you selected On, the path will be updated automatically; if you chose On (verify), a prompt will appear. If **On (verify)** is chosen, do as follows:

1. Click OK if the prompt appears.
2. Click on a picture name in the Missing/Modified Pictures dialog box **2**, and note its current Status (see the sidebar at left).
3. *Optional:* Click Show to see the picture selected in the document.
4. Click Update.
5. For a Modified or Wrong Type picture, click OK when the prompt appears.
   or
   For a Missing picture, locate and choose the picture in the Find "[ ]" dialog box, then click Open **3**.
6. Repeat for any other pictures, then click Close.

The path to a picture file can be updated at any time using Utilities menu > Usage > Pictures folder tab. If a picture is updated using Auto Picture Import or the Usage dialog box, the scale, rotation, color, and other attributes that were previously applied to the picture are retained.

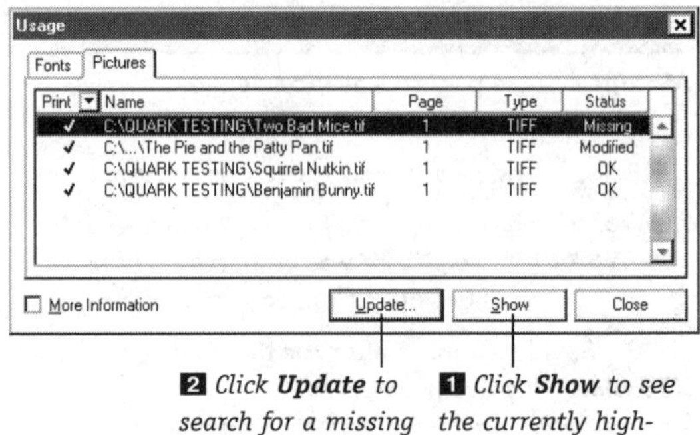

2 *Click **Update** to search for a missing picture file.*

1 *Click **Show** to see the currently highlighted picture selected in the document.*

To update the path to a picture using Picture Usage:

1. *Optional:* Choose the Content tool, then click on the picture that you want to update in the document window.
2. Choose Utilities menu > Usage.
3. Click the Pictures folder tab.
4. Click any file name whose Status is listed as Missing or Modified. If you clicked on a picture for step 1, its name will highlight automatically. Otherwise, you can click Show, if desired, to see the picture selected in the document window **1**.
5. Click Update **2**.
6. For a missing picture, choose the picture file name in the Find "[ ]" dialog box, **3** then click Open.

   Note: If you update a picture using the Usage > Pictures folder tab or by responding to an Auto Picture Import prompt and other missing pictures are located in the same folder, a prompt will appear. Click OK to update all the missing pictures in that folder at once. This won't work for a modified picture.

   For a modified picture, click OK.
7. Click Close.

TIP If you need to replace one picture with another using the Get Picture command and you want to keep the previously applied specifications, (scale, color, position, etc.), delete the current picture before importing the new one.

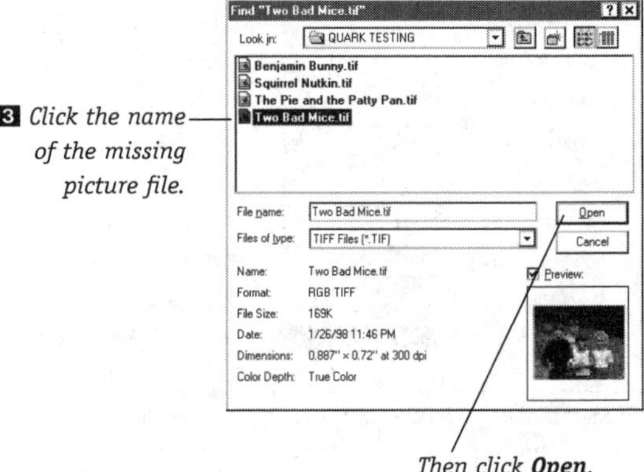

3 *Click the name of the missing picture file.*

*Then click **Open**.*

WHAT'S-ITS-NAME?

If you need to know a picture's name, click on the picture, then choose Utilities menu > Usage > Picture folder tab (Shift-F2). The name of the picture will be highlighted.

Pictures and text 10

1 *Click on the text box that you want to be in front.*

2 *Click the **Background** color icon.*

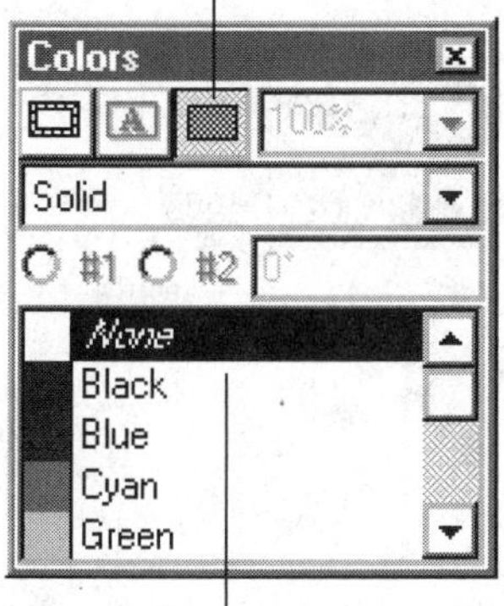

3 *Then click **None** to make the background of the top box transparent.*

4 *The text box is transparent.*

Pictures and text

There are many ways to combine text and pictures in QuarkXPress. For example, a picture can be placed behind a text box that has a transparent background. Or text can wrap partly or completely around the irregular contours of a picture—even within the same column—or around the perimeter of a picture box.

Text can wrap around the outer bounding box of the picture itself or QuarkXPress can create an editable clipping path to control precisely which parts of a picture will or will not print. A clipping path can even be created from an embedded path or alpha channel that was saved with a picture in another application. You no longer have to drive yourself insane trying to prevent a picture's white background from printing!

You can layer a text box over a picture box (or layer multiple picture or text boxes).

To layer text over a picture or other item:

1. Choose the Item or Content tool.
2. Click on the text box that is to be in front. If it's not yet in front, choose Item menu > Bring to Front (F5) **1**.
3. Choose View menu > Show Colors (F12).
4. Click the Background color icon on the Colors palette **2**.
5. Click None **3**–**4**. Do not select Black with a shade of 0%—you won't achieve transparency.

TIP Make sure the bottommost item isn't so dark that the text becomes unreadable, or make the text white.

To wrap text around a box:

1. A picture box must be on top of a text box if you want text to wrap around it. If the picture box is not on top, select it and choose Item menu > Bring to Front (F5).
2. Choose the Item or Content tool.
3. Select the picture box.
4. Choose Item menu > Runaround (Ctrl-T).
5. Choose Type: Item **1**.
6. To adjust the space between each side of a rectangular picture box and the text that's wrapping around it, enter numbers in the Top, Left, Bottom, and Right fields. If any other picture box shape is selected, enter a number in the Outset field.
7. Note the preview in the dialog box and click Apply to preview the text wrap in the document window.
8. Click OK or press Enter.

TIP The current Margin color is also used to denote the picture's bounding box. Similarly, the current Ruler color is used to denote the clipping path, and the current Grid color denotes the Runaround border. You can change any of these colors via Edit menu > Preferences > Application > Display folder tab (Ctrl-Alt-Shift-Y).

1 *Choose Type: **Item** in the Modify > **Runaround** folder tab.*

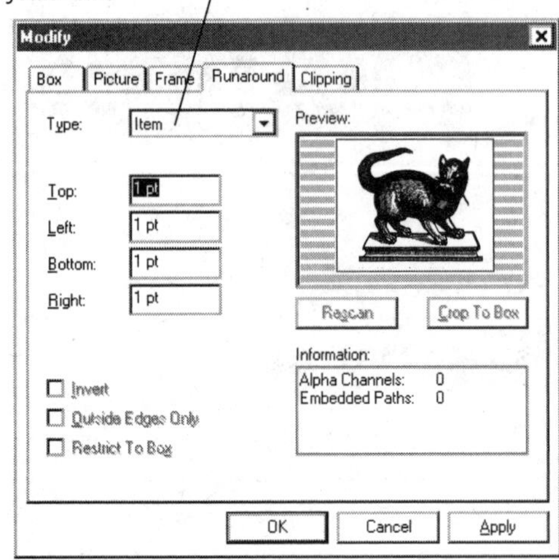

With my aversion to this cat, however, its partiality for myself seemed to increase. It followed my footsteps with a pertinacity which it would be difficult to make the reader comprehend. Whenever I sat, it would crouch beneath my chair, or spring upon my knees, covering me with its loathsome caresses. If I arose to walk it would get between my feet and thus nearly throw me down, or, fastening its long and sharp claws in my dress, clamber, in this manner to, to my breast. At such times, although I longed to destroy it with a blow, I was yet withheld from so doing, partly by a memory of my former crime, but chiefly—let me confess it at once—by absolute *dread* of the beast...

This dread was not exactly a dread of physical evil—and yet... *Edgar Allan Poe*

Normally, text will only wrap around three sides of a box that is placed within a column. Text will wrap around all four sides of a box if it straddles two columns or if the Run Text Around All Sides option is turned on for the text box in Item menu > Modify > Text folder tab.

ue to follow them."
just a little anxious
animals in front of
Intent. And Piglet
wished very much that his grandfather T.W. e

*Before a clipping path is created, the white area around the photo is **opaque**.*

*An XPress **clipping path** is used to make the photograph opaque and the **white** area around it **transparent**. The text is still running behind the photo, though—it's not wrapping around it.*

"Pooh!" cried Piglet.
"Do you think it is
another Woozle?"
"No," said Pooh,
"because it makes
different marks. It is
either Two Woozles
and one, as it might be,
Wizzle, or Two, as it might be, Wizzles and
one, if so it is, Woozle. Let us continue to fol-

*Finally, **Runaround** is turned on with the Type: **Same As Clipping** option for the photo to force the **text** to **wrap** around the image.*

What is a clipping path?

A clipping path is a device that controls which parts of a picture will print. Areas of the picture within the clipping path will be visible and will print; areas outside the clipping path will be transparent and won't print. You may already know how to create a clipping path in another application, like Photoshop. In that type of clipping path, the clipping information is saved in the image itself. In XPress, a clipping path that's saved with an image in another application is referred to as an embedded path.

Clipping paths in QuarkXPress work a little bit differently. While they are also used to control which parts of an image will print, they don't permanently clip areas of the image that extend outside it. Clipping path information in QuarkXPress is saved with the document, not the image itself. This means that you can create a different clipping path for each instance in which you use an image, which offers great flexibility. If you *want* to reuse a picture and its clipping path, on the other hand, you can simply drag-and-drop the picture box from one document to another; a copy will appear in the destination document.

Another compelling reason to use an XPress clipping path is that as you reshape it or choose different settings for it, you can see immediately how it looks within your overall layout. What's more, you can tweak the shape of a clipping path to your heart's delight using any technique you'd use to adjust a Bézier path.

In QuarkXPress, you can create a simple clipping path based on the shape or silhouette of the picture itself or you can create an irregular, customized path. QuarkXPress can also generate a new, editable clipping path based on an alpha channel or an embedded path if it was saved with the picture file in its original application (i.e. Adobe Photoshop).

Runaround vs. clipping in a nutshell

A clipping path controls which parts of a picture will **display** and **print**. Runaround controls how **text wraps** around a picture. The runaround text wrap or a clipping path can be controlled by any of the following parameters 1–2:

Item: The edge of the picture box.

Picture Bounds: The picture's bounding box (the outer edge of the picture).

Non-White Areas: The non-white edge of a picture (the path will follow the silhouette of an image if it has a white background).

Embedded Path or **Alpha Channel**: An embedded alpha channel or path that was created and saved with the picture in a graphics application. You can use an embedded path in an imported picture in any of these formats: TIFF, EPS, BMP, JPEG, PCX, PICT, and Scitex CT. You can also use an alpha channel in a TIFF.

To make matters even more confusing, for each Type there are additional options for controlling the placement of the clipping path or the runaround text wrap.

And there's one more Runaround option, **Auto Image**, which does a better job than its predecessor in earlier application versions. With Auto Image chosen, text will wrap around the edge of the image (not its bounding box). The runaround is created from the high-resolution image using Bézier curves, and works effectively on an image that has a clearly defined border and a flat, light background. A combined, uneditable clipping and runaround path is created in one step (the edit clipping and runaround functions are nullified).

Though they may at first seem confusing, the new runaround and clipping path options offer a lot of control and flexibility, so they're worth spending some time to learn.

Choose Type: **None** in the Runaround folder tab to turn off runaround altogether.

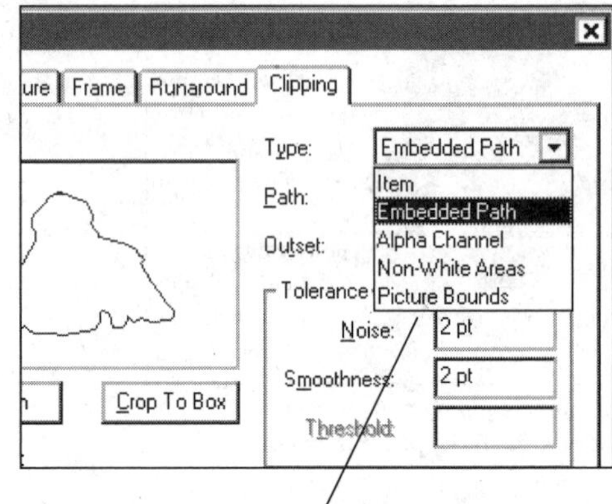

1 *The **Type** options in the **Clipping** dialog box.*

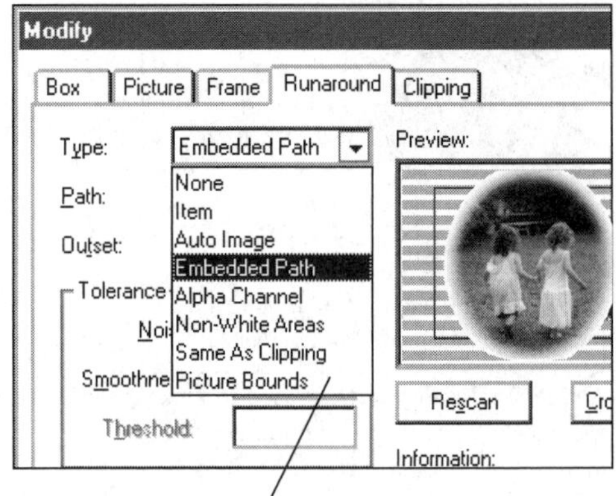

2 *The **Type** options in the **Runaround** dialog box.*

1 *Choose a clipping path type from the **Type** drop-down menu.*

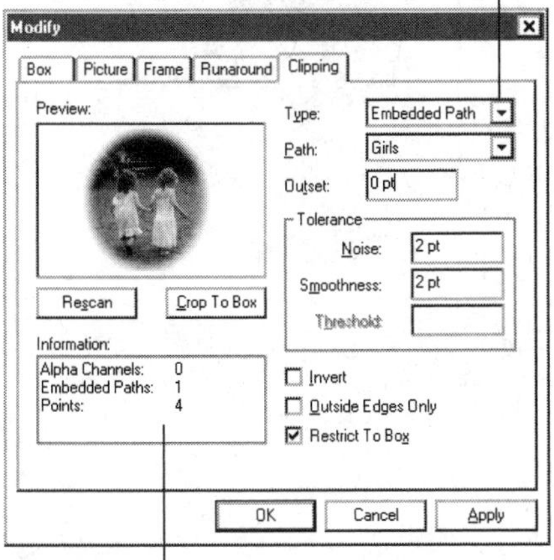

*The **Information** box displays the number of **Alpha Channels** and **Embedded Paths** contained in the picture file and the number of **points** that will be created for the QuarkXPress clipping path.*

2a *Clipping Type: **Item**. The clipping path conforms to the box.*

2b *Clipping Type: **Picture Bounds**. The clipping path conforms to the outer perimeter of the image (its bounding box).*

To create a clipping path:

1. Import an EPS, TIFF, or PICT file into a rectangular picture box. While you can use a picture that has a colored or textured background, for your first attempt, consider using a picture that's silhouetted on a white background.
2. To layer a picture, make sure its box has a background of None. (Select the box, click the background (third) icon on the Colors palette, then click None.)
3. Choose Item menu > Clipping (Ctrl-Alt-T).
4. Note the green line around the image in the preview window, which denotes the clipping path, as you choose from the **Type** drop-down menu **1**:

   (Choose **Item** to turn off the clipping path function **2a**. The picture will only be cropped by the picture box. To turn off Runaround, see page 156.)

   Choose **Picture Bounds** to conform the path to the rectangular outer boundary of the picture (its bounding box) **2b**. If Restrict to Box is unchecked, any areas of the picture that the picture box is cropping will become visible, and may block out other items beneath it.

   Choose **Embedded Path** to create a clipping path based on a clipping path that was saved with the picture in another application (**2c**, next page). Choose Alpha Channel to create a clipping path based on the non-black parts of an alpha channel that was saved with the picture in an image editing program. *Note:* If the picture was saved with more than one alpha channel or path, choose the desired channel or path name from the **Alpha** or **Path** drop-down menu.

   Choose **Non-White Areas** to create a clipping path that follows the contours of the actual image and ignores non-white areas of the picture. The white areas can be close to white (i.e. very light gray) or absolute white.

5. As you choose any of these *optional* settings, click **Apply** at any time to preview the current settings in the document:

   Click **Crop To Box** if you want the clipping path to stop at the edge of the box. Click **Rescan** to restore the original clipping path.

   Check **Invert** to switch what is cropped and what is visible **3a**. This option won't be available if the Item or Picture Bounds Type is chosen.

   Check **Outside Edges Only** for an Alpha Channel, Embedded Path, or Non-White Areas (not Item or Picture Bounds) clipping path if the picture contains a blank hole or holes where the background white shows through and you don't want the clipping path to include them. With Outside Edges Only unchecked, an additional clipping path will be created for each hole **3b**.

   Check **Restrict To Box** if you want only those areas of the picture that are within the picture box to display and print (**3c–d**, next page).

   With any Type option except Item chosen, you can further expand or contract the clipping path to print more or less of the picture by entering a positive or negative number, respectively, in the **Outset** field. For the Picture Bounds Type option, enter values in the Top, Left, Bottom, or Right fields. For a clipping path using the Embedded Path or Alpha Channel Type option, the Outset value will expand or contract the entire clipping path relative to the original path or alpha channel. For the Non-White Areas type of clipping path, the Outset value will expand or contract the entire clipping path relative to the original non-white areas (**4a–b**, page 160).

6. Choose Tolerance settings for an Embedded Path, Alpha Channel, or Non-White Areas type of clipping path:

2c *Clipping Type:* ***Embedded Path****. The clipping path conforms to a path that was saved with the image in its original application.*

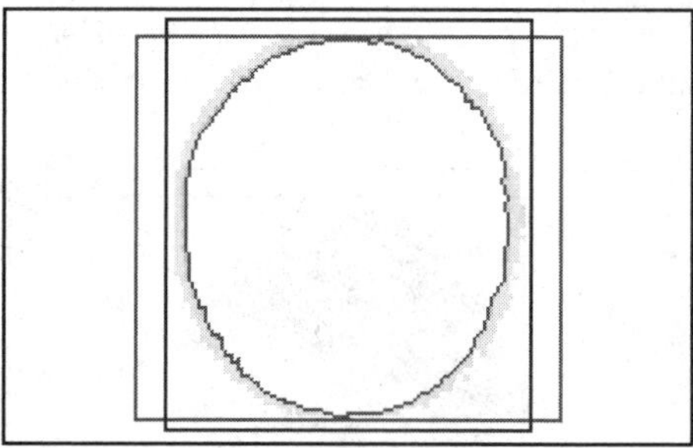

3a *Clipping Type:* ***Non-White Areas, Invert*** *option* ***on****. Only pixels in the outer fringe will print.*

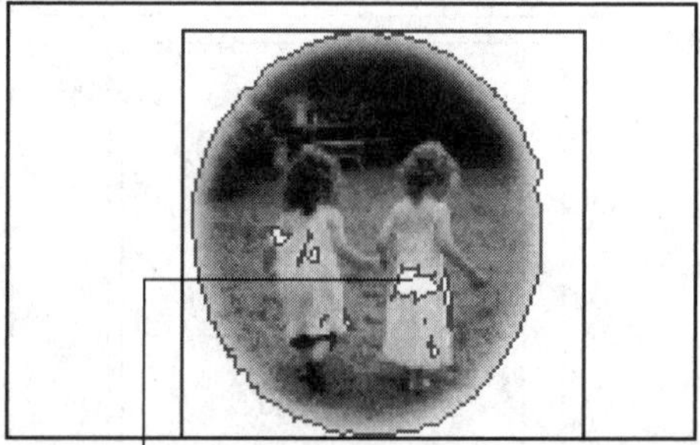

3b *Clipping Type:* ***Non-White Areas, Outside Edges*** *turned* ***off****. The clipping path or paths surround any non-white areas in the image.*

Create a Clipping Path

3c *Clipping Type:* ***Picture Bounds, Restrict to Box*** *turned on. Only areas of the picture that are inside the picture box will print.*

He trotted along happily, and by-and-by he crossed the stream and came to the place where his friends-and-rela-tions lived. There seemed to be even more of them about than usual this morning, and having nodded to a hedgehog or two, with whom he was too busy to shake hands, and having said, "Good morning, good morning," impor-tantly to some of the others, and "Ah, there you are," kindly, to the smaller ones, he waved a paw at them over his shoulder, and was gone; leaving such an air of excitement and I-don't-know-what behind him, that several members

3d *Clipping Type:* ***Picture Bounds, Restrict to Box*** *turned off. Areas outside the picture box will print, even if they overlap the text.*

He trotted along happily, and by-and-by he crossed the stream and came to the place where tions lived. There seemed to be more of them about than usual morning, and having nodded hedgehog or two, with whom he wa busy to shake hands, and having "Good morning, good morning," im tantly to some of the others, and there you are," kindly, to the sm ones, he waved a paw at them ove shoulder, and was gone; leaving such an air of excitement and I-don't-know-what behind him, that several members

For an alpha channel clipping path, the **Noise** value controls the minimum size an area near the border of an alpha channel must be to be included in the clipping path (**5a–b**, next page). Use this setting if you don't want the path to include tiny, extraneous blobs from the background.

Smoothness (0–100) makes the clipping path more or less smooth by adding or decreasing points (**6a–b**, next page). The lower the Smoothness setting, the more points the clipping path will contain; the higher the Smoothness, the fewer points the path will contain and the more precise will be its shape. A low Smoothness may cause output problems, but XPress can automatically adjust the Smoothness setting during printing, if necessary.

Threshold works with an Alpha Channel or Non-White Areas clipping path (**7a–b**, page 161). It controls what percentage of gray on the alpha channel will be treated as white (and thus not mask the picture) and what percentages will be treated as black (and mask parts of the picture). A Threshold setting of 10% will cause gray values from 0–10% to be treated as white. Values between 11% and 100% will treated as black and mask out those parts of the picture. A Threshold setting of 40% will make more gray values treated as white and thus reveal more of the picture. For the Non-White Areas type of clipping path, the opposite is true: The Threshold is the percentage a color can be darker than white before it will be left outside the clipping path and thus won't print.

7. Click OK or press Enter. If you'd like to reshape the clipping path, follow the instructions on the page 163.

(Illustrations on the following two pages)

4a *Clipping Type:* ***Non-White Areas, Outset -15****.* *The clipping path shrinks slightly inward.*

4b *Clipping Type:* ***Non-White Areas, Outset 15****.* *The clipping path expands slightly outward.*

5a *Clipping Type:* ***Non-White Areas,*** *the default* ***Noise*** *setting of* ***2 pt****. The clipping path includes extraneous pixels outside the oval.*

5b *Clipping Type:* ***Non-White Areas, Noise 30.*** *The extraneous blobs aren't included in the clipping path.*

6a *Clipping Type:* ***Non-White Areas,*** *the default* ***Smoothness*** *setting of* ***2 pt****. The clipping path has many points, and hugs the image precisely.*

6b *Clipping Type:* ***Non-White Areas, Smoothness 75 pt.*** *The clipping path is smoother, but less accurate.*

7a *Clipping Type:* ***Non-White Areas, Threshold 2.*** *The clipping path includes the gray background.*

7b *Clipping Type:* ***Non-White Areas, Threshold 10.*** *The clipping path ignores the gray background.*

Runaround and clipping: How they work together

If different runaround and clipping Type options are chosen for the same picture, the picture edge and the text wrap won't match. For example, if Picture Bounds is chosen as the Runaround type and the picture's alpha channel or embedded path is chosen as the clipping type (and assuming the channel or path is smaller than the picture bounds), there will be a buffer area between the clipped picture and the text wrap.

And it can't hurt to say the obvious: Don't wrap your text *inside* a clipping path unless the text or the picture's contrast has been carefully adjusted to make the type readable.

If the Non-White Areas option is chosen for a picture in both the Runaround and the Clipping folder tabs, text will wrap to the edge of a silhouetted picture, plus or minus any Outset width that you specify.

You can also force text to flow into any hole or holes in a picture where the white background shows through by unchecking the Outside Edges Only option in both the Clipping and Runaround dialog boxes.

To wrap text around a picture:

1. Choose the Item or Content tool.
2. Select a picture box, and make sure it's on top of the text box. If it's not, choose Item menu > Bring to Front.
3. Choose Item menu > Runaround (Ctrl-T).
4. Choose Type: Non-White Areas.
5. Enter a number in points in the Outset field to adjust the space between the picture and its surrounding text.
   or
   Check the Same As Clipping box if you want the text runaround to conform to a QuarkXPress clipping path and to utilize all the options that were chosen for that clipping path.
6. Click Apply to preview.
7. Click OK or press Enter.
8. Press Shift-Esc to force the screen to redraw.

   Note: Normally, text will wrap around three sides of a picture or picture box within a column. To wrap text completely around a picture box or picture box, select the text box, choose Item menu > Modify (Ctrl-M) or right-click and choose Modify, click the Text folder tab, check the Run Text Around All Sides box, then click OK **1**–**2**.

TIP Beware: If you choose Picture Bounds as the clipping path type and choose Non-White Areas as the runaround type, the text will wrap to the edge of the image, but it will be obscured by the opaque background of the picture. A picture's bounding box usually isn't the same as the edge of the picture box.

Then, pray tell me what it is that you can infer from this hat?" He picked it up and gazed at it in the peculiar introspective fashion which was characteristic of him. "It is perhaps less suggestive than it might have been," he remarked, "and yet there are a few inferences which are very distinct, and a few others which represent at least a strong balance of probability. That the man was highly intellectual is of course obvious upon the face of it, and also that he was fairly well-to-do within the last three years, although he has now fallen upon evil days. He had foresight, but has less now than formerly, pointing to a moral retrogression, which, when taken with the decline of his fortunes, seems to indicate some evil influence, probably drink, at work upon him. This may account also for the obvious fact that his wife has ceased to love him..."

—*Sir Arthur Conan Doyle*

1 *In QuarkXPress version 4.0 or later, you can make text run completely around a picture within the same column. The text will be tiring to read, though, so don't use this option if you need to convey important information.*

Then, pray tell me what it is that you can infer from this hat?" He picked it up and gazed at it in the peculiar introspective fashion which was characteristic of him. "It is perhaps less suggestive than it might have been," he remarked, "and yet there are a few inferences which are very distinct, and a few others which represent at least a strong balance of probability. That the man was highly intellectual is of course obvious upon the face of it, and also that he was fairly well-to-do within the last three years, although he has now fallen upon evil days. He had foresight, but has less now than formerly, pointing to a moral retrogression, which, when taken with the decline of his fortunes, seems to indicate some evil influence, probably drink, at work upon him. This may account also for the obvious fact that his wife has ceased to love him..."

2 *To run text inside the holes of a picture, choose Non-White Areas for the runaround type and uncheck Outside Edges only.*

*Reshape a **clipping** path to change which parts of a picture will **print**:*

1 *Alt-click on a line segment to add an anchor point.*

2 *Alt-click an anchor point to delete it.*

*Reshape a **runaround** path to change how **text wraps** around the picture:*

3 *Dragging a segment.*

4 *The text re-wraps.*

Note: When QuarkXPress generates a clipping path, it's based on the original, high resolution picture file. If you manually edit that clipping path, you'll be working off the low-resolution screen preview of that picture, which means your adjustments may not be perfectly precise.

To reshape a runaround or clipping path:

1. Choose the Item or Content tool.
2. Click on a picture that has a clipping path. You can edit the runaround for any of these Types: Embedded Path, Alpha Channel, Non-White Areas, or Picture Bounds.
3. Choose Item menu > Edit > Runaround (Ctrl-F10).
   or
   Choose Item menu > Edit > Clipping Path (Ctrl-Shift-F10).
4. Use any of the techniques that you'd normally use to reshape a Bézier path (see pages 182–189) **1**–**4**. You can add or delete an anchor point, drag a point, segment, or control handle, or convert an anchor point from corner to curved (or vice versa).

   Note: If you edit a clipping path and then reopen the Clipping folder tab, the clipping path Type will be listed as User Edited Path. If you choose a different Type at this point and click OK, you'll **lose** your custom path edits.
5. When you're done editing the runaround or clipping path, turn off Item menu > Edit > Runaround (Ctrl-F10) or Clipping Path (Ctrl-Shift-F10).

TIP To update the picture on screen, move it using the Content tool or use the screen redraw keystroke, which is Shift-Esc. To update the text wrap as you move a picture, turn on Live Refresh in Edit menu > Preferences > Application > Interactive folder tab.

To wrap text inside a hidden picture:

1. Choose the Item or Content tool, and click on a silhouetted image on a flat white or off-white background **1**.
2. Make sure the picture box is in front of the text box. Choose Item menu > Bring to Front (F5) for the picture, if necessary.
3. Choose Item menu > Modify (Ctrl-M) or right-click and choose Modify.
4. Click the Clipping folder tab, and choose Clipping Type: Non-White Areas.
5. Check the Invert box.
6. Click the Runaround folder tab.
7. Choose Type: Same As Clipping.
8. Click OK.
9. Press Shift-Esc to force the screen to redraw **2**. Try using a small type size and justified horizontal alignment.

   Note: If the edge of the picture is showing (as in **2**) and you don't want it to print, click on the picture, choose Item menu > Modify, click the Box folder tab, and check the Suppress Printout box.

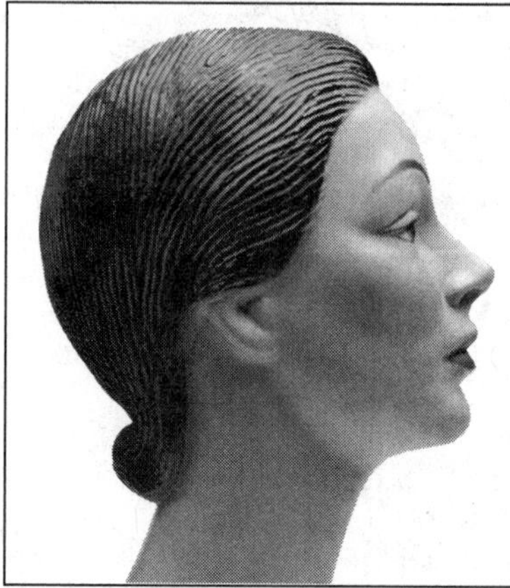

1 *Click on a picture that has a white background.*

brain *n.* **1** an organ of soft nervous tissue contained in the skull of vertebrates, functioning as the coordinating centre of sensation, and of intellectual and nervous activity. **2** (usu. in *pl.*; prec. by *the*) *colloq.* **a** the cleverest person in a group. **b** a person who originates a complex plan or idea. **brain** *n.* **1** an organ of soft nervous tissue contained in the skull of vertebrates, functioning as the coordinating centre of sensation, and of intellectual and nervous activity. **2** (usu.

2 *The text is wrapping inside the clipping path instead of outside it.*

Lines 11

NEED MORE THAN ONE?

- Use the Duplicate shortcut (Ctrl-D), or use the Step & Repeat command (Ctrl-Alt-D) if you want to control where the duplicates land.
- After you draw a line with a line tool, the tool automatically deselects. To keep a line tool selected so you can draw multiple lines, Alt-click the tool on the Tool palette. When you're finished using it, just choose a different tool.

1 *Choose the **Orthogonal Line** tool, then press and drag.*

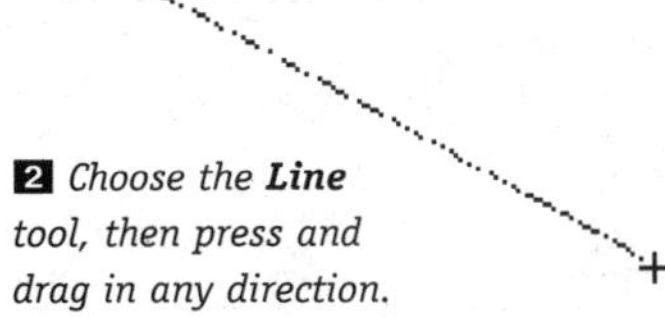

2 *Choose the **Line** tool, then press and drag in any direction.*

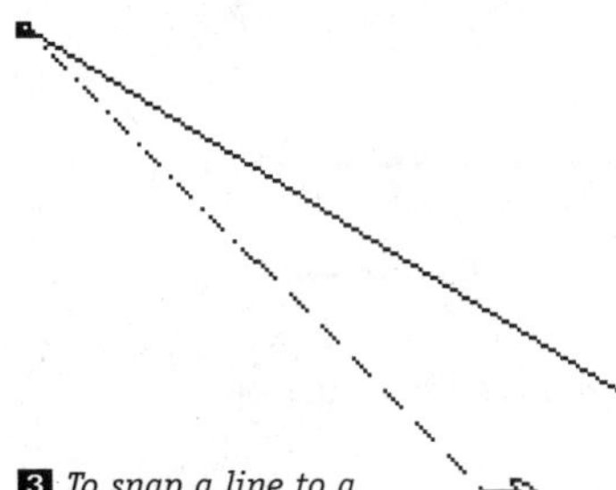

3 *To snap a line to a 45° increment from the existing angle, drag a handle with Shift held down.*

Lines

The line creation tools produce horizontal, vertical, or diagonal straight lines and arrows to which a variety of styles, endcaps, and of course colors, can be applied. Using the Dashes & Stripes feature, which is covered in this chapter, you can create custom line styles for use with the line tools, the Frame feature, or the paragraph Rules feature.

To place rules under type, use the paragraph Rules feature (see pages 90–92). To anchor a line, see page 127. Bézier lines (lines that have anchor points and curve handles) are covered in the next chapter.

To draw a straight horizontal or vertical line:

1. Choose the Orthogonal line tool.+
2. Press and drag the crosshair icon horizontally or vertically **1**.

TIP To convert an orthogonal line into a Bézier line, choose the wiggly line icon from the Item menu > Shape submenu.

To draw a straight line at any angle:

1. Choose the Line tool. ⁄
2. Press and drag the crosshair icon in any direction **2**.

TIP Hold down Shift while drawing a line to constrain the line to a 0°, 45°, or 90° angle. To reset an existing line, drag a handle with Shift held down **3**.

To change the width of a line using the keyboard:

1. Choose the Item or Content tool.
2. Click on a line (Bézier or standard).
3. Hold down Ctrl, Alt, Shift and press the > key to enlarge the line width or the < key to reduce the line width in 1-point increments. (Omit the Alt key to change the line width to preset increments, as listed on the Width drop-down menu on the Measurements palette).
   or
   Use the Ctrl-Shift-\ shortcut. The Line Width field in Item menu > Modify > Line folder tab will highlight automatically. Enter the desired width, then click OK.

To restyle a line using the Measurements palette:

1. Choose the Item or Content tool.
2. Click on a line (Bézier or standard).
3. In the Width field on the Measurements palette, enter up to 864 pt. in an increment as small as .001, then press Enter **1**–**3**. Or choose a preset line width from the drop-down menu.
   and/or
   Choose from the style drop-down menu. (To create custom lines, see page 169.)
   and/or
   Choose an arrowhead from the rightmost drop-down menu.

TIP You can also style a line using the Line Style, Arrowheads, Width, Color or Shade submenu under the Style menu. (Instructions for recoloring a line are on page 235.)

A Bézier line with an arrow endcap and a 10% black Gap Color.

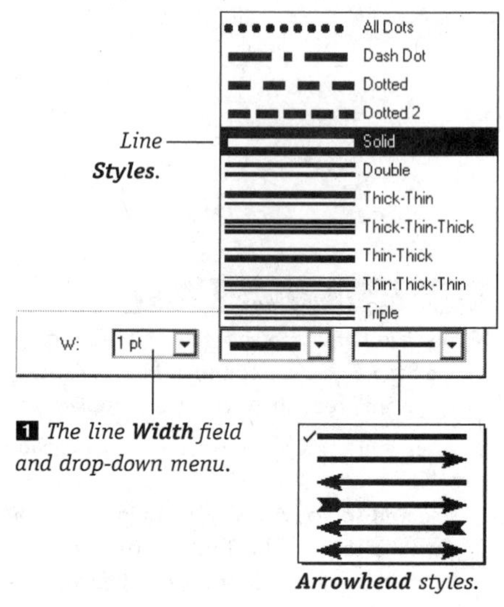

Line Styles.

1 *The line **Width** field and drop-down menu.*

***Arrowhead** styles.*

2 *A line is selected.*

Its width is increased.

A new style is applied.

An arrowhead is added.

Hairline

.5 pt

1 pt

2 pt

4 pt

6 pt

3 *A few sample line widths. A Hairline will print as one output device pixel.*

1 *Press and drag an* ***endpoint*** *to resize a line.*

To shorten or lengthen a line manually:

1. Choose the Item or Content tool.
2. Select a line.
3. Press and drag an endpoint to lengthen or shorten the line **1**.

TIP Shift-drag to preserve a line's angle as you change its length.

Diffusing,
dropping,
sideways-
darting,
in tiny
showers
of gold...

Diffusing,
dropping,
sideways-
darting,
in tiny
showers
of gold...

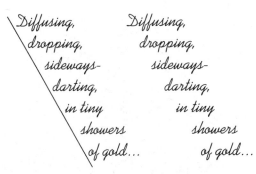

You can use a non-printing line to create an offbeat text shape. Click on a line, check the Suppress Printout box in Item menu > Modify > Line folder tab, click the Runaround folder tab, choose Type: Item, and specify an Outset.

To shorten or lengthen a line using the Measurements palette:

1. Choose the Item or Content tool.
2. Select a line.
3. Choose First Point (the beginning of the line), Midpoint, or Last Point from the mode drop-down menu on the Measurements palette. The line will be measured from this chosen point **2**.
4. Double-click the Length (L) field **3**, enter the desired length, then press Enter.

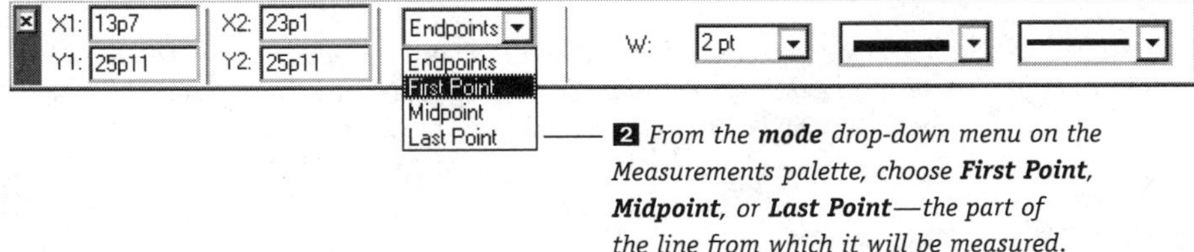

2 *From the* ***mode*** *drop-down menu on the Measurements palette, choose* ***First Point, Midpoint,*** *or* ***Last Point***—*the part of the line from which it will be measured.*

The line ***angle*** *field. This field is not available when Endpoints mode is chosen.*

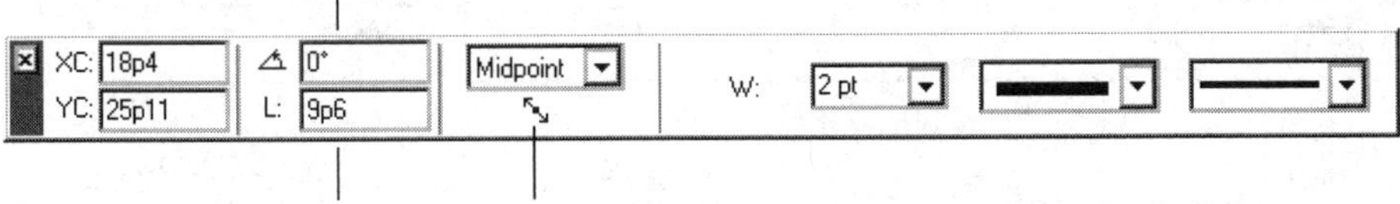

3 *The line* ***Length*** *field.*

This icon represents the currently chosen mode. The little square denotes the line's first point, midpoint, or last point.

To move a line manually:

1. Choose the Item or Content tool.
2. Drag any part of a line other than one of its endpoints **1**.

1 *A line being moved.*

To reposition a line using the Measurements palette:

1. Choose the Item or Content tool.
2. Click on a line.
3. Choose from the mode drop-down menu on the Measurements palette—the part of the line from which its position will be measured **2**–**3**.
4. Enter a number in the X and/or Y field. You can use math (add or subtract) in either field.
5. Press Enter.

TIP To rotate a line by dragging, use the Rotation tool. To rotate a line using the Measurements palette, choose any mode for the line except Endpoints, then enter a value in the angle field.

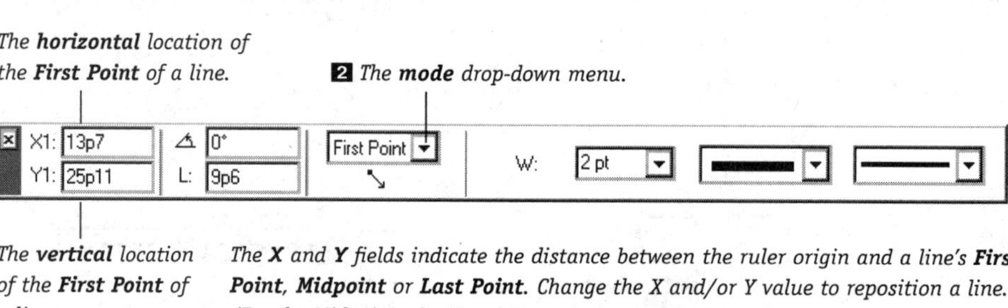

The **horizontal** location of the **First Point** of a line.
X1: 13p7
Y1: 25p11
0°
L: 9p6
First Point
W: 2 pt
The **vertical** location of the **First Point** of a line.
The **X** and **Y** fields indicate the distance between the ruler origin and a line's **First Point**, **Midpoint** or **Last Point**. Change the X and/or Y value to reposition a line. (For the Midpoint, the X and Y are designated by XC and YC.)

2 *The **mode** drop-down menu.*

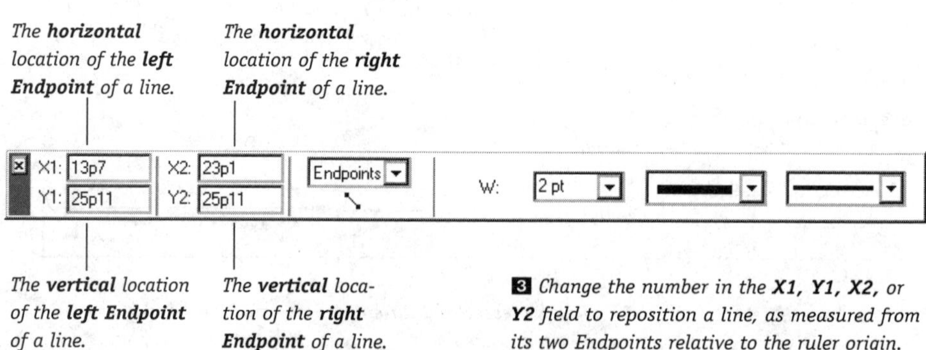

3 *Change the number in the **X1, Y1, X2,** or **Y2** field to reposition a line, as measured from its two Endpoints relative to the ruler origin.*

HOW TO APPLY DASHES/STRIPES

Once a dash or stripe style is saved, it will appear in the same document's **Frame** dialog box when a box is selected; on the Measurements palette style drop-down menu, on the Style menu > Line Style submenu, or in the Item menu > Modify > Line folder tab if a **line** is selected; and in Style menu > **Rules** if text is selected.

*To narrow down the selection of dashes and stripes that display in the scroll window, choose a category from the **Show** drop-down menu.*

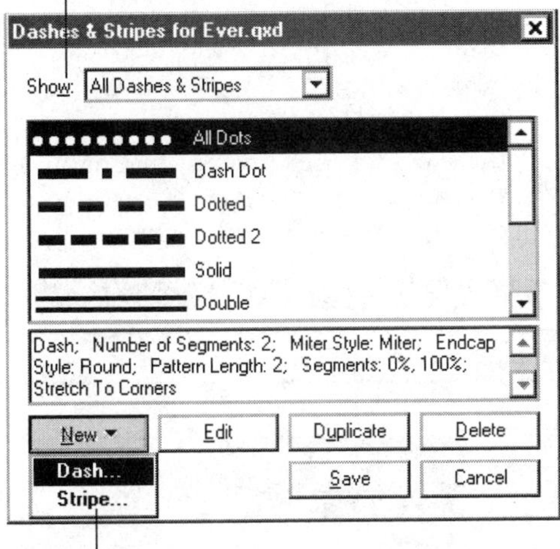

1 *To create a new style, choose **New: Dash** or **Stripe**.*

2 *Drag in the ruler to create a new stripe (or dash).*

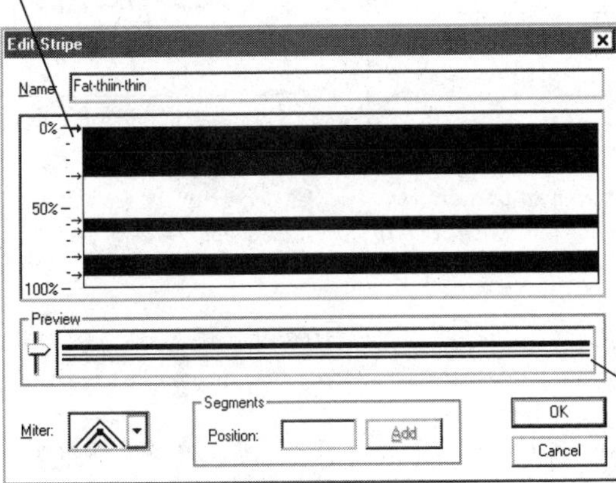

*The current stripe style **previews** here.*

Using the Dashes & Stripes dialog box, you can create custom, PostScript, dashed or multiple line styles for lines, frames, and paragraph rules. If you edit an existing dash or stripe style that is currently applied to an item in your document, the style will update on that item.

Note: To append a line style from one document to another, click Append in the Dashes & Stripes dialog box. Any dash or stripe style that's created when no documents are open will appear in all newly-created documents.

To create or edit dashes or stripes:

1. Choose Edit menu > Dashes & Stripes.
2. To create a new style, choose New: Dash or Stripe **1**, then type a name.
   or
   To edit an existing style, double-click it. Or click on its name, then click Edit.
   or
   To create a new dash or stripe style based on an existing style, click Duplicate, then change the name.
3. Press and drag in the ruler, then press and drag again in another part of the ruler to **create** more dash or stripe segments **2**. Note the Preview. (Five is the maximum for dashes.)

   To **move** a dash or a stripe, drag inside it with the hand cursor.

   To **shorten** or **lengthen** a dash or widen or narrow a stripe, drag either of its arrows.

   To **remove** a stripe, drag either of its arrows up or down off the ruler or drag the stripe itself right or left off the ruler. To remove a dash, drag either of its arrows right or left off the ruler or drag the dash itself up or down off the ruler.

(Continued on the following page)

If you want to specify the **distance** between dashes, enter a number in the Repeats Every field **3**. The higher the Repeats Every value, the further apart the dashes will be. If you choose "times width" from the Repeats Every drop-down menu, dash segments will spread to fit the dimensions of the line or frame to which that style is applied. If you choose "points" from the same drop-down menu, segments will maintain the same spacing no matter what.

Create a dash or stripe segment by entering the **ruler %** position where you want it to start in the Segments: Position field, then click Add.

4. Choose a **Miter** style for the corners of a frame or a multi-segment line: Pointed, rounded, or beveled **4**.

5. For dashes, you can choose a different **Endcap** style for the shape of the ends of the dash segments **5**. To enlarge the preview so you can see a closeup of how the endcap style looks, drag the Preview slider upward **6**.

6. *Optional:* Check the Stretch to Corners box to force the frame design to fit symmetrically around the corners of any box to which it is applied **7**.

7. Click OK or press Enter.

8. Click Save.

TIP To remove a dash or stripe style, click on it, click Delete, respond to the prompt, if it appears, then click OK.

TIP In the center of the Dashes & Stripes dialog box is an info field in which all the specs for the currently highlighted style are listed. Each gap between dashes or stripes counts as one segment.

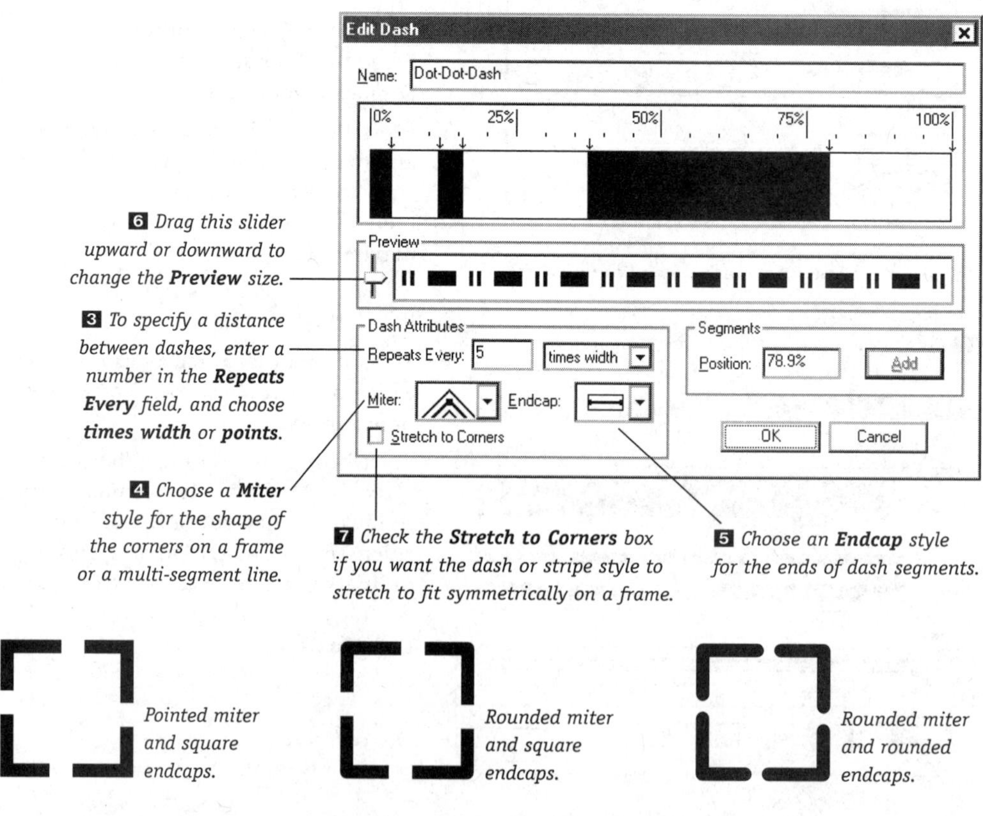

6 *Drag this slider upward or downward to change the **Preview** size.*

3 *To specify a distance between dashes, enter a number in the **Repeats Every** field, and choose **times width** or **points**.*

4 *Choose a **Miter** style for the shape of the corners on a frame or a multi-segment line.*

7 *Check the **Stretch to Corners** box if you want the dash or stripe style to stretch to fit symmetrically on a frame.*

5 *Choose an **Endcap** style for the ends of dash segments.*

Pointed miter and square endcaps.

Rounded miter and square endcaps.

Rounded miter and rounded endcaps.

Comparing specifications between two dashes and/or stripes

Ctrl-click two dashes and/or stripe styles in the scroll window in the Dashes & Stripes dialog box, then Alt-click the Append button (it will turn into a Compare button). Differences between the two styles will be listed in boldface.

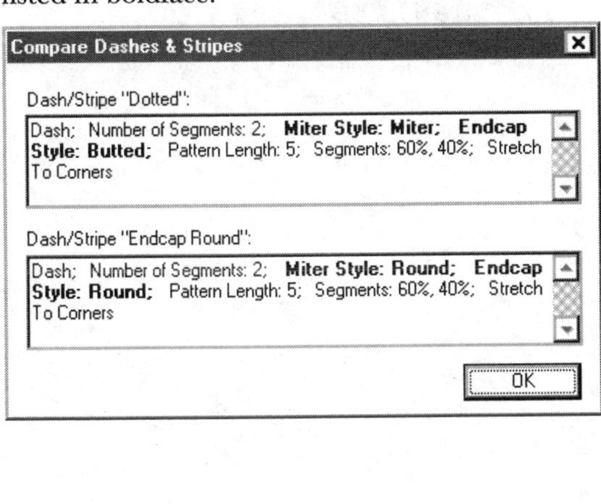

Stretch to corners

A custom dash style, with ***Stretch to Corners*** *turned* ***on.***

The same dash style with ***Stretch to Corners*** *turned* ***off.***

Dashes and stripes as paragraph rules

The possibilities are enormous! I expect to see a lot of creativity in this area, as designers start to experiment with this feature. Like any paragraph rule, a dash or stripe rule style can be applied via a style sheet.

❷ Subhead

The circle was created using a dash style as a paragraph Rule Above with a negative Offset. The dash style specifications are as follows, Number of Segments: 2; Miter Style: Round; Endcap Style: Round; Pattern Length: 20; Segments: 0.9%, 99.1%.

Subhead

A stripe style applied as a paragraph rule above with a 50% Shade. The specifications are: Number of Segments: 6; Miter Style: Miter; Segments: 1.6%, 42.7%, 1.6%, 42.7%, 1.6%.

Fill the gap

To color the white areas in a dash or stripe, choose Item menu > Modify > Box folder tab, then choose a Gap: Color and Shade.

*This is a dashed frame with a 15% Black **Gap** color.*

To polish it off, I added inner and outer frames in separate text boxes, both with a background color of None.

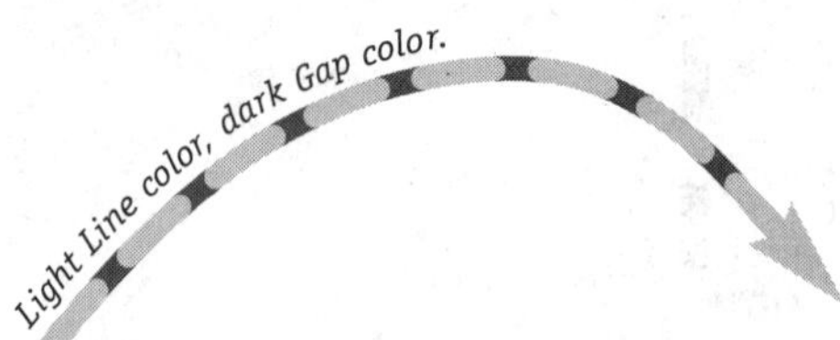

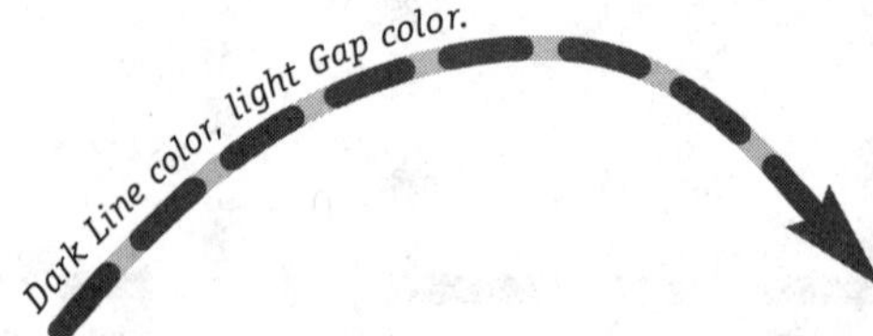

Béziers 12

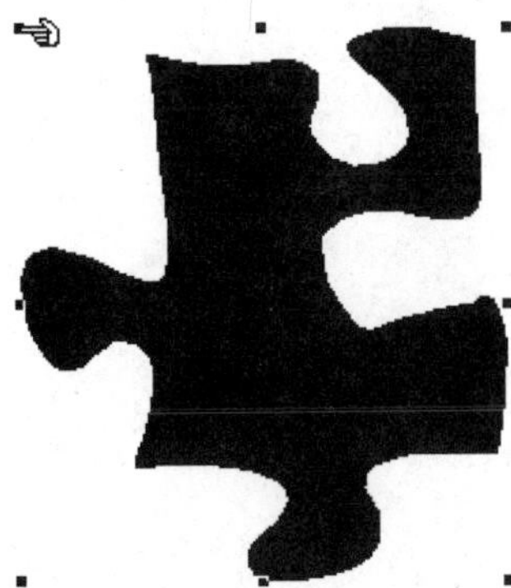

1 *With Item menu > Edit >* ***Shape off****, you can resize or reshape the overall shape by dragging any of the eight handles on the item's bounding box.*

Diamond- *shaped curve* ***handle***

Smooth point

Square*-shaped curve* ***handle***

Corner point

2 *With Item menu > Edit >* ***Shape on****, all of an item's individual points and curve handles are accessible for reshaping.*

Béziers

The most dramatic addition to QuarkXPress are the tools for creating Bézier boxes, lines, and text paths. A Bézier item is composed of straight and/or curved line segments that are connected by points. A point for a curve segment has two rabbit-ear curve handles attached to it that control the shape and direction of the curve. A Bézier item can be closed or open.

The many tools you can use to create and reshape Bézier items in QuarkXPress are shown on the following page. While each tool creates an item with a distinctive function—i.e., a closed shape to contain text or a picture or an open line on which to place text—the way Bézier points and handles are manipulated to reshape an item are the same for all items **1**–**2**.

How Béziers are used

In most ways a Bézier picture box functions like any other picture box. You can import a picture into it, apply a frame to it, color its background, and so on. Unlike a standard picture box, however, a Bézier box can be reshaped. Use an open Bézier item—a line—as a decorative element. If you like to draw using a freehand style, create a line or box using one of the freehand tools.

A Bézier text box also functions like a standard text box, except for its reshape-ability. A text path is a straight or curved line that you can type, paste, or import text onto.

And as you'll see by the end of this chapter, you can convert any type of shape into any other type of shape—a line into a box, a picture box into a text box, etc. Changing your mind is easy.

The Bézier tool chest

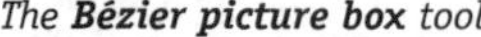

*The **Bézier picture box** tools*

Bézier picture box
Creates picture boxes by clicking or dragging

Freehand picture box
Creates picture boxes by dragging

*The **Bézier line** tools*

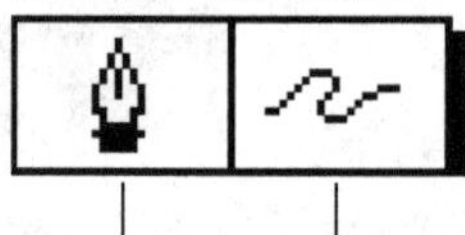

Bézier line
Creates lines by clicking

Freehand line
Creates lines by dragging

*The **Bézier text box** tools*

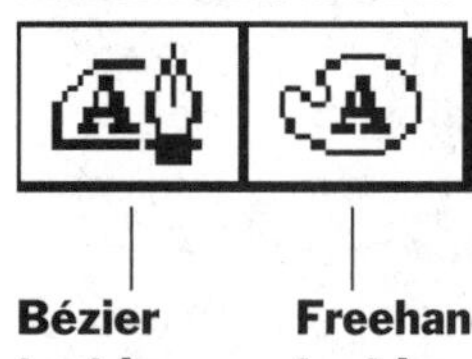

Bézier text box
Creates text boxes by clicking or dragging

Freehand text box
Creates text boxes by dragging

*The **Bézier text path** tools*

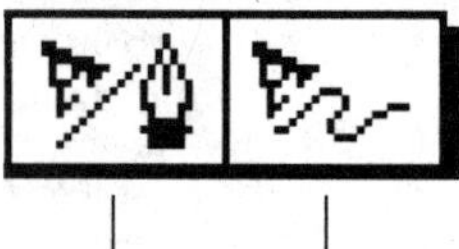

Bézier text path
Creates text paths by clicking or dragging

Freehand text path
Creates Bézier text paths by dragging

The Bézier settings on the Measurements palette

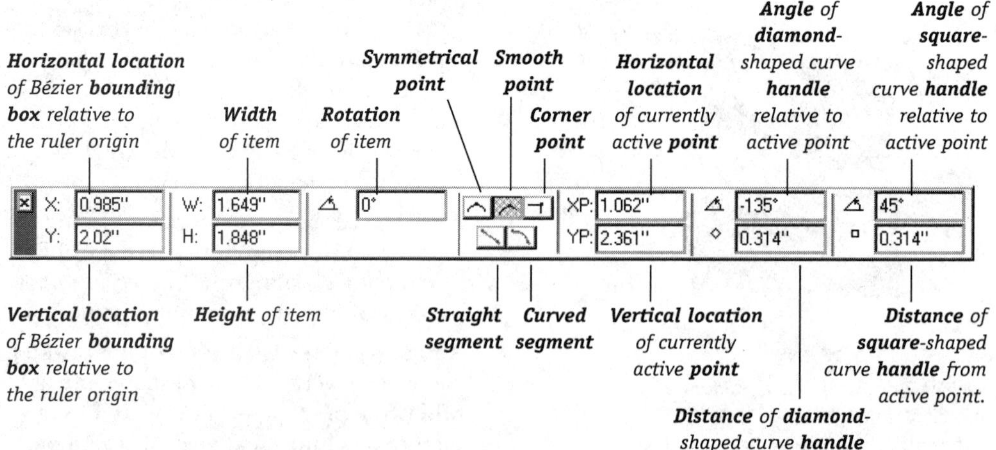

The Bézier shortcuts

This page is a reference guide. If you're new to Béziers, skip it for right now. Once you've learned the Bézier fundamentals, refer back to this page to speed things up.

Corner point	Select point, then Ctrl-F1
Smooth point	Select point, then Ctrl-F2
Symmetrical point	Select point, then Ctrl-F3
Add point	Alt-click line segment
Delete point	Alt-click point
Straight segment	Select segment, then Alt-Shift-F1
Curve segment	Select segment, then Ctrl-Shift-F2
Turn path editing on/off	F10
Select all the points in the shape	Double-click or click one point, then Ctrl-Shift-A
Select all the points in a merged paths item	Triple-click
Select multiple points individually	Shift-click
Make smooth/corner	Ctrl-Shift-drag curve handle
Snap point to 45° guides	Shift-drag point
Snap curve handle to 45° increments	Shift-drag curve handle
Retract one curve handle	Alt-click curve handle
Retract curve handles	Ctrl-Shift-click point
Expose curve handles	Ctrl-Shift-drag point
AS A PATH IS BEING DRAWN	
Toggle between corner and curve point	Ctrl-click point, then Ctrl-F1
Convert smooth point into a corner point joining a curve and a straight segment	Ctrl-Alt-click curve handle
Readjust point or drag a point or handle as you draw it	Ctrl

Bézier Shortcuts

To draw a straight-sided Bézier line or text path:

1. Choose the Bézier line or Bézier text path tool.
2. Click to create an anchor point.
3. Click to create additional anchor points **1**. Straight line segments will connect them.
4. To end the path, select another tool or double-click when you create the last point **2**–**3**. (More about text paths later in this chapter.)

TIP To delete a path as you're creating it: press Backspace (Ctrl-K).

TIP Hold down Shift to constrain a segment to a 0°, 45°, or 90° angle.

TIP Normally, a Bézier tool will switch to the Item or Content tool as soon as one path is completed. Alt-click a Bézier tool, and it will stay selected so you can draw multiple paths.

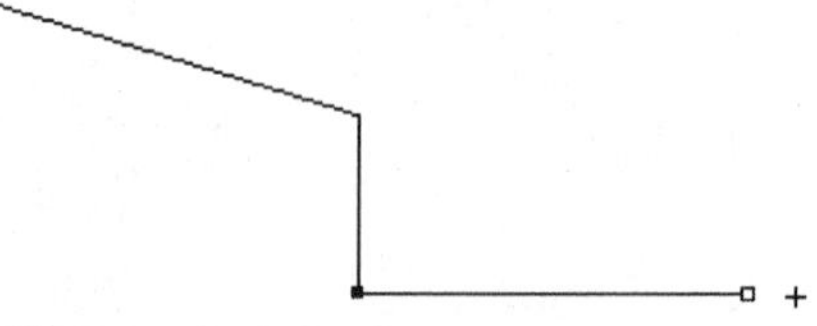

1 ***Click****—don't drag—to create points connected by straight segments.*

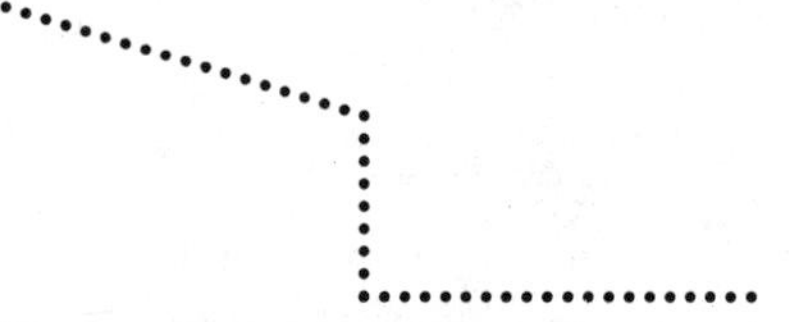

2 *Change the width, style, or color of a Bézier* ***line*** *as you would any other line—but first select it with the Item tool. See Chapter 11.*

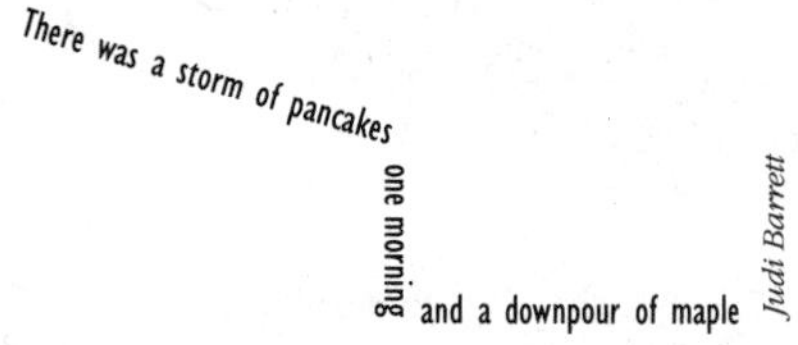

3 *If it's a* ***text path****, just enter and style your text as you would text in a box.*

To draw a straight-sided Bézier picture box or text box:

1. Choose the Bézier picture box or Bézier text box tool.
2. Click to create an anchor point.
3. Click to create additional anchor points. Straight line segments will connect them.
4. To close the box, choose another tool.
   or
   Double-click at the location where you want the last anchor point to appear (it doesn't have to be over the first point).
   or
   Click once back on the starting point **4**–**5**.

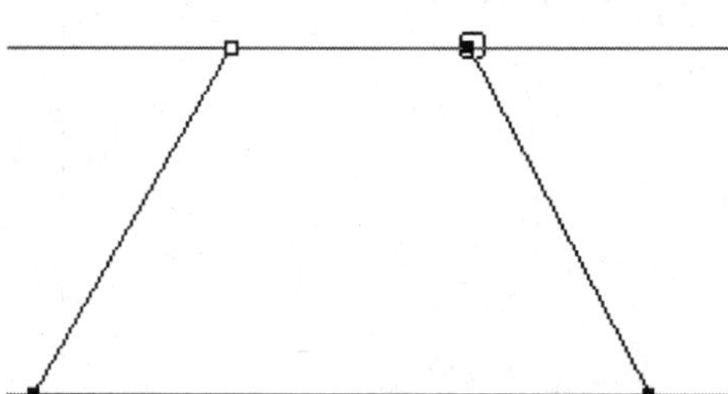

4 *One way to close a Bézier box is by clicking back on the starting point. You can use guides to help you place points.*

'After that I suppose we shall have pretty nearly finished rubbing off each other's angles,' he reflected; but the worst of it was that May's pressure was already bearing on the very angles whose sharpness he most wanted to keep. *Wharton*

5 *A Bézier text box.*

1 *To draw with any **freehand** tool, drag with the mouse button down for as long as you want the line to last.*

2 *If you're using a **Freehand picture** or **text box** tool, when you're ready to close a box, release the mouse or drag back over the starting point.*

3 *With the **Freehand line** or **Freehand text path** tool, you can make little separate marks or one long, wiggly string. Release the mouse to end an open path. Alt-choose either tool if you want to draw multiple, separate lines without having to reselect the tool.*

If you like to draw in a freeform manner, try using one of the freehand Bézier tools. They lend themselves to natural subjects—flora and fauna—more than to geometric subjects. Keep your mouse button down for as long as you want the line to last.

To draw a freehand box, line, or text path:

1. Choose the Freehand picture box, Freehand line, Freehand text box, or Freehand text path tool.
2. Press and drag to draw a path. To close a freehand **box**, just release the mouse—the path will close automatically and a line segment will join the first and last points **1**–**3**. Or, move the pointer back over the starting point and release the mouse.

   To end a **line**, just release the mouse.

TIP If you want to trace a picture, import the picture into a picture box, lock the box so you don't accidentally move it, put it on its own layer using a layer XTension, and lighten it using Style menu > Contrast or by applying a light tint to it via the Colors palette.

To delete a Bézier item:

1. Choose the Item tool.
2. Select the path you want to delete, and make sure no individual points are selected.
3. Choose Item menu > Delete (Ctrl-K).

   or

   Press Delete or Backspace.

   or

   Right-click the item and chose Delete from the pop-up menu.

   Note: You can also delete an item with the Content tool using Item menu > Delete (Ctrl-K).

Freehand Béziers; Delete a Bézier

A continuous curve has no abrupt twists or turns, and the curve handles for a point on a continuous curve move in tandem in a straight line. (To create handles that move independently of each other, see the next page.)

To draw continuous Bézier curves:

1. Choose the Bézier picture box, Bézier line, Bézier text box, or Bézier text path tool.
2. Press and drag to create a point. The shape of the curve segment and the angle of the curve handles that control the segment will be defined by the length and direction in which you drag the mouse.
3. Release the mouse and reposition it away from the first point. Press and drag in the direction in which you want the curve to follow to create a second point **1**. The points will now be connected by a curved segment. Remember, you can always reshape the curves later on.
4. Drag to create additional points and handles or click to create additional corner points.
5. There are three ways to close a Bézier picture or text box: Choose another tool; double-click at the location where you want the last point to appear; or click once back on the starting point (you'll see a close box pointer) **2**.

   If you're using the Bézier line or Bézier text path tool, select another tool or double-click to create the last point to end—not close—the path. (To join the endpoints of a line or text path and thus produce a closed shape, see page 191.)

TWEAK AS YOU GO

To adjust an existing point or curve handle as you draw, Ctrl-drag the point or handle, then release Ctrl to resume drawing.

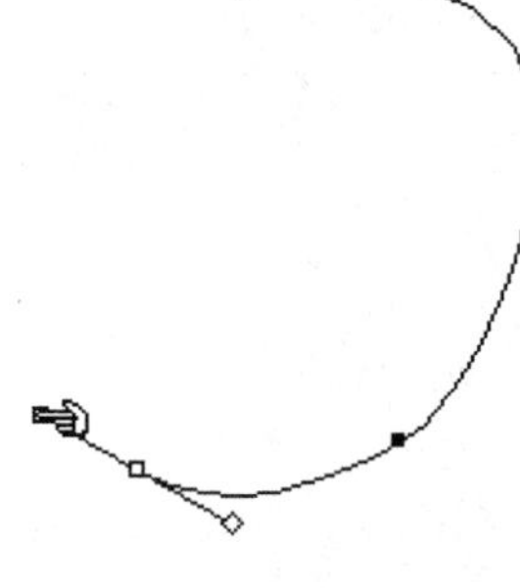

1 *To draw continuous curves, press and drag in the direction in which you want the curve to follow.*

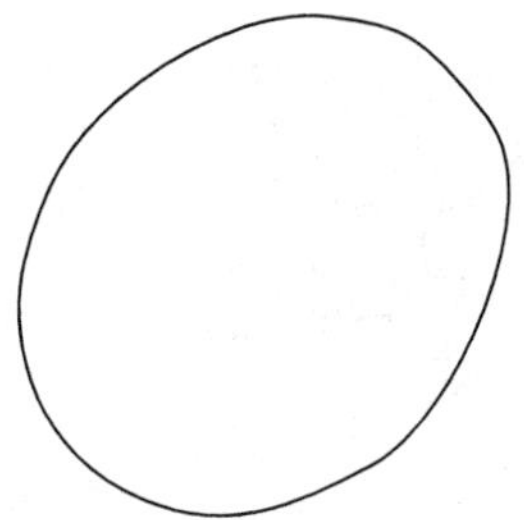

2 *The completed picture box.*

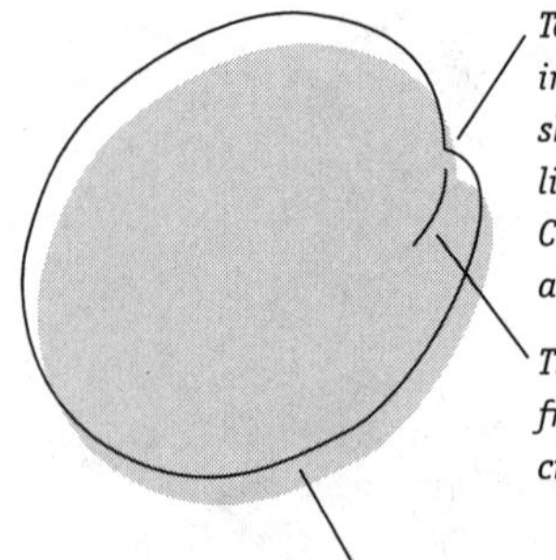

To pinch a curve inward to make the shape look more like an apricot, I Ctrl-Shift dragged a handle.

Then I added a freehand line to create a crease.

And finally, I duplicated the shape, removed the frame from the duplicate, applied a 10% black background, and sent it to the back (Shift-F5).

Continuous Curves

1 *If at any point while drawing a shape you want to pinch a curve, Ctrl-Shift-click one curve handle of the last created pair.*

2 *The handle disappears. Resume drawing the rest of the path.*

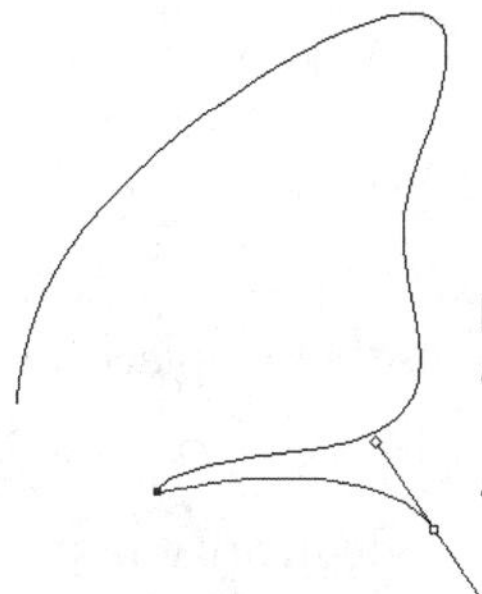

3 *In a pinched curve, two curved segments form a "v" shape rather than a smooth arc.*

On these pages I've broken down the drawing of straight, continuous, and pinched curves into separate instructions to make things as clear as possible. When you're actually drawing a shape, you'll more than likely use a combination of all these techniques—draw a straight segment, then a continuous curve, then another straight segment, then a pinched curve, and so on. Once you've mastered all three, go back and draw a puzzle piece, as illustrated on page 173.

To draw pinched curves:

1. Choose the Bézier picture box, Bézier line, Bézier text box, or Bézier text path tool.
2. Press and drag to create the first point.
3. Press and drag to create a second point **1**.
4. Ctrl-Alt click on the end of either of the last created curve handles (it will disappear) **2**.
5. To continue to draw non-continuous curves, repeat steps 3 and 4 **3**. You can, of course, also draw continuous curves (press and drag, but omit the Ctrl-Alt-click step) or straight segments (click without dragging).

TIP To pinch a point on a completed path, Ctrl-Shift-drag a curve handle.

HOW TO MAKE A POINT

If a smooth curve is your goal, the best place to place points is where a curve segment changes direction to meet another curve segment **4**, not at the peak of a curve **5**.

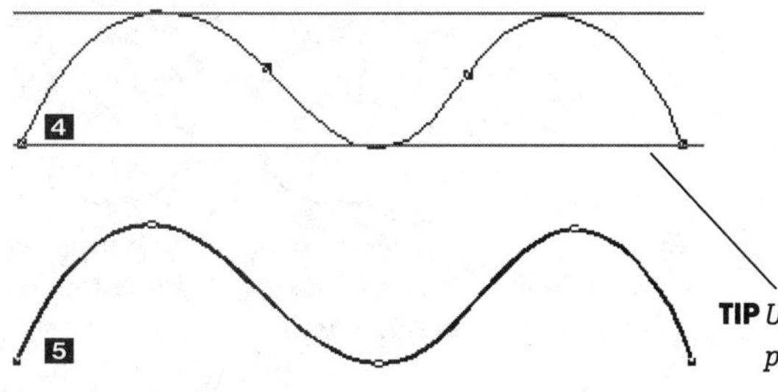

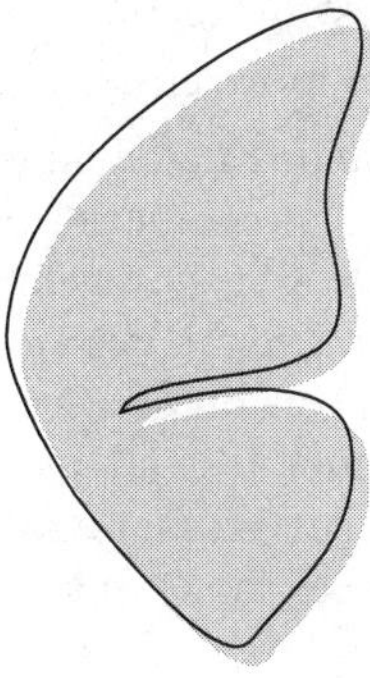

TIP *Use* ***guides*** *to place points symmetrically.*

It's not your imagination—shape conversion was discussed previously in this book. It's mentioned again here as a way to convert a standard box or line into a Bézier box or line.

To convert a standard box or line into a Bézier box or line:

1. Choose the Item or Content tool.
2. Select the item you want to convert.
3. Choose the freehand box icon from the Item menu > Shape submenu to convert the item into a closed Bézier box **1**–**3**. ***Note:*** See the tip on the next page before converting a standard line to a Bézier box. If you convert a standard oval into a Bézier box, the new Bézier box will have all corner points—not curve handles.

   or

   Choose the freehand line icon from the Item menu > Shape submenu to convert the item into a Bézier line. If you convert a text box into a line, you'll get an open path **4**. If you convert a picture box containing a picture into a line, you'll get a warning prompt. Click OK, and the picture will be deleted.

TIP If you convert a box into a line, one of the corner points of the box will be split into two points to form the line's two endpoints, and they will be positioned directly on top of each other (look in the lower-left corner). Select and move either point, if you like.

TIP The box that results from a standard oval box-to-Bézier box conversion may have an excessive number of points. Remove the extraneous points after the conversion **5**, or create the shape from scratch instead, using a Bézier tool. (A curved shape that's turned into a Bézier shape in a file that's converted from version 3.x to 4.0 will have many more points than are shown in my example.)

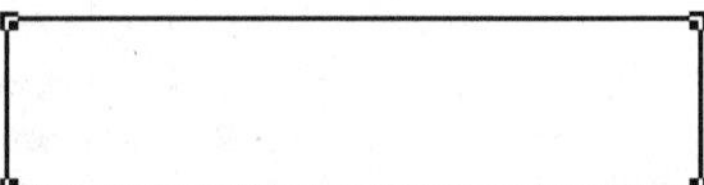
Education's purpose is to replace an empty mind with an open one.
—Malcolm S. Forbes

1 *A standard text box...*

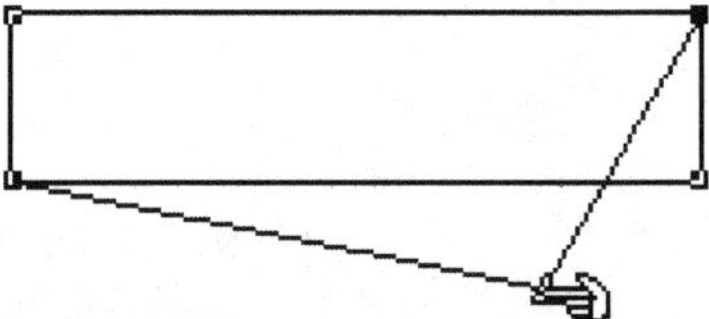

2 *...is converted into a Bézier box.*

3 *You can then reshape the Bézier box by any of the usual means: Drag a point or segment, convert a corner point to a smooth point, etc.*

Educa- tion's purpose is to replace an empty mind with an open one.

4 *If a standard text box is converted into a freehand line, an open text path is the result.*

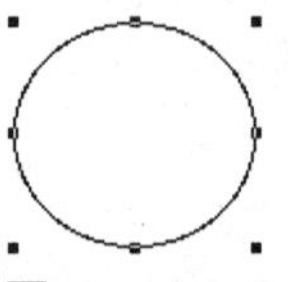

5 *The original standard oval text box.*

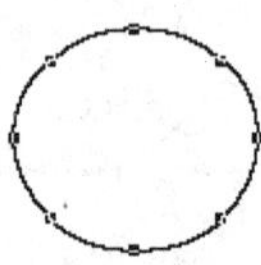

After it's converted into a Bézier box.

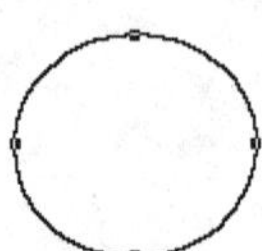

After removing four extraneous points.

TIP To convert a narrow line (less than 2 points wide) into a Bézier box, hold down Alt while choosing the freehand box shape 6–7. If you don't hold down Alt, you'll get a warning prompt 8. If you click OK, a very thin hollow line or lines will be created 9.

If the endpoints of a line are very close together or on top of each other and you choose the freehand box shape with Alt held down, the endpoints will be joined into a single point. Otherwise, they will be connected by a new line segment. Either way, a closed shape will be produced.

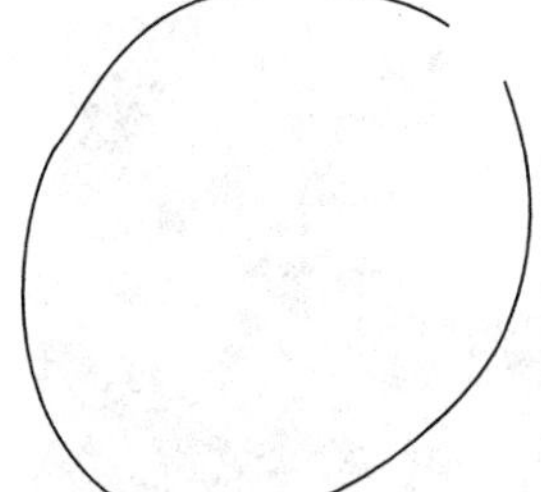

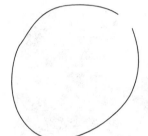

6 *A line with a .5 width is selected.*

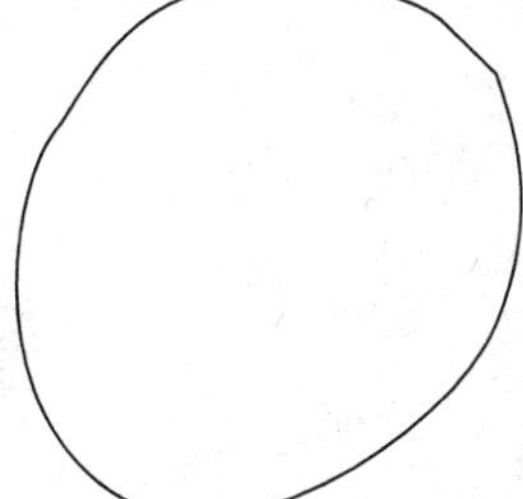

7 *After choosing the freehand box shape from the Item menu > Shape submenu with Alt held down, the line is converted into a closed shape. Its frame has the same width as the original line—.5 pt.*

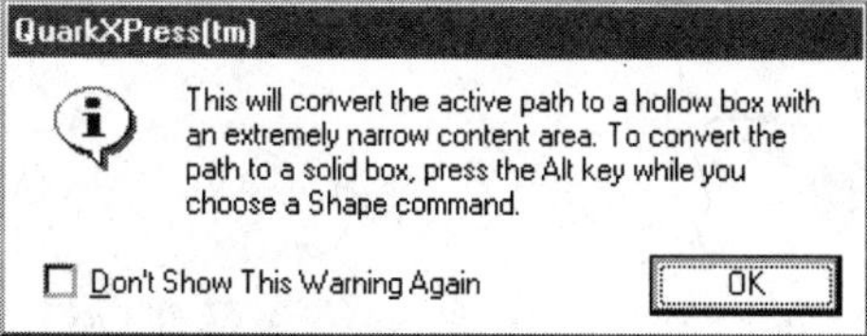

8 *This prompt will appear if you try to convert a narrow line into a freehand box.*

9 *If you choose the freehand box shape from the Item menu > Shape submenu without holding down Alt, you'll get a warning prompt. When you click OK, you'll get a very narrow box. You can choose Undo, if necessary.*

How to reshape a Bézier path

- Add or delete a point.
- Move a point or a segment.
- Rotate, lengthen, or shorten a curve handle to reshape a curve.
- Convert a point into a different type (symmetrical, smooth, or corner).
- Convert a curved segment into a straight segment (or vice versa).
- Move a handle of its bounding box.

First turn on path editing

If you want to manipulate the individual points, curve handles, or segments of a Bézier shape in order to reshape it, you must first turn on **Item** menu > **Edit** > **Shape** (**F10**—memorize this shortcut!) **1**. Turn this command off when you're finished reshaping so you don't inadvertently move a point or a segment.

To reshape or resize a whole path, turn off Item menu > Edit > Shape (re-choose the command), then drag one of the eight handles of its bounding box **2**.

1 *With Item menu > Edit > **Shape editing on**, a Bézier item's individual points and curve handles are accessible for reshaping.*

2 *With Item menu > Edit > **Shape editing off**, a Bézier item's outer bounding box and eight handles are visible.*

To add or delete a point:

1. Choose the Item or Content tool.
2. Alt-click a point to delete it **3**.
   or
   Alt-click a segment where you want a new point to appear **4**.

TIP If the Item tool is currently chosen, you can select the point or points you want to remove, then press Delete or Backspace. To select more than one point at a time, see "Get the points" on the next page.

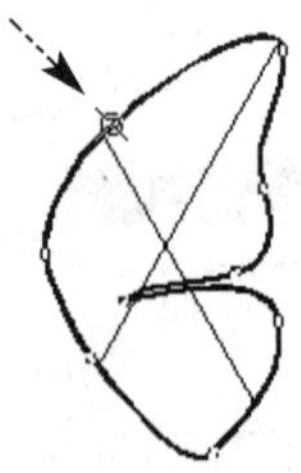

3 *Alt-click a point to delete it.*

The point is deleted.

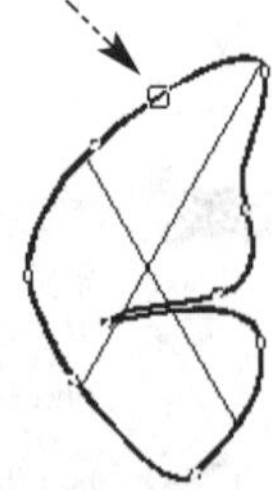

4 *Alt-click a segment to add a point.*

GET THE POINTS

Select all the points in an item	Double-click a point *or* click a point, then Ctrl-Shift-A
Select all the points in a merged item	Triple-click a point
Select multiple points individually	Shift-click a point
Select a segment's two connecting points	Click a segment

SPEED TIP

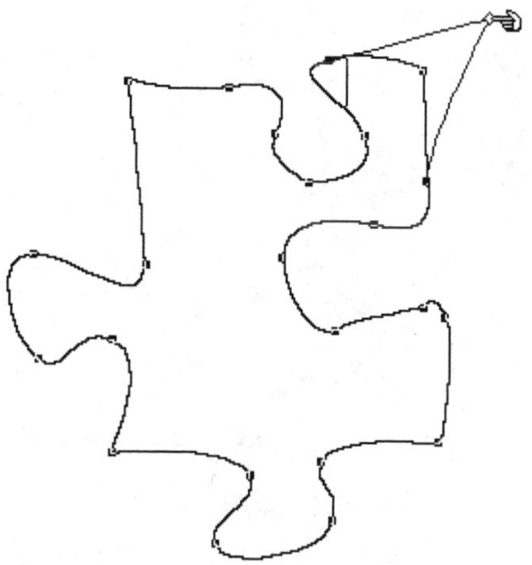

1 *To **move** a point, position the cursor over it, then press and drag.*

XP:	1.062"	⊿	-135	⊿	45
YP:	2.361"	◇	0.314"	□	0.314"

2 *Enter a new **XP** and/or **YP** location on the Measurements palette to reposition the currently selected point or points.*

To move a point:

1. Choose the Item or Content tool.
2. Click on the path to select it.
3. Position the cursor over a point (the cursor will change into a pointing finger with a little black square), then drag the point to reposition it **1**.
   or
   Click on the point to select it, then press an arrow key on the keyboard. (This works with the Item tool only, and constrains the movement of the point to the horizontal or vertical axis.)
   or
   Click on the point to select it, then enter the desired horizontal location in the XP field on the Measurements palette and/or the desired vertical location in the YP field **2**.

TIP To move multiple anchor points, use one of the shortcuts listed at left, then use a method in step 3, above. Entering a number in the XP or YP field will position all the currently selected points at the same XP or YP location.

To move a whole Bézier item:

1. Choose the Item tool. Or hold down Ctrl to move an item if the Content tool is selected.
2. Press inside a box, then drag. If Live Refresh is turned on in Edit menu > Preferences > Application > Interactive folder tab and you pause before dragging (wait for the cluster of arrows pointer to appear), the item's contents will display as you drag it.
   or
   To move a line or a text path, click on the line first to select it, position the pointer slightly off the line, then drag.

To move control handles to reshape a curve:

1. Choose the Item or Content tool.
2. Select a point on a curve segment **1**.
3. Press and drag a curve handle toward or away from the point to change the height of the curve **2**. The angle of a handle affects the slope of the curve into the point. The handles on a smooth point move in tandem, but can be different in length. The pair of handles on a symmetrical point move in tandem and are always equal in length.
   or
   Rotate the handle around the point **3**.
   or
   On the Measurements palette, enter a number in the angle field for the diamond-shaped curve handle or in the angle field for the square-shaped curve handle **4**.
   or
   On the Measurements palette, enter a position in the distance field for the diamond-shaped curve handle or in the distance field for the square-shaped curve handle to adjust the distance from the point to that handle **5**. To make the handles of equal length, enter the same number in both fields **6**.

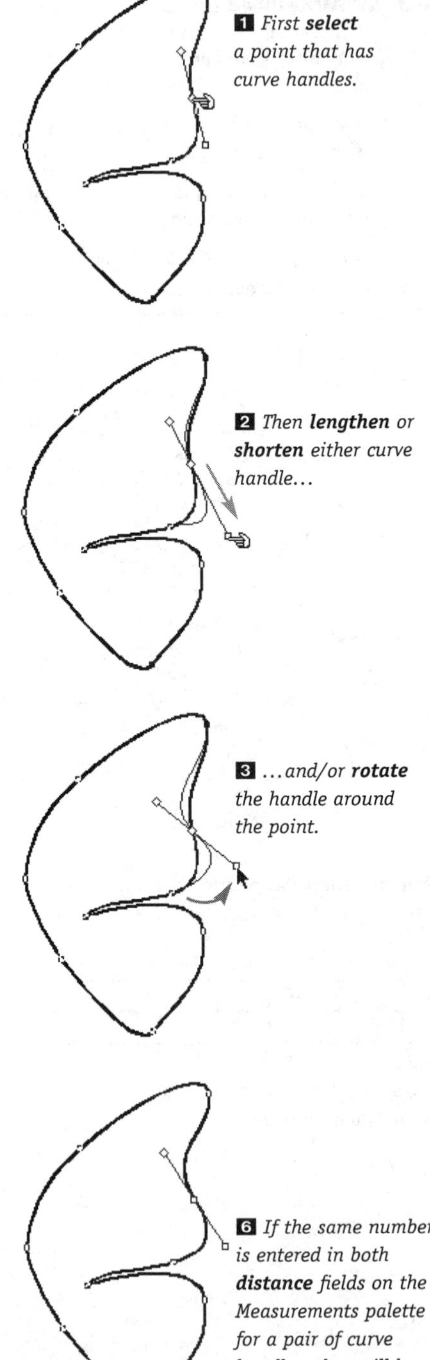

1 *First **select** a point that has curve handles.*

2 *Then **lengthen** or **shorten** either curve handle…*

3 *…and/or **rotate** the handle around the point.*

6 *If the same number is entered in both **distance** fields on the Measurements palette for a pair of curve handles, they will be **equal** in **length**.*

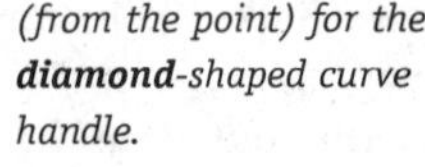

4 *Enter a new **angle** for the **diamond**-shaped curve handle.*

*Or enter a new **angle** for the **square**-shaped curve handle.*

5 *Enter a new **distance** (from the point) for the **diamond**-shaped curve handle.*

*Or enter a new **distance** (from the point) for the **square**-shaped curve handle.*

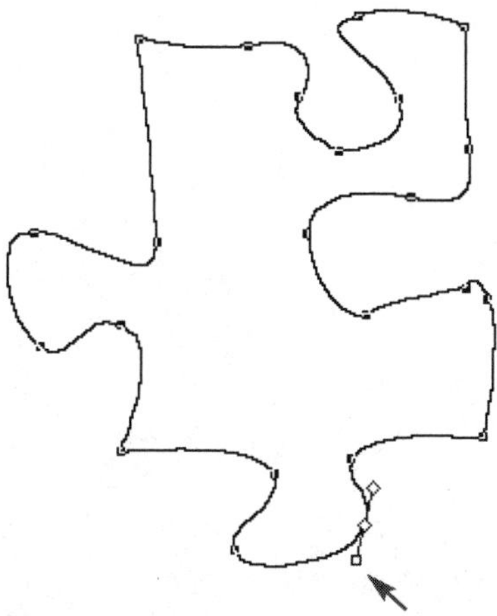

■1 *Click on the point to select it, then* ***Alt****-click a curve handle.*

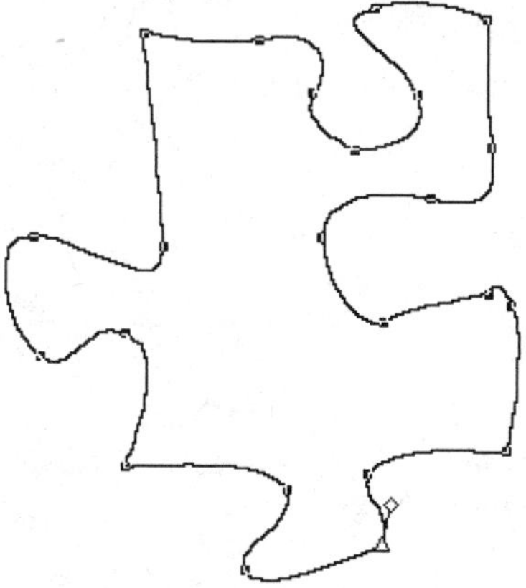

■2 *The handle disappears.*

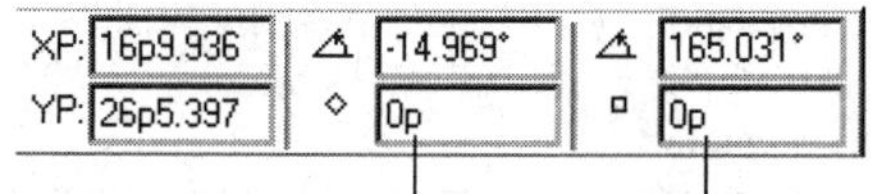

XP:	16p9.936	⦣	-14.969°	⦣	165.031°
YP:	26p5.397	◇	0p	□	0p

■3 *Enter* ***0*** *in the* ***distance*** *field for the diamond-shaped or square-shaped curve handle.*

When you retract a curve handle, it disappears and the curve becomes pinched.

To retract one curve handle:

1. Choose the Item or Content tool.
2. Select a point on a curve segment.
3. Alt-click a curve handle ■1. The handle disappears ■2.

   or

   On the Measurements palette, enter 0 in the distance field for the diamond-shaped or square-shaped handle ■3.

TIP To pinch a curve as you draw a path, Ctrl-Alt click one of the curve handles in the last created pair.

TIP To restore a retracted curve handle, select the point, then click the Symmetrical or Smooth point icon on the Measurements palette.

TIP To retract both curve handles, Ctrl-Shift-click the point. To expose them again, Ctrl-Shift-drag a point.

To reshape a segment by dragging:

1. Choose the Item or Content tool.
2. Click on the box, line, or text path to select it.
3. Drag a straight segment. The anchor points that touch it will move with it **1**.
   or
   Drag a curve segment. Only the curve will move, not its connecting points **2**.

   Note: If Live Refresh is turned on in Edit menu > Preferences > Application > Interactive folder tab and you pause before dragging a segment, the shape will redraw instantly as you drag. If you drag without pausing first, regardless of whether Live Refresh is on or not, the new shape will preview as you drag a segment, so you can compare it with the original shape.

TIP Hold down Shift while dragging to constrain the movement to 0°, 45°, or 90°.

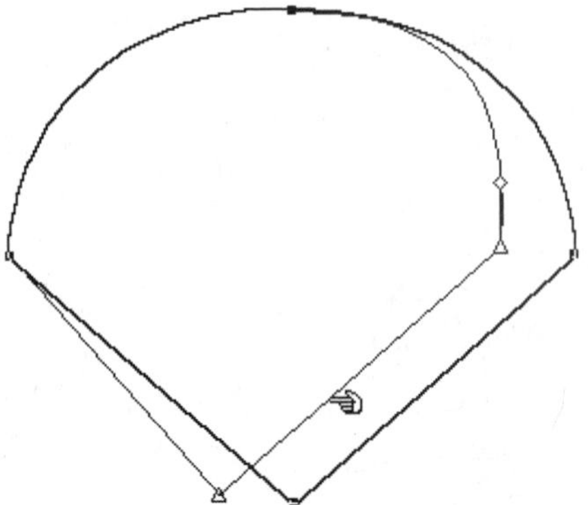

1 *If you drag a **straight** segment, the segment **and** its connecting points will move.*

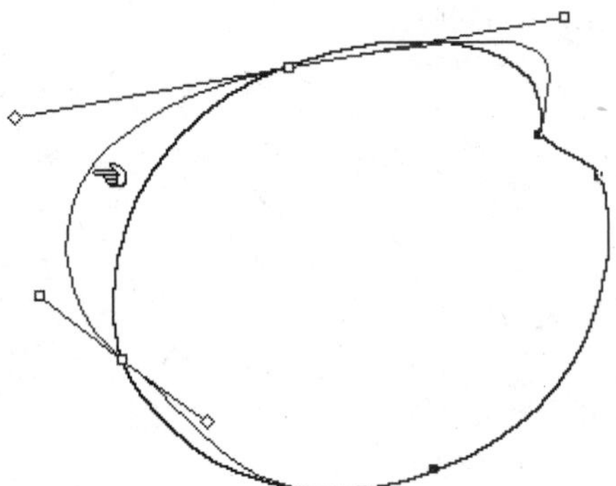

2 *If you drag a **curve** segment, only the curve will move—**not** its connecting points.*

SCALE THE HEIGHTS

To resize an item by a percentage, rather than manually, use the ResizeXT XTension from Vision's Edge, Inc.

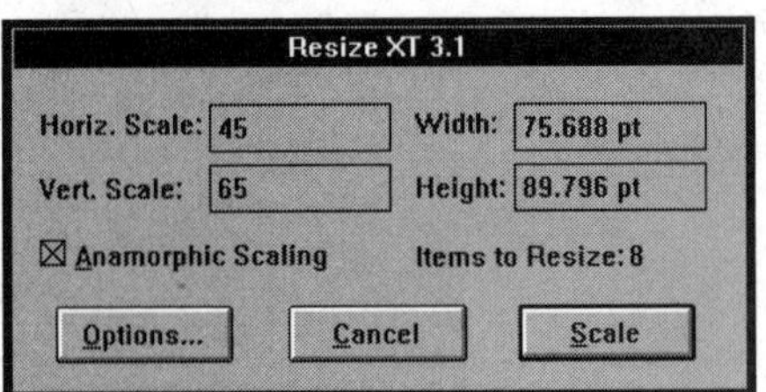

*The **ResizeXT** dialog box.*

CONVERT A SEGMENT

To straight	Select segment, then Alt-Shift-F1
To curve	Select segment, then Alt-Shift-F2

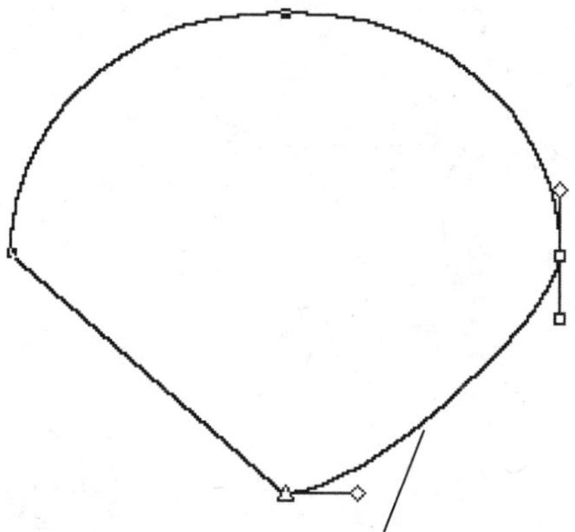

1 *A **curve** segment is selected.*

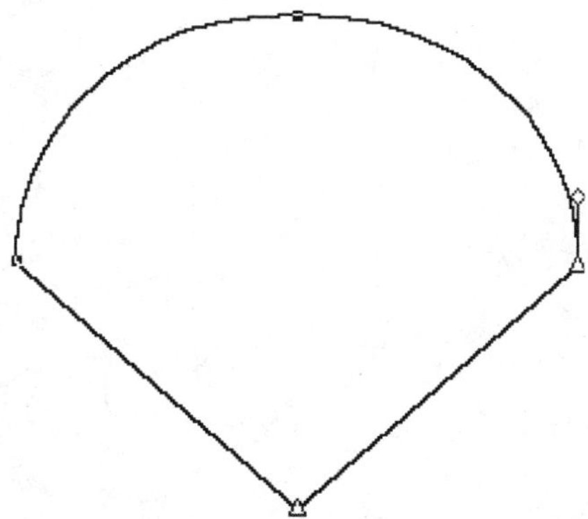

2 *After clicking the **Straight** segment button on the Measurements palette, the curve segment is converted into a straight segment.*

WHOLESALE CONVERSION

To convert all the points and segments on a path into curves or straights, double-click a point to select all the points and segments on the path, then click the Straight or Curve segment button on the Measurements palette.

Use buttons on the Measurements palette to convert a curve segment into a straight segment, or vice versa, in an existing box, line, or text path. Easy.

To convert a curve segment into a straight segment, or vice versa:

1. Choose the Item or Content tool.
2. Click on the box or line to select it, then click on the segment that you want to convert (make sure its points are selected) **1**.
3. Click the Straight segment button on the Measurements palette (Ctrl-Shift-F1). A curve handle on each of the two points that are adjacent to the segment will disappear **2**.
   or
   Click the Curve segment button on the Measurements palette (Ctrl-Shift-2). A curve handle will appear on each of the two points that are adjacent to the segment.

TIP You can also convert a segment by selecting it and then choosing Item menu > Point/Segment Type > Straight Segment or Curved Segment.

To change a point's style:

1. Choose the Item or Content tool.
2. Select one or more anchor points.
3. On the Measurements palette:
   Click the Corner button (Ctrl-F1). Corner point handles can be rotated or lengthened/shortened independently of each other. Choose this option to pinch a curve **1**.
   or
   Click the Smooth button (Ctrl-F2). Smooth point handles can be of different lengths, but they always remain in a straight-line relationship. The curve will be smooth **2**.
   or
   Click the Symmetrical button (Ctrl-F3). Symmetrical curve handles always work in tandem and are always of equal length **3**.

TIP You can also convert a point by selecting it and then choosing Item menu > Point/Segment Type > Corner Point, Smooth Point, or Symmetrical Point.

CHANGING THE POINT

To corner	Select point, then Ctrl-F1
To smooth	Select point, then Ctrl-F2
To symmetrical	Select point, then Ctrl-F3
Smooth/corner toggle	Ctrl-Shift-drag a handle

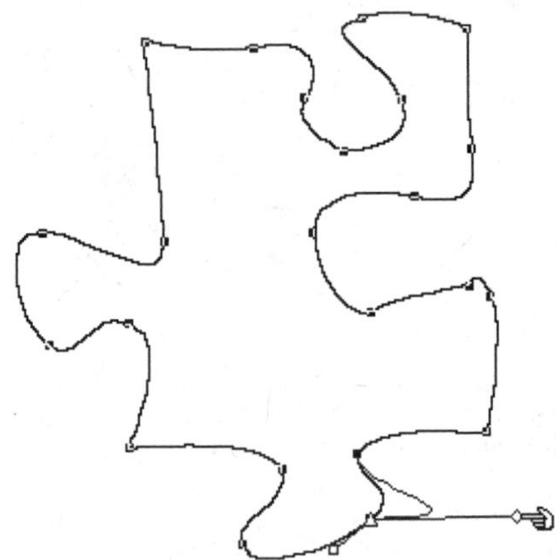

1 *In a **Corner** point, the handles move **independently** of each other.*

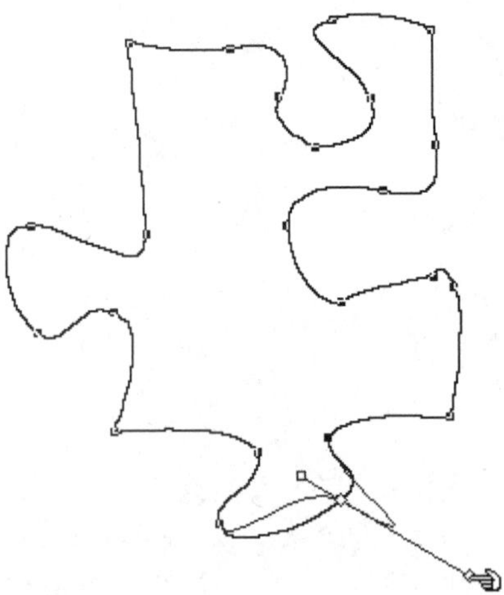

2 *In a **Smooth** point, the handles always stay in a **straight-line** relationship, but they can be of **different lengths**.*

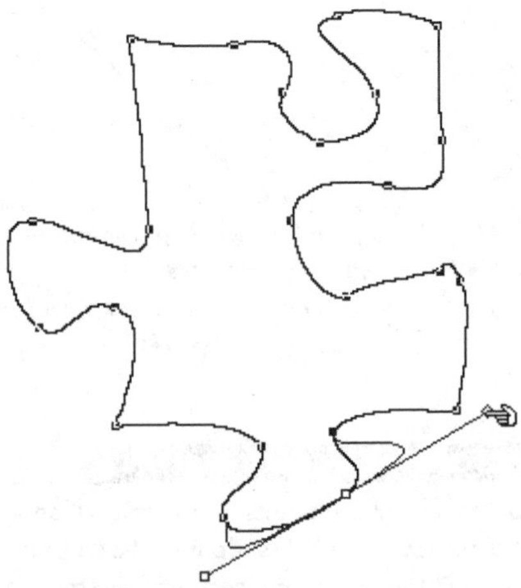

3 *In a **Symmetrical** point, the handles always stay in a **straight-line** relationship and are always of **equal length**.*

1 *With Shape editing turned off, an item has a bounding box with eight handles.*

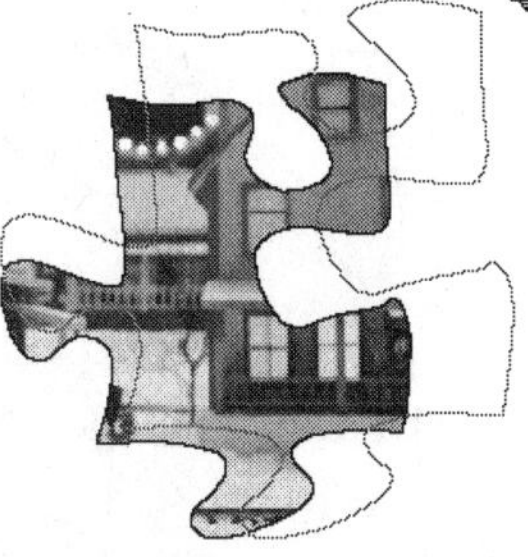

2 *Alt-Shift drag or Ctrl-Alt-Shift drag a handle of an item's bounding box.*

3 ***Alt-Shift*** *drag a handle of the bounding box to resize the* ***item only****—not its contents.*

4 ***Ctrl-Alt-Shift*** *drag a handle of the bounding box to resize the* ***item and*** *its* ***contents****, if any.*

To resize a whole Bézier box, line, or text path:

1. Choose the Item or Content tool.
2. Make sure Item menu > Edit > Shape is turned off (F10).
3. Click on the Bézier box, line, or text path **1**.
4. To resize the item proportionally, but not its contents, if any (picture or text), Alt-Shift-drag one of the handles of its bounding box **2**–**3**.
   or
   To resize the item *and* its contents (if any) proportionally, Ctrl-Alt-Shift-drag a handle **4**.
   or
   To resize the item proportionally, but not its contents, enter a new number in the W and/or H field on the Measurements palette **5**. Or use the Ctrl-M shortcut to open the Modify dialog box (or right-click and choose Modify), click the Box folder tab, then enter numbers in the Width and/or Height fields.

TIP If you resize a Bézier shape, unless it's part of a group, the width of any applied frame won't change. Use the Item menu > Frame dialog box to adjust the frame width, if desired. If you resize a group containing a Bézier with Ctrl, Alt, and Shift held down, the frame width will adjust accordingly.

X: 1.773" W: 12p
Y: 1.984" H: 1.63"

5 *To resize a Bézier numerically, enter a new number in the* ***W*** *and/or* ***H*** *field on the Measurements palette.*

The powerful Merge commands can be used to build a complex shape from two or more individual shapes. All the Merge commands produce a single Bézier shape. In all cases, the final shape will have the color attributes and contents of the original backmost item, including any text, picture, or background color that it contained.

To merge two or more items:

1. Choose the Item or Content tool.
2. Select two or more items. An item can be a line, box, or text path. If you're going to apply any Merge command except Union, arrange them so they at least partially overlap.
3. Choose Item menu > Merge.
4. Choose one of the following:

   UNION

   All items are combined into one overall new item. Items don't have to overlap for the Union effect to work. Use this option to create a complex item from a combination of simple items **1**.

   DIFFERENCE

   Only the backmost item will remain. All items above the backmost item are deleted. Parts of any item that are on top of and overlap the backmost item are cut out of the backmost item **2**.

   INTERSECTION

   Any part of an item that overlaps the backmost item will be preserved; parts of items that don't overlap the backmost item are cut away. If you copy the backmost item and place it behind other items, you can then use the Intersection option to trim away (clip) parts of the upper items that extend beyond the backmost item **3**.

   REVERSE DIFFERENCE

   The backmost item is deleted. Items above the former backmost item are united, and only parts of those items that overlapped the backmost item are cut out of the resulting item. Use this

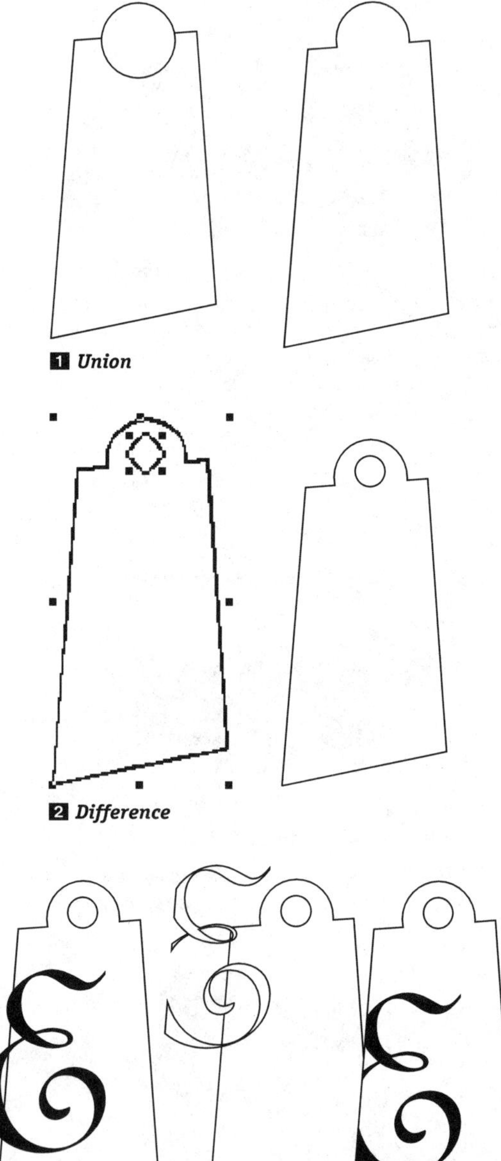

1 ***Union***

2 ***Difference***

3 ***Intersection.*** *To produce this picture, the background (hangtag) shape was duplicated and set aside. A letter was turned into a box (Style menu > Text to Box) and positioned on top of the hangtag. The Intersection command produced the cropped letter shape, which was then filled with black and placed on top of the duplicate hangtag shape.*

Merge Commands

option when you want to produce a shape from items that extend beyond the edge of the backmost item.

EXCLUSIVE OR

All items are combined into one new item. Any areas that overlap the backmost item are cut out from the resulting item. The corners of the cutout areas will have two sets of points—one to control the edge of the cutout item (the hole) and one to control the edge of the background item. Use to create unusual contour shapes on an item and cutout areas on the backmost item. The cutout can be reshaped separately from other parts of the item.

COMBINE

Like Exclusive Or, except that extra points aren't added to the corners of the cutout areas, so you can't adjust the corners of the cutout shapes unless you add corner points.

Note: Difference, Exclusive Or, and Combine will produce the same results if the original overlapping items do not extend beyond the edge of the backmost item.

JOIN ENDPOINTS

The Join Endpoints command **4** will join a pair of endpoints of two separate text paths (but not boxes, since they have no endpoints) at a time—as long as the points for each pair are positioned near each other. The endpoints will join into one point, and the resulting line will take on the attributes/characteristics (style, weight, color, etc.) of the backmost line. The distance between two endpoints within which the Join Endpoints command works is specified in the Snap Distance field in Edit menu > Preferences > Document > General folder tab.

4 *The gap between two freehand lines is joined using the* ***Join Endpoints*** *command.*

The Text to Box command converts a copy of one or more standard text characters into a single Bézier picture box. What's more, you can make this conversion and anchor the new Bézier box into its text block—all in one fell swoop!

The new Bézier box can be filled with a color, a gradient, or a picture; it can be converted into a text box and filled with text; or it can be reshaped using any of the techniques that were previously discussed in this chapter.

To convert text characters into a Bézier picture box:

1. Choose the Content tool.
2. Highlight the characters that you want to convert **1** (no more than one line). The larger and fatter, the better.
3. Choose Style menu > Text to Box. A duplicate of the text will be converted into a single picture box **2**–**4**.
   or
   To convert the text into a picture box and *anchor* it in its current location in the text, hold down Alt and choose Style menu > Text to Box. More about anchored boxes on pages 127–129.

TIP To change the content of the newly created picture box, choose Item menu > Content > Text (to enter text inside the lettershapes), or None (to fill the letter shapes with color only).

1 *The original characters.*

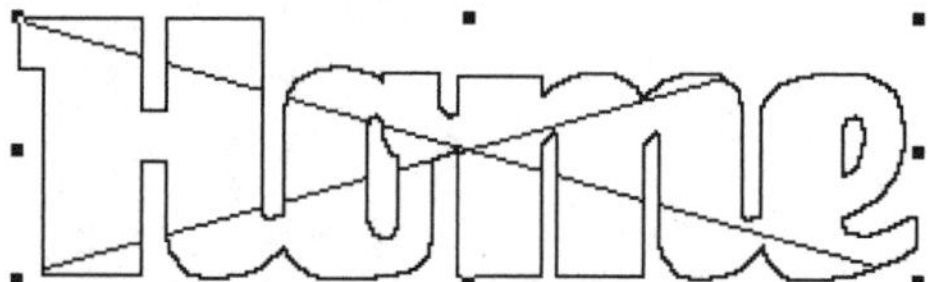

2 *After choosing Style menu > Text to Box, a copy of the characters are converted into a single Bézier picture box.*

3 *To apply an outline to the newly created picture box, use the Item menu > Frame command. You can even use a custom dash or stripe style. You can also fill the box with a picture, a flat color, or a gradient.*

4 *And, like any Bézier box, you can reshape it.*

■1 *The original picture box (from the FuturaStencil font).*

■2 *After choosing Item menu > Split >* ***Outside Paths****, the box is broken down into separate, individual items. Each stand-alone item can be filled with a different picture, repositioned, reshaped, or recolored.*

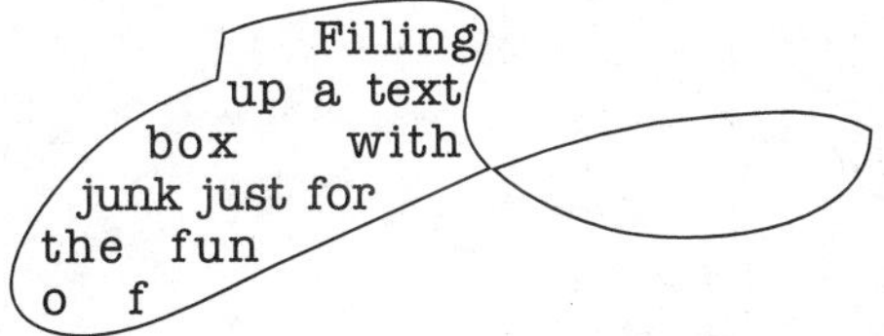

■3 *The original text box, with a criss-cross in it.*

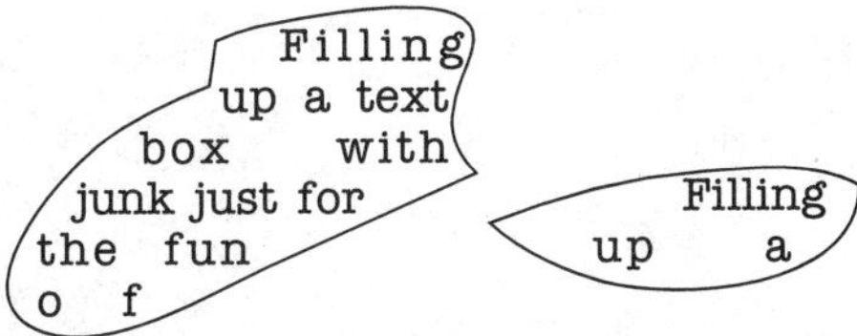

■4 *After choosing the Split > Outside Paths command, the box is divided in two (moved apart just to illustrate). The same text automatically fills both boxes.*

The Split command is really an un-merge command. It divides a text-to-box item or an item merged via the Combine or Exclusive Or command into individual, separate items. It can also be used to split up a complex box that contains paths within paths or a box whose border criss-crosses itself. Once an item is split, each component can be manipulated or recolored individually.

If you split a box that was created using the Text to Box command into separate paths, you can then select and recolor each letter individually. You can fill each of them with a different picture, or you can reshape each individual letter to create a custom character. Start with a box that was created from more than one letter.

To split a merged or text-to-box item:

1. Choose the Item or Content tool.
2. Select a complex (merged) item.
3. Choose Item menu > Split > Outside Paths to split only outside paths, not any paths contained within them ■1–■4.
   or
   Choose Item menu > Split > All Paths to split all of an item's paths, including any interior paths ■5–■6. If you apply this to Text to Box lettershapes, any counter (hole) within a letter will become a separate shape (as in an "O" or a "P"), which then can be treated as a separate item.

TYPE INSIDE TYPE

To type inside type, highlight text in a chunky font, choose Style menu > Text to Box, choose Item menu > Content > Text, then enter text. Before turning on Run Text Around All Sides, the text only wraps on one side of the interior oval ■5. To produce figure ■6, the Run Text Around All Sides box was checked in Item menu > Modify > Text folder tab.

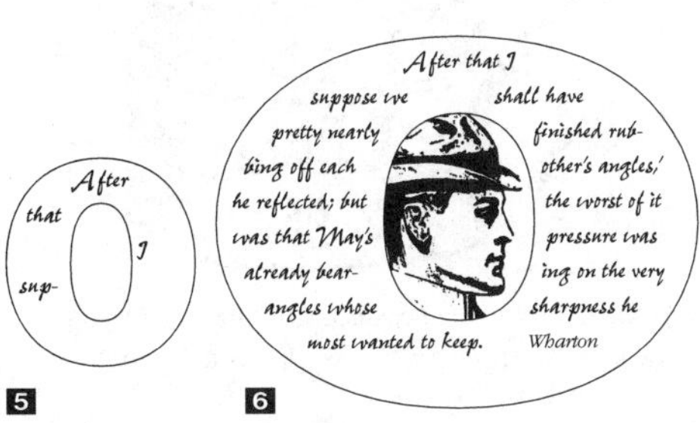

■5 ■6

Another way to produce a text path is by converting an existing line. For this, you can use a line that was created using the Orthogonal line, Line, Bézier line, or Freehand line tool. Other conversion methods are discussed on the next page.

To convert a line into a text path:

1. Choose the Item or Content tool.
2. Select the line **1**.
3. Choose Item menu > Content > Text.
4. Choose the Content tool, if necessary, then type, paste, or import text onto the path **2**.

1 *Select a line, then choose Item menu > Content > Text.*

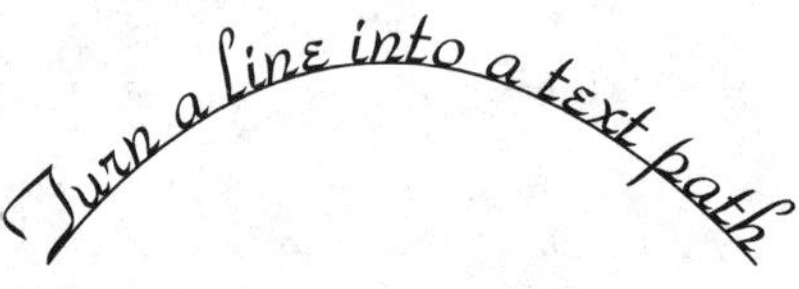

2 *The line becomes a text path.*

Reversed text on a path

I converted a round text box into a freehand line, made the path 100% black and very wide in Item > Modify > Line folder tab, created white type, and in the Item > Modify > Text Path folder tab, chose Align Text: Descent and Align with Line: Bottom.

Tip for drawing text paths

Try not to create acute concave angles when you draw a text path—the letters will bunch together and be unreadable.

Try to draw smooth, shallow curves instead.

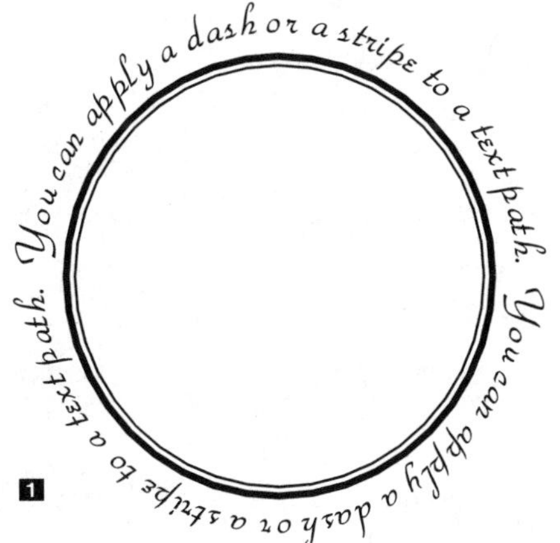

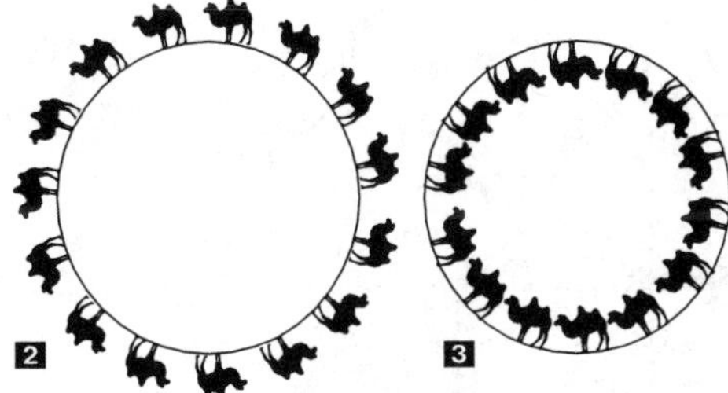

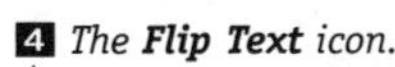

4 *The **Flip Text** icon.*

Other things you can do with a text path

To **Recolor** a text path, select it with the Item tool and use the Style menu > Color and Shade submenus. Or select it with the Item or Content tool and use the Colors palette (line color icon). If you don't want the path to show at all, click the line color icon, then click **None**. Recoloring a path has no effect on the text that's on it.

To change the **width** and other attributes of a text path: Select it using the Item tool, then choose attributes from the Style menu or the Item menu > Modify > Line folder tab (right-click and choose Modify > Line folder tab). You can apply any dash or stripe style to a text path **1**.

Change **text attributes** as you would text in a box: Select it using the Content tool and choose attributes from the Style menu or the right side of the Measurements palette.

To **flip** text to the opposite side of a path, click on the path with the Content tool, then click the Flip Text button on the Measurements palette **2**–**4** or choose Style menu > Flip Text. Or click on the path with the Item or Content tool, then check or uncheck the Flip Text box in Item menu > Modify > Text Path folder tab.

To turn a text **box** into a **text path**, select the box, then choose the Line (straight diagonal) icon or Orthogonal line (straight vertical) icon from the Item menu > Shape submenu. An open text path will be created on that angle **5**. If you choose the Bézier line (wiggly line) icon instead, a path will be created in the shape of the original box **6**.

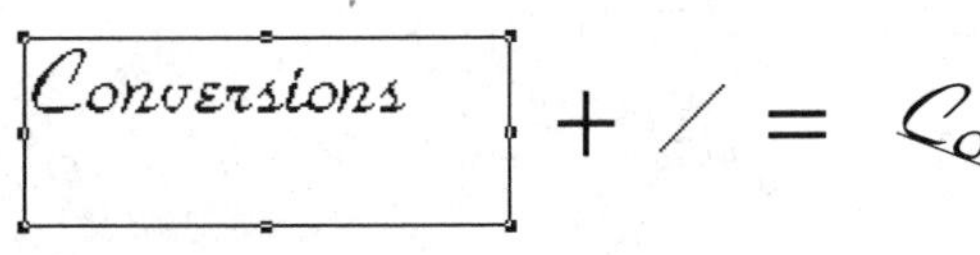

5 *Convert a text box into a text path by choosing the Line icon from the Item menu > Shape submenu.*

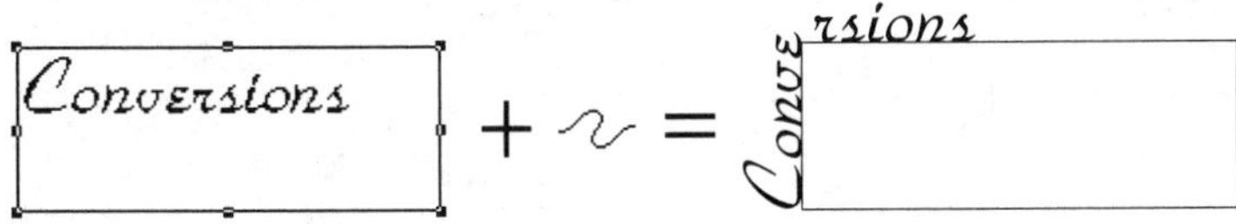

6 *Or convert a text box into a text path by choosing the Bézier line icon from the Item menu > Shape submenu.*

To change the orientation of text on a curvy path:

1. Choose the Item or Content tool.
2. Click on the text path.
3. Choose Item menu > Modify (Ctrl-M) or right-click and choose Modify, and click the Text Path folder tab.
4. Click one of the four Text Orientation buttons **1**.
5. Click Apply to preview.
6. Click OK or press Enter.

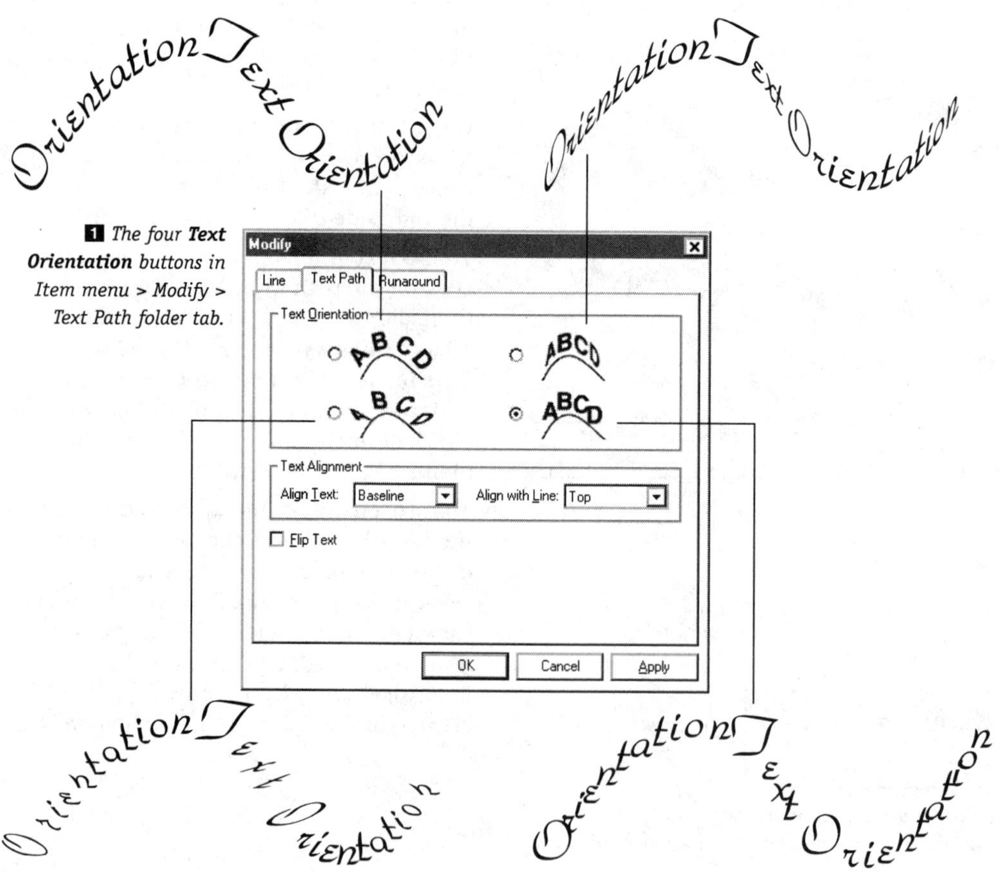

1 *The four* ***Text Orientation*** *buttons in Item menu > Modify > Text Path folder tab.*

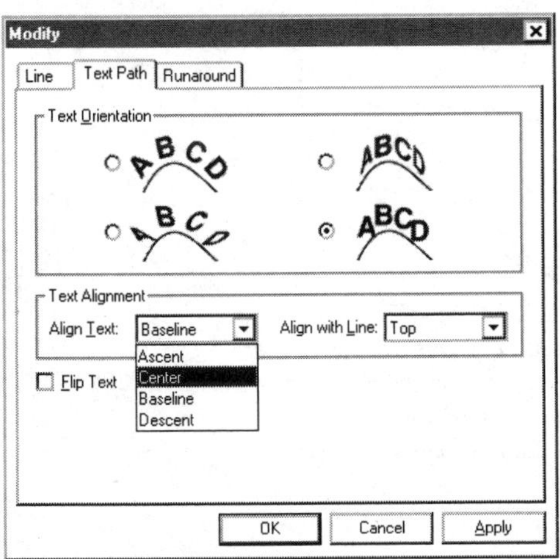

1 *The **Text Alignment: Align Text** and **Align with Line** drop-down menus in Item menu > Modify > Text Path folder tab.*

To raise or lower text on its path:

1. Choose the Item or Content tool.
2. Click on the text path.
3. Choose Item menu > Modify (Ctrl-M), and click the Text Path folder tab.
4. Choose Align Text: Ascent, Center, Baseline, or Descent **1**–**3** (the part of the text that touches the path).
5. Choose Align with Line: Top, Center, or Bottom (the part of path the text connects to). The wider the path, the more dramatic the shift.
6. Click Apply to preview.
7. Click OK or press Enter.

TIP You can use the Baseline Shift feature to further raise or lower text on a path.

2

Align text

*Align Text **Ascent**.*

Align text

*Align Text **Center**.*

Align text

*Align Text **Baseline**.*

Align text

*Align Text **Descent**.*

3

Align text

*Align with Line: **Top**.*

Align text

*Align with Line: **Center**.*

Align text

*Align with Line: **Bottom**.*

To flip a box:

1. *Optional:* To create a mirror image, duplicate the box (Ctrl-D) before you flip it.
2. Choose the Item or Content tool.
3. Click on the item, and turn off Item menu > Edit > Shape (F10).
4. So you'll be able to restore the original dimensions to the box after it's flipped, on the Measurements palette, highlight the W or H field, depending on which way you want to flip the box—horizontally (W field) or vertically (H field)—and copy the current value (Ctrl-C).
5. If you copied the W field, drag a side midpoint handle all the way across the item to the other side **1**–**2**. Drag the top or bottom midpoint handle if the H field was copied.
6. Re-highlight the field that was chosen for step 3 above, paste (Ctrl-V), then press Enter **3**.

TIP To flip the *contents* of a selected box, Choose Style menu > Flip or click the right-pointing or upward-pointing arrow on the Measurements palette **4**.

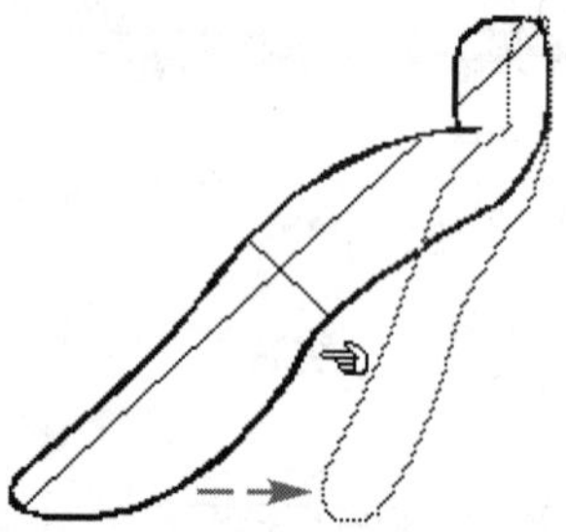

1 *After copying the item's width or height from the Measurements palette, drag a midpoint handle all the way across the shape.*

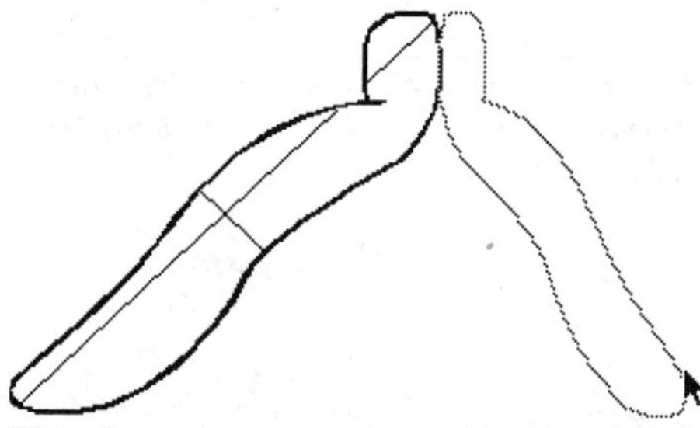

2 *Continue dragging to the opposite side.*

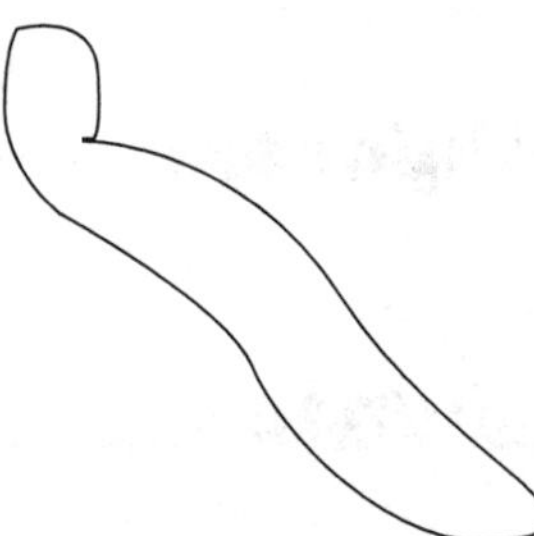

3 *Click in the Width or Height field on the Measurements palette (whichever you copied from),* ***paste*** *(Ctrl-V), then press Enter.*

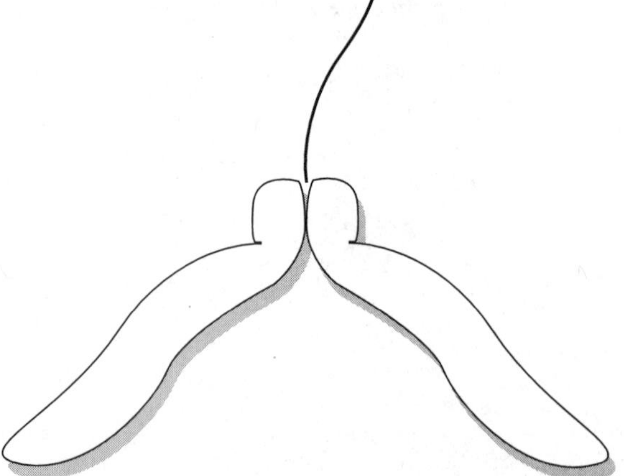

Flip Horizontal.

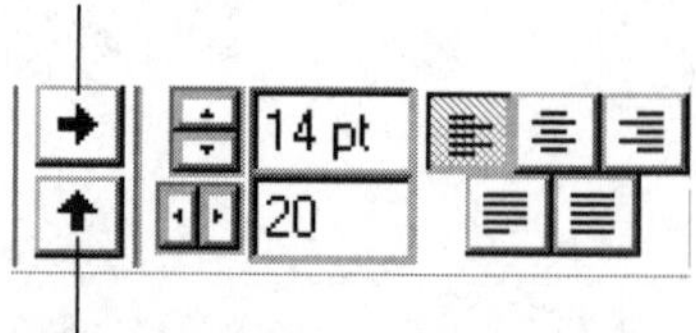

4 ***Flip Vertical.***

Flip a Box

Style sheets 13

Style sheets

A style sheet is a set of paragraph or character formatting specifications that can be applied to highlighted text via a user-assigned shortcut or by clicking the style sheet name on the Style Sheets palette. If a style sheet is modified, all paragraphs or text blocks to which it was previously applied will reformat instantly. A document can contain up to 1,000 style sheets.

I'm surprised when I encounter a long-time QuarkXPress user who doesn't use style sheets. Style sheets save zillions of man hours of tedious styling and restyling, and they ensure typgraphic consistency on a document-wide and project-wide basis. Whether you're working on a one-page letter or a massive catalogue, you can take advantage of this tremendous time-saver.

A headline style.

THE BILL OF RIGHTS

AMENDMENT I

Religious establishment prohibited. Freedom of speech, of the press, and right to petition

Congress shall make no law respecting an establishment of religion, or prohibiting the free exercise thereof; or abridging the freedom of speech, or of the press; or the right of the people peaceably to assemble, and to petition the Government for a redress of grievances.

AMENDMENT II

Right to keep and bear arms

A well-regulated militia, being necessary to the security of a free State, the right of the people to keep and bear arms, shall not be infringed.

AMENDMENT III — *A subhead style.*

Conditions for quarters for soldiers — *A small subhead style.*

No soldier shall, in time of peace be quartered in any house, without the consent of the owner, nor in time of war, but in a manner to be prescribed by law. — *A body text style.*

AMENDMENT IV

Right of search and seizure regulated

The right of the people to be secure in their persons, houses, papers, and effects, against unreasonable searches and seizures, shall not be violated, and no warrants shall issue, but upon probable cause, supported by oath or affirmation, and particularly describing the place to be searched, and the persons or things to be seized.

Prevent carpal tunnel syndrome: Use style sheets to apply repetitive type specifications quickly. ***Paragraph*** *style sheets are used in this illustration. A* ***character*** *style sheet is illustrated on the next page.*

Every new paragraph style sheet automatically has a default character style sheet associated with it that defines its character attributes. You can also create independent character style sheets **1**. If you're unsure of the difference between paragraph and character style sheets, see "What's the difference?" on the next page and study the illustrations on page 206.

To create a new style sheet:

1. For a paragraph style sheet, highlight either the first word of, or an entire paragraph, and apply any character or paragraph attributes, such as font, point size, type style, color, horizontal scaling, tracking, indents, leading, space after, H&J, horizontal alignment, tabs, rules, etc. that you want to be part of the style sheet. I'll refer to this as the "sample" paragraph.
   or
   For a character style sheet, highlight and style a word or a string of words.
2. With the paragraph or text string still highlighted, choose Edit menu > Style Sheets (Shift-F11), then choose New: Paragraph or Character **2**. Or click the word "New" to create a paragraph style.
   or
   Right-click on a paragraph or character style sheet name on the Style Sheets palette and choose New from the pop-up menu **3**.
3. Enter as descriptive a name as you can think of for the new style sheet in the Name field (**4**, next page).
4. *Optional:* Press Tab to move the cursor to the Keyboard Equivalent field, then press a number on the keypad alone or with the Ctrl key down.
5. *Optional:* To apply successive paragraph style sheets automatically as you input text, you can chain one style sheet to another. To do this, choose from the Next Style drop-down menu. When you enter a paragraph return as you input

> **"It is a very odd thing that Ribby's pie was not in the oven when I put mine in! And I can't find it anywhere; I have looked all over the house. I put my pie into a nice hot oven at the top. I could not turn any of the other handles; I think that they are all shams," said Duchess, "but I wish I could have removed the pie made of mouse! I cannot think what she has done with it? I heard Ribby coming and I had to run out by the back door!"** *Beatrix Potter*

1 *A character style sheet was used to style the words "not" and "my."*

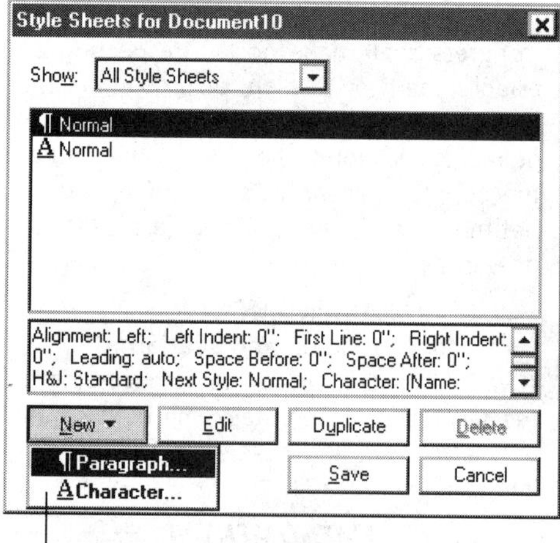

2 *Choose **New: Paragraph** or **Character**.*

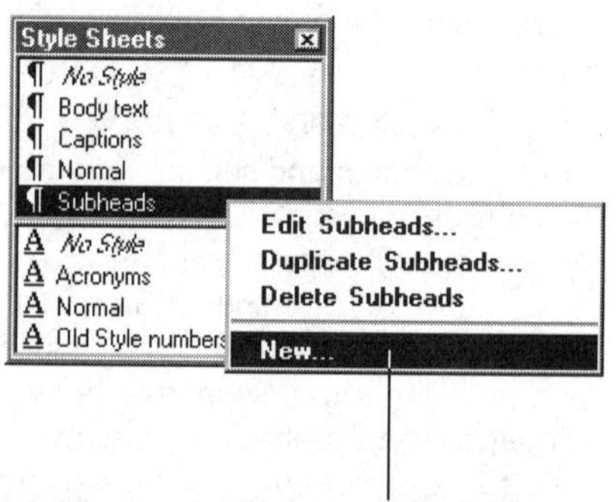

3 ***Right-click** a style sheet name, then choose **New** from the pop-up menu that opens.*

WHAT'S THE DIFFERENCE?

A **character** style sheet contains only character attributes: font, type style, point size, color, shade, horizontal/vertical scale, tracking, and baseline shift. A character style sheet can be applied to one or more characters.

A **paragraph** style sheet, on the other hand, contains paragraph formats, tabs, and rules. It derives its character attributes from the character style sheet that's currently associated with it. A paragraph style sheet can only be applied to entire paragraphs.

text, the Next Style sheet will apply automatically to the next paragraph you type.

6. Click OK or press Enter (and click Save, if necessary, to exit the Style Sheets dialog box **5**). Be sure to apply the new style sheet to the sample paragraph, in addition to any other paragraphs (next page). Two other methods for creating a style sheet are on page 203.

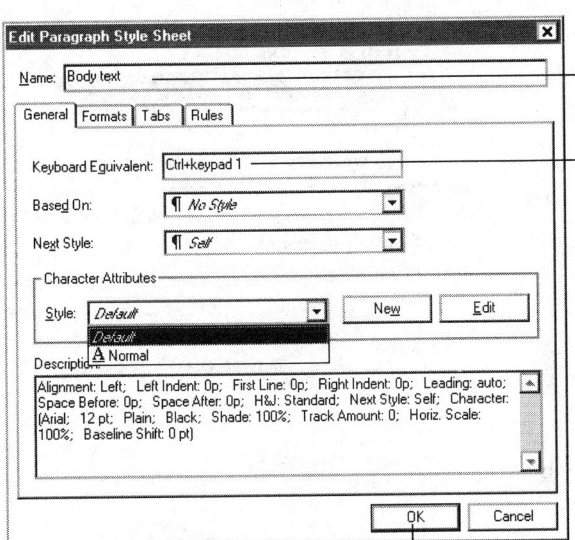

4 *Enter a **Name** for the style sheet. (Assign a descriptive name, such as "Body Text," or "Headline.") Enter a number before the name, if you like (i.e. 01Header, 02Subhead).*

*Enter a **Keyboard Equivalent** on the keypad for the style sheet. Make sure Num Lock is on. Note: You can also use a Function (F) key with or without Ctrl, Alt, or Shift. The F keys already have default commands assigned to them, though, so if you choose an F key as a style sheet keyboard equivalent, the style sheet shortcut will override the pre-assigned command. I suggest you stick to the keypad numbers unless you really need more options.*

*Click **OK** or press Enter to exit the Edit Style Sheet dialog box.*

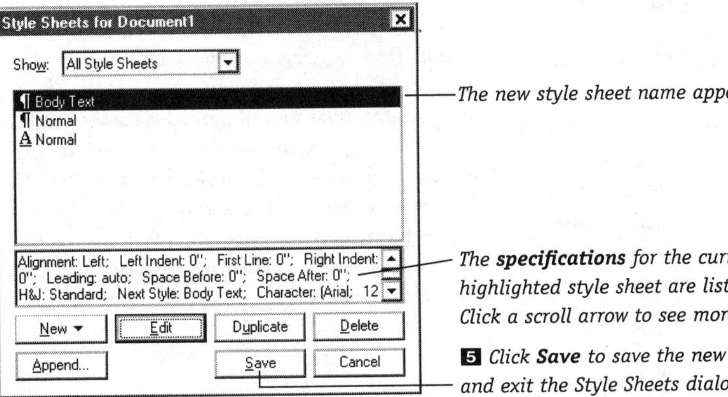

The new style sheet name appears here.

*The **specifications** for the currently highlighted style sheet are listed here. Click a scroll arrow to see more.*

5 *Click **Save** to save the new style sheet and exit the Style Sheets dialog box.*

To apply a style sheet:

1. Display the Style Sheets palette (View menu > Show Style Sheets or F-11).
2. Choose the Content tool.
3. To apply a paragraph style sheet, click in a paragraph or press and drag through a series of paragraphs.
   or
   To apply a character style sheet, highlight a word or a string of words.
4. Click a paragraph style sheet name on the top portion of the Style Sheets palette **1**. The paragraph(s) will reformat instantly.
   or
   Click a character style sheet name on the bottom portion of the Style Sheets palette. The highlighted text will reformat instantly.
   or
   Perform the keyboard equivalent, if any, that was assigned to the chosen style sheet. The keyboard equivalent for each style sheet is listed next to its name on the Style Sheets palette.
   Note: The case of the disappearing text? If you press a number key that was not asssigned to a style sheet, any currently highlighted text will be replaced by that number character. Keep track of which numbers have assigned shortcuts and which don't!

TIP Text formatted using a style sheet can be locally formatted at any time using the keyboard, the Measurements palette, or the Style menu. If you insert the cursor in or highlight locally styled text, a plus sign will appear on the Style Sheets palette next to the name of the style sheet that is associated with that paragraph. You'll also see a plus sign before a paragraph style sheet name if your cursor is inserted in text to which a character style sheet has been applied.

1 *To **apply** a style sheet, click its name on the Style Sheets palette or use the keyboard shortcut if any, that was assigned to the style sheet. The shortcuts are listed on the palette.*

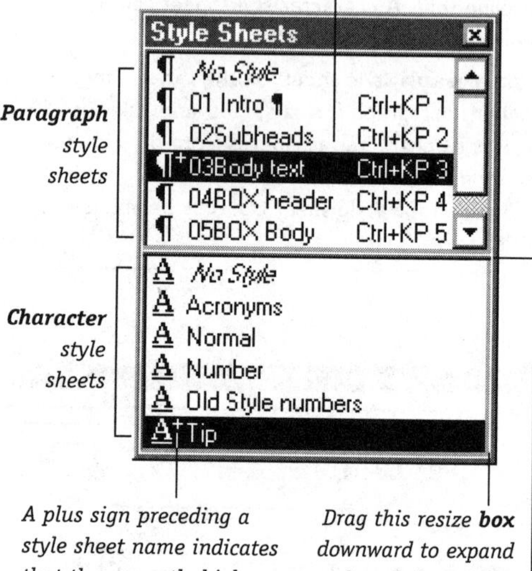

***Paragraph** style sheets*

***Character** style sheets*

*A plus sign preceding a style sheet name indicates that the currently highlighted characters contain **local formatting**.*

*Drag this resize **box** downward to expand the **whole** palette.*

*Drag the split **bar** downward to expand the **paragraph** style sheets area of the palette (expand the whole palette first).*

LOCAL STRIPPING

To strip a paragraph style sheet and all local formatting from a paragraph, including any character style sheets, and apply a new style sheet (or reapply the same style sheet) in one keystroke, click in the paragraph, then Alt-click the style sheet you want to apply on the Style Sheets palette. To do the same thing with a character style sheet, first highlight only the characters from which you want to strip local formatting, then Alt-click a character style sheet.

Apply a Style Sheet

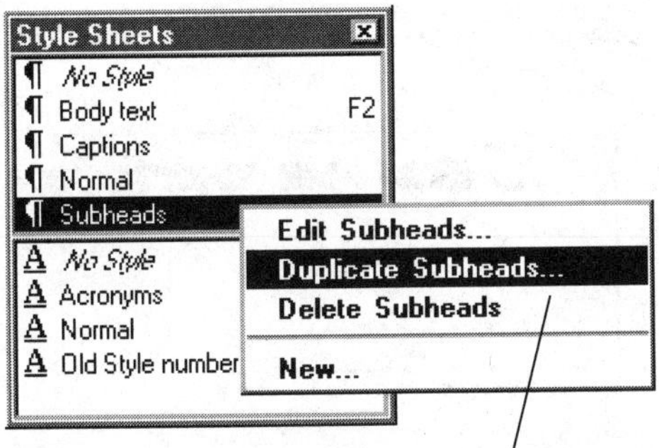

1 *Right-click a style sheet name and choose Duplicate [style sheet name] from the pop-up menu, then click OK.*

SPEED TIP

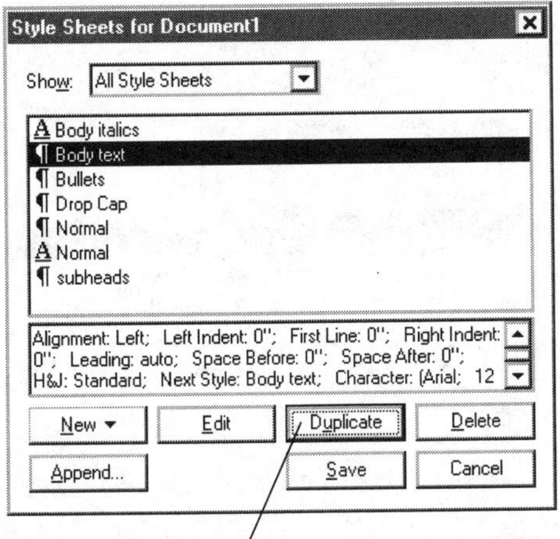

2 *Or, click a style sheet name, then click* ***Duplicate****. The words "copy of" will precede the style sheet name. Change the name, if you like.*

The Duplicate command simply creates a copy of an existing style sheet. Unlike a Based On style sheet, there is no linkage between a duplicate style sheet and the original from which it is generated. It's a fast way to create a variation on an existing style sheet.

To create a new style sheet by duplication:

1. On the Style Sheets palette, right-click the name of the style sheet you want to duplicate, then choose Duplicate [style sheet name] from the pop-up menu that opens **1**.
   or
   Choose Edit menu > Style Sheets (Shift-F11), choose a style sheet name, then click Duplicate **2**.
2. The Edit Style Sheet dialog box will open, and the words "copy of" will precede name of the style sheet in the Name field. Edit the name, if desired.
3. Edit the new style sheet, if desired (see the next page).
4. Click OK.
5. Click Save.

You can always create a style sheet from scratch

To create a new style sheet from scratch without clicking in a sample paragraph, choose Edit menu > Style Sheets, choose New: Character or Paragraph, enter a name for the new style sheet, then follow steps 2–3 on the next page to assign character and paragraph attributes to the style sheet.

To edit a style sheet:

1. Open the Style Sheets palette, click in a text box to activate it, right-click a style sheet name on the palette, then click Edit.
   or
   Choose Edit menu > Style Sheets (Shift-F11), click the name of the style sheet you want to edit, then click Edit **1**. To narrow the number of style sheets on the list, choose a category from the Show drop-down menu.
   or
   Right-click the name of a paragraph style sheet on the Style Sheets palette and choose Edit [style sheet name] to go directly to the General folder tab of the Edit Style Sheet dialog box. Or do the same for a character style sheet to go directly to Edit Character Style Sheet dialog box **2**.
2. For a paragraph style sheet, use the General folder tab to **rename** the style sheet, assign or change its **Keyboard Equivalent**, or assign a **Next Style**. To modify **character** attributes (i.e., font, color), click Edit in the General folder tab. To modify paragraph **formats**, click the Formats folder tab. To add, delete, or modify **tabs**, click the Tabs folder tab. To add, delete, or edit a **rule**, click the Rules folder tab (**3**, next page).
   or
   For a character style sheet, modify character attributes in the Edit Character Style Sheet dialog box. (**4**, next page).
3. Click OK or press Enter to exit the Formats, Rules, or Tabs folder tab (click OK or press Enter twice if you're in the Character Attributes dialog box), then click Save. If you got to the Edit Style Sheet dialog box via the right-click shortcut, just click OK once to exit that dialog box.

   Text to which the style sheet was previously applied will reformat instantly.

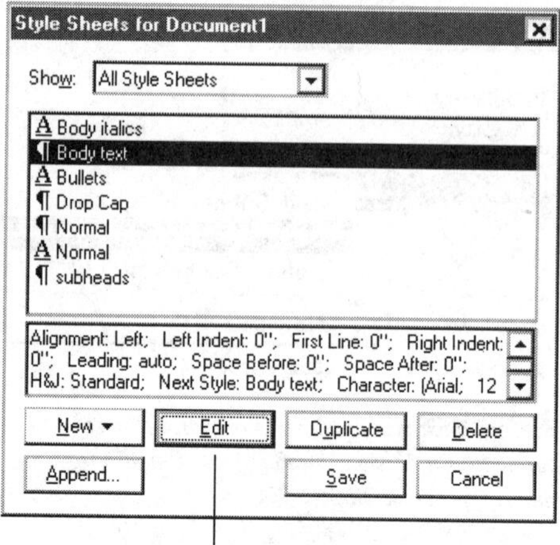

1 *Choose a style sheet name then click* ***Edit*** *(or double-click a style sheet name) to open the Edit Style Sheet dialog box.*

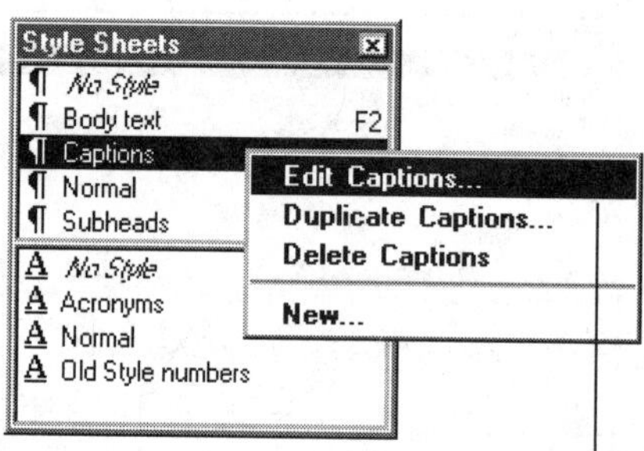

2 ***Right-click*** *a paragraph style sheet name and choose Edit [style sheet name] to go directly to the* ***General*** *folder tab of the Edit Style Sheet dialog box. Or do the same for a character style sheet to go directly to the Edit Character Style Sheet dialog box. You can only edit* ***one*** *style sheet at a time using this method, but it's fast.*

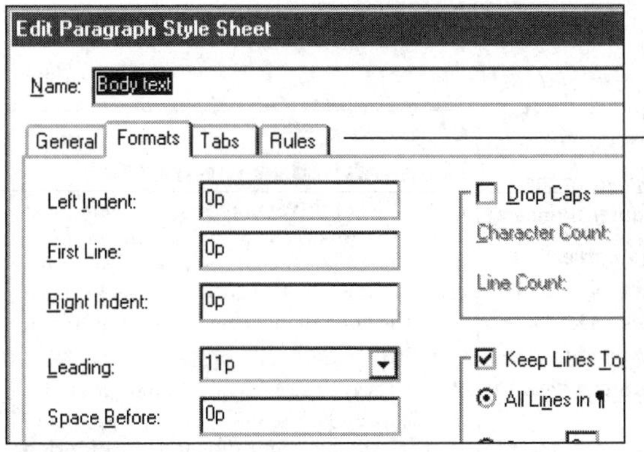

3 *For a paragraph style sheet, click the **Formats, Tabs,** or **Rules** folder tab to open the corresponding dialog box. Click **Edit** in the **General** folder tab to change **Character** attributes.*

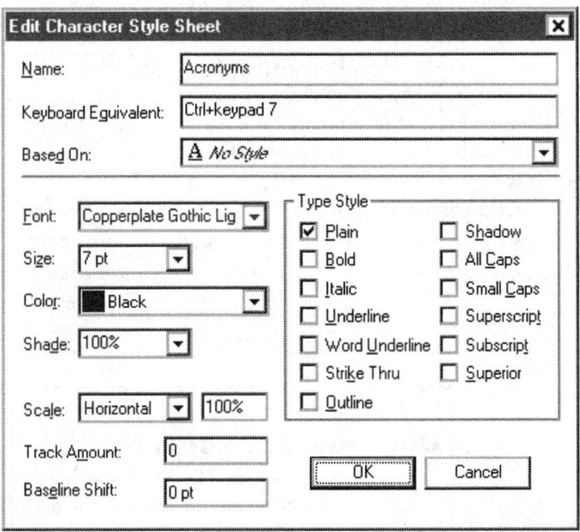

4 *For a **character** style sheet, change the **Name, Keyboard Equivalent, Font, Size, Color, Shade, Scale, Track Amount, Baseline Shift,** or **Type Style** attributes in the **Edit Character Style Sheet** dialog box.*

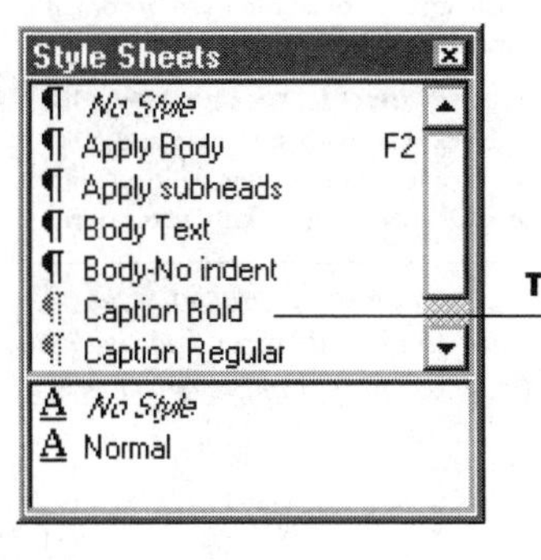

TIP *If the currently highlighted text is associated with more than one style sheet, the symbol next to those style sheet names will be grayed out on the Style Sheets palette.*

SPEED TIP

*It's easy to typeset bulleted lists or numbered paragraphs: Use a **character** style sheet for the bullet or number and a paragraph style sheet for the body text.*

Applying style sheets by example

Chapter xiv

Household economy

Clean paper walls = The very best method is to sweep off lightly all the dust, then rub the paper with stale bread—cut the crust off very thick, and wipe straight down from the top, then begin at the top again, and so on.

Wash carpets = The oftener these are taken up and shaken, the longer they will wear, as the dust and dirt underneath grind them out. Sweep carpets with a stiff hair brush, instead of an old corn broom, if you wish them to wear long or look well.

Black a brick hearth = Mix some black lead with soft soap and a little water, and boil it—then lay it on with a brush. Or mix the lead with water only.

2 Then another style sheet is applied to the chapter number.

3 Another paragraph style sheet is assigned to the chapter name.

1 A paragraph body text style sheet is applied first to all the body text.

Chapter xiv

Household economy

CLEAN PAPER WALLS — The very best method is to sweep off lightly all the dust, then rub the paper with stale bread—cut the crust off very thick, and wipe straight down from the top, then begin at the top again, and so on.

WASH CARPETS — The oftener these are taken up and shaken, the longer they will wear, as the dust and dirt underneath grind them out. Sweep carpets with a stiff hair brush, instead of an old corn broom, if you wish them to wear long or look well.

BLACK A BRICK HEARTH — Mix some black lead with soft soap and a little water, and boil it—then lay it on with a brush. Or mix the lead with water only.

4 A character style sheet is applied to each subhead.

5 To apply a character style sheet for the ornament, Find/Change was used to search for and replace "=".

Chapter xiv

Household economy

I CLEAN PAPER WALLS — The very best method is to sweep off lightly all the dust, then rub the paper with stale bread—cut the crust off very thick, and wipe straight down from the top, then begin at the top again, and so on.

2 WASH CARPETS —The oftener these are taken up and shaken, the longer they will wear, as the dust and dirt underneath grind them out. Sweep carpets with a stiff hair brush, instead of an old corn broom, if you wish them to wear long.

3 BLACK A BRICK HEARTH — Mix some black lead with soft soap and a little water, and boil it—then lay it on with a brush. Or mix the lead with water only.

6 A drop cap is added to the paragraph style sheet. The drop caps are colored 20% gray and changed to the Adobe Garamond Expert font using a new character style sheet.

Chapter xiv

Household economy

I **CLEAN PAPER WALLS** — The very best method is to sweep off lightly all the dust, then rub the paper with stale bread—cut the crust off very thick, and wipe straight down from the top, then begin at the top again, and so on.

2 **WASH CARPETS** —The oftener these are taken up and shaken, the longer they will wear, as the dust and dirt underneath grind them out. Sweep carpets with a stiff hair brush, instead of an old corn broom, if you wish them to wear long.

3 **BLACK A BRICK HEARTH** —Mix some black lead with soft soap and a little water, and boil it—then lay it on with a brush. Or mix the lead with water only.

7 The font in the subhead character style sheet is changed to Bodoni Poster and the font in the body text paragraph style sheet is changed to Gill Sans.

THE COLOR GREEN

Here's a technique that you can use to help yourself learn how to use style sheets. Assign various colors to paragraph and character style sheets, and make changing color part of editing a style sheet. This way, it will be easy to see which paragraphs or characters are affected by the changes and to remember what those changes were.

Let's say you want to use this technique to learn about embedded style sheets. Make the text in a paragraph style sheet blue and the text in a separate character style sheet red. Embed the red character style sheet into the blue paragraph style sheet and apply the paragraph style sheet to a paragraph. The text turns red. Next, change the red in the character style sheet to green. The text turns green.

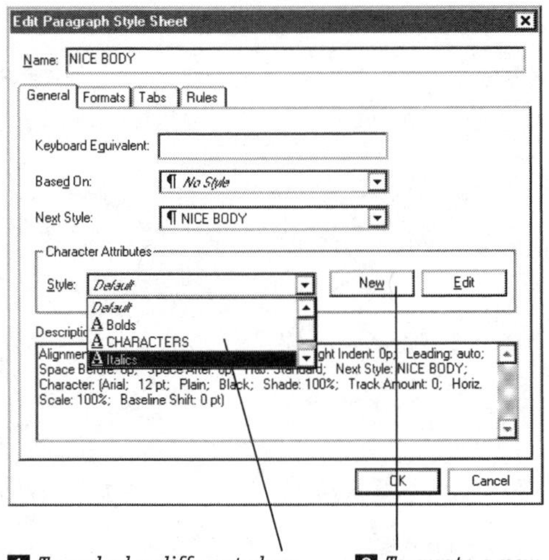

1 *To embed a different character style sheet into a paragraph style sheet, choose from the **Style** drop-down menu.*

2 *To create a new character style sheet, click **New**.*

A default character style sheet is automatically embedded into every paragraph style sheet. It's from the character style sheet that a paragraph style sheet's character attributes are derived. You can change the individual character attributes of the default character style sheet for its associated paragraph style sheet (choose a different font or point size, for example).

If you want to change multiple character attributes for a paragraph style sheet all at once, you can embed a different character style sheet into it or create a new character style sheet to associate with it. The same character style sheet can be embedded into many paragraph style sheets. This means, however, that if you change the specifications for the independent character style sheet, the character attributes for any paragraph style sheets into which it is embedded will update accordingly. If this seems like too much to keep track of, don't do it!

To embed a different character style sheet into a paragraph style sheet:

1. Choose Edit menu > Style Sheets (Shift-F11).
2. Click the name of the paragraph style sheet into which you want to embed the character style sheet.
3. Click Edit.
4. Choose an existing character style sheet from the Style drop-down menu in the Character Attributes area **1**.

   or

   Click New **2**, type a name for a new character style sheet, choose character attributes, then click OK.
5. Click OK to exit the Edit Style Sheet dialog box.
6. Click Save.

One degree of separation

When one style sheet is Based On an existing style sheet, the two remain associated. If the original style sheet is modified, any style sheets that are based on it will also change, except for any specifications that are unique to the Based On style sheet. To base one style sheet on another, choose from the Based On drop-down menu in the Edit Style Sheet dialog box **1**.

For example, you could create a style sheet called Drop Cap that's based on a Body Text style sheet, and then make a deviation in the Drop Cap style sheet—turn on the automatic Drop Cap option in the Formats folder tab. If you then change the Body Text style sheet (change the font, size, etc.), those changes will also occur in the Drop Cap style sheet.

How does this differ from embedding a character style sheet in a paragraph style sheet, you wonder? The Based On option associates two paragraph style sheets; it doesn't associate a character style sheet with a paragraph style sheet.

Styling the master

A style sheet can be applied to any text box on a master page. You can even apply a style sheet to the automatic text box, though you can't enter text into it. The style sheet will then apply automatically to any text that is subsequently typed into that box on any associated document page. It won't apply automatically to text that is imported into the box using Get Text, however.

Using Find/Change to apply or change style sheets

To apply a style sheet to locally styled text using the Find/Change palette, uncheck Ignore Attributes, choose character attributes on the Find What side of the palette, and choose the desired style sheet on the Change To side of the palette.

1 *Choose a style sheet from the* ***Based On*** *drop-down menu.*

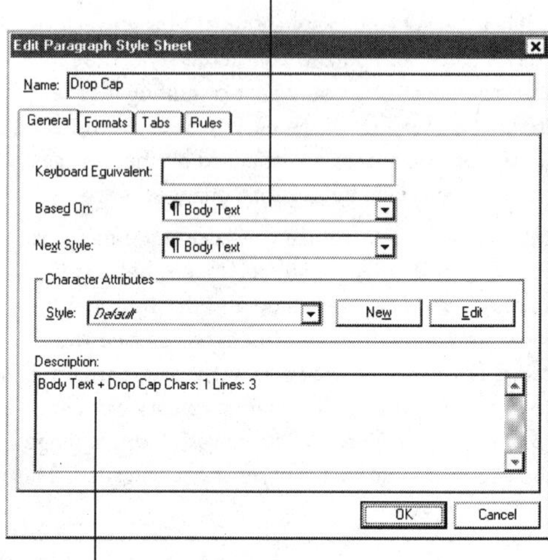

This ***Description*** *indicates that the Drop Cap style sheet consists of the Body text style sheet plus the Drop Cap option.*

You can use Find/Change to selectively find and change style sheets on a paragraph-by-paragraph basis by choosing a Find What style sheet and a Change To style sheet (as opposed to deleting/replacing a style, which causes all occurrences of the style sheet to change). This strategy makes phenomenal sense if you stop to think about it. See pages 250–254.

What is Normal?

The Normal paragraph and character style sheets are the default style sheets for all newly created text boxes. If the Normal style sheet is modified with a file open, any text with which the Normal style sheet is associated will update within that document only.

If the Normal paragraph or character style sheet is modified when no documents are open, the modified style sheet will become the default for all subsequently created documents. Similarly, any new style sheet that is created when no documents are open will appear automatically on the Style Sheets palette of all subsequently created documents.

Appending style sheets

To append style sheets from one document to another, follow the instructions on pages 34–36. Or to append a style sheet the quick-and-dirty way, drag a text box that contains text to which the desired style sheet has been applied from a library or from another document into the current document—the applied style sheet(s) will copy along with the item.

Note: You can't undo the deletion of a style sheet. If you save your document ahead of time and then delete the wrong style sheet or change your mind, you can choose File menu > Revert to Saved.

To delete a style sheet:

1. On the Style Sheets palette, right-click on the name of the style sheet that you want to delete and choose Delete [style sheet name] from the pop-up menu **1**.
2. If the style sheet that you're deleting is not currently applied to any text in your document, click OK **2**.

   If the style sheet is currently applied to any characters or paragraphs in your document, a prompt will appear. Choose a replacement style sheet from the "Replace with" drop-down menu or choose No Style, then click OK **3**.

   Note: If you choose a replacement style sheet, any local formatting will be preserved. If you choose No Style and then apply a new style sheet, on the other hand, all local formatting will be removed.

TIP To delete a style sheet using another method, choose Edit menu > Style Sheets (Shift-F11), click on the name of the style sheet you want to delete, then click Delete. Choose a replacement font if a warning prompt appears, click OK, then click Save.

TIP The Normal style sheet can be edited, but it cannot be deleted.

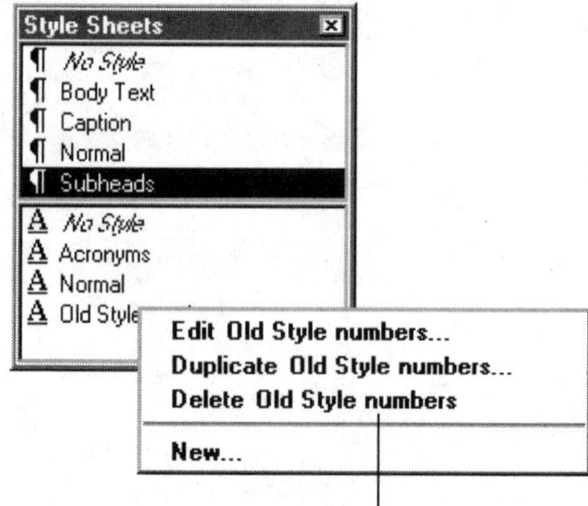

1 ***Right-click*** *a style sheet name and choose* ***Delete*** *[style sheet name] from the pop-up menu.*

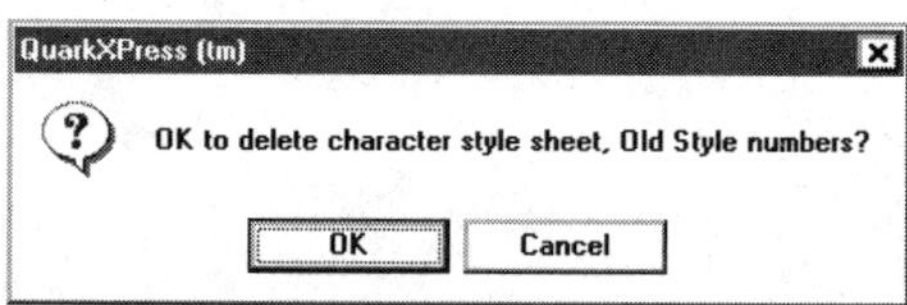

2 *If this prompt appears, click OK.*

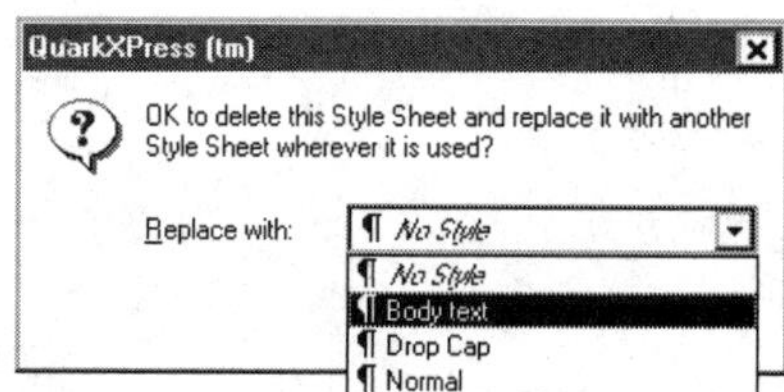

3 *If this prompt appears, choose a replacement style sheet or choose No Style from the* ***Replace with*** *drop-down menu.*

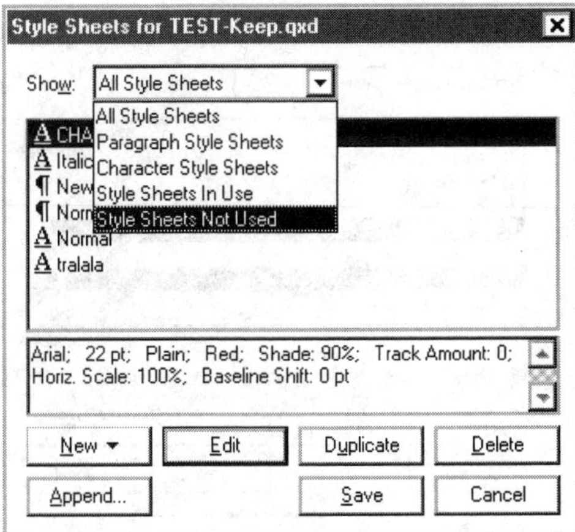

1 *Choose **Show: Style Sheets Not Used.***

To delete all unused style sheets:

1. Choose Edit menu > Style Sheets (Shift-F11).
2. Choose Show: Style Sheets Not Used **1**.
3. Hold down Shift and drag upward or downward through the names to highlight them.
   or
   Click on the first name in a series of contiguous names to be deleted, then Shift-click on the last name in the series.
4. *Optional:* Ctrl-click the names of any style sheets that you don't want to delete.
5. Click Delete.
6. Click Save.

To compare the specifications of two style sheets:

1. Choose Edit menu > Style Sheets (Shift-F11).
2. Ctrl-click the two style sheets that you want to compare **1**.
3. Alt-click the Append button (it will turn into a Compare button). The Compare Paragraph (or Character) Style Sheets dialog box will open **2**. Any specifications that differ between the two style sheets will be listed in boldface. Click OK when you're finished, and then click Cancel.

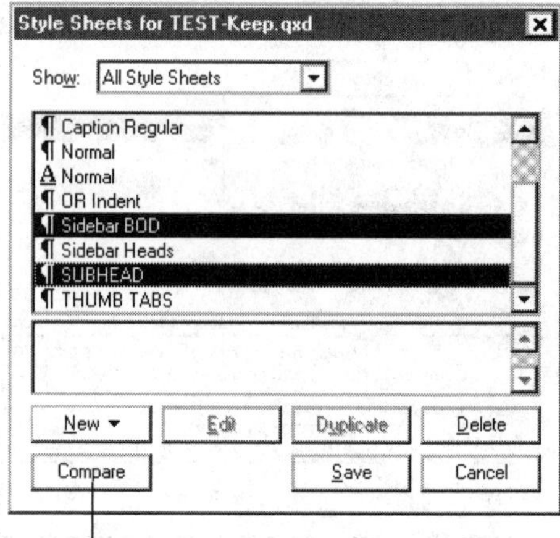

1 *In the Style Sheets dialog box,* ***Ctrl****-click two style sheets, then* ***Alt****-click* ***Append****.*

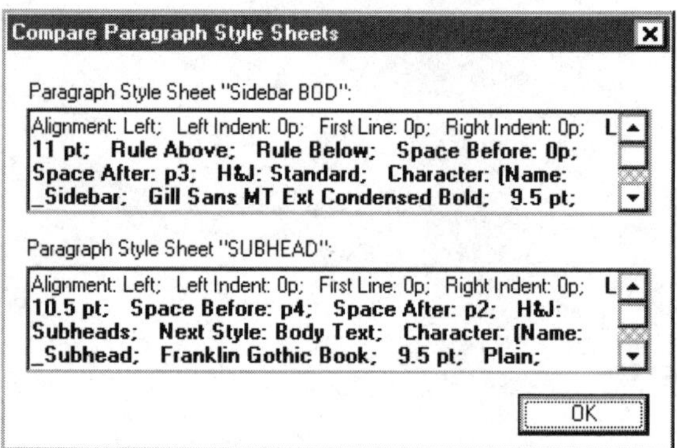

2 *When you're finished* ***comparing*** *the style sheets, click OK.*

Master pages 14

Master pages

Master pages are like style sheets for page layout. Items on a master page automatically appear on every document page to which that master is applied. If you change a master page item, that item will update automatically on any associated document pages. What's more, you can edit an item that originated from a master page on any associated document page.

Master pages help to expedite the production of documents that contain repetitive elements, such as headers, footers, picture boxes, logos, or lines. Master pages are also used for automatic page numbering. Every new document automatically contains a Master A page; an unlimited number of master pages can be added.

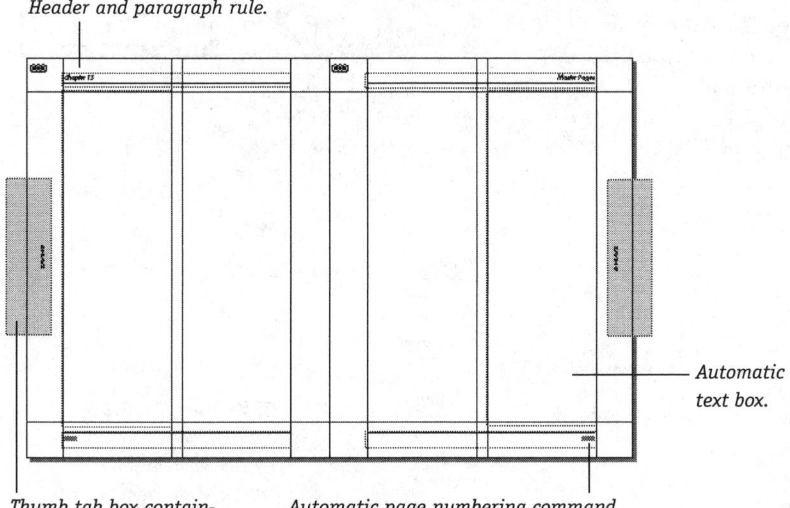

This is a screenshot of the left and right facing master pages that were used to produce this book.

Before you can learn how to use master pages, you need to learn how to navigate between master page and document page display. Master pages are created, modified, and applied using the Document Layout palette. Choose View menu > Show Document Layout (F4) to display it.

To switch between master page and document page display:

Double-click a master page icon or document page icon on the Document Layout palette **1**–**2**. The number of the currently displayed page will switch to boldface.

or

Choose a document or master page from the Go-to-page pop-up menu at the bottom of the document window **3**–**4**.

or

Choose Document or a master page name from the Page menu > Display submenu **5**. If you choose Document when a master page is displayed, the last displayed document page will redisplay.

or

To display the master page that's applied to the currently displayed document page (or the previously displayed document page if a master page is currently displayed), use this shortcut: Shift-F4. To display the next master if a master page is displayed: Ctrl-Shift-F4. To display the previous master: Ctrl Shift-F3.

WHERE ARE YOU?

The easiest way to tell whether you're on a document page or a master page is to glance at the lower left-hand corner of the document window. If you're on a document page, the readout will say "Page: Such-and-such." If a master page is displayed, it will say "A-Master A," or whatever the name of the master page is.

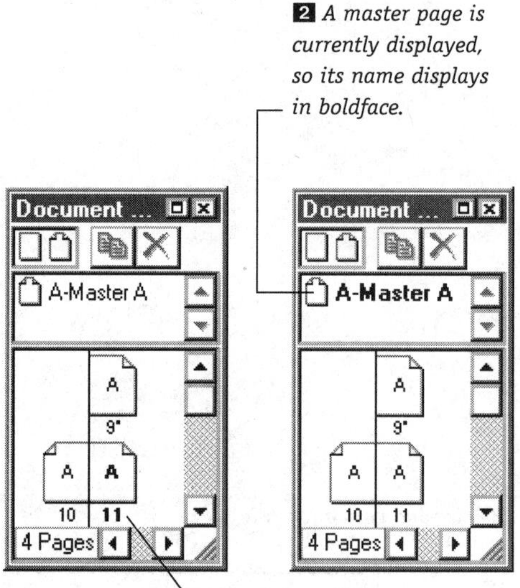

2 *A master page is currently displayed, so its name displays in boldface.*

1 *The number of the currently displayed document page displays in* ***boldface.***

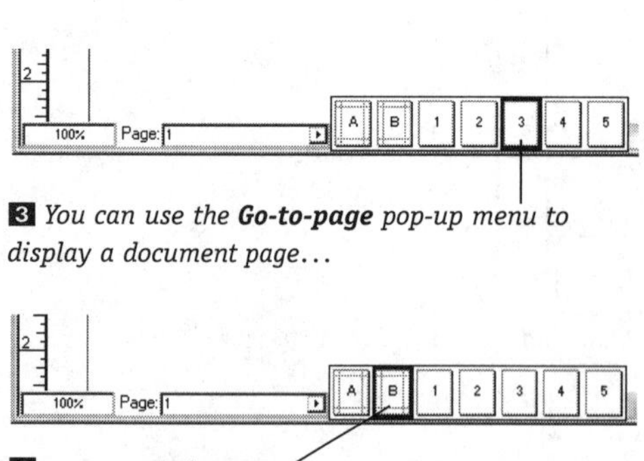

3 *You can use the* ***Go-to-page*** *pop-up menu to display a document page...*

4 *...or a master page.*

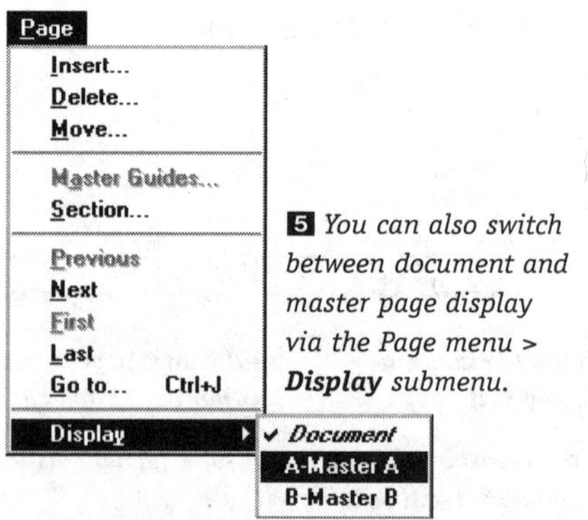

5 *You can also switch between document and master page display via the Page menu >* ***Display*** *submenu.*

Blank single-sided page *icon.*

Blank facing-pages *icon.*

Master page *icon.*

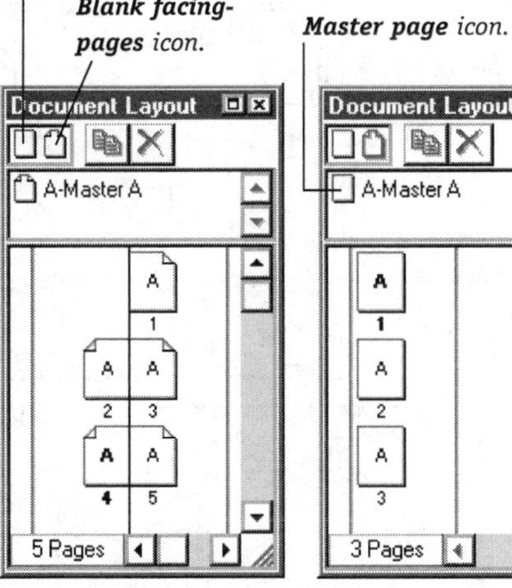

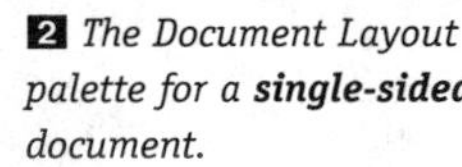

1 *The Document Layout palette for a* ***facing-pages*** *document.*

2 *The Document Layout palette for a* ***single-sided*** *document.*

Single-sided vs. facing-pages

If you check the Facing Pages box in the New dialog box, you can specify Inside and Outside margins instead of Left and Right margins. In this type of document, the first page is positioned by itself on the right side and any subsequent pages are arranged in pairs along a central spine **1** (that is, unless you've applied an even starting page number via the Section command). Facing master page and document page icons have turned-down corners. This format is used for book and magazine layouts.

If you uncheck the Facing Pages box in the New dialog box, you will create a single-sided document in which single pages are stacked vertically. Single-sided master page and document page icons have square corners **2**. To create a spread in a single-sided document, you can arrange document page icons so they're side by side (see page 66). To convert a document from single-sided to facing-pages, or vice versa, see page 32.

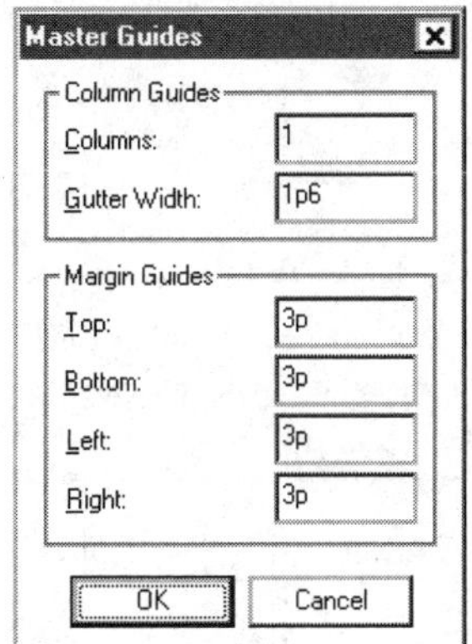

3 *Change the non-printing* ***Margin Guides*** *and/or* ***Column Guides*** *in the* ***Master Guides*** *dialog box.*

If you modify the margin or column guides on a master page, all the document pages with which that master is associated will display the updated guides. In addition, any automatic text box that fit exactly within the margin guides before you modified them will resize to fit perfectly within the new margin guides and will contain the new number of columns.

To modify the non-printing margin and column guides:

1. Double-click a master page icon on the Document Layout Palette.
2. Choose Page menu > Master Guides.
3. Change the numbers in the Column Guides and/or Margin Guides fields **3**.
4. Click OK or press Enter **4**–**5**.

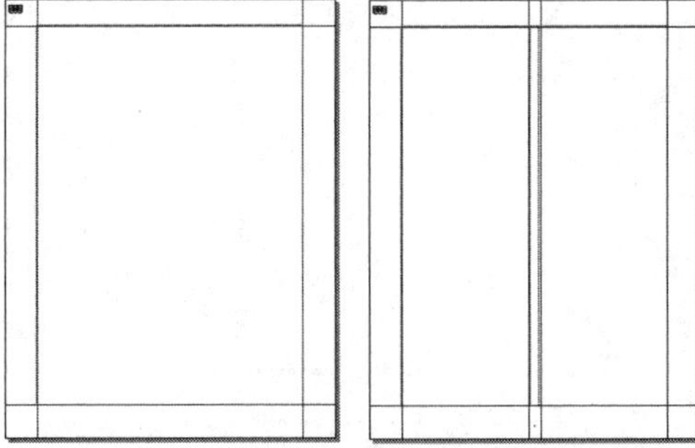

4 *A one-column master...*

5 *...is changed to a two-column master.*

If you enter the Current Page Number command on a master page, the current page number will appear on any document pages to which that master is applied. If you then add or delete pages from the document, the page numbers will update automatically.

Note: Many of the procedures discussed in this chapter can't be undone, like applying a master page or adding or deleting pages. Save your document before you start working with master pages and the Document Layout palette so you'll have the Revert to Saved command to fall back on.

To number pages automatically:

1. Double-click the Master A icon on the Document Layout palette **1**. The words "A-Master A" will appear in the lower left corner of the document window.
2. Choose the Rectangle text box tool.
3. Press and drag to create a small text box for the page number.
4. Hold down Ctrl and press "3" **2**. You can type a prefix, such as "Page," before the page numbering command. Enter the command on both the left and right master pages for a facing-pages document (see **4**–**5**, next page).
5. Highlight the numbering command, then style it like a regular character (choose a font, point size, etc.).

   Note: You can also place a header, picture box, vertical rule, or any other item on a master page. More about this on page 218.
6. To display a document page when you're finished editing the master, double-click a document page icon on the Document Layout palette or use the Shift-F4 shortcut **3**.

TIP Unfortunately, the automatic page numbers can't be manually kerned and they are unaffected by the Kerning Table Editor. You can track the Current

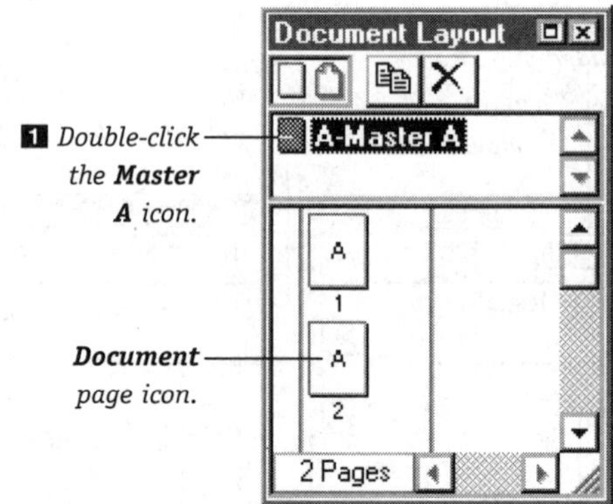

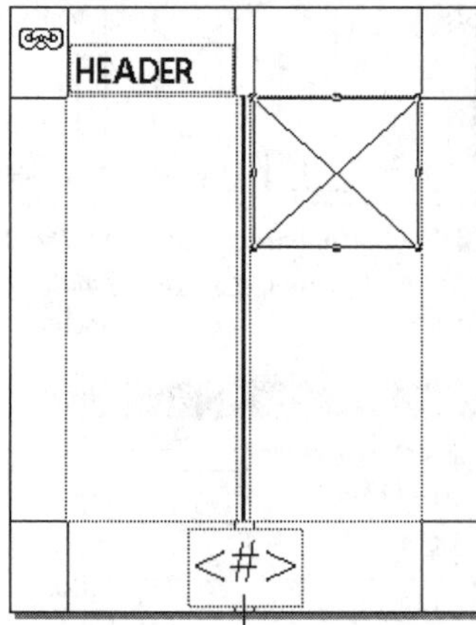

2 *The **Current Page Number** command displays as "<#>" on the master page.*

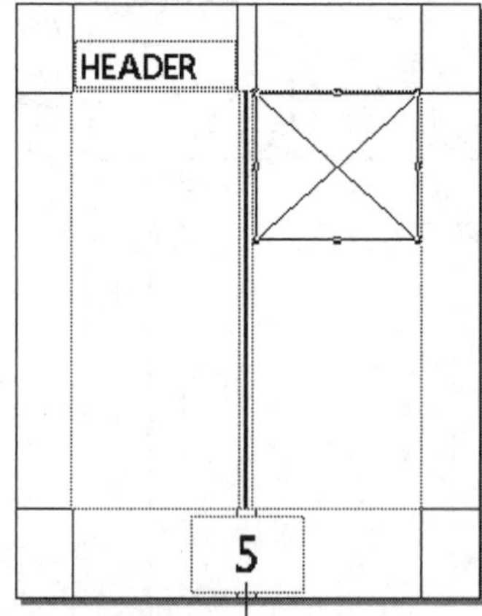

3 *The **Current Page Number** command displays as the **actual** page number on a document page.*

ALIGN THE NUMBERS

To make sure the two boxes that hold the page numbering command align vertically on the left and right master page in a facing-pages document, use Item menu > Step and Repeat (Horizontal Offset 10p, Vertical Offset 0) to duplicate the box, then hold down Shift as you move the duplicate to the right page.

Or, you could Duplicate the first box, select both boxes, and then use Item menu > Space/Align (Vertical, Space 0, Between Top Edges) to align their top edges. Another way to align the boxes vertically is to enter matching numbers in the Y field on the Measurements palette. Remember to choose right paragraph alignment for the command on the right facing page.

Page Number command on the master page, but doing so will cause all the document's automatic page numbers to be tracked by the same value.

TIP You can enter the Current Page Number command on a document page, but the page number will only appear on that individual page.

TIP To print a master page (or a set of facing-pages masters), just make sure it's displayed before choosing File menu > Print (Ctrl-P).

TIP Break with tradition. If your page design lends itself to experimentation, instead of automatically placing the page numbering command at the bottom of the page, try it in a new location. Then embellish it: Apply a color to it, make it very large, add a paragraph rule above and/or below it, etc.

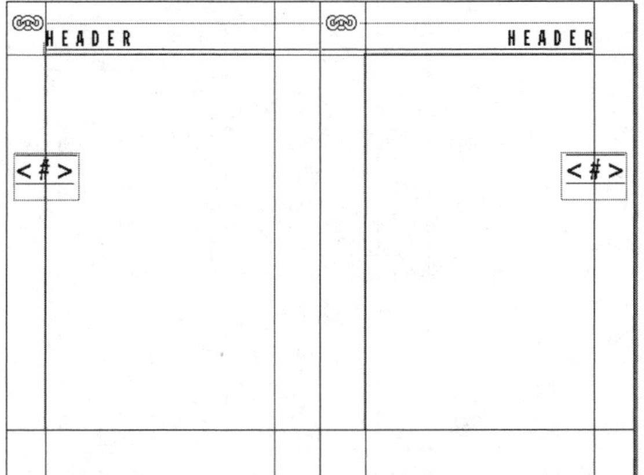

4 *In a facing-pages document, you must enter the Current Page Number command on both the left and right facing master pages.*

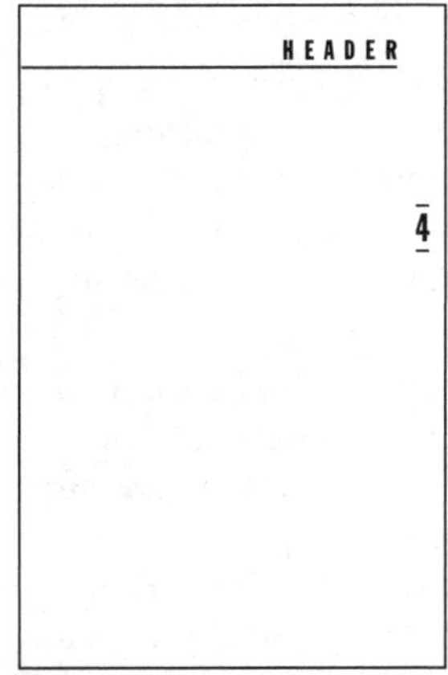

5 *This is what the document page looks like.*

To modify a master page:

1. Double-click a master page icon on the Document Layout palette **1** or choose a master page icon from the Go-to-page pop-up menu at the bottom of the document window.
2. Add or modify any master item—i.e., header, footer, line, ruler guide, or picture box. You can also drag any item from a library onto a master page.
3. To redisplay a document page, double-click a document page icon on the Document Layout palette or choose a document page number from the Go-to-page pop-up menu.

TIP Pages to which the master has already been applied will be modified. See "Keep or Delete Changes?" on pages 220–223.

TIP If Automatic Text Box was turned on in the New Document dialog box when the document was created, an automatic text box will appear on the default Master A and on any document pages that are associated with Master A. Text cannot be entered into the automatic text box on a master page, but text can be entered into any other text box on a master page. You *can* reshape the auto text box.

TIP You can preformat any text box on a master page by applying a style sheet or individual type specifications. Text that you subsequently type into the box will take on those specifications; imported text will not.

TIP In a facing-pages document, every master page has a left and a right page. Items on the left master page will appear only on left (even-numbered) document pages; items on the right master page will appear only on right (odd-numbered) document pages.

LOCK 'EM UP

Once your master items are positioned exactly where you want them, lock them to prevent them from being moved (Item menu > Lock or F6).

SPEEDTIP

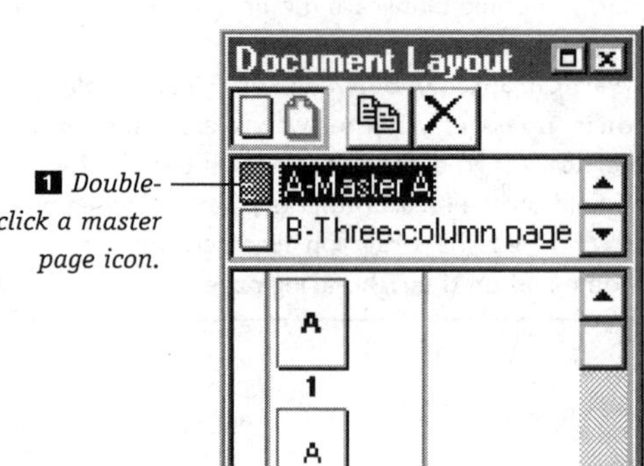

1 *Double-click a master page icon.*

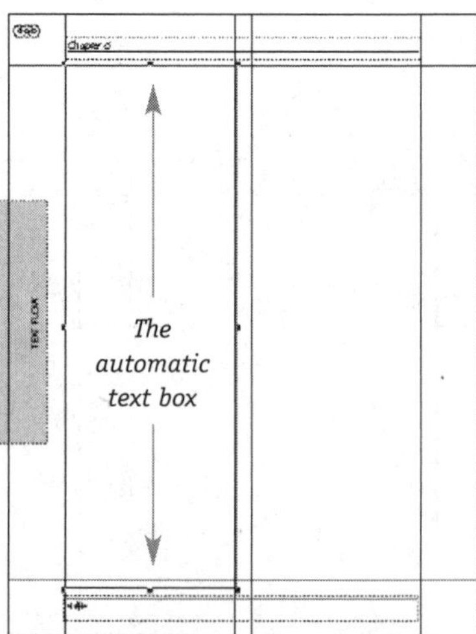

This is the left master page for this book. The automatic text box was resized to fit into one column, and then its number of columns was reduced to one.

Modify a Master Page

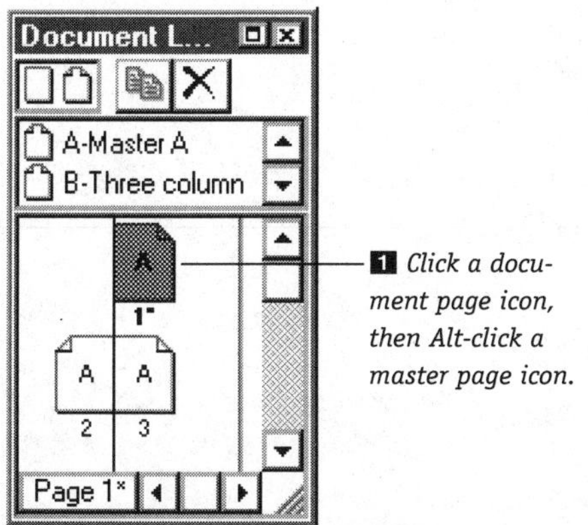

1 *Click a document page icon, then Alt-click a master page icon.*

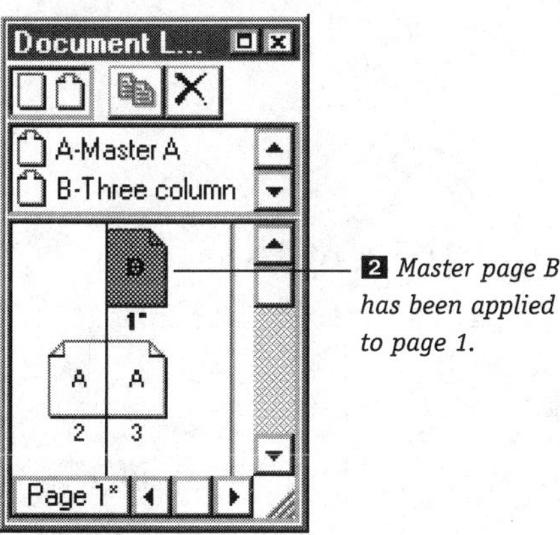

2 *Master page B has been applied to page 1.*

To apply a master page to a document page:

Click on a document page icon on the Document Layout palette **1**, then Alt-click a master page icon **2**.

or

Drag a master page icon over a document page icon.

or

To apply a master page to multiple pages, click on the page icon of the first page in the series, hold down Shift and click on the last page icon in the series **3**, then Alt-click the master page icon. Or Ctrl-click instead to highlight non-consecutive page icons **4**.

TIP If you drag a page or pages from one file to another in Thumbnails view, any applied master pages will also append.

TIP If an odd number of pages is added to, deleted from, or moved within a facing-pages document and document pages are reshuffled as a result, the corresponding left and right master pages will be applied to the reshuffled pages automatically.

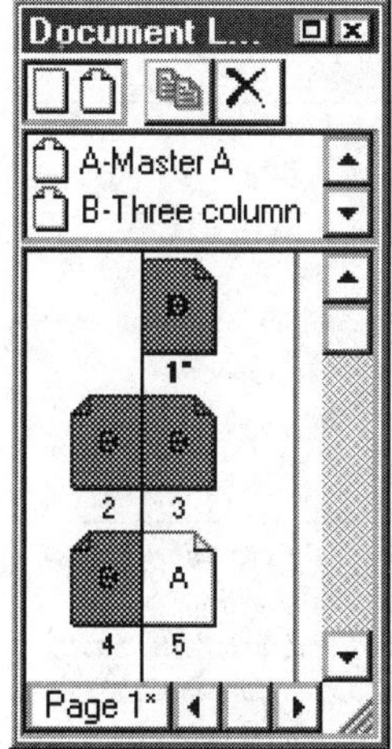

3 *Click on the first in a series of consecutive document page icons, then Shift-click on the last icon in the series.*

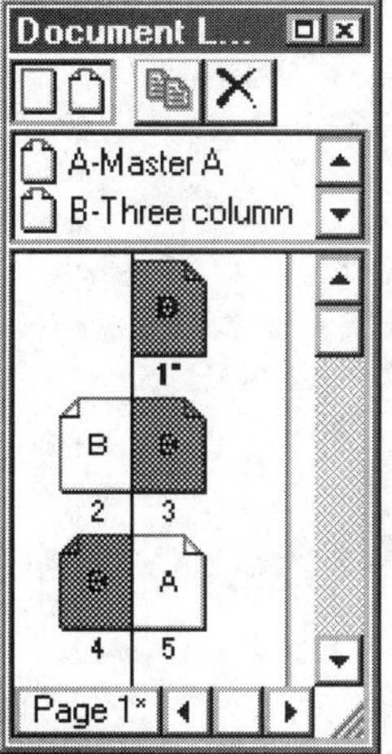

4 *Or Ctrl-click on individual document page icons.*

Keep or delete changes?

If Master Page Items: Delete Changes is chosen in Edit menu > Preferences > General folder tab (Ctrl-Y) and a master page is applied or reapplied to a document page, locally modified and unmodified master items will be deleted from the document page 1–3. If Keep Changes is chosen from the same drop-down menu, only unmodified master items will be deleted 4. Confused?

To learn the difference between these two settings, put a couple of items on a master page and then locally modify one of those master page items on a document page. Reapply the master page to the same document page. If the item you modified disappeared, Delete Changes is the current setting. Then do the same procedure with the opposite Master Page Items setting chosen. See the difference?

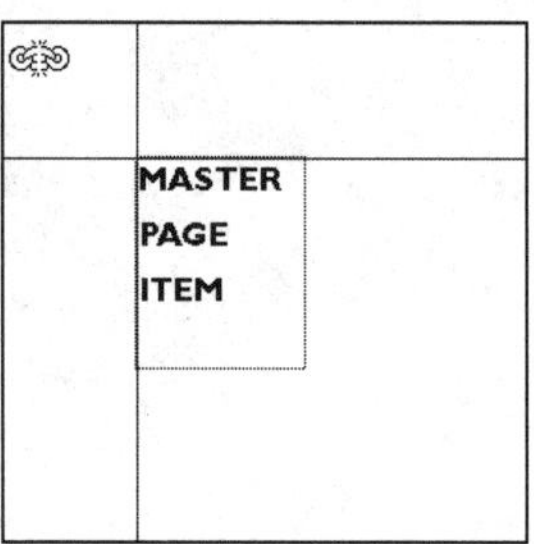

1 *This is an item on a master page.*

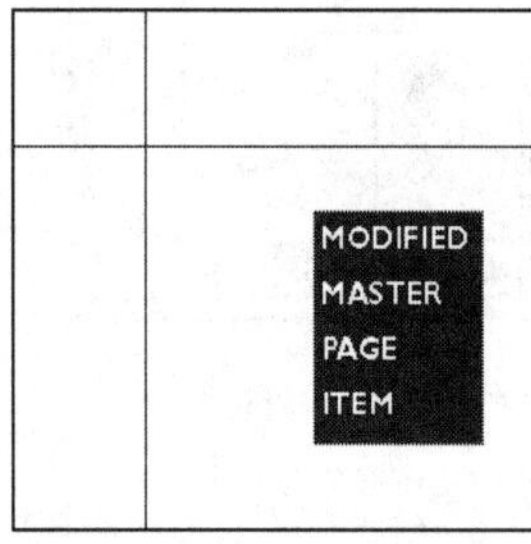

2 *The master page item is moved and modified on an associated document page.*

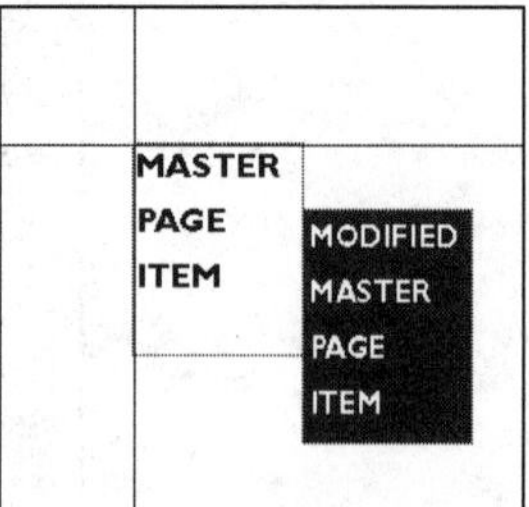

3 *With **Keep Changes** as the default setting, after the master page is reapplied, the modified item remains.*

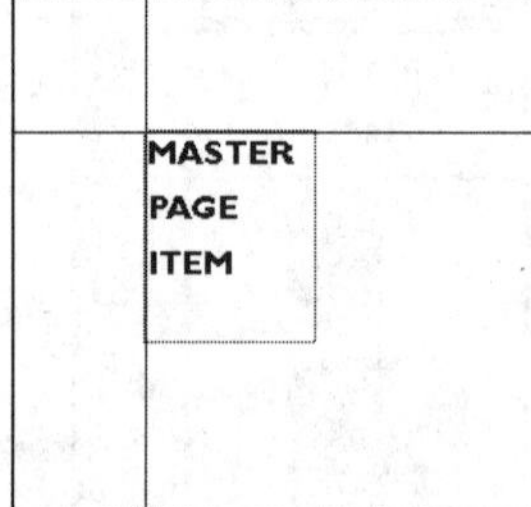

4 *With **Delete Changes** as the default setting, on the other hand, after the master is reapplied, the modified master item is deleted.*

To further confuse matters

If you're going to edit items that originated from a master page and then the master is reapplied, you'll need to keep one more thing in mind: Reapplying the master can affect an item and its contents differently.

The unmodified master page.

The contents are modified on a document page.

Delete Changes is in effect and the same master page is reapplied. The modified contents are replaced.

Scenario 1

You edit the contents of a text box that originated from a master page on a document page but you don't recolor or resize the box itself. Then you reapply the same master page and Master Page Items: Delete Changes is the current Preferences setting. The result: The locally modified text in the box on the document page is deleted.

The unmodified master page.

The contents are modified on a document page.

Keep Changes is in effect and the same master page is reapplied. The master item appears behind the modified item.

Scenario 2

You edit the contents of an item that originated from a master page on a document page, but the item itself isn't moved or edited. Then you reapply the same master page and Keep Changes is in effect. The result: The reapplied master page items will appear behind the modified document page items, which means they could be partially or completely hidden from view.

Scenario 3

You edit a box (item) on the master page but *not* its contents and you edit the contents of that box on the document page. You then reapply the master and Keep Changes is in effect. The result: The box updates on the document page and the edited contents on the document page remain.

The unmodified master page.

The contents on an associated document page are modified.

The item background is modified on the master page.

Keep Changes is in effect. The background is changed; the modified contents remain.

Scenario 4

You edit an item *and* its contents on a master page. Then you reapply the same master page and Delete Changes is in effect. The result: Both the item and its contents on the document page will be replaced completely by the new master page item, regardless of whether they were modified on that document page or not.

The unmodified master page.

The item and its contents are modified on the master page.

The contents of the item are modified on the document page.

Delete Changes is in effect and the same master is reapplied. The item is completely replaced on the document page.

Use the following method if you want to create a variation on an existing master page. The new, duplicate master page will contain all the items from the master from which it is copied, including an automatic text box or the Current Page Number command, if there is one. You can then make any additions or changes to the duplicate.

To duplicate a master page:

1. On the Document Layout palette, click on the icon of the master page that you want to copy **1**.
2. Click the Duplicate icon **2**–**3**.

TIP To copy a master page from one document to another, choose Thumbnails view for both, then drag-copy a page to which the master you want to copy has been applied. The master page will copy along with the document page.

SPEED TIP

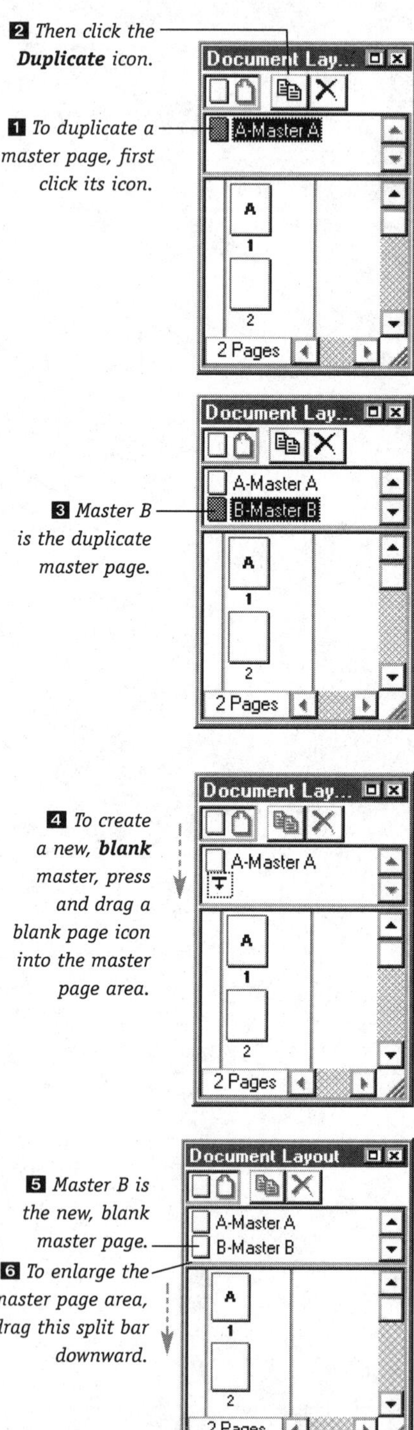
2 *Then click the* ***Duplicate*** *icon.*
1 *To duplicate a master page, first click its icon.*
Document Lay...
A-Master A
A
1
2
2 Pages
3 *Master B is the duplicate master page.*
Document Lay...
A-Master A
B-Master B
A
1
2
2 Pages
4 *To create a new,* ***blank*** *master, press and drag a blank page icon into the master page area.*
Document Lay...
A-Master A
A
1
2
2 Pages
5 *Master B is the new, blank master page.*
6 *To enlarge the master page area, drag this split bar downward.*
Document Layout
A-Master A
B-Master B
A
1
2
2 Pages

To create a new, blank master page:

Press and drag a blank single-sided or facing-pages icon into the blank part of the master page icon area on the Document Layout palette **4**. Move the split bar downward to enlarge the top portion of the palette, if necessary **5**–**6**. The new master page will be labeled with the next letter of the alphabet.

Note: If you intentionally or inadvertently drag a new master page icon over an existing master page icon, an alert dialog box will open. Click OK to replace the existing master with the new, blank one or click Cancel if you change your mind. You can't undo this, so do it only if you really mean to do it.

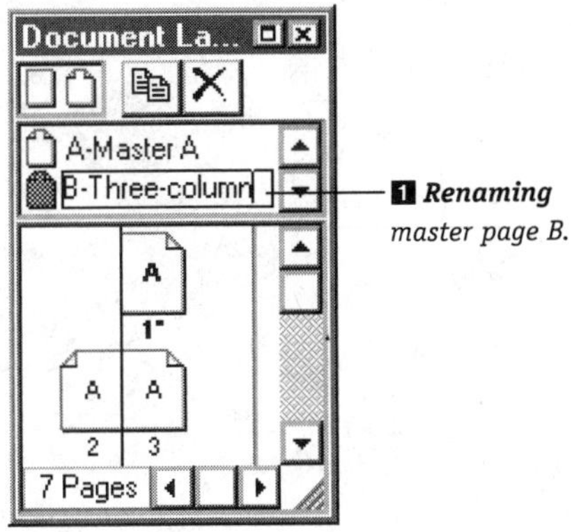

1 ***Renaming*** *master page B.*

To rename a master page:

1. Double-click a master page name on the Document Layout palette.
2. Highlight and change the characters after the hyphen **1**.
   or
   Change all the characters, including the prefix. The next letter in the alphabet and a hyphen will be reinserted automatically as the first two characters.
   or
   Enter a new prefix (up to three characters long). Make sure to leave a hyphen between the prefix and the master page name.

2 *To delete a master page, click its icon, then click the* ***brushstroke-X*** *icon.*

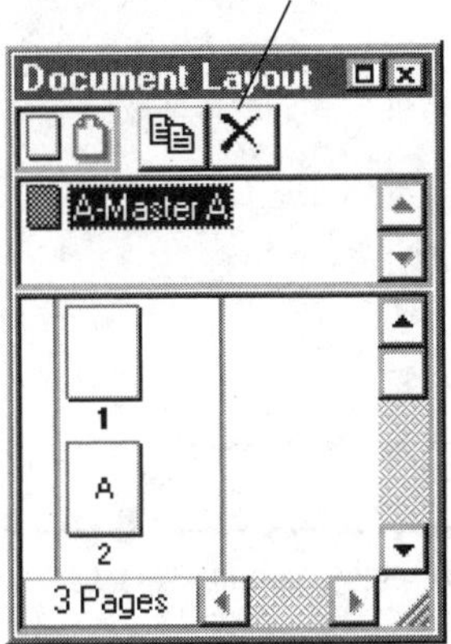

Note: If you delete a master page, any unmodified master items on any associated document pages will be deleted. If a document page associated with the deleted master page contains an automatic text box from the deleted master and that text box isn't resized, it will be deleted—even if it contains text! If it is resized, and the current Edit menu > Preferences > General > Master Page Items setting is Keep Changes, the box will be retained.

To delete a master page:

1. Click a master page icon on the Document Layout palette.
2. Click the brushstroke-X icon on the palette **2**.
3. If the master page is in use, an alert prompt will appear. Click OK or press Enter. You can't undo this! Choose File menu > Revert to Saved if you make a mistake.

To create your own automatic text box:

1. Display the master page on which you want to create an automatic text box, and choose Fit in Window view (Ctrl-0 or right-click and choose Fit in Window).
2. Choose the Rectangle text box tool, and draw a text box **1**.
3. Choose the Linking tool.
4. Click on the link icon in the upper left corner of the page **2**.
5. Click on the text box **3**, then click the Item or Content tool to turn off linking. That's all there is to it!

   Note: If the automatic text box fits perfectly within the current margin guides and you later change the margin guides, the auto text box will resize automatically to fit within the new guides.

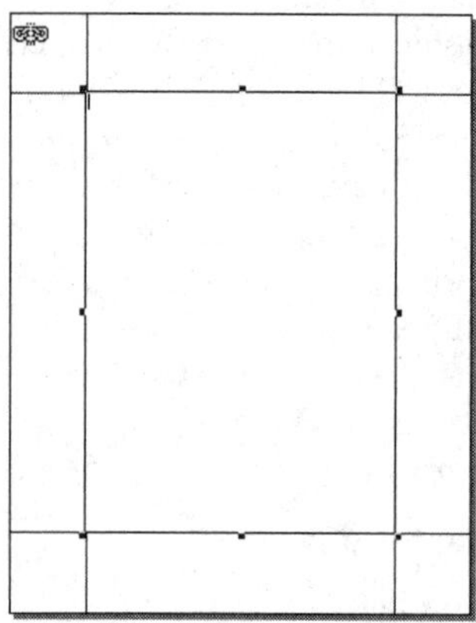

1 *To create an auto text box, first draw a text box of any size on the master page with the Rectangle text box tool.*

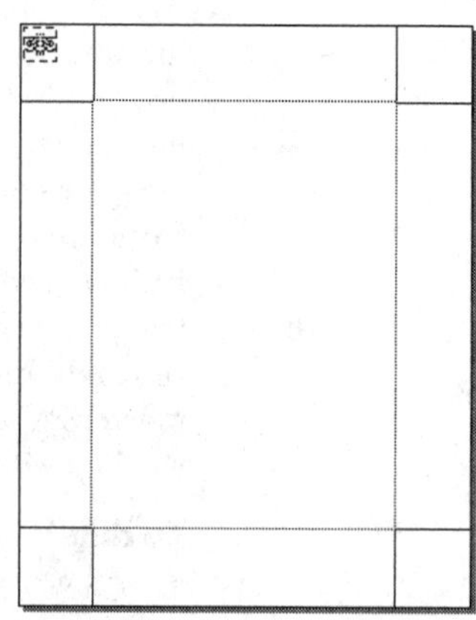

2 *Choose the Linking tool, then click on the link icon in the upper left corner of the master page.*

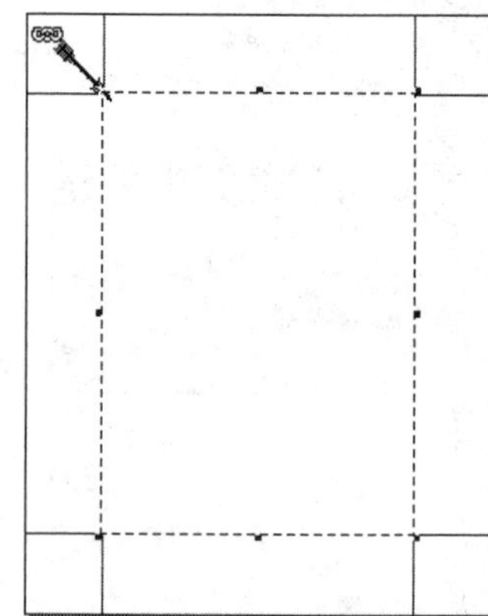

3 *Finally, click on the text box.*

Color 15

THE COLOR MODELS

RGB
The computer's native color model. Use for video or on-screen (World Wide Web) output.

HSB
The traditional artist's method for mixing colors based on their individual hue (H), saturation (S), and brightness (B) components.

CMYK
Four-color process printing model in which a multitude of colors are simulated by printing tiny dots of Cyan (C), Magenta (M), Yellow (Y), and Black (K) ink.

Hexachrome
Six-color process printing model, also known as high fidelity or hi-fi color, because it produces very vibrant color. Orange (O) and green (G) inks, in addition to C, M, Y, and K inks, bring the total to six.

Focoltone, Trumatch
Four-color process matching systems for choosing predefined, pre-named process colors (not spot colors). Focoltone colors were designed to lessen the need for trapping colors.

Pantone
The standard spot color matching system. Pantone also has its own process color matching systems.

Toyo, DIC
Spot color matching systems that are primarily used in the Far East.

Multi-ink
A color that is composed of multiple spot and/or process colors.

Trapping is covered in Chapter 20. Color management is discussed in Chapter 19.

Color

Two basic methods are used for printing color: Spot color and process color. Spot and process colors can be combined in the same color palette in QuarkXPress. Up to 1,000 colors can be created per file, and they're saved with the file.

A separate plate is used to print each spot color. Spot color inks are mixed according to specifications defined in a color matching system, such as PANTONE.

Four plates are used in process color printing: One each for cyan (C), magenta (M), yellow (Y), and black (K). A layer of tiny colored dots is printed from each plate, and the overlapping dots create a wide variety of colors. If your layout contains photographs or other continuous-tone images, the four-color process must be used.

Computer monitors display additive color by projecting light, whereas printers produce subtractive color using ink. Because computer monitors don't accurately display ink equivalents, colors for print output should be specified using formulas defined in a process or spot color matching system guide. Colors should not be mixed based on how they look on screen.

What you can recolor

- Text characters
- Text paths, with or without text
- Pictures in some file formats
- Lines
- Frames
- Paragraph rules
- Gaps between dashes or stripes
- The background of a text box, picture box, or contentless box.

A new spot color will appear on the Colors palette for the current document and in any dialog box where colors are chosen (Frame, Character Attributes, etc.).

To create a spot color:

1. Choose Edit menu > Colors (Shift-F12).
2. Click New **1**.
3. Choose Model: PANTONE Coated or PANTONE Uncoated (spot colors for coated or uncoated stock) **2**.
4. Click a color swatch **3**.
   or
   Enter a number from a PANTONE color guide in the PANTONE field.
5. Check the Spot Color box **4**.
6. Click OK or press Enter.
7. Click Save (**5**, next page).

TIP To access a PANTONE color or a color from any other matching system, that matching system file must be in the Color folder inside the QuarkXPress folder when the application is launched.

TIP TOYO and DIC spot color inks are used in Japan. Ask your print shop if they can mix either of these inks before you consider using them. An asterisk next to a Toyo or DIC color number indicates that that color isn't displayed accurately on screen. Two asterisks signifies an even wider discrepancy.

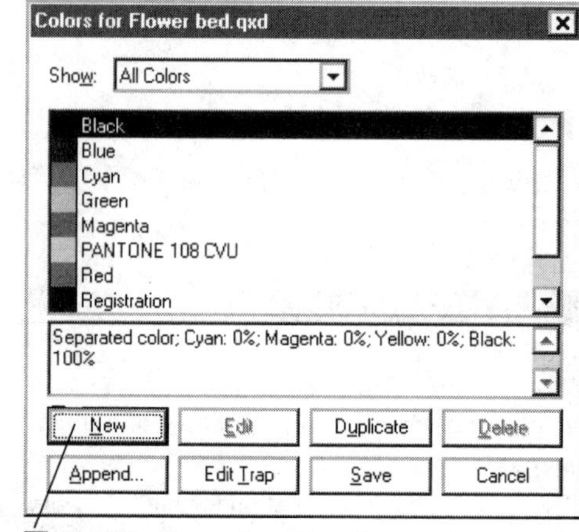

1 *Click* ***New*** *to create a new color.*

2 *Choose* ***Model: PANTONE Coated*** *or* ***PANTONE Uncoated*** *in the Edit Color dialog box.*

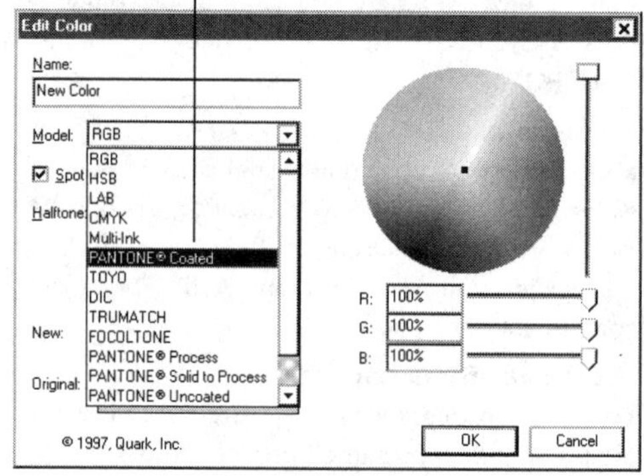

3 *Click a color* ***swatch****. (Click a scroll arrow to scroll through the swatches.)*

4 *Make sure the* ***Spot Color*** *box is* ***checked****. (If the Spot Color box is unchecked, the spot color will be converted into a process color.)*

The Halftone drop-down menu is discussed on the next page.

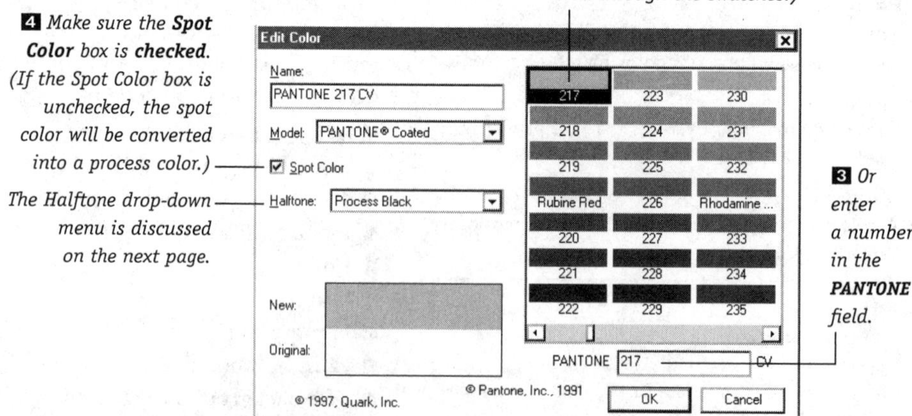

3 *Or enter a number in the* ***PANTONE*** *field.*

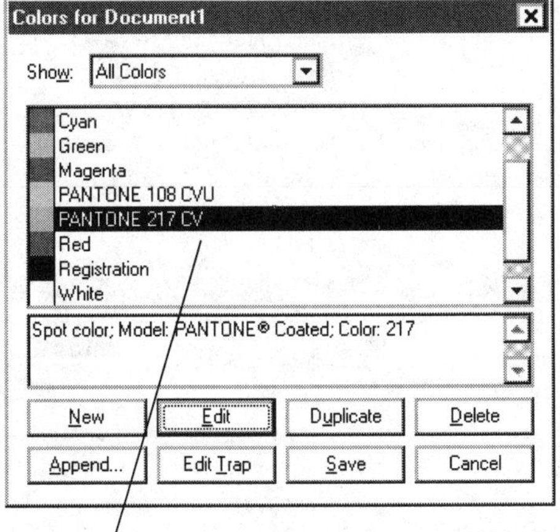

5 *The new PANTONE color is now listed in the Colors dialog box, and it will appear on the Colors palette when you click* ***Save****.*

Default colors

If you create a color when no document is open, that color will appear on the Colors palette of any subsequently created documents.

Append colors

To append colors from one document to another, click Append in the Colors dialog box or choose File menu > Append (Ctrl-Alt-A) (see page 34). Or quick-append by dragging an item to which the desired color has been applied from a library into a document window or from one document to another.

If you import an EPS picture into QuarkXPress, any spot colors in the picture will append to the QuarkXPress Colors palette.

Halftoning options

The Halftone Angle, Frequency, and Dot Function Halftone options that are currently set for each process color (C, M, Y, or K) can be assigned to a selected spot color via the Halftone drop-down menu in the Edit Color dialog box. To view the current settings, choose File menu > Print > Output folder tab (Ctrl-P), and check the Separations box in the Document folder tab. For more information, see page 301. Changes made in the Print dialog box override settings in the Edit Color dialog box.

Compare colors

To compare the components of two colors, in the Colors dialog box, Ctrl-click two color names, then hold down Alt and click the Append button (it will turn into a Compare button).

Note: In process color printing, a wide range of colors are produced by printing tiny dots from four plates, one each for Cyan, Magenta, Yellow, and Black. In the Hexachrome matching system by Pantone, Inc., two additional plates are used—orange and green—bringing the total to six plates. The additional plates in Hexachrome color (commonly referred to as "HiFi" or "high fidelity" color) expand the range of printable colors and also produce brighter and more vibrant colors than are possible using the standard four process plates. QuarkXPress can also color separate an RGB TIFF using high fidelity colors. Consult with your print shop before using HiFi colors. Their higher cost is justified only in certain cases.

(Trapping is discussed on pages 310–318.)

To create a process color:

1. Choose Edit menu > Colors (Shift-F12).
2. Click New.
3. Choose Model: TRUMATCH, FOCOLTONE, PANTONE Process (four-color process colors), or PANTONE Solid to Process (four-color process colors that simulate spot colors for coated stock), Hexachrome Uncoated, or Hexachrome Coated **1**, then enter the desired color number in the TRUMATCH, FOCOLTONE, or PANTONE field or scroll through the swatches and click a swatch **2**.
   or
   Choose Model: CMYK **3**, enter percentages from a color matching book in the Cyan, Magenta, Yellow, and Black fields **4**, and type a name for the color in the Name field **5**.
4. Make sure the Spot Color box is unchecked **6**.
5. Click OK or press Enter.
6. Click Save. The color will be added to the Colors palette.

A name will appear automatically after you choose a color.

1 *To choose a process color from a matching system, choose* ***Model: TRUMATCH, FOCOLTONE, PANTONE Process, PANTONE Solid to Process, Hexachrome Uncoated,*** *or* ***Hexachrome Coated.***

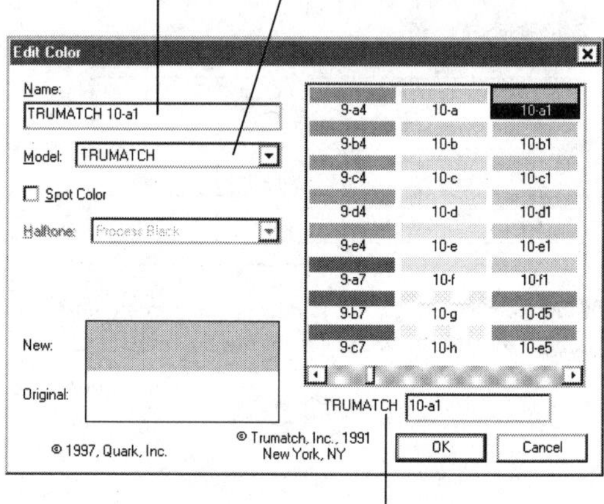

2 *Then enter a number in the TRUMATCH, FOCOLTONE, or PANTONE field or click a color swatch.*

3 *To mix your own process color, first choose* ***Model: CMYK.***

5 *Type a* ***Name*** *for the new* ***CMYK*** *color.*

6 *For any process color, make sure the* ***Spot Color*** *box is* ***unchecked.*** *(If the Spot Color box is checked, the process color will be converted into a spot color.)*

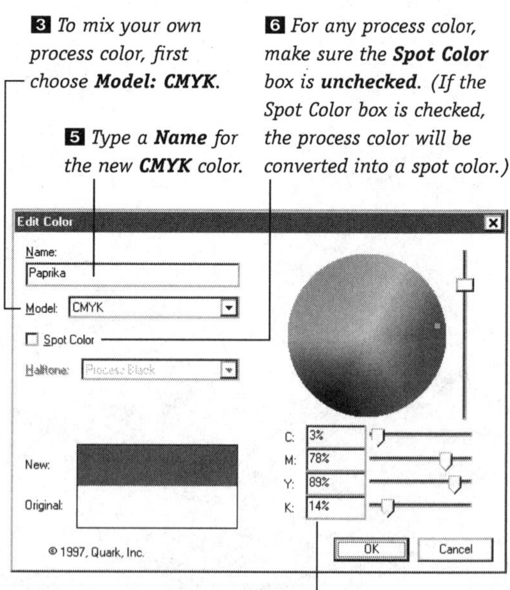

4 *For a* ***CMYK*** *model color, enter* ***Cyan, Magenta, Yellow,*** *and* ***Black*** *percentages.*

■1 *Double-click the name of the color that you want to edit.*

*To limit the colors that appear on the scroll list, choose a category from the **Show** drop-down menu.*

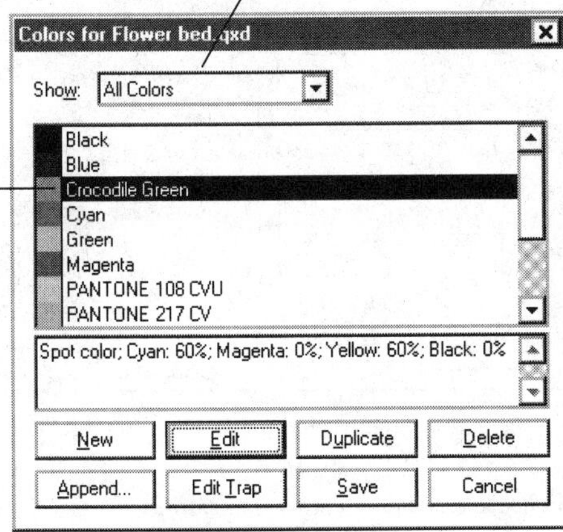

*The color **Name** can be changed.*

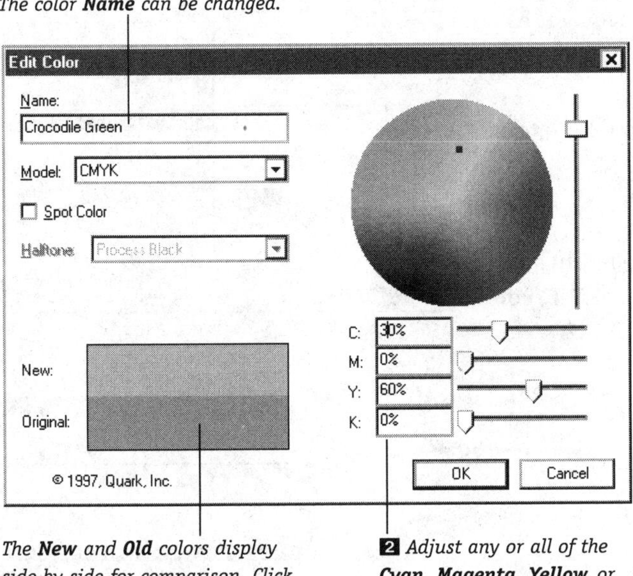

*The **New** and **Old** colors display side-by-side for comparison. Click the Original color swatch to restore the color to its original formula.*

■2 *Adjust any or all of the **Cyan, Magenta, Yellow,** or **Black** percentages.*

To edit a CMYK color:

1. Choose Edit menu > Colors (Shift-F12), then double-click the name of the color you want to edit (or click the color name, then click Edit) ■1.
   or
   Ctrl-click a color on the Colors palette, then click Edit.
2. Adjust any of the Cyan, Magenta, Yellow or Black percentages ■2.
3. Click OK.
4. Click Save. The color will update immediately in any item to which it has already been applied.

TIP To create a rich black, you can add some magenta (M) or cyan (C) to your black (K). Ask your commercial printer for advice.

Multi-ink is a new color model in which you can create new colors from a combination of process and/or spot colors. For example, you could create a new color by combining 50% of a PANTONE color and 20% of a CMYK color. Multi-ink colors print to more than one plate.

Note: Talk to your print shop before using multi-ink colors, as they can produce moiré patterns and other printing problems if the proper screen angles are not used.

To create a multi-ink color:

1. Choose Edit menu > Colors (Shift-F12).
2. Click New.
3. Choose Model: Multi-Ink **1**.
4. Click a color, then choose a Shade for that color **2**.
5. Repeat step 4 for the colors that you want to combine with the first color **3**.
6. Type a Name for the multi-ink color.
7. Click OK or press Enter.
8. Click Save **4**. The color will be added to the Colors palette.

TIP To preview how color mixes look when printed, get either or both of these PANTONE swatch books: Color+Black (spot colors plus black) or Color+Color (spot color combinations).

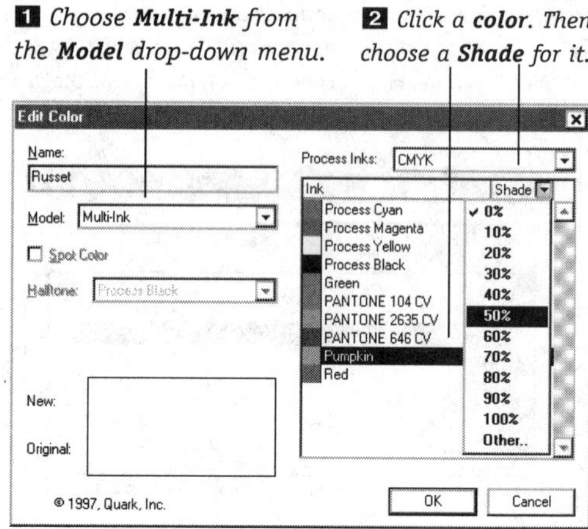

1 *Choose* ***Multi-Ink*** *from the* ***Model*** *drop-down menu.*

2 *Click a* ***color****. Then choose a* ***Shade*** *for it.*

3 *Choose additional* ***colors*** *and* ***shades****.*

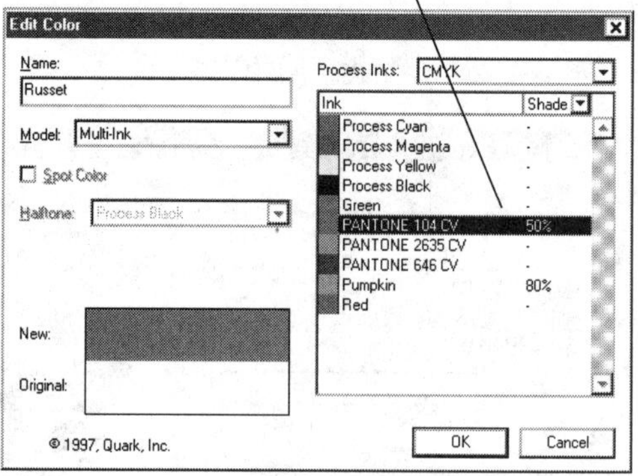

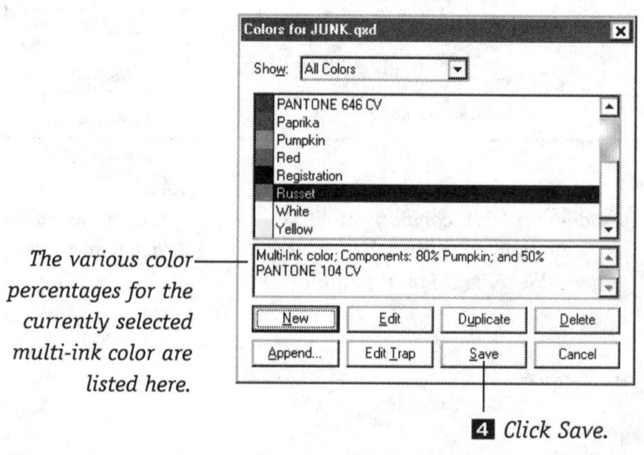

The various color percentages for the currently selected multi-ink color are listed here.

4 *Click Save.*

— The text color icon for text on a path.

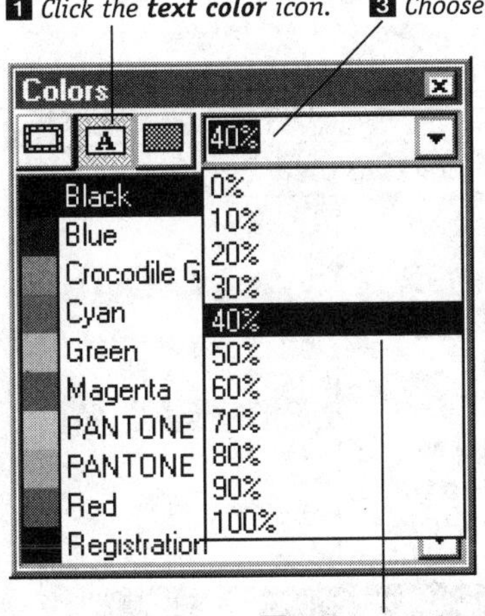

*The Colors palette when **text** is selected.*

Use the following method to recolor a unique area of text, like a headline. Since you can apply color to text using the Character Attributes dialog box, you can recolor repetitive text most efficiently via a style sheet (click Character Attributes: Edit in the Edit Style Sheets dialog box). And you can use Find/Change to apply a new color via a style sheet.

To recolor text:

1. Choose View menu > Show Colors to display the Colors palette (F12).
2. Choose the Content tool.
3. Highlight the text to which you want to apply a color.
4. Click the text color (middle) icon on the Colors palette 1.
5. Click a color 2.
6. Choose a percentage from the shade drop-down menu 3–4. To apply a custom shade, choose Style menu > Shade > Other, enter a percentage, then click OK.

TIP A color or shade can also be applied to text via the Character Attributes dialog box (Ctrl-Shift-D) or via the Style menu > Color or Shade submenu.

TIP If you're coloring type white or restoring reversed type to black-on-white, change the type color first and then change the background color, so the text will be easy to highlight 5.

There is no such thing as a non-working mother.

Hester Mundis

TWENTYPERCENT
THIRTYPERCENT
FORTY PERCENT
FIFTY PERCENT
SIXTY PERCENT
SEVENTYPERCENT
EIGHTYPERCENT
NINETYPERCENT
HUNDREDPERCENT

4 A range of shades can be applied to type.

If you create reversed type, use a bold, chunky typeface to enhance legibility, especially if it's going to be printed on porous paper stock.

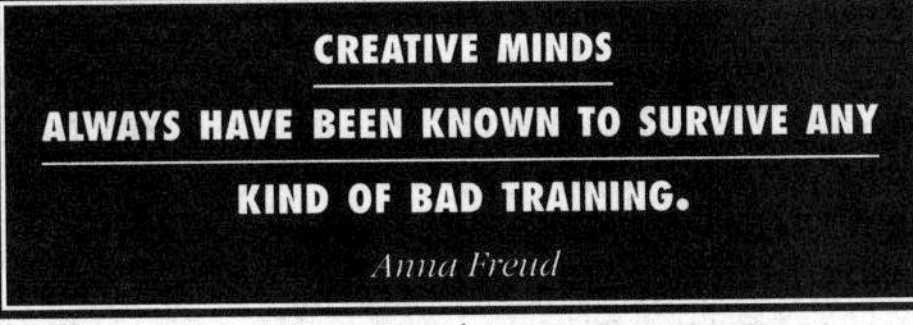

CREATIVE MINDS
ALWAYS HAVE BEEN KNOWN TO SURVIVE ANY
KIND OF BAD TRAINING.
Anna Freud

5 Reversed serif letters can look wispy.

Recolor Text

In the following instructions, you will learn how to recolor the background of any kind of box. Want to have some fun? Create playful or dramatic graphic elements using empty or contentless standard or Bézier boxes (or lines). Use your imagination! To create multiples of any item, use Item menu > Step and Repeat.

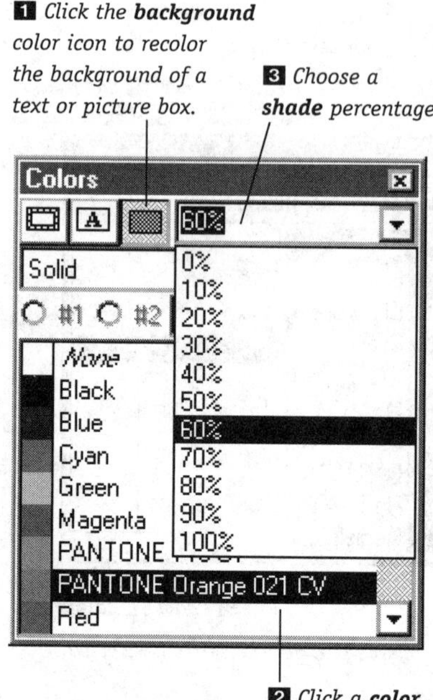

*The Colors palette when a **text box, picture box,** or **contentless box** is selected.*

To recolor the background of an item:

1. Choose View menu > Show Colors to display the Colors palette (F12).
2. Choose the Item or Content tool.
3. Click on a text box, picture box, contentless box, group, or multiple-item selection.
4. Click the background color (rightmost) icon on the Colors palette **1**.
5. Click a color **2**.
6. Choose a percentage from the Shade drop-down menu **3**.

TIP You can also recolor a box by dragging a color swatch (see page 237) or in the Item menu > Modify > Box or Group folder tab.

A text ornament on top of a 30% black & white picture, which has a 10% black background.

White and 30% black type on a 100% black background.

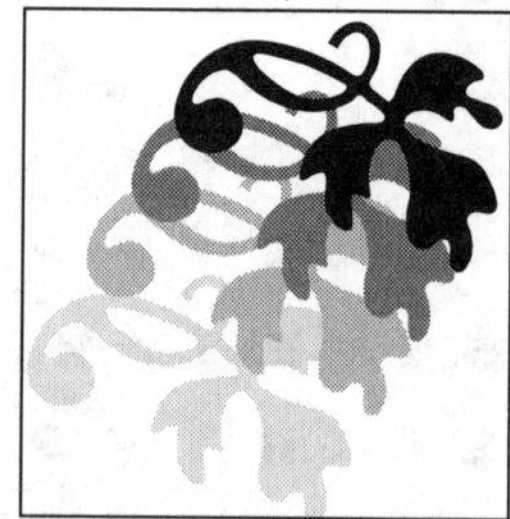

Bézier shapes in varying shades of black on a white background.

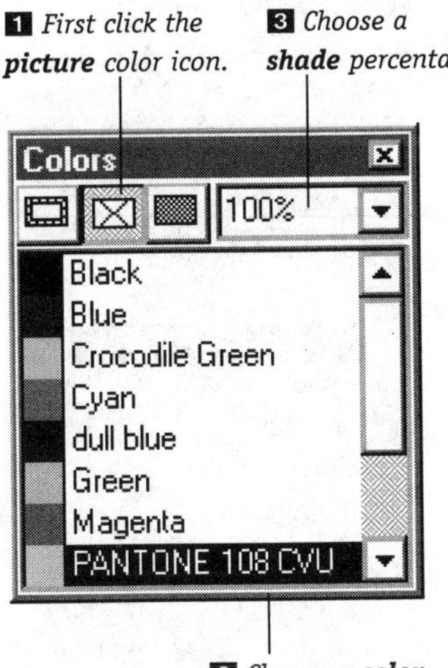

1 *First click the **picture** color icon.*

3 *Choose a **shade** percentage.*

2 *Choose a **color**.*

*The Colors palette when a **picture** is selected.*

4 *A TIFF line art picture with a 30% shade.*

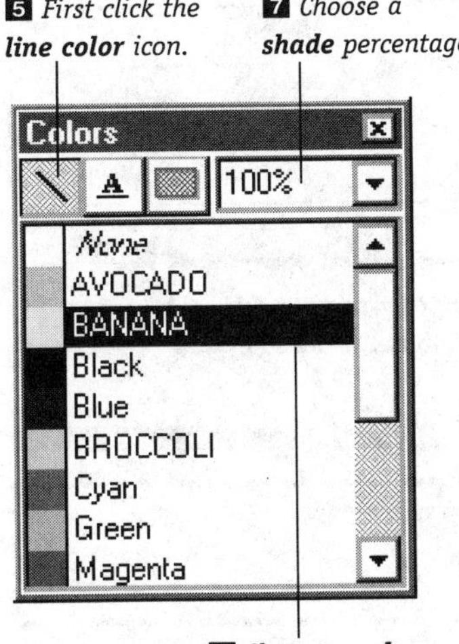

5 *First click the **line color** icon.*

7 *Choose a **shade** percentage.*

6 *Choose a **color**.*

*The Colors palette when a **line** is selected.*

To recolor a picture:

1. Choose View menu > Show Colors to display the Colors palette (F12).
2. Choose the Content tool.
3. Click on a JPEG grayscale, OS/2 1-bit bitmap, or PAINT picture, or a 1-bit or grayscale PICT, TIFF, or bitmap (BMP)/PCX picture (but not an EPS or a TIFF with a 16- or 32-bit preview).
4. Click the picture color (middle) icon in the Colors palette **1**.
5. Click a color **2**.
6. Choose a percentage from the Shade drop-down menu **3**–**4**.

TIP A color or shade can also be applied to a picture using the Style menu > Color or Shade submenu or the Item menu > Modify > Picture folder tab (Ctrl-M or right-click and choose Modify).

TIP You can color adjust a color JPEG, OS/2 bitmap, bitmap PICT, Scitex CT, TIFF, or Windows bitmap (BMP)/PCX picture via Style menu > Contrast.

To recolor a line or a text path:

1. Choose View menu > Show Colors to display the Colors palette (F12).
2. Choose the Item or Content tool.
3. Select a standard line, a Bézier line, or a text path, or create a multiple-item selection.
4. Click the line (leftmost) color icon on the Colors palette **5**.
5. Click a color **6**.
6. Choose a percentage from the Shade drop-down menu **7**.

TIP A color can also be applied to a line using the Style menu > Color submenu.

Note: Specifying a color for a frame using the Colors palette doesn't actually place the frame on the box. To make the frame appear, you must specify a frame width other than zero in the Item menu > Frame dialog box (Ctrl-B). You can apply a frame color before or after assigning a width.

To recolor a frame:

1. Choose View menu > Show Colors to display the Colors palette (F12).
2. Choose the Item or Content tool.
3. Click on a text box, picture box, or group of items, or create a multiple-item selection.
4. Click the frame (leftmost) color icon on the Colors palette **1**.
5. Click a color **2**.
6. Choose a percentage from the Shade drop-down menu **3**.

1 *First click the **frame** icon.*

3 *Choose a **shade** percentage.*

2 *Choose a **color**.*

*The **frame** icon is available on the Colors palette when a text or picture box is selected.*

To recolor the gaps in a line or frame:

1. Choose the Item or Content tool.
2. Select the box or line that contains the gaps that you want to recolor.
3. For a box, choose Item menu > Modify > Frame folder tab (Ctrl-B).

   For a line, choose Item menu > Modify > Line folder tab (Ctrl-M) or right-click and choose Modify.

   The gap color can't be changed for a paragraph rule.
4. Choose from the Gap: Color drop-down menu **4**.
5. Choose or enter a Gap: Shade percentage.
6. Click Apply to preview, then OK or press Enter.

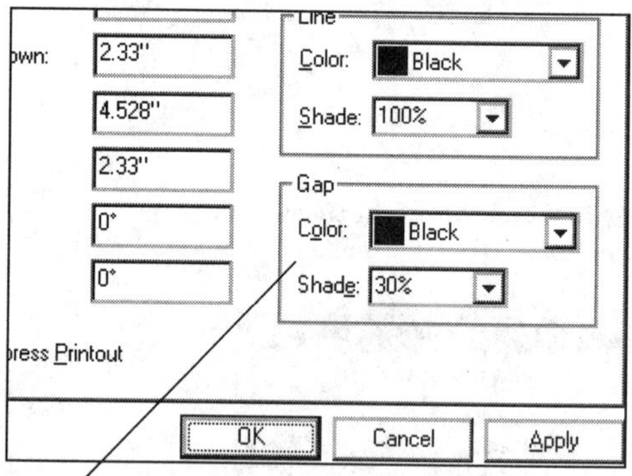

4 *Choose a **Gap Color** and **Shade** in the Item menu > Modify **Line** (or Frame) folder tab.*

This gap color is Black, 25%.

Use the Drag Color feature to preview or apply color to the background of a picture box, text box, or frame, or to recolor a line or text path. You can't recolor text or a picture this way.

1 *Drag a swatch from the Colors palette to the item you want to recolor.*

2 *The background of the box is recolored.*

To recolor by dragging:

1. Select any item in your document.
2. Drag a swatch (not the swatch name) from the Colors palette over a text box, picture box, frame, line, or text path **1**.
3. Release the mouse over the item to apply the color **2**. If you're applying a color to a frame, line, or text path, release the mouse when the *tip* of the arrow is directly over the component that you want to recolor.
   or
   Keep the mouse button down and move the cursor away from the item to leave its color unchanged.

TIP A color will be applied in the default shade percentage of an item if you have not changed its color, or in the shade of the color that was last applied to the item. If that shade is 0%, it will remain so. To apply a new shade, click the line or background color icon on the Colors palette, then choose a shade percentage.

TIP Alt-drag a swatch to apply a color at a 100% shade.

A two-color linear blend can be applied to the background of a text or picture box, but not to text, a line, or a frame.

To help prevent banding in a QuarkXPress blend (noticeable stripes instead of smooth color transitions), apply it to a box that is no larger than five inches in either dimension, and don't use two very similar colors. One of the colors can be white or 0% of a spot color. If you don't want to risk banding, create your blend in Photoshop and import it into a picture box in QuarkXPress.

Note: To apply a blend to text, use the Style menu > Text to Box command first to convert a copy of it into a picture box.

To apply a blend to a box:

1. Choose the Item tool.
2. Click on a text box, picture box, group, or multiple-item selection.
3. Choose View menu > Show Colors to open the Colors palette (F12).
4. Click the Background icon **1**.
5. Choose Linear, Mid-Linear, Rectangular, Diamond, Circular, or Full Circular from the fill-type drop-down menu **2**. (If Linear is the only available option, it means the Cool Blends XTension isn't enabled. Use the XTensions Manager to enable it, then re-launch XPress.)
6. Click the #1 button, then choose a color and a shade percentage **3**.
7. Click the #2 button, then choose a color and a shade percentage (**4**, this page and **5**–**9** on the next page).
8. *Optional:* Enter an angle between -360° and 360° in an increment as small as .001° in the angle field (remember to press Enter).

TIP To render blends on an 8-bit monitor without banding, check the Accurate Blends box in Edit menu > Preferences > Document > General folder tab (Ctrl-Y). Screen redraw may be slower with this option checked.

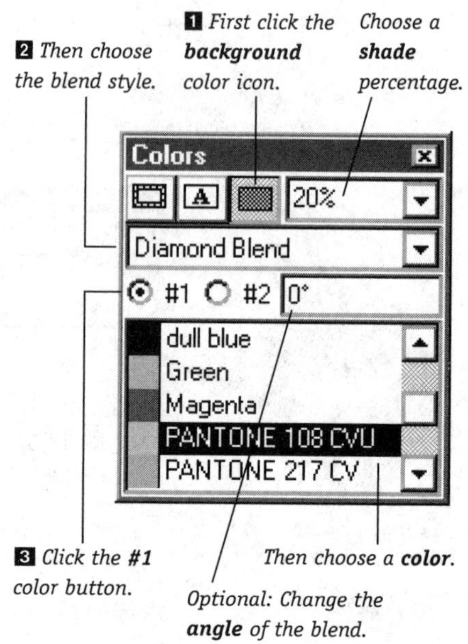

1 *First click the* ***background*** *color icon.*
2 *Then choose the blend style.*
Choose a ***shade*** *percentage.*
Colors
20%
Diamond Blend
#1
#2
0°
dull blue
Green
Magenta
PANTONE 108 CVU
PANTONE 217 CV
3 *Click the* ***#1*** *color button.*
Then choose a ***color****.*
Optional: Change the ***angle*** *of the blend.*

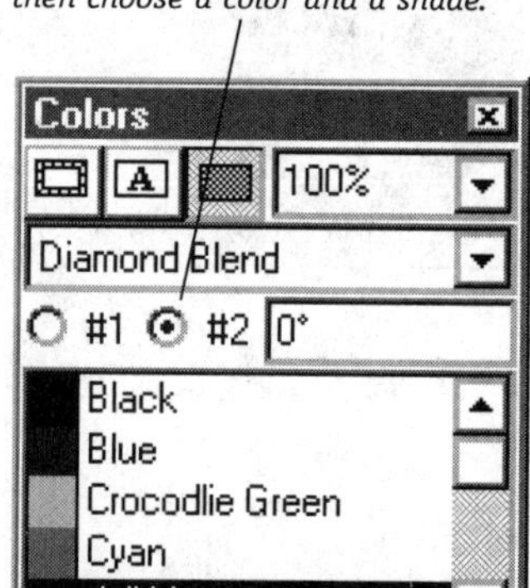

4 *Click the* ***#2*** *color button, then choose a color and a shade.*
Colors
100%
Diamond Blend
#1
#2
0°
Black
Blue
Crocodlie Green
Cyan
dull blue

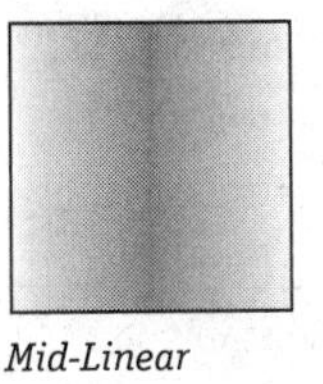

Mid-Linear

Mid-Linear (45°)

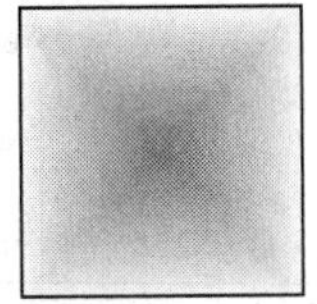

Rectangular

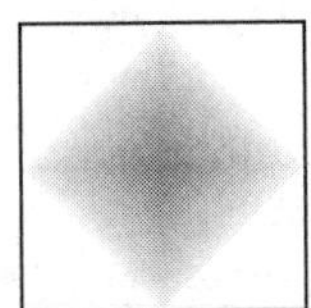

Diamond

Linear

Linear (125°)

Circular

Full Circular

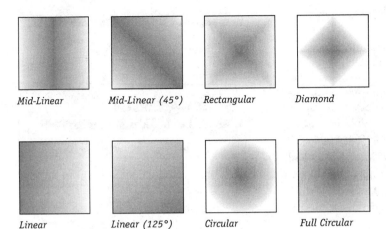

5

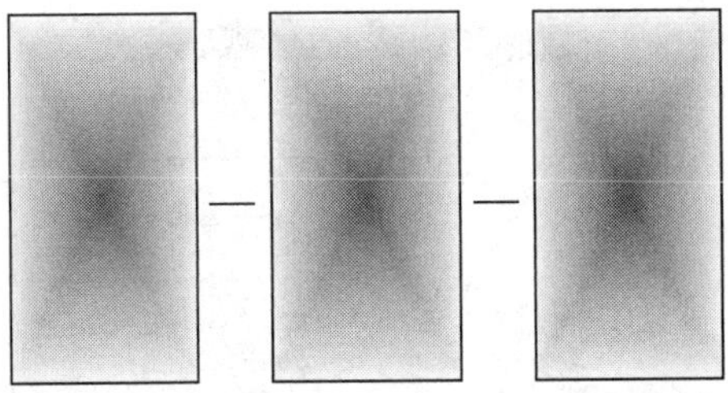

6 *A rectangular blend applied to each individual item.*

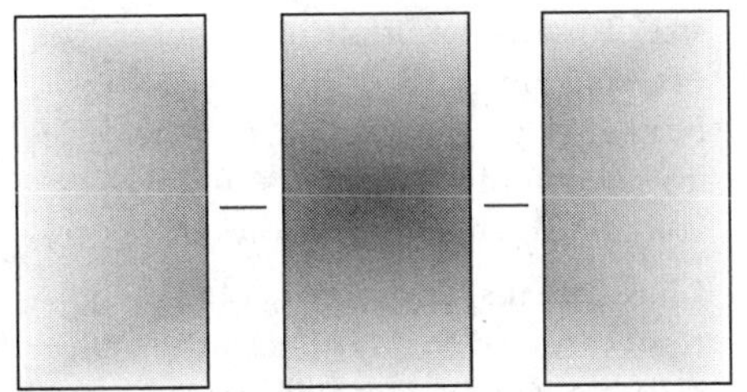

7 *The same blend applied to a multiple-item selection that was merged via Item menu > Merge >* ***Union****.*

8 *A linear blend applied to each individual item.*

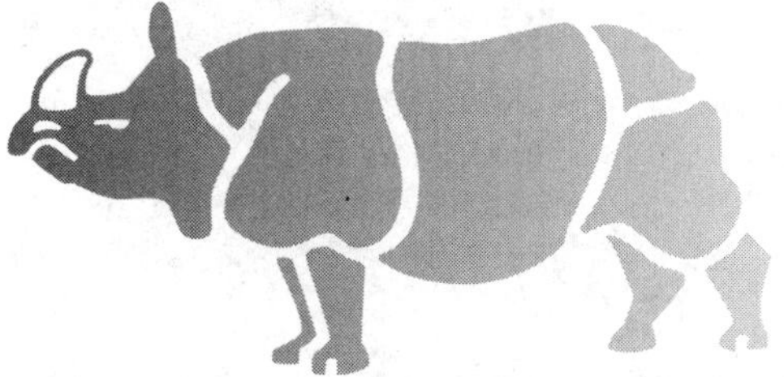

9 *The same blend applied to a multiple-item selection that was merged via Item menu > Merge >* ***Union****.*

To delete colors from the Colors palette:

1. To delete a color from a document, open the document now.
   or
   To delete a color from the default Colors palette (the palette that appears when you create a new document), make sure no documents are open.
2. Choose Edit menu > Colors (Shift-F12).
3. Click on the name of the color that you want to delete. Cyan, Magenta, Yellow, Black, White, and Registration cannot be deleted.
   or
   To delete all the colors that are not currently being used in the document, choose Show: Colors Not Used **1**, then select the colors you want to delete. This can reduce the document's file size. To select multiple, contiguous colors, click on the first in a series, then Shift-click on the last color in the series. To select multiple, non-contiguous colors, Ctrl-click them individually.
4. Click Delete. If a deleted color is currently applied to any item in the active document, a prompt will appear. Choose a replacement color from the "Replace with" drop-down menu **2**, then click OK.
5. Click Save.

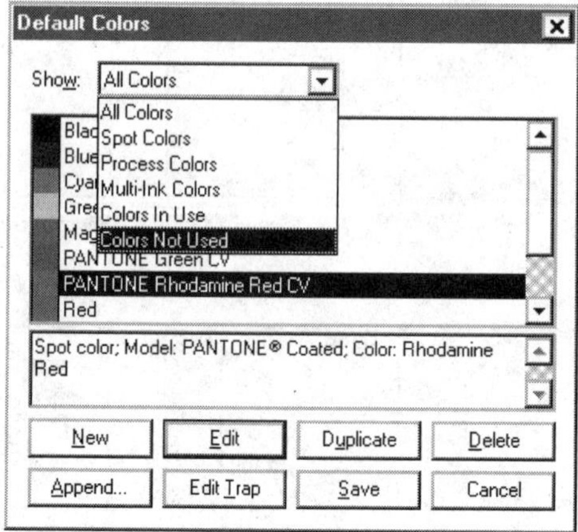

1 *In the* ***Default Colors*** *dialog box, click the name of the color that you want to delete, then click* ***Delete.*** *To delete all the colors that are not currently being used in the document, choose Show:* ***Colors Not Used,*** *select the colors you want to delete, then click Delete.*

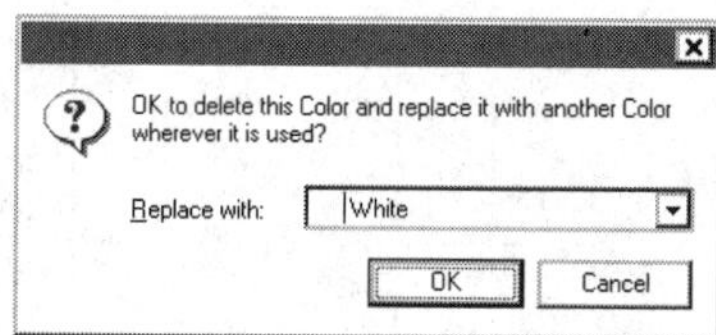

2 *Choose a replacement color from the* ***Replace with*** *drop-down menu.*

FIND/CHANGE COLORS

You can use the Color Change XTension from Vision's Edge, Inc. to search for and replace colors in a document.

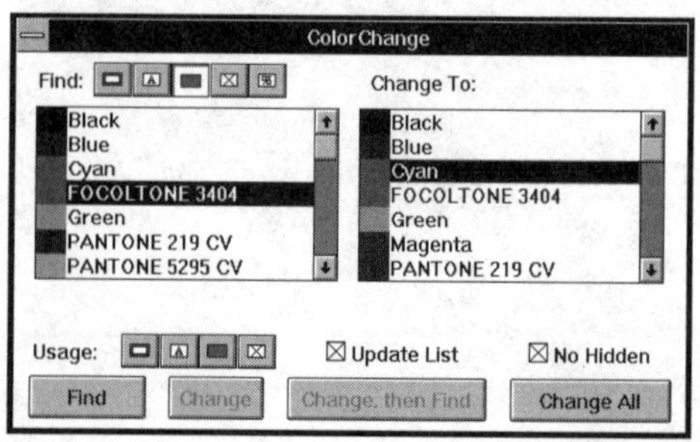

Libraries 16

QUICK-APPEND FROM A LIBRARY

When an item with a color applied to it is retrieved from a library, the color is appended to the color palette of the active file. Ditto for text with a style sheet applied—the style sheet is appended to the active file (unless its name matches that of an existing style sheet).

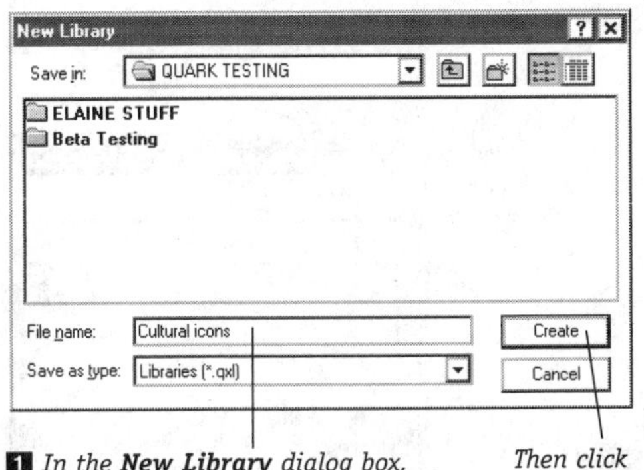

1 *In the* ***New Library*** *dialog box, enter a name in the* ***File name*** *field.*

Then click ***Create.***

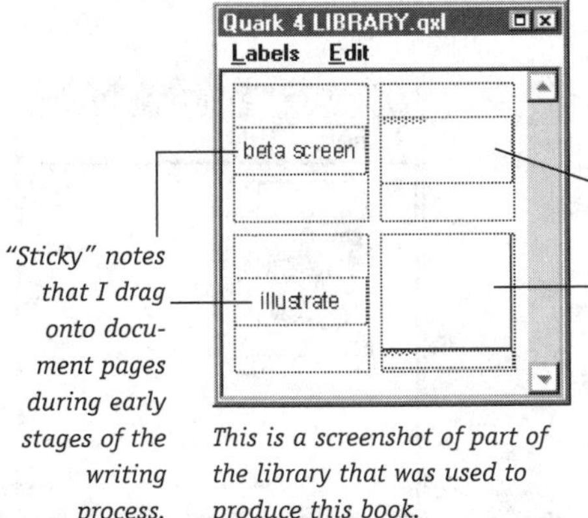

"Sticky" notes that I drag onto document pages during early stages of the writing process.

This is a screenshot of part of the library that was used to produce this book.

A box for a sidebar with style sheets applied to it.

A group, composed of a picture box with no frame and a caption box with the caption style sheet applied to it. This library also includes a picture box with a frame.

Libraries

A library is a special kind of file that is used to organize and store repetitively used items, such as empty boxes, boxes with text or picture contents, lines, text paths, or groups. Each library is displayed as a floating palette. You can drag an entry from a floating library palette into any open QuarkXPress document window. An unlimited number of libraries can be created.

Note: A picture that originates from a library is merely a TIFF preview. In fact, because of its relatively small file size, a library is easily portable and can be used like a picture thumbnail catalog. If you send a document containing library elements for imagesetting, however, you'll still need to supply the original picture files.

To create a library:

1. Choose File menu > New > Library (Ctrl-Alt-N).
2. Type a name for the library in the File name field **1**.
3. Select a drive or folder in which to save the library.
4. Click Create. A new library palette will appear on your screen.

To add an entry to a library:

1. Create a new library or open an existing library.
2. Choose the Item tool (or hold down Ctrl with the Content tool).
3. Press and drag any item, group, or multiple-item selection into the library 1–3. You can even drag an entry from one library to another. A thumbnail of the item will appear in the library; the original item will stay on your page.

1 *Press and drag an item into a library with the **Item** tool.*

2 *The cursor turns into an **eyeglasses** icon as an entry is dragged into a library.*

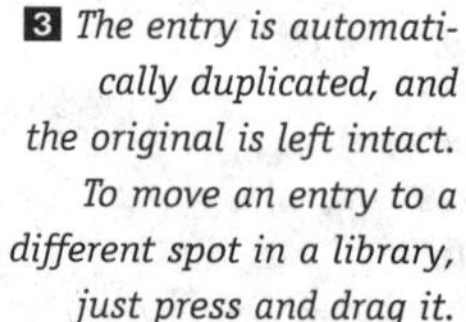

3 *The entry is automatically duplicated, and the original is left intact. To move an entry to a different spot in a library, just press and drag it.*

AUTO LIBRARY SAVE

A library is saved each time an entry is added to it if the Auto Library Save box is checked in Edit menu > Preferences > Application > Save folder tab. When this option is unchecked, a library is saved only when it's closed.

■1 *Double-click a **library** file or type the name in the File name box and press Enter.*

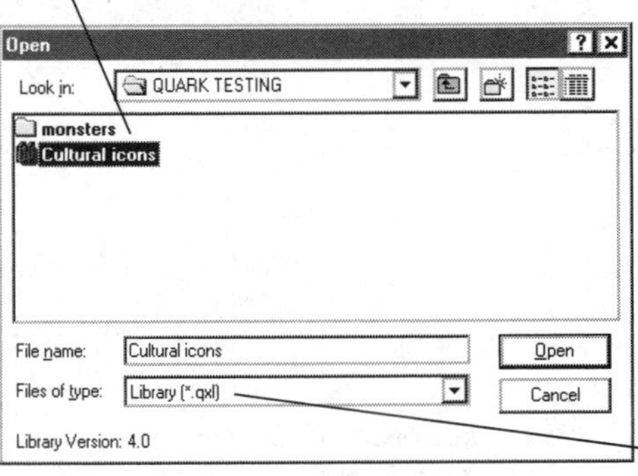

To display only library files, choose Library (.qxd) from the **Files of Type** drop-down list.*

Click the library palette maximize button to expand the palette to full-screen size.

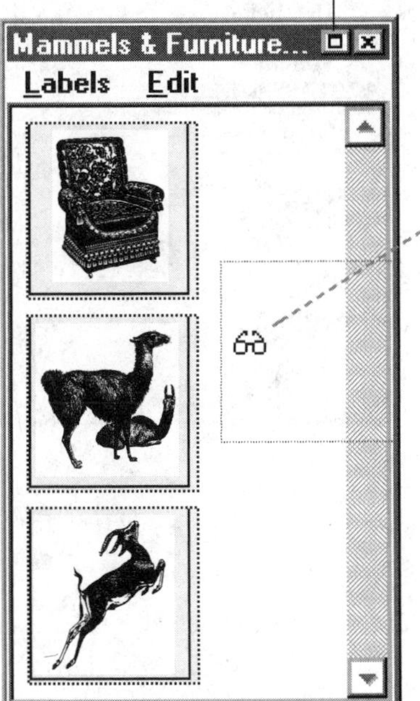

To reshape a library palette, drag the lower right-hand corner.

■2 *Press and drag an entry onto a document page.*

To open an existing library:

1. Choose File menu > Open (Ctrl-O).
2. Locate and highlight the name of the library that you want to open ■1, then click Open. Library files have a book icon.
   or
   Double-click a library file name.

TIP To open a library from the Desktop or Explorer, double-click the library file icon.

TIP To close a library palette, click its close box.

Note: When a picture is added to a library, info about the path to the original picture file is stored with the library entry. When a picture is retrieved from a library, the picture's path info is also stored with the document. The original picture file must be retained for the image to print properly.

To retrieve an entry from a library:

1. Choose the Item or Content tool.
2. Press and drag an item from a library onto a document page ■2.

Labeling related library entries helps to organize them and enables you to display them selectively. The same label can be applied to more than one entry.

To label a library entry:

1. Double-click a library entry.
2. Enter a name in the Label field **1**.
   or
   Choose an existing label from the Label drop-down menu **2**.
3. Click OK or press Enter. If you created a new label, it will appear on the Labels menu on the palette.

TIP You can retype the same label for various entries, but it's easier to just select an existing label, and you'll be less likely to make a typing error.

1 *Type a new label in the **Label** field.*

2 *Or choose an existing label from the **Label** drop-down menu.*

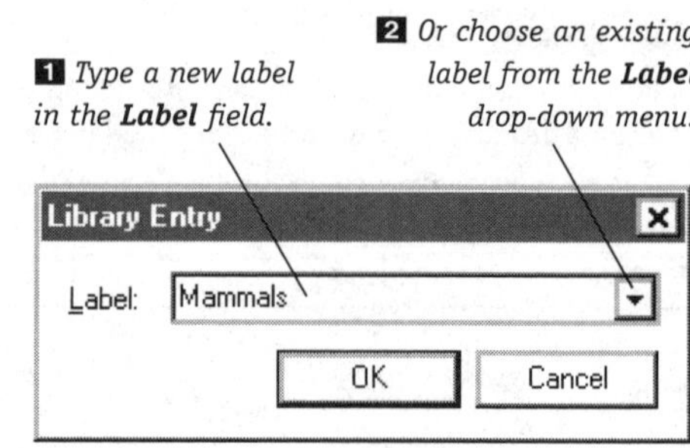

To display entries with the same label:

Choose a label from the Labels menu on the library palette. More than one label category can be displayed at a time **3**.

Choose All to display all the entries in the library.

Choose Unlabeled to display only those entries that are unlabeled.

3 *A **check mark** indicates that all the entries bearing that label are currently displayed.*

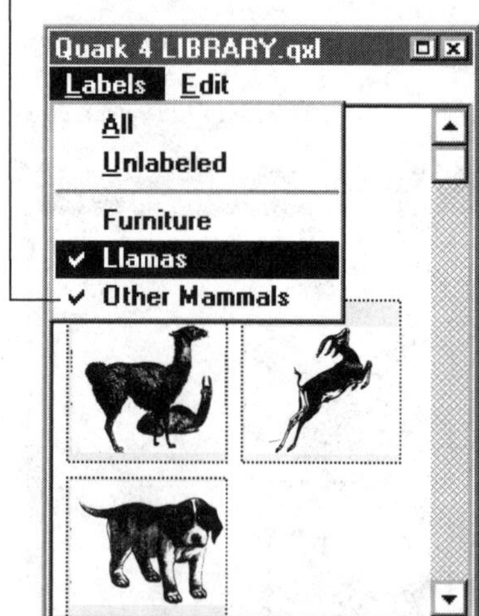

To hide entries with the same label:

Re-select a selected label from the Labels menu on the library palette to uncheck it. A check mark indicates that that label category is displayed.

To delete an entry from a library:

1. Choose the Item or Content tool.
2. Click on a library entry.
3. Choose Delete from the Edit menu on the library palette.
4. Click OK or press Enter. You can't undo a library entry deletion.

Search and replace 17

This chapter covers QuarkXPress' global search and replace features: Check Spelling, Find/Change, and Font Usage.

A word, story, or document can be checked for spelling accuracy. By default, the Check Spelling feature checks words against the QuarkXPress dictionary, which contains 120,000 words and cannot be edited. However, a custom auxiliary dictionary can be created or an existing auxiliary dictionary can be opened to be used in conjunction with the QuarkXPress dictionary.

1 *Neither the word "borogoves" nor similar words are found in the QuarkXPress dictionary.*

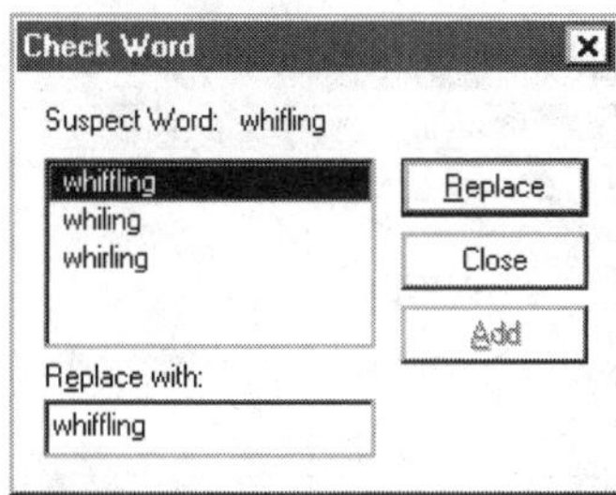

2 *Double-click a replacement word. The only way to tell whether the word in the document is spelled correctly is to compare it, letter by letter, to a word on the scroll list. (I wish an icon or the words "You're wrong!" would appear if a word is spelled incorrectly.)*

To check the spelling of a word:

1. Choose the Content tool.
2. Click or double-click a suspect word.
3. Choose Utilities menu > Check Spelling > Word (Ctrl-W).
4. If the Suspect Word is not found in the QuarkXPress dictionary or any open auxiliary dictionary and no similar words are found, the Check Word dialog box will display "No similar words found" **1**.

   If the Suspect Word and/or similar words are found in the QuarkXPress dictionary or in any open auxiliary dictionary, they will be listed, and the Suspect Word, if found, will be highlighted. Double-click a replacement word **2**; or highlight a word and click Replace; or click Close to leave the Suspect Word unchanged.
5. *Optional:* Click Add if you want to add the Suspect Word to the currently open auxiliary dictionary (see the next page).
6. Click Close.

An auxiliary dictionary is a user-defined dictionary that can be created to work in conjunction with the QuarkXPress dictionary. Unlike the QuarkXPress dictionary, an auxiliary dictionary can be edited. Only one auxiliary dictionary can be open at a time, but a document can be checked for spelling several times, each time with a different auxiliary dictionary open. And the same auxiliary dictionary can be used with any number of documents.

The last auxiliary dictionary that you create or open for a document will remain associated with that document until you close the auxiliary or open another auxiliary while that document is open. An auxiliary dictionary will also become disassociated from a document if you move it from its original location. If an auxiliary dictionary is created when no document is open, it will become the default auxiliary dictionary for any subsequently created documents.

1 *Type a name for the auxiliary dictionary.*

2 *Then click **New**.*

To create an auxiliary dictionary:

1. Choose Utilities menu > Auxiliary Dictionary.
2. Type a name in the File name field **1**.
3. Choose a location in which to save the dictionary, then click New **2**.

To open an existing auxiliary dictionary:

1. Choose Utilities menu > Auxiliary Dictionary.
2. Locate and highlight the auxiliary dictionary that you want to open **3**.
3. Click Open or press Enter **4**.

TIP Click Close to disassociate the currently open auxiliary dictionary from the active document.

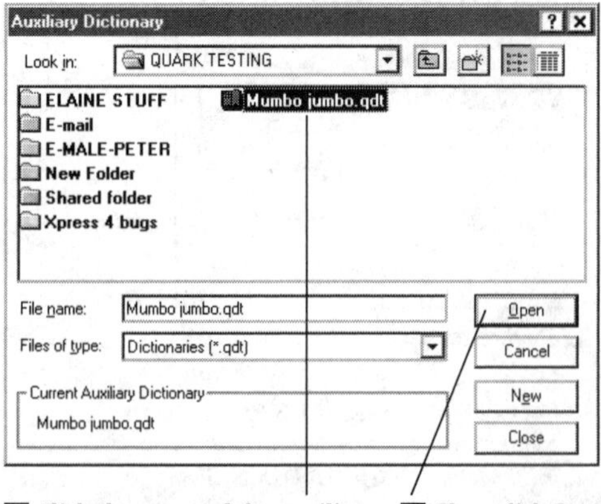

3 *Click the name of the auxiliary dictionary that you want to open.*

4 *Then click **Open**.*

Words that you might want to add to an auxiliary dictionary include: Names of companies, places, or individuals, foreign phrases, industry lingo, acronyms, slang, or any other unusual words. Check Spelling won't consider any word added to the auxiliary as suspect, and this speeds up the spelling-checking process. Words cannot actually be edited in the Edit Auxiliary Dictionary dialog box—they can only be deleted or added. It's a simple little system.

To edit an auxiliary dictionary:

1. Open the auxiliary dictionary that you want to edit via Utilities menu > Auxiliary Dictionary.
2. Choose Utilities menu > Edit Auxiliary.
3. Type a new word in the entry field **1**, then click Add. No spaces or compound words (i.e. on-screen) are permitted, and all characters are saved in lowercase. Punctuation is not permitted, except for an apostrophe in a contraction (i.e. can't). Enter the singular and plural forms of a word as separate entries, as in "kid" and "kids."
   or
   To delete a word, click on it, then click Delete **2**.
4. Click Save.

TIP A Suspect Word can also be added to an open auxiliary dictionary by clicking Add in the Check Word, Check Story, or Check Document dialog box.

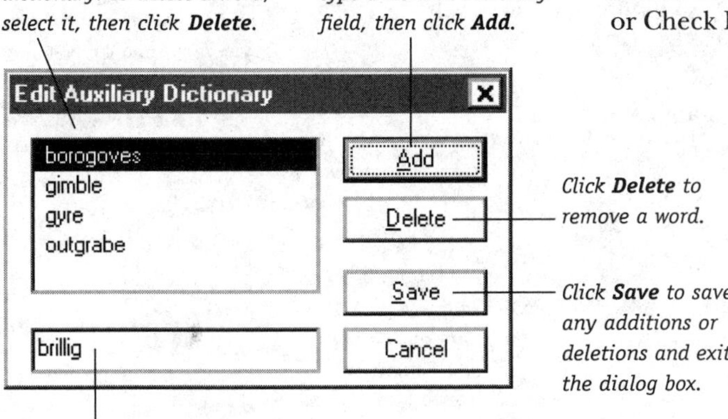
2 *This scroll list displays all the words in the auxiliary dictionary. To delete a word, select it, then click **Delete**.*
*To add a new word, type a word in the entry field, then click **Add**.*
Edit Auxiliary Dictionary
borogoves
gimble
gyre
outgrabe
brillig
Add
Delete
Save
Cancel
*Click **Delete** to remove a word.*
*Click **Save** to save any additions or deletions and exit the dialog box.*

1 *Type a **new** word in the entry field, then click Add.*

Edit Auxiliary Dictionary

To check the spelling of a story or a document:

1. *Optional:* Choose a large display size for your document so you'll be able to decipher words easily, and make the window smaller so it scrolls quickly.
2. Open (or close) the auxiliary dictionary that was last used with the document, if any. You can also create a new auxiliary dictionary (instructions on page 246).
3. Choose the Content tool.
4. To check spelling in a **story**, click in the story. Then choose Utilities menu > Check Spelling > Story (Ctrl-Alt-W).
   or
   To check spelling in a **document**, choose Utilities menu > Check Spelling > Document (Ctrl-Alt-Shift-W). Spelling will automatically be checked from the beginning of the document.
   or
   To check spelling on a **master page**, display that master page now, then choose Utilities > Check Spelling > Masters (Ctrl-Alt-Shift-W).

   Note: If, when you try to choose a Check Spelling command, you get a prompt saying "Cannot find the auxiliary dictionary," choose Utilities menu > Auxiliary Dictionary, locate and highlight the auxiliary dictionary that was created for the document, then click Open. Then you'll be able to access the Check Spelling commands.
5. When the Word Count box appears, click OK or press Enter **1**.

CHECK SPELLING IN SWEDISH?

If you're using QuarkXPress **Passport** for version 4.0 or later, you can choose any one of 11 languages for the application interface (menus, palettes, and dialog boxes), and a different language, if you wish, for hyphenation and spelling-checking. The available languages include Danish, Dutch, French, German, Italian, Norwegian, Spanish, Swedish, Swiss-German, U.S. English, and International English.

Choose a language for the **interface** from the Edit menu > Program Language submenu.

Choose a language in which to **hyhenate** or **check spelling** in selected text from the Language drop-down menu in the Style menu > Formats dialog box. Make sure the SpellChecker XTension software is enabled.

To assign a **hyphenation method** to a language, choose Edit menu > Preferences > Document > Paragraph folder tab, click a Hyphenation Language, then choose a Mode.

To **save** a document in a format that can be opened only in the multilingual version of QuarkXPress Passport, choose Multiple Languages from the Save as type drop-down menu in File menu > Save As. To save a document so it can be opened only in a single-language version of Passport or in QuarkXPress, choose Single Language from the same drop-down menu.

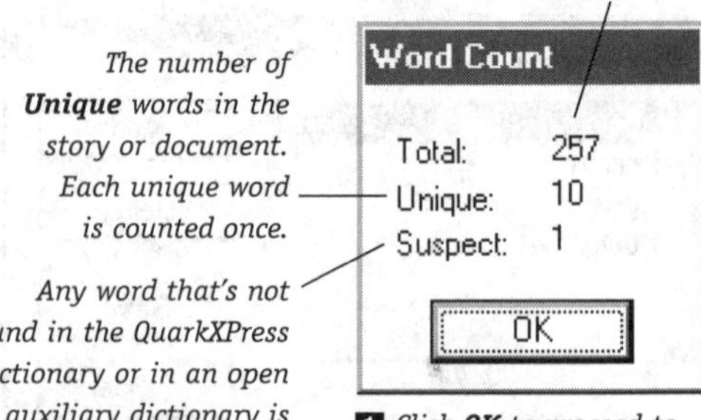
The **Total** number of words in the story. Tip: You can use this dialog box to get a tally of the length of a story if you're writing copy.
The number of **Unique** words in the story or document. Each unique word is counted once.
Any word that's not found in the QuarkXPress dictionary or in an open auxiliary dictionary is considered to be **Suspect**.
Word Count
Total: 257
Unique: 10
Suspect: 1
OK

1 *Click **OK** to proceed to the Check Story or Check Document dialog box.*

*2 **Instances** is the total number of times the Suspect Word appears in the story.*

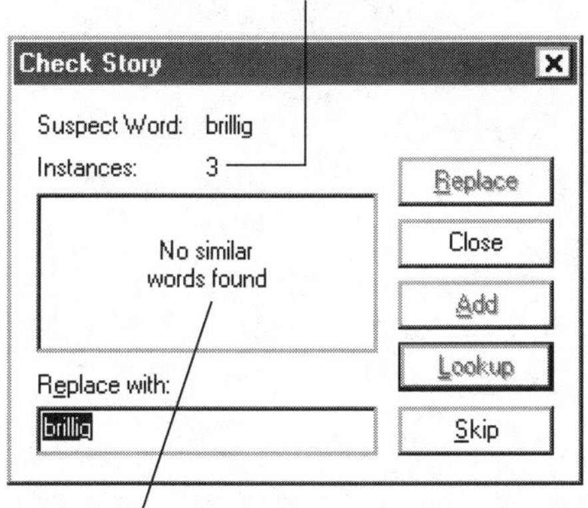

***No similar words found** indicates that no close approximation of the word was found in the QuarkXPress dictionary or in an open auxiliary dictionary.*

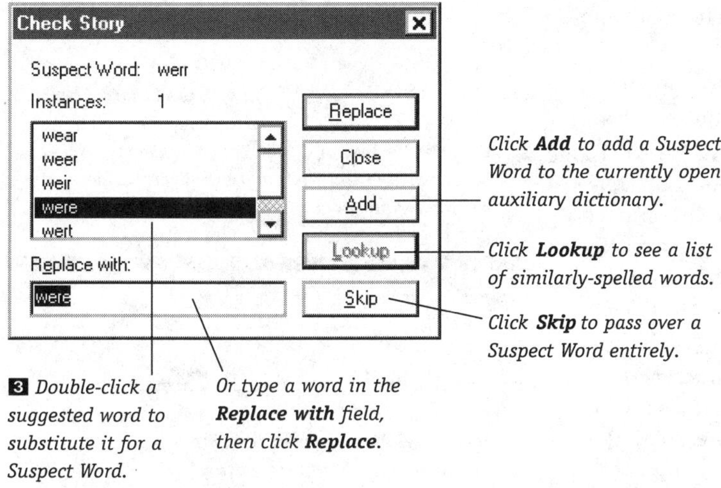

*Click **Add** to add a Suspect Word to the currently open auxiliary dictionary.*

*Click **Lookup** to see a list of similarly-spelled words.*

*Click **Skip** to pass over a Suspect Word entirely.*

3 Double-click a suggested word to substitute it for a Suspect Word.

*Or type a word in the **Replace with** field, then click **Replace**.*

6. Click Lookup (Alt-L) to see a list of similar words. Double-click a similar word, or click a similar word and click Replace 2–3.
or
Click Skip (Alt-S) to skip over a word.
or
Click Add (Alt-A) to add the Suspect Word to the currently open auxiliary dictionary.
or
Correct the spelling of the Suspect Word in the "Replace with" field, then click Replace (Alt-R).
or
To end the check spelling process at any time, click Close (Alt-F4).

TIP After the spelling of a word is checked once, all other instances of the word are treated in the same manner.

TIP Text can't be edited manually in the document while the Check Story or Check Document dialog box is open. Wish it could.

TIP Alt-Shift-click the Close button to add *all* the suspect words to the currently open auxiliary dictionary. If you do this, be sure to open the auxiliary dictionary and inspect it for misspellings (Utilities menu > Edit Auxiliary).

The Find/Change palette is used to search for and replace text, attributes, and paragraph or character style sheets. The fields and check boxes on the left side of the Find/Change palette define the text or attributes to be searched for; the fields and check boxes on the right side define what the text or attributes will be changed to.

Note: You can leave the Find/Change palette open while you edit your document, and you can zoom in or out on your document while you're using the Find/Change palette.

To find and change spaces, characters, style sheets, or attributes:

1. To limit the search to a story, choose the Content tool and click in a story. Also choose a decent-sized view size for the document so you'll be able to see the highlighted text on screen without squinting, and make the document window smaller so the Find/Change palette won't get in the way.

   If you're going to search for type attributes, like point size, style, etc., click in a word that contains those attributes. They will automatically register in the "Find what" area of the Find/Change palette if you uncheck the Ignore Attributes box.
2. Choose Edit menu > Find/Change (Ctrl-F).
3. *Optional:* Check the Document box to search the entire document.
4. *Note:* To find/change only text characters, follow this step and skip step 5. To find/change attributes only—not text characters—skip this step. To find/change text characters and attributes, follow steps 4 and 5.

   To change **text characters**, enter a maximum of 80 characters or spaces in the Find What field (the text that will be searched for) **1**. If the Ignore Attributes box is unchecked,

*Uncheck the **Ignore Attributes** box to expand the palette to Find/Change style sheets and/or individual font, size, and style attributes.*

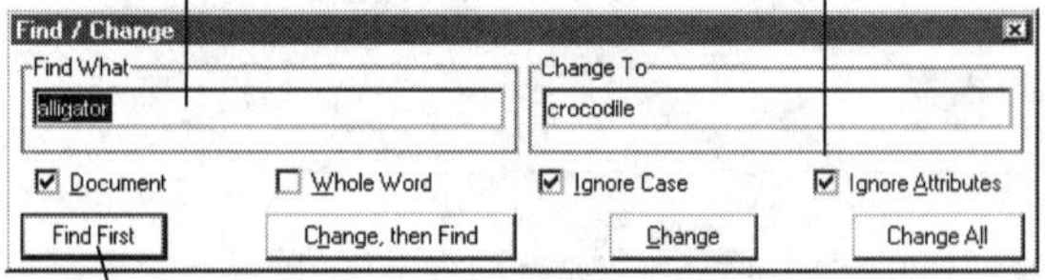

1 *Enter the text to be searched for in the **Find What** field.*

*Hold down **Alt** to convert the **Find Next** button into the **Find First** button.*

FINDING NON-PRINTING CHARACTERS

Character	*Keystroke*	*Field will display*
Tab	Ctrl-Tab	\t
New paragraph	Ctrl-Enter	\p
New line	Ctrl-Shift-Return	\n
Next column	\c	\c
Next box	\b	\b
Current page #	Ctrl 3	\3
Next box page #	Ctrl 4	\4
Previous box page #	Ctrl 2	\2
Wild card (Find only)	Ctrl ?	\?
Space	Space bar	
Flex space	Ctrl Shift-F	\f
Punctuation space	Ctrl . (period)	\.
Backslash	Ctrl \	\\

check the Text box, then enter the Find What text in the Text field.

Optional: Uncheck the Whole Word box to also search for any instances of the Find What text that may be embedded in a larger word.

Optional: Uncheck the Ignore Case box to search for only an exact match of the upper and lowercase configuration that was entered in the Find What field.

5. To Find/Change **attributes**, uncheck the Ignore Attributes box **2**, then do any of the following:

To search for instances of a character- or paragraph-based **style sheet**, check the Style Sheet box, then choose from the drop-down menu.

To search for a **font**, check the Font box or boxes, then choose from the font drop-down menu. Only fonts used in the document will appear on the Find What font drop-down menu.

To search for a specific **point size**, check the Size box, then enter a size.

To search for **type styles**, check the Type Style box, then activate a style to search for or leave it inactive if you want it to be excluded from the search. (If necessary, click twice on a style to make it highlight in black.) A grayed style, if found, won't be changed. Click Plain to deactivate all the styles.

Uncheck the boxes for any categories that you don't want to be included in the search.

(Continued on the following page)

*The **Find what** area.*

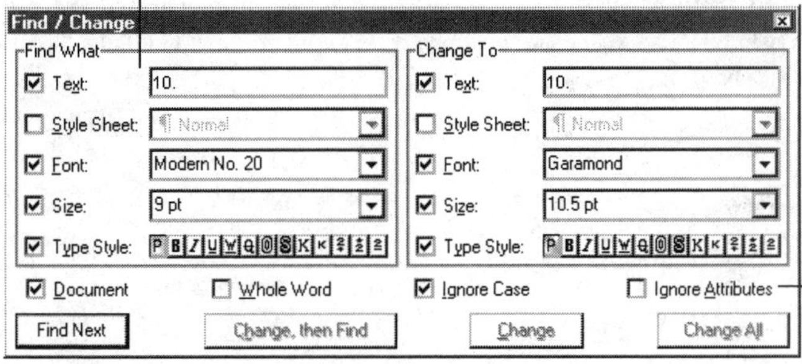

Find / Change
Find What
Text: 10.
Style Sheet: Normal
Font: Modern No. 20
Size: 9 pt
Type Style:
Change To
Text: 10.
Style Sheet: Normal
Font: Garamond
Size: 10.5 pt
Type Style:
Document
Whole Word
Ignore Case
Ignore Attributes
Find Next
Change, then Find
Change
Change All

2 *Uncheck the **Ignore Attributes** box to include Font, Size, and Style attributes in the search.*

Find/Change

6. In the **Change To** portion of the dialog box, do any of the following **3**:

   Check the Text box, if necessary, then enter a maximum of 80 characters or spaces in the Text field or leave the Text field blank to delete the Find What text altogether.

   If you unchecked the Ignore Attributes box, you can then choose a replacement style sheet, font, point size, or type style. An activated (black) Type Style will be applied to the text; an inactive style will be removed from the text; a grayed style will not be changed either way.

7. Hold down Alt and click Find First to find the first instance in the document of the Find What text.
   or
   Click Find Next to find the next instance of the Find What text from the current location of the cursor forward.

   TIP If the Find/Change palette is in the way, you can move it by dragging its title bar. To shrink the palette, double-click the palette title bar. Double-click it again to restore its previous size.

8. Click "Change, then Find" to change an instance and find the next instance.
   or
   Click Change to change the first instance, then click Find Next to resume the search.
   or
   Click Change All to change all the instances in one fell swoop. A prompt displaying the number of found instances will appear **4**. Click OK.

9. *Optional:* Close the Find/Change palette (Ctrl-Alt-F).

TIP Find/Change modifications can't be undone via the Undo command.

3 *In the **Change To** portion of the **Find/Change** palette, enter replacement **Text** characters and/or choose a **Style Sheet**, **Font**, **Size**, or **Type Style**.*

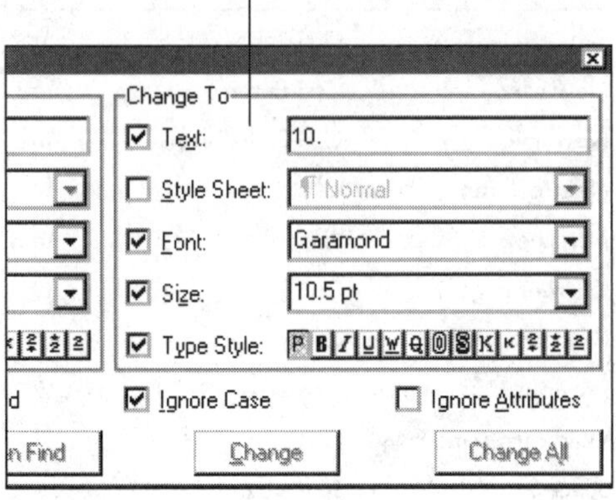

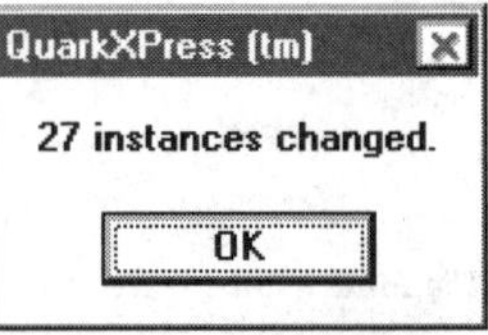

4 *This prompt will appear if you click **Change All**.*

Find/Change

Use Find/Change to apply a style sheet

You can use Find/Change to apply a character style sheet to type that has already been locally formatted. On the left side of the Find/Change palette, choose the font and other type attributes that you want to search for **1**, and on the right side, choose the character style sheet that you want to apply to that locally formatted text **2**.

If, in addition to applying a style sheet, you also choose other text attributes on the Change To side of the palette, the attributes that you choose will override the style sheet specs **3**. For example, let's say you want to apply a subhead character style sheet but you don't like the style sheet's 12-pt. font size. Just check the Size box in the Change To area of the palette and enter the desired size. In essence you'll be applying a style sheet and local formatting in one lightening-quick step.

If you want to search for locally formatted text in addition to a style sheet, choose those individual text attributes in the Find What area of the Find/Change palette.

1 *To apply a character style sheet to already formatted text, choose the attributes you want to search for in the* ***Find What*** *area.*

2 *And choose the* ***style sheet*** *you want to apply to the found text on the* ***Change To*** *side of the palette.*

Find / Change

Find What
Text:
Style Sheet: ¶ Body-No Indent
Font: Gill Sans MT Ext Condense
Size: 9.25 pt
Type Style:

Change To
Text:
Style Sheet: ¶ Sidebar body
Font:
Size: 9.25 pt
Type Style: P B I U W

Document
Whole Word
Ignore Case
Ignore Attributes

Find Next
Change, then Find
Change
Change All

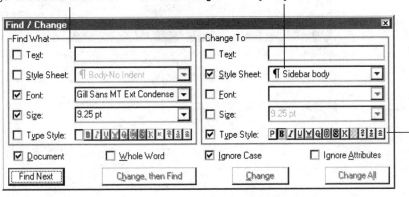

3 *Any other Change To attributes that are chosen will* ***override*** *the style sheet.*

Notes: Usage > Fonts replaces *all* instances of an individual font. To replace font instances on a case-by-case basis, use the Find/Change palette.

To find and change fonts only:

1. Choose Utilities menu > Usage, then click the Fonts folder tab (F2). The names of all the fonts used in the document will display. A minus sign before a font name indicates that that font is currently unavailable on the system.
2. Click the name of the font that you want to replace **1**, then click Replace **2**.
   or
   Double-click the name of the font that you want to replace.
3. Choose a replacement font, then click OK twice.
4. Repeat steps 2–3 for any other fonts that you want to replace.
5. *Optional:* Click Show First to display the first instance of the currently highlighted font in the document, click Show Next to see the next instance, or hold down Alt to turn the Show Next button into a Show First button.
   All instances of a given font will be replaced, regardless of which instance is currently displayed.
6. Click Close when you're finished.

TIP To replace more than one font at a time, before clicking Replace, click on the first in a series of consecutively listed fonts, then Shift-click on the last font in the series, or Ctrl-click them individually.

TIP Usage > Fonts doesn't list fonts used in any imported EPS files.

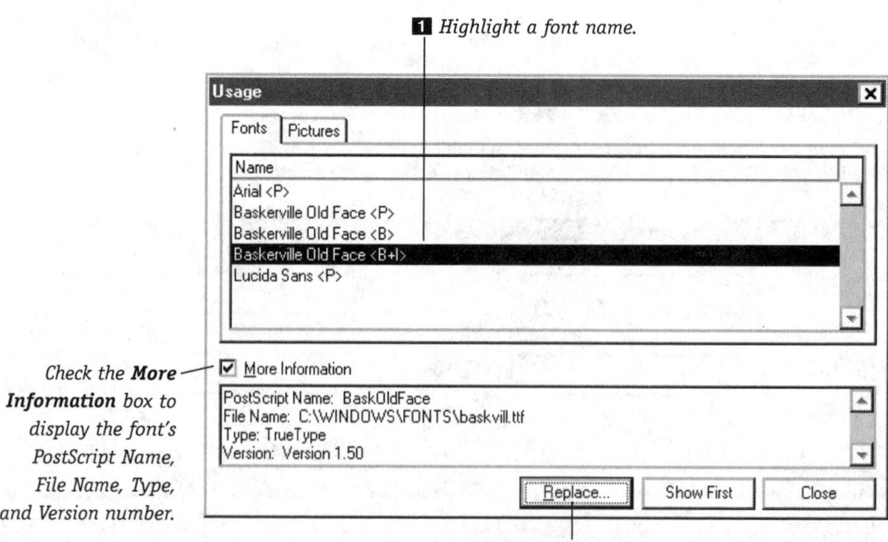

1 *Highlight a font name.*

*Check the **More Information** box to display the font's PostScript Name, File Name, Type, and Version number.*

2 *Click **Replace** to choose a replacement font.*

Books 18

Books, lists, and indexes

Roll out the red carpet, ring bells throughout the land. With its new books, lists, and indexing features, QuarkXPress ventures forth into the world of automating the creation of multi-file publications.

In QuarkXPress, a book is an umbrella file whose function is to organize multiple chapter files. In truth, a book can be any kind of publication that is comprised of more than one QuarkXPress file. When they're united into a book, the style sheets, colors, H&Js, lists, and dashes & stripes used in individual book chapter files will match the specifications of those in the file that you designate as the master. Page numbering also flows continuously from file to file. A book can contain up to 1,000 chapters. Each book has its own palette **1**.

ELAINE's BOOK.qxb

Like a library, a book palette has its own file icon in Explorer, and can be opened using File menu > Open.

In a workgroup situation, individual chapters of a book can be open and edited simultaneously on a network. If the book itself is edited at one station, any open copies of the same book palette on other stations will update automatically.

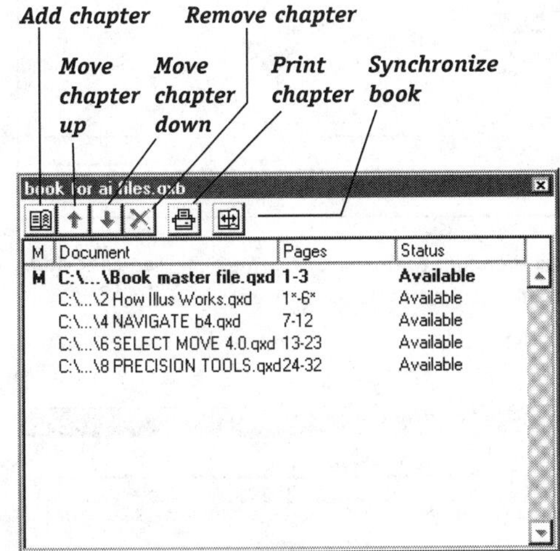

1 *The **Book** palette, displaying a master file and several chapter files.*

A list is a compilation of text from one or more documents that are associated with the same paragraph style sheet. Optional features that can be included in a list are page numbers and alphabetization, and they are assigned via the Lists palette. An example of a list is a table of contents.

Indexing is accomplished by manually tagging each individual entry in the document itself and then assigning an indent level and other formats to each entry via the Index palette.

To create a book:

1. Decide which file will be the master. The master file specifications will be applied to all the book chapters. To create a master file:

   Create a new file that contains only the master page(s), style sheets, colors, H&Js, lists, and dashes and stripes that you want all the chapter files to share. Save the file. Include the word "master" in the title, if you like, to help prevent confusion later on. Apply the Current Page Number command (Ctrl-3) to a text box on the master page.
   or
   Open an existing file, and use File menu > Save As to save a copy of it (use the word "master" in the name). Then delete all the text and all the pages except the first page and re-save the file. As with a new file, make sure it contains only the master pages, style sheets, colors, H&Js, lists, and dashes & stripes that you want all the chapter files to share and make sure it contains the Current Page Number command in a text box on the master page.

   You can use the File menu > Append command to append style sheets, lists, colors, etc. from any other file to the master.
2. Choose File menu > New > Book.
3. Choose a location in which to save the book **1**. (To create a new folder, click the Create New Folder button, type a name, press Enter, then click Open.)
4. Type a name for the book in the File name field, then click Create.
5. On the book palette that opens, click the Add Chapter (leftmost) icon **2**.
6. Locate and highlight the name of the file that you want to be the master **3**, then click Add or press Enter **4**. Now you can start adding chapters to the book (next page).

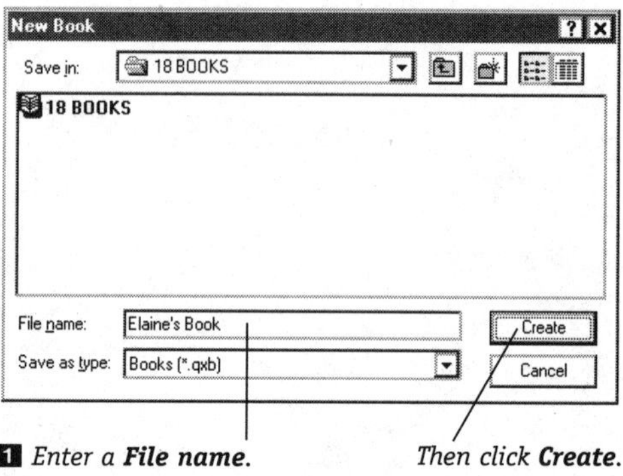

1 *Enter a **File name**.* *Then click **Create**.*

2 *Click the **Add Chapter** icon.*

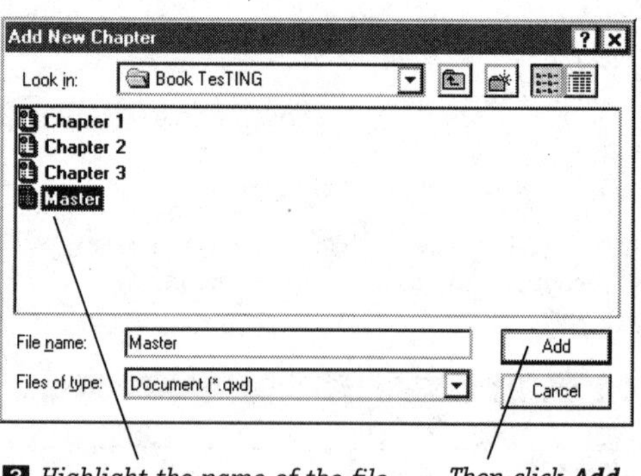

3 *Highlight the name of the file that you want to be the master.* *Then click **Add**.*

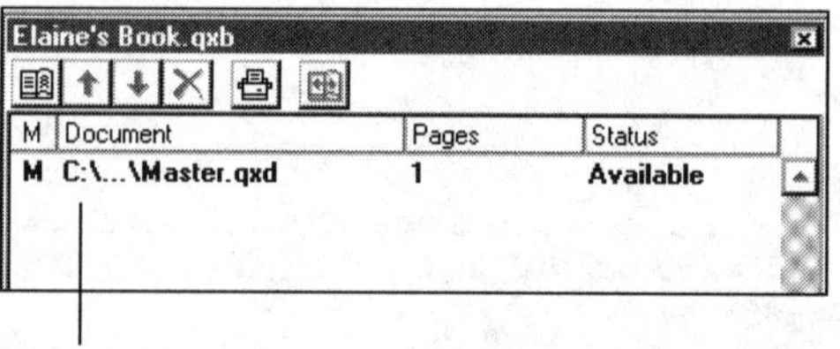

4 *The master file appears on the book palette.*

Create a Book

■1 *Click the **Add chapter** icon.*

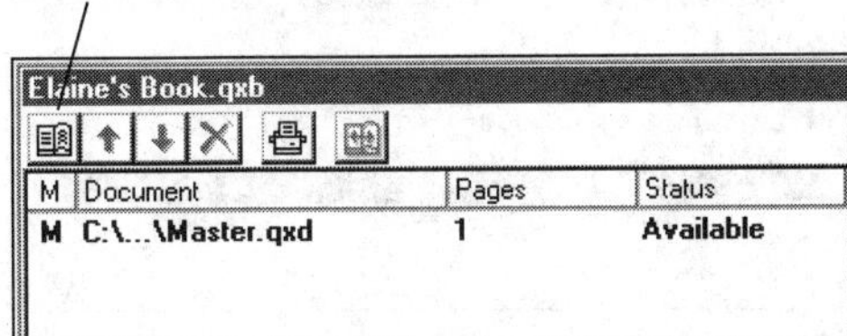

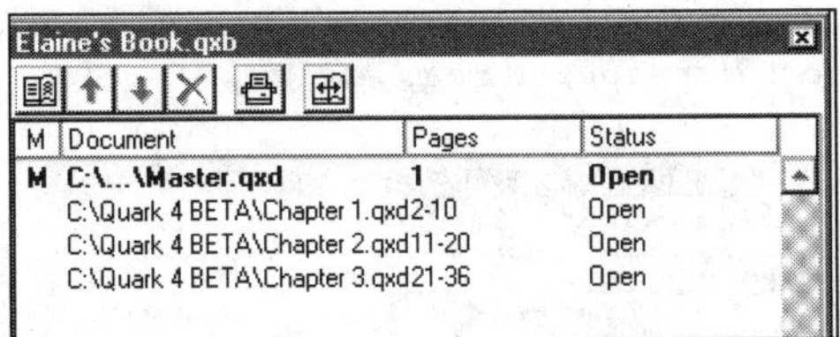

■2 *Three chapters have been added to the book.*

■3 *Click the **Synchronize Book** icon.*

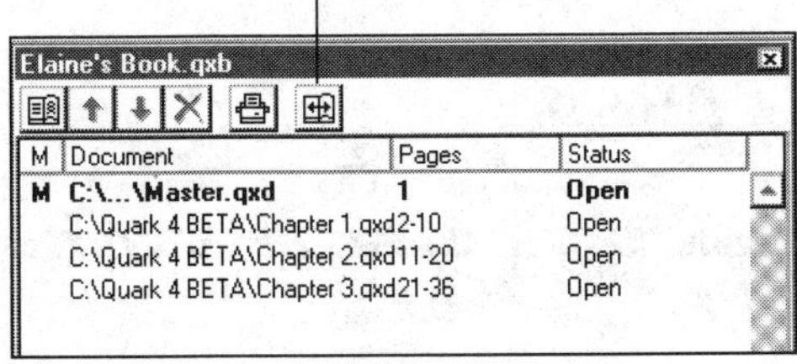

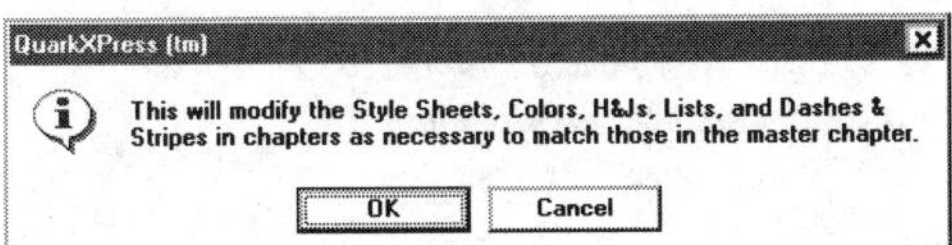

■4 *This prompt will appear after you click the Synchronize Book icon.*

NO BACKING OUT

Book changes, such as adding or rearranging chapters, cannot be undone, nor can the Revert to Saved command be used to restore a book to an earlier version.

Edits to a book are saved when you close the book palette or exit QuarkXPress. Save edits to an individual chapter as you would any other document.

Once chapters have been added to a book, all you have to do is double-click a chapter name on the palette to open that chapter.

To add chapters to a book:

1. Get the chapter files ready. You can use File menu > Save As to generate copies of the master file or you can use existing files. Make sure they all have the same page size.
2. Click the Add Chapter (leftmost) icon on the book palette ■1, locate and highlight the name of a file that you want to become a chapter in the book, then click Add or press Enter ■2. Repeat this step for any other files that you want to become chapters. The actual files don't have to be open. If you add a pre-4.0 version file, you'll get an alert prompt (click OK).

   Note: If no chapter name is highlighted when you click the Add Chapter icon, the new chapter will be added to the end of the book. If a chapter name is highlighted when you click the Add Chapter icon, the new chapter will be added directly above the highlighted one.
3. Click the Synchronize Book (left/right arrow) icon ■3 to apply the style sheets, colors, H&Js, etc. from the master chapter to all the chapter files. Page numbering will advance incrementally though the chapter files (unless any contain section numbering). Click OK or press Enter when the warning prompt appears ■4.
4. Close the Book palette (click the close box). All open book chapters will also close. You will be prompted to save changes, if there were any.

TIP Each chapter file can only be part of one book. To get around this, you can copy a chapter using File menu > Save As. Or use Edit > Copy (Ctrl-C or right-click and choose copy in Explorer). Then you can use the copy in a different book.

To change the chapter order:

Click a chapter name, then click the Move Chapter Up or Move Chapter Down icon at the top of the book palette **1**–**2**.

or

Alt-drag a chapter name upward or downward on the palette **3**.

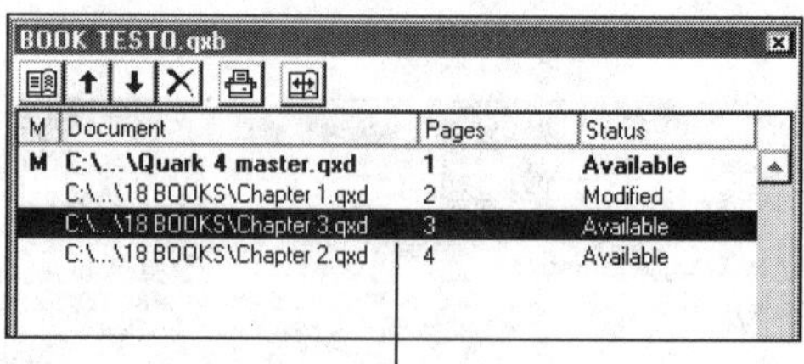

1 *Click on the chapter that you want to move.*

2 *After clicking the* ***Move Chapter Down*** *icon, chapter three is moved downward.*

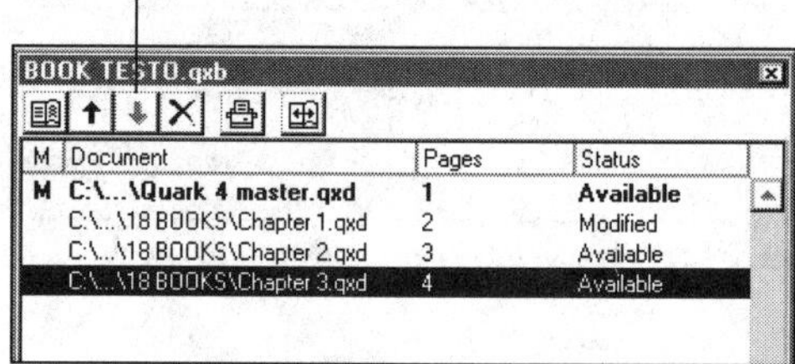

If you're working on a network, you'll need to check in the Status column on the book palette to find out if someone else on the network has a chapter open. Chapters should always be opened and closed from the server.

Deciphering the Status column

Available means that the chapter can be opened.

Open means that the chapter is open at your station.

[**Other station name**] means that the chapter is open at another station on a network.

Modified means that the chapter was opened and edited outside the book when the book palette was closed. To update it, double-click the chapter name on the book palette, and then close the document window.

Missing means that the chapter was moved. To re-link the chapter to the book, double-click its name on the palette, then locate and open the file.

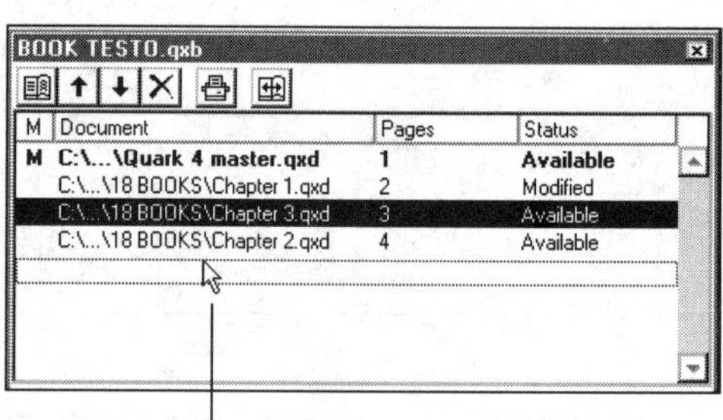

3 *You can also move a chapter to a different spot by* ***Alt****-dragging it.*

To delete a chapter from a book:

1. On the book palette, click the name of the chapter that you want to delete.
2. Click the Remove Chapter (brush-stroke-X) icon **4**.
3. Click OK or press Enter.

4 *To delete a chapter file, click on it, then click the* ***Remove Chapter*** *icon.*

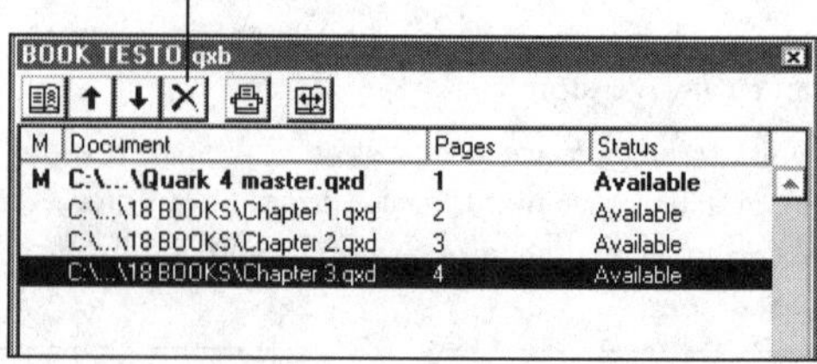

OUT OF SYNC?

You may add style sheets, colors, and so on to any individual chapter file. But bear in mind that those added elements will not appear in any other chapter file unless they're added to the master file and the chapters are synchronized.

If you re-synchronize, any style sheet, color, etc. in an individual chapter file that doesn't have a double in the master file will be untouched. A style sheet, color, etc. that has a matching name in the master file but whose specifications do not match will be updated in the chapter file to match the master file. A component that is present in the master but not in a chapter file will be added to the chapter file.

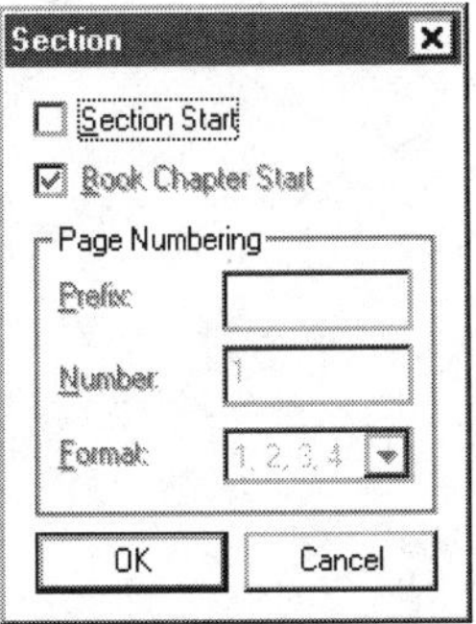

1 *This is the default setting in the **Section** dialog box for a book.*

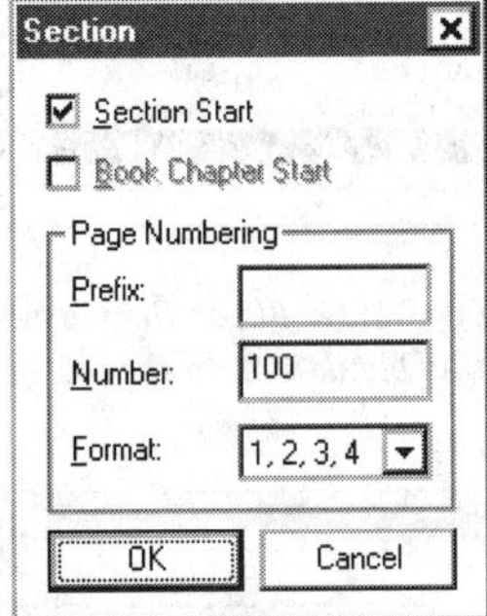

2 *For custom page numbering, click the **Section Start** box, and enter a starting page **Number**. You can also enter a **Prefix** and choose an alternative **Format**.*

To edit the master file:

1. Double-click the master file on the book palette.
2. Create new style sheets, colors, H&Js, lists, and dashes and stripes in the master file or use the File menu > Append command to add any of those elements from another file to the master.
3. Make sure all the chapters in the book have a status of Available. If a chapter has a Modified status, double-click it, then close it.
4. Click the Synchronize book icon to add the new elements from the master file to all the book chapters.
5. Click OK or press Enter.

Book page numbering

There are two ways to number pages in a book. In either case, for any numbering to show up on any document pages, the current page number command (Ctrl-3) must be inserted into a text box on the master page of the master file.

Option 1: Let the page numbering occur automatically without doing anything. Chapters will be numbered sequentially, and the Book Chapter Start box will be checked in the Section dialog box for each one **1**.

Option 2: Control the numbering yourself. On the book palette, double-click the chapter name that is to begin a section, choose Page menu > Section, check the Section Start box **2**, then enter a number in the Number field. Choose other options just as you would for a normal document. Section numbering will proceed through subsequent chapters up to the next section start, if there is one. You can make the first chapter (not the master) the beginning of the section and keep the master outside the main flow of pages.

To print book chapters:

1. To print an individual chapter in a book, click on its name on the book palette. Only a chapter file with a status of Available or Open will print. The chapter doesn't have to be open.
   or
   To selectively print more than one chapter, Ctrl-click individual chapter names.
   or
   To print a whole book, highlight all the chapters by clicking on the first chapter and then Shift-clicking on the last chapter, or press and drag over all the chapters. If you've just opened the book and you haven't clicked any of the chapters yet, follow the next two steps.

   Make sure no chapters have a Missing or Modified status or are open at another station on the network.
2. Click the Print Chapter icon **1**.
3. Choose the desired Print settings, including a Print Style, if desired, then click OK or press Enter.

1 *The **Print Chapter** icon.*

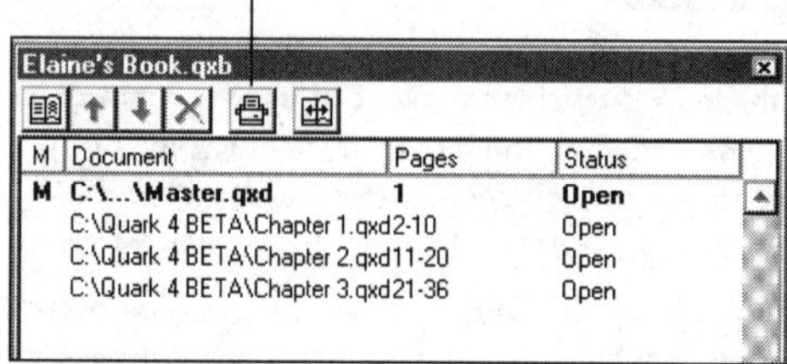

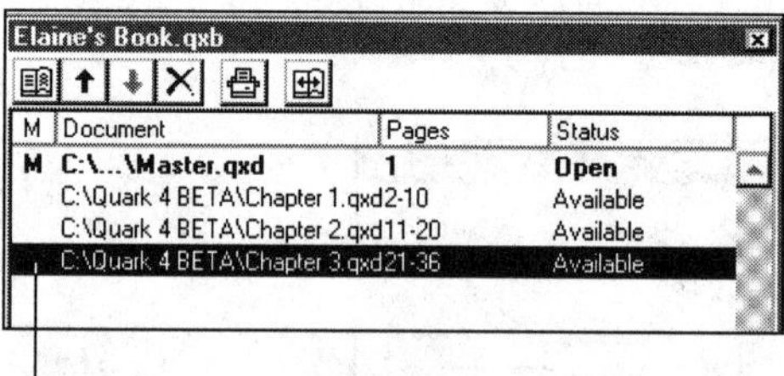

2 *To designate a different chapter file as the master, click on it, then click in this blank area to the left of it.*

To designate a different chapter as the master:

1. On the book palette, click on the name of the chapter that you want to be the new master **2**.
2. Click in the blank area to the left of the chapter name **3**.

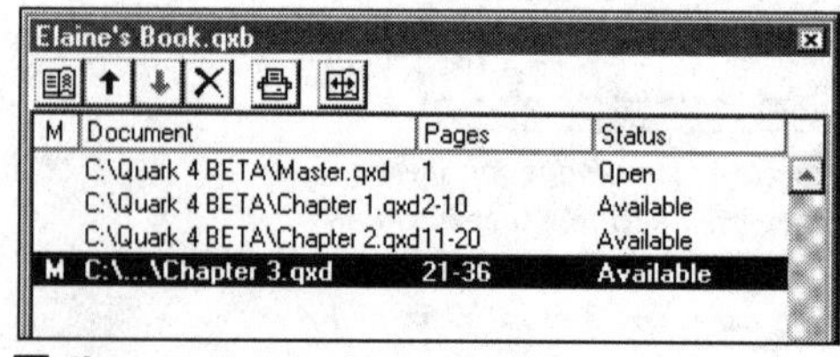

3 *Chapter 3 is now the **master** file.*

allspice	cloves	paprika
basil	coriander	parsley
bay leaf	cumin	red pepper
caraway seed	dill	rosemary
cardamom	ginger	saffron
cayenne	lavender	sage
chervil	mace	savory
chives	mint	tarragon
cilantro	nutmeg	thyme
cinnamon	oregano	turmeric

*A **list** can consist of anything from an alphabetized shopping list to a table of contents for a book.*

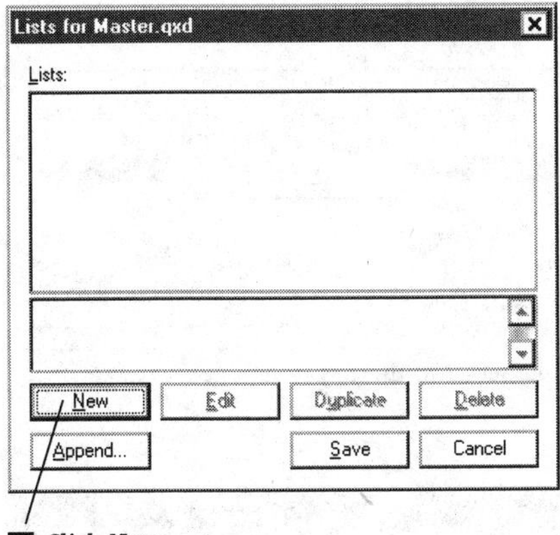

1 *Click **New**.*

2 *Enter a name.*

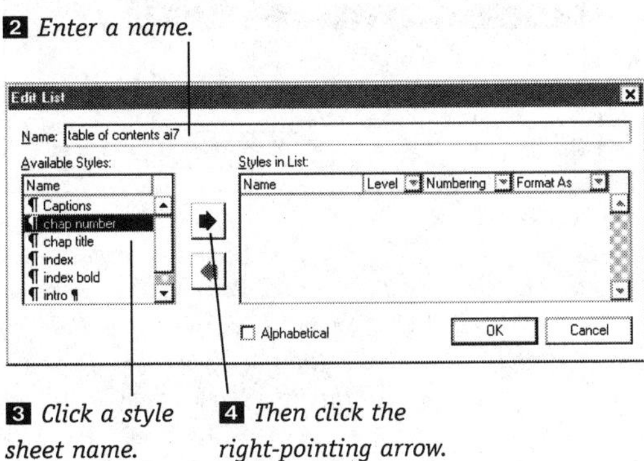

3 *Click a style sheet name.*

4 *Then click the right-pointing arrow.*

The function of the Lists feature is to generate a table of contents or other list, with or without page reference numbers, and with or without alphabetization. It works by grabbing chapters names and numbers, section subheads, captions, sidebars, reference tables, etc. from a document based on a style sheet that is assigned to those paragraphs. For example, let's say you want all your text that has been assigned a subhead style to be gathered into a table of contents. First you add the style sheets that are to be searched for in the Edit List dialog box. Then you decide how the list will be formatted. And finally, you use the Lists palette to preview and build the actual list.

To create a new list:

1. Create separate style sheets for styling the list itself. And make sure your document style sheets are consistent and are applied correctly to the categories of text that you want to appear on the table of contents.
2. If you're generating a table of contents from one file, open that file now. For a book, just open the master file.
3. Choose Edit menu > Lists.
4. Click New **1**, then enter a Name for the list **2**.
5. On the Available Styles scroll list, click the style sheet name (text category) that you want the document to be searched for **3**, then click the right-pointing arrow to add that style sheet to the Styles in List window **4**. Or just double-click the style sheet name.

   To add multiple style sheets at a time, Shift-click to select a contiguous series or Ctrl-click to select multiple style sheet names individually, then click the right-pointing arrow. (Click the left-pointing arrow if you need to remove a style sheet from the Styles in List window.)

(Continued on the following page)

6. Individually highlight each style sheet in the Styles in List window, then choose:

   The **Level** of indent text you want that style sheet to have in the list (1, 2, 3, and so on) **5**. For example, assign number 1 to chapter names, the number 2 to headers, the number 3 to subheads, and so on.

   A page **Numbering** style **6**. Choose Text...Page # if you want the page number to follow the text; choose Page #...Text if you want the page number to precede the text. Choose "Text only" if you don't want page numbers to appear at all.

   Which style sheet will be applied to that text category (**Format As** drop-down menu) **7**. This should be a style sheet you created specifically for the list.

7. *Optional:* Check the Alphabetical box to have the list entries appear in alphabetical order rather than the order in which they appear in the document **8**.
8. Click OK or press Enter.
9. Click Save. Follow the instructions on the next page to build (generate) the list.

TIP Click Duplicate to duplicate the currently highlighted list if you want to create a variation of it. Click Delete to remove the currently highlighted list. To append a list from another document, follow the instructions on pages 34–36.

TIP The maximum number of style sheets that can be chosen for a list is 32; the maximum number of characters per paragraph that a list can contain is 256.

TIP For a list level with page number references, choose a style sheet with a right tab and a dot leader. The tab character will be inserted automatically.

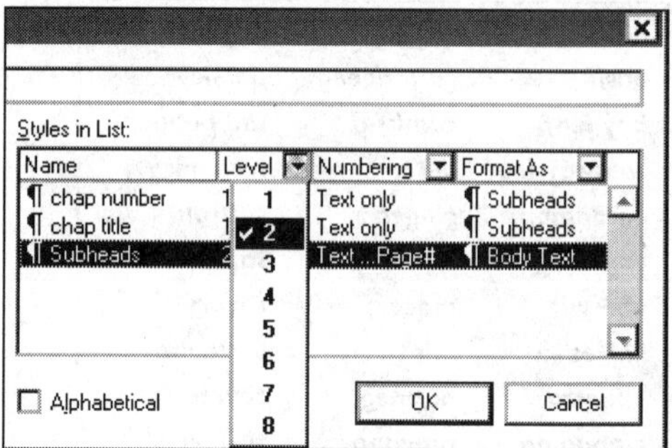

5 *For each style sheet category, choose an indent **Level**,...*

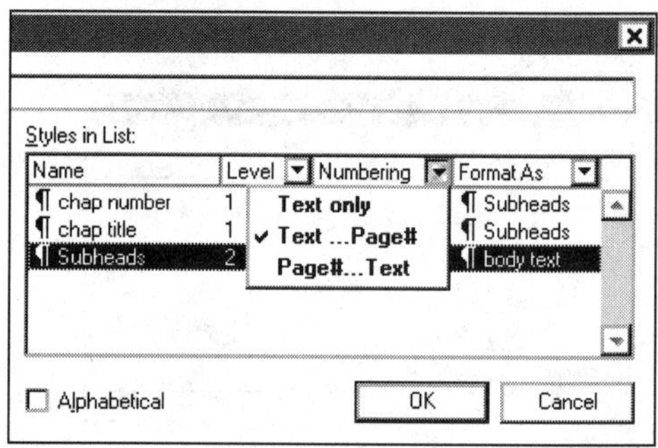

6 *...choose a **Numbering** option,...*

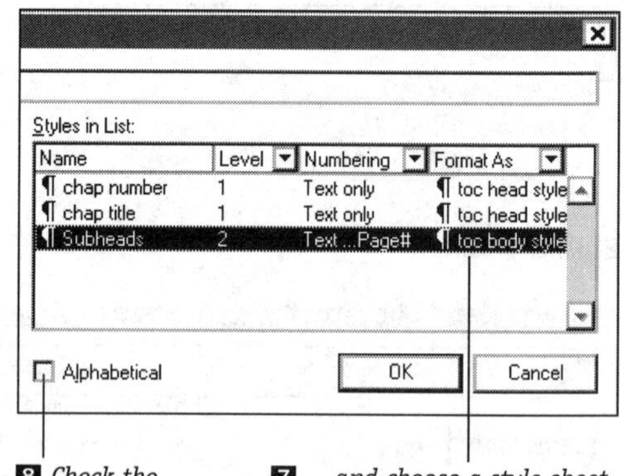

8 *Check the **Alphabetical** box if you want your list to be alphabetized.*

7 *...and choose a style sheet from the **Format As** drop-down menu. In our exmaple, the Format As styles are different from the Name styles.*

Lists
Show List For:
Current Document
Current Document
book for ai files.qxb
List Name:
Find:
Update
Build

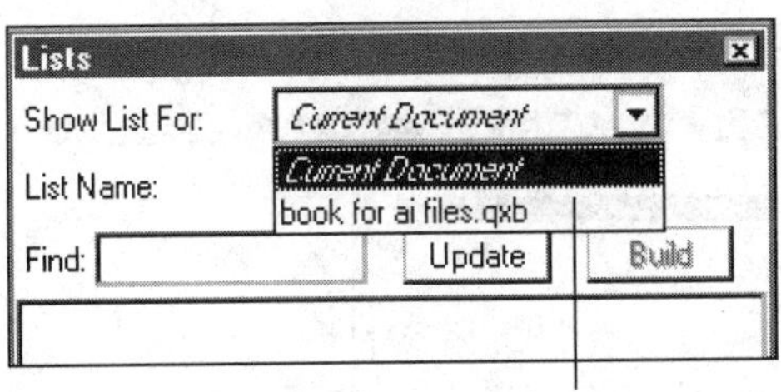

1 *Choose a document name from the* ***Show List For*** *drop-down menu.*

Lists
Show List For:
book for ai files.qxb
List Name:
table of contents ai7
Find:
Update
Build

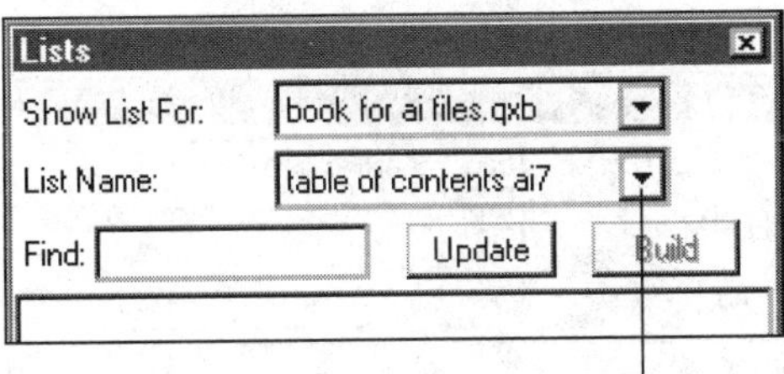

2 *Choose an existing list from the* ***List Name*** *drop-down menu.*

Lists
Show List For:
Current Document
List Name:
table of contents ai7
Find:
Update
Build
howillustratorworks
2
Illustrator is primarily an object-oriented program
How objects are made
Type
How objects are modified
Coloring
On the screen
When your illustration is finished
How to use this book

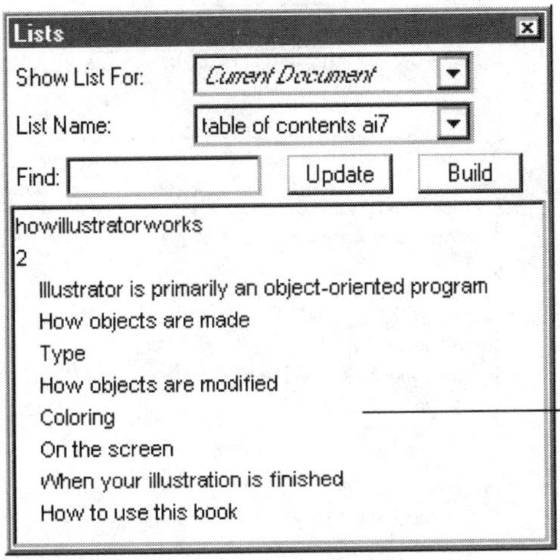

If you double-click a line of text on the Lists palette, that text will display and highlight in the document window.

3 *The Lists palette, displaying a document's table of contents.*

Once a list has been created, you've chosen Level, Numbering, and Format As options for it, and it's been saved, it's time to use the Lists palette to preview and build (generate) the actual list.

To preview and build a list:

1. Open the document or book for which you want to build a list.
2. Choose View menu > Show Lists (Ctrl-F11).
3. Choose Show List For: *Current Document,* or choose the name of any currently open book **1**.
4. Choose the name of the list that you want to build from the List Name drop-down menu **2**. The list will preview in the scroll window on the palette.
5. In the same document, choose the Content tool and click in an empty text box to create an insertion point. It can be a new box or the first of a series of linked text boxes.
6. Click Build on the Lists palette **3**. A list will be generated in that text box or in a series of linked boxes using the formatting options that were chosen in the Lists dialog box.

TIP Be careful not to delete from the document any Styles in List style sheet. If you do, text to which that style sheet was assigned won't appear on the list when you build it.

Note: Before following the instructions on this page, make sure the master book file contains all the style sheets that are used in the book and a list format has been created for that master. Also make sure that all the book chapters have a status of Available.

To generate a list for a book:

1. Close all open files.
2. Open the book file. The palette for that book will open.
3. Choose Edit menu > Lists.
4. Click Append, then locate and open the file that contains the list that you want to use.
5. Click the desired list format, click the right-pointing arrow to append that list, then click OK **1**.
6. Respond to any name conflicts, then click Save.
7. On the Lists palette (View menu > Show Lists or Ctrl-F11), make sure the book file is chosen in the Show List For field.
8. Click the Synchronize button on the Book palette, then click OK.
9. Make sure the correct list is chosen in the List Name field on the Lists palette, then click Update. The list that was generated from all the chapters will display on the Lists palette **2**–**3**. (If the correct list doesn't appear on the List Name drop-down menu or if it doesn't preview correctly, try opening the master file first.)

TIP If you renumber or rearrange pages in a book, you will have to update and rebuild the list.

1 *Click the right-pointing arrow to **append** the list.*

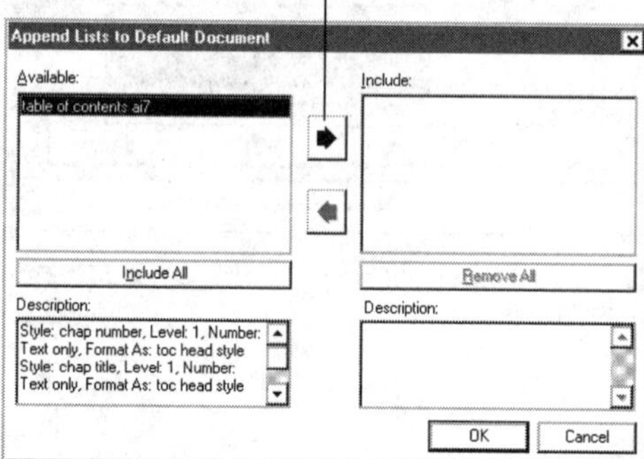

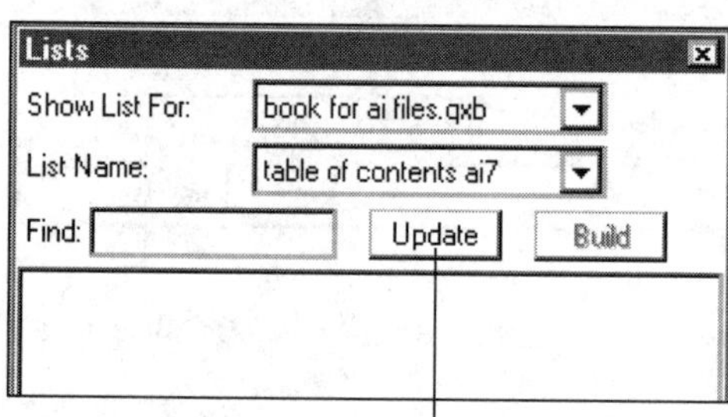

2 *Click **Update** to display the list.*

3 *The list will preview on the **Lists** palette.*

*A **built list** (table of contents) generated from a book using style sheets that were created specifically for the list and assigned via the Edit List dialog box.*

Perform the following steps after you generate a list for the book file (instructions on the previous page).

To build a list for a book file:

1. Create a new chapter for the book. One way to do this is by opening the master file and generating a copy of it using File menu > Save As. Strip out the text from the new chapter. If it's going to be a table of contents and you want it to have its own numbering format, choose Page menu > Section, check the Section Start box, enter a Number, and choose a Format.
2. Add the new chapter to the book. (Click the Add Chapter icon on the book palette, then locate and open the new chapter.)
3. Click the Synchronize button on the book palette to copy the style sheets, colors, etc. from the master file to the new file, then click OK.
4. Click in a blank text box in the newly created chapter file.
5. On the Lists palette, choose Show List For: [book name].
6. *Optional:* Turn on Auto Page Insertion in Edit menu > Document > General folder tab for the new chapter if you want overflow text from the list, if any, to flow into linked boxes on additional pages.
7. Click Build. The list will be appear in the text box or boxes.

To revise a list:

1. Open the document and open the Lists palette (Ctrl-F11).
2. Choose a List Name.
3. For a non-book file, double-click an entry—that text will highlight in the document window **1**. If you double-click an entry from a chapter file, the chapter file will open, but the correct text will not be highlighted.
4. Make any modifications to the text in the document. To prevent text from appearing on the list, for example, apply a style sheet to it that is not being used in the list.
5. Click Update on the Lists palette to update the list preview.
6. If you're going to rebuild the list in the same document, click in the text box that contains the list. If you're going to insert the re-built list and leave the old list unchanged, click exactly where you want the new one to appear. If the list is in a separate chapter of a book, open that chapter now.
7. Click Build.
8. Click Replace to replace the current list with the new list **2**. You can't undo this.
   or
   Click Insert to build a new list and leave the old list unchanged **3**. You can't undo this either.

TIP You can reformat a built list or apply different style sheets to it, but such changes will be lost if you rebuild the list using the Replace option.

TIP If the list is long and you want to quickly find a particular line, type the first word of the line in the Find field **4**. QuarkXPress will search from the first word of all the entries as you type. Keep typing until enough of the entry is typed in to differentiate it from similar entries. Only whole lines will highlight.

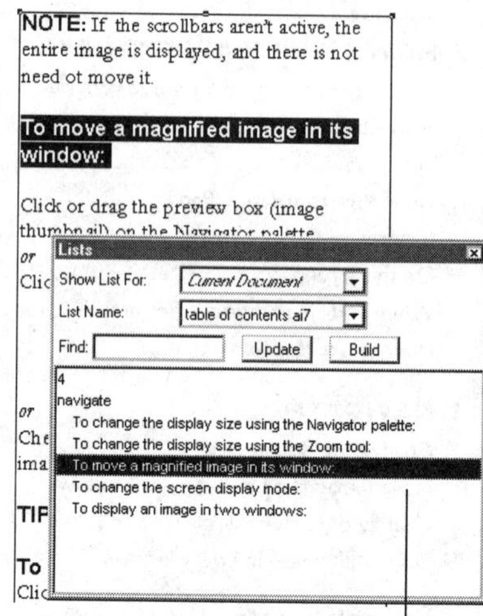

1 *For a non-book file, double-click an entry on the Lists palette to view that entry in the* ***document***.

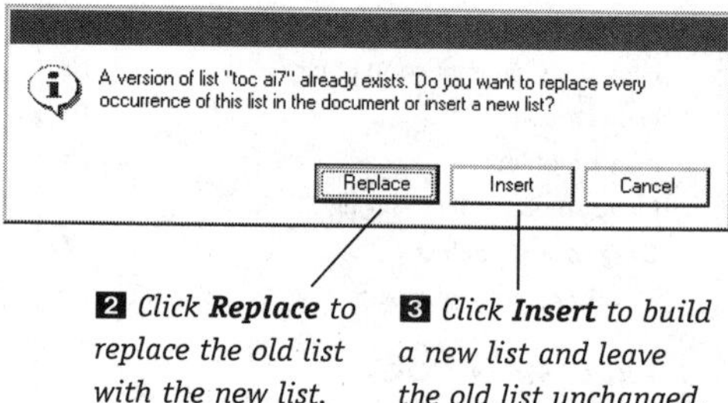

2 *Click* ***Replace*** *to replace the old list with the new list.*

3 *Click* ***Insert*** *to build a new list and leave the old list unchanged.*

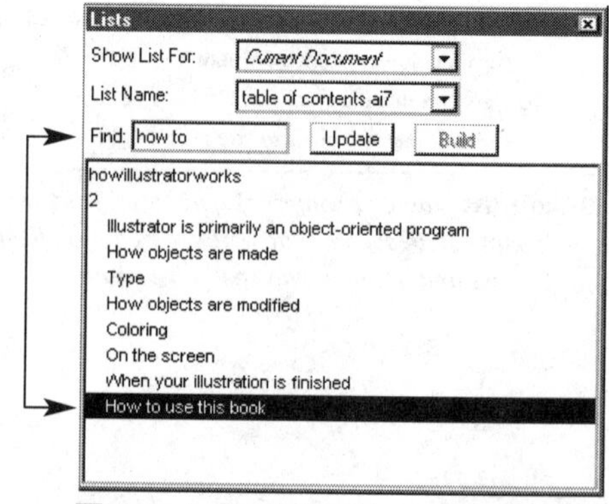

4 *An entry that's typed into the* ***Find*** *field on the Lists palette is searched for in the list.*

Use the Index palette to mark and format index references for individual text strings in a document. This is a time-consuming process. Then you'll build the index itself in the same file or in a separate file.

Note: Enable Quark's Index XTension.

To mark a document for indexing:

1. Open an existing document to mark for indexing or create a new document to be marked as you enter text.
2. If you're going to do any "see also" cross-referencing or if you want page number references to appear in a different style from the index entries, create the character style sheet(s) that you want to apply to those references.

   This is also a good time to create all the other style sheets that you want to use in the built index. An index can have a nested or run-in format (see the illustrations on page 274). You can edit the style sheets later.

   For a nested index, you'll need a style sheet for the first level text strings and a style sheet for each subsequent indent level. You can use the Based On option for this, and apply progressively larger Left Indent values for the second, third, and fourth level styles.

   Also create a style sheet for letter headings if you're going to use them (A, B, C, etc.). Apply a Space Before value via the Paragraph Attributes > Formats folder tab, and make it a bolder font than the body text so it stands out.
3. Choose View menu > Show Index.
4. In the document, highlight a word or a phrase that you want to include in the index **1**. You'll be choosing settings for each individual entry separately.
5. On the Index palette, review the text in the Text field, and change any capitalization or word endings, if desired **2**.

1 *Highlight a word or a phrase in a document that you want to include in the index.*

2 *The text that's currently highlighted in the document will also display in the **Text** field.*

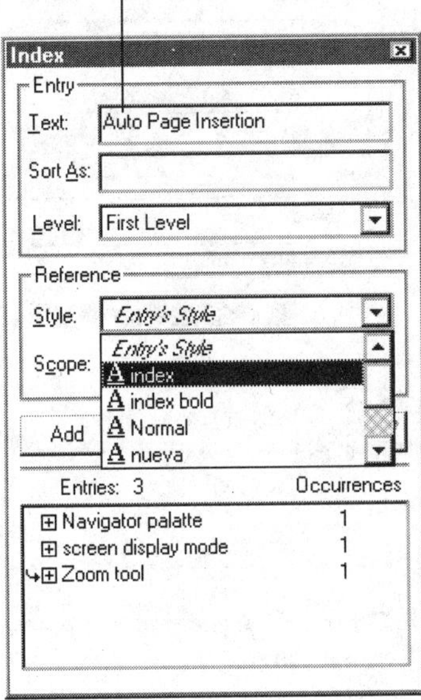

(Continued on the following page)

6. *Optional:* Enter a different method for sorting (alphabetizing) the text string in the index Sort As field **1**. For example, if you spell out a number in this field (i.e., "Seven-Up" instead of "7-Up"), the number will sort alphabetically in the index rather than be placed at the top of the index.
7. Choose indent Level: First Level **2**.
8. *Optional:* From the Style drop-down menu, **3** choose a style sheet to be applied to cross-referenced words entered in the Scope field or to index entry page numbers.
9. To specify the range of paragraphs or pages QuarkXPress will look through for other instances of the current text string, choose from the Scope drop-down menu **4**:

   Selection Start to search from the open bracket to the end of that page.

   Selection Text to search from the open bracket to the closed bracket (it may span more than one page).

   To Style to search to the next instance of the style sheet you choose from the adjoining drop-down menu.

   Specified # of ¶s to search through the exact number of paragraphs that you enter in the adjoining field.

   To End Of to search to the end of the *Story* or *Document,* whichever you choose from the drop-down menu. Choose this option for the title of a section that you want listed as a range of pages (i.e. "42–58").

   Choose **Suppress Page #** to suppress the page number.

   Choose **X-Ref:** *See, See also,* or *See herein* to create a cross-reference for the current text string. Enter the reference in the text field to the right.

1 *Optional: Re-alphabetize an entry by retyping it differently in the* ***Sort As*** *field.*

2 *Choose a* ***Level*** *of indentation for each entry.*

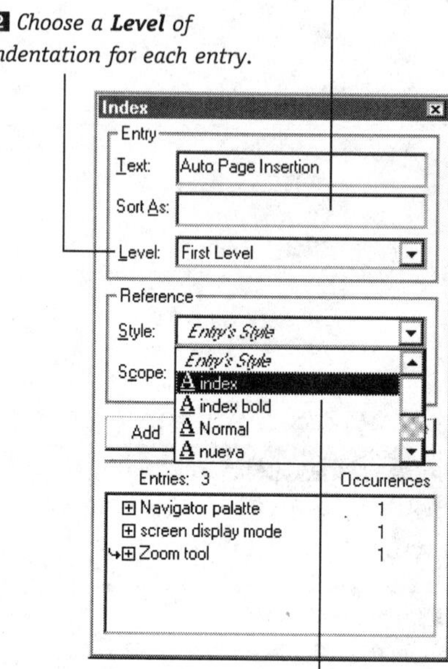

3 *Choose a character style sheet for each entry.*

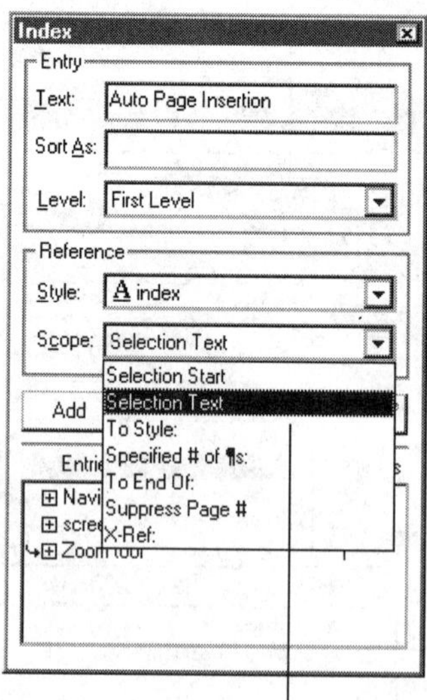

4 *Choose a* ***Scope*** *(range of pages) for the entry.*

INDEXING SHORTCUTS

Display palette	Ctrl-Alt-I
Highlight Text field	Ctrl-Alt-I
Click Add button	Ctrl-Alt-Shift-I

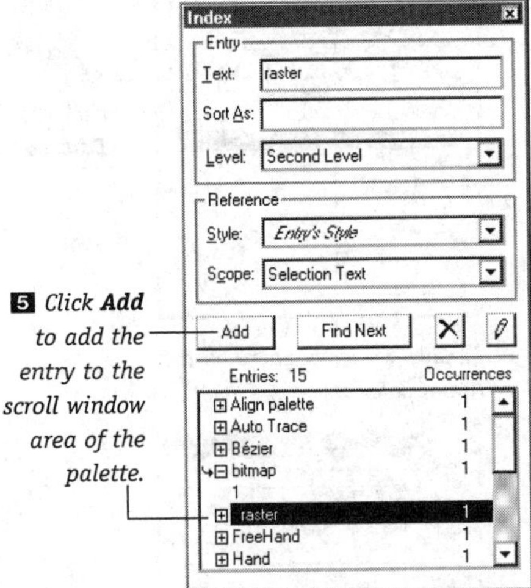

5 *Click **Add** to add the entry to the scroll window area of the palette.*

The "raster" entry has been specified as a second-level indent. Note the position of the indent arrow and the indentation of the "raster" entry in the scroll window area of the palette.

ocument can contain u
e[Auto Page Insertion]
n the General Preferen
your document contai

6 *If you highlight a word or a phrase in a document with the Index palette open, left and right **index marker brackets** will surround that text string.*

10. Click Add. The newly added entry will preview at the bottom of the palette **5** and will be listed alphabetically in its chosen indent level. An index marker (red brackets) will surround the text string in the document—but only while the Index palette is open **6**.

11. Repeat steps 4–9 for all the remaining text strings in the document that you want to include in the index.

TIP If you double-click an index entry's page number on the palette, the entry will display and highlight in the document.

TIP To delete an index entry, click on it in the scroll window on the palette, click the brushstroke-X icon on the palette, then click OK. You don't have to highlight the text in the document—the bracket will be removed automatically. You can't undo this.

TIP To zip through a *story* to make sure you've marked all the desired text strings, keep clicking Find Next on the Index palette. Hold down Alt to turn the Find Next button into a Find First button.

To create nested (indented) entries:

Follow the instructions on the previous two pages, except for this additional step: Click in the palette scroll window to the left of an existing first level entry to move the indent arrow to that entry, then choose Level: Second Level, Third Level, or Fourth Level. When you add the entry, it will appear below and indented from the chosen first level entry.

To edit an index entry:

1. Click an index entry in the scroll window on the Index palette **1**.
2. Click the Edit icon **2**. The pencil will turn gray **3**.
3. Edit the text in the Text field and/or the Sort As field **4**. The entry will update immediately.
   and/or
   Click the entry's reference (page number or X-ref) in the scroll window (click the downward-pointing arrow to reveal it, if necessary), then edit the Reference: Style or Scope. The reference will update immediately.
4. Click on and edit any other entries.
5. Click the Edit icon again when you're finished editing.

TIP In case you're wondering, you can't edit the Level for an existing entry; you can only delete the existing one and add it again at the desired new Level.

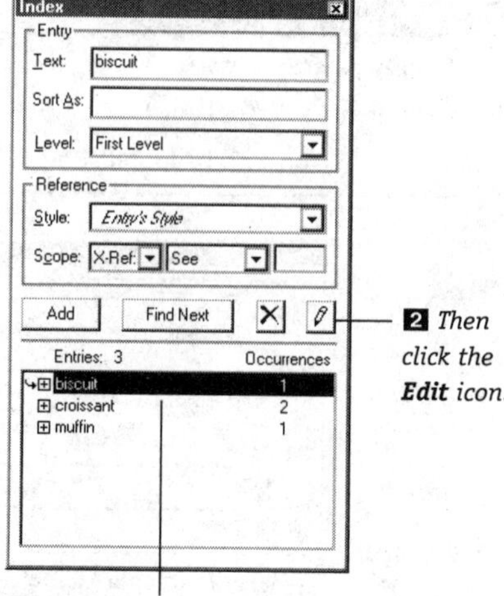

2 *Then click the* ***Edit*** *icon.*

1 *Click an index* ***entry*** *on the* ***Index*** *palette.*

Let's say you want to add the same text string as a second level entry under a different First Level entry. You can't simply add it, because you can't add the same text string twice. Here's a workaround.

To add an already marked word again to an index:

1. Click in the original marked word in the document.
2. Click in the Text field on the Index palette, then retype the entry.
3. Choose other Entry and Reference options.
4. To create a nested entry, click in the insertion arrow (leftmost) column next to the entry below which you want the new entry to nest.
5. Click Add. A small box will display inside the index marker brackets **5**.

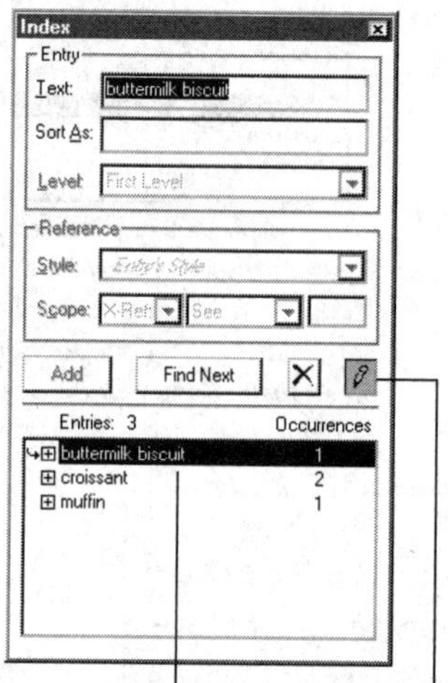

4 *The entry is edited in the* ***Text*** *field, and updates here.*

3 *The* ***Edit*** *icon turns gray.*

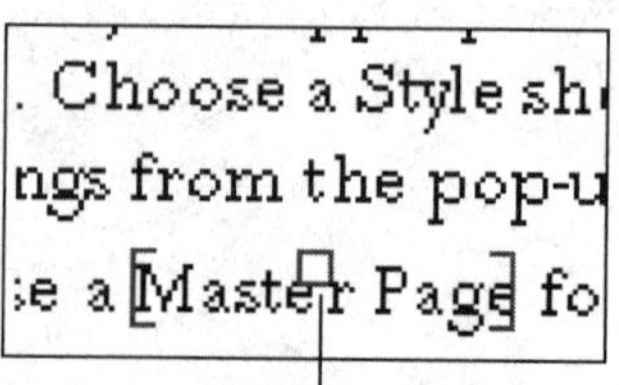

5 *The* ***second*** *index entry marker box displays if the same word is indexed twice.*

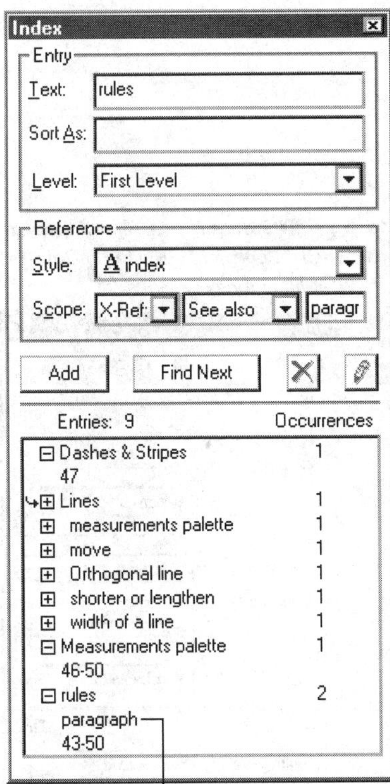

1 *A **see reference** added to an index.*

**As of this writing, an en dash can't be used as the Between Page Range punctuation. As a workaround, you can enter a unique character, and then use the Find/Change palette later to change it.*

Index Preferences
Index Marker Color
Separation Characters
Following Entry:
Between Page #s:
Between Page Range:
Before X-ref:
Between Entries:
OK
Cancel

2 *Choose **Index Preferences** before building or rebuilding an index.*

To X-ref an existing index entry:

1. Click in the text box in the document that contains the indexed word.
2. Click the entry in the scroll window on the Index palette.
3. Choose Scope: X-Ref, choose an option from the "See also" drop-down menu, then type in the X-Ref word.
4. Click Add. Click the downward-pointing arrow next to the entry to preview **1**.

Before you build or rebuild an index, you can use the Index Preferences dialog box to specify which punctuation marks the index will contain.

To choose Index Preferences:

1. Choose Edit menu > Preferences > Index.
2. *Optional:* To change the Index Marker Color (the brackets in marked text), click on the color square, choose a new color, then click OK.
3. Change any or all of the settings in the Separation Characters fields **2**:

   Following Entry is the punctuation following the index entry (as in "Biscuit,").

   Between Page #s is the punctuation between non-continuous page numbers (as in "34, 77").

   Between Page Range is the punctuation in a range of pages (as in "24–102"). Use an en dash (Ctrl-Alt-Shift-hyphen).*

   Before X-ref is the punctuation used before a "See" cross-reference (as in "Biscuit, 20. See also Rolls"). (This character will replace the chosen Following Entry character when necessary.)

   Between Entries is the punctuation between entries in a run-in style index (as in "frog, 17; toad, 18") and the ending punctuation in a paragraph in a nested style index.
4. Click OK or press Enter.

Follow these instructions to generate the actual index once the document or documents have been marked for indexing and pagination is finalized.

Note: Before building an index, you can choose Index Preferences (previous page).

To build an index:

1. For a book, create a new chapter file to hold the index. Make it the last chapter (see the first tip on the next page). Or open a non-book file in which you want the index to appear.
2. Turn on Auto Page Insertion on in Edit menu > Preferences > General folder tab if you're building a large index.
3. *Optional:* If you haven't already done so, create style sheets for each level of indentation and for alphabet letter headings. For a book, do this in the master file and Synchronize.
4. Choose Utilities menu > Build Index.
5. Choose Format: Nested to indent each progressive level in the index **1**.
   or
   Choose Format: Run-in to string the index entry levels together in paragraph form following the first level entry. They will be separated by the Between Entries punctuation mark that you chose in Index Preferences.
6. *Do any of these optional steps:*
   Click Entire Book to index an entire set of book files **2**.
   Click Replace Existing Index to replace an existing, previously built index with the newly built index.
   Click Add Letter Headings to separate each alphabetical group of index entries by the appropriate alphabet letter **3**. Choose a Style sheet for the headings from the drop-down menu.
7. Choose a Master Page for the index **4**.

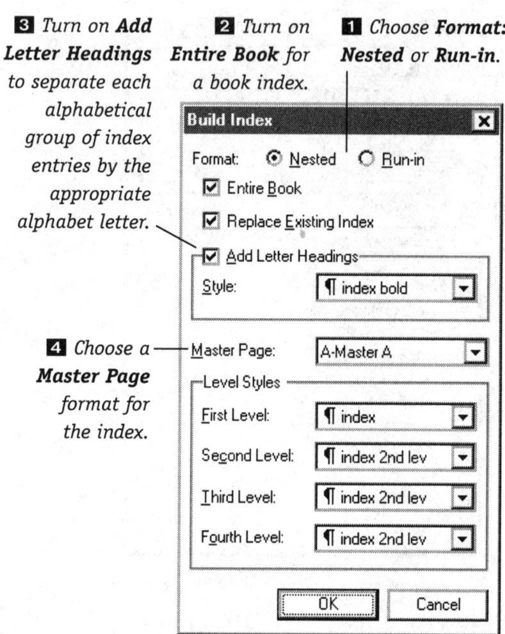

8. For the Nested Format, choose a paragraph style sheet for each level of indent (First Level, Second Level, Third Level, or Fourth Level). For the Run-in Format, choose a First Level Style.
9. Click OK or press Enter (see the illustrations on the next page). The index will be generated and a new page will be added to the end of your document. (You don't have to select a text box.)

TIP Before building an index for a book, create a separate file for it with the correct master page, headers, and footers, add it as a chapter to the book palette, and Synchronize it into the book. Be sure to check the Entire Book box in the Build Index dialog box.

TIP If you manually restyle an index using style sheets that are different from those that were selected in the Build Index dialog box, you will lose those changes if you then rebuild the index with the Replace Existing Index option checked. Keep the final, restyled index in a separate document so you don't accidentally build over it.

TIP Use a built index if you want to edit the style sheets specified in the Build Index dialog box. Since the index is based on the Level Styles chosen in the Build Index dialog box, you will actually be editing the style sheets chosen in that dialog box. You'll see the new style immediately in the built index, and the new style will be a part of any rebuilt index.

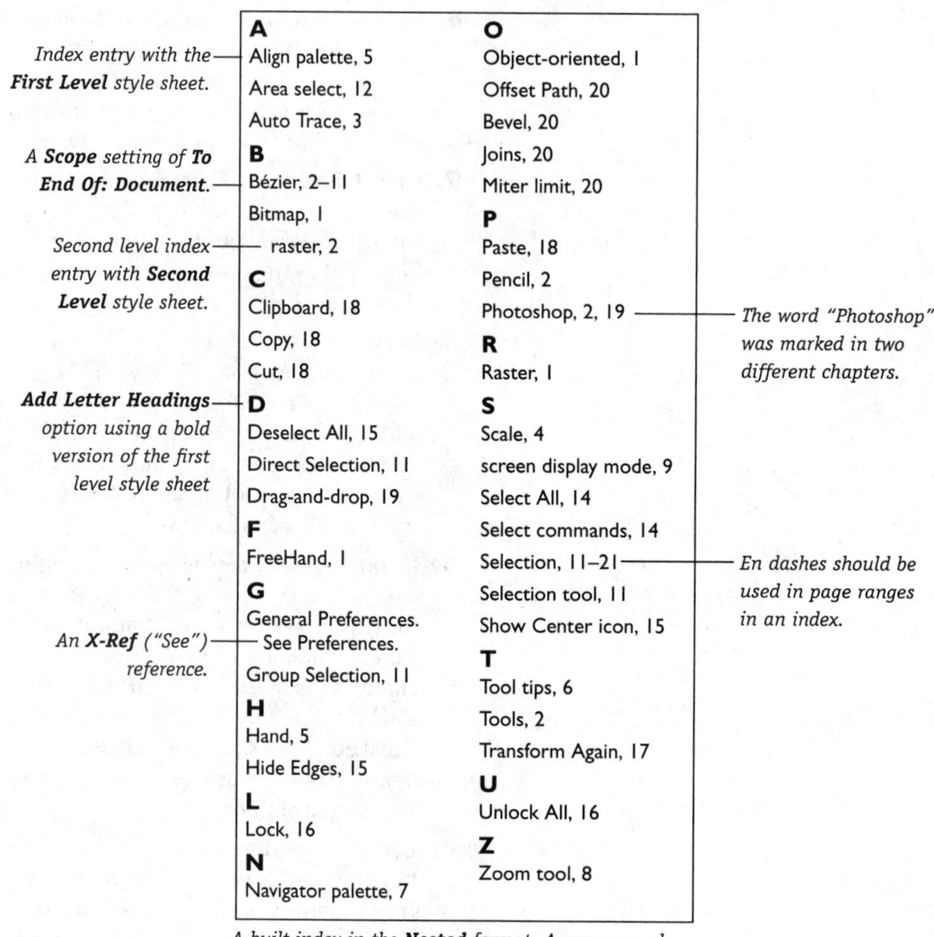

A
Align palette, 5
Area select, 12
Auto Trace, 3
B
Bézier, 2–11
Bitmap, 1
  raster, 2
C
Clipboard, 18
Copy, 18
Cut, 18
D
Deselect All, 15
Direct Selection, 11
Drag-and-drop, 19
F
FreeHand, 1
G
General Preferences.
  See Preferences.
Group Selection, 11
H
Hand, 5
Hide Edges, 15
L
Lock, 16
N
Navigator palette, 7
O
Object-oriented, 1
Offset Path, 20
Bevel, 20
Joins, 20
Miter limit, 20
P
Paste, 18
Pencil, 2
Photoshop, 2, 19
R
Raster, 1
S
Scale, 4
screen display mode, 9
Select All, 14
Select commands, 14
Selection, 11–21
Selection tool, 11
Show Center icon, 15
T
Tool tips, 6
Tools, 2
Transform Again, 17
U
Unlock All, 16
Z
Zoom tool, 8

*Index entry with the **First Level** style sheet.*
*A **Scope** setting of **To End Of: Document.***
*Second level index entry with **Second Level** style sheet.*
***Add Letter Headings** option using a bold version of the first level style sheet*
*An **X-Ref** ("See") reference.*
The word "Photoshop" was marked in two different chapters.
En dashes should be used in page ranges in an index.

*A built index in the **Nested** format. A comma and space ", " was specified as the Separation Characters: Following Entry in Index Preferences.*

A
anchor points, 2-3
I
Illustrator, 1-6; Adobe, 1; closed paths, 2; FreeHand, 1; Macintosh, 1; object-oriented, 1; Objects, 1; precision tools, 5; Stroke, 3; tools, 2; vector image, 1; Windows, 1
O
object-oriented, 1 vector, 3; versus raster, 4; paths, 5; Pen tool, 5-7; printing, 8; resolution, 7
P
Pencil. See tool

*Portions of a built index in the **Run-in** format.*

Preferences 19

PREFERENCES SHORTCUTS

Application Preferences	Ctrl-Alt-Shift-Y
Document Preferences	Ctrl-Y
Document > Paragraph tab	Ctrl-Alt-Y
Document > Trapping tab	Ctrl-Shift-F12
Document > Tool tab	Double-click item creation or Zoom tool

The Preferences dialog boxes

Preferences are the default values that automatically apply when a feature or a tool is used. For example, when the Line tool is used, a line is automatically drawn in a particular width. That width is one of its default settings. Other default settings for a line include its color and style.

Some preferences—such as the current unit of measure for the rulers, dialog boxes, and palettes—if chosen when a document is open, will apply only to that document. To set document defaults for all future documents, make sure no documents are open when you open the Document Preferences dialog box. Other preferences, such as whether the XTensions Manager displays at startup, apply application-wide, regardless of whether any documents are open when you choose them.

Like many other QuarkXPress features, preferences are chosen via folder tabs from two central dialog boxes. The General, Paragraph, Character, Tool, and Trapping preferences folder tabs are in Document Preferences **1** and the Display, Interactive, Save, and XTensions folder tabs are in Application Preferences **2**. Open a preferences dialog box from the Edit menu > Preferences submenu or via its keyboard shortcut (listed at upper left). The Color Management Preferences, which are profiles for coordinating color display and output, are in a separate dialog box. The Index Preferences are discussed on page 271, and Trapping Preferences are discussed on pages 311–313.

1 *The **General, Paragraph, Character, Tool,** and **Trapping** folder tabs are in **Document Preferences.***

Document Preferences for PREFERENCES.qxd
General | Paragraph | Character | Tool | Trapping
Leading — Auto Leading: 20% — Mode: Typesetting
Hyphenation — Method: Enhanced

2 *The **Display, Interactive, Save,** and **XTensions** folder tabs are in **Application Preferences.***

Application Preferences
Display | Interactive | Save | XTensions
Guide Colors — Margin: — Ruler: — Grid:

Other kinds of preferences

In addition to the preferences that you can choose via the Preferences dialog boxes, you can also set other kinds of very useful defaults for the application. For example, any paragraph or character style sheet that is created when no documents are open will appear on the Style Sheets palette of any subsequently created documents. The same holds true for colors, H&Js, lists, dashes & stripes, and the default auxiliary dictionary. Normal, which is the default style sheet that automatically appears in every new document and in any text box to which type specifications have not yet been applied, can be edited for all future documents when no documents are open. Don't overlook these kinds of defaults—they are enormous time-savers.

Tracking and kerning table settings, custom frame data, and hyphenation exceptions are stored in individual documents and in the QuarkXPress application folder in a file called XPress Preferences. If, upon opening a file, the document settings do not match the XPress Preferences settings, an alert dialog box will appear. Click Use XPress Preferences to apply the Preferences resident on that machine or click Keep Document Settings to leave the document as is.

If you trash your XPress Preferences file, the application will create a new one automatically, but in the process all custom settings will be lost. Trash the Preferences file only under extreme duress (i.e., the application becomes corrupted and unusable) or if you intentionally want to restore the program defaults for some reason. You can copy your Preferences file and stash it away for safe-keeping. And it can be copied to the QuarkXPress folder on another computer.

The XTensions Manager is also covered in this chapter because it controls, among other things, which XTensions are enabled when the application is launched.

INSIDE XPRESS PREFERENCES

Saves in XPress Preferences and affects all documents immediately

Application Preferences (Display, Interactive, Save, and XTensions)

XTensions Manager

PPD Manager

Saves in document and in XPress Preferences

Kerning Table Edit, Tracking Edit, Hyphenation Exceptions, Frame Editor

Saves only in active document

Document Preferences (General, Character, Paragraph, Tool, and Trapping), open or create auxiliary dictionary

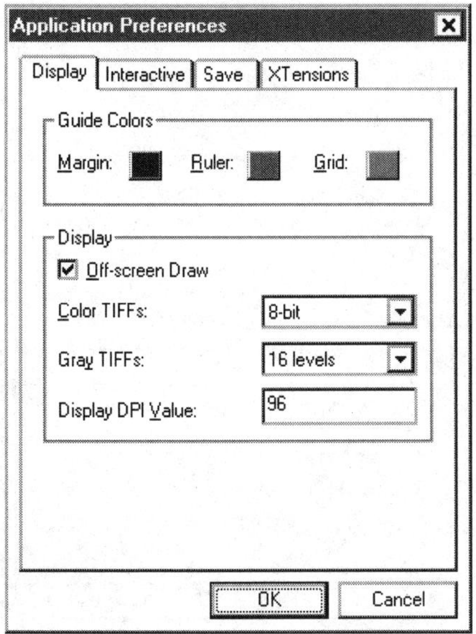

Application Preferences

Display

To choose Margin, Ruler, or Grid **Guide Colors**, click the appropriate square, then choose a color from the Color Picker. The Margin color is also used to represent the item boundary in the Runaround and Clipping dialog boxes, the Ruler color also represents the clipping path, and the Grid color also represents the runaround path.

With **Off-screen Draw** turned on, the screen will redraw all at once, not gradually in sections. The overall redraw speed is the same whether this option is on or off.

Choose a **Color TIFFs** resolution for the screen preview that is created for imported color TIFFs. A picture's screen preview affects its redraw speed and the storage size of the document into which it's imported, so choose 8-bit (256 possible colors) whenever it's practical to do so. Style menu > Contrast is not available for a picture with a 16-bit (thousands of possible colors) or 32-bit (millions of possible colors) preview. Choose 32-bit if you're using a non-PostScript printer.

TIP The Color TIFFs setting affects subsequently imported pictures only—not already imported pictures. To reimport all the pictures in a document using a new Color TIFFs setting, close the document, choose File menu > Open, locate and highlight the document name, then Ctrl-click Open.

Choose a **Gray TIFFs** resolution for the screen preview for imported grayscale TIFFs.

The **Display DPI Value** is the monitor's resolution. Read more about this setting in QuarkXPress on-screen Help.

Application Preferences

Interactive

Move the **Scrolling** slider to choose a rate of speed for the document window scroll arrows and boxes.

With **Speed Scroll** turned on, pictures and blends may be greeked (display as solid gray) while you scroll, and will redraw when you stop scrolling.

With **Live Scroll** turned on, the document will redraw as you drag a scroll box. This could slow things down to a crawl on a slow machine. Alt-drag a scroll box to temporarily turn this option on or off. The Page Grabber is always live scroll.

With **Smart Quotes** turned on, smart (curly) quotation marks are inserted automatically when you press the ' (or ") key. Choose a Format (style) for the quotes. Smart Quotes are absolutely essential for professional typesetting. Un-smart quotes look, well—un-smart (see page 110).

Click Delayed Item Dragging: **Show Contents** to temporarily display the full contents of a picture or text box as you drag it, even if the item is behind other items (pause for the Delay period before dragging). Turn on **Live Refresh** to see an item as it really looks in its layer as you pause-drag it, with an instantly updated text wrap. Enter the number of seconds (or fraction of a second) in the Delay field that you want to pause before dragging.

With **Drag and Drop Text** turned on, you can highlight text and drag it to a new location in the same story (one or more linked boxes).

If **Show Tool Tips** is turned and you rest the pointer on a tool or palette icon, the tool or icon name will display.

The **Pasteboard Width** is the percentage of the total document width that is allocated to the pasteboard. 48" is the maximum total width. 100% is the default.

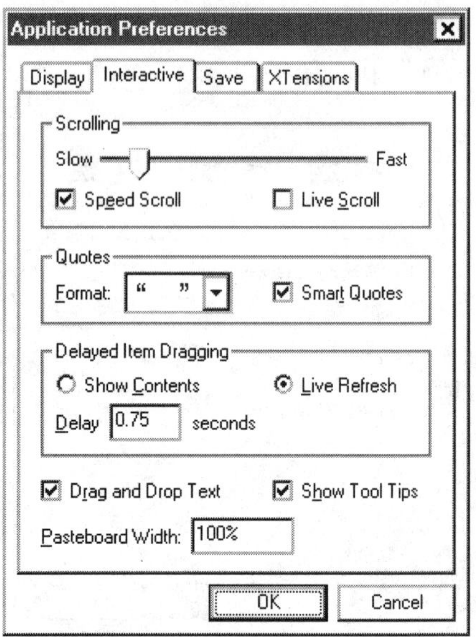

SCREEN REDRAW SHORTCUTS

Forced redraw	Shift-Esc
Stop redraw	Esc *or* perform another operation (select an item, choose another command, etc.)

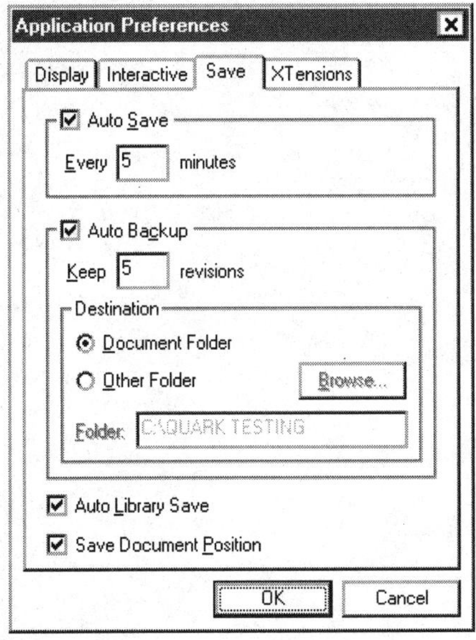

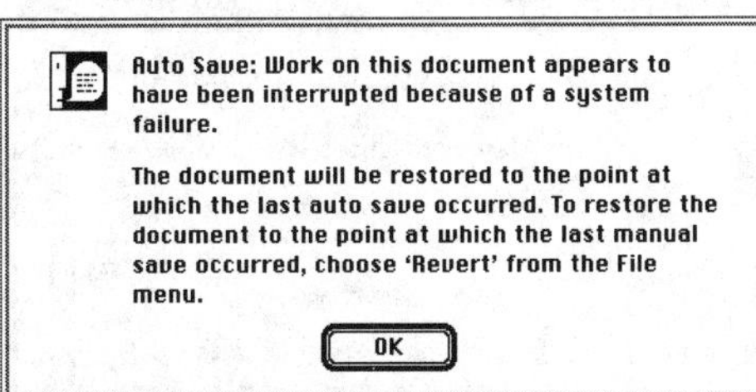

1 *The* ***Auto Save*** *prompt.*

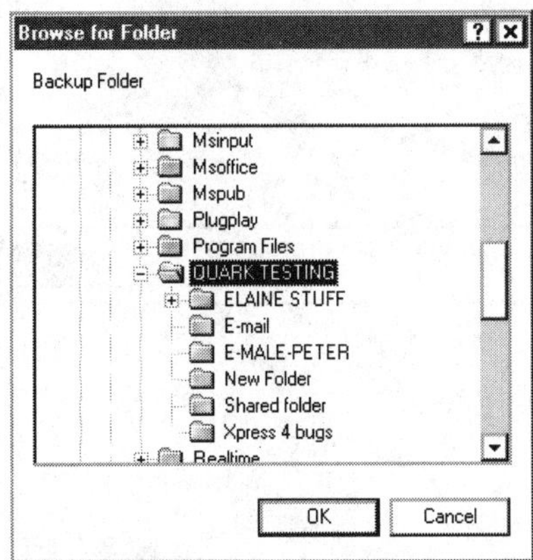

2 *In the* ***Backup Folder*** *dialog box, choose an existing folder for the backups, then click* ***OK****.*

Application Preferences

Save

Auto Save and Auto Backup are like system or power failure insurance. With the **Auto Save** option enabled, modifications are saved in a temporary file every five minutes or at an alternative interval that you specify in the "Every [ ] minutes" field. There may be a short interruption in processing while an Auto Save occurs. If a system or power failure occurs while you are modifying a document and you restart and then reopen the document, a prompt will appear **1**. Click OK to reopen the last Auto saved version. ***Note:*** Auto Save cannot retrieve a document that's never been saved.

To restore the last manually saved version of an open document, choose File menu > Revert to Saved. To restore the last auto-saved version of your document, hold down Alt while choosing the Revert to Saved command.

Unlike Auto Save, which saves only modifications made to a document in a temporary file, **Auto Backup** creates a backup version of the entire document when you execute the Save command. Progressively higher numbers are appended to the backup names. You can specify how many backup versions will be created before the oldest backup version is deleted.

Enter a number between 1 and 100 in the "Keep [ ] revisions" field. Auto Backups are saved in the current document folder, unless you specify a different destination. Designating a different location for the backups can help prevent file management confusion **2**. If you want to designate a different Destination, click Other Folder, click Browse to display the Backup Folder dialog box, locate and open an existing folder, then click OK. *Note:* You cannot create a new folder in the Backup Folder dialog box. To create a new folder,

(Continued on the following page)

exit Application Preferences, then use Explorer or choose File menu > Open (Ctrl-O).

With **Auto Library Save** turned on, a library will be saved whenever an item is added to it. With Auto Library Save off, a library will be saved only when it's closed.

With **Save Document Position** turned on, a document will reopen in the same display size and in the same document window size and position that it was in when it was last closed. *Note:* This feature may not work.

Application Preferences

XTensions

With **Show XTensions Manager at startup: Always** on, the XTensions Manager will automatically open when the application is launched.

With **When: XTension folder changes** on, the XTensions Manager will open during launch only if you have added or removed an XTension or XTensions from your XTension folder since the application was last open.

With **When: Error loading XTensions occurs** on, the XTensions Manager will open during launch only if QuarkXPress encounters a problem while loading the XTensions.

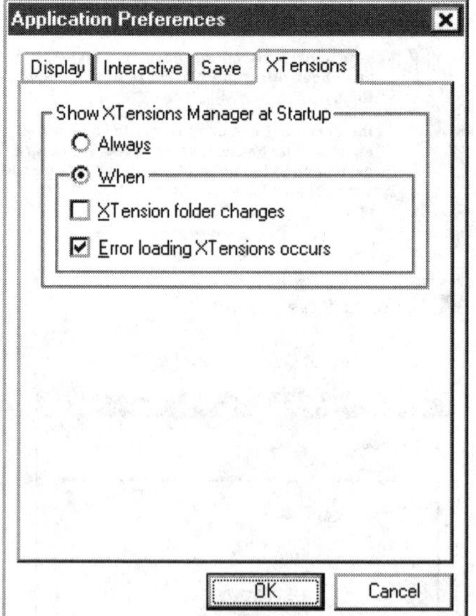

Document Preferences

General

Choose the default **Horizontal** and **Vertical Measure** separately: Inches, Inches Decimal, Picas, Points, Millimeters, Centimeters, Ciceros, or Agates (see page 21). These increments are used for the Measurements palette, rulers, and dialog boxes (except for font size, leading, frame width, and line width, which always display in points).

With **Auto Page Insertion** on, pages can be added to an auto text box chain at End of Story, End of Section, End of Document, or not at all (Off) (see pages 61–63).

Framing is added to the Inside (the default) or Outside edges of a box. A frame added to the Outside of a box will increase its dimensions (and thus change its x/y location). A changed Framing setting will affect only subsequently created boxes.

Set ruler **Guides** to display In Front of or Behind page elements (see page 135).

With **Item Coordinates**: Spreads chosen, horizontal ruler increments progress uninterrupted across a multi-page spread. Choose Page for normal ruler display.

The **Auto Picture Import** options, Off, On, and On (verify), are for reimporting pictures that were modified or moved since a document was last opened. Choose On to reimport pictures automatically or On (verify) to reimport selectively (see page 151).

The **Master Page Items** options, Keep Changes and Delete Changes, affect whether modified items from the previously applied master page are kept or deleted when a new master page is applied to a document page (see page 220).

72/inch is now the standard **Points/Inch** ratio in desktop publishing, so there's no need to change it. Ditto for Ciceros/cm, the ciceros-to-centimeter conversion ratio (2.197 is the default).

The **Snap Distance** is the range in pixels within which an item will snap to a guide if View menu > Snap to Guides is turned on.

Greek Below is the point size below which text will display as solid gray bars. Greeking is also affected by the current view size.

With **Greek Pictures** on, an unselected picture will display as solid gray; a selected picture will display normally. Greeking speeds up screen redraw—but turn it on only if you really need it.

With **Accurate Blends** on, blends look smoother on screen—but render more slowly—on an 8-bit monitor. Blends are always accurate on a 16- or 24-bit monitor.

With **Auto Constrain** on, each newly created item (child) is constrained by the dimensions of an existing (parent) item—a holdover from the early days of XPress.

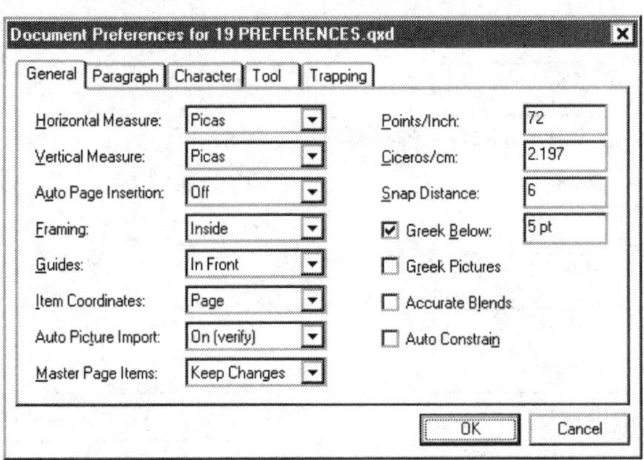

Document Preferences

Paragraph

Auto Leading is primarily calculated as a percentage of the point size of the current font, and it is enabled when "auto" or "0" is entered in the Leading field on the Measurements palette or in the Formats dialog box. The spacing between each line in an auto-leaded paragraph will vary according to the point size of the largest character in each line. You can also enter an increment in this field. Enter an Auto Leading amount of +2, for example, and two points will be added to the point size of the text to arrive at the leading amount. This means 10-point text will have 12-point leading, and so on. This setting affects both newly created *and* existing text.

In Typesetting leading **Mode**, leading is measured from baseline to baseline—the method that is traditionally preferred by typesetters. In Word Processing mode, leading is measured from ascent to ascent.

If **Maintain Leading** is turned on and an item is positioned within a column of text, the first line of text that is forced below the item will snap to the nearest leading increment.

The **Baseline Grid** is the underlying, non-printing grid that's used to precisely align text or items in a layout across columns to ensure page symmetry and uniformity. To use the Baseline Grid feature for text, specify an Increment that is equal to or a multiple of the text leading. The Start value should match the vertical (*y*) position of the first baseline of the text. To snap text to the grid lines, choose Style menu > Formats, then check the Lock to Baseline Grid box. To display the grid, choose View menu > Show Baseline Grid. If vertical justification is on, only the first and last lines in the column will lock to the grid.

Note: To align text without using the Baseline Grid, make sure the sum of the space before and after any subheads or between paragraphs is a multiple of the leading value. For example, if your body text has 14-pt. leading, add eight points before each subhead and six points after. Use style sheets to ensure that your body text leading is uniform.

The **Hyphenation Methods** are, in order of appearance from earlier versions of QuarkXPress to the current version: Standard, Enhanced, and Expanded.

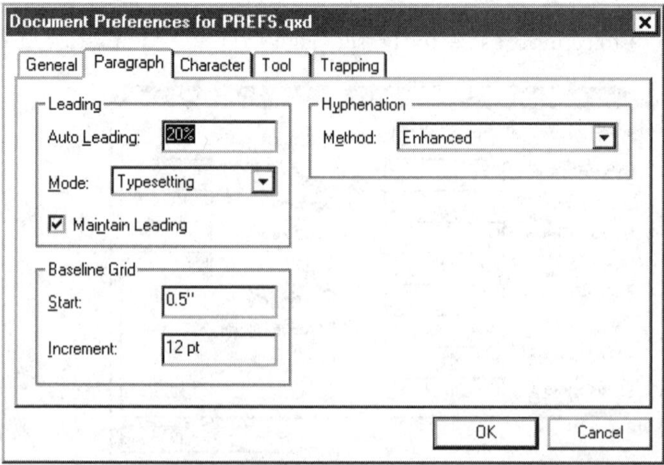

Document Preferences

Character

The **Superscript** Offset is the distance a superscript character is raised above the baseline, and is measured as a percentage of the current point size. The **Subscript** Offset is the distance a character is lowered below the baseline. The Superscript, Subscript, and Small Caps VScale (height) and HScale (width) are calculated as a percentage of a normal uppercase letter.

TIP Try increasing the HScale for Small Caps, or better yet, use an expert font with built-in small caps.

The **Auto Kern Above** value is the point size above which characters will be kerned automatically based on each particular font's built in kerning values, as well as any user-defined QuarkXPress Tracking Edit or Kerning Table Edit values. Kerning is essential for professional-looking type.

The **Flex Space Width** is a specified percentage of an en space in the current font. To enter a breaking flex space in your text, use this keystroke: Ctrl-Shift-5. To enter a non-breaking flex space: Ctrl-Alt-Shift-5. (To make the flex space the same width as an em space, enter 200%.)

With **Standard em space** turned on, an em space equals the point size of the text into which it's inserted. With this option off, an em space equals the width of two zeros in the current font.

Turn on **Accents for All Caps** to use foreign language accent marks in small caps or all caps text **1**. All-caps accents are considered kosher in some languages but not in others.

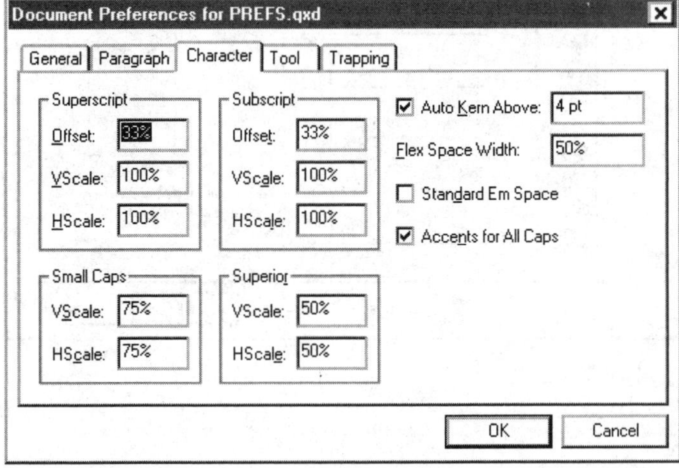

ALL CAPS ACCENTS

Ä	Alt-0196
À	Alt-0192
Ã	Alt-0195
É	Alt-0201
Ñ	Alt-0209
Ö	Alt-0214
Õ	Alt-0213
Ü	Alt-0220

Accent *n.*: a mark (as **É, À, Õ, Ü**) used in writing or printing to indicate a specific sound value, stress, or pitch.

1 *With Accents for All Caps on, accents can be inserted above uppercase characters in the All Caps style.*

Document Preferences

Tool

To choose default settings for a tool, click the tool's icon in the Tool folder tab or double-click the tool on the Tool palette. To set preferences for more than one tool at a time, first Ctrl-click their icons individually or Shift-click a range of icons. Or click one tool icon, then click **Select Similar Types** or **Select Similar Shapes** to change the default settings for related tools. Fewer Modify dialog box settings may be available when more than one tool icon is highlighted.

Click **Modify** to change the default settings for the currently highlighted item creation tool or tools. Tool settings that you can change include: The background color for picture boxes or text boxes (I use Black 0%), frame width, text inset, Line tool width, and the runaround Type.

To restore the default *settings* for the currently highlighted tool or tools, click **Use Default Prefs**. Click **Default Tool Palette** to restore the default *arrangement* of tools on the Tool palette.

The **View Scale** Minimum and Maximum percentages apply only to the Zoom tool. The Increment is the percentage the display size of the document will be enlarged or reduced with each click of the Zoom tool in the document window.

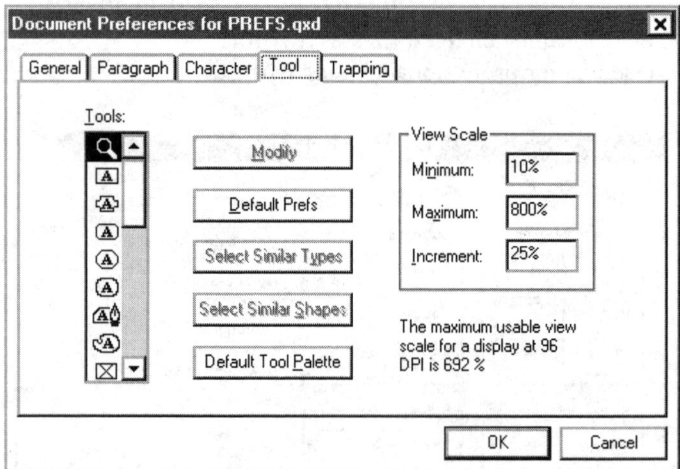

WHAT DOES "!ERROR" MEAN?

The word !Error in the Status column for an XTensions is a warning that QuarkXPress had a problem loading that XTension. Disable any XTension that has an error status.

Choose an XTensions set from the **Set** drop-down menu.

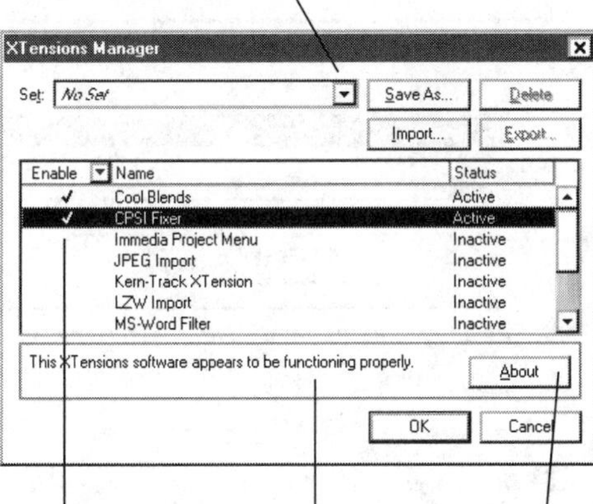

*Click in the **Enable** column in the **XTensions Manager** to enable or disable a Quark XTension, import/export filter, or third-party XTension.*

More information about the status of the currently highlighted XTension.

*Click **About** to learn more about an XTension, such as its version number and whether it's optimized for QuarkXPress version 4.0.*

XTensions are add-ons to QuarkXPress that extend the program's capabilities. Using the XTensions Manager, you can enable or disable Quark XTensions from within the application, as long as they are located in the XTension folder (not the XTension Disabled folder). You should disable any that you don't need, as they utilize memory. You can also use this utility to save, export, import, or delete user-defined XTension sets (XTension groups).

Note: XTensions Manager changes go into effect when QuarkXPress is re-launched.

To enable/disable XTensions or import/export filters:

1. Choose Utilities menu > XTensions Manager.
2. Click the name of the XTension or filter that you want to turn on or off.
3. Click a check mark to disable that XTension or click an absent check mark to enable it. Repeat for any other XTensions that you want to turn on or off.
   or
   Choose an XTensions set from the Set drop-down menu (see the next page).
4. *Optional:* Click About to display information about the currently highlighted XTension. Click in this info dialog box to return to the Manager.
5. Click OK, then exit and re-launch QuarkXPress.

TIP To turn more than one XTension on or off at a time, click on the name of the first XTension in a consecutive series, then Shift-click the name of the last XTension in the series, or Ctrl-click individual XTension names, then choose Yes or No from the Enable drop-down menu.

TIP For information on purchasing XTensions, see page 19.

Enable/Disable XTensions

You can save your custom XTensions Manager settings (this XTension on, that XTension off, etc.) as a set, and you can choose which set will be in effect when the application is launched. XTensions sets are saved in the XPress Preferences file.

Note: XTensions Manager changes don't take effect until you exit and restart QuarkXPress.

To create a custom XTensions set:

1. Choose Utilities menu > XTensions Manager.
2. Disable any XTensions that you don't want to include in your set and enable any XTensions that you do want to include.
3. Click Save As **1**.
4. Enter a name for current set **2**.
5. Click Save. Your custom set will appear on the Set drop-down menu in the XTensions Manager **3** and it will also be enabled when the application is re-launched. (You can choose a different set to be in effect upon relaunch from the Set drop-down menu.)
6. Click OK or press Enter.

TIP To enable all the XTensions, choose Set: All XTensions Enabled. To disable them all, choose All XTensions Disabled from the same drop-down menu. Choose 4.0-Optimized XTensions to enable only the XTensions that have been written or upgraded for Quark 4.0.

TIP To delete the current set (the one that's listed on the Set drop-down menu), click Delete. You can't delete any set that shipped with QuarkXPress.

1 *Click **Save As** in the **XTensions Manager** to create a custom set.*

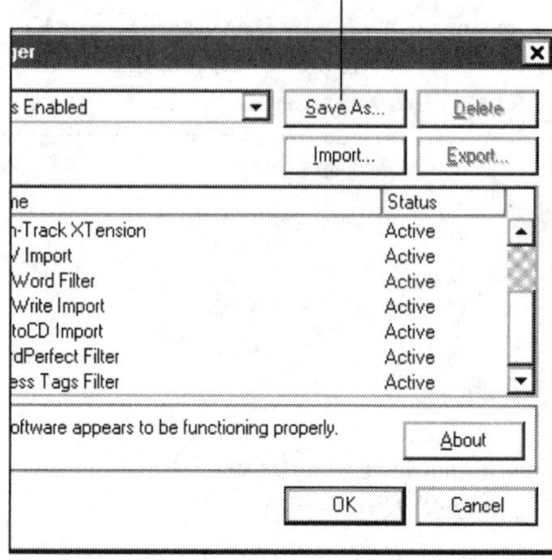

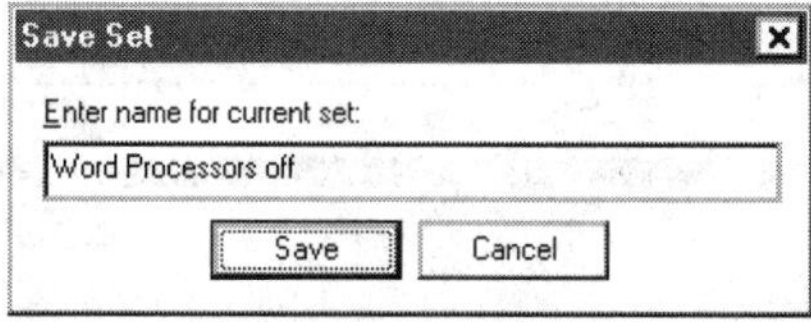

2 *Enter a **name** for a custom XTensions set.*

3 *The new custom set will appear on the **Set** drop-down menu.*

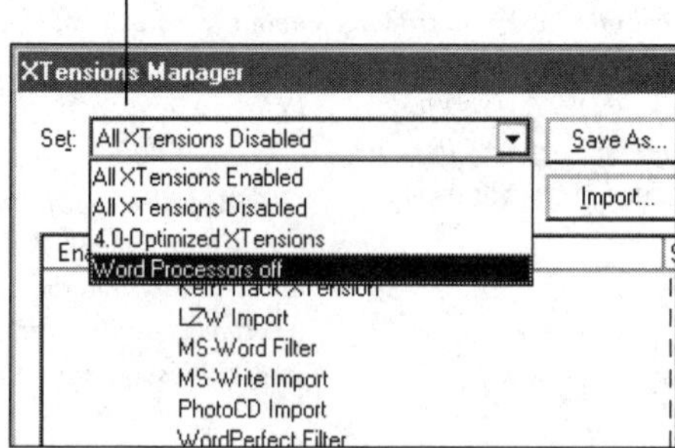

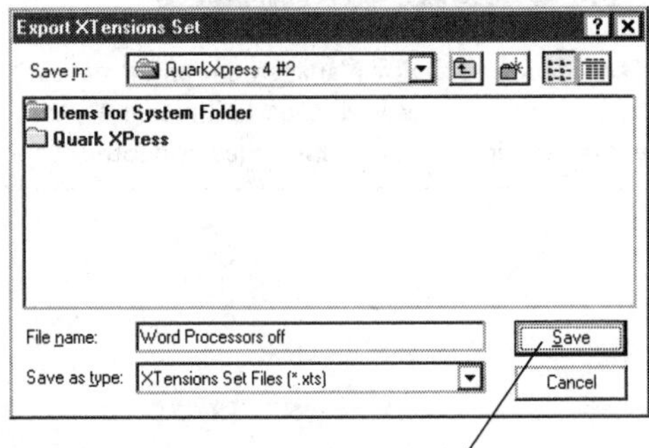

1 *Choose a location in which to save the XTensions file, then click **save**.*

Elaine's set.xts

2 *This is what an XTensions set file icon looks like.*

As a safety measure, you can save any custom XTensions set to a separate file using the Export command. Then, if you need to delete the XPress Preferences file for some reason, where XTensions sets are stored, you can import any saved XTensions set using the XTensions Manager.

To save an XTensions set as a separate file:

1. Choose Utilities menu > XTensions Manager.
2. Create a new custom set (instructions on the previous page).
   or
   Choose an existing custom set from the Set drop-down menu.
3. Click Export.
4. Choose a location in which to save the file, then click Save **1** or press enter.
5. Click OK.

TIP To import a previously saved custom set file that's not listed on the Set drop-down menu, click Import, locate and highlight the file that you want to import, then click Open **2**.

XTENSIONS MANAGER AT STARTUP

If you want the XTensions Manager to always open automatically upon launching the application, choose Edit menu > Preferences > Application, click the XTensions folder tab, then check the Show XTensions Manager at startup: Always button.

If the Show XTensions Manager at startup preference is off, you can open the XTensions Manager as you launch QuarkXPress by holding down Space bar. Keep the Space bar pressed until the Manager opens.

What is color management?

Color management helps to ensure consistent color between screen and final output. Color management is necessary because each device, whether it's a monitor or a printer, defines color within its own unique color range (gamut) when it represents or reproduces color. A monitor can't display, nor can a printing device output, all the colors in the visible spectrum. Color management systems aim to coordinate and match color between various device gamuts—from monitor color (RGB) to final print output color (CMYK). If color on a source device (monitor or scanner) is within the gamut of the destination device (printer), then color matching is straightforward. If color on a source device is outside the gamut of the destination device, then the color management system adjusts the color (alters its hue, lightness, or saturation) to match color between devices.

The Quark Color Management System (CMS), helps to ensure color accuracy between monitor representation and final output by taking into account color variations between different color models (RGB and CMYK) and device gamuts.

Let's say you have a picture that was created in Photoshop and then is imported into a QuarkXPress document. If you choose the same profiles (particularly the monitor profile) in both applications, the picture hopefully will look the same on screen in QuarkXPress as it does in Photoshop, and in both applications it should match as closely as possible the final output color. Once this color consistency is established, if you then change the monitor or the final output printer type, you must choose new profiles within each application.

Two critical steps in color matching are monitor calibration (generating and maintaining accurate screen characteristics, such as the white point and gamut) and

FROM THE HORSE'S MOUTH

The "Guide to Color Management and Prepress" booklet that comes with QuarkXPress 4.0 explains color management issues in depth.

INSTALLING CMS

The Quark Color Management System (CMS) XTension must be specially selected during installation; it isn't part of the standard installation set. If you didn't select it during installation, you must do a custom installation. Click Customize in the installation program, double-click the XTensions folder, click the Quark Color Management System Files folder, check the Install Highlighted Items box, click OK, and continue with the installation.

choosing the correct color profile for each device.

Color in QuarkXPress

Two kinds of color are used in a QuarkXPress document: Color that is applied to an item that's created within the application and color that was saved in an imported picture. In the case of color that's applied in QuarkXPress, the CMS generates color data based on the monitor profile or the profile for the output device the color is intended for. Item color profiles are assigned in the CMS Color Management Preferences dialog box.

When a picture is imported, the CMS searches for an included profile, if any, that is contained in that picture. The profile can be for the scanning device, the monitor used in the image creation program, or the final output device that was chosen for the picture. If no profile is included with an imported picture, you can use the CMS to assign a source profile. For an RGB picture, this will be a scanning device or monitor profile—whichever is appropriate. For a CMYK picture, this will be the profile for the final output device. ***Note:*** The CMS may not detect an embedded TIFF profile.

An imported picture to which no profile was assigned will be assigned a default profile as per the current settings in the Color Management Preferences dialog box. The default profile can be overridden via the Profile Information palette or the Get Picture dialog box.

Color management is accessed in XPress via Edit menu > Preferences > Color Management (if you don't see Color Management listed, see the note on page 288). This dialog box makes QuarkXPress aware of your choice for source and destination profiles, and your choice of parameters for on-screen color correction.

To turn on color management:

1. Choose Edit menu > Preferences > Color Management.
2. Check the Color Management Active box to turn on color management **1**.
3. Choose from the Destination Profiles drop-down menus for the target color output device **2**:

   Choose from the Monitor pop-up menu for monitor output. The profile names come from the System > Preferences > ColorSync Profiles folder. If the correct monitor name isn't listed, choose a monitor that closely approximates your target screen size.

   For composite printer output (all colors printing on one sheet), choose a Composite Printer. This type of printer is usually used for a limited run or to produce color proofs for review before producing separations.

   For color separations, choose a Separation Printer.
4. Choose a Default Source Profile, the source device that created the pictures you've imported into QuarkXPress **3**. Choose profiles to manage specific color spaces (models) for colors and pictures in three categories: RGB, CMYK and Hexachrome (six-plate printing).

   For the RGB color source, click the RGB folder tab, and from the Color drop-down menu, choose the exact monitor or the closest match that you can find. This kind of color derives

1 *Check here to turn on color management.*

2 *Choose Destination profiles.*

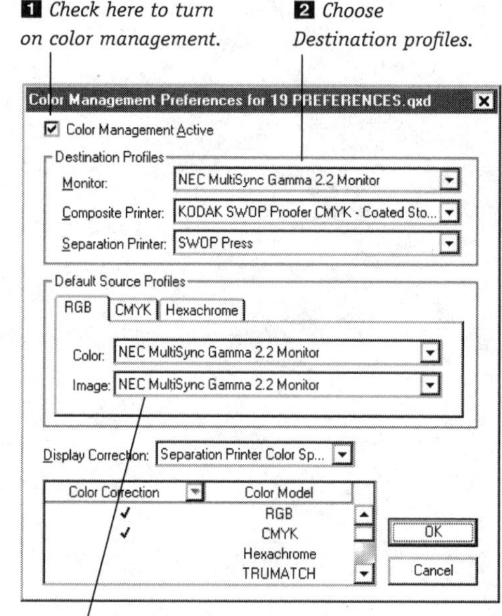

3 *Choose a Default Source profile for each color model.*

from the monitor profile used by the program that created the color.

For a scanned picture, choose the scanner profile from the Image drop-down menu. For a picture created in a graphics application, from the Image drop-down menu, choose the Monitor profile used by that graphics application.

For the CMYK color source, click the CMYK folder tab and choose the desired printer for color proofing or final output.

For the Hexachrome color source, click the Hexachrome folder tab, and choose the target output printer.

5. Under Display Correction, choose the device profile (and thus what device gamut or color range) that you want the CMS to use for on-screen color correction. The bottom three categories on the drop-down menu match the three Destination Profile categories. For each Display Correction choice, the profile you chose in the matching Destination Profile category will be used. Choose Off if or when you need to turn off on-screen color correction.
6. You can use the Color Model list to include/exclude individual color models from on-screen color correction. A check mark to the left of a color model name signifies that that model will be on-screen color corrected. Click a color model name and then click in the leftmost column to display or remove a check mark.
7. Click OK or press Enter to close the dialog box and save your changes.

TIP Profiles assigned using the CMS are saved in the QuarkXPress document.

QuarkXPress' Profile Information palette displays a selected picture's characteristics and gives the user a limited means for modifying on-screen color correction for that picture.

To use the Profile Information palette:

1. Open the palette by choosing View menu > Show Profile Information.
2. Click on a picture box that contains an imported picture.
3. Examine the three information fields to learn about:

   The current picture's Picture Type—Color, Grayscale, or Line Art (black-and-white).

   The File type: TIFF, EPS, etc.

   The Color Space: RGB, CMYK, Unknown (for an EPS file whose exact color space information is not accessable to QuarkXPress), etc.
4. If necessary, choose from the Profile drop-down menu **1** to alter the source profile for the selected picture from the embedded or default profile currently chosen in Color Management Preferences. For an RGB picture, the Profile drop-down menu will display monitor or scanner names. For a CMYK picture, the Profile drop-down menu will display output device names. (The defaults were set up in the Default Source Profiles section of the Color Management Preferences.
5. Check the Color Correction box to turn on QuarkXPress' on-screen color correction for the selected picture **2**.

   Choosing a different profile name when Color Correction is checked will immediately alter the on-screen appearance of the currently selected picture.

   The Profile drop-down menu and Color Correction box will be grayed out for a grayscale or EPS picture. In the case of the former, there is no color

*The **Profile Information** palette.*

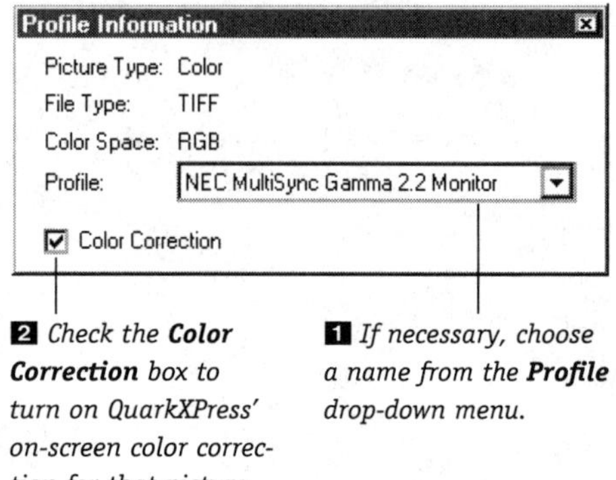

2 *Check the **Color Correction** box to turn on QuarkXPress' on-screen color correction for that picture.*

1 *If necessary, choose a name from the **Profile** drop-down menu.*

Profile Information Palette

to correct. And an EPS picture is encapsulated, which means its color information cannot be altered using any QuarkXPress command.

TIP A profile chosen from the Profile Information palette will override the default profile assigned to the picture via the Color Management Preferences dialog box.

You can also view an imported picture's characteristics and modify its profile in the Get Picture dialog box.

To turn on color management for a picture as it's imported:

1. Choose the Content tool, then click on a picture box.
2. Choose File menu > Get Picture.
3. Locate and highlight the name of the picture that you want to import.
4. The picture's Name, Format, File Size, Date, Dimensions (and resolution), and Color Depth will be listed.
5. Either the profile that was assigned to the picture in an image editing application or the default profile that was assigned to its picture type via the Color Management Preferences will display on the Profile drop-down menu. To override that profile, choose another profile from the drop-down menu **1**.

   Check the Color Correction box to turn on QuarkXPress' color correction for that picture.
6. Click Open to import the picture. (Click Cancel to close the dialog box and disregard changes.)

TIP A profile chosen in the Get Picture dialog box will override any default profile assigned to the picture via the Color Management Preferences dialog box.

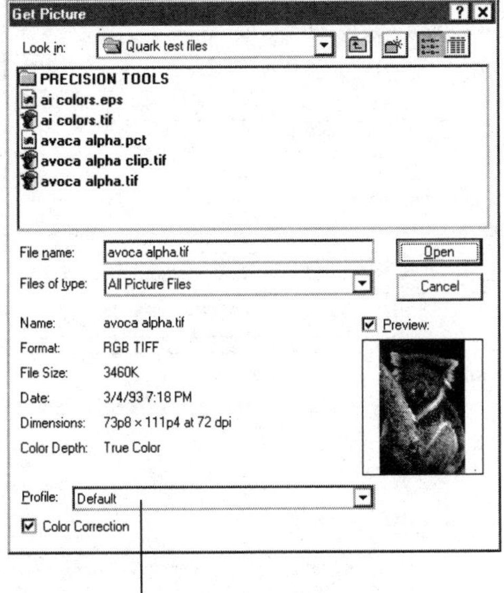

1 *You can choose a different profile for an imported picture in the **Get Picture** dialog box.*

The Profile Manager is used to view which profiles are currently installed in your system and/or to include or exclude individual profiles for use with the CMS.

To include/exclude profiles in QuarkXPress:

1. Choose Utilities menu > Profile Manager.
2. Click a check mark to the left of a profile name to exclude that profile from the CMS or click on the blank space under the Include column to produce a check mark and include that profile. By default, all profiles in the system are automatically included (checked).
3. Click OK or press Enter.

TIP Click Update if you have just installed/uninstalled profiles in your system and you want the Profile Manager to update its list of current system profiles.

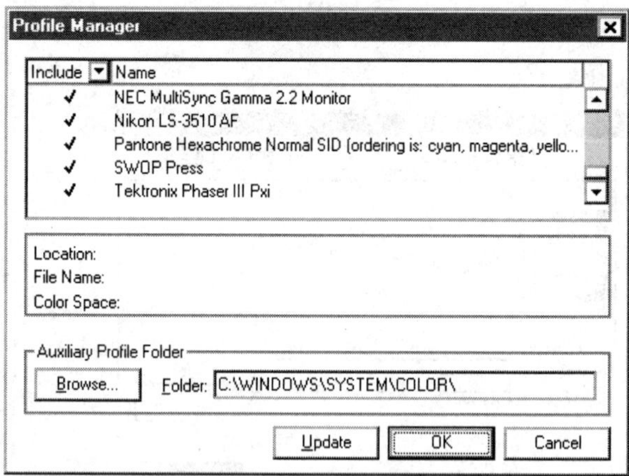

The ***Profile Manager****.*

Output 20

QUICK-AND-DIRTY PRINT

Once you've established your Print dialog box settings and you want to print an entire document: Ctrl-P, then press Enter. Or, to specify a range of pages, press Tab, type the starting page number, type a hyphen, type the ending page number, then press Enter.

SPEED TIP

1 *Enter the number of **Copies** to be printed. 1 is the default.*

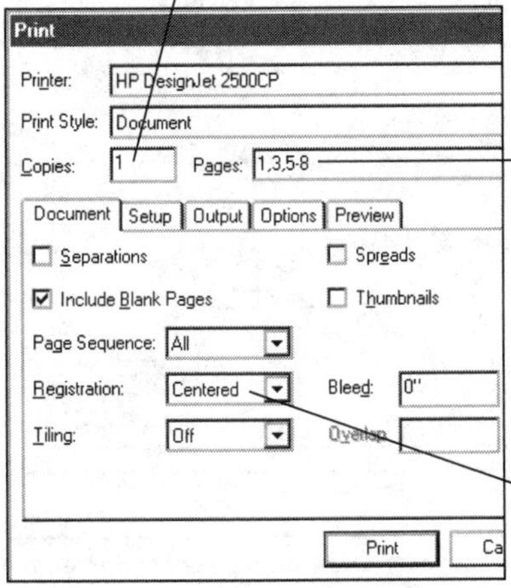

Print
Printer: HP DesignJet 2500CP
Print Style: Document
Copies: 1 Pages: 1,3,5-8
Document | Setup | Output | Options | Preview
☐ Separations ☐ Spreads
☑ Include Blank Pages ☐ Thumbnails
Page Sequence: All
Registration: Centered Bleed: 0"
Tiling: Off Overlap:
Print Ca

*To specify which pages will print, leave the default **Pages** setting on All, or enter non-consecutive page numbers divided by commas, or enter a range of numbers divided by a hyphen. You can type "end" after a hyphen to print to the end of a document.*

*Choose **Centered: Registration** to print crop and registration marks.*

*The left side of the **Print > Document** dialog box.*

To print from QuarkXPress:

1. Open the Print dialog box by choosing File menu > Print (Ctrl-P) or File menu > Page Setup (Ctrl-Alt-P).
2. *Optional:* Choose an existing print style from the **Print Style** drop-down menu (see page 299). If you want to override the current print style settings, enter new settings via the folder tabs in the Print dialog box and then print. These changes will be only temporary and won't affect the original print style. (A bullet will appear before the original print style name to signal that a temporary change was made.)
3. Enter the number of **Copies** of each page you want to print **1**. 1 is the default.
4. In the **Pages** field, enter the pages to be printed. For continuous pages, separate the starting and ending page numbers with a "-" (hyphen). For non-continuous pages, separate each page number with a "," (comma). See the tip on page 297 regarding page numbering.

(Continued on the following page)

5. Click the **Document** folder tab if you want to turn on Separations, Spreads, Include Blank Pages, Registration (crop marks), and other settings.

   Click the **Setup** folder tab to choose the correct Printer Description 2, which will automatically set up the default Page Size, Page Width, and Height settings. You can change the printout size (Reduce or Enlarge), Page Positioning, and Orientation.

   Click the **Output** folder tab to choose a Print Colors setting (Black & White, Grayscale, or Color Composite), Halftoning, and printer Resolution options. The Print Colors options are controlled by the current Printer Description under the Setup folder tab.

   Click the **Options** folder tab if you want to turn on the Quark PostScript Error Handler (QuarkXPress' alert boxes), type of Output (Normal, Low, or Rough), data encoding, OPI, TIFF image Output, and other settings.

   Click the **Preview** folder tab to view a thumbnail of the current page with the chosen printing parameters 3.

6. You can return to any tab folder at any time. Click **Print** or press Enter when you're ready to print.

   If a missing pictures prompt appears, click **List Pictures**, click Update, locate and highlight the missing picture(s), click Open, then click Print.

   Note: Click **Properties** to display the printer's Properties dialog box 4. Settings chosen in this dialog box will override the current QuarkXPress print settings.

   Changes made to settings in QuarkXPress' Print dialog box Setup folder tab—such as Copies and Orientation—update automatically in the Paper folder tab in the Properties dialog box, and vice versa. A Paper Size

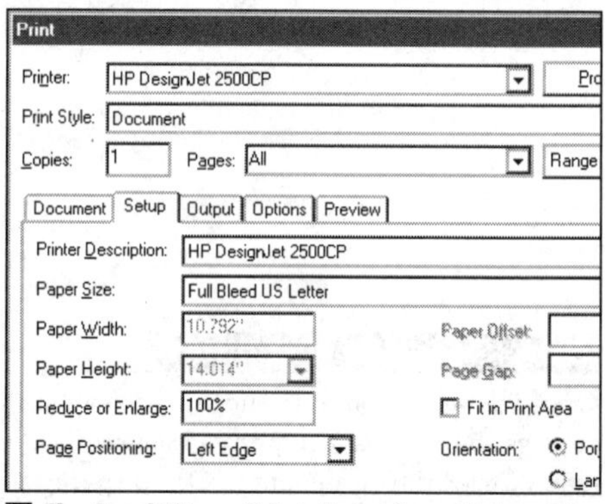

2 *The QuarkXPress **Print** dialog box > **Setup** tab.*

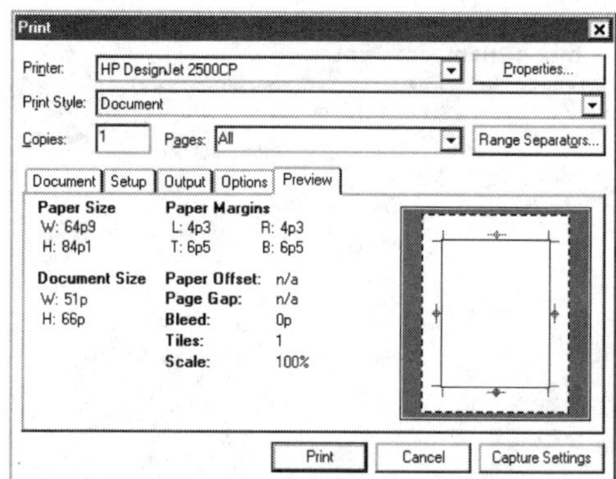

3 *The print preview in the **Print** > **Preview** tab.*

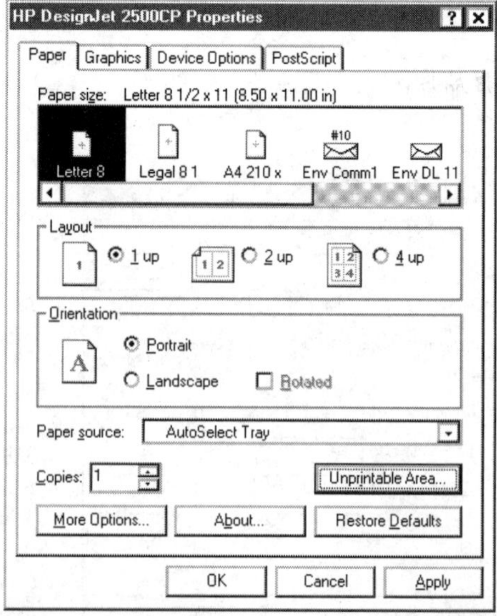

4 *Choose **Layout**, **Orientation**, **Paper source**, and **Unprintable Area** options in the **Paper** folder tab.*

BLEED REDEFINE DEFINED

With the Bleed Redefine XTension *installed,* QuarkXPress handles bleeds as in pre-4.0 versions of the application: Items that extend off the page *won't* be trimmed at the crop marks, regardless of the current Bleed value in File > Print > Document folder tab **1**.

If the Bleed Redefine XTension is *not* installed and the Bleed value in the File > Print > Document folder tab is 0, any item that extends off the page as a bleed *will* be trimmed at the crop marks **2**. At a Bleed value greater than 0, bleed objects will print into the bleed value area, and cut and registration marks will appear six points beyond the Bleed value. If the Bleed value is ten points, for example, objects can print up to ten points beyond the edge of the page, and registration marks will appear six points beyond the Bleed value.

The Bleed Redefine XTension can be downloaded from the Quark web site (Quark.com). Install it in the XTension folder in the QuarkXPress application folder and then relaunch the application. *Note:* Bleed Redefine becomes part of the XPress Preferences file, and it can only be deleted by deleting the XPress Preferences file; removing the XTension from the XTension folder will not remove it. Duplicate your XPress Preferences file before you install the XTension if you want to reserve a copy of it without the XTension.

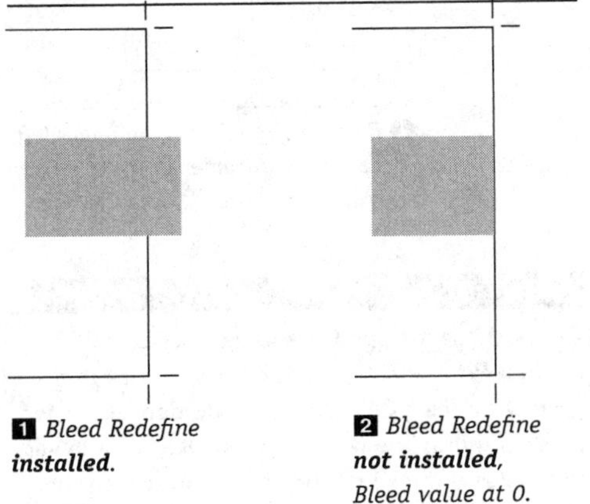

1 *Bleed Redefine* ***installed.***

2 *Bleed Redefine* ***not installed,*** *Bleed value at 0.*

change, on the other hand, will **not** update in the other dialog box.

Options in the printer's **Properties** dialog box will vary depending on the currently selected printer. For a PostScript printer, there are four folder tabs: Paper, Graphics, Device Options and PostScript.

Use the **Paper** tab to format the Layout, Orientation, Paper source, and Unprintable Area of the page. Click More Options to select the type of paper you'll be printing on.

Use the **Graphics** tab to choose Resolution, image color matching, Halftoning, and Scaling settings. You can also choose to print a negative or a mirror image here.

Use the **Device Options** tab to change Color Correction settings.

Use the **PostScript** tab to set the PostScript Output format.

When you're done choosing settings, click OK from any folder tab to return to the Print dialog box.

TIP If your page numbers contain hyphens, you'll need to choose a different range separator for the Pages field. To do this, click Range Separators, then type a character in the Continuous and Noncontinuous fields.

If your document contains section numbering, enter the page number accurately, including any prefix, as in "Page xii." To enter the number of the position of the page within the document instead (the absolute page number), enter a plus sign before it. To print the third and fourth pages in a document, for example, enter "+3-+4."

Capture the setting

Click Capture Settings to save the current print settings to the generic Document print style and also close the Print dialog box. The next time you choose Print, the captured settings will be listed under the generic Document print style. If you choose another print style or choose other print options and click Capture Settings again, the Document print style will take on the new settings.

Some custom Halftoning options can also be saved to the generic Document print style when you click Capture Settings. If you want to create a print style with Halftoning options for use with other documents, use Edit menu > Print Styles (see the next page).

THE DOCUMENT PRINT STYLE

Don't confuse the Document print style with the Default print style. The Document print style is listed in the Print dialog box. The Default print style is listed in the Edit menu > Print Styles dialog box.

To save the Default print style as the Document print style, choose Edit menu > Print Styles, click the Default style, click Duplicate, click OK, then click Save. Choose File menu > Print, choose the Default Copy print style, then click Capture Settings. The Document style now matches the Default style.

An oversized document (a page size that's larger than the printer's paper size) can be printed in sections on more than one sheet of paper using automatic or manual Tiling. To print an oversized document on one sheet of paper, reduce the printout size percentage (Setup tab) until it fits.

To print using automatic tiling:

1. Choose File menu>Print (Ctrl-P).
2. Choose the appropriate Orientation button in the Setup folder tab.
3. Choose Tiling: Automatic in the Document folder tab.
4. Enter a number in the Overlap field. 3" (18p) is the default.
5. Adjust any other print settings. Click the Preview folder tab to preview.
6. Click Print.

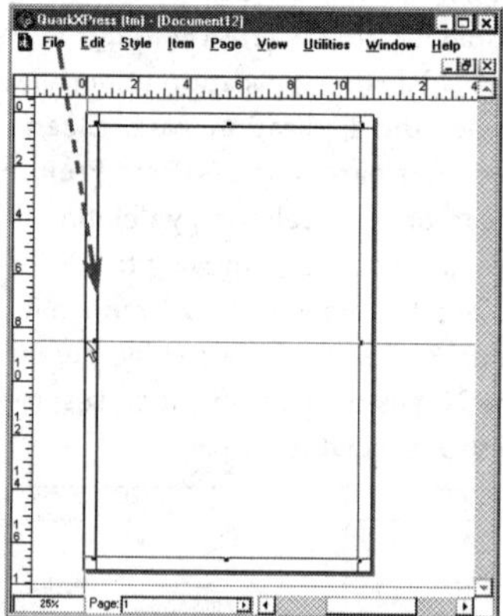

1 *Press and drag from the upper left corner of the document window to move the* ***ruler origin*** *for* ***Manual Tiling.***

PRINT 11 X 17 PAGE ON TWO SHEETS

Check the landscape Orientation button in File menu > Print > Setup folder tab and print the page with Tiling Off (Document folder tab). Then press and drag the ruler origin to 8.5" on the vertical ruler to move the position from which the document will begin printing **1**, and print again with Tiling set to Manual.

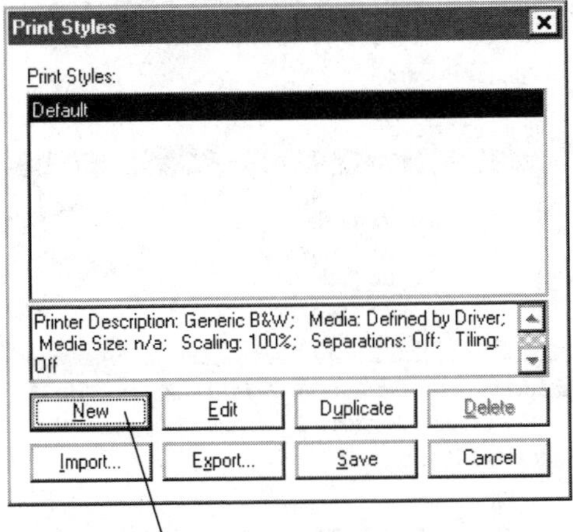

1 *Click **New** in the **Print Styles** dialog box.*

2 *In this example, a new print style has been created with an Output setting of Rough for faster printing (the pictures won't print).*

Print styles are like style sheets for printers. Each print style can contain custom Print dialog box settings. Once you've created a print style, you can then choose it from the Print Styles drop-down menu in the Print dialog box for *any* QuarkXPress document. To temporarily override the saved settings in a print style, simply choose new settings from any folder tab in the Print dialog box.

To create or edit a print style:

1. Choose Edit menu > Print Styles.
2. Click an existing print style, then click Edit to modify it or click Duplicate to edit a copy of it.
   or
   Click New to create a new print style **1**.
3. For a new or duplicate print style, type a name in the Name field.
4. Click the Document, Setup, Output, and Options folder tabs, and choose the desired settings.
5. Click OK, then click Save **2**.

TIP To remove a print style from the list, click on it, then click Delete. The Default print style can't be deleted.

TIP Click Export to save the current print style to a separate file. If that style is inadvertently deleted (or if the XPress Preferences file, where print styles are stored, is deleted), you can restore it via the Import button in the Print Styles dialog box.

Suppress picture printing: Picture Usage

Choose Utilities menu > Usage > Pictures folder tab (Shift-F2), then click to delete the check mark in the Print column to suppress printing of that picture **1**. The picture won't print, but a frame, if applied to the box, will print. (Click again in the same column to restore the check mark and turn printing back on.) Click Close when you're finished.

To suppress the printing of multiple pictures, click on the first picture in a series of consecutively listed pictures, then Shift-click on the last picture in the series, or Ctrl-click non-consecutive pictures individually, then choose No from the Print drop-down menu.

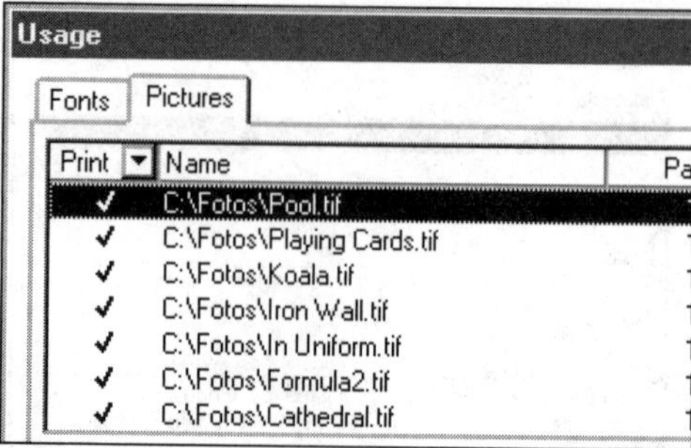

1 *Click a check mark in the **Print** column in Utilities menu > Usage > **Pictures** folder tab to suppress the printing of that picture.*

Suppress item printing: Modify dialog box

To completely suppress printing of any individual item (a line, a box, or a text path) including its frame, if any, check the Suppress Printout box in Item menu > Modify > Box folder tab (Ctrl-M or right-click and choose Modify) **2**. You can add non-printing notes to your document this way.

Or, to print a frame on a picture box but not the picture, check the Suppress Picture Printout box in Item menu > Modify > Picture folder tab.

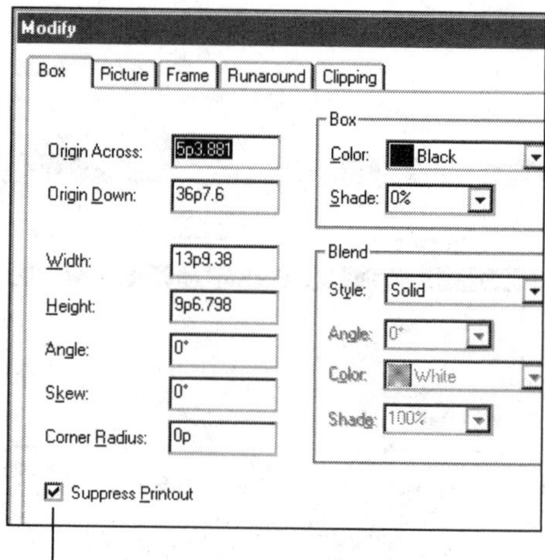

2 *Check the **Suppress Printout** box in Item > Modify > **Box** folder tab to prevent a picture and frame, if any, from printing.*

Suppress printing of all pictures: Print dialog box

Choose File menu > Print > Options folder tab, then choose Output: Rough **3**. On the printout, an "x" will appear in each picture box, and any applied frames will also print.

Another option for a document that seems to be taking an eternity to print is to choose Output: Low Resolution. The low resolution version of the picture that was saved automatically with the QuarkXPress file will print instead of the original picture.

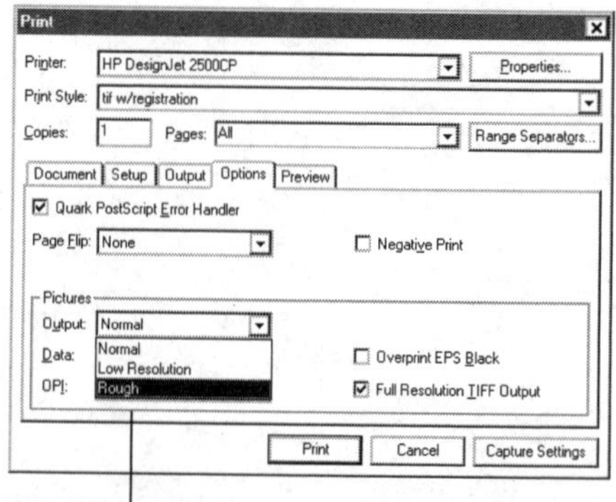

3 *Choose **Output: Low Resolution** or **Rough** in File menu > Print > **Options** folder tab.*

READ ALL ABOUT IT

To read more about the complicated world of scanning and color separation, there are many excellent reference books to choose from, such as *Real World Scanning and Halftones* by David Blatner and Stephen Roth or *Start with a Scan* by Janet Ashford and John Odam, both from Peachpit Press. Or take a look at *Production Essentials* from Adobe Press.

To modify the halftoning used by QuarkXPress

In the File menu > Print > Output folder tab, choose Halftoning: Conventional, then click on the name of the plate to be modified. At the top of the Frequency, Angle, and Function columns are drop-down menus from which you can make additional choices. Be sure to check with your output service provider before choosing any new settings.

If you check the Separations box in the Print > Document folder tab, a Plates drop-down menu will appear in the Output folder tab **1**. Choose Process & Spot to choose halftoning options for individual plates or choose Convert to Process to convert spot colors to process colors. Further down in the dialog box you'll see several columns. Use the Print drop-down menu to turn the printing of individual plates on or off. Use the Halftone drop-down menu to specify the print parameters for R, G, and B colors and spot colors in the file. (If Printer is chosen from the Halftoning drop-down menu, no halftone information is sent to the printer by QuarkXPress.)

TIP To save yourself from repetitive setup work, you can create a print style containing halftoning options. Then all you have to do is choose that style from the Print Style drop-down menu in the Print dialog box.

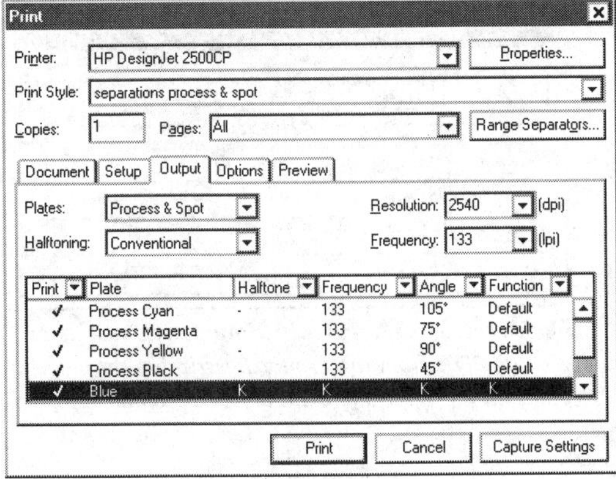

1 *Click on a color plate name and choose different settings for that plate from the **Halftone**, **Frequency**, **Angle**, and **Function** column drop-down menus. But check with your service provider first.*

PPD, which stands for PostScript Printer Description, is a text file that contains information about a particular printer's parameters—its default resolution, usable paper and page sizes, PostScript version number, etc. The PPD Manager—which facilitates loading of PPDs into QuarkXPress—is useful in any setting where more than one kind of printer is used. It can be used to control which of the System's PPDs (and thus printer names) are available on the Printer Description drop-down menu (File menu > Print > Setup folder tab, or Edit menu > Print Styles > New, or Print Styles > Edit > Setup folder tab). You can limit the Setup lists to only the printers you print to from QuarkXPress. An unlimited number of PPDs can be loaded at a time, but the fewer the better, because they affect the speed at which the Print dialog box opens. The PPD Manager's current settings update on all QuarkXPress' Printer Description drop-down menus immediately.

To use the PPD manager:

1. Choose Utilities menu > PPD Manager.
2. Click on a printer name to select it **1**.
3. Click the check mark to remove that printer name from any Setup folder tab list or click in that spot to add the printer name.
   or
   To highlight multiple, consecutively listed printer names, click a name, then Shift-click the last name you want to select. Ctrl-click to highlight non-consecutive names. Press and hold on the Include column and choose Yes or No from the drop-down menu to include or exclude the highlighted PPDs.
4. Click OK or press Enter. The Printer Description drop-down menu in the File menu > Print > Setup folder tab will update.

WHERE TO PUT YOUR PPDS

Windows stores PPDs in C:\WINDOWS\SYSTEM. QuarkXPress uses this location as its default setting, and it's a good idea to leave PPDs in this location so they can be found and accessed by all your applications. If the PPD list gets to be too long, use the PPD Manager to exclude printer names that aren't currently being used in your QuarkXPress projects. Changes made using the PPD Manager will only affect QuarkXPress—not any other applications.

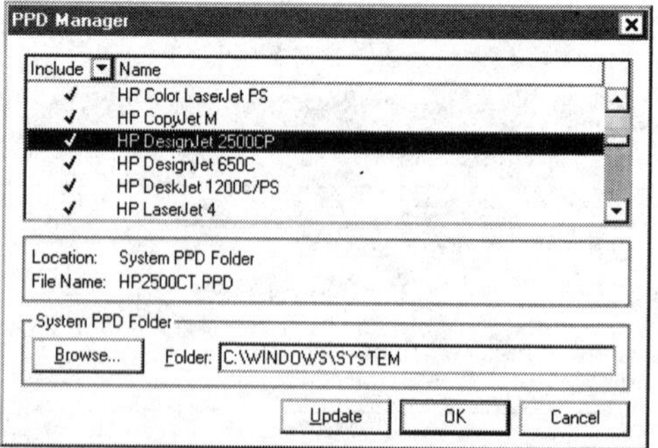

1 *Use the QuarkXPress* ***PPD Manager*** *to include or exclude PPDs from the Printer Description drop-down menu in the Print and Print Styles dialog boxes.*

To add PPDs to the PPD manager list:

1. Install the PPDs in the C:\WINDOWS\SYSTEM.
2. If QuarkXPress isn't open, launch the application now.
3. Choose Utilities menu > PPD Manager.
4. Make sure the Folder path for the PPD folder is the same as the location that was used for step 1. If it is, skip to step 5.

   If it's not the same path, click Browse, and locate the folder that contains the System's PPD files (C:\WINDOWS\SYSTEM, in our example). When the correct folder name is highlighted, click OK.
5. In the PPD Manager, click Update. Any PPDs that were just added to the System folder will also be added to the current PPD list.
6. Make sure a check mark appears in the Include column for any PPD that you want to appear on the Printer Description drop-down menu in the File menu > Print > Setup folder tab.
7. Click OK.

TIP QuarkXPress can only look to one PPD folder at a time. If you have different folders containing different PPD files, then only one of those folders will be accessable to the PPD Manager (and thus, the QuarkXPress Setup folder tab list) at a time.

Some print shops may request or require that you furnish a PostScript file of your document for output. To do this, first prepare your document as per your service provider's instructions.

Note: Before creating a PostScript file, make sure the proper Printer Description file is in the PPD Manager so it's available in the Print dialog box > Setup folder tab.

To create a PostScript file:

1. Click Start button > Settings > Printers.

(Continued on the following page)

2. Right-click on the name of your printer and choose Properties.
3. Click the Details folder tab.
4. Choose "FILE: (creates a file on disk)" from the "Print to the following port" drop-down menu **1**, then click OK.
5. Click in the QuarkXPress document window, and choose File menu > Print (Ctrl-P).
6. Ask your service provider what settings to choose in the Setup and Output folder tabs.
7. Click Properties, and click the PostScript folder tab.
8. From the PostScript output format drop-down menu, choose Encapsulated PostScript (EPS) **2**. (A warning will appear if you haven't selected Print to the following port: FILE, as described in steps 1–4, above.)
9. Click OK, then click Print. In the Print To File dialog box, type a name for and choose a folder in which to save the output file in the File name field **3**. If you want an extension, you must type it; none will be added automatically.

   Reminder: Be sure to go back into Printer Settings and change the "Print to the following port" setting back to LPT1: (Printer Port) in order to print normally.

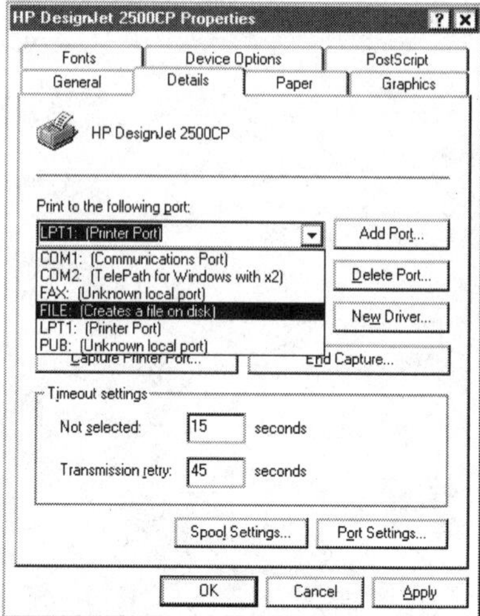

1 *Choose* ***FILE: (creates a file on disk)*** *from the* ***Print to the following port*** *drop-down menu.*

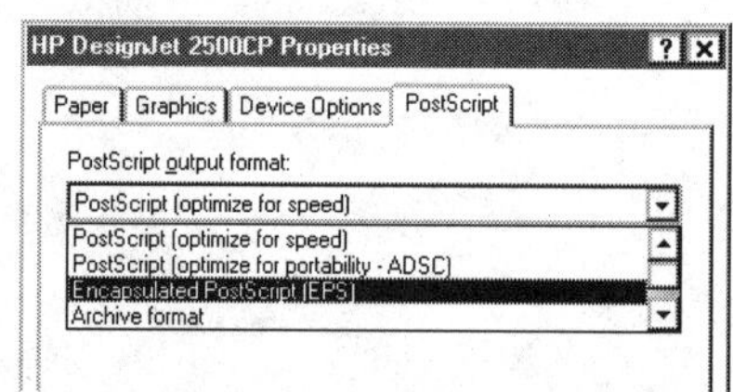

2 *Choose* ***Encapsulated Postscript (EPS)*** *from the* ***PostScript output format*** *drop-down menu.*

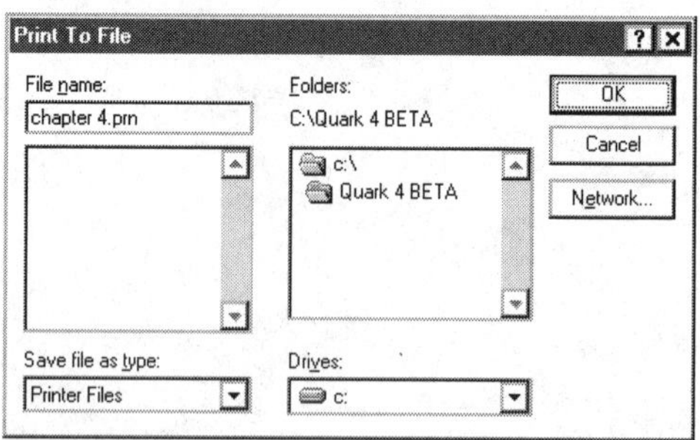

3 *In the* ***Print to File*** *dialog box, type a name for and choose a folder in which to save the output file.*

The **Save Page as EPS** command converts a QuarkXPress page into a single picture. There are a few reasons why you might need to do this. Your service provider or commercial printer might ask you to save a page as an EPS file in order to color separate it. Second, a file produced using this feature can be imported into another application, like Photoshop or Illustrator. And finally, you can use Save Page as EPS to create a resizable page-within-a-page.

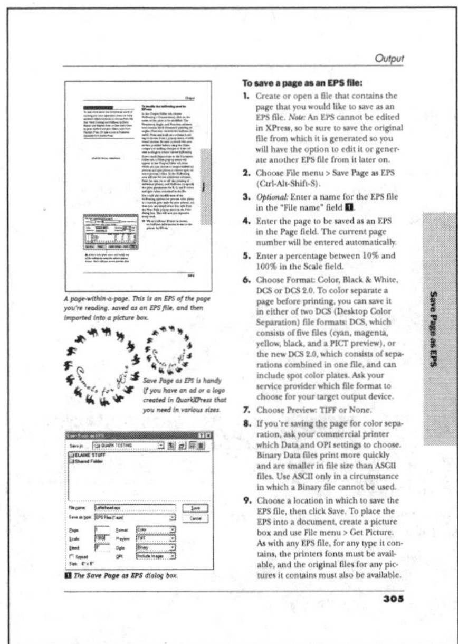

A page-within-a-page. This is an EPS of the page you're reading, saved as an EPS file, and then imported into a picture box.

Save Page as EPS is handy if you have an ad or a logo that was created in QuarkXPress that you need in various sizes.

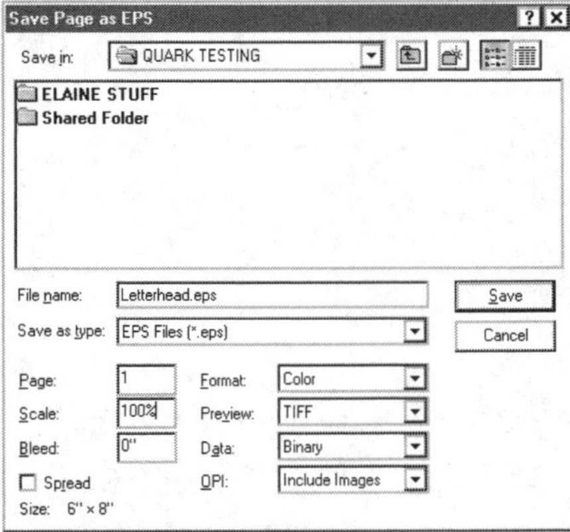

1 *The **Save Page as EPS** dialog box.*

To save a page as an EPS file:

1. Create or open a file that contains the page that you would like to save as an EPS file. *Note:* An EPS cannot be edited in XPress, so be sure to save the original file from which it is generated so you will have the option to edit it or generate another EPS file from it later on.
2. Choose File menu > Save Page as EPS (Ctrl-Alt-Shift-S).
3. Enter a name for the EPS file in the "File name" field **1**.
4. Enter the page to be saved as an EPS in the Page field. The current page number will be entered automatically.
5. Enter a percentage between 10% and 100% in the Scale field.
6. Choose Format: Color, Black & White, DCS or DCS 2.0. To color separate a page before printing, you can save it in either of two DCS (Desktop Color Separation) file formats: DCS, which consists of five files (cyan, magenta, yellow, black, and a PICT preview), or DCS 2.0, which consists of separations combined in one file, and can include spot color plates. Ask your service provider which file format to choose for your target output device.
7. Choose Preview: TIFF or None.
8. If you're saving the page for color separation, ask your commercial printer which Data and OPI settings to choose. Binary Data files print more quickly and are smaller in file size than ASCII files. Use ASCII only in a circumstance in which a Binary file cannot be used.
9. Choose a location in which to save the EPS file, then click Save. To place the EPS into a document, create a picture box and use File menu > Get Picture. As with any EPS file, for any type it contains, the printers fonts must be available, and the original files for any pictures it contains must also be available.

If you send a document to a service provider, you must send along with it the original picture files used in the document. You also need to include written information about the document, such the file name, date, dimensions, and fonts used. The Collect for Output command gathers copies of all the required elements together for you automatically and also produces a text report that contains information about the file, such as the names of the fonts and colors it contains.

To collect for output:

1. Save the document, then choose File menu > Collect for Output.

   If any pictures cannot be located or were modified after they were imported into the QuarkXPress file, the Missing/Modified Pictures dialog box will open. Click List Pictures, update the pictures, then click Collect (see page 152).
2. Choose a location for the folder.
3. Click the New Folder icon **1**.
4. *Optional:* Change the folder name.
5. Double-click on the folder icon to open it.
6. *Optional:* Change the Report Name.
7. Click Collect or press Enter. A folder containing the current document, associated picture files, and a detailed report file will appear in the location you chose.

   Note: To have the Collect function produce a report only, and not gather any files, check the **Report Only** box before you click Collect. Choosing File menu > Collect for Output with Alt held down does the same thing.

1 *New Folder icon*

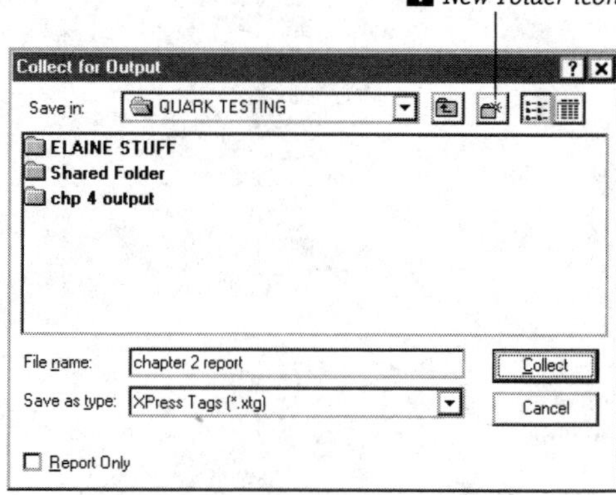

*The **Collect for Output** dialog box.*

1 *Fill out this form.*

ELECTRONIC OUTPUT REQUEST

CLIENT INFORMATION
Contact Person: ______
Company: ______
Address: ______
City, ST, Zip: ______
Office Phone: ______
Home Phone: ______

DELIVERY INFORMATION
__ Deliver __ Hold For Pickup __ Call When Complete
Delivery Address: ______
City, ST, Zip: ______

TURNAROUND INFORMATION
__ Normal __ Rush __ Emergency

FONT INFORMATION
__ Adobe/Linotype __ Font Company __ Agfa Compugraphic
__ Bitstream __ Monotype __ ______

COPYRIGHT INFORMATION
All that appears on the enclosed medium (including, but not limited to, floppy disk, modem transmission, removable media) is unencumbered by copyrights. We, the customer, have full rights to reproduce the supplied content.
Signature: ______
Date: ______

OUTPUT MEDIA (CHECK ALL THAT APPLY)
__ Film __ RC Paper __ Color Proof
__ Laser Print __ Color Slides __ ______
__ Negative -or- __ Positive
__ Emulsion Down -or- __ Emulsion Up

OUTPUT SPECIFICATION
__ Output All Pages
__ Output The Following Specified Pages…
From: ______ To: ______

CROP MARKS
__ Yes __ No

RESOLUTION/DPI
__ 1200/1270 __ 2400/2540 __ 3000+

SCREEN RULING/LPI
__ 65 __ 85 __ 120
__ 133 __ 150 __ ______

COLOR SEPARATION PLATES
__ Cyan __ Magenta __ Yellow __ Black
__ ______ __ ______ __ ______ __ ______

COLOR PROOF SPECIFICATION
__ Proof All Pages
__ Proof The Following Specified Pages…
From: ______ To: ______

LASER PROOF PROVIDED WITH JOB?
__ Yes __ No

OTHER INFORMATION
Type information about the job here.

QUARK REPORT
@doc info: Source Pathname: ANITA: QUARK 3.2 UPGRADE:GAMMA 3.2 DOCUMENTS:Quark 3.2
Destination Pathname: ANITA:Desktop Folder:Report folder:
Last modified: 12:23 PM; 7/7/93
Document Size: 116K
Most recently saved version: 3.20G2
Document has been saved by the following versions of QuarkXPress:
3.20G1
3.20G2
Total Pages: 2
Page Width: 51p
Page Height: 66p

REQUIRED XTENSIONS:
Cool Blends

2 *And import the **report file** into the bottom box.*

*Any fonts used in EPS graphics will be listed in the **Picture Fonts** category.*

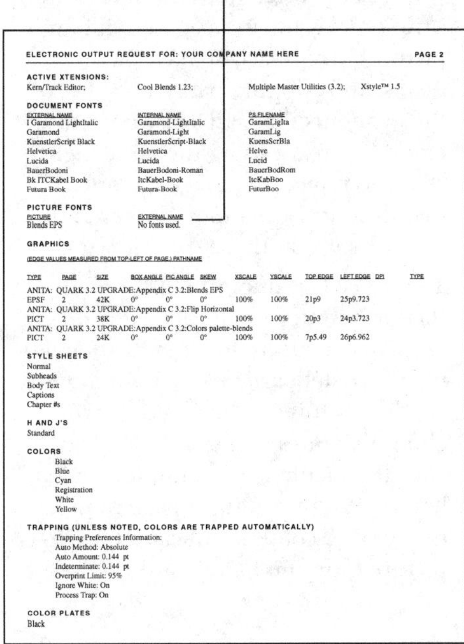

ELECTRONIC OUTPUT REQUEST FOR: YOUR COMPANY NAME HERE PAGE 2

ACTIVE XTENSIONS:
Kern/Track Editor; Cool Blends 1.23; Multiple Master Utilities (3.2); Xstyle™ 1.5

DOCUMENT FONTS

EXTERNAL NAME	INTERNAL NAME	PS FILENAME
I Garamond LightItalic	Garamond-LightItalic	GaramLigIta
Garamond	Garamond-Light	GaramLig
KuenstlerScript Black	KuenstlerScript-Black	KuensScrBla
Helvetica	Helvetica	Helve
Lucida	Lucida	Lucid
BauerBodoni	BauerBodoni-Roman	BauerBodRom
Bk ITCKabel Book	ItcKabel-Book	ItcKabBoo
Futura Book	Futura-Book	FuturBoo

PICTURE FONTS

PICTURE	EXTERNAL NAME
Blends EPS	No fonts used.

GRAPHICS
(EDGE VALUES MEASURED FROM TOP-LEFT OF PAGE.) PATHNAME

TYPE	PAGE	SIZE	BOX ANGLE	PIC ANGLE	SKEW	XSCALE	YSCALE	TOP EDGE	LEFT EDGE	DPI	TYPE
ANITA: QUARK 3.2 UPGRADE:Appendix C 3.2:Blends EPS											
EPSF	2	42K	0°	0°	0°	100%	100%	21p9	25p9.723		
ANITA: QUARK 3.2 UPGRADE:Appendix C 3.2:Flip Horizontal											
PICT	2	38K	0°	0°	0°	100%	100%	20p3	24p3.723		
ANITA: QUARK 3.2 UPGRADE:Appendix C 3.2:Colors palette-blends											
PICT	2	24K	0°	0°	0°	100%	100%	7p5.49	26p6.962		

STYLE SHEETS
Normal
Subheads
Body Text
Captions
Chapter #s

H AND J'S
Standard

COLORS
Black
Blue
Cyan
Registration
White
Yellow

TRAPPING (UNLESS NOTED, COLORS ARE TRAPPED AUTOMATICALLY)
Trapping Preferences Information:
Auto Method: Absolute
Auto Amount: 0.144 pt
Indeterminate: 0.144 pt
Overprint Limit: 95%
Ignore White: On
Process Trap: On

COLOR PLATES
Black

After using the Collect for Output command, you can flow the report file into the Output Request template, print that report, and then give the printout to your service provider along with your computer file.

Note: In order to import the report file, the XPress Tags filter must be enabled. Use the XTensions Manager to do this, and then re-launch QuarkXPress.

To create an output request form:

1. Choose File menu > Open (Ctrl-O), and locate and open the Output Request template. Unless it was moved, you'll find it in the Documents folder in the QuarkXPress folder.
2. Choose File menu > Save As (Ctrl-Alt-S), type a name for the report, then click Save. For simplicity's sake, save the request form to your new Collect for Output folder.
3. Fill out the top portion of the Electronic Output Request **1**.
4. Choose the Content tool.
5. Click in the text box at the bottom of page 1 **2**.
6. Choose File menu > Get Text (Ctrl-E).
7. Locate and highlight the report file, and check the Include Style Sheets box.
8. Click Open or press Enter. New pages will be added automatically to accommodate all the text.

Imagesetting tips

An imagesetter is a device that produces high resolution (1,250–3,540 dpi) paper or film output from electronic files. A commercial printer uses paper or film output to produce plates. Nowadays, some printers output directly to plate, skipping the intermediary film output step. The following is a checklist of things to do to help your imagesetting run successfully:

- Find out if your commercial printer can output your electronic files. Since they're intimately familiar with the printing press—its quirks and its requirements—they're often the best imagesetting choice.
- If you're outputting the file at an output service, ask your commercial printer for specific advice regarding the following settings: Lpi (lines per inch), emulsion up or down, and negative or positive. Also ask whether you should set trapping values yourself or the output service should do the trapping on their high-end system. Tell your output service what setting your commercial printer specified, and they will enter the correct values in the Print dialog box > Output folder tab when they output your file. Don't guess on this one. And don't hestiate to ask your commercial printer to talk directly with your service provider.
- Make sure any pictures in the document were saved at final printout size and at the appropriate resolution for the final output device, which means approximately 1½ times the final lpi for a black-and-white or grayscale picture and 2 times the final lpi for a color picture. If a picture requres cropping, rotating, or scaling down, do so in the picture's original application, if possible—it will output more quickly.
- Use the File menu > Collect for Output command to collect your document and associated images and to produce a report file. If you don't supply your service bureau with the original picture files, the low resolution versions will be used for printing. The report file lists important specifications that they need in order to output your file properly, such as the fonts used in the document.
- If your output service needs a PostScript file of your document, ask them for specific instructions.
- Some service bureaus will supply the fonts—at least the Adobe fonts—but some printers prefer that you supply them all. Include both the screen and the printer fonts, and don't forget to include fonts used in any imported EPS pictures.
- Include laser printouts of your file (unless you're modem-ing the file), with Registration marks turned on.
- If your document doesn't print or takes an inordinately long time to print on your laser printer, don't assume it will print quickly on an imagesetter. Large pictures, irregularly-shaped picture boxes, and clipping paths are some of the elements that can cause a printing error. If you are using the same high resolution picture more than once but in different sizes, import copies of the picture saved at those specific sizes.

To reduce the amount of information the imagesetter has to calculate, delete any extraneous items from the document's pasteboard. To find out if there are any pictures on the pasteboard, choose Utilities menu > Usage, and click the Pictures tab (Shift-F2). The letters "PB" preceding a page number in the page column indicates that that picture is on the Pasteboard.

WHAT'S ON YOUR PLATE?

In standard four-color process printing, a document is color separated onto four plates, one each for Cyan, Yellow, Magenta, and Black. The many other potential combinations include printing a spot color and black on two separate plates or printing a spot color and the four process colors, bringing the total to five plates.

Hexachrome (high fidelity) colors color separate onto six process color plates, with the result being greater color fidelity due to the wider range of printable colors. An RGB picture can also be color separated using this method.

PRINTING A SPOT

Make sure the Spot Color box in the Edit Color dialog box is checked for any spot color that you want to color separate onto a separate plate. To output a particular color, choose File menu > Print, check the Separations box, then, in the Output folder tab, choose Process & Spot from the Plates drop-down menu and Conventional from the Halftoning drop-down menu.

Spot colors, if they are saved in an Illustrator or FreeHand file in the EPS format, will append to the Colors dialog box in the QuarkXPress document and will also display in the plate scroll window in the File menu > Print > Output folder tab. Make sure the name that is assigned to any spot color that is used both in QuarkXPress and Illustrator is exactly the same in each program, otherwise two plates will print instead of the desired single plate.

Color separation tips

- *Don't* choose colors based on how they appear on screen, because a computer screen can only simulate printed colors. Always use a matching system booklet to choose colors.
- To apply a spot color tint—whether as a background color in an item or as type color—choose a shade percentage from the Colors palette or choose a Trumatch or Focoltone color that has the desired value in Edit menu > Colors (Shift-F12).
- If your document contains bitmapped pictures, ask your service bureau or commercial printer in which file format (TIFF, EPS, etc.) and image mode (CMYK, RGB, etc.) those pictures should be saved. You can use Photoshop to easily change a picture's file format, resolution, or image mode.
- Ask your output service whether to use Photoshop or QuarkXPress to convert any color pictures from RGB to CMYK for separations. A picture scanned into CMYK color mode doesn't need to be converted.
- QuarkXPress will convert any RGB spot color from an imported Illustrator EPS file into a CMYK process color. To output an Illustrator RGB spot color on a separate plate, first convert it into a CMYK spot color in Illustrator.
- If your document contains hand-drawn registration or crop marks, apply the Registration color to them to ensure that they appear on all the separation plates.
- For color work, order a color proof—an IRIS or a 3M Rainbow—of the document so you can inspect it for color accuracy.

What is trapping?

Trapping is the ever-so-slight overlapping of colors to prevent gaps from occurring during printing as a result of paper shift, paper stretch, or plate misalignment on press. In QuarkXPress, trapping is applied according to the way an object color—an item or text—interacts with the color in an item in the background. Use the mini-glossary at right to familiarize yourself with trapping terminology.

Before exploring the circumstances in which trapping is necessary, I'll discuss a couple of circumstances in which trapping is unnecessary.

When not to apply trapping

Trapping is unnecessary when black type or a black item or frame is on top of a light background color. In this circumstance, the black type will overprint (print on top of) the background color. You can specify a minimum percentage of black to control when and if overprinting will occur (see page 313).

Trapping is also unnecessary if process colors and adjacent or overlapping colors contain a common color component (C, M, Y, or K). Let's say you have a red containing a percentage of magenta that touches a blue area that also contains a small percentage of magenta. The two colors both contain magenta, so trapping is unnecessary.

When to apply trapping

Trapping is necessary when you print spot colors, print process colors that don't have a common color component, or print a light color on a dark background.

In QuarkXPress, trapping values are assigned to the foreground color. A light foreground color spreads into the background color by a specified amount, and a light background color chokes the foreground color. To produce a choke trap in QuarkXPress, the foreground color is assigned a negative trapping value.

TRAPPING MINI-GLOSSARY

Overprint
The foreground object color prints on top of the background color, so inks actually mix together. Overprint is used if black is the foreground object color or if ink mixing is used intentionally to produce a third (overlap) color.

Knockout
To prevent inks from overprinting, the foreground object color shape is cut out (knocked out) of the underlying background color area on the background color plate. While this eliminates the problem of ink mixing, it creates a potential problem of a gap between the edges of the foreground and background colors. Trapping closes this gap.

Spread
The spread method of trapping is used when colors knock out and the foreground color is lighter than the background color. The edge of the foreground color object is enlarged slightly to make the foreground color spread into the background color on press **1**.

Choke
The choke method of trapping is employed when the foreground color is darker than the background color. The edge of the background color object (the cutout shape that matches up with the foreground color area) is slightly reduced, which causes the background color to spread into (choke) the foreground color on press.

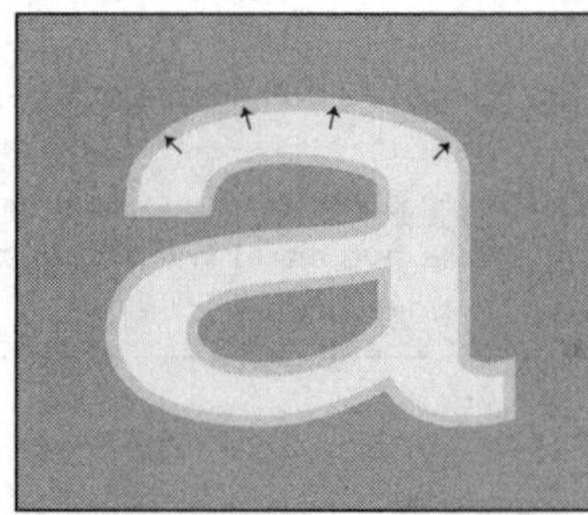

1 *In a spread trap, the foreground object color spreads into the background object color.*

What is Trapping

SHUT YOUR TRAP!

If you are unsure about setting traps in XPress, let your service provider do the trapping.

To turn off trapping, choose Trapping Method: Knockout All in the Edit menu > Preferences > Document > Trapping folder tab. Choose this option if you're producing a PostScript file for a high-end separation system or for some color composite printers.

*Two process color objects. Both the letters and the art work contain magenta. Because they have a **color in common**, trapping is unnecessary.*

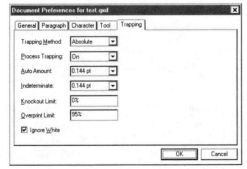

Document Preferences for test.qxd

General | Paragraph | Character | Tool | Trapping

Trapping Method: Absolute

Process Trapping: On

Auto Amount: 0.144 pt

Indeterminate: 0.144 pt

Knockout Limit: 0%

Overprint Limit: 95%

☑ Ignore White

OK | Cancel

1 *The Edit menu > Preferences > Document >* ***Trapping*** *folder tab.*

In XPress, trapping can be controlled on a default document-wide basis (Document Preferences > Trapping folder tab), on an individual color basis (Edit menu > Colors > Edit Trap > Trap Specifications dialog box), or on an individual item basis (Trap Information palette). Colors > Edit Trap trap settings override settings in Document preferences. Trap Information palette settings override the Colors > Edit Trap and Document Preferences settings.

To define automatic trap values and specify the defaults used by QuarkXPress for trapping object colors, choose the settings in the Trapping folder tab in the Document Preferences dialog box.

To choose trapping preferences for a whole document:

1. Choose Edit menu > Preferences > Document > Trapping folder tab (Ctrl-Shift-F12) **1**.
2. From the Trapping Method drop-down menu, choose **Absolute** to use the trapping value entered in the Auto Amount or Indeterminate field. The Auto Amount value is used if the foreground color is on top of a flat color. The Indeterminate value is used if the foreground color is on top of multiple shades or colors or over an imported picture. When the object color is darker, the background color chokes into the object color by the Auto Amount. When the foreground object color is lighter, the object color spreads into the background color by the Auto Amount.
   or
   Choose **Proportional** to use the trapping value entered in the Auto Amount field, multiplied by the difference in luminosity (lights and darks) between the foreground object color and the background color. The width of the trap will vary and be determined by multiplying the Auto Amount value by

(Continued on the following page)

the difference in luminosity between the object and background colors.

or

Choose **Knockout All** to turn trapping off for all objects. Objects will print with 0 trapping **2**.

3. Choose On or Off from the Process Trapping drop-down menu. With Process Trapping on, each process component (cyan, magenta, yellow, and black) is spread or choked depending which is darker—the foreground object or the background color. For example, if the cyan in the foreground object color is lighter than the cyan in the background color, the foreground object cyan is spread into the background cyan—but only on the cyan plate.

   The trap width is equal to half the Auto Amount value when Absolute trapping is specified. When Proportional trapping is specified, the amount of trap is the Auto Amount value multiplied by the difference in luminosity values between the foreground object and background colors.

   When Process Trapping is off, all process components trap by the same amount and use the trapping settings for those colors, as determined in the Colors > Edit Trap area.

4. Enter a trapping value in the Auto Amount field **3** or choose Overprint from the drop-down menu. Either the value entered or the Overprint setting will be used in the Trap Specifications dialog box (Edit menu > Colors > Edit Trap) and on the Trap Information palette whenever a field in either of these two locations is set to Auto Amount (+/-).

5. Enter a trapping value in the Indeterminate field or choose Overprint from the drop-down menu. If a foreground object is over a background

2 *Choose a trapping method from the* ***Trapping Method*** *drop-down menu.*

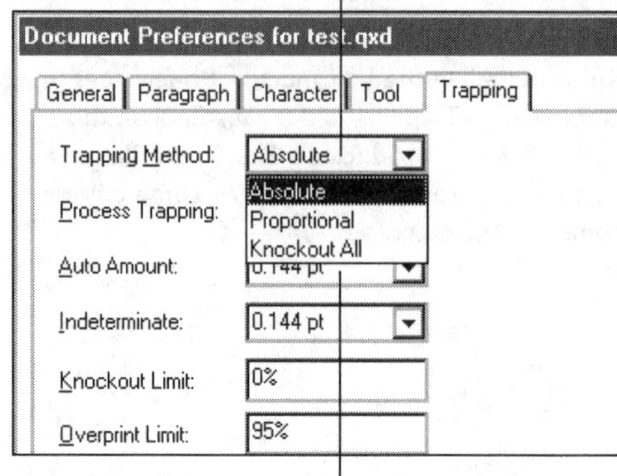

3 *Enter a trapping value in the* ***Auto Amount*** *field.*

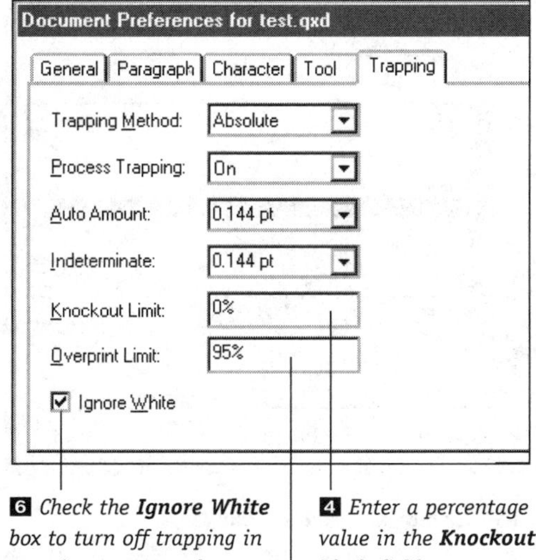

6 *Check the **Ignore White** box to turn off trapping in any circumstance where the foreground object is on top of a white background.*

4 *Enter a percentage value in the **Knockout Limit** field.*

5 *Enter a percentage value in the **Overprint Limit** field.*

that consists of multiple shades or colors or is over an imported picture, either the value you entered or the Overprint setting will be used.

6. Enter a percentage value in the Knockout Limit field 4 to set the luminosity (light and dark) value limit at which a foreground object color knocks out the background color. The luminosity value is the percentage difference in luminosity between the foreground object color and the background color.

7. Enter a value in the Overprint Limit field 5. This value sets the shade percentage limit below which the foreground object color will not overprint the background color. For example, if the Overprint Limit is set to 92%, a foreground object colored with a black value of 85% will not overprint, even if that color or object is set to overprint (via the Edit Trap > Trap Specifications dialog box). The object will trap using the value in the Auto Amount field.

   An Overprint setting chosen on the Trap Information palette will cause the selected object to overprint, regardless of the current trap settings or any Overprint Limit value entered in any other dialog box.

8. Leave the Ignore White box checked 6 to turn off trapping for any instance in which the foreground object color is on top of white and other color areas in the background. This is the preferred situation, since the white area won't be considered when the trap is calculated for the other colors.

   When this box is unchecked, all objects on a white background will overprint. If an object is set to spread over a background color, then the Indeterminate value will be used for the spread.

9. Click OK to close the Document Preferences dialog box.

The Trap Specifications dialog box controls trapping on a color-by-color basis. The default settings for each color display and can be modified using this dialog box.

To choose trapping values for a color (Trap Specifications):

1. Choose Edit menu > Colors (Shift-F12).
2. Click a color, then click Edit Trap **1**.
3. The name of the foreground color you chose will appear in the title bar of the Trap Specifications dialog box. Click one of the remaining colors, any of which can be a potential background color **2**.
4. Choose a setting from the Trap drop-down menu **3**:

   Default to have QuarkXPress determine how colors trap. With Default, black always overprints.

   Overprint to have the foreground color overprint the selected background color when the foreground color is equal to or greater than the Overprint Limit value in the Trapping tab dialog box.

   Knockout to have the foreground color knock out the selected background color.

   Auto Amount (+/-) to use the auto spread/auto choke value for the foreground color.

   Custom to enter a custom spread or choke (negative) value for the foreground color.

   The Auto Amount and Overprint Limit settings were established in Edit menu > Preferences > Document > Trapping folder tab.
5. Choose Dependent traps (the default) from the drop-down menu in the middle column to create the reverse trap situation for the colors you chose in steps 2 and 3 based on the current Trap column setting. Or choose Independent traps to create a unique

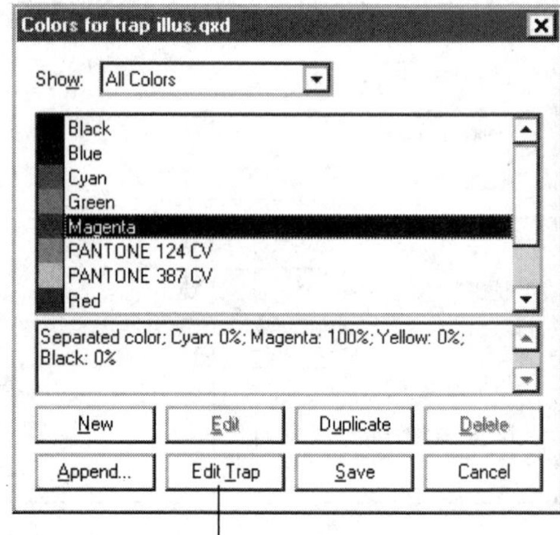

1 *Click a color, then click **Edit Trap**.*

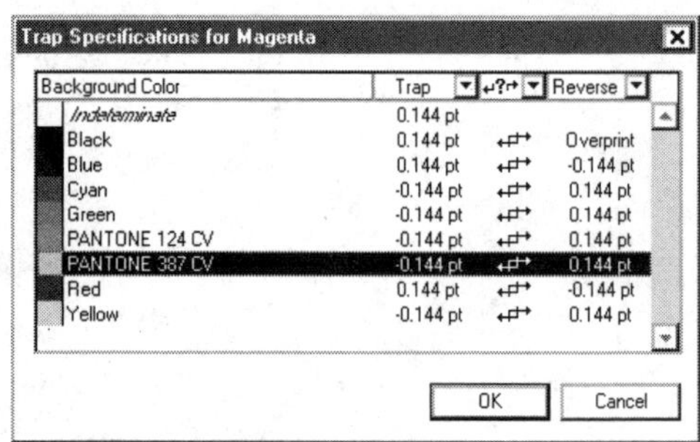

2 *The **Trap specifications** dialog box for the color selected when Edit Trap was clicked.*

3 *Choose an option from the **Trap** drop-down menu.*

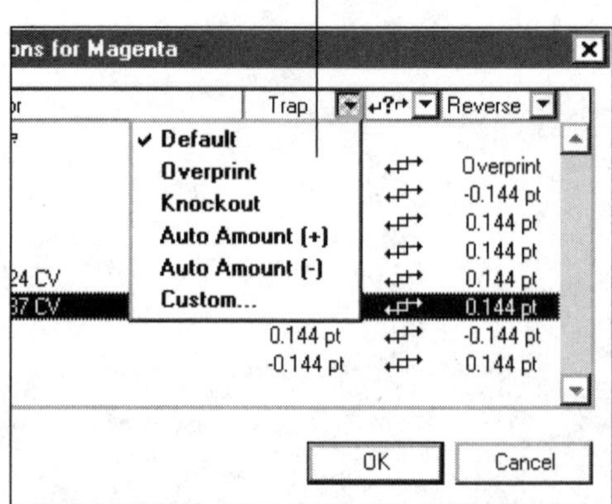

4 *Choose* ***Dependent Traps*** *or* ***Independent Traps*** *from this drop-down menu.*

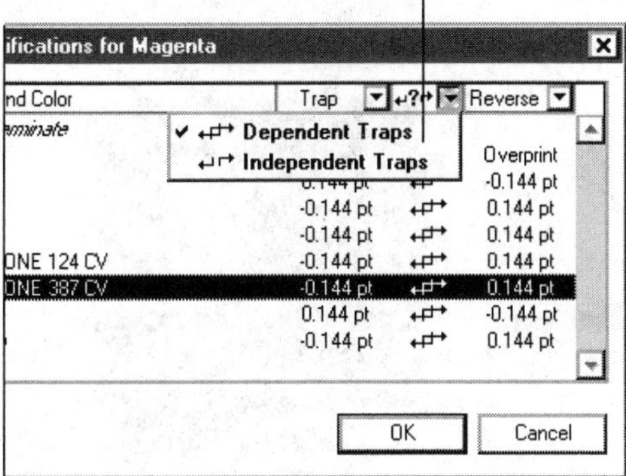

5 *Choose an option from the* ***Reverse*** *drop-down menu.*

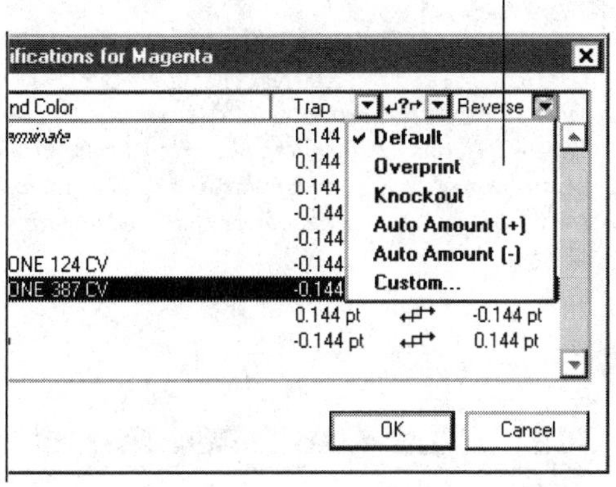

trap setting in the Reverse column for these two colors **4**.

6. To set the trap situation for a circumstance in which the current background color (from step 3) becomes the foreground color over the color (from step 2) listed in the title bar of the dialog box, choose a different setting from the Reverse drop-down menu **5**. The options are the same as in step 4, above. Remember that when traps have a Dependent relationship, the Reverse column setting automatically derives from the current Trap column setting, and vice versa. Change either of these columns, and the other will change automatically. When traps have an independent relationship, then unique settings can be set in these two columns.
7. Click OK, then click Save, to close the Default Colors dialog box.

TIP Settings in the Trap Specifications dialog box override the settings in the Edit menu > Document > Preferences > Trapping folder tab.

TIP If a document is open when Edit menu > Colors is chosen, Edit Trap changes will apply only to the current document. If no document is open, changes will apply to any newly created documents.

Note: The Trap Information palette overrides settings chosen in the Trap Preferences and Trap Specifications dialog boxes.

To choose trapping values for an object (Trap Information palette):

1. Choose View menu > Show Trap Information to open the palette (Ctrl-F12) **1**.
2. Select the item to which you want to apply trapping.
3. Choose a new trap setting from the drop-down menu on the left side of the palette (the options will vary depending on the type of item chosen) **2**:

   Default to have the settings in Trapping tab preferences or Edit Trap Specifications be used to determine how colors will trap.

   Overprint to have the foreground item color overprint any background color.

   Knockout to have the foreground item color knock out any background color.

   Auto Amount (+/-) to use the auto spread/auto choke value for the foreground color. Auto Amount settings are established in the Edit menu > Preferences > Document > Trapping folder tab.

   Custom to enter a custom spread or choke (negative) value for the foreground color.

TIP Choosing Overprint from the palette will cause that item to overprint, regardless of the foreground or background color shade or the Overprint Limit value.

TIP To set trapping for text, highlight the text—the Text option on the palette will become available.

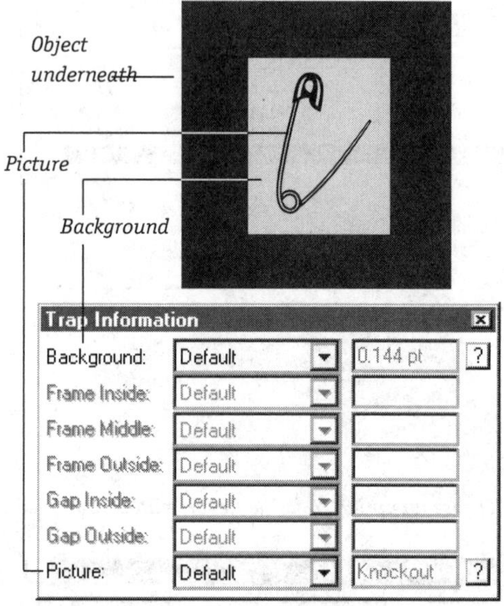

1 *The **Trap Information** palette with a picture box selected. In this example, the Background color of the picture box (20% Black) defaults to a spread trap of the Auto Amount over the darker color underneath.*

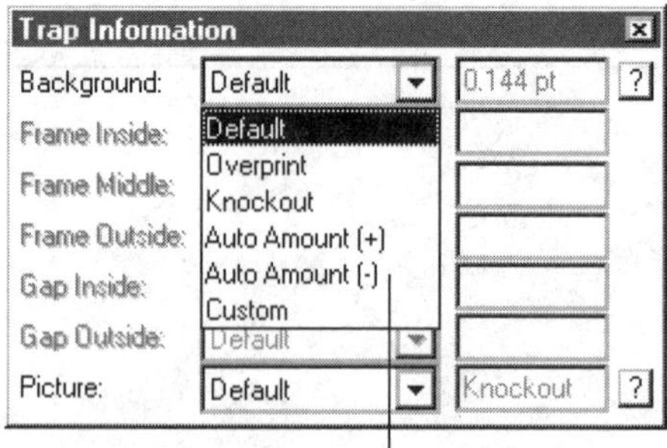

2 *The drop-down menu for trapping the **Background** color of a picture box.*

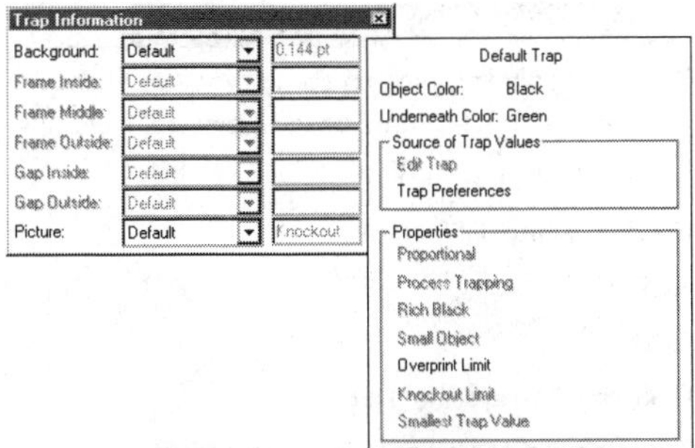

Pressing on the ? icon on the Trap Information palette displays an explanation of the Default Trap setting. The two object colors are named, the Edit Trap or Preferences dialog box shows as the source of the trap decision, and the significant trap option (Property) is singled out.

1 *In this example, the text only partially overlaps a background color.*

What follows are guidelines for common trapping situations that may occur.

Trapping type

When it comes to trapping, a text box is treated like a single foreground object. The text box color will trap to background color based on the current trap settings. When a text box with a background of None is on top of a background color, QuarkXPress will trap the type even if the type itself is not overlapping the background color **1**. This can occur with type that appears inside a large text box.

To control how text traps, select the text and set it to Overprint or Knockout via the Trap Information palette. You can also highlight individual characters or words and apply a unique trap setting to them that's different from the remaining characters in the box. Any box that's layered on top of a text box will trap to the background color of the text box—not the type itself.

QuarkXPress regards type that is partially on top of a paragraph rule as trapping to an indeterminate background color. If the type is completely within the paragraph rule, then the type traps based on the type color-to-rule color relationship from the Edit menu > Colors trap settings. This relationship can only be changed using Edit menu > Colors > Edit trap.

Trapping a frame

A frame is layered on top of the contents of the box the frame is attached to. Using the Trap Information palette, different trapping settings can be applied to the inside, middle, and outside parts of a single line or multi-line frame, and to the gaps in a dashed frame.

Trapping imported pictures

In QuarkXPress, a picture cannot be spread or choked to a background color.

Trapping adjustments that are made to a vector (object-oriented) picture in a drawing program, like Adobe Illustrator, will successfully output from QuarkXPress. The Trap Information palette provides no trapping controls for the picture itself. But don't scale an imported vector picture that was created with built-in trapping, because such scaling will also resize the trapping areas in the picture.

You can specify that a raster (bitmap) picture knock out or overprint a background color using the Trap Information palette. Using the Trap Information palette, you can set the image of a picture to overprint or knock out a background. This is helpful if you're colorizing a Grayscale TIFF picture in QuarkXPress. Click on a picture, then choose Overprint or Knockout from the Picture drop-down menu on the Trap Information palette—whichever your commercial printer tells you to choose.

A line art (black and white) picture that has been colored black in QuarkXPress with a shade of black equal or greater than the overprint limit will overprint any background color(s) it is positioned on top of. Use the Trap Information palette to set the picture to knock out, if desired.

Lines and boxes in QuarkXPress can knock out, overprint, or trap to pictures that are underneath them. Use the Trap Information palette to set the type of trap. Type can knock out, overprint, or spread to a picture underneath it.

TRAPPING A BITMAP PICTURE

You can apply trapping to some types of bitmap pictures via the Trap Information palette, including:

Grayscale TIFF (8-bit)

Black & white TIFF (1-bit)

RGB TIFF

CMYK TIFF

Colorized Grayscale TIFF

Trapping cannot be applied to an EPS in QuarkXPress.

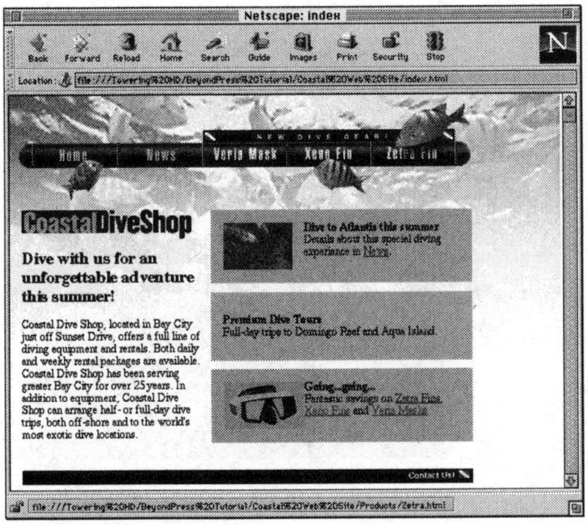

QuarkXPress to the World Wide Web

In this section, I briefly discuss methods for outputting a QuarkXPress document to the World Wide Web for on-line viewing. For more specific instructions, please consult the XTension documentation. The Web page you create can consist of words and pictures only or it can contain animation, QuickTime movies, and/or Java applets. You can also create links in the form of text or image icons for a viewer to click on to get to another Web page.

When you're designing a Web page, keep in mind that what looks good on print output may not be suitable for on-line viewing. To build a successful Web page, you may have to adjust such elements as your color choices, the volume of text and its point size, the size and number of images, and the size of the page layout on screen. Your aim should be to design a Web page that communicates clearly, doesn't display any unexpected color changes, and downloads quickly. A page that meets those requirements is outputing well.

A common typeface will be readable by a browser and display reliably on-line. If you want to display an unusual typeface, you may need to convert it into an image. Choose RGB colors for your text and backgrounds. Choose a resolution of 72 ppi for your imported images, and save them at the proper size in RGB color mode in the GIF or JPEG file format.

To convert QuarkXPress document text and imported pictures to an HTML file, you must use an XTension, such as Extensis' BeyondPress or Quark's Immedia, both of which are discussed briefly on the following pages.

Note: As of this writing, BeyondPress is not yet available for Windows. It should be available sometime in 1998. The illustrations on these pages are from the Macintosh version.

This is a Web page that was created in QuarkXPress using the tutorial in Extensis' ***BeyondPress*** *XTension.*

BeyondPress

Using Extensis' BeyondPress XTension, you can create and export a QuarkXPress page as an HTML file. BeyondPress offers many features for controlling the creation of the HTML file.

In Document Conversion Mode, once page items are added to the Document Content palette, you can then use this palette to rearrange the placement of various elements for the Web page, apply HTML style tags, and create links to other URLs. The palette elements are then exported by BeyondPress to create the HTML file. This mode works well when you want to convert an existing QuarkXPress document into Web pages with minimal reworking.

You can also create a multi-page Web site by first creating items on a QuarkXPress document page and then adding items to the Document Conent palette one by one in BeyondPress' Authoring Mode. You can even add live media elements (i.e. QuickTime movies or Shockwave animations) or Java applets simply by dragging those elements onto a QuarkXPress page. Media elements are conveniently opened and stored on the Elements palette (along with images and reusable HTML elements), from which they are available to all QuarkXPress pages.

Using BeyondPress' Document Content palette, you can toggle between Authoring and Conversion mode to switch between various Web site pages and modify Web page elements. Each page in a QuarkXPress document will become a separate Web page. You can easily link between pages or to other sites using the Link Destination palette. BeyondPress will export the QuarkXPress page(s) to create an HTML file and HTML tables will be used to recreate the QuarkXPress layout.

Using BeyondPress' image control options, you can convert groups of images all at once or choose settings for each image

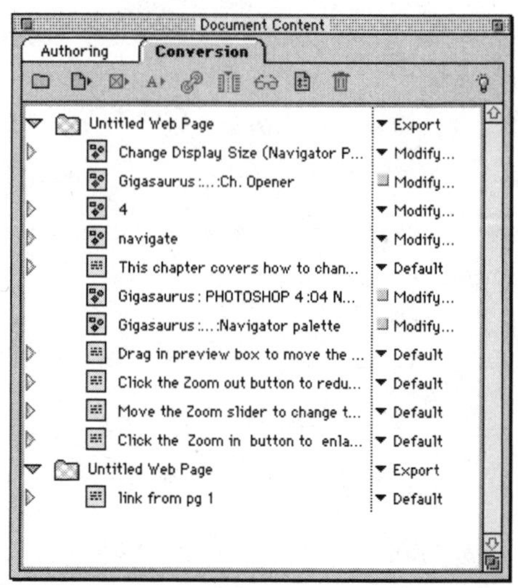

*The **Document Content** palette in **Conversion** mode. QuarkXPress items are individual, editable elements.*

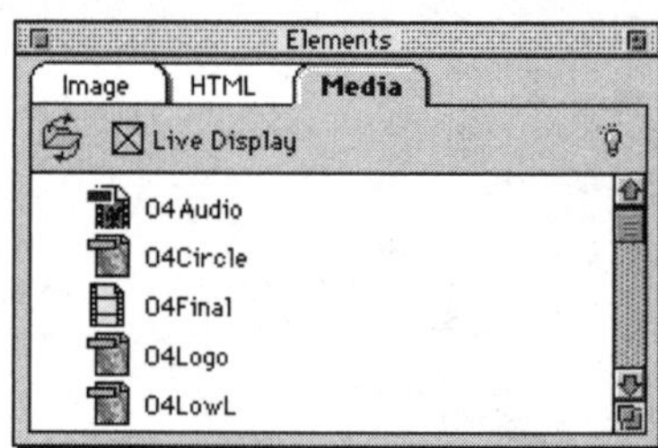

*The **Elements** palette. Various media files are displayed and available for dragging onto the QuarkXPress page.*

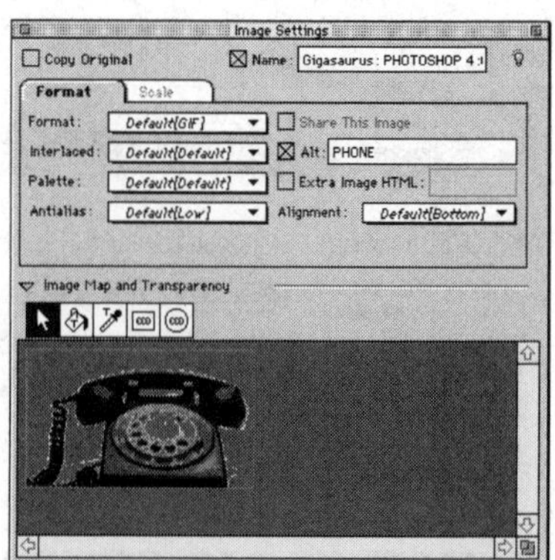

*Using the **Image Settings** palette, a picture can be formatted using various menu options and its background can be rendered transparent.*

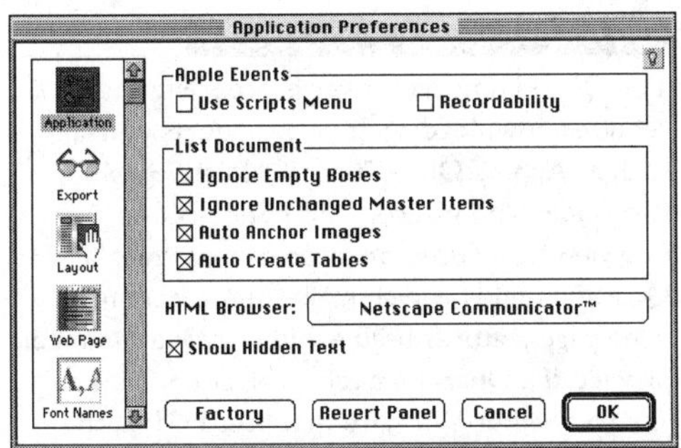

The BeyondPress' ***Application Preferences*** *dialog box.*

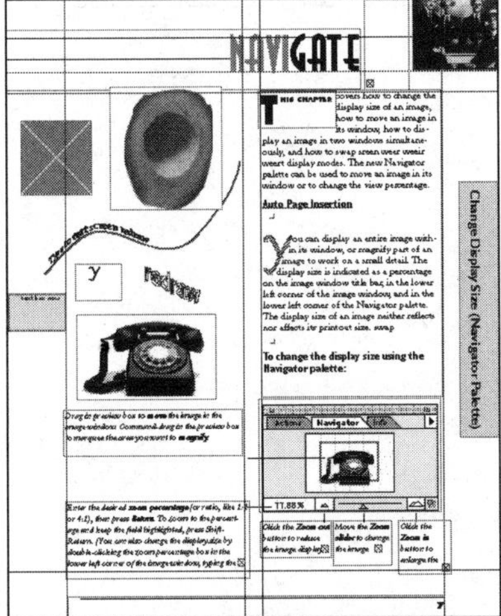

The original QuarkXPress page layout.

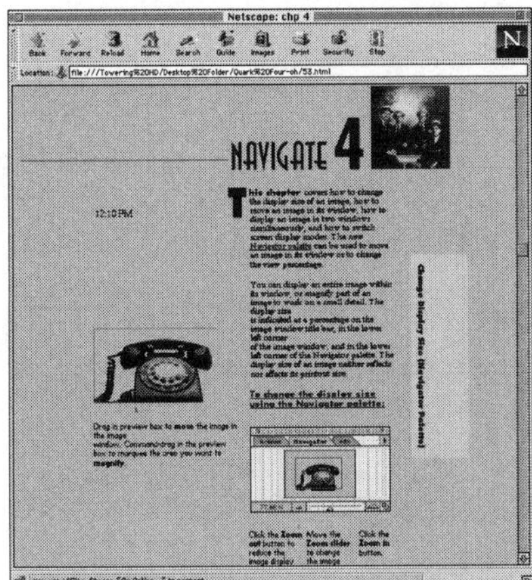

A QuarkXPress page (see the previous figure) exported as an HTML file and viewed in the ***Netscape Navigator*** *browser. (Not all the pictures were exported to the Web page.)*

individually. Color areas in an image can also be rendered transparent. A color palette can be created and optimized for each image, or one color palette can be created for all the imported images in a file. A browser searches for a color palette to help interpret image color. If no color palette is present, the browser will remap the image to the browser's color palette. This usually doesn't produce pleasing results.

BeyondPress can also be used to perform any of the following tasks:

- Export images in the JPEG format (including progressive JPEG, in which image detail builds up over several passes).
- Generate multiple articles from one QuarkXPress document with HTML authoring control.
- Create a tiled background for a Web page.
- Quickly preview and re-export Web pages.
- Format tables and lists on an individual basis.
- Easily create links to other pages on your site or other sites. Create client-side and server-side image maps by which a person viewing your page on the Web can click on a page element to jump to another Web page.
- Map style sheets to HTML styles using automation tools. HTML styles are also accessible from the Document Content palette.
- View an estimate of download times for various ISDN and T1 lines and modem speeds on the Export palette. This palette also lists problems encountered when converting type and layout to the HTML file. I discovered, using this palette, that rotated text, baseline-shifted text, and drop caps will not export successfully unless the text is first converted into an image in BeyondPress.

QuarkImmedia

The function of QuarkImmedia is to convert a QuarkXPress document into an interactive multimedia project. QuarkXPress typography and layout features are used to create an Immedia project. Immedia provides multiple output paths for a single project. You can export the same project to a CD-ROM, a hard drive, or the Web with minimal deviations from the original document, and the same QuarkImmedia project can be viewed on both the Mac and Windows operating systems.

In addition to text and graphics, you can also incorporate sound, video, and simple animation into a QuarkImmedia project. And you can create interactivity by creating objects such as windows, buttons, sound, or video elements that respond to an event (a mouse click) and assign an action to that event (the window opens, the button turns sound on or off or links to another page or another Web site, etc.). QuarkImmedia has a library of pre-made buttons for various actions that can be dragged right onto a QuarkXPress page.

Objects are created and positioned as items on specific pages in XPress, and any typography on the page is preserved. Using the Immedia dialog box and its various folder tabs and drop-down menus, you can name an object, assign an event to an object, assign an action to that event, assign timing, transitions, and sounds to occur when an object appears or disappears, and various other operations. More advanced scripts can also be produced using the menus (to create variables, use functions, test conditions, etc.).

The QuarkImmedia viewer is used to preview the project as you develop it. The final project is exported in the chosen delivery format. It can be viewed only through the QuarkImmedia viewer, which must be downloaded and installed in the system. This royalty-free viewer acts like a browser for viewing on the Web.

QUARKIMMEDIA'S VIEWER

The QuarkImmedia viewer is proprietary and requires downloading. It also supports plug-ins such as Apple's QuickTime, RealNetworks' RealAudio, and Macromedia's ShockWave (for viewing a Director piece from within QuarkImmedia), which makes these common Web page features usable within a QuarkImmedia project. If a QuarkImmedia project contains a link to another Web site that uses HTML, the QuarkImmedia viewer will launch the resident browser to view that link.

Keyboard shortcuts A

Show/hide palettes

Tools	F8
Measurements	F9
Document Layout	F4
Style Sheets	F11
Colors	F12
Find/Change	Ctrl F
Trap Information	Ctrl F12
Lists	Ctrl F11

Dialog boxes

OK (or heavy bordered button)	Enter
Display next tab	Ctrl Tab
Display previous tab	Ctrl Shift Tab
Cancel	Esc
Apply	Alt A
Continuous apply (not Space/Align)	Ctrl click Apply
Yes	Y
No	N
Highlight field	Double-click

Dialog boxes and palettes

Highlight next field	Tab
Highlight previous field	Shift Tab
Add	+
Subtract	-
Multiply	*
Divide	/
Revert to original values	Ctrl Z

Tools palette

Show Tools or select next tool	Ctrl Alt Tab
Show Tools or select previous tool	Ctrl Alt Shift Tab
Item tool/Content tool toggle	Shift F8
Keep a tool selected	Alt click tool

Open Tool folder tab of Document Preferences	Double-click Zoom tool or any creation tool

Measurements palette

Display Measurements palette and highlight first field	Ctrl Alt M
Highlight field	Double-click
Highlight next field	Tab
Highlight previous field	Shift Tab
Cancel/Exit	Esc
Apply/Exit	Enter
Highlight font field/display palette	Ctrl Alt Shift M
Highlight font field	Shift F9

Clipboard

Cut	Ctrl X
Copy	Ctrl C
Paste	Ctrl V

Whole document

New...	Ctrl N
New Library	Ctrl Alt N
Open...	Ctrl O
Save	Ctrl S
Save As...	Ctrl Alt S
Exit	Ctrl Q
Append...	Ctrl Alt A
Revert to last Auto Save	Alt Revert to Saved
Document Setup	Ctrl Alt Shift P
Close active document	Ctrl F4

Undo

Undo	Ctrl Z

Display

Fit in Window view	Ctrl 0 (zero)
Page/spread and pasteboard	Ctrl Alt 0 (zero)
Any view to 200%	Ctrl Alt click
200% to Actual size	Ctrl Alt click
Any view to Actual size	Ctrl 1
Enlarge view size	Ctrl Space bar click or drag
Reduce view size	Ctrl Alt Space bar click or drag
Highlight view percent field	Ctrl Alt V
Thumbnails	Shift F6 or enter "T" in view percent field

Halt redraw	Esc
Force redraw	Shift Esc

Rulers, guides, grid

Show/hide Guides	F7
Snap to Guides	Shift F7
Show/hide Rulers	Ctrl R
Delete all horizontal ruler guides	Alt click horizontal ruler
Delete all vertical ruler guides	Alt click vertical ruler
Show/hide Baseline Grid	Ctrl F7

Navigate through a document

Go To Page...	Ctrl J
Start of document	Ctrl Home
End of document	Ctrl End
Up one screen	Page Up
Down one screen	Page Down
To first page	Ctrl Page Up
To last page	Ctrl Page Down
To previous page	Shift Page Up
To next page	Shift Page Down
Page Grabber Hand	Alt drag
To previous spread	Alt Page Up
To next spread	Alt Page Down
Display master pages/document pages	Shift F4
Display next master page	Ctrl Shift F4
Display previous master page	Ctrl Shift F3
Enable Live Scroll (Interactive Preference off) or Disable Live Scroll (Interactive Preference on)	Alt drag scroll box

Items

Frame...	Ctrl B
Modify...	Ctrl M or double-click item with Item tool
Lock/Unlock	F6
Delete item	Ctrl K
Constrain rotation to 0°, 45°, 90°	Shift click with Rotation tool
Move item (Content tool)	Ctrl drag
Nudge item 1 point	Arrow keys
Nudge item 1/10 point	Alt arrow keys
Constrain movement to horizontal/vertical (Item tool)	Shift drag

Constrain movement to horizontal/ vertical (Content tool)	Ctrl Shift drag

Highlight text

Show/Hide Invisibles	Ctrl I
One word (no punctuation mark)	Double-click
One word (with punctuation mark)	Double-click between word and punctuation
One line	Triple-click
One paragraph	Click four times quickly
Entire story (Select All) Content tool	Click five times quickly or Ctrl A
Previous character	Shift left arrow
Next character	Shift right arrow
Previous line	Shift up arrow
Next line	Shift down arrow
Previous word	Ctrl Shift left arrow
Next word	Ctrl Shift right arrow
Previous paragraph	Ctrl Shift up arrow
Next paragraph	Ctrl Shift down arrow
Start of line	Ctrl Alt Shift left arrow or Shift Home
End of line	Ctrl Alt Shift right arrow or Shift End
Start of story	Ctrl Alt Shift up arrow or Ctrl Shift Home
End of story	Ctrl Alt Shift down arrow or Ctrl Shift End

Text insertion point

Character-by-character	Left and right arrows
Line-by-line	Up and down arrows
Word-by-word	Ctrl left and right arrows
Paragraph-by-paragraph	Ctrl up and down arrows
Start of line	Ctrl Alt left arrow or Home
End of line	Ctrl Alt right arrow or End
Start of story	Ctrl Alt up arrow or Ctrl Home
End of story	Ctrl Alt down arrow or Ctrl End

Drag and drop

Drag-copy text (Interactive Preference on)	Shift drag

Delete text

Previous character	Backspace
Next character	Delete
Previous word	Ctrl Backspace
Next word	Ctrl Delete
Highlighted characters	Delete or Space bar

Resize text interactively

Resize text and box	Ctrl drag handle
Resize text and box proportionally	Ctrl Alt Shift drag handle

Text flow

Get text...	Ctrl E
Current page number (use on master page or document page)	Ctrl 3
Previous text box page number	Ctrl 2
Next text box page number	Ctrl 4
Next column	Enter (Keypad)
Next box	Shift Enter (Keypad)
Reflow text in current version of QuarkXPress	Alt Open in Open dialog box
Save Text	Ctrl Alt E
Open Section dialog box for currently displayed page	Click page number in lower left corner of Document Layout palette
Open Insert Pages dialog box	Alt drag master page into document page area

Paragraph formats

Formats...	Ctrl Shift F
Leading...	Ctrl Shift E
Tabs...	Ctrl Shift T
Rules...	Ctrl Shift N
Increase leading 1 point	Ctrl Shift "
Decrease leading 1 point	Ctrl Shift :
Increase leading 1⁄10 point	Ctrl Alt Shift "
Decrease leading 1⁄10 point	Ctrl Alt Shift :
Delete all tab stops	Alt click on tabs ruler
Right-indent tab	Shift Tab
Suggested Hyphenation	Ctrl H
Set button in Tabs (in Paragraph Attributes)	Alt S
H&Js...	Ctrl Shift F11
Copy formats within the same text chain	Highlight paragraph to be formatted then Alt Shift click in paragraph that contains the desired formats

Fonts

Character...	Ctrl Shift D
Select next font	Highlight text, then Ctrl F9
Select previous font	Highlight text, then Ctrl Shift F9

Display Measurements palette/ highlight Font field	Ctrl Alt Shift M
Insert one Zapf Dingbats character	Ctrl Shift Z, then type character
Insert one Symbol character	Ctrl Shift Q, then type character

Baseline shift

Baseline Shift up 1 point	Ctrl Alt Shift)
Baseline Shift down 1 point	Ctrl Alt Shift (

Style text

Plain text	Ctrl Shift P
Bold	Ctrl Shift B
Italic	Ctrl Shift I
Underline	Ctrl Shift U
Word Underline	Ctrl Shift W
Outline	Ctrl Shift O
Shadow	Ctrl Shift S
All Caps	Ctrl Shift K
Small Caps	Ctrl Shift H
Superscript	Ctrl Shift 0 (zero)
Subscript	Ctrl Shift 9
Superior	Ctrl Shift V

Horizontal alignment of text

Left alignment	Ctrl Shift L
Right alignment	Ctrl Shift R
Center alignment	Ctrl Shift C
Justified alignment	Ctrl Shift J
Forced justify	Ctrl Alt Shift J

Tracking and kerning

Increase Kerning/Tracking 10 units	Ctrl Shift }
Decrease Kerning/Tracking 10 units	Ctrl Shift {
Increase Kerning/Tracking 1 unit	Ctrl Alt Shift }
Decrease Kerning/Tracking 1 unit	Ctrl Alt Shift {

Horizontal/vertical type scale

Decrease scale 5%	Ctrl [
Increase scale 5%	Ctrl]
Decrease scale 1%	Ctrl Alt [
Increase scale 1%	Ctrl Alt]

Word space tracking

For use with the Type Tricks XTension

Increase Word Space 10 units	Ctrl Shift }
Decrease Word Space 10 units	Ctrl Shift {
Increase Word Space 1 unit	Ctrl Alt Shift }
Decrease Word Space 1 unit	Ctrl Alt Shift {

Special text characters

New paragraph	Enter
New line	Shift Enter
Indent here	Ctrl \
Discretionary new line	Ctrl Enter
Breaking em dash	Ctrl Shift =
Nonbreaking em dash	Ctrl Alt Shift =
Nonbreaking en dash	Ctrl Alt Shift - (hyphen)
Discretionary hyphen	Ctrl - (hyphen)
Nonbreaking standard hyphen	Ctrl =
Break at discretionary hyphen only	Ctrl - (hyphen) before first character in word
Nonbreaking standard space	Ctrl 5
Breaking en space	Ctrl Shift 6
Nonbreaking en space	Ctrl Alt Shift 6
Breaking flex space	Ctrl Shift 5
Nonbreaking flex space	Ctrl Alt Shift 5
Breaking punctuation space	Shift Space bar or Ctrl 6
Nonbreaking punctuation space	Ctrl Shift Space bar or Ctrl Alt 6

Import a picture

Get Picture... (Item or Content tool)	Ctrl E
Reimport all pictures in document	Ctrl Open in Open dialog box

In Get Picture dialog box

TIFF line art to grayscale	Ctrl Open
TIFF grayscale to black-and-white	Ctrl Open
TIFF color to grayscale	Ctrl Open

Pictures and picture boxes or Béziers

Center picture in box	Ctrl Shift M
Move picture in box 1 point	Arrow keys
Move picture in box 1/10 point	Alt arrow keys
Fit picture to box	Ctrl Shift F
Fit picture to box (maintain aspect ratio)	Ctrl Alt Shift F

Enlarge picture in 5% increments	Ctrl Alt Shift >
Reduce picture in 5% increments	Ctrl Alt Shift <
Constrain box to square or circle	Shift drag
Resize box (maintain aspect ratio)	Alt Shift drag
Scale picture and box (Edit > Shape off)	Ctrl drag
Scale picture and box (maintain aspect ratio)	Ctrl Alt Shift drag

Picture styling

Picture Contrast...	Ctrl Shift C
Negative	Ctrl Shift - (hyphen)
Halftone (grayscale, line art only)	Ctrl Shift H

Runaround/clipping

Runaround...	Ctrl T
Edit runaround	Ctrl F10
Clipping...	Ctrl Alt T
Edit clipping path	Ctrl Shift F10

Bézier box or line (or clipping path)

Add a point	Alt click line segment
Delete a point	Alt click point or Backspace (Item tool)
Delete selected Bézier point while drawing shape	Backspace
Edit Bézier while drawing it	Ctrl
Constrain line, point, or handle movement to 0°, 45°, 90°	Shift drag
Retract curve handles	Ctrl Shift click point
Expose/create curve handle	Ctrl Shift drag point
Select all points in active shape	Ctrl Shift A or triple-click point
Select all points in active path	Double-click point
Convert Bézier line to filled-center Bézier box	Alt Item menu > Shape > freehand picture box icon
Edit Shape	F10

Convert Bézier segment

Straight segment	Ctrl Shift F1
Curved segment	Ctrl Shift F2

Convert Bézier point

Corner point	Ctrl F1
Smooth point	Ctrl F2
Symmetrical point	Ctrl F3

Corner to smooth/smooth to corner	Ctrl Shift drag curve handle
Smooth to corner while drawing shape	Ctrl click point, then press Ctrl F1

Line or text

Increase width/size to preset size	Ctrl Shift >
Decrease width/size to preset size	Ctrl Shift <
Increase width/size by 1 point	Ctrl Alt Shift >
Decrease width/size by 1 point	Ctrl Alt Shift <
Proportional resize	Ctrl Alt Shift drag
Constrain resize/rotate to 0°, 45°, 90°	Ctrl Shift drag
Nonproportional resize	Ctrl drag

Style sheets

Style Sheets...	Ctrl click style sheet name on Style Sheets palette or Shift F11
Display Edit Style Sheet pop-up menu	Right-click style sheet name
Apply No Style, then style sheet	Alt click style sheet name

Color

Colors...	Ctrl click color on Colors palette or Shift F12

Multiple items

Select All (Item tool)	Ctrl A
Select multiple items (Item tool)	Shift click or marquee
Group	Ctrl G
Ungroup	Ctrl U
Duplicate	Ctrl D
Step and Repeat...	Ctrl Alt D
Select through layers	Ctrl Alt Shift click
Bring to Front	F5
Send to Back	Shift F5
Bring Forward one level	Ctrl F5
Send Backward one level	Ctrl Shift F5
Space/Align...	Ctrl , (comma)

Anchored boxes

Text to box (anchor box and delete text)	Alt choose Style menu > Text to Box

Check spelling

Check Word...	Ctrl W
Check Story...	Ctrl Alt W
Check Document...	Ctrl Alt Shift W
Lookup	Alt L
Skip	Alt S

Add	Alt A
Add all suspect words to current auxiliary dictionary	Alt Shift Close

Find/Change

Find/Change...	Ctrl F
Change Find Next button to Find First	Alt
Close Find/Change	Ctrl Alt F
Wild card (Find what)	Ctrl ? (question mark)
Space	Space bar
Tab	Ctrl Tab
New paragraph	Ctrl Enter
New line	Ctrl Shift Enter
New column	\c
New box	\b
Punctuation space	Ctrl . (period)
Flex space	Ctrl Shift F
Backslash	Ctrl \
Previous box page number	Ctrl 2
Current box page number	Ctrl 3
Next box page number	Ctrl 4

Indexing

Display palette	Ctrl Alt I
Highlight text field	Ctrl Alt I
Add highlighted entry	Ctrl Alt Shift I
Edit highlighted index entry	Double-click

Compare components

Compare two style sheets, colors, lists, H&Js, dashes & stripes, print styles	Open dialog box from edit menu, Ctrl-click two components, then Alt click Append (Import button in Print Styles)

Preferences

Document Preferences...	Ctrl Y
Document > Paragraph folder tab	Ctrl Alt Y
Tool Preferences	Double-click item creation or Zoom tool
Application Preferences...	Ctrl Alt Shift Y

Output

Page Setup...	Ctrl Alt P
Print...	Ctrl P
Save Page as EPS...	Ctrl Alt Shift S

Note: If an F key is chosen as a Keyboard Equivalent for a style sheet, it will override the default F key command.

Index

C

D

E

S

T